Introduction to Ethical Theory

edited by
Kenneth F. Rogerson
Florida International University

Holt, Rinehart and Winston, Inc.
Fort Worth   Chicago   San Francisco   Philadelphia
Montreal   Toronto   London   Sydney   Tokyo

Publisher: Ted Buchholz
Acquisitions Editor: Jo-Anne Weaver
Editorial Assistant: Wendy Ludgewait
Project Editor: Catherine Townsend
Production Manager: Ken Dunaway
Art & Design Supervisor: Guy Jacobs
Text Designer: Leon Bolognese & Associates, Inc.
Cover Designer: Richard Hannus
Compositor: P&M Typesetting, Inc.

Library of Congress Cataloging-in-Publication Data

Introduction to ethical theory / edited by Kenneth F. Rogerson.
    p.   cm.
  ISBN 0-03-023094-2
  1. Ethics. I. Rogerson, Kenneth F., 1948–
BJ1025.I56 1991
171—dc20   90-43129
                                CIP

ISBN: 0-03-023094-2

Address Editorial Correspondence To: 301 Commerce Street, Suite 3700, Fort Worth, TX 76102

Address Orders To: 6277 Sea Harbor Drive, Orlando, FL 32887
1-800-782-4479, or 1-800-433-0001 (in Florida)

Printed in the United States of America

1 2 3 4   090   9 8 7 6 5 4 3 2 1

Holt, Rinehart and Winston, Inc.
The Dryden Press
Saunders College Publishing

Preface

Students are not initially receptive to philosophy generally or ethical theory more specifically. There are several reasons for this. Students rarely have had any formal exposure to philosophy before college. Or, worse yet, to the extent they have some idea about philosophy it is often a misleading stereotype. Typically, students believe that philosophy is a matter of spinning out wild speculations in complete abstraction from everyday life. So conceived, philosophy seems irrelevant to contemporary students who are increasingly drawn toward practical, job-related majors. Accordingly, students are suspicious of any "far fetched" theoretical reasoning. These are serious obstacles toward teaching philosophy to undergraduates, particularly nonmajors.

A central goal of this text is to overcome such obstacles to studying a philosophical treatment of ethics. Each chapter of the text begins with a "Current Discussion," a nontechnical, popular essay. These essays are chosen as a common, everyday expression of the ethical theory to be discussed in the chapter. The function of this popular essay is twofold. First, it shows students that the ethical theories they will read are based upon more everyday reasoning about ethics—that, for example, Kant's Categorical Imperative is a sophisticated version of the much more familiar idea of the "Golden Rule." But, additionally, as discussed in the introductory chapters, the Current Discussions show the need for a sophisticated, philosophical expression of everyday positions on ethics. Philosophical expressions of ethical ideas are needed to overcome problems and objections inherent in everyday expressions. In short, a guiding premise of the text is that ethical theories are more careful, consistent, and coherent versions of familiar ethical ideas. In this respect students will be encouraged to see that philosophical ethics is not divorced from everyday concerns.

As discussed in the General Introduction, this text has a comparatively narrow focus. Many ethics texts attempt to cover the full range of philosophical ethics: meta-ethics, normative ethics, applied ethics, and more. The result is often disappointing. In order to cover such a broad domain, the treatment of individual issues tends to be far too sketchy. The present text makes no pretense of covering all the interesting issues in ethics, but rather focuses on the arguably central topic of normative ethics.

This is primarily a text on normative ethical theories. However, a qualification is needed here. As one would expect, there are chapters on utilitarianism and Kantianism, as well as a chapter on virtue theories, reflecting recently renewed interest in such an approach to ethics. Yet, perhaps unexpectedly, roughly half of the text considers theories often discussed under the heading of political philosophy: rights theory and social contract theory as well as a discussion of the relation of law and morality. There are several reasons for the inclusion of these "political theories" in a text on normative ethics. To the extent that rights theory and social contract theory have direct implications for the sorts of actions one ought and ought not perform, they are relevant to a broad normative theory of actions. More narrowly, however, much contemporary work in normative ethics is done from the vantage point of these traditional political theories (e.g., Rawls, Nozick, and Gauthier). As such, neglecting rights theory and social contract theory would fail to account for some fruitful contemporary work. Additionally, the readings chosen for this text tend to concentrate not simply on normative ethics but normative ethics as relevant to our social relations with others and to social policy governing these social relations. Again, rights theory, social contract theory, and the final chapter on the relation of law and morality help students to see the relevance of ethics to their daily concerns about social policy.

Editing an anthology can be a time-consuming and sometimes frustrating affair. These problems were mitigated to a large measure by financial assistance from Florida International University, helpful clerical work from my student assistant Frances Comeau, and considerable patience and moral support from Jo-Anne Weaver at Holt, Rinehart and Winston. I also want to thank the reviewers whose detailed criticisms on earlier drafts greatly improved the final product:

Donna Bestock
Skyline College

William Davie
University of Oregon

Michael Gorr
Illinois State University

George Graham
University of Alabama–Birmingham

Mary Hines
Catonsville Community College

David Johnson
Bucks County Community College

Lutz Kramer
Rogue Community College

Bruce Miller
Michigan State University

William Nelson
University of Houston

William Nietmann
University of Northern Arizona

Tom Phillips
California State University–Northridge

Anita Silvers
San Francisco State

Contents

ETHICS OF VIRTUE   159

RIGHTS THEORIES   235

SOCIAL CONTRACT THEORIES   325

LAW AND MORALITY   407

General Introduction

What Is Ethics?

The topic of this book is ethical theory. But before we begin to study the various theories, we need to say something about the nature of the enterprise. The terms *ethics* and *morality* are not always used with a clear meaning in ordinary contexts, nor do the ordinary meanings correspond exactly to the academic or philosophical uses of the terms. On the one hand, *ethics* is often used these days in connection with professional codes of conduct. These are rules or guidelines for how persons ought to conduct themselves on their job, for example. *Morality,* on the other hand, is often used to prescribe conduct for our personal life—sometimes it has the even more restricted usage of pertaining to sexual behavior. For example, if a person is tried on a morals charge, we understand that they have been accused of some kind of sexual misconduct. These uses of the terms *ethics* and *morality* are not so much incorrect, by philosophical standards, as they are too limited. Both professional ethics and sexual morality are examples of the wider domain that interests us. The first is concerned with the right and proper way to act in one's professional life, while the second is concerned with the right and proper personal behavior. Our interest in the theoretical study of ethics or morality is with the idea of right and proper conduct generally speaking—an idea that can be applied to a wide variety of cases.

For our present purposes we will not make a distinction between *ethics* and *morality*. The terms will be used interchangeably to refer to ideas or principles recommending how we ought to act. We can be just slightly more specific here. As we have seen above, it may be possible to distinguish issues of proper conduct in areas that mostly concern our relations with other people, and areas that mostly concern our own lives. The main focus of this text will be upon the former question. Our study of ethics will be a study, for the most part, of those ideas or principles that tell us how we ought to act toward other people. The qualification "for the most part" is important since in the final chapter of this book we will take a look at the difference between actions that concern oneself and actions that concern others. The issue covered in the final chapter will be the extent to which society ought to concern itself exclusively with the former sorts of actions.

While the above discussion gives an idea of the nature of ethics, there is perhaps a preliminary question that needs to be addressed. Why study ethics? There are a numer of answers that can be given here, but we will concentrate on a few that are most important. For most day-to-day concerns the theoretical study of ethics is most probably not necessary. Most of us carry around with us a serviceable collection of moral do's and don't's. It is wrong to lie. It is good to help people. It is wrong to kill. It is good to keep promises. If these moral notions are correct, and there is little reason to doubt that they are, then perhaps we do not need to study ethics. If the study of ethics is to tell us the right way to act and the list of do's and don't's cited above does the job, then there is no need to go farther. Yet there is a need, however. Consider the idea that it is wrong to kill. Does this mean that capital punishment is wrong? Or that killing in self-defense is wrong? Or that abortion or mercy-killing is wrong? When we press our everyday moral notions for details, particularly in controversial cases, answers are not forthcoming. We need to dig deeper, and this is just what a theoretical study of ethics is intended to do.

The answer given above to the question of why we study ethics may not be entirely satisfying. On the assumption that we want to know whether abortion, mercy-killing and so on are right or wrong, then theoretical ethics has a role. However, a person may not be convinced that such knowledge is terribly important. Perhaps sophisticated knowledge about ethics is not terribly important to everyone in all circumstances. Consider an extreme example. A person stranded alone on a desert island for the rest of his or her life would have little use for a sophisticated knowledge of ethics. After all, if ethics is interested in the proper way to act toward others and our friend will not be running into anyone else, then study of ethics would be "academic" in the popular sense of that term. Or, to take a different example, if we were serfs in the Middle Ages with little power to decide how to run our own lives, then studying rules for how to act would again have few practical consequences. Decisions about how to run our lives would be made for us. However, circumstances are different for us. We live in a large, interdependent society. It seems at every turn other people's actions affect our lives and our actions affect theirs. Rules to regulate peoples' actions toward another are important in these circumstances. It is not just that there must *be* such rules, but given the fact that we live in a political democracy, each of us is responsible for deciding which rules ought to be adopted. As citizens of a democracy, we must decide whether abortion, mercy-killing, and capital punishment are morally wrong or wrong enough to pass laws prohibiting them.

Issues in Ethical Theory

Ethics, we have seen, is concerned with the proper treatment of other people. However, this broad characterization contains a number of more specific issues that are studied under the general heading of ethics. For simplicity's sake the field of ethics can be subdivided into three smaller areas. *Meta-ethics* is a branch of ethics whose issues are most remote to daily questions of what to do. The term *meta* as applied to ethics refers to an inquiry into issues more basic or fundamental than concerns about particular values or standards in human conduct. Specifically, in meta-ethics scholars are primarily concerned to find out how ethical principles are ultimately justified. Are they factual statements supported by hard data? Are they commands issued by some authority? Are they expressions of personal preference? As these questions suggest, the topic of ultimate justification is closely connected to the proper analysis of the meaning of ethical statements. If they are statements of fact or commands of a legitimate authority, it makes sense to look for objective justification. However, if they are more expressions of preference, then perhaps this does not make sense. While the issues of meta-ethics are rather remote from daily experience, moral psychology and moral education are much closer to home. In the latter cases we are interested in the following. Assuming we know the right and wrong ways to act, what would motivate people to do the right thing and avoid doing wrong things? How might we educate people about morality so that it is more likely that they will be better people?

Both meta-ethics and moral psychology are interesting fields of study well deserving of our attention. However, the focus of this text will be upon a third set of issues that lies midway between the comparatively remote study of meta-ethics and the more practical issue of moral psychology. We will study what is called *normative ethics*. While meta-ethics is concerned with the ultimate justification of ethical principles, and moral psychology is concerned with the employment of these principles, normative ethics searches for the principles themselves. Simply put, the study of normative ethics is intended to uncover the principle (or principles) that should be used to decide the rightness or wrongness of particular actions. It is the search for a criterion or "norm" for moral actions.

A Procedure for Normative Ethics

The task of a normative ethical theory is to defend principles of proper conduct. However, while a normative theory requires justification, we have already said that the task of giving an "ultimate" justification for ethics belongs to the subfield of meta-ethics. This brings into question just how we are to go about doing normative ethics. It might seem that it is impossible to argue for normative principles unless we are prepared to offer an "ultimate," meta-ethical justification of the principles. Fortunately, this is not the case. There is a lot that can be said for or against an ethical principle short of an "ultimate" justification. In this subsection we will touch briefly on a procedure for doing normative ethics even when we have not entirely settled on a best meta-ethical theory. For students who wish more discussion on this topic, see the selection from Michael Tooley that immediately follows this introduction.

There is a rough-and-ready way to proceed in order to defend a position on normative ethics without having to reach definitive conclusion about meta-ethics. As suggested above, one of the best reasons for doing normative ethics is to find a principle that helps us to decide what to do in difficult, controversial cases. While there are surely controversial cases in ethics, however, there are just as surely cases where we are clear about the right thing to do. Stealing a new car just for the fun of driving it or cheating on an exam to get a higher grade are not controversial cases. I take it that we are as certain as we are certain of anything that these actions are wrong. Many more such examples exist. In fact, it is likely that noncontroversial cases far outnumber the controversial ones.

If we can accept that there are clear ethical cases, then there is a way to proceed in normative ethics. An adequate normative theory should help to explain why the clear cases are, in fact, clear ones, while also helping us to decide the controversial cases. An example will help to clarify this point. The first theory we will study is utilitarianism. The normative principle proposed by utilitarianism is that the right thing to do in a particular situation is that which promotes the greatest amount of "happiness" (human good) for all persons involved. Utilitarianism goes a long way toward explaining why we judge car stealing and cheating to be morally wrong. It is fairly obvious that in these cases we do more harm than good. Not only can a theory like utilitarianism explain why we judge the way we do in clear cases, but it can also give us answers in difficult cases. Consider this example. In order to decide whether capital punishment is a good policy, a utilitarian will find out whether the consequences of the policy, overall, are more beneficial than harmful. If yes, then, according to utilitarianism, we should judge the policy as morally correct. If not, then we should condemn the policy.

Clear cases in ethics can be used not only to support a normative theory, but also to criticize one. If a normative theory recommends that we cheat, lie, or steal in circumstances where it is certain that these actions are wrong, or if the theory recommends against doing something that is clearly correct in the circumstances, then this is evidence that points against the theory—we have found a counterexample to the theory. The theory gives the wrong answers when compared to our firm beliefs in clear cases. In this respect a normative ethical theory can be tested in a way rather similar to the way we test scientific theory. Scientific theories can be shown to be mistaken if they predict a result different from what we actually observe. Normative ethical theories can be shown to be mistaken if they render moral judgments different from what we are convinced is the right answer in clear cases.

Some Problems with Normative Ethics

The procedure we have outlined for justifying or criticizing normative theories is not *ultimately* satisfying, however. Any, possibly all, of our firmest convictions about particular cases can be challenged. Someone could ask us to justify further our conviction that cheating on an exam or stealing a car is a morally wrong thing to do. To demand such a justification is to raise a meta-ethical issue. It is to ask for a justification of clear cases. Although the readings we will consider are not entirely free of such meta-ethical questions, for the most part we will assume that there is some justification for clear cases and proceed with the business of normative ethics. However, something must be said about meta-ethics in order to allow our enquiry to go forward. As a matter of practice it is permissible to argue for normative theories short of an ultimate justification of clear cases. This is a reasonable procedure only if we have some assurance that there is some ultimate justification—even if we are not prepared to give the justification. (Again, see the reading from Michael Tooley for a more detailed discussion of these matters.) However, there are a couple of meta-ethical positions that cast doubt upon the very possibility of justifying of clear cases. Subjectivism and relativism are two meta-ethical positions that, if accepted, would disallow us from claiming that our so-called "clear-case moral judgments" truly tell us what is right and wrong.

Subjectivism holds that moral judgments are nothing more than statements of personal preferences. Typically, proponents hold that ethical statements are merely expressions of pro or con feelings or emotions toward certain kinds of behavior. When I say "cheating on an exam is wrong," the subjectivist holds that all I am really doing is expressing my feeling of disapproval for cheating. This is perfectly compatible with another person saying "cheating is permissible," since the other person is merely expressing her feelings of approval for cheating. Subjectivism in ethics holds that moral judgments about right and wrong are rather like statements of personal tastes in food. Jim says that catsup is good. Jill says that catsup is awful. They can both be right, since taste for catsup is merely subjective.

A full-blown refutation of subjectivism would take us further into meta-ethics than we want to go. However, on the face of it, there are some good reasons to reject the theory. Perhaps the chief reason is that subjectivism does not square well with the way we actually use moral judgments. If subjectivism were correct, then it would be absurd to have disputes about ethics. It does not make any sense for Jim and Jill to dispute the merits of catsup. Taste for catsup is merely a matter of personal preference. If moral judgments are subjective in the same way that judgments about catsup are subjective, however, then it would be equally absurd to dispute about moral judgments. When Jim says that abortion is morally wrong and Jill says that it is morally permissible, there is no genuine disagreement. Both are merely stating feelings of personal preference. And yet, the meta-ethical position of subjectivism does not reflect what we actually do about moral issues. People take a firm stand on issues like abortion. They argue against others' positions and attempt to convince others that their position is correct. They argue for a law of the land that reflects their considered judgments. In short, people do not act as if moral judgments are just a matter of personal preference.

This is not a conclusive argument against subjectivism. It is conceivable that subjectivism is correct and that our practice of disputing moral issues is pointless. However, the burden of proof lies with the subjectivist. The subjectivist must convince us, in the face of practice that runs counter to the position, that subjectivism is yet correct. It is an uphill battle.

There is another meta-ethical position that is similar to subjectivism: *relativism*. Although there can be many kinds of relativism the most typical meta-ethical position is called *social* or *cultural relativism*. Whereas subjectivism holds that moral judgments are a matter of personal preferences, social relativism holds that they are matters of social preferences. For a social relativist, saying "cheating is wrong" merely means that "cheating is wrong for our particular society." And this claim is compatible with people in another society saying that "cheating is permissible." The latter claim, after all, just means that "cheating is permissible in their society." Again, the burden of proof lies with the relativist since, as before, the position does not square well with practice. If social relativism were the correct meta-ethical position, then it would be absurd to praise or condemn the moral code of another society. And yet we do this all the time. We criticize the Soviet Union's stand on dissidents or South Africa's apartheid policy, and we praise other countries for their progress on human rights. Not only do we compare one society to another on moral grounds, but we also make judgments about the moral direction of our own society historically. We take seriously claims that our society is morally improving or deteriorating when compared to an earlier stage in our history. If social relativism is correct, however, then each stage of society has its own standards and we cannot make such comparisons—contrary to actual practice. Again, like subjectivism, our practical use of moral judgments suggests that social relativism is not the correct meta-ethical position.

There is an additional problem with social relativism that is not shared with subjectivism. Social relativists often assume that it is easy to determine a society's moral judgment on a particular issue. It is not. It might be said that in the 1930s, Germans (as a society) judged that sending people to concentration camps was morally permissible. However, it is clear that not all Germans held this view (e.g., those sent to the camps did not). As such, a relativist must say that a society's moral position is determined by what most (but not all) of the people in the society hold. However, this position has an unsavory consequence. A minority moral opinion in a society cannot be correct. If relativism holds that the correctness of a moral judgment is determined by what most people in that society hold, then any contrary minority view is necessarily incorrect. In our example, the relativist would have to say that those who objected to concentration camps in Germany held a morally incorrect position. This is an implausible result. Surely, as in the concentration camp example, there are some occasions when a minority moral opinion is correct.

Ethics and Religion

We need to consider another issue before beginning work on normative ethics. In many people's minds there is a close connection between ethics and religion. There is good reason for this belief. For nearly all of us the way we look at ethics is influenced by the religious culture around us. This is true even for those people who may not be actively religious. We live in a predominately Judeo-Christian culture, and no doubt some of the specific moral concepts we use have their source in this religious heritage. The notion of the Golden Rule, which we shall consider in Chapter II, is a moral principle that most of us know because of religion. Similarly, the idea that we should guide our lives by certain "virtues" (discussed in Chapter III) such as temperance and charity is prominent in religious teachings. Judeo-Christianity is not the only religious tradition that is closely associated with ethics. It is safe to say that all major world religions currently practiced are "moral religions"—they have moral principles central to their religious doctrine.

On the basis of the above it is clear that there is some kind of connection between religion and ethics. However, we must be careful not to overstate the connection. For example, sometimes it is claimed that a person must be religious (or even subscribe to one particular religion) in order to be moral. This claim can mean a number of different things. There are theistic positions on the ultimate justification of moral principles. One such position is the *divine command theory*. This theory states that what makes a principle a truly moral principle (that is, one which we ought to obey) is the fact that God has commanded it. This is not the place for a detailed examination of this theory. This is clearly a meta-ethical issue. It is important, however, to point out that even if it is true, it does not follow that one must be religious in order to be moral. For example, one may believe (perhaps falsely) that there is some different ultimate justification for moral principles. One might even believe that there is no God. However, as argued above, as long as we hold that there are clear cases in ethics and believe there is some kind of ultimate justification for those cases, then we can do normative ethics. The point of these remarks is this: Even if the divine command theory is correct, it need not play a central role in our present task of normative ethics.

While divine command theory offers an ultimate justification of moral principles, there is another version of the connection between religion and ethics. Even if we could waive the question of ultimate justification, the following argument could be made for the importance of religion when doing normative ethics. As stated above, the job of normative ethics is to discover the correct set of moral principles. And, it could be argued, religion has an important role to play. In divine command theory, not only does God ultimately justify moral principles, but knowledge of God's commands is knowledge of the right moral principles— exactly the goal of normative ethics. Accordingly, the religious person seems to have an edge. By consulting his or her religion a person can find the principles of normative ethics. Unfortunately, matters are not so simple. Again, for the sake of argument, let's grant that the divine command theory is correct. Even so, there are yet problems specifying a good normative theory since there is a problem *knowing* exactly what the commands of God are. Obviously religions differ with respect to what they consider to be the moral commands of God (different holy texts, different interpretations of the same texts, and so on). If we knew which is the "true" religion (i.e., the religion that taught God's actual commands), then we would know the proper normative principles. Unfortunately, knowing which is the "true" religion seems to require that we first know the proper normative principles. This is a requirement since a criterion for being the "true" religion is that it teaches the morally correct commands of God. Unless we already know what is morally correct, however, we cannot find the "true" religion. Accordingly it still makes sense to do normative ethics independently from the question of religion.

There is yet another way to understand the claim that one must be religious to be moral. Instead of being a meta-ethical theory of ultimate justification or an assertion about how to know normative principles, it is a claim about moral psychology. Specifically the claim is that only a religious person is motivated to act morally. This seems too strong. One need not go far afield to find nonreligious people who act quite morally. Perhaps the claim could be toned down to say that religious belief and education are particularly good training for a moral life. And, on the average, religious people are better equipped to act morally. This is a factual claim that is worthy of consideration, but, like the meta-ethical version of the claim, it is not directly relevant to our enquiry. We want to uncover the most plausible candidate for a highest moral principle. We will leave it to others to argue for the best way of motivating people to accept and live by this principle. Both tasks are important, but we have chosen to confine ourselves to the first. It should be mentioned that it is impossible to maintain an absolutely rigid distinction between normative ethics and meta-ethics and moral psychology. As we shall see shortly, some meta-ethical theories threaten the possibility of doing normative ethics. Similarly, in extreme cases, some facts about moral psychology may tell against a particular normative theory. For example, someone might propose that people ought to act in accordance with a moral principle that is so extremely demanding that no one, or virtually no one, could possibly live up to such a high standard. If this were so, then we might rightfully criticize the proposed principle as unworkable. Even though there will be occasions when issues in meta-ethics and moral psychology intrude upon a study of normative ethics, let's turn to some suggestions as to how we can do normative ethics in comparative isolation from these other issues.

A Point of Procedure

This is a text on the philosophical treatment of ethics. Saying only this much can be off-putting. There is a widespread idea that anything that has to do with philosophy is abstract, obtuse, and wholly unconnected with everyday life. There is only a little bit of truth in this characterization. A philosophical treatment of ethics is abstract, but only because it is one level removed from everyday concerns. Our everyday moral concern is to make correct judgments and act upon them. Our philosophical concern is to find those principles upon which we make moral judgments. This project is not divorced from everyday life, however. Just the contrary—if there is a grander point to make in this text it is that normative ethical theories are careful, detailed, sophisticated statements of root ideas that are part of everyday moral reasoning. To illustrate this point, each chapter, which is devoted to a particular normative theory, begins with a nonacademic, popular essay. These nonacademic essays illustrate the idea that is the basis for the philosophical theory expressed in the philosophical readings.

The role of a philosopher doing normative ethics, then, is much different from the popular image. It is not as though philosophers sit in armchairs and cook up wild, fantastic theories disregarding everyday concerns. Instead, the philosopher works with ideas whose home base is everyday life. This may seem to give philosophers an unimportant role in ethics. For example, one could argue that if philosophers merely restate ideas that common people have, then philosophers have nothing new and interesting to say. If we add to this the fact that philosophical essays are often difficult to read, then there may be good reason to avoid philosophical ethics altogether. The glitch in this argument is that philosophers do not merely restate the ideas of common people. Rather, as we shall see, a plausible root idea for a moral principle (like utilitarianism or the Golden Rule), needs to be stated much more specifically and carefully if it is to be an acceptable moral principle. The job of the philosopher is to take a plausible root moral idea and refine it in such a way that it is immune from criticism.

There is one more remark that needs to be made before we begin. The organization of this text is slightly unusual in the following respect. The first three chapters discuss familiar normative ethical theories: utilitarianism, Kantianism, and virtue theories of ethics. No one would doubt that knowledge of each of these theories is crucial to a good understanding of normative ethics. However, Chapters IV through VI consider topics more often discussed in a course on political philosophy than in an ethics course: rights theory, social contract theory, and law and morality. There are several reasons why the latter topics are important to a study of ethical theory. First, as suggested above, one of the most important reasons for studying ethics is to help us as citizens in a democracy. As citizens, we are all called upon to decide issues of right and wrong for the purpose of making laws that are fair and just for everyone. Accordingly, it is not out of place to consider those political theories that attempt to formulate morally grounded social rules. Second, rights theory and social contract theory play a special role these days in discussions of ethics. Often debates about what is right or wrong turn upon claims about the rights of others. Who has a "right to life" and what does that right entail? Or do people have a "right" to public health care? Given the abundance of rights talk in current ethical discussions, a text on ethical theory would be inadequate without a consideration of rights theory. For rather different reasons, social contract theory has become particularly important to ethical theory. As we shall see in Chapter V, some contemporary writers argue that the best technique for discovering proper ethical principles is to find which principles we would be willing to impose upon ourselves for the purpose of the betterment of everyone. This is the root idea of a social contract.

The final chapter, Law and Morality, is directly relevant to the idea that issues in ethics are particularly important to us when they are incorporated into laws of the land. The topic of the final chapter is the legitimacy of enforcing ethical principles by law. Are there some things that people do that are considered to be immoral or unethical, and yet should not be made illegal? Or should all moral wrongs carry with them a legal sanction?

MICHAEL TOOLEY

Ethics, Meta-ethics, and Philosophical Thinking

1.2 Ethics

The questions we shall be concerned with here fall within the branch of philosophy known as ethics. A brief general survey of this area of philosophy will, I believe, help the reader to place subsequent discussions in their proper settings. . . . Three aspects of philosophy mentioned above are . . . encountered within the field of ethics. First, analysis. Philosophers working in ethics have devoted considerable attention to questions of analysis. Such questions can be seen as falling into two main groups. First, there are questions concerning the analysis of specific ethical terms. What does it mean to say that an action is *right*, or that it is *wrong*? That one *ought*, or ought not, do something? What does it mean to say that some state of affairs is *good*? Or that it is *valuable*, or *desirable*? What does it mean to say that someone has a *right* to something? Can such terms be analysed? If some of them can be analysed, what will the analysis involve? Will it be in terms of other ethical expressions, or is it possible to offer an analysis that is free of ethical terms?

Second, and also within the general area of analysis, there are questions concerning the meaning of ethical *statements*. What sort of meaning do ethical statements have? How do they function? Does an ethical statement, such as "It is wrong to cause suffering," serve to put forward some claim about the nature of the world, or about some transcendent realm of values? Does it, in short, say something which is either true or false? Or does it have some very different sort of function?

Many philosophers maintain that ethical statements say something which is either true or false—that their primary function, at least, is to describe certain states of affairs, to formulate propositions, expressing moral facts. Many other philosophers, however, think that this view is mistaken, and a variety of alterna-tive positions have been advanced concerning the meaning of ethical statements. One view, known as emotivism, suggests that moral statements function to express one's feelings or attitudes towards acts of the sort in question.[1] To say that murder is wrong, on this view, is just to express a certain negative attitude towards acts of murder.

Another view, known as prescriptivism, maintains that ethical statements are, in effect, universalized imperatives—imperatives directed not at any particular person, but at people in general.[2] On this view, a statement such as "Euthanasia is wrong" is, as a first approximation, to be analysed as equivalent to "Everyone, refrain from euthanasia."

What is the significance of these two areas of ethical analysis for the discussion that follows? As regards the analysis of particular ethical terms, this assumes importance only in one place . . . [Later] I shall be considering the question of the conditions that something must satisfy in order to have a right to life, and I shall be advancing an argument in which the question of the correct analysis of the concept of a right is quite crucial.

The analysis of the meaning of ethical statements, in contrast, has no bearing upon specific arguments. On the other hand, the fact that this question has not been satisfactorily re-

[1]A brief statement of an emotivist view of ethical language can be found in chapter 6 of A. J. Ayer's *Language, Truth and Logic*, 1936. A more detailed statement and defence is contained in Charles L. Stevenson's *Ethics and Language*, 1944.

[2]For a lucid defence of a prescriptivist approach to the analysis of ethical language, see R. M. Hare's *The Language of Morals*, 1952.

solved has important implications for the justi-fication of ethical principles, and this in turn raises some critical questions about the appro-priate method for the discussion of ethical issues. Some of these questions will be consid-ered in the next three sections.

Let us now turn to the second aspect of phi-losophy—that of justification. In the field of ethics, this involves two main tasks. One of these is concerned with general issues of justi-fication within ethics. Are some ethical state-ments correct, and other incorrect? Can ethical statements be justified, or criticized? Can one give reasons either for accepting some ethical statements, or for rejecting others? If so, how can this be done?

The answers one offers to these questions will depend, among other things, upon the ac-count that one accepts of the meaning of ethical statements. If ethical statements possess fac-tual meaning, then to say that an ethical state-ment is justified will, presumably, just be to say that the available evidence makes it likely that it is true. The really serious questions, of course, remain. Is it possible for one to know that some ethical statements are true, and others false? Is it possible for there to be evi-dence that would make some ethical state-ments reasonable and others not? If so, what sort of evidence is relevant?

The situation is, none the less, very differ-ent if ethical statements are neither true nor false, if they do not function to make asser-tions. Then it is, to say the least, much less clear what could be meant by saying that some moral principles are correct, or justified, and others not. Most philosophers, in fact, tend to assume that if ethical statements do not pos-sess factual meaning, it makes no sense to speak of some as justified and others not.

This inference may seem very plausible. I want to urge, however, that it not be embraced too quickly. It rests upon the assumption that it cannot be appropriate to speak of ethical princi-ples as being capable of objective justification unless it is possible for there to be grounds that can make it likely that an ethical principle is true. But perhaps there is some other accept-able model of objective justification that may be applicable to ethical statements even if they are not such as can be either true or false? This possibility will be considered in section 1.4.

The other main undertaking in ethics that is connected with the problem of justification is that of formulating, and subjecting to critical scrutiny, competing sets of general ethical principles that will, ideally, provide a compre-hensive account of when actions are right or wrong, and of when states of affairs are good or bad. How this task is to be viewed will de-pend upon the general question of the jus-tifiability of ethical statements. If objective justification is possible, then one should be aim-ing at a comprehensive set of general principles that are objectively justified. But suppose, on the other hand, that it should turn out that ethi-cal principles are not susceptible to any sort of objective justification. What implications would this have for the philosophical discussion of the merits of competing ethical systems? Would it imply, in particular, that rational discussion of ethical issues was impossible, and that what passes for rational discussion in this area must be nothing more than an exercise in propa-ganda, an attempt to persuade others to adopt one's views through the use of various emo-tional appeals?

It is important to see that the impossibility of any sort of objective justification would not have such implications. The reason is that ob-jective *criticism* of ethical systems is possible even if objective justification is not. In the first place, an ethical system can be criticized on purely *logical* grounds, since it may incorporate principles that are, possibly in quite subtle ways, mutually inconsistent. Second, as will become clear shortly, most actual ethical sys-tems involve moral principles some of which rest upon *non-ethical* claims. A demonstration that some of those non-ethical claims are im-plausible may thus provide a person with a good reason for abandoning the ethical princi-ples that presuppose them.

These possibilities will be explored more fully in the next section. The important point here is merely that there are types of criticism that can be brought to bear upon ethical sys-tems regardless of whether it is possible to of-fer any sort of objective justification for ethical claims. The enterprise of comparing and evalu-ating ethical systems thus remains a sound and valuable undertaking—albeit a more limited one—even if moral scepticism should turn out to be the correct view to take on the question of the possibility of an objective justification of ethical claims.

Let us turn, now, to the final philosophical undertaking—that of setting out a synoptic vision of reality, of offering a general account of what there is. The relevance of ethics to this enterprise is connected with the question of the meaning of ethical statements. If ethical statements function to make assertions, if they say something which is either true or false, this may have implications with respect to what sorts of things there are.

The reason is this. Suppose that some ethical statements, such as "It is wrong to cause suffering," are true. What account is to be offered of the truth of such statements? The answer will depend upon how the concept of truth is to be analysed in general. But consider a view that many would accept, to the effect that a statement (or proposition) is true in virtue of its standing in some appropriate relation to some corresponding fact, or state of affairs. If this view is adopted, the question becomes one of what the truth-maker is for the statement, "It is wrong to cause suffering." Again, different answers are possible. One view, however, is that the state of affairs that makes this statement true involves what have been referred to as *non-natural* properties or relations—where a non-natural property or relation is one that cannot be reduced to, or analysed in terms of, the physical and psychological properties (and relations) which characterize entities, including people, in the natural world. If this view is adopted, the resulting picture of reality is quite different from what it would otherwise be. It is clear, then, that the questions, first, of whether ethical statements are such as are either true or false, and, if so, what account is to be given of their truth, raise issues that have an important bearing upon the philosophical task of constructing a comprehensive and unified picture of the world.

1.3 The Clarification and Evaluation of Ethical Positions

There are a variety of techniques that philosophers typically employ in examining systems of ethical principles. The discussion in this section will be confined to those techniques whose employment does not presuppose that ethical statements can be objectively justified.

The examination of an ethical position usually involves two aspects: clarification and evaluation. Let us begin by considering some techniques of clarification. The first two aspects of clarification are connected with ways in which individual ethical statements may be unclear. One obvious way is that a statement may contain terms that are *vague or ambiguous*. An important illustration of this in the present context is afforded by principles that contain the expression "human being". We shall see later that this expression is often used in significantly different senses by people debating the morality of abortion. When this ambiguity goes unnoticed, as it usually does, the result is a discussion in which people talk past one another, generating considerable heat, but very little illumination. In approaching moral questions philosophically it is important to be sensitive to such ambiguity, and to attempt to make explicit the different possible meanings of crucial terms. When this is done, fruitful discussion becomes possible.

The second reason that individual ethical statements often stand in need of clarification is that the moral principles that people advance often involve *tacit restrictions of scope*. If, for example, someone says that killing is wrong, it is unlikely that he intends that statement to be interpreted in an unrestricted way. First, because he probably does not object to the killing of non-human animals, let alone to the killing of plants. Second, because he may very well not even think that the killing of humans is always wrong. He may hold, for example, that there is nothing wrong with capital punishment, or with killing in self-defence. Thus, one of the first tasks, when confronted with a statement such as "Killing is wrong," is to determine precisely what is being affirmed. The result will be a somewhat more complex statement, in which the scope restrictions implicit in the original statement are made explicit.

Two other important techniques of clarification are concerned not with individual ethical statements, but with the over-all structure of the moral principles that underlie an individual's moral point of view. Many such principles can be arrived at in a very direct fashion. In the first place, people are usually prepared to advance a number of general principles that they believe represent their moral outlook. Second, one can propose other general principles, and see whether the individual is prepared to accept them. There are, however, two other, less direct methods of eliciting general principles. The first of these turns upon the fact that, in addition to feelings about the correctness or incorrectness of general moral principles, individuals also have feelings about what is right or wrong in a number of concrete situations. In many cases, these feelings about particular cases will be explicable by reference to general principles that the person himself would advance, or immediately assent to once they were proposed. But in other cases, these feelings may point to restrictions upon the individual's general moral principles, or even to other general moral principles that the individual might be hesitant about accepting when first proposed, but that seem to underlie the person's moral judgements in a wide range of concrete cases.

The second less direct method involves the application of a similar procedure in order to discover moral principles of greater generality that seem to underlie a number of the individual's less general principles. Thus, just as one can ask an individual who says that an action of a certain type is right in one concrete situation but wrong in another, what the difference is, so also if it is held that all actions of one type are right, and all actions of another type wrong, one can ask what the morally relevant difference is between the two types of actions. And the answer will be provided by another general moral principle, albeit of a deeper sort, since it will serve to explain the general moral principles which assert that actions of the one type are right, and actions of the other type wrong. We shall see later that this technique of searching for deeper general principles is a very important one.

But must it always be possible to formulate general moral principles? May one not have to be content with moral judgements that arise in concrete situations—as some existentialists have urged—at least some of the time? Is there any reason for supposing that there must be general moral principles that could in princi-

ple be discovered? Most philosophers think that there is. If a judgement is to be a moral judgement, rather than merely an expression of one's momentary likes and dislikes, enthusiasms or revulsions, it must be based upon features of the situation. One cannot justifiably advance different moral judgements in two situations unless one is prepared to hold that there is some morally relevant feature, present in the one case and not in the other. It may be difficult, of course, to say precisely what that feature is. But the mere fact that there must be such a feature, if one's differing moral judgements are to be justified, means that it must be in principle possible to formulate general moral principles that will capture what it is that is different about the two situations.

The second main technique for clarifying the overall structure of an individual's ethical position turns upon an important distinction between moral principles that are *basic for an individual* and those that are *derived*.[3] This distinction can be explained as follows. Consider, for example, the claim that adultery is wrong. To say that this is a derived moral principle for a certain individual is to say that the reason that that person accepts it is that he thinks it follows from some other ethical principle that he accepts, together with some factual claim of a *non-ethical* sort. Suppose, for example, that a person believes that adultery is wrong because, and only because, he believes that God forbids adultery, and that what God forbids is wrong. The claim that adultery is wrong then represents a derived moral principle for the person in question. Similarly, it would be a derived principle for a person who accepts it because he believes that adultery causes unhappiness, and that what causes unhappiness is wrong. In contrast, a person might hold that adultery is wrong without thinking that the principle can be derived from some other moral principle together with some factual belief of a non-ethical sort. In that case the principle would be a basic one for that person.

[3]This distinction was set out by Amartya K. Sen in his article, "The Nature and Classes of Prescriptive Judgments," *Philosophical Quarterly*, Volume 17, Number 66, 1967, pp. 46–62. See pp. 50–1.

This distinction between moral principles that are basic for a given individual, and those that are derived, points immediately to an important way in which the underlying structure of a person's moral outlook can be clarified. It will involve determining, first, which of a person's moral principles are basic for him, and which are derived, and second, in the case of those principles that are derived, what the derivation is. The latter will involve the specification of relevant basic moral principles, and relevant factual claims of a non-ethical sort, together with some argument which is thought to lead from those claims to the derived moral principle in question.

To sum up, then, the principal techniques of clarification are as follows. First, there is the detection, and elimination, of any crucial vagueness or ambiguity. Second, there is the technique of making explicit any tacit scope restrictions involved in individual statements. Third, there is the eliciting of general ethical claims that underlie less general ones. Finally, there is the technique of distinguishing between moral principles that are basic for the person, and those that are derived, and of determining what underlying assumptions and arguments the individual believes provide the grounds for the derived moral principles.

Let us now consider methods that can be used to evaluate ethical positions, and whose application does not presuppose that ethical principles can be objectively justified. At bottom, there are really only two such methods. The one involves showing that a certain ethical position is logically inconsistent in some respect. The other involves showing that there is good reason for rejecting one or more of the factual claims of a non-ethical sort that underlie some of the person's derived moral principles.

The first method can, however, take somewhat different forms, which it may be helpful to distinguish. One of the more important is the method of *counter-examples*. Suppose that a person holds that all actions of a certain type are wrong. A counter-example would consist of some situation involving an action of the relevant type, but which the individual would not judge to be wrong. Confronted with such a situation, the person will need to revise some aspect of his over-all ethical outlook. Either he

will have to hold that his judgement about the particular case is mistaken, or he will have to modify, or abandon completely, the general moral claim that actions of the relevant type are wrong.

This is straightforward. However there is an aspect of the method of counter-examples that sometimes evokes suspicion. This is the use of purely hypothetical, or imaginary counter-examples—a practice that is quite common in philosophical discussions of ethical questions. What is the rationale underlying such counter-examples? After all, if a person claims that all swans are white, it is no refutation to say that one can imagine a black swan. One must be able to point to an actual case of a non-white swan. How then can purely imaginary cases provide any reason for rejecting general ethical principles?

The key to understanding what is going on in the use of hypothetical counter-examples lies in the distinction, set out above, between moral principles that are basic for an individual and those that are derived. When a moral principle is a derived one for an individual, appeals to what would be right or wrong in purely hypothetical situations may very well not provide any reason for questioning the principle. For it may be that the apparent conflict between the hypothetical case and the general moral principle is due to the fact that certain factual beliefs of a non-ethical sort, which are in fact true, would not be true in the hypothetical situation being considered. If any of those beliefs are used by the individual in his derivation of the moral principle in question, the hypothetical case will provide no ground for rejecting the derived moral principle, any more than it would give one reason for questioning the underlying non-ethical beliefs.

Suppose, for example, that Mary holds that it is wrong to pull cats' tails, and that she does so because she believes that it is wrong to cause pain, and that pulling cats' tails causes them pain. One will not provide Mary with any reason for giving up her derived moral belief that it is wrong to pull cats' tails by asking her to consider a world in which cats enjoy having their tails pulled.

When the moral principle is a basic one for the individual, the situation is quite different.

Here purely hypothetical cases are relevant. For when the principle is a basic one, it does not rest upon any non-ethical beliefs about the nature of the world. The principle should thus be applicable not merely to the world as it actualy is, but to any world that one can imagine. So if one can specify some *conceivable* situation that falls under a principle that is basic for a given individual, and where the individual's moral feelings are not what they ought to be given the moral principle in question, some revision in the individual's moral outlook is in order. One possibility is for the person to cease regarding the principle that rests upon some other moral principle or principles, together with some non-ethical, purely factual assumptions about the nature of the world. A second possibility is for the individual to abandon the general principle completely. The final possibility is for him to retain the general principle as a basic one, and to hold that his moral feelings about the hypothetical case are somehow mistaken, and that they ought to be rejected, rather than the general ethical principle.

To sum up, the crucial point is this. Moral principles that are basic for an individual, in contrast to those that are derived, do not rest upon any non-ethical beliefs about what the world is like. As a consequence, moral principles that are basic for an individual function to pick out those features of situations or actions that the individual judges to be morally relevant regardless of what is the case. This means that an appeal to hypothetical counter-examples is perfectly in order when one is examining moral principles that are basic for an individual. This deserves to be emphasized, since the use of hypothetical counter-examples is both quite common, and very important, in philosophical thinking.

The strategy of searching for counter-examples is an important one in examining a person's ethical position. Another technique that is also very useful involves carefully working out the consequences of a given position. In the case of some very simple ethical positions, it will be quite obvious what principles follow from those that are explicitly stated. Often, however, a person's ethical outlook may be quite complex, either because it involves a large number of independent principles, or be-

cause some of the principles are complicated ones. It may then be quite difficult to see precisely what one is committed to in accepting the position. The construction of carefully formulated deductive arguments will enable one to determine the precise implications of the explicitly stated principles.

This, in turn, may enable one to see that the person's over-all ethical outlook is inconsistent in some respect. For example, it may be possible to deduce contradictory conclusions from the position in question, thereby showing that it is implicitly inconsistent. A second possibility is that, although the position does not entail contradictory conclusions, it does entail some consequence that the individual cannot accept. This means that the person's over-all ethical outlook, of which the explicitly formualted position is only a part, is logically inconsistent.

Let us now turn to the second way in which ethical positions can be criticized even if it turns out that ethical claims cannot be objectively justified. This second method arises out of the distinction between principles that are basic for an individual, and those that are derived. When a moral principle is a derived one, the person in question accepts it only because he thinks that it follows from some other moral principle together with some non-ethical beliefs about the world. As a consequence, there are two questions that can be raised about any derived moral belief. The first concerns the argument to which the person is appealing to get from the more basic ethical principle and the non-ethical belief to the derived moral principle: Is the argument valid? The second concerns the non-ethical belief involved in the derivation: Is this belief a reasonable one? If the answer to either question is no, the person has a good reason for abandoning the derived moral principle in question.

This second method of criticizing an ethical position has, I believe, considerable scope, owing to two factors. On the one hand, most people accept many ethical principles that they are unable to view as basic moral principles, since they are not such as they would accept no matter what changes in the world one envisages. But on the other hand, the justifications that they propose for those principles are often extremely shaky—either because they involve bad arguments, or, more commonly, because they rest upon some highly speculative non-ethical claims about the world that will not really stand up under critical scrutiny.

1.4 The Problem of Objective Justification

In the previous section we saw that ethical positions can be subject to rational criticism even if ethical principles cannot be objectively justified. First, because some of the ethical principles that a person accepts may be mutually inconsistent. And second, because some of the derivations upon which the individual's acceptance of some of his ethical principles rests may in fact be unsound, either owing to faulty logic, or owing to non-ethical beliefs that are not supported by the available evidence.

Philosophical reflection can show, then, that many moral positions are untenable. This will still leave one, however, with many possible sets of moral principles that do not suffer from either of the above two defects. How is one to choose among these alternatives? Is it ultimately just a matter of taste, or can there be objective grounds for ruling out at least some of the alternatives, and perhaps even for viewing one moral system as the correct one?

The issue of whether ethical principles can be objectively justified is very difficult. Essentially, there are three main alternatives. The first, which I shall refer to as the view that ethical principles can be *epistemically justified,* involves three claims—a semantical claim, an ontological claim, and an epistemological claim. The semantical claim concerns the sort of meaning possessed by ethical statements. The contention is that such statements do function to describe reality; they say something which is either true or false. The ontological claim is that there are, in reality, states of affairs that serve to make at least some "positive" ethical statements true. Finally, the epistemological claim is that it is possible for humans to know that some "positive" ethical statements are true, or at least, for them to have rationally justified ethical beliefs.

The claim that moral principles can be epistemically justified has both been accepted, and rejected, by many philosophers. Most of those who reject it adopt the position often referred to as *moral scepticism.* This is the view that ethical claims cannot be objectively justified at all, whether epistemically or otherwise.

Moral scepticism takes somewhat different forms. Most commonly, perhaps, it rests upon the contention that ethical statements do not function descriptively. This claim that ethical statements are neither true nor false may strike many as very implausible, given that most people certainly believe that some ethical statements are true, and others false. This claims is, however, by no means groundless, and a variety of considerations have been advanced in support of it. Of these, one of the most important concerns an apparent conceptual connection between accepting moral claims and being motivated to act in certain corresponding ways. Could a person, for example, believe that it was prima facie wrong not to keep one's promises, and yet be completely indifferent as to whether he or any other people ever kept their promises? Wouldn't one be tempted to say that such a person did not really believe that it was wrong to break one's promises? Yet how could there possibly be such a conceptual connection if ethical statements functioned descriptively? For to believe that some state of affairs is the case is not necessarily to be motivated to act in any particular way. A person who learns that he is drinking contaminated water will usually stop, but this is because he will usually have a desire not to get sick. Beliefs, unaccompanied by relevant desires, do not, it would seem, affect what one is likely to do. Therefore, if ethical beliefs *necessarily* imply the presence of an inclination to act in certain ways, or to encourage others to do so, it would seem that an ethical belief cannot be a matter, or at least not simply a matter, of believing that something is the case.

Some philosophers who are moral sceptics do not, however, appeal to the view that ethical statements are neither true nor false. Rather than challenging the semantical claim involved in the view that ethical judgements can be epistemically justified, they challenge either the ontological claim or the epistemological one. The result is what John Mackie has referred to as an "error theory".[4] According to this theory, ethical statements are such as are either true or false. However, every ethical statement that could possibly be used in formulating a moral outlook is, as a matter of fact, either false, or at least such as one has no reason to believe it true. For statements such as "One should not cause suffering," or "Pain is a bad thing," can only be true if there are objective values, in a broad sense, somewhere in reality, and according to the error theory, either there are no objective values, or if there are, at least we have no reason at all to believe that this is so.

Why might one adopt the error theory of morality? Mackie mentions a number of supporting considerations. One is connected with the relativity of values[5]—the fact that individuals accept quite different moral principles, and, moreover, that the principles that individuals accept tend to be very closely related to those accepted by their parents or society. If there were objective values, and if it were possible for people to be aware of them, would one expect there to be this sort of relativity of values?

Second, there is the ontological peculiarity of objective values.[6] Suppose that there are moral standards that are somehow written into reality. Confronted with such standards, wouldn't it always be possible to wonder whether there was any reason for accepting those standards, rather than some others? And might it not be the case that one found oneself in no way motivated to act in accordance with those standards? Yet the concept of objective values appears, in contrast, to be the concept of entities that both provide one with good reasons for accepting certain moral principles, and that tend to motivate one to act in accordance with those principles. It is not easy to grasp how there could be states of affairs with these unusual properties.

Another aspect of the ontological peculiarity is this. If there is some state of affairs that makes it wrong to cause suffering, then that state of affairs must presumably involve, on the one hand, the property of being an action that causes suffering, and, on the other, some moral property—such as the property of being wrong. How are we to conceive of the relation between these properties? Could it be thought of as a matter of one property having another property: the first-order property of being an action that causes suffering has a certain second-order property, namely, that of being a wrong-making property? But this takes us only part of the way. The crucial point is that the relation between the two properties must somehow be a *necessary* one: if it is prima facie wrong to cause suffering, it is wrong not merely in this world, but in every conceivable world. How are we to make sense of this necessity? What account of it can be offered? As yet, no halfway satisfactory answer to this question has been advanced.

These problems, of course, may turn out not to be insurmountable. But they do pose serious difficulties for the view that ethical statements can be epistemically justified, and it is easy to undertand why many philosophers feel that moral scepticism is correct. But one needs to ask, at this point, whether there are just the two alternatives. Is one forced to hold either that ethical statements can be epistemically justified, or that they cannot be objectively justified at all? Might there not be some third alternative? In particular, might it not be the case that there are grounds that make it reasonable to choose some ethical systems over others, even if ethical statements are neither true nor false, or even if there are no objective values?

But what might such grounds be? One possibility is some relation to the interests of people living together in society. It seems true, for example, that most systems of morality, though they usually involve some rules that appear to impair the interests of people in general, do, on the whole, result in societies that most people would find preferable to societies with no moral rules at all. One can therefore say that, given the desires that people normally have, they have a reason for preferring a soci-

[4]The error theory was originally set out by John L. Mackie in his article, "A Refutation of Morals," the *Australasian Journal of Philosophy,* Volume 24, 1946, pp. 77–90. For a more detailed discussion, see John L. Mackie, *Ethics—Inventing Right and Wrong,* 1977, chapter 1.
[5]Mackie, *Ethics,* pp. 36–8.
[6]Ibid., pp. 39–40.

ety with moral rules to one without. Similarly, it seems true that systems of moral rules vary considerably with respect to the impact they have upon the interests of people in general. If so, then people have a reason for preferring some systems of moral rules to others. And as this is quite independent of the question of whether any ethical statements are true, it suggests that there may be a way in which systems of morality can be rationally compared even if it is the case either that moral statements do not function to make assertions, or that there are not, as a matter of fact, any objective values.

A very clear exposition of this general approach to the justification of moral principles can be found in Michael Scriven's book, *Primary Philosophy*:

> *Roughly, then, it will be argued that there is a particular conception of morality which can be shown to be an extension of rationality. This conception is relevant to many decisions about actions and attitudes that affect more than one person, and where it is relevant, we shall see that immorality can be said to be irrational. This does not mean that any immoral act by any person is irrational in terms of that person's current goals; it means that having moral goals is rationally preferable to not having them.*[7]

The basic idea, then, is that it may be possible to justify ethical principles by showing that it is *rational* to accept them. Rational, however, not in the sense that there is evidence that makes it likely that they are true, but in the sense that it is in the interest of people in general to accept them. In short, ethical principles may be such as can be *non-epistemically* justified, even if they cannot be epistemically justified.

This approach avoids virtually all of the difficulties that the other response to moral scepticism encounters. It does so, however, at a cost. Perhaps the most important point in this respect is that it is not really possible to show that certain ethical principles are non-epistemically justified *simpliciter*. The reason is that it need not be in absolutely everyone's interest to have moral goals. A person with unlimited power, certainly, would have no reason for accepting moral principles. The most that can be shown, then, is that certain moral principles are non-epistemically reasonable for appropriately specified sorts of societies. The idea of objective moral rules that are universally binding must, in a sense, be set aside.

Some philosophers feel that this is a serious defect in a non-epistemic approach to the justification of morality. Others, such as Scriven, argue that it is not, on the ground that a non-epistemic justification can be offered for any group of individuals that is likely to exist:

> *Morality, Nietzsche said, is for the weak. This is true enough, but in the relevant sense we are all weak. To be precise, we are all less powerful than any significantly probable opposing combination of human and natural forces, and for that reason there is great advantage in the moral compromise for every human being.*[8]

Where does this leave us? Should we adopt the view that ethical claims can be epistemically justified? Or the view that they can be non-epistemically justified? Or should we be moral sceptics? The position that I am inclined to accept is that ethical principles can be non-epistemically justified, and, . . . acceptance of a non-epistemic approach to the justification or morality would provide additional support for some specific ethical claim that I am advancing. On the other hand, it seems to me that the issues raised by the question of the objective justifiability of ethical claims are puzzling indeed, and that, as a consequence, it would be foolish to rest anything of importance . . . upon the adoption of a particular view on the foundations of morality. The meta-ethical stance adopted will thus be, in effect, one of neutrality.

---

[7]Michael Scriven, *Primary Philosophy*, 1966, p. 230.   [8]Ibid., p.

Chapter I

Utilitarianism

ERNEST VAN DEN HAAG

Death and Deterrence

P rofessor Stephen K. Layson, an economist at the University of North Carolina at Greensboro, has published in the *Southern Economic Journal* (July 1985) a statistical study of the effects of executions on the murder rate. He concluded that every execution of a murderer deters, on the average, 18 murders that would have occurred without it.

Layson also inquired into the effects of the arrest and conviction of murderers on the murder rate. His correlations indicate that a 1 per cent increase in the clearance (arrest) rate for murder would lead to 250 fewer murders per year. Currently the clearance rate is 75 per cent. Further, a 1 per cent increase in murder convictions would deter about 105 murders. Currently 38 per cent of all murders result in a conviction; 0.1 per cent of murders result in an execution.

Attempts to correlate murder to punishment rates have been made for a long time. Most had flagrant defects. Some correlated murder rates to the presence or absence of capital-punishment statutes—not to executions, which alone matter. Others failed properly to isolate murder rates from variables other than punishment, even when these variables were known to influence murder rates. For instance, changes in the proportion of young males in the population do influence murder rates regardless of executions, since most murders are committed by young males. The first major statistical analysis that properly handled all variables was published by Isaac Ehrlich in the *American Economic Review* (June 1975). Ehrlich found that from 1933 to 1969 "an additional execution per year . . . may have resulted on the average in seven or eight fewer murders."

Ehrlich's study went against the cherished beliefs of most social scientists (after all, it confirmed what common sense tells us). A whole cottage industry arose to refute him. In turn he refuted the refuters. The verdict is inconclusive. As is often the case in statistical matters, if a different period is analyzed, or some technical assumptions are changed, a different result is produced. Thus the testimony of Professor Thorsten Sellin, given in 1953—long before Ehrlich wrote—to the Royal Commission on Capital Punishment in Great Britain, still stands. Asked whether he could "conclude . . . that capital punishment has no deterrent effect," Sellin, an ardent but honest opponent of capital punishment, replied, "No, there is no such conclusion." Despite considerable advances in methods of analysis I think that, as yet, it has not been proved conclusively that capital punishment deters more than life imprisonment, or that it does not. However, the preponderance of evidence now does tend to show that capital punishment deters more than alternative punishments. Professor Layson's paper will add to that preponderance. But many attempts will be made to refute it, and, in all likelihood, the verdict will still be that the statistics are not conclusive.

What are we to deduce? Obviously people fear death more than life imprisonment. Only death is final. Where there is life there is hope. Actual murderers feel that way: 99.9 per cent prefer life imprisonment to death. So will prospective murderers. What is feared most deters most. Possibly, statistics do not show this clearly, because there are so few executions compared to the number of murders. It is even possible that the uncertain prospect of execution deters so few not already deterred by the prospect of life imprisonment that there is no statistical trace. Yet, if by executing convicted murderers there is any chance, even a mere possibility, of deterring future murderers, I think we should execute them. The life even of a few victims who may be spared seems infinitely precious to me. The life of the convicted murderer has but negative value. His crime has forfeited it.

Opponents of capital punishment usually admit that their opposition has little to do with statistical data. When asked whether they would favor the death penalty if it were shown conclusively that each execution deters, say, one hundred murders, such opponents as Ramsey Clark (former U.S. attorney general) or Henry Schwarzschild (ACLU) resoundingly say no. But neither likes the inference that must be drawn: that he is more interested in keeping murderers alive than in sparing their victims, that he values the life of a convicted murderer more than the life of innocent victims. Those who do not share this bizarre valuation will favor capital punishment.

For beyond deterrence, or possible deterrence, there is justice. The thought that the man who cruelly and deliberately slaughtered your child for fun or profit is entitled peacefully to live out his days at taxpayers' expense, playing tennis or baseball or enjoying the prison library, is hard to stomach. Wherefore about 75 per cent of Americans favor the death penalty, for the sake of justice, and to save innocent lives. I think they are right.

On occasion I have been presented with a hypothetical. Suppose, I have been asked, that each execution were shown to raise rather than reduce the murder rate. Of course this is quite unlikely (wherefore there is no serious evidence): The more severe and certain the punishment, the less often the crime occurs, all other things being equal. The higher the price of anything, the less is bought. But, if one accepts, *arguendo,* the hypothetical, the answer depends on whether one prefers justice—which demands the execution of the murderer—or saving the lives that, by this hypothesis, could be saved by not executing him. I love justice, but I love innocent lives more. I would prefer to save them.

Fortunately we do not face this dilemma. On the contrary. Capital punishment not only satisfies justice but is also more likely to save innocent lives than life imprisonment.

Utilitarianism

In this chapter we will look closely at the ethical theory called *utilitariansim*. A simple way to state utilitarianism is the following: An action is right (obligatory) if it produces the greatest total amount of good for all persons affected by the action (maximum utility). And an action is wrong if it fails to maximize utility. The root idea of utilitarianism is that the rightness of our actions is determined by the effects these actions have on the well-being of ourselves and other people. An example will help to clarify this general idea. My neighbor, Jim, has a brand new Porsche that I covet to the depths of my soul. I consider taking the car for a long, tortuous weekend drive and abandoning it when I have got my fill. If I were to judge the morality of my action along utilitarian lines, I would compute the effects my actions have on the "utility" of all persons affected. The action would, no doubt, give me a great deal of pleasure (assuming I am not arrested). In the language of utilitarian theory, my pleasure counts as "positive utility." However, Jim, who has spent many thousands of dollars on the car, will be greatly upset by my action (this weighs on the balance as "negative utility"). Although Jim and I are the only persons directly affected by my action, there will be others indirectly affected; for example, Jim's insurance company may suffer a loss from my recklessness. There are other, more far-reaching effects to consider. My action of stealing a car may set an example for others, perhaps contributing to an increase in car theft. If we sum up the positive utility of the act (in this case my happiness) and weigh it against all of the negative utility cited, the overall result (the "net" utility) of my action is less happiness in the world than had I not stolen the car. Thus, according to utilitarian theory, stealing the car is morally wrong (assuming that the utilitarian's calculations of positive and negative utility are correct). It is an action I am obliged not to perform.

Utilitarian reasoning about ethics should be familiar to us. It is similar to a cost–benefit analysis used in business. A businessperson must calculate the monetary costs and benefits of various decisions with the goal of maximizing profits. Utilitarianism also asks us to calculate the costs and benefits of our actions with the goal of maximizing the result. However, the "commodity" we wish to maximize is the well-being or happiness of persons. For any action some people may end up worse off and some better off, but the right action is the one where the net utility (computed by subtracting the negative effects from the positive ones) is the greatest.

The reason why people find utilitarianism an attractive theory is easy to see. Each of us wants out of life the largest amount of personal happiness we can obtain. The problem, of course, is that we live in a society with many other people who also want the most out of life. And these self-interested pursuits come into conflict—like my wanting to steal the Porsche and Jim wanting to keep it. If all persons vigorously pursued their own self-interest without regard for the interests of others, society would be a horrible place to live. If we want to live in a society where there is a reasonable chance to live the "good life," then we need to think of a principle that limits the self-interested pursuits of each to make society a better place for all. Utilitarianism asks us to limit our self-interested pursuits by acting in such a way as to maximize the net well-being of everyone affected by our actions. Utilitarianism does not demand total self-sacrifice, however. If everyone acts according to utilitarianism, then our collective interests are promoted—including our own self-interest, we would hope.

The above sort of reasoning motivated the utilitarian theorists we will be studying. Contemporary utilitarianism began in nineteenth-century England (Bentham, Mill, and Sidgwick are from that period) as a social reform movement. As the utilitarians saw it, moral thinking in their society was a muddled affair at best. Specifically, the utilitarians saw two major problems with the sort of morality their society had inherited. First, some "moral" dictums actually made society a worse place to live than if there were no such dictums or if there were some alternative principles adopted. Highly restrictive, Victorian sexual morality is an example where people would be better off without "moral" intervention. Severe penal practices, discussed by Jeremy Bentham, is another case where an alternative policy would better serve society as a whole. Second, other rules, while generally acceptable, were too inflexible to account for various circumstances. People tend to think that lying, promise breaking, and killing are always wrong. However, the utilitarians hold, we are mistaken if we believe these principles are absolute. Lying is generally wrong, but lying to an enemy in time of war may be the right thing to do. Breaking a promise is generally wrong, but canceling a dinner date to help a seriously ill friend should be an exception to the rule. These examples suggested a couple of things to the utilitarian. Lying, promise breaking, and killing are not wrong in themselves, but they are generally wrong because they cause more harm than good. And, the reason we make the exceptions to the general guidelines is that in some cases lying, promise breaking, and so on, cause more good than harm. If this analysis is correct, then what seems to be at the heart of moral reasoning is just the utilitarian principle of maximizing utility.

There is a technical way to describe the difference between utilitarianism and the sort of moral theory that the utilitarians wish to replace. Utilitarianism is a "consequentialist" theory. It judges the moral worth of actions by the effects they have on the well-being of persons. As it is sometimes said, utilitarianism is a "forward-looking" theory; it looks to see where an action will lead. This contrasts with an ethical theory that regards certain act-types (lying, promise keeping, or killing) as right, wrong or indifferent *in themselves*—regardless of the consequences. We consider a version of such a nonconsequentialist theory in the next chapter. A distinction between consequentialist and nonconsequentialist theories is a simple way to begin to place utilitarianism. However, it should be noted that everyone is happy with such a stark distinction. It is not always easy to distinguish an action "in itself" from the consequences that action produces. Consider the case "Jane beat up on Bill, giving him a black eye so he couldn't go to the dance."

Which is the action and which is the consequence? It is tempting to say the "beating up" is the action while "getting a black eye" and "not going to the dance" are the consequences of the action. But couldn't we also describe the situation as "Jane beating up Bill by giving him a black eye" with "not going to the dance" as the consequence? Or even this: "Jane bringing her fists in contact with Jim's face" with the consequences that "Jim was beaten up," "Jim's eye was blackened," and "Jim couldn't go to the dance." We need only note here that the distinction between consequentialist and nonconsequentialist theories may not be as easy to make as it seems.

While the above is a brief history of the utilitarian movement, it would be misleading to think that utilitarianism is some relic of the past. There are a large number of contemporary philosophers who count themselves as utilitarians and continue to refine the basic theory. But neither should we think of utilitarian reasoning as exclusive to professional philosophers. As our popular reading illustrates, utilitarianism is part of the way nonphilosophers think about real-life moral issues. Ernest Van Den Haag uses utilitarian reasoning to justify capital punishment. Van Den Haag claims that capital punishment does not actually conflict with our usual (nonconsequentialist) notion of "just punishment." Even if it did conflict, however, Van Den Haag argues that there is yet a compelling reason to accept capital punishment. It is morally proper to execute people for certain high crimes (typically extraordinary cases of first-degree murder) since the positive utility of deterring crime outweighs the negative utility of taking the life of the criminal. To be sure, not everyone (not even every utilitarian) agrees with Van Den Haag that capital punishment is so effective as a deterrent that this benefit offsets its negative effects. The point here, however, is that arguments for and against capital punishment are often utilitarian in nature. They are arguments concerning whether the good effects of capital punishment outweigh its bad effects. This is utilitarian reasoning.

Even if we agree that there is something compelling about the claim that actions are right the extent to which they promote the general good, we need to do some close philosophical work on the utilitarian principle. As it stands, it is far too vague. For example, we do not know what the utilitarian principle "promote the general good" means unless we know what counts as "good." From our readings we see that utilitarians disagree about what constitutes the good life. Jeremy Bentham holds that the only good for people is pleasure (or the absence of pain). This theory is called *hedonistic utilitarianism* from the Greek term for pleasure. According to Bentham, then, an action is right if it produces more pleasure (or less pain) than any alternative action we could perform. And as such, maximizing utility is maximizing the total amount of pleasure (the amount of pleasure for each person multiplied by the number of persons).

However, John Stuart Mill criticizes Bentham's hedonistic utilitarianism on the grounds that Bentham only compared pleasures by their quantity (primarily intensity and duration), ignoring differences in quality. Eating ice cream cones may give greater pleasure than reading a good novel or seeing a film, but the latter makes us "happier" because the quality of pleasure is higher. Accordingly, Mill argues that we should formulate utilitarianism as maximizing the total amount of "happiness" where happiness takes into account the fact that some pleasures are qualitatively better than others. This form is called *eudaimonistic utilitarianism,* again from the Greek term for happiness.

Yet, there is a disadvantage to Mill's theory that Henry Sidgwick points out. It seems a reasonable task to compute a sum total of utility if we are adding up units of the same sort of thing (qualitatively identical "pleasures"). If there are qualitative differences between pleasures, however, it is unclear how to compare one to another in order to compute net utility. How do we figure the net utility of an action that, for example, has the effects of depriving two persons of the pleasure of an ice cream cone and giving one person the pleasure of attending a film— assuming qualitative differences between the two pleasures? Isn't this like trying to compare apples with oranges?

These are the two main ways of specifying the "good" that we are obligated to maximize, but there are other candidates. In the final reading Tziporah Kasachkoff argues for what is called *ideal utilitarianism.* Following the twentieth-century English philosopher G. E. Moore, Kasachkoff favors a version of utilitarianism where "goodness" is defined in terms of various objects, states of affairs, or experiences that have their own special "intrinsic" value (something has intrinsic value if it is considered good for its own sake). On this theory there is not a single commodity like pleasure or happiness that is exclusively good, but rather all sorts of things have "intrinsic value" and make up part of the good life. To be sure, pleasure and happiness are intrinsic values, but, the ideal utilitarian holds, there are others. For example, one could argue that the excitement of scientific discovery gives neither pleasure nor happiness, but is nonetheless a valuable experience in its own right.

There is considerable disagreement among utilitarians over the notion of good, but there are other differences as well. Classical utilitarianism talks about the rightness of *acts* (their rightness depends upon their consequences). This version of utilitarianism usually goes by the name *act utilitarianism* (although J. J. C. Smart uses the tag *extreme utilitarianism*). Act utilitarianism requires us to evaluate the consequences of each of our actions in order to see if they maximize utility in their specific circumstances. Some contemporary utilitarians, however, have been dissatisfied with this way of stating the theory and have proposed an alternative—*rule utilitarianism* (or what Smart calls *restricted utilitarianism*). Generally speaking, a rule utilitarian holds that rightness (or wrongness) of an action is determined by whether it conforms (or fails to conform) to some rule—where the rule, not the specific act, is justified on utilitarian grounds. For example, we can justify a rule against theft on the grounds that were the rule to be adopted (or generally obeyed), more net utility would be produced than were any alternative rule governing property use adopted. A specific act of theft, according to the rule utilitarian, should be judged by whether it conforms to the rule that maximizes utility, not whether the single action is maximizing. Typically act and rule utilitarianism will give us the same answers in specific cases. For example, both would tell me not to steal Jim's Porsche—the particular act does not maximize utility and it does not conform to a maximizing rule (like don't steal). Presumably, however, there will be cases where the two diverge. Act utilitarianism might license a public official to lie about foreign policy if the lie promotes the larger interests of the country. Assuming rule utilitarianism would support a rule against lying generally, however, lying would be wrong even in the circumstances described.

There are various reasons why rule utilitarianism has been thought a better moral theory than act utilitarianism. Act utilitarianism, it is sometimes charged, is much too cumbersome to use. Instead of having some general guidelines to make decisions about what to do, we must calculate the consequences of *each* act *every time* we do it. The calculations can be quite complex since we must judge our actions in terms of the utility of everyone affected, even people in the distant future. Because the calculations are so complex, there is a considerable chance that people will make so many mistakes that general utility will suffer.

Beyond the practical problems for act utilitarianism, however, there is something morally unsavory about the theory. Consider the so-called "free rider" problem discussed by Smart. Assume we live in a city with law-abiding, public-spirited people and our city happens to be in the middle of a bad drought. The situation has become so worrisome that the city council has passed severe water-use restrictions. Let's say I'm a dedicated act utilitarian who would dearly love to water his lawn, wash his car, and take long showers. According to act utilitarianism, would it be wrong for me to violate the restrictions and use the water? I know that most of the townspeople will obey the restrictions and because they will obey, more than enough water will be conserved to cope with the drought. I also know that there is only a small chance of my being punished for violating the restrictions since restrictions are not vigorously enforced. Of course, my well being would be considerably improved were I to use as much water as I wished. Thus, it would seem that according to act utilitarianism not only would it be permissible to violate the restrictions; it would actually be my duty. My violating the restrictions would result in more net utility than my obeying them since none of the other townspeople would be worse off and I would be considerably better off.

The point of this example is that it seems wrong to use all the water we want when our neighbors are sacrificing so much. It counts against a moral theory to tell us that such an action is no less than our moral duty. The rule utilitarian position tries to avoid this problem. The rule, "obey the water restrictions" has more utility than the rule "don't obey the water restrictions"; that is, obeying water restrictions better provides for social welfare than not doing so. Since the rule utilitarian holds that we ought to act according to utilitarianly optimal rules, then each of us should obey the restrictions. "Free rider" problems seem to disappear.

The considerations mentioned above underlie the rule utilitarian position advocated, in different forms, by R. B. Brandt and Tziporah Kasachkoff in the readings. But not all contemporary utilitarians have been converted to rule utilitarianism. J. J. C. Smart argues that act utilitarianism is still a better theory than rule utilitarianism. He claims that the differences between the two theories are not nearly as extreme as many have thought, especially when the act utilitarian takes into account all the indirect and long-range effects of his actions. Smart also goes on to argue that when there are legitimate differences between the two theories, act utilitarianism gives the better advice.

The debate between act and rule utilitarians is something of a family quarrel since despite their differences both are still utilitarians. Criticisms of the broad utilitarian theory still exist, however, regardless of subtle differences in formulation. Perhaps the most long-standing criticism of the theory concerns the apparent conflict between the principle of utilitarianism and a common sense notion of justice. The criticism is usually directed against act utilitarianism, but, if Kasachkoff is correct, it applies to most versions of rule utilitarianism as well.

In the example above it seems unfair or unjust that one person gets to use all the water he or she wants while the rest of us must conserve. Utilitarianism seems to want us to act unjustly. The utilitarian seeks to maximize total utility—to get the largest amount of good. Notice, though, that the principle doesn't say anything about how the good is to be distributed among the people in the society. Let's say you are a parent deciding how to distribute four pieces of candy to four children. There are a number of ways to do this, but we can restrict ourselves to the extreme alternatives. You could give one piece to each child or four pieces to one child and none to the others. It may well be that from a utilitarian standpoint it makes no difference which alternative you choose. The egalitarian alternative yields four instances of moderate happiness. The nonegalitarian result yields one case of great happiness and three cases of mild to moderate unhappiness (the extent of the unhappiness may depend upon whether the "deprived" children know how the candy is being distributed). If the net utility is the same in each case, the utilitarian must say that there is no moral difference between the alternatives. There is a difference, however—the first alternative conforms to our sense of justice and the second does not.

There have been a number of utilitarian responses to the problem of justice. Mill and Sidgwick, in the selections that follow, attempt to show that despite appearances, utilitarianism squares with common-sense notions of morality such as justice. And at least it must be admitted that utilitarianism incorporates one element thought crucial to justice, namely, the idea of impartiality. A utilitarian calculation is impartial because, to use Bentham's phrase, "everyone counts as one and no more than one." Everyone's interests are given equal consideration when computing the net utility of an action—no one's well-being is more important than anyone else's. However, even if this is so, it does not seem enough to reconcile utilitarianism with justice. The examples above are all consistent with the slogan "everyone counts for one" and yet at odds with our notion of justice.

There are other responses utilitarians can make. They can argue that for any alleged case where the utilitarian result appears to conflict with justice, we have failed to consider all the relevant consequences of our actions. For instance, in the candy example, we have not considered the long-range (negative) effects that such unequal treatment may have on the children who are deprived. In short, one utilitarian defense is to argue that for any real-life cases where the issue of justice is involved, common-sense justice and the principle of utilitarianism give the same answer.

Tziporah Kasachkoff in the final selection reviews the usual solutions to the problem of justice and finds them wanting. In the place of classical utilitarianism Kasachkoff pursues a kind of ideal utilitarianism. According to Kasachkoff's version of ideal utilitarianism, our goal should be to maximize the total amount of "intrinsic values." Assuming that justice has intrinsic value, then justice is part of the utilitarian goal, not something in competition with it. For Kasachkoff, then, justice is one of the "goods" that a utilitarian should promote. It is arguable, however, whether Kasachkoff has solved the problem of justice within utilitarian theory or offered a theory not exclusively utilitarian. A general way to stage utilitarianism is to say that moral goodness consists in maximizing nonmoral goodness (things people find to be useful for the "good life," independent of their notions of right and wrong). It is the nonmoral good of each individual, their "well-being" as we have been calling it, that is the basis of our utilitarian calculation. However, Kasachkoff's ideal utilitarianism says something different. The theory actually combines classical utilitarianism (maximizing nonmoral goods) with another *moral* value (justice). Perhaps this is a more acceptable theory, but it begins to stray from classical utilitarianism.

Hedonistic Utilitarianism

Jeremy Bentham

OF THE PRINCIPLE OF UTILITY

I. Nature has placed mankind under the governance of two sovereign masters, *pain* and *pleasure*. It is for them alone to point out what we ought to do, as well as to determine what we shall do. On the one hand the standard of right and wrong, on the other the chain of causes and effects, are fastened to their throne. They govern us in all we do, in all we say, in all we think: every effort we can make to throw off our subjection, will serve but to demonstrate and confirm it. In words a man may pretend to abjure their empire: but in reality he will remain subject to it all the while. The *principle of utility*[1] recognises this subjection, and assumes it for the foundation of that system, the object of which is to rear the fabric of felicity by the hands of reason and of law. Systems which attempt to question it, deal in sounds instead of sense, in caprice instead of reason, in darkness instead of light.

But enough of metaphor and declamation: it is not by such means that moral science is to be improved.

II. The principle of utility is the foundation of the present work: it will be proper therefore at the outset to give an explicit and determinate account of what is meant by it. By the principle[2] of utility is meant that principle which approves or disapproves of every action whatsoever, according to the tendency which it appears to have to augment or diminish the happiness of the party whose interest is in question: or, what is the same thing in other words, to promote or to oppose that happiness. I say

From Jeremy Bentham, Chapters I, IV, and XIII from *An Introduction to the Principles of Morals and Legislation* (London 1789, revised edition 1923).

[1]Note by the Author, July 1822.

To this denomination has of late been added, or substituted, by the *greatest happiness* or *greatest felicity* principle: this for shortness, instead of saying at length *that principle* which states the greatest happiness of all those whose interest is in question, as being the right and proper, and only right and proper and universally desirable, end of human action: of human action in every situation, and in particular in that of a functionary or set of functionaries exercising the powers of Government. The word *utility* does not so clearly point to the ideas of *pleasure* and *pain* as the words *happiness* and *felicity* do; nor does it lead us to the consideration of the *number,* of the interests affected; to the *number,* as being circumstance, which contributes, in the largest proportion, to the formation of the standard here in question; the *standard of right and wrong,* by which alone the propriety of human conduct, in every situation, can with propriety be tried. This want of a sufficiently manifest connexion between the ideas of *happiness* and *pleasure* on the one hand, and the idea of *utility* on the other, I have every now and then found operating, and with but too much efficiency, as a bar to the acceptance, that might otherwise have been given, to this principle.

[2]The word principle is derived from the Latin *principium*: which seems to be compounded of the two words *primus,* first, or chief, and *cipium,* a termination which seems to be derived from *capio,* to take, as in *mancipium, municipium;* to which are analogous, *auceps, forceps,* and others. It is a term of very vague and very extensive signification: it is applied to any thing which is conceived to serve as a foundation or beginning to any series of operations: in some cases, of physical operations; but of mental operations in the present case.

The principle here in question may be taken for an act of the mind; a sentiment; a sentiment of approbation; a sentiment which, when applied to an action, approves of its utility, as that quality of it by which the measure of approbation or disapprobation bestowed upon it ought to be governed.

of every action whatsoever; and therefore not only of every action of a private individual, but of every measure of government.

III. By utility is meant that property in any object, whereby it tends to produce benefit, advantage, pleasure, good, or happiness (all this in the present case comes to the same thing) or (what comes again to the same thing) to prevent the happening of mischief, pain, evil, or unhappiness to the party whose interest is considered: if that party be the community in general, then the happiness of the community: if a particular individual, then the happiness of that individual.

IV. The interest of the community is one of the most general expressions that can occur in the phraseology of morals: no wonder that the meaning of it is often lost. When it has a meaning, it is this. The community is a fictitious *body,* composed of the individual persons who are considered as constituting as it were its *members.* The interest of the community then is, what?—the sum of the interests of the several members who compose it.

V. It is in vain to talk of the interest of the community, without understanding what is the interest of the individual.[3] A thing is said to promote the interest, or to be *for* the interest, of an individual, when it tends to add to the sum total of his pleasures: or, what comes to the same thing, to diminish the sum total of his pain.

VI. An action then may be said to be comformable to the principle of utility, or, for shortness sake, to utility (meaning with respect to the community at large) when the tendency it has to augment the happiness of the community is greater than any it has to diminish it.

VII. A measure of government (which is but a particular kind of action, performed by a particular person or persons) may be said to be comformable to or dictated by the principle of utility, when in like manner the tendency which it has to augment the happiness of the community is greater than any which it has to diminish it.

VIII. When an action, or in particular a measure of government, is supposed by a man to be comformable to the principle of utility, it may be convenient, for the purposes of discourse, to imagine a kind of law or dictate, called a law or dictate of utility: and to speak of the action in question, as being comformable to such law or dictate.

IX. A man may be said to be a partizan of the principle of utility, when the approbation or disapprobation he annexes to any action, or to any measure, is determined by and proportioned to the tendency which he conceives it to have to augment or to diminish the happiness of the community: or in other words, to its conformity or uncomformity to the laws or dictates of utility.

X. Of an action that is conformable to the principle of utility one may always say either that it is one that ought to be done, or at least that it is not one that ought not to be done. One may say also, that it is right it should be done; at least that it is not wrong it should be done; that it is a right action; at least that it is not a wrong action. When thus interpreted, the words *ought,* and *right* and *wrong,* and others of that stamp, have a meaning: when otherwise, they have none.

XI. Has the rectitude of this principle been ever formally contested? It should seem that it had, by those who have not known what they have been meaning. Is it susceptible of any direct proof? it should seem not: for that which is used to prove every thing else, cannot itself be proved: a chain of proofs must have their commencement somewhere. To give such proof is as impossible as it is needless.

---

[3]Interest is one of those words, which not having any superior *genus,* cannot in the ordinary way be defined.

XII. Not that there is or ever has been that human creature breathing, however stupid or perverse, who has not on many, perhaps on most occasions of his life, deferred to it. By the natural constitution of the human frame, on most occasions of their lives men in general embrace this principle, without thinking of it: if not for the ordering of their own actions, yet for the trying of their own actions, as well as those of other men. There have been, at the same time, not many, perhaps, even of the most intelligent, who have been disposed to embrace it purely and without reserve. There are even few who have not taken some occasion or other to quarrel with it, either on account of their not understanding always how to apply it, or on account of some prejudice or other which they were afraid to examine into, or could not bear to part with. For such is the stuff that man is made of: in principle and in practice, in a right track and in a wrong one, the rarest of all human qualities is consistency.

XIII. When a man attempts to combat the principle of utility, it is with reasons drawn, without his being aware of it, from that very principle itself.[4] His arguments, if they prove any thing, prove not that the principle is *wrong,* but that, according to the applications he supposes to be made of it, it is *misapplied.* Is it possible for a man to move the earth? Yes; but he must first find out another earth to stand upon.

XIV. To disprove the propriety of it by arguments is impossible; but, from the causes that have been mentioned, or from some confused or partial view of it, a man may happen to be disposed not to relish it. Where this is the case, if he thinks the settling of his opinions on such a subject worth the trouble, let him take the following steps, and at length, perhaps, he may come to reconcile himself to it.

1. Let him settle with himself, whether he would wish to discard this principle

---

[4]"The principle of utility (I have heard it said) is a dangerous principle: it is dangerous on certain occasions to consult it." This is as much as to say, what? that it is not consonant to utility, to consult utility: in short, that it is *not* consulting it, to consult it.

Addition by the Author, July 1822.

Not long after the publication of the Fragment on Government, anno 1776, in which, in the character of an all-comprehensive and all-commanding principle, the principle of *utility* was brought to view, one person by whom observation to the above effect was made was *Alexander Wedderburn*, at that time Attorney or Solicitor General, afterwards successively Chief Justice of the Common Pleas, and Chancellor of England, under the successive titles of Lord Loughborough and Earl of Rosslyn. It was made—not indeed in my hearing, but in the hearing of a person by whom it was almost immediately communicated to me. So far from being self-contradictory, it was a shrewd and perfectly true one. By that distinguished functionary, the state of the Government was thoroughly understood: by the obscure individual, at that time not so much as supposed to be so: his disquisitions had not been as yet applied, with any thing like a comprehensive view, to the field of Constitutional Law, nor therefore to those features of the English Government, by which the greatest happiness of the ruling *one* with *or* without that of a favoured few, are now so plainly seen to be the only ends to which the course of it has at any time been directed. The *principle of utility* was an appellative, at that time employed—employed by me, as it had been by others, to design that which, in a more perspicuous and instructive manner, may as above be designated by the name of the *greatest happiness principle.* "This principle (said Wedderburn) is a dangerous one." Saying so, he said that which, to a certain extent, is strictly true: a principle, which lays down, as the only *right* and justifiable end of Government, the greatest happiness of the greatest number—how can it be denied to be a dangerous one? dangerous it unquestionably is, to every government which has for its *actual* end or orbject, the greatest number of others, whom it is matter of pleasure or accommodation to him to admit, each of them, to a share in the concern, on the footing of so many junior partners. *Dangerous* it therefore really was, to the interest—the sinister interest—of all those functionaries, himself included, whose interest it was, to maximize delay, vexation, and expense, in judicial and other modes of procedure, for the sake of the profit, extractible out of the expense. In a Government which had for its end in view the greatest happiness of the greatest number. Alexander Wedderburn might have been Attorney General and then Chancellor; but he would not have been Attorney General with £15,000 a year, nor Chancellor, with a peerage with a veto upon all justice, with £25,000 a year, and with 500 sinecures at his disposal, under the name of Ecclesiastical Benefices, besides *et cœteras.*

altogether; if so, let him consider what it is that all his reasonings (in matters of politics especially) can amount to?

2. If he would, let him settle with himself, whether he would judge and act without any principle, or whether there is any other he would judge and act by?

3. If there be, let him examine and satisfy himself whether the principle he thinks he has found is really any separate intelligible principle; or whether it be not a mere principle in words, a kind of phrase, which at bottom expresses neither more nor less than the mere averment of his own unfounded sentiments; that is, what in another person he might be apt to call caprice?

4. If he is inclined to think that his own approbation or disapprobation, annexed to the idea of an act, without any regard to its consequences, is a sufficient foundation for him to judge and act upon, let him ask himself whether his sentiment is to be a standard of right and wrong, with respect to every other man, or whether every man's sentiment has the same privilege of being a standard to itself?

5. In the first case, let him ask himself whether his principle is not despotical, and hostile to all the rest of human race?

6. In the second case, whether it is not anarchical, and whether at this rate there are not as many different standards of right and wrong as there are men? and whether even to the same man, the same thing, which is right today, may not (without the least change in its nature) be wrong tomorrow? and whether the same thing is not right and wrong in the same place at the same time? and in either case, whether all argument is not at an end? and whether, when two men have said, "I like this," and "I don't like it," they can (upon such a principle) hae any thing more to say?

7. If he should have said to himself, No: for that the sentiment which he proposes as a standard must be grounded on reflection, let him say on what particulars the reflection is to turn? if on particulars having relation to the utility of the act, then let him say whether this is not deserting his own principle, and borrowing assistance from that very one in opposition to which he sets it up: or if not on those particulars, on what other particulars?

8. If he should be for compounding the matter, and adopting his own principle in part, and the principle of utility in part, let him say how far he will adopt it?

9. When he has settled with himself where he will stop, then let him ask himself how he justifies to himself the adopting it so far? and why he will not adopt it any farther?

10. Admitting any other principle than the principle of utility to be a right principle, a principle that it is right for a man to pursue; admitting (what is not true) that the word *right* can have a meaning without reference to utility, let him say whether there is any such thing as a *motive* that man can have to pursue the dictates of it: if there is, let him say what that motive is, and how it is to be distinguished from those which enforce the dictates of utility: if not, then lastly let him say what it is this other principle can be good for? . . .

VALUE OF A LOT OF PLEASURE OR PAIN, HOW TO BE MEASURED

I. Pleasures then, and the avoidance of pains, are the *ends* which the legislator has in view: it behooves him therefore to understand their *value*. Pleasures and pains are the *instruments* he has to work with: it behooves him therefore to understand their force, which is again, in other words, their value.

II. To a person considered *by himself,* the value of a pleasure or pain considered *by itself,* will be greater or less, according to the four following circumstances:[5]

1. Its *intensity*.
2. Its *duration*.
3. Its *certainty* or *uncertainty*.
4. Its *propinquity* or *remoteness*.

III. These are the circumstances which are to be considered in estimating a pleasure or a pain considered each of them by itself. But when the value of any pleasure or pain is considered for the purpose of estimating the tendency of any *act* by which it is produced, there are two other circumstances to be taken into the account; these are,

5. Its *fecundity,* or the chance it has of being followed by sensations of the *same* kind: that is, pleasures, if it be a pleasure: pains, if it be a pain.

6. Its *purity,* or the chance it has of *not* being followed by sensations of the *opposite* kind: that is, pains, if it be a pleasure: pleasures, it if be a pain.

These two last, however, are in strictness scarcely to be deemed properties of pleasure or the pain itself; they are not, therefore, in strictness to be taken into the account of the value of that pleasure or pain. They are in strictness to be deemed properties only of the act, or other event, by which such pleasure or pain has been produced; and accordingly are only to be taken into the account of the tendency of such act or such event.

IV. To a *number* of persons, with reference to each of whom the value of a pleasure or a pain is considered, it will be greater or less, according to seven circumstances: to wit, the six preceding ones; *viz.*

1. Its *intensity*.
2. Its *duration*.
3. Its *certainty* or *uncertainty*.
4. Its *propinquity* or *remoteness*.
5. Its *fecundity*.
6. Its *purity*.

And one other; to wit:

7. Its *extent;* that is, the number of persons to whom it *extends;* or (in other words) who are affected by it.

[5]These circumstances have since been denominated *elements* or *dimensions* of *value* in a pleasure or a pain.

Not long after the publication of the first edition, the following memoriter verses were framed, in the view of lodging more effectually, in the memory, these points, on which the whole fabric of morals and legislation may be seen to rest.

Intense, long, certain, speedy, fruitful, pure—
Such marks in *pleasure* and in *pains* endure.
Such pleasures seek of *private* be thy end:
If it be *public,* wide let them *extend.*
Such *pains* avoid, whichever be thy view:
If pains *must* come, let them *extend* to few.

V. To take an exact account then of the general tendency of any act, by which the interests of a community are affected, proceed as follows. Begin with any one person of those whose interests seem most immediately to be affected by it: and take an account,

1. Of the value of each distinguishable *pleasure* which appears to be produced by it in the *first* instance.

2. Of the value of each *pain* which appears to be produced by it in the *first* instance.

3. Of the value of each pleasure which appears to be produced by it *after* the first. This constitutes the *fecundity* of the first *pleasure* and the *impurity* of the first *pain*.

4. Of the value of each *pain* which appears to be produced by it after the first. This constitutes the *fecundity* of the first *pain,* and the *impurity* of the first pleasure.

5. Sum up all the values of all the *pleasures* on the one side, and those of all the pains on the other. The balance, if it be on the side of pleasure, will give the *good* tendency of the act upon the whole, with respect to the interests of that *individual* person; if on the side of pain, the *bad* tendency of it upon the whole.

6. Take an account of the *number* of persons whose interests appear to be concerned; and repeat the above process with respect to each. *Sum up* the numbers expressive of the degrees of *good* tendency, which the act has, with respect to each individual, in regard to whom the tendency of it is *good* upon the whole: do this again with respect to each individual, in regard to whom the tendency of it is *good* upon the whole: do this again with respect to each individual, in regard to whom the tendency of it is *bad* upon the whole. Take the *balance;* which, if on the side of *pleasure,* will give the general *good tendency* of the act, with respect to the total number or community of individuals concerned; if on the side of pain, the general *evil tendency,* with respect to the same community.

VI. It is not to be expected that this process should be strictly pursued previously to every moral judgment, or to every legislative or judicial operation. It may, however, be always kept in view: and as near as the process actually pursued on these occasions approaches to it, so near will such process approach to the character of an exact one.

VII. The same process is alike applicable to pleasure and pain, in whatever shape they appear: and by whatever denomination they are distinguished: to pleasure, whether it be called *good* (which is properly the cause or instrument of pleasure), or *profit* (which is distant pleasure, or the cause or instrument of distant pleasure), or *convenience,* or *advantage, benefit, emolument, happiness,* and so forth: to pain, whether it be called *evil* (which corresponds to *good*) or *mischief,* or *inconvenience,* or *disadvantage,* or *loss,* or *unhappiness,* and so forth.

VIII. Nor is this a novel and unwarranted, any more than it is a useless theory. In all this there is nothing but what the practice of mankind, wheresoever they have a clear view of their own interest, is perfectly conformable to. An article of property, an estate in land, for instance, is valuable, on what account? On account of the pleasures of all kinds which it enables a man to produce, and what comes to the same thing the pains of all kinds which it enables him to avert. But the value of such an article of property is universally understood to rise or fall according to the length or shortness of the time which a man has in it: the certainty or uncertainty of its coming into possession: and the nearness or remoteness of the time at which, if at all, it is to come into possession. As to the *intensity* of the pleasures which a man may derive from it, this is never thought of, because it depends upon the use which each particular person may come to make of it; which cannot be estimated till the particular pleasures he may come to derive from it, or the particular pains he may come to exclude by means of it, are brought to view. For the same reason, neither does he think of the *fecundity* or *purity* of those pleasures. . . .

CASES UNMEET FOR PUNISHMENT

1. General View of Cases Unmeet for Punishment

I. The general object which all laws have, or ought to have, in common, is to augment the total happiness of the community; and therefore, in the first place, to exclude, as far as may be, every thing that tends to subtract from that happiness: in other words, to exclude mischief.

II. But all punishment is mischief: all punishment in itself evil. Upon the principle of utility, if it ought at all to be admitted, it ought only to be admitted in as far as it promises to exclude some greater evil.[6]

III. It is plain, therefore, that in the following cases punishment ought not to be inflicted.

1. Where it is *groundless:* where there is no mischief for it to prevent; the act not being mischievous upon the whole.

2. Where it must be *inefficacious:* where it cannot act so as to prevent the mischief.

3. Where it is *unprofitable,* or too *expensive:* where the mischief it would produce would be greater than what it prevented.

4. Where it is *needless:* where the mischief may be prevented, or cease of itself, without it: that is, at a cheaper rate.

---

[6]What follows, relative to the subject of punishment, ought regularly to be preceded by a distinct chapter on the ends of punishment. But having little to say on that particular branch of the subject, which has not been said before, it seemed better, in a work, which will at any rate be but too voluminous, to omit this title, reserving it for another, hereafter to be published, entitled *The Theory of Punishment*. To the same work I must refer the analysis of the several possible modes of punishment, a particular and minute examination of the nature of each, and of its advantages and disadvantages, and various other disquisitions, which did not seem absolutely necessary to be inserted here. A very few words, however, concerning the *ends* of punishment, can scarcely be dispensed with.

The immediate principal end of punishment is to control action. This action is either that of the offender, or of others: that of the offender it controls by its influence, either on his will, in which case it is said to operate in the way of *reformation;* or on his physical power, in which case it is said to operate by *disablement:* that of others it can influence no otherwise than by its influence over their wills; in which case it is said to operate in the way of *example.* A kind of collateral end, which it has a natural tendency to answer, is that of affording a pleasure or satisfaction to the party injured, where there is one, and, in general, to parties whose ill-will, whether on a self-regarding account, or on the account of sympathy or antipathy, has been excited by the offence. This purpose, as far as it can be answered *gratis,* is a beneficial one. But no punishment ought to be allotted merely to this purpose, because (setting aside its effects in the way of control) no such pleasure is ever produced by punishment as can be equivalent to the pain. The punishment, however, which is alloted to the other purpose, ought, as far as it can be done without expense, to be accommodated to this. Satisfaction thus administered to a party injured, in the shape of a dissocial pleasure, may be styled a vindictive satisfaction or compensation: as a compensation, administered in the shape of a self-regarding profit, or stock of pleasure, may be styled a lucrative one. Example is the most important end of all, in proportion as the *number* of the persons under temptation to offend is to *one.*

2. Cases in Which Punishment Is Groundless

These are,

IV. 1. Where there has never been any mischief: where no mischief has been produced to any body by the act in question. Of this number are those in which the act was such as might, on some occasions, be mischievous or disagreeable, but the person whose interest it concerns gave his *consent* to the performance of it. This consent, provided it be free, and fairly obtained, is the best proof that can be produced, that, to the person who gives it, no mischief, at least no immediate mischief, upon the whole, is done. For no man can be so good a judge as the man himself, what it is gives him pleasure or displeasure.

V. 2. Where the mischief was *outweighed:* although a mischief was produced by that act, yet the same act was necessary to the production of a benefit which was of greater value than the mischief. This may be the case with any thing that is done in the way of precaution against instant calamity, as also with any thing that is done in the exercise of the several sorts of powers necessary to be established in every community, to wit, domestic, judicial, military, and supreme.

VI. 3. Where there is a certainty of an adequate compensation: and that in all cases where the offence can be committed. This supposes two things: 1. That the offence is such as admits of an adequate compensation: 2. That such a compensation is sure to be forthcoming. Of these suppositions, the latter will be found to be a merely ideal one: a supposition that cannot, in the university here given to it, be verified by fact. It cannot, therefore, in practice, be numbered amongst the grounds of absolute impunity. It may, however, be admitted as a ground for an abatement of that punishment, which other considerations, standing by themselves, would seem to dictate.[7]

3. Cases in Which Punishment Must Be Inefficacious

These are,

VII. 1. Where the penal provision is *not established* until after the act is done. Such are the cases. 1. Of an *ex-post-facto* law; where the legislator himself appoints not a punishment till after the act is done. 2. Of a sentence beyond the law; where the judge, of his own authority, appoints a punishment which the legislator had not appointed.

VIII. 2. Where the penal provision, though established, is *not conveyed* to the notice of the person on whom it seems intended that it should operate. Such is the case where the law has omitted to employ any of the expedients which are necessary, to make sure that every person whatsoever, who is within the reach of the law, be apprized of all the cases whatsoever, in which (being in the station of life he is in) he can be subjected to the penalties of the law.

IX. 3. Where the penal provision, though it were conveyed to a man's notice, *could produce no effect* on him, with respect to the preventing him from engaging in any act of the *sort* in question. Such is the case, 1. In extreme *infancy;* where a man has not yet attained that state or disposition of mind in which the prospect of evils so

---

[7]This, for example, seems to have been one ground, at least, of the favour shown by perhaps all systems of laws, to such offenders as stand upon a footing of responsibility: shown, not directly indeed to the persons themselves; but to such offences as none but responsible persons are likely to have the opportunity of engaging in. In particular, this seems to be the reason why embezzlement, in certain cases, has not commonly been punished upon the footing of theft; nor mercantile frauds upon that of common sharping.

distant as those which are held forth by the law, has the effect of influencing his conduct. 2. In *insanity;* where the person, if he has attained to that disposition, has since
been deprived of it through the influence of some permanent though unseen cause.
3. In *intoxication;* where he has been deprived of it by transient influence of a visible
cause: such as the use of wine, or opium, or other drugs, that act in this manner on
the nervous system: which condition is indeed neither more nor less than a temporary
insanity produced by an assignable cause.[8]

X. 4. Where the penal provision (although, being conveyed to the party's notice, it might very well prevent his engaging in acts of the sort in question, provided
he knew that it related to those acts) could not have this effect, with regard to the *individual* act he is about to engage in: to wit, because he knows not that it is of the number of those to which the penal provision relates. This may happen, 1. In the case of
unintentionality; where he intends not to engage, and thereby knows not that he is
about to engage, in the *act* in which eventually he is about to engage. 2. In the case of
unconsciousness; where, although he may know that he is about to engage in the *act*
itself, yet from not knowing all the material *circumstances* attending it, he knows not
of the *tendency* it has to produce that mischief, in contemplation of which it has been
made penal in most instances. 3. In the case of *missupposal;* where, although he may
know of the tendency the act has to produce that degree of mischief, he supposes it,
though mistakenly, to be attended with some circumstance, or set of circumstances,
which, if it had been attended with, it would either not have been productive of that
mischief, or have been productive of such a greater degree of good, as has determined the legislator in such a case not to make it penal.

XI. 5. Where, though the penal clause might exercise a full and prevailing influence, were it to act alone, yet by the *predominant* influence of some opposite cause
upon the will, it must necessarily be ineffectual; because the evil which he sets himself
about to undergo, in the case of his *not* engaging in the act, is so great, that the evil
denounced by the penal clause, in case of his engaging in it, cannot appear greater.
This may happen, 1. In the case of *physical danger;* where the evil is such as appears
likely to be brought about by the unassisted powers of *nature.* 2. In the case of a
threatened mischief; where it is such as appears likely to be brought about through the
intentional and conscious agency of *man.*[9]

---

[8]Notwithstanding what is here said, the cases of infancy and intoxication (as we shall see hereafter) cannot
be looked upon in practice as affording sufficient grounds for absolute impunity. But this is no objection to
the propriety of the rule in point of theory. The ground of the exception is neither more nor less than the
difficulty there is of ascertaining the matter of fact: viz, whether at the requisite point of time the party was
actually in the state in question; that is, whether a given case comes really under the rule. Suppose the matter of fact capable of being perfectly ascertained, without danger or mistake, the impropriety of punishment
would be as indubitable in these cases as in any other.

The reason that is commonly assigned for the establishing an exemption from punishment in favour of
infants, insane persons, and persons under intoxication, is either false in fact, or confusedly expressed. The
phrase is, that the will of these persons concurs not with the act; that they have no vicious will; or, that they
have not the free use of their will. But suppose all this to be true? What is it to the purpose? Nothing: except
in as far as it implies the reason given in the text.

[9]The influences of the *moral* and *religious* sanctions, or, in other words, of the motives of *love of reputation*
and *religion,* are other causes, the force of which may, upon particular occasions, come to be greater than
that of any punishment which the legislator is *able,* or at least which he will *think proper,* to apply. These,
therefore, it will be proper for him to have his eye upon. But the force of these influences is variable and
different in different times and places: the force of the foregoing influences is constant and the same, at all
times and every where. These, therefore, it can never be proper to look upon as safe grounds for establishing absolute impunity: owing (as in the above-mentioned cases of infancy and intoxication) to the impracticability of ascertaining the matter of fact.

XII. 6. Where (though the penal clause may exert a full and prevailing influence over the *will* of the party) yet his *physical faculties* (owing to the predominant influence of some physical cause) are not in a condition to follow the determination of the will: insomuch that the act is absolutely *involuntary*. Such is the case of physical *compulsion* or *restraint,* by whatever means brought about; where the man's hand, for instance, is pushed against some object which his will disposes him *not* too touch; or tied down from touching some object which his will disposes him to touch.

4. Cases Where Punishment Is Unprofitable

These are,

XIII. 1. Where, on the one hand, the nature of the offence, on the other hand, that of the punishment, are, *in the ordinary state of things,* such, that when compared together, the evil of the latter will turn out to be greater than that of the former.

XIV. Now the evil of the punishment divides itself into four branches, by which so many different sets of persons are affected. 1. The evil of *coercion* or *restraint:* or the pain which it gives a man not to be able to do the act, whatever it be, which by the apprehension of the punishment he is deterred from doing. This is felt by those by whom the law is *observed.* 2. The evil of *apprehension:* or the pain which a man, who has exposed himself to punishment, feels at the thoughts of undergoing it. This is felt by those by whom the law has been *broken,* and who feel themselves in *danger* of its being executed upon them. 3. The evil of *sufferance:* or the pain which a man feels, in virtue of the punishment itself, from the time when he begins to undergo it. This is felt by those by whom the law is broken, and upon whom it comes actually to be executed. 4. The pain of sympathy, and the other *derivative* evils resulting to the persons who are in *connection* with the several classes of original sufferers just mentioned. Now of these four lots of evil, the first will be greater or less, according to the nature of the act from which the party is restrained: the second and third according to the nature of the punishment which stands annexed to that offence.

XV. On the other hand, as to the evil of the offence, this will also, of course, be greater or less, according to the nature of each offence. The proportion between the one evil and the other will therefore be different in the case of each particular offence. The cases, therefore, where punishment is unprofitable on this ground, can by no other means be discovered, than by an examination of each particular offence; which is what will be the business of the body of the work.

XVI. 2. Where, although in the *ordinary state* of things, the evil resulting from the punishment is not greater than the benefit which is likely to result from the force with which it operates, during the same space of time, towards the excluding the evil of the offences, yet it may have been rendered so by the influence of some *occasional circumstances*. In the number of these circumstances may be, 1. The multitude of delinquents at a particular juncture; being such as would increase, beyond the ordinary measure, the *quantum* of the second and third lots, and thereby also of a part of the fourth lot, in the evil of the punishment. 2. The extraordinary value of the services of some one delinquent; in the case where the effect of the punishment would be to deprive the community of the benefit of those services. 3. The displeasure of the *people;* that of an indefinite number of the members of the *same* community, in cases where (owing to the influence of some occasional incident) they happen to conceive, that the offence or the offender ought not to be punished at all, or at least ought not to be punished in the way in question. 4. The displeasure of *foreign powers;* that is, of the governing body, or a considerable number of the members of some *foreign* community or communities, with which the community in question is connected.

5. Cases Where Punishment Is Needless

These are,

XVII. 1. Where the purpose of putting an end to the practice may be attained as effectually at a cheaper rate: by instruction, for instance, as well as by terror: by informing the understanding, as well as by exercising an immediate influence on the will. This seems to be the case with respect to all those offences which consist in the disseminating pernicious principles in matters of *duty;* of whatever kind the duty be; whether political, or moral, or religious. And this, whether such principles be disseminated *under,* or even *without,* a sincere persuasion of their being beneficial. I say, even *without:* for though in such a case it is not instruction that can prevent the writer from endeavouring to inculcate his principles, yet it may keep the readers from adopting them: without which, his endeavouring to inculcate them will do no harm. In such a case, the sovereign will commonly have little need to take an active part: if it be the interest of *one* individual to inculcate principles that are pernicious, it will as surely be the interest of *other* individuals to expose them. But if the sovereign must needs take a part in the controversy, the pen is the proper weapon to combat error with, not the sword.

Utilitarianism
What Utilitarianism Is

John Stuart Mill

The creed which accepts as the foundation of morals "utility" or the "greatest happiness principle" hold that actions are right in proportion as they tend to promote happiness; wrong as they tend to produce the reverse of happiness. By happiness is intended pleasure and the absence of pain; by unhappiness, pain and the privation of pleasure. To give a clear view of the moral standard set up by the theory, much more requires to be said; in particular, what things it includes in the ideas of pain and pleasure, and to what extent this is left an open question. But these supplementary explanations do not affect the theory of life on which this theory of morality is grounded—namely, that pleasure and freedom from pain are the only things desirable as ends; and that all desirable things (which are as numerous in the utilitarian as in any other scheme) are desirable either for pleasure inherent in themselves or as means to the promotion of pleasure and the prevention of pain.

From John Stuart Mill, *Utilitarianism* (1863), excerpts from Chapters II, IV, and V.

Now such a theory of life excites in many minds, and among them in some of the most estimable in feeling and purpose, inveterate dislike. To suppose that life has (as they express it) no higher end than pleasure—no better and nobler object of desire and pursuit—they designate as utterly mean and groveling, as a doctrine worthy only of swine, to whom the followers of Epicurus were, at a very early period, contemptuously likened; and modern holders of the doctrine are occasionally made the subject of equally polite comparisons by its German, French, and English assailants.

When thus attacked, the Epicureans have always answered that it is not they, but their accusers, who represent human nature in a degrading light, since the accusation supposes human beings to be capable of no pleasures except those of which swine are capable. If this supposition were true, the charge could not be gainsaid, but would then be no longer an imputation; for if the sources of pleasure were precisely the same to human beings and to swine, the rule of life which is good enough for the one would be good enough for the other. The comparison of the Epicurean life to that of beasts is felt as degrading, precisely because a beast's pleasures do not satisfy a human being's conceptions of happiness. Human beings have faculties more elevated than the animal appetites and, when once made conscious of them, do not regard anything as happiness which does not include their gratification. I do not, indeed, consider the Epicureans to have been by any means faultless in drawing out their scheme of consequences from the utilitarian principle. To do this in any sufficient manner, many Stoic, as well as Christian, elements require to be included. But there is no known Epicurean theory of life which does not assign to the pleasures of the intellect, of the feelings and imagination, and of the moral sentiments a much higher value as pleasures than to those of mere sensation. It must be admitted, however, that utilitarian writers in general have placed the superiority of mental over bodily pleasures chiefly in the greater permanency, safety, uncostliness, etc., of the former—that is, in their circumstantial advantages rather than in their intrinsic nature. And on all these points utilitarians have fully proved their case; but they might have taken the other and, as it may be called, higher ground with entire consistency. It is quite compatible with the principle of utility to recognize the fact that some kinds of pleasure are more desirable and more valuable than others. It would be absurd that, while in estimating all other things quality is considered as well as quantity, the estimation of pleasure should be supposed to depend on quantity alone.

If I am asked what I mean by difference of quality in pleasures, or what makes one pleasure more valuable than another, merely as a pleasure, except its being greater in amount, there is but one possible answer. Of two pleasures, if there be one to which all or almost all who have experience of both give a decided preference, irrespective of any feeling of moral obligation to prefer it, that is the more desirable pleasure. If one of the two is, by those who are competently acquainted with both, placed so far above the other that they prefer it, even though knowing it to be attended with a greater amount of discontent, and would not resign it for any quantity of the other pleasure which their nature is capable of, we are justified in ascribing to the preferred enjoyment a superiority in quality so far outweighing quantity as to render it, in comparison, of small account.

Now it is an unquestionable fact that those who are equally acquainted with and equally capable of appreciating and enjoying both do give a most marked preference to the manner of existence which employs their higher faculties. Few human creatures would consent to be changed into any of the lower animals for a promise of the fullest allowance of a beast's pleasures; no intelligent human being would consent to be a

fool, no instructed person would be an ignoramus, no person of feeling and conscience would be selfish and base, even though they should be persuaded that the
fool, the dunce, or the rascal is better satisfied with his lot than they are with theirs.
They would not resign what they possess more than he for the most complete satisfaction of all the desires which they have in common with him. If they ever fancy they
would, it is only in cases of unhappiness so extreme that to escape from it they would
exchange their lot for almost any other, however undesirable in their own eyes. A being of higher faculties requires more to make him happy, is capable probably of more
acute suffering, and certainly accessible to it at more points, than one of an inferior
type; but in spite of these liabilities, he can never really wish to sink into what he feels
to be a lower grade of existence. We may give what explanation we please of this unwillingness; we may attribute it to pride, a name which is given indiscriminately to
some of the most and to some of the least estimable feelings of which mankind are capable; we may refer it to the love of liberty and personal independence, an appeal to
which was with the Stoics one of the most effective means for the inculcation of it; to
the love or power or to the love of excitement, both of which do really enter into and
contribute to it; but its most appropriate appellation is a sense of dignity, which all human beings possess in one form or other, and in some, though by no means in exact,
proportion to their higher faculties, and which is so essential a part of the happiness
of those in whom it is strong that nothing which conflicts with it could be otherwise
than momentarily an object of desire to them. Whoever supposes that this preference
takes place at a sacrifice of happiness—that the superior being, in anything like equal
circumstances, is not happier than the inferior—confounds the two very different
ideas of happiness and content. It is indisputable that the being whose capacities of
enjoyment are low has the greatest chance of having them fully satisfied; and a highly
endowed being will always feel that any happiness which he can look for, as the world
is constituted, is imperfect. But he can learn to bear its imperfections, if they are at all
bearable; and they will not make him envy the being who is indeed unconscious of
the imperfections, but only because he feels not at all the good which those imperfections qualify. It is better to be a human being dissatisfied than a pig satisfied; better to
be Socrates dissatisfied than a fool satisfied. And if the fool, or the pig, are of a different
opinion, it is because they only know their own side of the question. The other party
to the comparison knows both sides.

   It may be objected that many who are capable of the higher pleasures occasionally, under the influence of temptation, postpone them to the lower. But this is quite
compatible with a full appreciation of the intrinsic superiority of the higher. Men often, from infirmity of character, make their election for the nearer good, though they
know it to be the less valuable; and this no less when the choice is between two bodily
pleasures than when it is between bodily and mental. They pursue sensual indul-
gences to the injury of health, though perfectly aware that health is the greater good.
It may be further objected that many who begin with youthful enthusiasm for everything noble, as they advance in years, sink into indolence and selfishness. But I do not
believe that those who undergo this very common change voluntarily choose the
lower description of pleasures in preference to the higher. I believe that, before they
devote themselves exclusively to the one, they have already become incapable of the
other. Capacity for the nobler feelings is in most natures a very tender plant, easily
killed, not only by hostile influences, but by mere want of sustenance; and in the majority of young persons it speedily dies away if the occupations to which their position
in life has devoted them, and the society into which it has thrown them, are not favor-

able to keeping that higher capacity in exercise. Men lose their high aspirations as they lose their intellectual tastes, because they have not time or opportunity for indulging them; and they addict themselves to inferior pleasures, not because they deliberately prefer them, but because they are either the only ones to which they have access or the only ones which they are any longer capable of enjoying. It may be questioned whether anyone who has remained equally susceptible to both classes of pleasures ever knowingly and calmly preferred the lower, though many, in all ages, have broken down in an ineffectual attempt to combine both.

From this verdict of the only competent judges, I apprehend there can be no appeal. On a question which is the best worth having of two pleasures, or which of two modes of existence is the most grateful to the feelings, apart from its moral attributes and from its consequences, the judgment of those who are qualified by knowledge of both, or, if they differ, that of the majority among them, must be admitted as final. And there needs be the less hesitation to accept this judgment respecting the quality of pleasures, since there is no other tribunal to be referred to even on the question of quantity. What means are there of determining which is the acutest of two pains, or the intensest of two pleasurable sensations, except the general suffrage of those who are familiar with both? Neither pains nor pleasures are homogeneous, and pain is always heterogeneous with pleasure. What is there to decide whether a particular pleasure is worth purchasing at the cost of a particular pain, except the feelings and judgment of the experienced? When, therefore, those feelings and judgment declare the pleasures derived from the higher faculties to be preferable *in kind,* apart from the question of intensity, to those of which the animal nature, disjoined from the higher faculties, is susceptible, they are entitled on this subject to the same regard.

I have dwelt on this point as being a necessary part of a perfectly just conception of utility or happiness considered as the directive rule of human conduct. But it is by no means an indispensable condition to the acceptance of the utilitarian standard; for that standard is not the agent's own greatest happiness, but the greatest amount of happiness altogether; and if it may possibly be doubted whether a noble character is always the happier for its nobleness, there can be no doubt that it makes other people happier, and that the world in general is immensely a gainer by it. Utilitarianism, therefore, could only attain its end by the general cultivation of nobleness of character, even if each individual were only benefited by the nobleness of others, and his own, so far as happiness is concerned, were a sheer deduction from the benefit. But the bare enunciation of such an absurdity as this last renders refutation superfluous.

According to the greatest happiness principle, as above explained, the ultimate end, with reference to and for the sake of which all other things are desirable— whether we are considering our own good or that of other people—is an existence exempt as far as possible from pain, and as rich as possible in enjoyments, both in point of quantity and quality; the test of quality and the rule for measuring it against quantity being the preference felt by those who, in their opportunities of experience, to which must be added their habits of self-consciousness and self-observation, are best furnished with the means of comparison. This, being according to the utilitarian opinion the end of human action, is necessarily also the standard of morality, which may accordingly be defined "the rules and precepts for human conduct," by the observance of which an existence such as has been described might be, to the greatest extent possible, secured to all mankind; and not to them only, but, so far as the nature of things admits, to the whole sentient creation. . . .

I must again repeat what the assailants of utilitarianism seldom have the justice to acknowledge, that the happiness which forms the utilitarian standard of what is right in conduct is not the agent's own happiness but that of all concerned. As between his own happiness and that of others, utilitarianism requires him to be as strictly impartial as a disinterested and benevolent spectator. In the golden rule of Jesus of Nazareth, we read the complete spirit of the ethics of utility. "To do as you would be done by," and "to love your neighbor as yourself," constitute the ideal perfection of utilitarian morality. As the means of making the nearest approach to this ideal, utility would enjoin, first, that laws and social arrangements should place the happiness or (as, speaking practically, it may be called) the interest of every individual as nearly as possible in harmony with the interest of the whole; and, secondly, that education and opinion, which have so vast a power over human character, should so use that power as to establish in the mind of every individual an indissoluble assocation between his own happiness and the good of the whole, especially between his own happiness and the practice of such modes of conduct, negative and positive, as regard for the universal happiness prescribes; so that not only he may be unable to conceive the possibility of happiness to himself, consistently with conduct opposed to the general good, but also that a direct impulse to promote the general good may be in every individual one of the habitual motives of action, and the sentiments connected therewith may fill a large and prominent place in every human being's sentient existence. If the impugners of the utilitarian morality represented it to their own minds in this its true character, I know not what recommendation possessed by any other morality they could possibly affirm to be wanting to it; what more beautiful or more exalted developments of human nature any other ethical system can be supposed to foster, or what springs of action, not accessible to the utilitarian, such systems rely on for giving effect to their mandates.

The objectors to utilitarianism cannot always be charged with representing it in a discreditable light. On the contrary, those among them who entertain anything like a just idea of its disinterested character sometimes find fault with its standard as being too high for humanity. They say it is exacting too much to require that people shall always act from the inducement of promoting the general interests of society. But this is to mistake the very meaning of a standard of morals and confound the rule of action with the motive of it. It is the business of ethics to tell us what are our duties, or by what test we may know them; but no system of ethics requires that the sole motive of all we do shall be a feeling of duty; on the contrary, ninety-nine hundredths of all our actions are done from other motives, and rightly so done if the rule of duty does not condemn them. It is the more unjust to utilitarianism that this particular misapprehension should be made a ground of objection to it, inasmuch as utilitarian moralists have gone beyond almost all others in affirming that the motive has nothing to do with the morality of the action, though much with the worth of the agent. He who saves a fellow creature from drowning does what is morally right, whether his motive be duty or the hope of being paid for his trouble; he who betrays the friend that trusts him is guilty of a crime, even if his object be to serve another friend to whom he is under greater obligations. But to speak only of actions done from the motive of duty, and in direct obedience to principle: it is a misapprehension of the utilitarian mode of thought to conceive it as implying that people should fix their minds upon so wide a generality as the world, or society at large. The great majority of good actions are intended not for the benefit of the world, but for that of individuals, of which the good of the world is made up; and the thoughts of the most virtuous man need not on these occasions travel beyond the particular persons concerned, except so far as is necessary to assure himself that in benefiting them he is not violating the rights, that is, the legitimate and authorized expectations, of anyone else. The multiplication of happiness is, according to the utilitarian ethics, the object of virtue: the occasions on which any person (except one in a thousand) has it in his power to do this on an extended scale—in other words, to be a public benefactor—are but exceptional; and on these occasions alone is he called on to consider public utility; in every other case, private utility, the interest or happiness of some few persons, is all he has to attend to. Those alone the influence of whose actions extends to society in general need concern themselves habitually about so large an object. In the case of abstinences indeed—of things which people forbear to do from moral considerations, though the consequences in the particular case might be beneficial—it would be unworthy of an intelligent agent not to be consciously aware that the action is of a class which, if practiced generally, would be generally injurious, and that this is the ground of the obligation to abstain from it. The amount of regard for the public interest implied in this recognition is no greater than is demanded by every system of morals, for they all enjoin to abstain from whatever is manifestly pernicious to society. . . .

It may not be superfluous to notice a few more of the common misapprehensions of utilitarian ethics, even those which are so obvious and gross that it might appear impossible for any person of candor and intelligence to fall into them; since persons, even of considerable mental endowment, often give themselves so little trouble to understand the bearings of any opinion against which they entertain a prejudice, and men are in general so little conscious of this voluntary ignorance as a defect that the vulgarest misunderstandings of ethical doctrines are continually met with in the deliberate writings of persons of the greatest pretensions both to high principle and to philosophy. We not uncommonly hear the doctrine of utility inveighed against as a *godless* doctrine. If it be necessary to say anything at all against so mere an assumption, we may say that the question depends upon what idea we have formed of the moral character of the Deity. If it be a true belief that God desires, above all things, the happiness of his creatures, and that this was his purpose in their creation, utility is not only not a godless doctrine, but more profoundly religious than any other. If it be meant that utilitarianism does not recognize the revealed will of God as the supreme law of morals, I answer that a utilitarian who believes in the perfect goodness and wisdom of *God* necessarily believes that whatever God has thought fit to reveal on the subject of morals must fulfill the requirements of utility in a supreme degree. But others besides utilitarians have been of opinion that the Christian revelation was intended, and is fitted, to inform the hearts and minds of mankind with a spirit which should enable them to find for themselves what is right, and incline them to do it when found, rather than to tell them, except in a very general way, what it is; and that we need a doctrine of ethics, carefully followed out, to *interpret* to us the will of God. Whether this opinion is correct or not, it is superfluous here to discuss; since whatever aid religion, either natural or revealed, can afford to ethical investigation is as open to the utilitarian moralist as to any other. He can use it as the testimony of God to the usefulness or hurtfulness of any given course of action by as good a right as others can use it for the indication of a transcendental law having no connection with usefulness or with happiness.

Again, utility is often summarily stigmatized as an immoral doctrine by giving it the name of "expediency," and taking advantage of the popular use of that term to contrast it with principle. But the expedient, in the sense in which it is opposed to the right, generally means that which is expedient for the particular interest of the agent himself; as when a minister sacrifices the interests of his country to keep himself in place. When it means anything better than this, it means that which is expedient for some immediate object, some temporary purpose, but which violates a rule whose observance is expedient in a much higher degree. The expedient, in this sense, instead of being the same thing with the useful, is a branch of the hurtful. Thus it would often be expedient, for the purpose of getting over some momentary embarrassment, or attaining some object immediately useful to ourselves or others, to tell a lie. But inasmuch as the cultivation in ourselves of a sensitive feeling on the subject of veracity is one of the most useful, and the enfeeblement of that feeling one of the most hurtful, things to which our conduct can be instrumental; and inasmuch as any, even unintentional, deviation from truth does that much toward weakening the trustworthiness of human assertion, which is not only the principal support of all present social well-being, but the insufficiency of which does more than any one thing that can be named to keep back civilization, virtue, everything on which human happiness on the largest scale depends—we feel that the violation, for a present advantage, of a rule of such transcendent expediency is not expedient, and that he who, for the sake of convenience to himself or to some other individual, does what depends on him to deprive mankind of the good, and inflict upon them the evil, involved in the greater or less reliance which they can place in each other's word, acts the part of one of their worst enemies. Yet that even this rule, sacred as it is, admits of possible exceptions is acknowledged by all moralists; the chief of which is when the withholding of some fact (as of information from a malefactor, or of bad news from a person dangerously ill) would save an individual (especially an individual other than oneself) from great and unmerited evil, and when the withholding can only be effected by denial. But in order that the exception may not extend itself beyond the need, and may have the least possible effect in weakening reliance on veracity, it ought to be recognized and, if possible, its limits defined; and, if the principle of utility is good for anything, it must be good for weighing these conflicting utilities against one another and marking out the region within which one or the other preponderates.

Again, defenders of utility often find themselves called upon to reply to such objections as this—that there is not time, previous to action, for calculating and weighing the effects of any line of conduct on the general happiness. This is exactly as if anyone were to say that it is impossible to guide our conduct by Christianity because there is not time, on every occasion on which anything has to be done, to read through the Old and New Testaments. The answer to the objection is that there has been ample time, namely, the whole past duration of the human species. During all that time mankind have been learning by experience the tendencies of actions; on which experience all the prudence as well as all the morality of life are dependent. People talk as if the commencement of this course of experience had hitherto been put off, and as if, at the moment when some man feels tempted to meddle with the property or life of another, he had to begin considering for the first time whether murder and theft are injurious to human happiness. Even then I do not think that he would find the question very puzzling; but, at all events, the matter is now done to his hand. It is truly a whimsical supposition that, if mankind were agreed in considering utility to be the test of morality, they would remain without any agreement as to what *is* useful, and would take no measures for having their notions on the subject taught to the young and enforced by law and opinion. There is no difficulty in proving any ethical standard whatever to work ill if we suppose universal idiocy to be conjoined with it; but on any hypothesis short of that, mankind must by this time have acquired positive beliefs as to the effects of some actions on their happiness; and the beliefs which have thus come down are the rules of morality for the multitude, and for the philosopher until he has succeeded in finding better. That philosophers might easily do this, even now, on many subjects; that the received code of ethics is by no means of divine right; and that mankind have still much to learn as to the effects of actions on the general happiness, I admit or rather earnestly maintain. The corollaries from the principle of utility, like the precepts of every practical art, admit of indefinite improvement, and, in a progressive state of the human mind, their improvement is perpetually going on. But to consider the rules of morality as improvable is one thing; to pass over the intermediate generalization entirely and endeavor to test each individual action directly by the first principle is another. It is a strange notion that the acknowledgement of a first principle is inconsistent with the admission of secondary ones. To inform a traveler respecting the place of his ultimate destination is not to forbid the use of landmarks and direciton-posts on the way. The proposition that happiness is the end and aim of morality does not mean that no road ought to be laid down to that goal, or that persons going thither should not be advised to take one direction rather than another. Men really ought to leave off talking a kind of nonsense on this subject, which they would neither talk nor listen to on other matters of practical concernment. Nobody argues that the art of navigation is not founded on astronomy because sailors cannot wait to calculate the Nautical Almanac. Being rational creatures, they go to sea with it ready calculated; and all rational creatures go out upon the sea of life with their minds made up on the common questions of right and wrong, as well as on many of the far more difficult questions of wise and foolish. And this, as long as foresight is a human quality, it is to be presumed they will continue to do. Whatever we adopt as the fundamental principle of morality, we require subordinate principles to apply it by; the impossibility of doing without them, being common to all systems, can afford no argument against any one in particular; but gravely to argue as if no such secondary principles could be had, and as if mankind had remained till now, and always must remain, without drawing any general conclusions from the experience of human life is as high a pitch, I think, as absurdity has ever reached in philosophical controversy.

The remainder of the stock arguments against utilitarianism mostly consist in laying to its charge the common infirmities of human nature, and the general difficulties which embarrass conscientious persons in shaping their course through life. We are told that a utilitarian will be apt to make his own particular case an exception to moral rules, and, when under temptation, will see a utility in the breach of a rule, greater than he will see in its observance. But is utility the only creed which is able to furnish us with excuses for evil-doing and means of cheating our own conscience? They are afforded in abundance by all doctrines which recognize as a fact in morals the existence of conflicting considerations, which all doctrines do that have been believed by sane persons. It is not the fault of any creed, but of the complicated nature of human affairs, that rules of conduct cannot be so framed as to require no exceptions, and that hardly any kind of action can safely be laid down as either always obligatory or always condemnable. There is no ethical creed which does not temper the rigidity of its laws by giving a certain latitude, under the moral responsibility of the agent, for accommodation to peculiarities of circumstances; and under every creed, at the opening thus made, self-deception and dishonest casuistry get in. There exists no moral system under which there do not arise unequivocal cases of conflicting obligation. These are the real difficulties, the knotty points both in the theory of ethics and in the conscientious guidance of personal conduct. They are overcome practically, with greater or with less success, according to the intellect and virtue of the individual; but it can hardly be pretended that anyone will be the less qualified for dealing with them, from possessing an ultimate standard to which conflicting rights and duties can be referred. If utility is the ultimate source of moral obligations, utility may be invoked to decide between them when their demands are incompatible. Though the application of the standard may be difficult, it is better than none at all; while in other systems, the moral laws all claiming independent authority, there is no common umpire entitled to interfere between them; their claims to precedence one over another rest on little better than sophistry, and, unless determined, as they generally are, by the unacknowledged influence of consideration of utility, afford a free scope for the action of personal desires and partialities. We must remember that only in these cases of conflict between secondary principles is it requisite that first principles should be appealed to. There is no case of moral obligation in which some secondary principle is not involved; and if only one, there can seldom be any real doubt which one it is, in the mind of any person by whom the principle itself is recognized. . . .

Of What Sort of Proof the Principle of Utility Is Susceptible

It has already been remarked that questions of ultimate ends do not admit of proof, in the ordinary acceptation of the term. To be incapable of proof by reasoning is common to all first principles, to the first premises of our knowledge, as well as to those of our conduct. But the former, being matters of fact, may be the subject of a direct appeal to the faculties which judge of fact—namely, our senses and our internal consciousness. Can an appeal be made to the same faculties on questions of practical ends? Or by what other faculty is cognizance taken of them?

Questions about ends are, in other words, questions what things are desirable. The utilitarian doctrine is that happiness is desirable, and the only thing desirable, as an end; all other things being only desirable as means to that end. What ought to be required of this doctrine, what conditions is it requisite that the doctrine should fulfill—to make good its claim to be believed?

The only proof capable of being given that an object is visible is that people actually see it. The only proof that a sound is audible is that people hear it; and so of the other sources of our experience. In like manner, I apprehend, the sole evidence it is possible to produce that anything is desirable is that people do actually desire it. If the end which the utilitarian doctrine proposes to itself were not, in theory and in practice, acknowledged to be an end, nothing could ever convince any person that it was so. No reason can be given why the general happiness is desirable, except that each person, so far as he believes it to be attainable, desires his own happiness. This, however, being a fact, we have not only all the proof which the case admits of, but all which it is possible to require, that happiness is a good to that person, and the general happiness, therefore, a good to the aggregate of all persons. Happiness has made out its title as *one* of the ends of conduct and, consequently, one of the criteria of morality.

But it has not, by this alone, proved itself to be the sole criterion. To do that, it would seem, by the same rule, necessary to show, not only that people desire happiness, but that they never desire anything else. Now it is palpable that they do desire things which, in common language, are decidedly distinguished from happiness. They desire, for example, virtue and the absence of vice no less really than pleasure and the absence of pain. The desire of virtue is not as universal, but it is as authentic a fact as the desire of happiness. And hence the opponents of the utilitarian standard deem that they have a right to infer that there are other ends of human action besides happiness, and that happiness is not the standard of approbation and disapprobation.

But does the utilitarian doctrine deny that people desire virtue, or maintain that virtue is not a thing to be desired? The very reverse. It maintains not only that virtue is to be desired, but that it is to be desired disinterestedly, for itself. Whatever may be the opinion of utilitarian moralists as to the original conditions by which virtue is made virtue, however they may believe (as they do) that actions and dispositions are only virtuous because they promote another end than virtue, yet this be granted, and it having been decided, from considerations of this description, what *is* virtuous, they not only place virtue at the very head of the things which are good as means to the ultimate end, but they also recognize as a psychological fact the possibility of its being, to the individual, a good in itself, without looking to any end beyond it; and hold that the mind is not in a right state, not in a state conformable to utility, not in the state most conducive to the general happiness, unless it does love virtue in this manner—as a thing desirable in itself, even although, in the individual instance, it should not produce those other desirable consequences which it tends to produce, and on account of which it is held to be virtue. This opinion is not, in the smallest degree, a departure from the happiness principle. The ingredients of happiness are very various, and each of them is desirable in itself, and not merely when considered as swelling an aggregate. The principle of utility does not mean that any given pleasure, as music, for instance, or any given exemption from pain, as for example health, is to be looked upon as means to a collective something termed happiness, and to be desired on that account. They are desired and desirable in and for themselves; besides being means, they are a part of the end. Virtue, according to the utilitarian doctrine, is not naturally and originally part of the end, but it is capable of becoming so; and in those who live it disinterestedly it has become so, and is desired and cherished, not as a means to happiness, but as a part of their happiness.

To illustrate this further, we may remember that virtue is not the only thing originally a means, and which if it were not a means to anything else would be and remain indifferent, but which by association with what it is a means to comes to be desired for itself, and that too with the utmost intensity. What, for example, shall we say of the love of money? There is nothing originally more desirable about money than about any heap of glittering pebbles. Its worth is solely that of the things which it will buy; the desires for other things than itelf, which it is a means of gratifying. Yet the love of money is not only one of the strongest moving forces of human life, but money is, in many cases, desired in and for itself; the desire to possess it is often stronger than the desire to use it, and goes on increasing when all the desires which point to ends beyond it, to be compassed by it, are falling off. It may, then, be said truly that money is desired not for the sake of an end, but as part of the end. From being a means to happiness, it has come to be itself a principal ingredient of the individual's conception of happiness. The same may be said of the majority of the great objects of human life: power, for example, or fame, except that to each of these there is a certain amount of immediate pleasure annexed, which has at least the semblance of being naturally inherent in them—a thing which cannot be said of money. Still, however, the strongest natural attraction, both of power and of fame, is the immense aid they give to the attainment of our other wishes; and it is the strong association thus generated between them and all our objects of desire which gives to the direct desire of them the intensity it often assumes, so as in some characters to surpass in strength all other desires. In these cases the means have become a part of the end, and a more important part of it than any of the things which they are means to. What was once desired as an instrument for the attainment of happiness has come to be desired for its own sake. In being desired for its own sake it is, however, desired as *part* of happiness. The person is made, or thinks he would be made, happy by its mere possession; and is made unhappy by failure to obtain it. The desire of it is not a different thing from the desire of happiness any more than the love of music or the desire of health. They are included in happiness. They are some of the elements of which the desire of happiness is made up. Happiness is not an abstract idea but a concrete whole; and these are some of its parts. And the utilitarian standard sanctions and approves their being so. Life would be a poor thing, very ill provided with sources of happiness, if there were not this provision of nature by which things originally indifferent, but conducive to, or otherwise associated with, the satisfaction of our primitive desires, become in themselves sources of pleasure more valuable than the primitive pleasures, both in permanency, in the space of human existence that they are capable of covering, and even in intensity.

Virtue, according to the utilitarian conception, is a good of this description. There was no original desire of it, or motive to it, save its conduciveness to pleasure, and especially to protection from pain. But through the association thus formed it may be felt a good in itself, and desired as such with as great intensity as any other good; and with this difference between it and the love of money, of power, or of fame—that all of these may, and often do, render the individual noxious to the other members of the society to which he belongs, whereas there is nothing which makes him so much a blessing to them as the cultivation of the disinterested love of virtue. And consequently, the utilitarian standard, while it tolerates and approves those other acquired desires, up to the point beyond which they would be more injurious to the general happiness than promotive of it, enjoins and requires the cultivation of the love of virtue up to the greatest strength possible, as being above all things important to the general happiness.

It results from the preceding considerations that there is in reality nothing desired except happiness. Whatever is desired otherwise than as a means to some end beyond itself, and ultimately to happiness, is desired as itself a part of happiness, and is not desired for itself until it has become so. Those who desire virtue for its own sake desire it either because the consciousness of it is a pleasure, or because the consciousness of being without it is a pain, or for both reasons united; as in truth the pleasure and pain seldom exist separately, but amost always together—the same person feeling pleasure in the degree of virtue attained, and pain in not having attained more. If one of these gave him no pleasure, and the other no pain, he would not love or desire virtue, or would desire it only for the other benefits which it might produce to himself or to persons whom he cared for.

We have now, then, an answer to the question, of what sort of proof the principle of utility is susceptible. If the opinion which I have now stated is psychologically true—if human nature is so constituted as to desire nothing which is not either a part of happiness or a means of happiness—we can have no other proof, and we require no other, that these are the only things desirable. If so, happiness is the sole end of human action, and the promotion of it the test by which to judge of all human conduct; from whence it necessarily follows that it must be the criterion of morality, since a part is included in the whole.

And now to decide whether this is really so, whether mankind do desire nothing for itself but that which is a pleasure to them, or of which the absence is a pain, we have evidently arrived at a question of fact and experience, dependent, like all similar questions, upon evidence. It can only be determined by practiced self-consciousness and self-observation, assisted by observation of others. I believe that these sources of evidence, impartially consulted, will declare that desiring a thing and finding it pleasant, aversion to it and thinking of it as painful, are phenomena entirely inseparable or, rather, two parts of the same phenomenon—in strictness of language, two different modes of naming the same psychological fact; that to think of an object as desirable (unless for the sake of its consequences) and to think of it as pleasant are one and the same thing; and that to desire anything except in proportion as the idea of it is pleasant is a physical and metaphysical impossibility.

So obvious does this appear to me that I expect it will hardly be disputed; and the objection made will be, not that desire can possibly be directed to anything ultimately except pleasure and exemption from pain, but that the will is a different thing from desire; that a person of confirmed virtue or any other person whose purposes are fixed carries out his purposes without any thought of the pleasure he has in contemplating them or expects to derive from their fulfillment, and persists in acting on them, even though these pleasures are much diminished by changes in his character or decay of his passive sensibilities, or are outweighed by the pains which the pursuit of the purposes may bring upon him. All this I fully admit and have stated it elsewhere as positively and emphatically as anyone. Will, the active phenomenon, is a different thing from desire, the state of passive sensibility, and, though originally an offshoot from it, may in time take root and detach itself from the parent stock, so much so that in the case of a habitual purpose, instead of willing the thing because we desire it, we often desire it only because we will it. This, however, is but an instance of that familiar fact, the power of habit, and is nowise confined to the case of virtuous actions. Many indifferent things which men originally did from a motive of some sort they continue to do from habit. Sometimes this is done unconsciously, the consciousness coming only after the action; at other times with conscious volition, but volition which has become habitual and is put in operation by the force of habit, in opposition perhaps to the deliberate preference, as often happens with those who have contracted habits of vicious or hurtful indulgence. Third and last comes the case in which the habitual act of will in the individual instance is not in contradiction to the general intention prevailing at other times, but in fulfillment of it, as in the case of the person of confirmed virtue and of all who pursue deliberately and consistently any determinate end. The distinction between will and desire thus understood is an authentic and highly important psychological fact; but the fact consists solely in this—that will, like all other parts of our constitution, is amenable to habit, and that we may will from habit what we no longer desire for itself, or desire only because we will it. It is not the less true that will, in the beginning, is entirely produced by desire, including in that term the repelling influence of pain as well as the attractive one of pleasure. Let us take into consideration no longer the person who has a confirmed will to do right, but him in whom that virtuous will is still feeble, conquerable by temptation, and not to be fully relied on;

by what means can it be strengthened? How can the will to be virtuous, where it does not exist in sufficient force, be implanted or awakened? Only by making the person *desire* virtue—by making him think of it in a pleasurable light, or of its absence in a painful one. It is by associating the doing right with pleasure, or the wrong with pain, or by eliciting and impressing and bringing home to the person's experience the pleasure naturally involved in the one or the pain in the other, that it is possible to call forth that will to be virtuous which, when confirmed, acts without any thought of either pleasure or pain. Will is the child of desire, and passes out of the dominion of its parent only to come under that of habit. That which is the result of habit affords no presumption of being intrinsically good; and there would be no reason for wishing that the purpose of virtue should become independent of pleasure and pain were it not that the influence of the pleasurable and painful associations which prompt to virtue is not sufficiently to be depended on for unerring constancy of action until it has acquired the support of habit. Both in feeling and in conduct, habit is the only thing which imparts certainty; and it is because of the importance to others of being able to rely absolutely on one's feelings and conduct, and to oneself of being able to rely on one's own, that the will to do right ought to be cultivated into this habitual independence. In other words, this state of the will is a means to good, not intrinsically a good; and does not contradict the doctrine that nothing is a good to human beings but in so far as it is either itself pleasurable or a means of attaining pleasure or averting pain.

But if this doctrine be true, the principle of utility is proved. Whether it is so or not must now be left to the consideration of the thoughtful reader.

On the Connection between Justice and Utility

In all ages of speculation one of the strongest obstacles to the reception of the doctrine that utility or happiness is the criterion of right and wrong has been drawn from the idea of justice. The powerful sentiment and apparently clear perception which that word recalls with a rapidity and certainty resembling an instinct have seemed to the majority of thinkers to point to an inherent quality in things; to show that the just must have an existence in nature as something absolute, generically distinct from every variety of the expedient and, in idea, opposed to it, though (as is commonly acknowledged) never, in the long run, disjoined from it in fact. . . .

To throw light upon this question, it is necessary to attempt to ascertain what is the distinguishing character of justice, or of injustice; what is the quality, or whether there is any quality, attributed in common to all modes of conduct designated as unjust (for justice, like many other moral attributes, is best defined by its opposite), and distinguishing them from such modes of conduct as are disapproved, but without having that particular epithet of disapprobation applied to them. If in everything which men are accustomed to characterize as just or unjust some one common attribute or collection of attributes is always present, we may judge whether this particular attribute or combination of attributes would be capable of gathering round it a sentiment of that peculiar character and intensity by virtue of the general laws of our emotional constitution, or whether the sentiment is inexplicable and requires to be regarded as a special provision of nature. If we find the former to be the case, we shall, in resolving this question, have resolved also the main problem; if the latter, we shall have to seek for some other mode of investigating it. . . .

In the first place, it is mostly considered unjust to deprive anyone of his personal liberty, his property, or any other thing which belongs to him by law. Here, therefore, is one instance of the application of the terms "just" and "unjust" in a perfectly definite sense, namely, that it is just to respect, unjust to violate, the *legal rights* of anyone. But this judgment admits of several exceptions, arising from the other forms in which the notions of justice and injustice present themselves. For example, the person who suffers the deprivation may (as the phrase is) have *forfeited* the rights which he is so deprived of—a case to which we shall return presently. But also—

Secondly, the legal rights of which he is deprived may be rights which *ought* not to have belonged to him; in other words, the law which confers on him these rights may be a bad law. When it is so or when (which is the same thing for our purpose) it is supposed to be so, opinions will differ as to the justice or injustice of infringing it. Some maintain that no law, however bad, ought to be disobeyed by an individual citizen; that his opposition to it, if shown at all, should only be shown in endeavoring to get it altered by competent authority. This opinion (which condemns many of the most illustrious benefactors of mankind, and would often protect pernicious institutions against the only weapons which, in the state of things existing at the time, have any chance of succeeding against them) is defended by those who hold it on grounds of expediency, principally on that of the importance to the common interest of mankind, of maintaining inviolate the sentiment of submission to law. Other persons, again, hold the directly contrary opinion that any law, judged to be bad, may blamelessly be disobeyed, even though it be not judged to be unjust but only inexpedient, while others would confine the license of disobedience to the case of unjust laws; but, again, some say that all laws which are inexpedient are unjust, since every law imposes some restriction on the natural liberty of mankind, which restriction is an injustice unless legitimated by tending to their good. Among these diversities of opinion it seems to be universally admitted that there may be unjust laws, and that law, consequently, is not the ultimate criterion of justice, but may give to one person a benefit, or impose on another an evil, which justice condemns. When, however, a law is thought to be unjust, it seems always to be regarded as being so in the same way in which a breach of law is unjust, namely, by infringing somebody's right, which, as it cannot in this case be a legal right, receives a different appelation and is called a moral right. We may say, therefore, that a second case of injustice consists in taking or withholding from any person that to which he has a *moral right*.

Thirdly, it is universally considered just that each person should obtain that (whether good or evil) which he *deserves,* and unjust that he should obtain a good or be made to undergo an evil which he does not deserve. This is, perhaps, the clearest and most emphatic form in which the idea of justice is conceived by the general mind. As it involves the notion of desert, the question arises what constitutes desert? Speaking in a general way, a person is understood to deserve good if he does right, evil if he does wrong; and in a more particular sense, to deserve good from those to whom he does or has done good, and evil from those to whom he does or has done evil. The precept of returning good for evil has never been regarded as a case of the fulfillment of justice, but as one in which the claims of justice are waived, in obedience to other considerations.

Fourthly, it is confessedly unjust to *break faith* with anyone: to violate an engagement, either express or implied, or disappoint expectations raised by our own conduct, at least if we have raised those expectations knowingly and voluntarily. Like the other obligations of justice already spoken of, this one is not regarded as absolute, but as capable of being overruled by a stronger obligation of justice on the other side, or by such conduct on the part of the person concerned as is deemed to absolve us from our obligation to him and to constitute a *forfeiture* of the benefit which he has been led to expect.

Fifthly, it is, by universal admission, inconsistent with justice to be *partial*—to show favor or preference to one person over another in matters to which favor and preference do not properly apply. Impartiality, however, does not seem to be regarded as a duty in itself, but rather as instrumental to some other duty; for it is admitted that favor and preference are not always censurable, and, indeed, the cases in which they are condemned are rather the exception than the rule. A person would be more likely to be blamed than applauded for giving his family or friends no superiority in good office over strangers when he could do so without violating any other duty; and no one thinks it unjust to seek one person in preference to another as a friend, connection, or companion. Impartiality where rights are concerned is of course obligatory, but this is involved in the more general obligations of giving to everyone his right. A tribunal, for example, must be impartial because it is bound to award, without regard to any other consideration, a disputed object to the one of two parties who has the right to it. There are other cases in which impartiality means being solely influenced by desert, as with those who, in the capacity of judges, perceptors, or parents, administer reward and punishment as such. There are cases, again, in which it means being solely influenced by considerations for the public interest, as in making a selection among candidates for a government employment. Impartiality, in short, as an obligation of justice, may be said to mean being exclusively influenced by the considerations which it is supposed ought to influence the particular case in hand, and resisting solicitation of any motives which prompt to conduct different from what those considerations would dictate.

Nearly allied to the idea of impartiality is that of *equality,* which often enters as a component part both into the conception of justice and into the practice of it, and, in the eyes of many persons, constitutes its essence. But in this, still more than in any other case, the notion of justice varies in different persons, and always conforms in its variations to their notion of utility. Each person maintains that equality is the dictate of justice, except where he thinks that expediency requires inequality. The justice of giving equal protection to the rights of all is maintained by those who support the most outrageous inequality in the right themselves. Even in slave countries it is theoretically admitted that the rights of the slave, such as they are, ought to be as sacred as those of the master, and that a tribunal which fails to enforce them with equal strictness is wanting in justice; while, at the same time, institutions which leave to the slave scarcely any rights to enforce are not deemed unjust because they are not deemed inexpedient. Those who think that utility requires distinctions of rank do not consider it unjust that riches and social privileges should be unequally dispensed; but those who think this inequality inexpedient think it unjust also. Whoever thinks that government is necessary sees no injustice in as much inequality as is constituted by giving to the magistrate powers not granted to other people. Even among those who hold leveling doctrines, there are differences of opinion about expediency. Some communists consider it unjust that the produce of the labor of the community should be shared on any other principle than that of exact equality; others think it just that those should receive most whose wants are greatest; while others hold that those who work harder, or who produce more, or whose services are more valuable to the community, may justly claim a larger quota in the division of the produce. And the sense of natural justice may be plausibly appealed to in behalf of every one of these opinions. . . .

We have seen that the two essential ingredients in the sentiment of justice are the desire to punish a person who has done harm and the knowledge or belief that there is some definite individual or individuals to whom harm has been done.

Now it appears to me that the desire to punish a person who has done harm to some individual is a spontaneous outgrowth from two sentiments, both in the highest degree natural and which either are or resemble instincts: the impulse of self-defense and the feeling of sympathy.

It is natural to resent and to repel or retaliate any harm done or attempted against ourselves or againt those with whom we sympathize. The origin of this sentiment it is not necessary here to discuss. Whether it be an instinct or a result of intelligence, it is, we know, common to all animal nature; for every animal tries to hurt those who have hurt, or who it thinks are about to hurt, itself or its young. Human beings, on this point, only differ from other animals in two particulars. First, in being capable of sympathizing, not solely with their offspring, or, like some of the more noble animals, with some superior animal who is kind to them, but will all human, and even with all sentient, beings; secondly, in having a more developed intelligence, which gives a wider range to the whole of their sentiments, whether self-regarding or sympathetic. By virtue of his superior intelligence, even apart from his superior range of sympathy, a human being is capable of apprehending a community of interest between himself and the human society of which he forms a part, such that any conduct which threatens the security of the society generally is threatening to his own, and calls forth his instinct (if instinct it be) of self-defense. The same superiority of intelligence, joined to the power of sympathizing with human beings generally, enables him to attach himself to the collective idea of his tribe, his country, or mankind in such a manner that any act hurtful to them raises his instinct of sympathy and urges him to resistance.

The sentiment of justice, in that one of its elements which consists of the desire to punish, is thus, I conceive, the natural feeling of retaliation or vengeance, rendered by intellect and sympathy applicable to those injuries, that is, to those hurts, which wound us through, or in common with, society at large. This sentiment, in itself, has nothing moral in it; what is moral is the exclusive subordination of it to the social sympathies, so as to wait on and obey their call. For the natural feeling would make us resent indiscriminately whatever anyone does that is disagreeable to us; but, when moralized by the social feeling, it only acts in the directions conformable to the general good: just persons resenting a hurt to society, though not otherwise a hurt to themselves, and not resenting a hurt to themselves, however painful, unless it be of the kind which society has a common interest with them in the repression of.

It is no objection against this doctrine to say that, when we feel our sentiment of justice outraged, we are not thinking of society at large or of any collective interest, but only of the individual case. It is common enough, certainly, though the reverse of commendable, to feel resentment merely because we have suffered pain; but a person whose resentment is really a moral feeling, that is, who considers whether an act is blamable before he allows himself to resent it—such a person, though he may not say expressly to himself that he is standing up for the interest of society, certainly does feel that he is asserting a rule which is for the benefit of others as well as for his own. If he is not feeling this, if he is regarding the act solely as it affects him individually, he is not consciously just; he is not concerning himself about the justice of his actions. This is admitted even by anti-utilitarian moralists. When Kant (as before remarked) propounds as the fundamental principle of morals, "So act that thy rule of conduct might be adopted as a law by all rational beings," he virtually acknowledges that the interest of mankind collectively, or at least of mankind indiscriminately, must be in the mind of the agent when conscientiously deciding on the morality of the act. Otherwise he uses words without a meaning; for that a rule even of utter selfishness could not *possibly* be adopted by all rational beings—that there is any insuperable obstacle in the nature of things to its adoption—cannot be even plausibly maintained. To give any meaning to Kant's principle, the sense put upon it must be that we ought to shape our conduct by a rule which all rational beings might adopt *with benefit to their collective interest*.

To recapitulate: the idea of justice supposes two things—a rule of conduct and a sentiment which sanctions the rule. The first must be supposed common to all mankind and intended for their good. The other (the sentiment) is a desire that punishment may be suffered by those who infringe the rule. There is involved, in addition, the concepton of some definite person who suffers by the infringement, whose rights (to use the expression appropriated to the case) are violated by it. And the sentiment of justice appears to me to be the animal desire to repel or retaliate a hurt or damage to oneself or to those with whom one sympathizes, widened so as to include all persons, by the human capacity of enlarged sympathy and the human conception of intelligent self-interest. From the latter elements the feeling derives its morality; from the former, its peculiar impressiveness and energy of self-assertion.

I have, throughout, treated the idea of a *right* residing in the injured person and violated by the injury, not as a separate element in the composition of the idea and sentiment, but as one of the forms in which the other two elements clothe themselves. Those elements are a hurt to some assignable person or persons, on the one hand, and a demand for punishment, on the other. An examination of our own minds, I think, will show that these two things include all that we mean when we speak of violation of a right. When we call anything a person's right, we mean that he has a valid claim on society to protect him in the possession of it, either by the force of law or by that of education and opinion. If he has what we consider a sufficient claim, on whatever account, to have something guaranteed to him by society, we say that he has a right to it. If we desire to prove that anything does not belong to him by right, we think this done as soon as it is admitted that society ought not to take measures for securing it to him, but should leave him to chance or to his own exertions. Thus a person is said to have a right to what he can earn in fair professional competition, because society ought not to allow any other person to hinder him from endeavoring to earn in that manner as much as he can. But he has not a right to three hundred a year, though he may happen to be earning it; because society is not called on to provide that he shall earn that sum. On the contrary, if he owns ten thousand pounds three-per-cent stock, he *has* a right to three hundred a year because society has come under an obligation to provide him with an income of that amount.

To have a right, then, is, I conceive, to have something which society ought to defend me in the possession of. If the objector goes on to ask why it ought, I can give him no other reason than general utility. If that expression does not seem to convey a sufficient feeling of the strength of the obligation, nor to account for the peculiar energy of the feeling, it is because there goes to the composition of the sentiment, not a rational only but also an animal element—the thirst for retaliation; and this thirst derives its intensity, as well as its moral justification, from the extraordinarily important and impressive kind of utility which is concerned. The interest involved is that of security, to everyone's feelings the most vital of all interests. All other earthly benefits are needed by one person, not needed by another; and many of them can, if necessary, be cheerfully foregone or replaced by something else; but security no human being can possibly do without; on it we depend for all our immunity from evil and for the whole value of all and every good, beyond the passing moment, since nothing but the gratification of the instant could be of any worth to us if we could be deprived of everything the next instant by whoever was momentarily stronger than ourselves. Now this most indispensable of all necessaries, after physical nutriment, cannot be had unless the machinery for providing it is kept unintermittedly in active play. Our notion, therefore, of the claim we have on our fellow creatures to join in making safe for us the very groundwork of our existence gathers feelings around it so much more intense than those concered in any of the more common cases of utility that the difference in degree (as is often the case in psychology) becomes a real difference in kind. The claim assumes that character of absoluteness, that apparent infinity and incommensurability with all other considerations which constitute the distinction between the feeling of right and wrong and that of ordinary expediency and inexpediency. The feelings concerned are so powerful, and we count so positively on finding a responsive feeling in others (all being alike interested) that *ought* and *should* grow into *must,* and recognized indispensability becomes a moral necessity, analogous to physical, and often not inferior to it in binding force.

If the preceding analysis, or something resembling it, be not the correct account of the notion of justice—if justice be totally independent of utility, and be a standard *per se,* which the mind can recognize by simple introspection of itself—it is hard to understand why that internal oracle is so ambiguous, and why so many things appear either just or unjust, according to the light in which they are regarded. . . .

The moral rules which forbid mankind to hurt one another (in which we must never forget to include wrongful interference with each other's freedom) are more vital to human well-being than any maxims, however important, which only point out the best mode of managing some department of human affairs. They have also the peculiarity that they are the main element in determining the whole of the social feelings of mankind. It is their observance which alone preserves peace among human beings; if obedience to them were not the rule, and disobedience the exception, everyone would see in everyone else an enemy against whom he must be perpetually guarding himself. What is hardly less important, these are the precepts which mankind have the strongest and the most direct inducements for impressing upon one another. By merely giving to each other prudential instruction or exhortation, they may gain, or think they gain, nothing; in inculcating on each other the duty of positive beneficence, they have an unmistakable interest, but far less in degree; a person may possibly not need the benefits of others, but he always needs that they should not do him hurt. Thus the moralities which protect every individual from being harmed by others, either directly or by being hindered in his freedom of pursuing his own good, are at once those which he himself has most at heart and those which he has the strongest interest in publishing and enforcing by word and deed. It is by a person's observance of these that his fitness to exist as one of the fellowship of human beings is tested and decided; for on that depends his being a nuisance or not to those with whom he is in contact. Now it is these moralities primarily which compose the obligations of justice.

The most marked cases of injustice, and those which give the tone to the feeling of repugnance which characterizes the sentiment, are acts of wrongful aggression or wrongful exercise of power over someone; the next are those which consist in wrongfully withholding from him something which is his due—in both cases inflicting on him a positive hurt; either in the form of direct suffering or of the privation of some good which he had reasonable ground, either of a physical or of a social kind, for counting upon.

The same powerful motives which command the observance of these primary moralities enjoin the punishment of those who violate them; and as the impulses of self-defense, of defense of others, and of vengeance are all called forth against such persons, retribution, or evil for evil, become closely connected with the sentiment of justice, and is universally included in the idea. Good for good is also one of the dictates of justice; and this, though its social utility is evident, and though it carries with it a natural human feeling, has not at first sight that obvious connection with hurt or injury which, existing in the most elementary cases of just and unjust, is the source of the characteristic intensity of the sentiment. But the connection, though less obvious, is not less real. He who accepts benefits and denies a return of them when needed inflicts a real hurt by disappointing one of the most natural and reasonable of expectations, and one which he must at least tacitly have encouraged, otherwise the benefits would seldom have been conferred. The important rank, among human evils and wrongs, of the disappointment of expectation is shown in the fact that it constitutes the principal criminality of two such highly immoral acts as a breach of friendship and a breach of promise. Few hurts which human beings can sustain are greater, and none wound more, than when that on which they habitually and with full assurance relied fails them in the hour of need; and few wrongs are greater than this mere withholding of good; none excite more resentment, either in the person suffering or in a sympathizing spectator. The principle, therefore, of giving to each what they deserve, that is, good for good as well as evil for evil, is not only included within the idea of justice as we have defined it, but is a proper object of that intensity of sentiment which places the just in human estimation above the simply expedient.

Most of the maxims of justice current in the world, and commonly appealed to in its transactions, are simply instrumental to carrying into effect the principles of justice which we have now spoken of. That a person is only responsible for what he has done voluntarily, or could voluntarily have avoided, that it is unjust to condemn any person unheard; that the punishment ought to be proportioned to the offense, and the like, are maxims intended to prevent the just principle of evil for evil from being perverted to the infliction of evil without that justification. The greater part of these common maxims have come into use from the practice of courts of justice, which have been naturally led to a more complete recognition and elaboration than was likely to suggest itself to others, of the rules necessary to enable them to fulfill their double function—of inflicting punishment when due, and of awarding to each person his right.

That first of judicial virtues, impartiality, is an obligation of justice, partly for the reason last mentioned, a being a necessary condition of the fulfillment of other obligations of justice. But this is not the only source of the exalted rank, among human obligations, of those maxims of equality and impartiality, which, both in popular estimation and in that of the most enlightened, are included among the precepts of justice. In one point of view, they may be considered as corollaries from the principles already laid down. If it is a duty to do to each according to his deserts, returning good for good, as well as repressing evil by evil, it necessarily follows that we should treat all equally well (when no higher duty forbids) who have deserved equally well of *us*, and that society should treat all equally well who have deserved equally well of *it*, that is, who have deserved equally well absolutely. This is the highest abstract standard of social and distributive justice, toward which all institutions and the efforts of all virtuous citizens should be made in the utmost possible degree to converge. But this great moral duty rests upon a still deeper foundation, being a direct emanation from the first principle of morals, and not a mere logical corollary from secondary or derivative doctrines. It is involved in the very meaning of utility, or the greatest happiness principle. That principle is a mere form of words without rational signification unless one person's happiness, supposed equal in degree (with the proper allowance made for kind), is counted for exactly as much as another's. Those conditions being supplied, Bentham's dictum, "everybody to count for one, nobody for more than one," might be written under the principle of utility as an explanatory commentary.[1] The equal claim of everybody to happiness, in the estimation of the moralist and of the legislator, involves an equal claim to all the means of happiness except in so far as the inevitable conditions of human life and the general interest in which that of every individual is included set limits to the maxim; and those limits ought to be strictly construed. As every other maxim of justice, so this is by no means applied or held applicable universally; on the contrary, as I have already remarked, it bends to every person's ideas of social expediency. But in whatever case it is deemed applicable at all, it is held to be the dictate of justice. All persons are deemed to have a *right* to equality of treatment, except when some recognized social expediency requires the reverse. And hence all social inequalities which have ceased to be considered expedient assume the character, not of simple inexpediency, but of injustice, and appear so tyrannical that people are apt to wonder how they ever could have been tolerated—forgetful that they themselves, perhaps, tolerate other inequalities under an equally mistaken notion of expediency, the correction of which would make that which they approve seem quite as

---

[1]This implication, in the first principle of the utilitarian scheme, of perfect impartiality between persons is regarded by Mr. Herbert Spencer (in his *Social Statics*) as a disproof of the pretensions of utility to be a sufficient guide to right; since (he says) the principle of utility presupposes the anterior principle that everybody has an equal right to happiness. It may be more correctly described as supposing that equal amounts of happiness are equally desirable, whether felt by the same or different persons. This, however, is not a *pre*supposition, not a premise needful to support the principle of utility, but the very principle itself; for what is the principle of utility if it be not that "happiness" and "desirable" are synonymous terms? If there is any anterior principle implied, it can be no other than this, that the truths of arithmetic are applicable to the valuation of happiness, as of all other measureable quantites.

(Mr. Herbert Spencer, in a private communication on the subject of the preceding note, objects to being considered an opponent of utilitarianism and states that he regards happiness as the ultimate end of morality; but deems that end only partially attainable by empirical generalizations from the observed results of conduct, and completely attainable only by deducing, from the law of life and the conditions of existence, what kinds of action necessarily tend to produce happiness, and what kinds to produce unhappiness. With the exception of the word "necessarily," I have no dissent to express from this doctrine; and (omitting that word) I am not aware that any modern advocate of utilitarianism is of a different opinion. Bentham, certainly, to whom in the *Social Statics* Mr. Spencer particularly referred, is, least of all writers, chargeable with unwillingness to deduce the effect of actions on happiness from the laws of human nature and the universal conditions of human life. The common charge against him is of relying too exclusively upon such deductions and declining altogether to be bound by the generalizations from specific experience which Mr. Spencer thinks that utilitarians generally confine themselves to. My own opinion (and, as I collect, Mr. Spencer's) is that in ethics, as in all other branches of scientific study, the consilience of the results of both these processes, each corroborating and verifying the other, is requisite to give to any general proposition the kind and degree of evidence which constitutes scientific proof.)

monstrous as what they have at last learned to condemn. The entire history of social improvement has been a series of transitions by which one custom or institution after another, from being a supposed primary necessity of social existence, has passed into the rank of a universally stigmatized injustice and tyranny. So it has been with the distinctions of slaves and freemen, nobles and serfs, patricians and plebeians; and so it will be, and in part already is, with the aristocracies of color, race, and sex.

It appears from what has been said that justice is a name for certain moral requirements which, regarded collectively, stand higher in the scale of social utility, and are therefore of more paramount obligation, than any others, though particular cases may occur in which some other social duty is so important as to overrule any one of the general maxims of justice. Thus, to save a life, it may not only be allowable, but a duty, to steal or take by force the necessary food or medicine, or to kidnap and compel to officiate the only qualified medical practitioner. In such cases, as we do not call anything justice which is not a virtue, we usually say, not that justice must give way to some other moral principle, but that what is just an ordinary case is, by reason of that other principle, not just in the particular case. By this useful accommodation of language, the character of indefeasibility attributed to justice is kept up, and we are saved from the necessity of maintaining that there can be laudable injustice.

The considerations which have now been adduced resolve, I conceive, the only real difficulty in the utilitarian theory of morals. It has always been evident that all cases of justice are also cases of expediency; the difference is in the peculiar sentiment which attaches to the former, as contradistinguished from the latter. If this characteristic sentiment has been sufficiently accounted for; if there is no necessity to assume for it any peculiarity of origin; if it is simply the natural feeling of resentment, moralized by being made co-existensive with the demands of social good; and if this feeling not only does but ought to exist in all the classes of cases to which the idea of justice corresponds—that idea no longer presents itself as a stumbling block to the utilitarian ethics. Justice remains the appropriate name for certain social utilities which are vastly more important, and therefore more absolute and imperative, than any others are as a class (though not more so than others may be in particular cases); and which, therefore, ought to be, as well as naturally are, guarded by a sentiment, not only different in degree, but also in kind; distinguished from the milder feeling which attaches to the mere idea of promoting human pleasure or convenience at once by the more definite nature of its commands and by the sterner character of its sanctions.

Problems in Utilitarianism
The Meaning of Utilitarianism

Henry Sidgwick

§1. The term Utilitarianism is, at the present day, in common use, and is supposed to designate a doctrine or method with which we are all familiar. But on closer examination, it appears to be applied to several distinct theories, having no necessary connexion with one another, and not even referring to the same subject-matter. It will be well, therefore, to define, as carefully as possible, the doctrine that is to be denoted by the term in the present Book: at the same time distinguishing this from other doctrines to which usage would allow the name to be applied, and indicating, so far as seems necessary, its relation to these.

By Utilitarianism is here meant the ethical theory, that the conduct which, under any given circumstances, is objectively right, is that which will produce the greatest amount of happiness on the whole; that is, taking into account all whose happiness is affected by the conduct. It would tend to clearness if we might call this principle, and the method based upon it, by some such name as "Universalistic Hedonism": and I have therefore sometimes ventured to use this term, in spite of its cumbrousness.

The first doctrine from which it seems necessary to distinguish this, is the Egoistic Hedonism expounded and discussed in Book ii. of this treatise. The difference, however, between the propositions (1) that each ought to seek his own happiness and (2) that each ought to seek the happiness of all, is so obvious and glaring, that instead of dwelling upon it we seem rather called upon to explain how the two ever came to be confounded, or in any way included under one notion. This question and the general relation between the two doctrines were briefly discussed in a former chapter.[1] Among other points it was there noticed that the confusion between these two ethical theories was partly assisted by the confusion with both of the psychological theory that in voluntary actions every agent does, universally or normally, seek his own individual happiness of pleasure. Now there seems to be no *necessary* connexion between this latter proposition and any ethical theory: but in so far as there is a natural tendency to pass from psychological to ethical Hedonism, the transition must be—at least primarily—to the Egoistic phase of the latter. For clearly, from the fact that every one actually does seek his own happiness we cannot conclude, as an immediate and obvious inference, that he ought to seek the happiness of other people.[2]

Nor, again, is Utilitarianism, as an ethical doctrine, necessarily connected with the psychological theory that the moral sentiments are derived, by "association of ideas" or otherwise, from experiences of the non-moral pleasures and pains resulting

---

[1] Book i, chap. vi. It may be worth while to notice, that in Mill's well-known treatise on Utilitarianism this confusion, though expressly deprecated, is to some extent encouraged by the author's treatment of the subject.

[2] I have already criticis ' (Book iii, chap. xiii.) the mode in which Mill attempts to exhibit this inference.

From Henry Sidgwick, *The Methods of Ethics* (first edition 1874, selections here from seventh edition, 1907). Reprinted courtesy of Hackett Publishing Company, Inc. Excerpts are from Book IV, Chapter I; Book II, Chapter II; and Book IV, Chapter III.

to the agent or to others from different kinds of conduct. An Intuitionist might accept this theory, so far as it is capable of scientific proof, and still hold that these moral sentiments, being found in our present consciousness as independent impulses, ought to possess the authority that they seem to claim over the more primary desires and aversions from which they have sprung: and an Egoist on the other hand might fully admit the altruistic element of the derivation, and still hold that these and all other impulses (including even Universal Benevolence) are properly under the rule of Rational Self-love: and that it is really only reasonable to gratify them in so far as we may expect to find our private happiness in such gratification. In short, what is often called the "utilitarian" theory of the origin of the moral sentiments cannot by itself provide a proof of the ethical doctrine to which I in this treatise restrict the term Utilitarianism. I shall, however, hereafter try to show that this psychological theory has an important though subordinate place in the establishment of Ethical Utilitarianism.[3]

Finally, the doctrine that Universal Happiness is the ultimate *standard* must not be understood to imply that Universal Benevolence is the only right or always best *motive* of action. For, as we have before observed, it is not necessary that the end which gives the criterion of rightness should always be the end at which we consciously aim: and if experience shows that the general happiness will be more satisfactorily attained if men frequently act from other motives than pure universal philanthropy, it is obvious that these other motives are reasonably to be preferred on Utilitarian principles.

§ **2.** Let us now examine the principle itself somewhat closer. I have already attempted (Book ii. chap. i.) to render the notion of Greatest Happiness as clear and definite as possible; and the results there obtained are of course as applicable to the discussion of Universalistic as to that of Egoistic Hedonism. We shall understand, then, that by Greatest Happiness is meant the greatest possible surplus of pleasure over pain, the pain being conceived as balanced against an equal amount of pleasure, so that the two contrasted amounts annihilate each other for purposes of ethical calculation. And of course, here as before, the assumption is involved that all pleasures included in our calculation are capable of being compared quantitatively with one another and with all pains; that every such feeling has a certain intensive quantity, positive or negative (or, perhaps, zero), in respect of its desirableness, and that this quantity may be to some extent known: so that each may be at least roughly weighed in ideal scales against any other. This assumption is involved in the very notion of Maximum Happiness; as the attempt to make "as great as possible" a sum of elements not quantitatively commensurable would be a mathematical absurdity. Therefore whatever weight is to be attached to the objections brough against this assumption (which was discussed in chap. iii. of Book ii.) must of course tell against the present method.

We have next to consider who the "all" are, whose happiness is to be taken into account. Are we to extend our concern to all the beings capable of pleasure and pain whose feelings are affected by our conduct? or are we to confine our view to human happiness? The former view is the one adopted by Bentham and Mill, and (I believe) by the Utilitarian school generally: and is obviously most in accordance with the universality that is characteristic of their principle. It is the Good *Universal,* interpreted and defined as "happiness" or "pleasure" at which a Utilitarian considers it his duty to aim: and it seems arbitrary and unreasonable to exclude from the end, as so conceived, any pleasure of any sentient being.

[3]Cf. *post,* chap. iv.

It may be said that by giving this extension to the notion, we considerably increase the scientific difficulties of he hedonistic comparison, which have already been pointed out (Book ii. chap. iii.): for if it be difficult to compare the pleasures and pains of other men accurately with our own, a comparison of either with the pleasures and pains of brutes is obviously still more obscure. Still, the difficulty is at least not greater for Utilitarians than it is for any other moralists who recoil from the paradox of disregarding altogether the pleasures and pains of brutes. But even if we limit our attention to human beings, the extent of the subjects of happiness is not yet quite determinate. In the first place, it may be asked, How far we are to consider the interests of posterity when they seem to conflict with those of existing human beings? It seems, however, clear that the time at which a man exists cannot affect the value of his happiness from a universal point of view; and that the interests of posterity must concern a Utilitarian as much as those of his contemporaries, except in so far as the effect of his actions on posterity—and even the existence of human beings to be affected—must necessarily be more uncertain. But a further question arises when we consider that we can to some extent influence the number of future human (or sentient) beings. We have to ask how, on Utilitarian principles, this influence is to be exercised. Here I shall assume that, for human beings generally, life on the average yields a positive balance of pleasure over pain. This has been denied by thoughtful persons: but the denial seems to me clearly opposed to the common experience of mankind, as expressed in their commonly accepted principles of action. The great majority of men, in the great majority of conditions under which human life is lived, certainly act as if death were one of the worst of evils, for themselves and for those whom they love: and the administration of criminal justice proceeds on a similar assumption.[4]

Assuming, then, that the average happiness of human beings is a positive quantity, it seems clear that, supposing the average happiness enjoyed remains undiminished, Utilitarianism directs us to make the number enjoying it as great as possible. But if we foresee as possible that an increase in numbers will be accompanied by a decrease in average happiness or *vice versa,* a point arises which has not only never been formally noticed, but which seems to have been substantially overlooked by many Utilitarians. For if we take Utilitarianism to prescribe, as the ultimate end of action, happiness on the whole, and not any individual's happiness, unless considered as an element of the whole, it would follow that, if the additional population enjoy on the whole positive happiness, we ought to weigh the amount of happiness gained by the extra number against the amount lost by the remainder. So that, strictly conceived, the point up to which, on Utilitarian principles, population ought to be encouraged to increase, is not that at which average happiness is the greatest possible—as appears to

---

[4]Those who held the opposite opinion appear generally to assume that the appetites and desires which are the mainspring of ordinary human action are in themselves painful: a view entirely contrary to my own experience, and, I believe, to the common experience of mankind. See chap. iv. § 2 of Book i. So far as their argument is not a development of this psychological error, any plausibility it has seems to me to be obtained by dwelling onesidedly on the annoyances and disappointments undoubtedly incident to normal human life, and on the exceptional sufferings of small minorities of the human race, or perhaps of most men during small portions of their lives.

The reader who wishes to see the paradoxical results of pessimistic utilitarianism seriously worked out by a thoughtful and suggestive writer, may refer to Professor Macmillan's book on the *Promotion of General Happiness* (Swan Sonnenschein and Co. 1890). The author considers that "the philosophical world is pretty equally divided between optimists and pessimists," and his own judgment on the question at issue between the two schools appears to be held in suspense.

be often assumed by political economists of the school of Malthus—but that at which the product formed by multiplying the number of persons living into the amount of average happiness reaches its maximum.

It may be well here to make a remark which has a wide application in Utilitarian discussion. The conclusion just given wears a certain air of absurdity to the view of Common Sense; because its show of exactness is grotesquely incongruous with our consciousness of the inevitable inexactness of all such calculations in actual practice. But, that our practical Utilitarian reasonings must necessarily be rough, is no reason for not making them as accurate as the the the case admits; and we shall be more likely to succeed in this if we keep before our mind as distinctly as possible the strict type of the calculation that we should have to make, if all the relevant considerations could be estimated with mathematical precision.

There is one more point that remains to be noticed. It is evident that there may be many different ways of distributing the same quantum of happiness among the same number of persons; in order, therefore, that the Utilitarian criterion of right conduct may be as complete as possible, we ought to know which of these ways is to be preferred. This question is often ignored in expositions of Utilitarianism. It has perhaps seemed somewhat idle, as suggesting a purely abstract and theoretical perplexity, that could have no practical exemplification; and no doubt, if all the consequences of actions were capable of being estimated and summed up with mathematical precision, we should probably never find the excess of pleasure over pain exactly equal in the case of two competing alternatives of conduct. But the very indefiniteness of all hedonistic calculations, which was sufficiently shown in Book ii., renders it by no means unlikely that there may be no *cognisable* difference between the quantities of happiness involved in two sets of consequences respectively; the more rough our estimates necessarily are, the less likely we shall be to come to any clear decision between two apparently balanced alternatives. In all such cases, therefore, it becomes practically important to ask whether any mode of distributing a given quantum of happiness is better than any other. Now the Utilitarian formula seems to supply no answer to this question: at least we have to supplement the principle of seeking the greatest happiness on the whole by some principle of Just or Right distribution of this happiness. The principle which most Utilitarians have either tacitly or expressly adopted is that of pure equality—as given in Bentham's formula, "everybody to count for one, and nobody for more than one." And this principle seems the only one which does not need a special justification; for, as we saw, it must be reasonable to treat any one man in the same way as any other, if there be no reason apparent for treating him differently.[5]

Empirical Hedonism

§ **1.** The first and most fundamental assumption, involved not only in the empirical method of Egoistic Hedonism, but in the very conception of "Greatest Happiness" as an end of action, is the commensurability of Pleasures and Pains. By this I mean that we must assume the pleasures sought and the pains shunned to have deter-

---

[5]It should be observed that the question here is as to the distribution of *Happiness,* not the *means of happiness.* If more happiness on the whole is produced by giving the same means of happiness to B rather than to A, it is an obvious and incontrovertible deduction from the Utilitarian principle that it ought to be given to B, whatever inequality in the distribution of the *means* of happiness this may involve.

minate quantitative relations to each other; for otherwise they cannot be conceived as possible elements of a total which we are to seek to make as great as possible. It is not absolutely necessary to exclude the supposition that there are some kinds of pleasure so much more pleasant than others, that the smallest conceivable amount of the former would outweigh the greatest conceivable amount of the latter; since, if this were ascertained to be the case, the only result would be that any hedonistic calculation involving pleasures of the former class might be simplified by treating those of the latter class as practically non-existent.[6] I think, however, that in all ordinary prudential reasoning, at any rate, the assumption is implicitly made that all the pleasures and pains that man can experience bear a finite ratio to each other in respect of pleasantness and its opposite. So far as this ratio can be made definite the Intensity of a pleasure (or pain) can be balanced against its Duration:[7] for if we conceive one pleasure (or pain), finite in duration, to be intensively greater than another in some definite ratio, it seems to be implied in this conception that the latter if continuously increased in extent—without change in its intensity—would at a certain point just balance the former in amount.

If pleasures, then, can be arranged in a scale, as greater or less in some finite degree; we are led to the assumption of a hedonistic zero, or perfectly neutral feeling, as a point from which the positive quantity of pleasures may be measured. And this latter assumption emerges still more clearly when we consider the comparison and balancing of pleasures with pains, which Hedonism necessarily involves. For pain must be reckoned as the negative quantity of pleasure, to be balanced against and subtracted from the positive in estimating happiness on the whole; we must therefore conceive, as at least ideally possible, a point of transition in consciousness at which we pass from the positive to the negative. It is not absolutely necessary to assume that this strictly indifferent or neutral feeling ever actually occurs. Still experience seems to show that a state at any rate very nearly approximating to it is even common: and we certainly experience continual transitions from pleasure to pain and *vice versa,* and thus (unless we conceive all such transitions to be abrupt) we must exist at least momentarily in this neutral state.

[6]We find it sometimes asserted by persons of enthusiastic and passionate temperament, that there are feelings so exquisitely delightful, that one moment of their rapture is preferable to an eternity of agreeable consciousness of an inferior kind. These assertions, however, are perhaps consciously hyperbolical, and not intended to be taken as scientific statements: but in the case of pain, it has been deliberately maintained by a thoughtful and subtle writer, with a view to important practical conclusions, that "torture" so extreme as to be "incommensurable with moderate pain" is an actual fact of experience. (See "A Chapter in the Ethics of Pain," by the late Edmund Gurney, in a volume of essays entitled *Tertium Quid.*) This doctrine, however, does not correspond to my own experience; nor does it appear to me to be supported by the common sense of mankind—at least I do not find, in the practical forethought of persons noted for caution, any recognition of the danger of agony such that, in order to avoid the smallest extra risk of it, the greatest conceivable amount of moderate pain should reasonably be incurred.

[7]Bentham gives four qualities of any pleasure or pain (taken singly) as important for purposes of Hedonistic calculation: (1) Intensity, (2) Duration, (3) Certainty, (4) Proximity. If we assume (as above argued) that Intensity must be commensurable with Duration, the influence of the other qualities on the comparative value of pleasures and pains is not difficult to determine: for we are accustomed to estimate the value of chances numerically, and by this method we can tell exactly (in so far as the degree of uncertainty can be exactly determined) how much the doubtfulness of a pleasure detracts from its value: and *proximity* is a property which it is reasonable to disregard except in so far as it diminishes uncertainty. For my feelings a year hence should be just as important to me as my feelings next minute, if only I could make an equally sure forecast of them. Indeed this equal and impartial concern for all parts of one's conscious life is perhaps the most prominent element in the common notion of the *rational*—as opposed to the merely *impulsive*—pursuit of pleasure.

In what I have just said, I have by implication denied the paradox of Epicurus[8] that the state of painlessness is equivalent to the highest possible pleasure; so that if we can obtain absolute freedom from pain, the goal of Hedonism is reached, after which we may vary, but cannot increase, our pleasure. This doctrine is opposed to common sense and common experience. But it would, I think, be equally erroneous, on the other hand, to regard this neutral feeling—hedonistic zero, as I have called it—as the normal condition of our consciousness, out of which we occasionally sink into pain, and occasionally rise into pleasure. Nature has not been so niggardly to man as this: so long as health is retained, and pain and irksome toil banished, the mere performance of the ordinary habitual functions of life is, according to my experience, a frequent source of moderate pleasures, alternating rapidly with states nearly or quite indifferent. Thus we may venture to say that the "apathy" which so large a proportion of Greek moralists in the post-Aristotelian period regarded as the ideal state of existence, was not really conceived by them as "without one pleasure and without one pain"; but rather as a state of placid intellectual contemplation, which in philosophic minds might easily reach a high degree of pleasure.

2. We have yet to give to the notions of pleasure and pain the precision required for quantitative comparison. In dealing with this point, and in the rest of the hedonistic discussion, it will be convenient for the most part to speak of pleasure only, assuming that pain may be regarded as the negative quantity of pleasure, and that accordingly any statements made with respect to pleasure may be at once applied, by obvious changes of phrase, to pain. . . .

Here, however, a new question comes into view. When I stated in the preceding chapter [Chapter I], as a fundamental assumption of Hedonism, that it is reasonable to prefer pleasures in proportion to their intensity, and not to allow this ground of preference to be outweighed by any merely qualitative difference. I implied that the preference of pleasures on grounds of quality as opposed to quantity—as "higher" or "nobler"—is actually possible: and indeed such non-hedonistic preference is commonly thought to be of frequent occurrence. But if we take the definition of pleasure just given—that it is the kind of feeling which we apprehend to be desirable or preferable—it seems to be a contradiction in terms to say that the less pleasant feeling can ever be thought preferable to the more pleasant.

This contradiction may be avoided as follows. It will be generally admitted that the pleasantness of a feeling is only directly cognisable by the individual who feels it at the time of feeling it. Thus, though (as I shall presently argue), in so far as any estimate of pleasantness involves comparison with feelings only represented in idea, it is liable to be erroneous through imperfections in the representation—still, no one is in a position to controvert the preference of the sentient individual, so far as the quality of the present feeling alone is concerned. When, however, we judge of the preferable quality (as "elevation" or "refinement") of a state of consciousness as distinct from its pleasantness,[9] we seem to appeal to some common standard which others can apply as well as the sentient individual. Hence I should conclude that when one kind of pleasure is judged to be qualitatively superior to another, although less pleasant, it is not really the feeling itself that is preferred, but something in the mental or physical

---

[8]Cf. Cic. *de Fin.* Book i. chap. xi p. 38.

[9]It was before observed that by saying that one pleasure is superior in *quality* to another we may mean that it is preferable when considered merely as pleasant: in which case difference in kind resolves itself into difference in degree.

conditions or relations under which it arises, regarded as cognisable objects of our common thought. For certainly if I in thought distinguish any feeling from all its conditions and concomitants—and also from all its effects on the subsequent feelings of the same individual or of others—and contemplate it merely as the transient feeling of a single subject; it seems to me impossible to find in it any other preferable quality than that which we call its pleasantness, the degree of which is only cognisable directly by the sentient individual.

It should be observed that if this definition of pleasure be accepted, and if, as before proposed, "Ultimate Good" be taken as equivalent to "what is ultimately desirable," the fundamental proposition of ethical Hedonism has chiefly a negative significance; for the statement that "Pleasure is the Ultimate Good" will only mean that nothing is ultimately desirable except desirable feeling, apprehended as desirable by the sentient individual at the time of feeling it. This being so, it may be urged against the definition that it could not be accepted by a moralist of stoical turn, who while recognising pleasure as a fact refused to recognise it as in any degree ultimately desirable. But I think such a moralist ought to admit an implied judgment that a feeling is *per se* desirable to be inseparably connected with its recognition as pleasure; while holding that sound philosophy shows the illusoriness of such judgments. This, in fact, seems to have been substantially the view of the Stoic school. . . .

4. I pass to consider [a] group of duties, often contrasted with those of Benevolence, under the comprehensive notion of Justice.

"That Justice is useful to society," says Hume, "it would be a superfluous undertaking to prove": what he endeavours to show at some length is "that public utility is the *sole* origin of Justice": and the same question of origin has occupied the chief attention of J. S. Mill.[10] Here, however, we are not so much concerned with the growth of the sentiment of Justice from experiences of utility, as with the Utilitarian basis of the mature notion; while at the same time if the analysis previously given be correct, the Justice that is commonly demanded and inculcated is something more complex than these writers have recognised. What Hume (e.g.) means by Justice is rather what I should call Order, understood in its widest sense: the observance of the actual system of rules, whether strictly legal or customary, which bind together the different members of any society into an organic whole, checking malevolent or otherwise injurious impulses, distributing the different objects of men's clashing desires, and exacting such positive services, customary or contractual, as are commonly recognised as matters of debt. And though there have rarely been wanting plausible empirical arguments for the revolutionary paradox quoted by Plato, that "laws are imposed in the interest of rulers," it remains true that the general conduciveness to social happiness of the habit of Order or Law-observance, is, as Hume says, too obvious to need proof; indeed it is of such paramount importance to a community, that even where particular laws are clearly injurious it is usually expedient to observe them, apart from any penalty which their breach might entail on the individual. We saw, however, that Common Sense sometimes bids us refuse obedience to bad laws, because "we ought to obey God rather than men" (though there seems to be no clear intuition as to the kind of degree of badness that justifies resistance); and further allows us, in special emergencies, to violate rules generally good, for "necessity has no law," and "salus populi suprema lex."

These and similar common opinions seem at least to suggest that the limits of

[10]*Utilitarianism,* chap. v.

the duty of Law-observance are to be determined by utilitarian considerations. While, again, the Utilitarian view gets rid of the difficulties in which the attempt to define intuitively the truly legitimate source of legislative authority involved us;[11] at the same time that it justifies to some extent each of the different views current as to the intrinsic legitimacy of governments. For, on the one hand, it finds the moral basis of any established political order primarily in its effects rather than its causes; so that, generally speaking, obedience will seem due to any *de facto* government that is not governing very badly. On the other hand, in so far as laws originating in a particular way are likely to be (1) better, or (2) more readily observed, it is a Utilitarian duty to aim at introducing this mode of origination: and thus in a certain stage of social development it may be right that (e.g.) a "representative system" should be popularly demanded, or possibly (in extreme cases) even introduced by force: while, again, there is expediency in maintaining an ancient mode of legislation, because men readily obey such: and loyalty to a dispossessed government may be on the whole expedient, even at the cost of some temporary suffering and disorder, in order that ambitious men may not find usurpation too easy. Here, as elsewhere, Utilitarianism at once supports the different reasons commonly put forward as absolute, and also brings them theoretically to a common measure, so that in any particular case we have a principle of decision between conflicting political arguments.

As was before said, this Law-observance, in so far at least as it affects the interests of other individuals, is what we frequently mean by Justice. It seems, however,[12] that the notion of Justice, exhaustively analysed, includes several distinct elements combined in a somewhat complex manner: we have to inquire, therefore, what latent utilities are represented by each of these elements.

Now, first, a constant part of the notion, which appears in it even when the Just is not distinguished from the Legal, is impartiality or the negation of arbitrary inequality. This impartiality, as we saw[13] (whether exhibited in the establishment or in the administration of laws), is merely a special application of the wider maxim that it cannot be right to treat two persons differently if their cases are similar in all material circumstances. And Utilitarianism, as we saw, admits this maxim no less than other systems of Ethics. At the same time, this negative criterion is clearly inadequate for the complete determination of what is just in laws, or in conduct generally; when we have admitted this, it still remains to ask, "What are the inequalities in laws, and in the distribution of pleasures and pains outside the sphere of law, which are not arbitrary and unreasonable? and to what general principles can they be reduced?"

Here in the first place we may explain, on utilitarian principles, why apparently arbitrary inequality in a certain part of the conduct of individuals . . . is not regarded as injustice or even—in some cases—as in any way censurable. For freedom of action is an important source of happiness to the agents, and a socially useful stimulus to their energies: hence it is obviously expedient that a man's free choice in the distribution of wealth or kind services should not be restrained by the fear of legal penalties, or even of social disapprobation, beyond what the interests of others clearly require; and therefore, when distinctly recognised claims are satisfied, it is *pro tanto* expedient that the mere preferences of an individual should be treated by others as legitimate grounds for inequality in the distribution of his property or services. Nay, as we have

---

[11]Cf. Book iii. chap. vi. §§ 2, 3.
[12]Cf. Book iii. chap. v.
[13]Book iii. chap. xiii. § 3.

before seen, it is within certain limits expedient that each individual should practically regard his own unreasoned impulses as reasonable grounds of action: as in the rendering of services prompted by such affections as are normally and properly spontaneous and unforced.

Passing to consider the general principles upon which "just claims" as commonly recognised appear to be based, we notice that the grounds of a number of such claims may be brought under the general head of "normal expectations"; but that the stringency of such obligations varies much in degree, according as the expectations are based upon definite engagements, or on some vague mutual understanding, or are merely such as an average man would form from past experience of the conduct of other men. In these latter cases Common Sense appeared to be somewhat perplexed as to the validity of the claims. But for the Utilitarian the difficulty has ceased to exist. He will hold any disappointment of expectations to be *pro tanto* an evil, but a greater evil in proportion to the previous security of the expectant individual, from the greater shock thus given to his reliance on the conduct of his fellow-men generally: and many times greater in proportion as the expectation is generally recognised as normal and reasonable, as in this case the shock extends to all who are in any way cognisant of his disappointment. The importance to mankind of being able to rely on each other's actions is so great, that in ordinary cases of absolutely definite engagements there is scarcely any advantage that can counterbalance the harm done by violating them. Still, we found[14] that several exceptions and qualifications to the rule of Good Faith were more or less distinctly recognised by Common Sense: and most of these have a utilitarian basis, which it does not need much penetration to discern. To begin, we may notice that the superficial view of the obligation of a promise which makes it depend on the assertion of the promiser, and not, as Utilitarians hold, on the expectations produced in the promisee, cannot fairly be attributed to Common Sense: which certainly condemns a breach of promise much more strongly when others have acted in reliance on it, than when its observance did not directly concern others, so that its breach involves for them only the indirect evil of a bad precedent—as when a man breaks a pledge of total abstinence. We see, again, how the utilitarian reasons for keeping a promise are diminished by a material change of circumstances,[15] for in that case the expectations disappointed by breaking it are at least not those which the promise originally created. It is obvious, too, that it is a disadvantage to the community that men should be able to rely on the performance of promises procured by fraud or unlawful force, so far as encouragement is thereby given to the use of fraud or force for this end.[16] We saw, again,[17] that when the performance would be injurious to the promisee, Common Sense is disposed to admit that its obligation is superseded; and is at least doubtful whether the promise should be kept, even when it is only the promiser who would be injured, if the harm be extreme—both which qualifications are in harmony with Utilitarianism. And similarly for the other qualifications and exceptions: they are turn out to be as clearly utilitarian, as the general utility of keeping one's word is plain and manifest.

---

[14]Book iii. chap. vi.

[15]Cf. *ante,* Book iii. chap. vi. § 8.

[16]In the case of force, however, there is the counterbalancing consideration that the unlawful aggressor may be led to inflict worse injury on his victim, if he is unable to rely on the latter's promise.

[17]Cf. Book iii. chap. vi. § 8.

But further, the expediency of satisfying normal expectations, even when they are not based upon a definite contract, is undeniable; it will clearly conduce to the tranquillity of social existence, and to the settled and well-adjusted activity on which social happiness greatly depends, that such expectations should be as little as possible baulked. And here Utilitarianism relieves us of the difficulties which beset the common view of just conduct as something absolutely precise and definite. For in this vaguer region we cannot draw a sharp line between valid and invalid claims; "injustice" shades gradually off into mere "hardship." Hence the Utilitarian veiw that the disappointment of natural expectations is an evil, but an evil which must sometimes be incurred for the sake of a greater good, is that to which Common Sense is practically forced, though it is difficult to reconcile it with the theoretical absoluteness of Justice in the Intuitional view of Morality.

The gain of recognising the relativity of this obligation will be still more felt, when we consider what I distinguished as Ideal Justice, and examine the general conceptions of this which we find expressed or latent in current criticisms of the existing order of Society.

We have seen that there are two competing views of an ideally just social order—or perhaps we may say two extreme types between which the looser notions of ordinary men seem to fluctuate—which I called respectively Individualistic and Socialistic. According to the former view an ideal system of Law ought to aim at Freedom, or perfect mutual non-interference of all the members of the community, as an absolute end. Now the general utilitarian reasons for leaving each rational adult free to seek happiness in his own way are obvious and striking: for, generally speaking, each is best qualified to provide for his own interests, since even when he does not know best what they are and how to attain them, he is at any rate most keenly concerned for them: and again, the consciousness of freedom and concomitant responsibility increases the average effective activity of men: and besides, the discomfort of constraint is directly an evil and *pro tanto* to be avoided. Still, we saw[18] that the attempt to construct a consistent code of laws, taking Maximum Freedom (instead of Happiness) as an absolute end, must lead to startling paradoxes and insoluble puzzles: and in fact the practical interpretation of the notion "Freedom," and the limits within which its realisation has been actually sought, have always—even in the freest societies—been more or less consciously determined by considerations of expediency. So that we may fairly say that in so far as Common Sense has adopted the Individualistic ideal in politics, it has always been as subordinate to and limited by the Utilitarian first principle.[19]

It seems, however, that what we commonly demand or long for, under the name of Ideal Justice, is not so much the realisation of Freedom, as the distribution of good and evil according to Desert: indeed it is as a means to this latter end that Freedom is often advocated; for it is said that if we protect men completely from mutual interference, each will reap the good and bad consequences of his own conduct, and so be happy or unhappy in proportion to his deserts. In particular, it has been widely held that if a free exchange of wealth and services is allowed, each individual will obtain from society, in money or other advantages, what his services are really worth. We saw, however, that the price which an individual obtains under a system or perfect

---

[18]Book iii. chap. v. § 4.

[19]In another work (*Principles of Political Economy,* Book iii. chap. ii.) I have tried to show that complete *laisser faire,* in the organisation of industry, tends in various ways to fall short of the most economic production of wealth.

free trade, for wealth or services exchanged by him, may for several reasons be not proportioned to the social utility of what he exchanges: and reflective Common Sense seems to admit this disproportion as to some extent legitimate, under the influence of utilitarian considerations correcting the unreflective utterances of moral sentiments.

To take a particular case: if a moral man were asked how far it is right to take advantage in bargaining of another's ignorance, probably his first impulse would be to condemn such a procedure altogether. But reflection, I think, would show him that such a censure would be too sweeping: that it would be contrary to Common Sense to "blame *A* for having, in negotiating with a strange *B,* taken advantage of *B*'s ignorance of facts known to himself, provided that *A*'s superior knowledge had been obtained by a legitimate use of diligence and foresight, which *B* might have used with equal success ... What prevents us from censuring in this and similar cases is, I conceive, a more or less conscious apprehension of the indefinite loss to the wealth of the community that is likely to result from any effective social restrictions on the free pursuit and exercise" of economic knowledge. And for somewhat similar reasons of general expediency, if the question be raised whether it is fair for a class of persons to gain by the unfavourable economic situation of any class with which they deal, Common Sense at least hesitates to censure such gains—at any rate when such unfavourable situation is due "to the gradual action of general causes, for the existence of which the persons who gain are not specially responsible."[20]

The general principle of "requiting good desert," so far as Common Sense really accepts it as practically applicable to the relations of men in society, is broadly in harmony with Utilitarianism; since we obviously encourage the production of general happiness by rewarding men for felicific conduct; only the Utilitarian scale of rewards will not be determined entirely by the magnitude of the services performed, but partly also by the difficulty of inducing men to perform them. But this latter element seems to be always taken into account (though perhaps unconsciously) by Common Sense: for, as we have been led to notice,[21] we do not commonly recognise merit in right actions, if they are such as men are naturally inclined to perform rather too much than too little. Again, in cases where the Intuitional principle that ill-desert lies in wrong intention conflicts with the Utilitarian view of punishment as purely preventive, we find that in the actual administration of criminal justice Common Sense is forced, however reluctantly, into practical agreement with Utilitarianism. Thus after a civil war it demands the execution of the most purely patriotic rebels; and after a railway accident it clamours for the severe punishment of unintentional neglects, which, except for their consequences, would have been regarded as very venial.

If, however, in any distribution of pleasures and privileges, or of pains and burdens, considerations of desert do not properly come in (i.e. if the good or evil to be distributed have no relation to any conduct on the part of the persons who are to receive either)—or if it is practically impossible to take such considerations into account—then Common Sense seems to fall back on simple equality as the principle of just apportionment. ... And we have seen that the Utilitarian, in the case supposed, will reasonably accept Equality as the only mode of distribution that is not arbitrary; and it may be observed that this mode of apportioning the means of happines is likely

---

[20]The quotations are from my *Principles of Political Economy,* Book iii. chap. ix; where these questions are discussed at somewhat greater length.

[21]Cf. *ante,* § 2, and Book iii, chap. ii. § 1.

to produce more happiness on the whole, not only because men have a disinterested aversion to unreason, but still more because they have an aversion to any kind of inferiority to others (which is much intensified when the inferiority seems unreasonable). This latter feeling is so strong that it often prevails in spite of obvious claims of desert; and it may even be sometimes expedient that it should so prevail.

Extreme and Restricted Utilitarianism

J. J. C. Smart

I

Utilitarianism is the doctrine that the rightness of actions is to be judged by their consequences. What do we mean by "actions" here? Do we mean particular actions or do we mean classes of actions? According to which way we interpret the word "actions" we get two different theories, both of which merit the appellation "utilitarian."

(1) If by "actions" we mean particular individual actions we get the sort of doctrine held by Bentham, Sidgwick, and Moore. According to this doctrine we test individual actions by their consequences, and general rules, like "keep promises," are mere rules of thumb which we use only to avoid the necessity of estimating the probable consequences of our actions at every step. The rightness or wrongness of keeping a promise on a particular occasion depends only on the goodness or badness of the consequences of keeping or of breaking, the promise on that particular occasion. Of course part of the consequences of breaking the promise, and a part to which we will normally ascribe decisive importance, will be the weakening of faith in the institution of promising. However, if the goodness of the consequences of breaking the rule is *in toto* greater than the goodness of the consequences of keeping it, then we must break the rule, irrespective of whether the goodness of the consequences of *everybody's* obeying the rule is or is not greater than the consequences of *everybody's* breaking it. To put it shortly, rules do not matter, save *per accidens* as rules of thumb and as de facto social institutions with which the utilitarian has to reckon when estimating consequences. I shall call this doctrine "extreme utilitarianism."

(2) A more modest form of utilitarianism has recently become fashionable. The doctrine is to be found in Toulmin's book *The Place of Reason in Ethics,* in Nowell-Smith's *Ethics* (though I think Nowell-Smith has qualms), in John Austin's *Lectures on Jurisprudence* (Lecture II), and even in J. S. Mill, if Urmson's interpretation of him is correct (*Philosophical Quarterly* 3 [January 1953], pp. 33–39. Part of its charm is that it appears to resolve the dispute in moral philosophy between intuitionists and utilitarians in a way which is very neat. The above philosophers hold, or seem to hold, that

From *The Philosophical Quarterly,* vol. 6 (1956), pp. 344–354. Reprinted, with revisions, by permission of the author and *The Philosophical Quarterly.*

moral rules are more than rules of thumb. In general the rightness of an action is *not* to be tested by evaluating its consequences but only by considering whether or not it falls under a certain rule. Whether the rule is to be considered an acceptable moral rule is, however, to be decided by considering the consequences of adopting the rule. Broadly, then, actions are to be tested by rules and rules by consequences. The only cases in which we must test an individual action directly by its consequences are *(a)* when the action comes under two different rules, one of which enjoins it and one of which forbids it, and *(b)* when there is no rule whatever that governs the given case. I shall call this doctrine "restricted utilitarianism."

It should be noticed that the distinction I am making cuts across, and is quite different from, the distinction commonly made between hedonistic and ideal utilitarianism. Bentham was an extreme hedonistic utilitarian and Moore an extreme ideal utilitarian, and Toulmin (perhaps) could be classified as a restricted ideal utilitarian. A hedonistic utilitarian holds that the goodness of the consequences of an action is a function only of their pleasurableness and an ideal utilitarian, like Moore, holds that pleasurableness is not even a necessary condition of goodness. Mill seems, if we are to take his remarks about higher and lower pleasures seriously, to be neither a pure hedonistic nor a pure ideal utilitarian. He seems to hold that pleasurableness is a necessary condition for goodness, but that goodness is a function of other qualities of mind as well. Perhaps we can call him a quasi-ideal utilitarian. When we say that a state of mind is good I take it that we are expressing some sort of *rational preference*. When we say that it is pleasurable I take it that we are saying that it is enjoyable, and when we say that something is a higher pleasure I take it that we are saying that it is more truly, or more deeply, enjoyable. I am doubtful whether "more deeply enjoyable" does not just mean "more enjoyable, even though not more enjoyable on a first look," and so I am doubtful whether quasi-ideal utilitarianism, and possibly ideal utilitarianism too, would not collapse into hedonistic utilitarianism on a closer scrutiny of the logic of words like "preference," "pleasure," "enjoy," "deeply enjoy," and so on. However, it is beside the point of the present paper to go into these questions. I am here concerned only with the issues between extreme and restricted utilitarianism and am ready to concede that both forms of utilitarianism can be either hedonistic or nonhedonistic.

The issue between extreme and restricted utilitarianism can be illustrated by considering the remark "But suppose everyone did the same." (Cf. A. K. Stout's article in *The Australasian Journal of Philosophy,* Vol. 32, pp. 1–29). Stout distinguishes two forms of the universalisation principle, the causal form and the hypothetical form. To say that you ought not to do an action A because it would have bad results if everyone (or many people) did action A may be merely to point out that while the action A would otherwise be the optimific one, nevertheless when you take into account that doing A will probably cause other people to do A too, you can see that A is not, on a broad view, really optimific. If this causal influence could be avoided (as may happen in the case of a secret desert island promise) then we would disregard the universalisation principle. This is the causal form of the principle. A person who accepted the universalisation principle in its hypothetical form would be one who was concerned only with what would happen *if* everyone did the action A: he would be totally unconcerned with the question of whether in fact everyone would do the action A. That is, he might say that it would be wrong not to vote because it would have bad results if everyone took this attitude, and he would be totally unmoved by arguments purporting to show that my refusing to vote has no effect whatever on other people's propensity to vote. Making use of Stout's distinction, we can say that an extreme utilitarian would apply the universalisation principle in the causal form, while a restricted utilitarian would apply it in the hypothetical form.

How are we to decide the issue between extreme and restricted utilitarianism? I wish to repudiate at the outset that milk and water approach which describes itself sometimes as "investigating what is implicit in the common moral consciousness" and sometimes as "investigating how people ordinarily talk about morality." We have only to read the newspaper correspondence about capital punishment or about what should be done with Formosa to realise that the common moral consciousness is in part made up of superstitious elements, of morally bad elements, and of logically confused elements. I address myself to good-hearted and benevolent people and so I hope that if we rid ourselves of the logical confusion the superstitious and morally bad elements will largely fall away. For even among good-hearted and benevolent people it is possible to find superstitious and morally bad reasons for moral beliefs. These superstitious and morally bad reasons, hide behind the protective screen of logical confusion. With people who are not logically confused but who are openly superstitious or morally bad I can of course do nothing. That is, our ultimate pro-attitudes may be different. Nevertheless I propose to rely on *my own* moral consciousness and to appeal to *your* moral consciousness and to forget about what people ordinarily say. "This obligation to obey a rule," says Nowell-Smith (*Ethics,* p. 239), "does not, *in the opinion of ordinary men*" (my italics), "rest on the beneficial consequences of obeying it in a particular case." What does this prove? Surely it is more than likely that ordinary men are confused here. Philosophers should be able to examine the question more rationally.

II

For an extreme utilitarian, moral rules are rules of thumb. In practice the extreme utilitarian will mostly guide his conduct by appealing to the rules ("do not lie," "do not break promises," etc.) of common sense morality. This is not because there is anything sacrosanct in the rules themselves but because he can argue that probably he will most often act in an extreme utilitarian way if he does not think as a utilitarian. For one thing, actions have frequently to be done in a hurry. Imagine a man seeing a person drowning. He jumps in and rescues him. There is no time to reason the matter out, but usually this will be the course of action which an extreme utilitarian would recommend if he did not reason the matter out. If, however, the man drowning had been drowning in a river near Berchtesgaden in 1938, and if he had had the well-known black forelock and moustache of Adolf Hitler, an extreme utilitarian would, if he had time, work out the probability of the man's being the villainous dictator, and if the probability were high enough he would, on extreme utilitarian grounds, leave him to drown. The rescuer, however, has not time. He trusts to his instincts and dives in and rescues the man. And this trusting to instincts and to moral rules can be justified on extreme utilitarian gounds. Furthermore, an extreme utilitarian who knew that the drowning man was Hitler would nevertheless praise the rescuer, not condemn him. For by praising the man he is strengthening a courageous and benevolent disposition of mind, and in general this disposition has great positive utility. (Next time, perhaps, it will be Winston Churchill that the man saves!) We must never forget that an extreme utilitarian may praise actions which he knows to be wrong. Saving Hitler was wrong, but it was a member of a class of actions which are generally right, and the motive to do actions of this class is in general an optimific one. In considering questions of praise and blame it is not the expediency of the praised or blamed action that is at issue, but the expediency of the praise. It can be expedient to praise an inexpedient action and inexpedient to praise an expedient one.

Lack of time is not the only reason why an extreme utilitarian may, on extreme utilitarian principles, trust to rules of common sense morality. He knows that in particular cases where his own interests are involved his calculations are likely to be biased in his own favour. Suppose that he is unhappily married and is deciding whether to get divorced. He will in all probability greatly exaggerate his own unhappiness (and possibly his wife's) and greatly underestimate the harm done to his children by the breakup of the family. He will probably also underestimate the likely harm done by the weakening of the general faith in marriage vows. So probably he will come to the correct extreme utilitarian conclusion if he does not in this instance think as an extreme utilitarian but trust to common sense morality.

There are many more and subtle points that could be made in connection with the relation between extreme utilitarianism and the morality of common sense. All those that I have just made and many more will be found in Book IV Chapters 3–5 of Sidgwick's *Methods of Ethics* [Chapter III is excerpted in this edition; see p. 62]. I think that this book is the best book ever written on ethics, and that these chapters are the best chapters of the book. As they occur so near the end of a very long book they are unduly neglected. I refer the reader, then, to Sidgwick for the classical exposition of the relation between (extreme) utilitarianism and the morality of common sense. One further point raised by Sidgwick in this connection is whether an (extreme) utilitarian ought on (extreme) utilitarian principles to propagate (extreme) utilitarianism among the public. As most people are not very philosophical and not good at empirical calculations, it is probable that they will most often act in an extreme utilitarian way if they do not try to think as extreme utilitarians. We have seen how easy it would be to misapply the extreme utilitarian criterion in the case of divorce. Sidgwick seems to think it quite probable that an extreme utilitarian should not propagate his doctrine too widely. However, the great danger to humanity comes nowadays on the plane of public morality—not private morality. There is greater danger to humanity from the hydrogen bomb than from an increase of the divorce rate, regrettable though that might be, and there seems no doubt that extreme utilitarianism makes for good sense in international relations. When France walked out of the United Nations because she did not wish Morocco discussed, she said that she was within her rights because Morocco and Algiers are part of her metropolitan territory and nothing to do with U.N. This was clearly a legalistic if not superstitious argument. We should not be concerned with the so-called "rights" of France or any other country but with whether the cause of humanity would best be served by discussing Morocco in U.N. (I am not saying that the answer to this is "Yes." There are good grounds for supposing that more harm than good would come by such a discussion.) I myself have no hesitation in saying than on extreme utilitarian principles we ought to propagate extreme utilitarianism as widely as possible. But Sidgwick had respectable reasons for suspecting the opposite.

The extreme utilitarian, then, regards moral rules as rules of thumb and as sociological facts that have to be taken into account when deciding what to do, just as facts of any other sort have to be taken into account. But in themselves they do not justify any action.

III

The restricted utilitarian regards moral rules as more than rules of thumb for short-circuiting calculations of consequences. Generally, he argues, consequences are not relevant at all when we are deciding what to do in a particular case. In general, they are relevant only to deciding what rules are good reasons for acting in a certain way in particular cases. This doctrine is possibly a good account of how the modern unreflective twentieth-century Englishman often thinks about morality, but surely it is monstrous as an account of how it is most rational to think about morality. Suppose that there is a rule *R* and that in 99% of cases the best possible results are obtained by acting in accordance with *R*. Then clearly *R* is a useful rule of thumb; if we have not time or are not impartial enough to assess the consequences of an action it is an extremely good bet that the thing to do is to act in accordance with *R*. But is it not monstrous to suppose that if we *have* worked out the consequences and if we have perfect faith in the impartiality of our calculations, and if we *know* that in this instance to break *R* will have better results than to keep it, we should nevertheless obey the rule? Is it not to erect *R* into a sort of idol if we keep it when breaking it will prevent, say, some avoidable misery? Is not this a form of superstitious rule-worship (easily explicable psychologically) and not the rational thought of a philosopher?

The point may be made more clearly if we consider Mill's comparison of moral rules to the tables in the nautical almanack. (*Utilitarianism*, Everyman's Edition pp. 22–23). This comparison of Mill's is adduced by Urmson as evidence that Mill was a restricted utilitarian but I do not think that it will bear this interpretation at all. (Though I quite agree with Urmson that many other things said by Mill are in harmony with restricted rather than extreme utilitarianism. Probably Mill had never thought very much about the distinction and was arguing for utilitarianism, restricted or extreme, against other and quite non-utilitarian forms of moral argument.) Mill says: "Nobody argues that the art of navigation is not founded on astronomy, because sailors cannot wait to calculate the Nautical Almanack. Being rational creatures, they go out upon the sea of life with their minds made up on the common questions of right and wrong, as well as on many of the far more difficult questions of wise and foolish. . . . Whatever we adopt as the fundamental principle of morality, we require subordinate principles to apply it by." Notice that this is, as it stands, only an argument for subordinate principles as rules of thumb. The example of the nautical almanack is misleading because the information given in the almanack is in all cases the same as the information one would get if one made a long and laborious calculation from the original astronomical data on which the almanack is founded. Suppose, however, that astronomy were different. Suppose that the behaviour of the sun, moon, and planets was very nearly as it is now, but that on rare occasions there were peculiar irregularities and discontinuities, so that the almanack gave us rules of the form "in 99% of cases where the observations are such and such you can deduce that your position is so and so." Furthermore, let us suppose that there were methods which enabled us, by direct and laborious calculation from the original astronomical data, not using the rough and ready tables of the almanack, to get our correct position in 100% of cases. Seafarers might use the almanack because they never had time for the long calculations and they were content with a 99% chance of success in calculating their positions. Would it not be absurd, however, if they *did* make the direct calculation, and, finding that it disagreed with the almanack calculation, nevertheless ignored it and stuck to the almannack conclusion? Of course the case would be altered if there were a high enough probability of making slips in the direct calculation: then we might stick to the almanack result, liable to error though we knew it to be, simply because the direct calculation would be open to error for a different reason, the fallibility of the computer. This would be analogous to the case of the extreme utilitarian who abides by the conventional rule against the dictates of his utilitarian calculations simply because he thinks that his calculations are probably affected by personal bias. But if the navigator were sure of his direct calculations would he not be foolish to abide by his almanack? I conclude, then, that if we change our suppositions about astronomy and the almanack (to which there are no exceptions) to bring the case into line with that of morality (to whose rules there are exceptions), Mill's example loses its appearance of supporting the restricted form of utilitarianism. Let me say once more that I am not here concerned with how ordinary men think about morality but with how they ought to think. We could quite well imagine a race of sailors who acquired a superstitious reverence for their almanack, even though it was only right in 99% of cases, and who indignantly threw overboard any man who mentioned the possibility of a direct calculation. But would this behaviour of the sailors be rational?

Let us consider a much discussed sort of case in which the extreme utilitarian might go against the conventional moral rule. I have promised to a friend, dying on a desert island from which I am subsequently rescued, that I will see that his fortune (over which I have control) is given to a jockey club. However, when I am rescued I decide that it would be better to give the money to a hospital, which can do more good with it. It may be argued that I am wrong to give the money to the hospital. But why? *(a)* The hospital can do more good with the money than the jockey club can. *(b)* The present case is unlike most cases of promising in that no one except me knows about the promise. In breaking the promise I am doing so with complete secrecy and am doing nothing to weaken the general faith in promises. That is, a factor which would normally keep the extreme utilitarian from promise breaking even in otherwise unoptimific cases does not at present operate. *(c)* There is no doubt a slight weakening in my own character as an habitual promise keeper, and moreover psychological tensions will be set up in me every time I am asked what the man made me promise him to do. For clearly I shall have to say that he made me promise to give the money to the hospital, and, since I am an habitual truth teller, this will go very much against the grain with me. Indeed I am pretty sure that in practice I myself would keep the promise. But we are not discussing what my moral habits would probably make me do; we are discussing what I ought to do. Moreover, we must not forget that even if it would be most rational of me to give the money to the hospital it would also be most rational of you to punish or condemn me if you did, most improbably, find out the truth (e.g. by finding a note washed ashore in a bottle). Furthermore, I would agree that though it was most rational of me to give the money to the hospital it would be most rational of you to condemn me for it. We revert again to Sidgwick's distinction between the utility of the action and the utility of the praise of it.

Many such issues are discussed by A. K. Stout in the article to which I have already referred. I do not wish to go over the same ground again, especially as I think that Stout's arguments support my own point of view. It will be useful, however, to consider one other example that he gives. Suppose that during hot weather there is an edict that no water must be used for watering gardens. I have a garden and I reason that most people are sure to obey the edict, and that as the amount of water that I use will be by itself negligible no harm will be done if I use the water secretly. So I do use the water, thus producing some lovely flowers which give happiness to various people. Still, you may say, though the action was perhaps optimific, it was unfair and wrong.

There are several matters to consider. Certainly my action should be condemned. We revert once more to Sidgwick's distinction. A right action may be rationally condemned. Furthermore, this sort of offence is normally found out. If I have a wonderful garden when everybody else's is dry and brown there is only one explanation. So if I water my garden I am weakening my respect for law and order, and as this leads to bad results an extreme utilitarian would agree that I was wrong to water the garden. Suppose now that the case is altered and that I can keep the thing secret: there is a secluded part of the garden where I grow flowers which I give away anonymously to a home for old ladies. Are you still so sure that I did the wrong thing by watering my garden? However, this is still a weaker case than that of the hospital and the jockey club. There will be tensions set up within myself: my secret knowledge that I have broken the rule will make it hard for me to exhort others to keep the rule. These psychological ill effects in myself may be not inconsiderable: directly and indirectly they may lead to harm which is at least of the same order as the happiness that the old ladies get from the flowers. You can see that on an extreme utilitarian view there are two sides to the question.

So far I have been considering the duty of an extreme utilitarian in a predominantly non-utilitarian society. The case is altered if we consider the extreme utilitarian who lives in a society every member, or most members, of which can be expected to reason as he does. Should he water his flowers now? (Granting, what is doubtful, that in the case already considered he would have been right to water his flowers.) As a first approximation, the answer is that he should not do so. For since the situation is a completely symmetrical one, what is rational for him is rational for others. Hence, by a reductio ad absurdum argument, it would seem that watering his garden would be rational for none. Nevertheless, a more refined analysis shows that the above argument is not quite correct, though it is correct enough for practical purposes. The argument considers each person as confronted with the choice either of watering his garden or of not watering it. However there is a third possibility, which is that each person should, with the aid of a suitable randomising device, such as throwing dice, give himself a certain probability of watering his garden. This would be to adopt what in the theory of games is called "a mixed strategy." If we could give numerical values to the private benefit of garden watering and to the public harm done by 1, 2, 3, etc., persons using the water in this way, we could work out a value of the probability of watering his garden that each extreme utilitarian should give himself. Let a be the value which each extreme utilitarian gets from watering his garden, and let $f(1), f(2), f(3)$, etc., be the public harm done by exactly 1, 2, 3, etc., persons respectively watering their gardens. Suppose that p is the probability that each person gives himself of watering his garden. Then we can easily calculate, as functions of p, the probabilities that exactly 1, 2, 3, etc., persons will water their gardens. Let these probabilities be p_1, $p_2 \ldots p_n$. Then the total net probable benefit can be expressed as

$$V = p_1 (a - f(1)) + p_2 (2a - f(2)) + \ldots p_n (na - f(n))$$

Then if we know the function $f(x)$ we can calculate the value of p for which $\dfrac{dV}{dp} = 0$.

This gives the value of p which it would be rational for each extreme utilitarian to adopt. The present argument does of course depend on a perhaps unjustified assumption that the values in question are measurable, and in a practical case such as that of the garden watering we can doubtless assume that p will be so small that we can take it near enough as equal to zero. However, the argument is of interest for the theoretical underpinning of extreme utilitarianism, since the possibility of a mixed strategy is usually neglected by critics of utilitarianism, who wrongly assume that the only relevant and symmetrical alternatives are of the form "everybody does X" and "nobody does X."

I now pass on to a type of case which may be thought to be the trump card of restricted utilitarianism. Consider the rule of the road. It may be said that since all that matters is that everyone should do the same it is indifferent which rule we have, "go on the left hand side" or "go on the right hand side." Hence the only *reason* for going on the left hand side in British countries is that this is the rule. Here the rule does seem to be a reason, in itself, for acting in a certain way. I wish to argue against this. The rule in itself is not a reason for our actions. We would be perfectly justified in going on the right hand side if *(a)* we knew that the rule was to go on the left hand side, and *(b)* we were in a country peopled by superanarchists who always on principle did the opposite of what they were told. This shows that the rule does not give us a reason for acting so much as an indication of the probable action of others, which helps us to find out what would be our own most rational course of action. If we are in a country not peopled by anarchists, but by non-anarchist extreme utilitarians, we expect, other things being equal, that they will keep rules laid down for them. Knowledge of the rule enables us to predict their behaviour and to harmonise our own actions with theirs. The rule "keep to the left hand side," then, is not a logical *reason* for action but an anthropological *datum* for planning actions.

I conclude that in every case if there is a rule R the keeping of which is in general optimific, but such that in a special sort of circumstances the optimific behaviour is to break R, then in these circumstances we should break R. Of course we must consider all the less obvious effects of breaking R, such as reducing people's faith in the moral order, before coming to the conclusion that to break R is right: in fact we shall rarely come to such a conclusion. Moral rules, on the extreme utilitarian view, are rules of thumb only, but they are not bad rules of thumb. But if we *do* come to the conclusion that we should break the rule and if we have weighed in the balance our own fallibility and liability to personal bias, what good reason remains for keeping the rule? I can understand "it is optimific" as a reason for action, but why should "it is a member of a class of actions which are usually optimific" or "it is a member of a class of actions which as a class are more optimific than any alternative general class" to be a good reason? You might as well say that a person ought to be picked to play for Australia just because all his brothers have been, or that the Australian team should be composed entirely of the Harvey family because this would be better than composing it entirely of any other family. The extreme utilitarian does not appeal to artificial feelings, but only to our feelings of benevolence, and what better feelings can there be to appeal to? Admittedly we can have a pro-attitude to anything, even to rules, but such artificially begotten pro-attitudes smack of superstition. Let us get down to realities, human happiness and misery, and make these the objects of our pro-attitudes and anti-attitudes.

The restricted utilitarian might say that he is talking only of *morality,* not of such things as rules of the road. I am not sure how far this objection, if valid, would affect my argument, but in any case I would reply that as a philosopher I conceive of ethics as the study of how it would be *most rational* to act. If my opponent wishes to restrict the word "morality" to a narrower use he can have the word. The fundamental question is the question of rationality of action *in general*. Similarly if the restricted utilitarian were to appeal to ordinary usage and say "it might be most rational to leave Hitler to drown but it would surely not be *wrong* to rescue him," I should again let him have the words "right" and "wrong" and should stick to "rational" and "irrational." We already saw that it would be rational not to have rescued Hitler. In ordinary langauge, no doubt, "right" and "wrong" have not only the meaning "most rational to do" and "not most rational to do" but also have the meaning "praiseworthy" and "not praiseworthy." Usually to the utility of an action corresponds utility of praise of it, but as we saw, this is not always so. Moral language could thus do with tidying up, for example by reserving "right" for "most rational" and "good" as an epithet of praise for the motive from which the action sprang. It would be more becoming in a philosopher to try to iron out illogicalities in moral language and to make suggestions for its reform than to use it as a court of appeal whereby to perpetuate confusions.

One last defense of restricted utilitarianism might be as follows. "Act optimifically" might be regarded as itself one of the rules of our system (though it would be odd to say that this rule was justified by its optimificality). According to Toulmin (*The Place of Reason in Ethics* [Cambridge: The University Press, 1950], pp. 146–48) if "keep promises," say, conflicts with another rule we are allowed to argue the case on its merits as if we were extreme utilitarians. If "act optimifically" is itself one of our rules then there will always be a conflict of rules whenever to keep a rule is not itself optimific. If this is so, restricted utilitarianism collapses into extreme utilitarianism. And no one could read Toulmin's book or Urmson's article on Mill without thinking that Toulmin and Urmson are of the opinion that they have thought of a doctrine which does *not* collapse into extreme utilitarianism, but which is, on the contrary, an improvement on it.

Some Merits of One Form of Rule Utilitarianism

R. B. Brandt

Utilitarianism is the thesis that the moral predicates of an act—at least its objective rightness or wrongness, and sometimes also its moral praiseworthiness or blameworthiness—are functions in some way, direct or indirect, of consequences for the welfare of sentient creatures, and of nothing else. Utilitarians differ about what precise

From *The University Study Series in Philosophy,* no. 3, © Colorado Associated University Press, 1965. Reprinted by permission of the Colorado Associated University Press.

function they are; and they differ about what constitutes welfare and how it is to be measured. But they agree that all one needs to know, in order to make moral appraisals correctly, is the consequences of certain things for welfare.

Utilitarianism is thus a normative ethical thesis and not, at least not necessarily, a meta-ethical position—that is, a position about the meaning and justification of ethical statements. It is true that some utilitarians have declared that the truth of the normative thesis follows, given the ordinary, or proper, meaning of moral terms such as "right." I shall ignore this further, meta-ethical claim. More recently some writers have suggested something very similar, to the effect that our concept of "morality" is such that we could not call a system of rules a "moral system" unless it were utilitarian in some sense. . . .

II

If an analysis of concepts like "morally wrong" and "morality" and "moral code" does not enable us to establish the truth of the utilitarian thesis, the question arises what standard a normative theory like utilitarianism has to meet in order for a reasonable presumption to be established in its favor. It is well known that the identity and justification of any such standard can be debated at length. In order to set bounds to the present discussion, I shall state briefly the standard I shall take for granted for purposes of the present discussion. Approximately this standard would be acceptable to a good many writers on normative ethics. However this may be, it would be agreed that it is worth knowing whether some form of utilitarianism meets this standard better than any other form of utilitarian theory, and it is this question which I shall discuss.

The standard which I suggest an acceptable normative moral theory has to meet is this: The theory must contain no unintelligible concepts or internal inconsistencies; it must not be inconsistent with known facts; it must be capable of precise formulation so that its implications for action can be determined; and—most important—its implications must be acceptable to thoughtful persons who have had reasonably wide experience, when taken in the light of supporting remarks that can be made and when compared with the implications of other clearly statable normative theories. It is not required that the implications of a satisfactory theory be consonant with the uncriticized moral intuitions of intelligent and experienced people, but only with those intuitions which stand in the light of supporting remarks, etc. Furthermore, it is not required of an acceptable theory that the best consequences would be produced by people adopting that theory, in contrast to other theories by which they might be convinced. (The theory might be so complex that it would be a good thing if most people did not try their hand at applying it to concrete situations!) It may be a moving *ad hominem* argument, if one can persuade an act-utilitarian that it would have bad consequences for people to try to determine the right act according to that theory, and to live by their conclusions; but such a showing would not be a reasonable ground for rejecting that normative theory. . . .

IV

The type of utilitarianism on which I wish to focus is a form of rule utilitarianism, as contrasted with act utilitarianism. According to the latter type of theory (espoused by Sidgwick and Moore), an act is objectively right if no other act the agent could perform would produce better consequences. (On this view, an act is blameworthy if and only if it is right to perform the act of blaming or condemning it; the principles of blame-worthiness are a special case of the principle of objectively right actions.) Act utilitari-anism is hence a rather atomistic theory: the rightness of a single act is fixed by its effect on the world. Rule utilitarianism, in contrast, is the view that the rightness of an act is fixed, not by its relative utility, but by the utility of having a relevant moral rule or of most or all members of a certain class of acts being performed.

The implications of act utilitarianism are seriously counterintuitive, and I shall ignore it except to consider whether some ostensibly different theories really are dif-ferent.

V

Rule utilitarianisms may be divided into two main groups, according as the rightness of a particular act is made a function of ideal rules in some sense, or of the actual and recognized rules of a society. The variety of theory I shall explain more fully is of the former type.

According to the latter type of theory, a person's moral duties or obligations in a particular situation are determined, with some exceptions, solely by the moral rules, or institutions or practices prevalent in the society, and not by what rules (etc.) it would ideally be best to have in the society. (It is sometimes held that actual moral rules, practices, etc., are only a necessary condition of an act's being morally obliga-tory or wrong.) Views roughly of this sort have been held in recent years by A. Mac-beath, Stephen Toulmin, John Rawls, P. F. Strawson, J. O. Urmson, and B. J. Diggs. Indeed, Strawson says in effect that for there to be a moral obligation on one is just for there to be a socially sanctioned demand on him, in a situation where he has an inter-est in the system of demands which his society is wont to impose on its members, and where such demands are generally acknowledged and respected by members of his society.[1] And Toulmin asserts that when a person asks, "Is this the right thing to do?" what he is normally asking is whether a proposed action "conforms to the moral code" of his group, "whether the action in question belongs to a class of actions gen-erally approved of in the agent's community." In deliberating about the question what is right to do, he says, "there is no more general 'reason' to be given beyond one which related the action . . . to an accepted social practice."[2]

So far the proposal does not appear to be a form of utilitarianism at all. The the-ory is utilitarian, however, in the following way: it is thought that what is relevant for a decision whether to try to change moral codes, institutions, etc., or for a justification of them, is the relative utility of the code, practice, etc. The recognized code or practice determines the individual's moral obligations in a particular case; utility of the code or practice determines whether it is justified or ought to be changed. Furthermore, it is sometimes held that utilitarian considerations have some relevance to the rightness of a particular action. For instance, Toulmin thinks that in case the requirements of the recognized code or practice conflict in a particular case, the individual ought (al-though strictly, he is not morally obligated) to do what will maximize utility in the situ-

---

[1]P. F. Strawson, "Social Morality and Individual Ideal," *Philosophy* 36 (1961), 1–17.

[2]Stephen Toulmin, *An Examination of the Place of Reason in Ethics* (Cambridge: The University Press, 1950), pp. 144–145. See various acute criticisms, with which I mostly agree, in Rawls's review, *Philos. Rev.* 60 (1951): 572–580.

ation, and that in case an individual can relieve the distress of another, he ought (strictly, is not morally obligated) to do so, even if the recognized code does not require him to.[3]

This theory, at least in some of its forms or parts, has such conspicuously counterintuitive implications that it fails to meet the standard for a satisfactory normative theory. In general, we do not believe that an act's being prohibited by the moral code of one's society is sufficient to make it morally wrong. Moral codes have prohibited such things as work on the Sabbath, marriage to a divorced person, medically necessary abortion, and suicide; but we do not believe it was really wrong for persons living in a society with such prohibitions, to do these things.[4]

Neither do we think it a necessary condition of an act's being wrong that it be prohibited by the code of the agent's society, or of an act's being obligatory that it be required by the code of his society. A society may permit a man to have his wife put to death for infidelity or to have a child put to death for almost any reason; but we still think such actions wrong. Moreover, a society may permit a man absolute freedom in divorcing his wife and recognize no obligations on his part toward her; but we think, I believe, that a man has some obligations for the welfare of a wife of thirty years' standing (with some qualifications), whatever his society may think.[5]

Some parts of the theory in some of its forms, however, appear to be correct. In particular, the theory in some forms implies that, if a person has a certain recognized obligation in an institution or practice (e.g., a child to support his aged parent, a citizen to pay his taxes), then he morally does have the obligation, with some exceptions, irrespective of whether in an ideal institution he would or would not have. This we do roughly believe, although we need not at the same time accept the reasoning which has been offered to explain how the fact of a practice or institution leads to the moral obligation. The fact that the theory seems right in this would be a strong point in its favor if charges were correct that "ideal" forms of rule utilitarianism necessarily differ at this point. B. J. Diggs, for instance, has charged that the "ideal" theories imply that:

> "one may freely disregard a rule if ever he discovers that action on the rule is not maximally felicific, and in this respect makes moral rules like 'practical maxims.' . . . It deprives social and moral rules of their authority and naturally is in sharp conflict with practice. On this alternative rule utilitarianism collapses into act utilitarianism. Surely it is a mistake to maintain that a set of rules, thought to

[3]Toulmin and Rawls sometimes go further and suggest that a person is morally free to do something which the actual code or practice of his society prohibits, if he is convinced that the society would be better off if the code or practice were rewritten so as to permit that sort of thing, and he is prepared to live according to the ideally revised code. If their theory were developed in this direction, it need not be different from some "ideal" forms of rule utilitarianism, although, as stated, the theory makes the recognized code the standard for moral obligations, with exceptions granted to individuals, who hold certain moral opinions. See Toulmin, *Reason in Ethics,* pp. 151–152, and Rawls, "Two Concepts of Rules," *Philos. Rev.* 64 (1955), pp. 28–29, especially ftnt. 25. It should be noticed that Rawls's proposal is different from Toulmin's in an important way. He is concerned with only a segment of the moral code, the part which can be viewed as the rules of practices. As he observes, this may be only a small part of the moral code.

[4]Does a stranger living in a society have a moral obligation to conform to its moral code? I suggest we think that he does not, unless it is the right moral code or perhaps at least he thinks it is, although we think that the offense he might give to the feelings of others should be taken into account, as well as the result his nonconformity might have in weakening regard for moral rules in general.

[5]It is a different question whether we should hold offenders in such societies seriously morally blameworthy. People cannot be expected to rise much above the level of recognized morality, and we condemn them little when they do not.

be ideally utilitarian or felicific, is the criterion of right action . . . If we are presented with a list [of rules], but these are not rules in practice, the most one could reasonably do is to try to get them adopted."[6]

I believe, however, and shall explain in detail later that this charge is without foundation.

VI

Let us turn now to "ideal" forms of rule utilitarianism, which affirm that whether it is morally obligatory or morally right to do a certain thing in a particular situation is fixed not by the actual code or practice of the society (these may be indirectly relevant, as forming part of the situation) but by some "ideal" rule—that is, by the utility of having a certain general moral rule or by the utility of all or most actions being performed which are members of a relevant class of actions.

If the rightness of an act is fixed by the utility of a relevant rule (class), are we to say that the rule (class) which qualifies must be the optimific rule (class), the one which maximizes utility, or must the rule (class) meet only some less stringent requirement (e.g., be better than the absence of any rule regulating the type of conduct in question)? And, if it is to be of the optimific type, are all utilities to be counted, or perhaps only "negative" utilities, as is done when it is suggested that the rule (class) must be the one which minimizes suffering?[7]

The simplest proposal—that the rule (class) which qualifies is the one that maximizes utility, with all utilities, whether "positive" or "negative," being counted—also seems to me to be the best, and it is the one I shall shortly explain more fully. . . .

VII

I propose, then, that we tentatively opt for an "ideal" rule utilitarianism, of the "maximizing utility" variety. This decision, however, leaves various choices still to be made between theories better or worse fitted to meet various problems. Rather than attempt to list alternatives and explain why one choice rather than another between them would work out better, I propose to describe in some detail the type of theory which seems most plausible. I shall later show how this theory meets the one problem to which the "actual rule" type theories seemed to have a nice solution; and I shall discuss its merits, as compared with another quite similar type of theory which has been suggested by Jonathan Harrison and others.

The theory I wish to describe is rather similar to one proposed by J. D. Mabbott in his 1953 British Academy lecture, "Moral Rules." It is also very similar to the view defended by J. S. Mill in *Utilitarianism,* although Mill's formulation is ambiguous at some points and he apparently did not draw some distinctions he should have drawn. (I shall revert to this historical point.)

---

[6]"Rules and Utilitarianism," *American Philosophical Quarterly* 1 (1964), 32–44.

[7]In a footnote to Chapter 9 of *The Open Society,* Professor Karl R. Popper suggested that utilitarianism would be more acceptable if its test were minimizing suffering rather than maximizing welfare, to which J. J. C. Smart replied (*Mind* (1958), pp. 542–543) that the proposal implies that we ought to destroy all living beings, as the surest way to eliminate suffering. It appears, however, that Professor Popper does not seriously advocate what seemed to be the position of the earlier footnote (Addendum to fourth edition, p. 386).

For convenience I shall refer to the theory as the "ideal moral code" theory. The essence of it is as follows. Let us first say that a moral code is "ideal" if its currency in a particular society would produce at least as much good per person (the total divided by the number of persons) as the currency of any other moral code. (Two different codes might meet this condition, but, in order to avoid complicated formulations, the following discussion will ignore this possibility.) Given this stipulation for the meaning of "ideal," the Ideal Moral Code theory consists in the assertion of the following thesis: *An act is right if and only if it would not be prohibited by the moral code ideal for the society; and an agent is morally blameworthy (praiseworthy) for an act if, and to the degree that, the moral code ideal in that society would condemn (praise) him for it*. It is a virtue of this theory that it is a theory both about objective rightness and about moral blameworthiness (praiseworthiness) of actions, but the assertion about blameworthiness will be virtually ignored in what follows.

VIII

In order to have a clear proposal before us, however, the foregoing summary statement must be filled out in three ways: (1) by explaining what it is for a moral code to have currency; (2) by making clear what is the difference between the rules of a society's moral code and the rules of its institutions; and (3) by describing how the relative utility of a moral code is to be estimated.

First, then, the notion of a moral code having currency in a society.

For a moral code to have currency in a society, two things must be true. First, a high proportion of the adults in the society must subscribe to the moral principles, or have the moral opinions, constitutive of the code. Exactly how high the proportion should be, we can hardly decide on the basis of the ordinary meaning of "the moral code"; but probably it would not be wrong to require at least ninety percent agreement. Thus, if at least 90 percent of the adults subscribe to principle *A,* and 90 percent to principle *B,* etc., we may say that a code consisting of *A* and *B* (etc.) has currency in the society, provided the second condition is met. Second, we want to say that certain principles *A, B,* etc., belong to the moral code of a society only if they are recognized as such. That is, it must be that a large proportion of the adults of the society would respond correctly if asked, with respect to *A* and *B,* whether most members of the society subscribed to them. (It need not be required that adults base their judgments on such good evidence a recollection of moral discussions; it is enough if for some reason the correct opinion about what is accepted is widespread.) It is of course possible for certain principles to constitute a moral code with currency in a society even if some persons in the society have no moral opinions at all, or if there is disagreement, e.g., if everyone in the society disagrees with every other person with respect to at least one principle.

The more difficult question is what it is for an individual to subscribe to a moral principle or to have a moral opinion. What is it, then, for someone to think sincerely that any action of the kind *F* is wrong? (1) He is to some extent motivated to avoid actions which he thinks are *F,* and often, if asked why he does not perform such an action when it appears to be to his advantage, offers, as one of his reasons, that it is *F*. In addition, the person's motivation to avoid *F*-actions does not derive entirely from his belief that *F*-actions on his part are likely to be harmful to him or to persons to whom he is somehow attached. (2) If he thinks he has just performed an *F*-action, he feels guilty or remorseful or uncomfortable about it, unless he thinks he has some ex-cuse—unless, for instance, he knows that at the time of action he did not think his ac-tion would be an *F*-action. "Guilt" (etc.) is not to be understood as implying some special origin such as interiorization of parental prohibitions, or as being a vestige of anxiety about punishment. It is left open that it might be an unlearned emotional re-sponse to the thought of being the cause of the suffering of another person. Any feel-ing which must be viewed simply as anxiety about anticipated consequences, for one's self or person to whom one is attached, is not, however, to count as a "guilt" feeling. (3) If he believes that someone has performed an *F*-action, he will tend to admire him less as a person, unless he thinks that the individual has a good excuse. He thinks that action of this sort, without excuse reflects on character—this being spelled out, in part, by reference to traits like honesty, respect for the rights of others, and so on. (4) He thinks that these attitudes of his are correct or well justified, in some sense, but with one restriction: it is not enough if he thinks that what justifies them is simply the fact that they are shared by all or most members of his society. This restriction corre-sponds with our distinction between a moral conviction and something else. For in-stance, we are inclined to think no moral attitude is involved if an Englishman disapproves of something but says that his disapproval is justified by the fact that it is shared by "well-bred Englishmen." In such cases we are inclined to say that the indi-vidual subscribes only to a custom or to a rule of etiquette or manners. On the other hand, if the individual thinks that what justifies his attitude unfavorable to *F*-actions is that *F*-actions are contrary to the will of God (and the individual's attitude is not merely a prudential one), or inconsistent with the welfare of mankind, or contrary to human nature, we are disposed to say the attitude is a moral attitude and the opinions expressed a moral one. And the same if he thinks his attitude justified, but can give no reason. There are perhaps other restrictions we should make on acceptable justifica-tions (perhaps to distinguish a moral code from a code of honor), and other types of justification we should wish to list as clearly acceptable (perhaps an appeal to human equality).

IX

It is important to distinguish between the moral code of a society and its institutions, or the rules of its institutions. It is especially important for the Ideal Moral Code the-ory, for this theory involves the conception of a moral code ideal for a society in the context of its institutions, so that it is necessary to distinguish the moral code which a society does or might have from its institutions and their rules. The distinction is also one we actually do make in our thinking, although it is blurred in some cases. (For in-stance, is "Honor thy father and thy mother" a moral rule, or a rule of the family insti-tution, in our society?)[8]

An institution is a set of positions or statuses, with which certain privileges and jobs are associated. (We can speak of these as "rights" and "duties" if we are careful to explain that we do not mean moral rights and duties.) That is, there are certain, usually

---

[8]The confusion is compounded by the fact that terms like "obligation" and "duty" are used sometimes to speak about moral obligations and duties, and sometimes not. The fact that persons have a certain legal duty in certain situations is a rule of the legal institutions of the society; a person may not have a moral duty to do what is his legal duty. The fact that a person has an obligation to invite a certain individual to dinner is a matter of manners or etiquette, and at least may not be a matter of moral obligation. See R. B. Brandt, "The Concepts of Duty and Obligation," *Mind* 73 (1964), especially pp. 380–384.

nameable, positions which consist in the fact that anyone who is assigned to the position is expected to do certain things, and at the same time is expected to have certain things done for him. The individuals occupying these positions are a group of cooperating agents in a system which as a whole is thought to have the aim of serving certain ends. (E.g., a university is thought to serve the ends of education, research, etc.) The rules of the system concern jobs that must be done in order that the goals of the institution be achieved; they allocate the necessary jobs to different positions. Take, for instance, a university. There are various positions in it: the presidency, the professorial ranks, the registrars, librarians, etc. It is understood that one who occupies a certain post has certain duties, say teaching a specified number of classes or spending time working on research in the case of the instructing staff. Obviously the university cannot achieve its ends unless certain persons do the teaching, some tend to the administration, some to certain jobs in the library, and so on. Another such system is the family. We need not speculate on the "purpose" of the family, whether it is primarily a device for producing a new generation, etc. But it is clear that when a man enters marriage, he takes a position to which certain jobs are attached, such as providing support for the family to the best of his ability, and to which also certain rights are attached, such as exclusive sexual rights with his wife and the right to be cared for should he become incapacitated.

If an "institution" is defined in this way, it is clear that the moral code of a society cannot itself be construed as an institution, nor its rules as rules of an institution. The moral code is society-wide, so if we were to identify its rules as institutional rules, we should presumably have to say that everyone belongs to this institution. But what is the "purpose" of society as a whole? Are there any distinctions of status, with rights and duties attached, which we could identify as the "positions" in the moral system? Can we say that moral rules consist in the assignment of jobs in such a way that the aims of the institution may be achieved? It is true that there is a certain analogy: society as a whole might be said to be aiming at the good life for all, and the moral rules of the society might be viewed as the rules with which all must conform in order to achieve this end. But the analogy is feeble. Society as a whole is obviously not an organization like a university, an educational system, the church, General Motors, etc.; there is no specific goal in the achievement of which each position has a designated role to play. Our answer to the above questions must be in the negative: morality is not an institution in the explained sense; nor are moral rules institutional expectations or rules.

The moral code of a society may, of course, have implications that bear on institutional rules. For one thing, the moral code may imply that an institutional system is morally wrong and ought to be changed. Moreover, the moral code may imply that a person has also a moral duty to do something which is his institutional job. For instance, it may be a moral rule that a person ought to do whatever he has undertaken to do, or that he ought not to accept the benefits of a position without performing its duties. Take for instance the rules, "A professor should meet his classes" or "Wives ought to make the beds." Since the professor has undertaken to do what pertains to his office, and the same for a wife, and since these tasks are known to pertain to the respective offices, the moral rules that a person is morally bound (with certain qualifications) to do what he has undertaken to do implies, in context, that the professor is morally bound to meet his classes and the wife to make the beds, other things being equal (viz., there being no contrary moral obligations in the situation). But these implications are not themselves part of the moral code. No one would say that a parent had neglected to teach his child the moral code of the society if he had neglected to teach him that professors must meet classes, and that wives must make the beds. A person becomes obligated to do these things only by participating in an institution, by taking on the status of professor or wife. Parents do not teach children to have guilt feelings about missing classes or making beds. The moral code consists only of more general rules, defining what is to be done in certain types of situations in which practically everyone will find himself. ("Do what you have promised!")

Admittedly some rules can be both moral and institutional: "Take care of your father in his old age" might be both an institutional rule of the family organization and also a part of the moral code of a society. (In this situation, one can still raise the question whether this moral rule is optimific in a society with that institutional rule; the answer could be negative.) . . .

X

It has been proposed above that an action is right if and only if it would not be prohibited by the moral code ideal for the society in which it occurs, where a moral code is taken to be "ideal" if and only if its currency would produce at least as much good per person as the currency of any other moral code.[9] We must now give more attention to the conception of an ideal moral code, and how it may be decided when a given moral code will produce as much good per person as any other. We may, however, reasonably bypass the familiar problems of judgments of comparative utilities, especially when different persons are involved, since these problems are faced by all moral theories that have any plausibility. We shall simply assume that rough judgments of this sort are made and can be justified.

(a) We should first notice that, as "currency" has been explained above, a moral code could not be current in a society if it were too complex to be learned or applied. We may therefore confine our consideration to codes simple enough to be absorbed by human beings, roughly in the way in which people learn actual moral codes.

(b) We have already distinguished the concept of an institution and its rules from the concept of a moral rule, or a rule of the moral code. (We have however, pointed out that in some cases a moral rule may prescribe the same thing that is also an institutional expectation. But this is not a necessary situation, and a moral code could condemn an institutional expectation.) Therefore, in deciding how much good the currency of a specific moral system would do, we consider the institutional setting as it is, as part of the situation. We are asking which moral code would produce the most good in the long run in this setting. One good to be reckoned, of course, might be that the currency of a given moral code would tend to change the institutional system.

(c) In deciding which moral code will produce the most per person good, we must take into account the probability that certain types of situation will arise in the society. For instance, we must take for granted that people will make promises and subsequently want to break them, that people will sometimes assault other persons in order to achieve their own ends, that people will be in distress and need the assistance

---

[9]Some utilitarians have suggested that the right act is determined by the total net intrinsic good produced. This view can have embarrassing consequences for problems of population control. The view here advocated is that the right act is determined by the per person, average, net intrinsic good produced.

of others, and so on. We may not suppose that, because an ideal moral code might have certain features, it need not have other features because they will not be required; for instance, we may not suppose, on the ground that an ideal moral system would forbid everyone to purchase a gun, that such a moral system needs no provisions about the possession and use of guns—just as our present moral and legal codes have provisions about self-defense, which would be unnecessary if everyone obeyed the provision never to assault anyone.

It is true that the currency of a moral code with certain provisions might bring about a reduction in certain types of situation, e.g., the number of assaults or cases of dishonesty. And the reduction might be substantial, if the moral code were current which prohibited these offenses very strongly. (We must remember that an ideal moral code might differ from the actual one not only in what it prohibits or enjoins, but also in how strongly it prohibits or enjoins.) But it is consistent to suppose that a moral code prohibits a certain form of behavior very severely, and yet that the behavior will occur, since the "currency" of a moral code requires only 90 percent subscription to it, and a "strong" subscription, on the average, permits a great range from person to person. In any case there must be doubt whether the best moral code will prohibit many things very severely, since there are serious human costs in severe prohibitions: the burden of guilt feelings, the traumas caused by the severe criticism by others which is a part of having a strong injunction in a code, the risks of any training process which would succeed in interiorizing a severe prohibition, and so on.

(d) It would be a great oversimplification if, in assessing the comparative utility of various codes, we confined ourselves merely to counting the benefis of people doing (refraining from doing) certain things, as a result of subscribing to a certain code. To consider only this would be as absurd as estimating the utility of some feature of a legal system by attending only to the utility of people behaving in the way the law aims to make them behave—and overlooking the fact that the law only reduces and does not eliminate misbehavior, as well as the disutility of punishment to the convicted, and the cost of the administration of criminal law. In the case of morals, we must weigh the benefit of the improvement in behavior as a result of the restriction built into conscience, against the cost of the restriction—the burden of guilt feelings, the effects of the training process, etc. There is a further necessary refinement. In both law and morals we must adjust our estimates of utility by taking into account the envisaged system of excuses. That *mens rea* is required as a condition of guilt in the case of most legal offenses is most important, and it is highly important for the utility of a moral system whether accident, intent, and motives are taken into account in deciding a person's liability to moral criticism. A description of a moral code is incomplete until we have specified the severity of condemnation (by conscience or the criticism of others) to be attached to various actions, along with the excuses to be allowed as exculpating or mitigating. . . .

XIII

It is sometimes thought that a rule utilitarianism rather like Mill's cannot differ in its implication about what is right or wrong from the act utilitarian theory. This is a mistake.

The contention would be correct if two dubious assumptions happened to be true. The first is that one of the rules of an optimific moral code will be that a person ought always to do whatever will maximize utility. The second is that when there is a conflict between the rules of an optimific code, when a person ought to do is to maximize utility. For then, either the utilitarian rule is the only one that applies (and it always will be relevant), in which case the person ought to do what the act utilitarian directs; or if there is a conflict among the relevant rules, the conflict-resolving principle takes over, and this, of course, prescribes exactly what act utilitarianism prescribes. Either way, we come out where the act utilitarian comes out.

But there is no reason at all to suppose that there will be a utilitarian rule in an optimific moral code. In fact, obviously there will not be. It is true that there should be a directive to relieve the distress of others, when this can be done, say, at relatively low personal cost; and there should be a directive not to injure other persons except in special situations. And so on. But none of this amounts to a straight directive to do the most good possible. Life would be chaotic if people tried to observe any such moral requirement.

The second assumption was apparently acceptable to Mill. But a utilitarian principle is by no means the only possible conflict-resolving principle. For if we say, with the Ideal Moral Code theory, that what is right is fixed by the content of the moral system with maximum utility, the possibility is open that the utility-maximizing moral system will contain some rather different device for resolving conflicts between lowest-level moral rules. The ideal system might contain several higher-level conflict-resolving principles, all different from Mill's. Or, if there is a single one, it could be a directive to maximize utility; it could be a directive to do what an intelligent person who had fully interiorized the rest of the ideal moral system would feel best satisfied with doing; and so on. But the final court of appeal need not be an appeal to direct utilities. Hence the argument that Mill-like rule utilitarianism must collapse into direct utilitarianism is doubly at fault.[10]

In fact, far from "collapsing" into act utilitarianism, the Ideal Moral Code theory appears to avoid the serious objections which have been leveled at direct utilitarianism. One objection to the latter view is that it implies that various immoral actions (murdering one's elderly father, breaking solemn promises) are right or even obligatory if only they can be kept secret. The Ideal Moral Code theory has no such implication. For it obviously would not maximize utility to have a moral code which condoned secret murders or breaches of promise. W. D. Ross criticized act utilitarianism on the ground that it ignored the personal relations important in ordinary morality, and he listed a half-dozen types of moral rule which he thought captured the main themes of thoughtful morality: obligations of fidelity, obligations of gratitude, obligations to make restitution for injuries, obligations to help other persons, to avoid injuring them, to improve one's self, and to bring about a just distribution of good things in life. An ideal moral code, however, would presumably contain substantially such rules in any society, doubtless not precisely as Ross stated them. So the rule utilitarian need not fail to recognize the personal character of morality.

---

[10]Could some moral problems be so unique that they would not be provided for by the set of rules it is best for the society to have? If so, how should they be appraised morally? Must there be some appeal to rules covering cases most closely analogous, as seems to be the procedure in law? If so, should we say that an act is right if it is not prohibited, either explicitly or by close analogy, by an ideal moral code? I shall not attempt to answer these questions.

Utilitarianism and Justice

Tziporah Kasachkoff

I

The main criticism of the utilitarian view that the rightness of an act depends entirely on the goodness of its consequences has been that it fails to recognize considerations of *justice* as relevant to the moral assessment of human actions. If the utilitarian bases the morality of an act solely on its utility, then what about the act which is unjust but of net positive utility? Or the act which is just but slightly disutilitarian? The utilitarian must conclude that in the first case the act is right and in the second case the act is wrong. The problem is not that we (supposing we are not utilitarians) will necessarily disagree with his conclusions: we may at times consider an act unjust but nevertheless the right thing to do, or regard an act as just but, everything considered, not the right thing to do. However, the trouble is that for most of us, the rightness or wrongness of an act depends, at least in part, on its justness while for the utilitarian the justness or unjustness of an act appears to have no relevance at all to its moral assessment.

This essay examines the utilitarian view in order to determine its susceptibility to the charge that it neglects considerations of justice. We shall gauge the force of this charge and the adequacy of the utilitarian reply by focusing on an issue to which considerations of both utility and justice apply, viz. *punishment*. We shall begin with the act-utilitarian view on punishment and the difficulties which it encounters and then examine various alternative utilitarian solutions. In the end we shall see that despite many moves in its defense, utilitarianism cannot answer the charge of injustice without sacrificing its integrity as a consistent principle of *utility*. . . .

II

Utilitarians begin with the premise that since pain is intrinsically evil, its infliction is justified when and only when it produces a good greater than the good of its non-infliction or presents an evil greater than the evil of the pain itself.

We can easily see how this applies to punishment: since punishment is the infliction of pain or hardship, it is justified when and only when it produces a good greater than that of not punishing or prevents an evil greater than the evil of the punishment. The good that punishment is generally thought to produce is the reform of the individual punished, and the evil it is thought to avert is further commission of crime, achieved through the deterrent effects of punishing offenders.

Critics argue that utilitarians lack a principle of justice, a deficiency most frequently illustrated by appeal to the following arguments:

(1) *Punishment of the innocent.* On the utilitarian view, punishment of a wrongdoer might be justified on the grounds that it will deter other would-be offenders. But the deterrence value remains the same *even if the individual punished is innocent,* provided that the fact of his innocence is not revealed. If punishing a person for the commission of an offense will deter others from committing similar offenses, then it is of no theoretical importance whether the accused is guilty.

(2) *Severe or unfair punishment.* If punishment is justified by appeal to its deterrent effects, minor offenses (like pilfering) might warrant severe penalties while more serious crimes (like murder) might warrant milder punishment if the culprits of minor offenses were in need of stronger deterring forces than those of major offenses. Utilitarianism could thus justify unduly harsh punishment for trivial offenses and mild punishment for grave ones.

(3) *The justification of deception.* The utilitarian justification of punishment is, most commonly, its deterrence value, but "it is publicity and not punishment which deters."[1] If someone commits a wrong, he need not be punished in order to deter others. All that is needed is that others *think* the offender has been punished. Deception rather than punishment is what is actually justified on utilitarian grounds. "For a Utilitarian apparent justice is everything, real justice is irrelevant."[2]

These difficulties arise, it is argued, precisely because utilitarianism lacks two essential elements of justice: (1) recognition of guilt as necessary for the justification of punishment, and (2) the requirement that the punishment fit the crime, i.e. be proportional to the gravity of the offense. . . .

Generally, the act-utilitarian meets the charge of injustice with one of the following two replies:

(1) Any conflict between the utilitarian principle and the interests of justice is only apparent, for acts which we call "just" are but one way of realizing the utilitarian ideal of maximizing the general welfare. Justice and benevolence are not separate moral obligations but two different ways of achieving the same end.

(2) Utility and justice are separate moral obligations—both of which are legitimate and non-reducible one to the other. But this is no problem for the utilitarian because conflict between the two is nearly impossible. In almost every situation where punishment is unjust, it is also of net *dis*-utilitarian value. And in those cases in which an unjust punishment has the greatest utility, the case will be such that even the non-utilitarian will agree that the punishment, though unjust, is justified.

Let us consider each of these replies in turn, first the claim that our concern for justice is, at bottom, a concern for the general welfare.[3] On this view, conflicts between what are usually taken to be the disparate moral concerns of justice and utility are really conflicts between concern for the production of one type of utility and concern for the production of another. Some utilitarians have interpreted justice as acts of long-range than short-term utility;[4] others have interpreted it as acts which are of general utility;[5] still others have claimed that just acts are acts which produce utilities only when others are doing the same.[6] But none of these suggestions succeeds.

If the translation of justice into utility is meant to be definitional, it is unacceptable because "justice" does not mean what these theories say it means. One can, with-

---

[1]J. D. Mabbott, "Punishment," in F. A. Olafson, ed., *Justice and Social Policy* (Prentice-Hall, 1961), p. 40.
[2]*Ibid.*
[3]Bentham, for example, held that "justice, in the only sense in which it has a meaning, is an imaginary personage, feigned for the convenience of discourse, whose dictates are the dictates of utility *applied to certain cases*. . . . The dictates of justice are nothing more than a part of the dictates of benevolence." *Op. cit.,* chap. x, § xl *n.* -

[4]See Ronald J. Glossop's review of *Distributive Justice* by Nicholas Rescher, in *The Journal of Philosophy,* LXVI (April 10, 1969), p. 220.

[5]John Austin, *The Province of Jurisprudence Determined* (1832), p. 263*n.*
[6]David Hume, *A Treatise on Human Nature,* III, ii, 2.

out any contradiction, assert that an act is useful in the ways specified but unjust nonetheless; and conversely, that an act is just but neither of long-range nor general utility, nor useful when combined with other acts of the same sort. On the other hand, if what is being asserted is that *as a matter of fact,* just acts will always produce utility in the ways specified, experience shows this to be false. Some just acts we perform have neither long-range nor general positive utilitarian effects; nor do just acts always produce utility when others are doing the same. The problem the utilitarian faces in deciding the morality of any act which is useful but unjust cannot be resolved by regarding "justice" as the name for a class of acts productive of the general good in some special sort of way.

Let us turn then to those utilitarians who argue that the problem of justice and utility is only theoretical because in fact the two never conflict, that any case of gross injustice will, on analysis, turn out to be of disutility as well. Generally, the argument is of the following sort:

> There are very obvious utilitarian reasons why we should avoid punishing people not guilty of definite offences defined by law. . . . The miserable insecurity produced by such unjust punishment has been sufficiently exemplified in certain states in the last years as well as in earlier history. But, it may be said, this will only apply if such action is taken frequently; there may well be occasional cases where the punishment of the innocent is useful. But the utilitarian has still a possible reply. He may admit that there are cases where this is so but deny that any human authority could be trusted to decide which these cases are. It is all very well to say that the innocence of the man punished might be kept secret, but could the authorities ever be quite sure that they would succeed in doing this (unless at least they imposed an extreme dictatorship, which would be open to other objections)? And, if they recognized that they might punish the innocent sometimes, would not there be a great danger of their going too far in this practice? Against the tangible advantages that they saw or might think they saw have to be set a number of considerations which are very important and yet hardly susceptible of measurement—the psychological effects of being punished when one knew oneself innocent, the risk of discovery, the effects on the relatives of the person punished, the bad psychological effects on the punisher. As with most cases of adopting means generally condemned morally in order to produce good results, we should realize that besides any definitely forseeable results there is reason to think that the unforseeable results of such action will tend to be bad rather than good and these ought to be allowed for. I think this generalization is supported by the empirical evidence.[7]

This argument has engendered a uniform response from critics of utilitarianism. They say that such a reply misses the essential point of criticism—viz. that whatever the fact of the matter, it is at least *possible,* though perhaps not likely, that an unjust act may be more useful than a just one and the inadequacy of utilitarianism is that, should this occur, injustice will be utilitarian-justified.

However, this point against utilitarianism is not well taken. The utilitarian need not shore up his criterion in such a way that possible counter cases are uncondition-

---

[7]A. C. Ewing, "Armstrong on the Retributive Theory," *Mind,* LXXII (January 1963), 122. Although Ewing believes that unjust punishments will never, in fact, be useful, he condemns them on other grounds as well.

ally precluded. What we want from a justifying principle of action is not that it preclude the possibility of injustice but that it allow it only under heavy constraints. The act-utilitarian offers us constraints which are empirical in the belief that utilitarianism will not easily condone an unjust punishment, for as a matter of fact, considerations of utility will not tally in favor of such punishment. But though the utilitarian's account of what justifies punishment both does not and need not preclude unjust punishments entirely, what still remains at issue is the *latitude* allowed for the justification of injustice. The constraints offered by the utilitarian—empirically based considerations of disutility—are far too weak. For in cases where we must decide between a punishment which yields utilitarian advantages and one which is just, a slight net balance of utility over disutility will tip the scales in favor of injustice. Though we cannot condemn the utilitarian principle because in some cases it permits unjust punishment, we can condemn it on account of the ease with which it permits it.

What is wrong with the utilitarian account is that is has no balance to the principle of utility, with the result that the principle ends up justifying many acts which, because they are unjust and of no *great* utilitarian advantage, are not morally justifiable.

In the end, then, the criticism of the utilitarian's position on punishment comes to this: it cannot recognize the justice or injustice of a punishment as a relevant feature of its justification. The non-utilitarian, on the other hand, though he may ultimately come to the same decision as the utilitarian on a question of whether or not to punish, not only considers the injustice of the punishment but regards it as counting *heavily* against its justification so that any utility which ultimately provides for its moral sanction must be such as to outweigh the evil of the injustice involved. Ordinarily "we determine what punishment ought to be inflicted by taking into account *firstly* what punishment is deserved, and then other considerations. . . . Production of the greatest good is obviously a relevant consideration when determining which punishment may properly be inflicted, *but the question as to which punishment is just is a much more basic and important consideration*."[8] . . .

We conclude that while any justification of punishment must consider (though perhaps not give priority to) the desert of the person to be punished, the utilitarian account does not. This failure of utilitarianism is a direct result of its inability to translate, in some way or another, the notion of desert into terms relating to the general good—the only terms which are, for the utilitarian, of any moral significance. Thus, the utilitarian account of punishment lacks a necessary feature—recognition of the moral significance of punishing according to desert regardless of the consequences which result.

III

A totally different defense of utilitarianism against the charge of injustice has been the reformulation of the utilitarian principle. Although there are many reformulations, all agree that the morality of an act depends not on the consequences which *it* produces (act-utilitarianism) but rather on the consequences of observing the *rule* under which it falls (rule-utilitarianism).[9] We shall examine three versions of rule-utilitarianism and show that none of them overcomes the difficulties of act-utilitarianism.

[8]H. J. McCloskey, "A Non-Utilitarian Approach to Punishment," *Inquiry*, VIII (Autumn 1965), 261. See also K. G. Armstrong, "The Retributivist Hits Back," *Mind*, LXX (October 1961), 471–490.

[9]Rule-utilitarianism is not, strictly speaking, a twentieth-century phenomenon as it is sometimes characterized. Nor has its adoption always come about as a response to the charge of injustice. The early champions

The most popular version of rule-utilitarianism holds that the morality of an act is determined by asking, "What would happen if everyone were to do the same?" According to this view, the morality of an individual act is to be judged by considering the utility of the hypothesized *general* performance of acts relevantly similar to the act in question.

To see how this version of rule-utilitarianism is supposed to be an improvement over act-utilitarianism, let us consider the following example. In a Southern town where racial tension runs high a white man is beaten by a Negro. This incident so incites the white townspeople that they demand that the sheriff hand over the black man he has in custody (and who the sheriff knows is innocent) so that they can "take justice into their own hands." They back their order with the threat that refusal will be met by retaliation against the entire black community. If the sheriff reasons as an act-utilitarian, his decision to hand over an innocent man to an angry mob for lynching will depend—supposing his act to have no other effects, either positive or negative—solely on whether or not lynching an innocent man is preferable to indiscriminate violence against many. Neither alternative is attractive, but since one (allowing many innocent people to be killed) is worse than the other (handing over one innocent person to be killed) the act-utilitarian must choose the latter.

The rule-utilitarian claims that his criterion will not yield this unjust conclusion, for according to him, the sheriff must balance not the consequences of his individual act against the consequences of his refusal, but rather, he must weigh the consequences of every sheriff in his situation capitulating to violence against the consequences of evey sheriff refusing. Were every sheriff to hand over an innocent prisoner at the threat of violence, the results would be disastrous; violence as a means of achieving one's wants would be encouraged, and there would be loss of respect for the law as redressor of wrong and loss of confidence that the law will protect those known to be innocent. Clearly the *practice* of punishing an innocent man will not be justified on rule-utilitarian grounds and so, it is argued, neither will any such particular act. It appears from this example that rule-utilitarianism may very well be the answer to the act-utilitarian's difficulty.

But it is not. It *seems* that we get one answer when we look at the sheriff's problem from the act-utilitarian's point of view (which evaluates his act in terms of its utility alone) and a different one when we look at it from the point of view of the rule-utilitarian (which evaluates his act in terms of the utility of its hypothesized general performance). But this is illusory. The utility—and so the moral assessment—of an action is

of the utilitarian principle were concerned not so much with the evaluation of individual acts as with the evaluation of laws and the sanctions to be applied when laws were violated. In fact, in Bentham's first published work, *Fragment on Government,* the principle of utility is specifically put forth as a criterion with which to distinguish good from bad laws (Paragraph 54 of the preface).

Mill, too, seems to be a rule-utilitarian in that he applies the principle of utility to rules and not to acts, leaving the justification of particular acts to depend on whether or not they are in accord with utilitarian-justified rules. But there is some controversy concerning his position. J. O. Urmson argues that Mill was indeed a rule-utilitarian in "The Interpretation of the Moral Philosophy of J. S. Mill," *The Philosophical Quarterly,* III (1953). J. D. Mabbott disagrees: "Interpretations of Mill's Utilitarianism," in the same journal, vi (1956). It seems to me that the most we can conclude is that Mill was an inconsistent rule-utilitarian, hardly surprising when we consider that the distinction between act- and rule-utilitarianism, although in evidence among the classical utilitarians, was not a self-consciously recognized and developed distinction until the middle of this century when rule-utilitarianism was first explicitly formulated as a version of the utilitarian theory.

not different when we consider the consequences of its generalized rather than its single performance.

Consider the following case: I am trying to decide whether or not to vote, knowing that a certain number of votes is required for the election of a particular candidate and that this number has already been reached. If I reason as an act-utilitarian, I will argue that since voting is inconvenient for me and, in this situation, of no positive consequence to others while not voting is convenient for me and of no negative consequence, I ought not to vote in these circumstances because voting would be disutilitarian. The rule-utilitarian replies that

> if Mr. Smith can reason that his vote won't make any difference to the outcome, so can Mr. Jones and Mr. Robinson and every other would-be voter; but if everyone reasoned this way, no one would vote and this would have bad effects. It is considered one's duty to vote, not because the consequences of one's not doing so are bad, but because the consequences of the general practice of not doing so are bad.[10]

It is easy to spot what's wrong here: the rule-utilitarian fails to see that it is impossible for *all* the people who are considering whether to vote to do the same when the act is relevantly described. The act is not simply *not voting;* it is *not voting when one knows one's vote is inconsequential.* But this is not something that everybody can know for it is not something which is true of everyone. Specifically, it is not true of all those voters who consider the question before the required number of votes for election is reached. The rule-utilitarian mistakenly describes as "the same" two classes of acts which are different; he ignores that some votes are cast before the election is decided and some are not—a relevant difference between them.

To assess an act correctly by the rule-utilitarian standard one must consider what would happen were everyone to do the act in question when that act is relevantly described, i.e. described with respect to all those circumstances which affect its performance and outcome. In the above case, the rule-utilitarian should ask, "What would happen were everyone not to vote *when he knows that his vote will be of no consequence in the election?"* And the answer, of course, is that nothing disutilitarian would result—the same answer one arrives at by assessing the utility of not voting at its consequences alone. The judgment of the utility of voting which is derived from applying the utilitarian principle to the consequences of that act's general performance is no different from the judgment arrived at by applying the principle directly to the consequences of the particular act—so long, that is, as the particular act is fully and relevantly described.

The argument illustrated by the voting case—that the utility of an act remains the same whether that act is performed singly or in the context of the performance of relevantly similar acts—is completely general. Whenever there is a difference between the effects produced by the single performance of an act and those produced by multiple performances of it, there is *ex hypothesi* a difference in the relevant descriptions of that act: one is done in the context of its general performance and one is not. For example, when Sammy, Susan, and Johnny *all* practice their drumrolls, the cumulative effect (a headache, say) may far exceed the effect of just one drumroll. Acts which have cumulative effects are acts which produce different effects when done in

[10]John Hospers, [p. 637 above].

concert from those they produce when done in isolation. The disproportionate difference in effects between the single performance of an act and the performance of that
act with other such acts results because the context of performance, i.e. what else is
taking place and what others are doing, is a causally relevant factor in the description
of these acts and is different for the isolated as opposed to repeated act.[11]

Thus, it is a mistake to evaluate a particular act in terms of its hypothesized general performance if in doing so the value of utility changes. For any difference in value
between the single performance of an act on the one hand, and its general performance on the other, reflects a difference in their causal properties and so a difference
in the acts themselves when they are fully and adequately described. To evaluate an act
in terms of its hypothesized general performance when the utility of the latter differs
from that of the former is to assess the morality of one act by reference to the utility of
another.

On the other hand, if the utility of the general performance of an act is the same
as the value of its single performance, then there is no difference at all between taking
a rule- as opposed to act-utilitarian view.

Let us apply this to the sheriff case. We saw that if the sheriff reasons as an act-
utilitarian he will conclude, knowing that his act will not lead to or reinforce a general
practice, that turning over an innocent prisoner to save the lives of many is preferable
to sacrificing many to save the life of one. If the sheriff now reasons *correctly* as a rule-
utilitarian, he will consider what would happen if every sheriff, when he knows that
his act will not lead to its becoming a general practice, were to sacrifice an innocent
person to save the lives of many; and as a utilitarian he will conclude that whatever the
injustice, the loss of one life is better than the loss of many and so he will choose the
former—the same choice as the act-utilitarian's. There is thus no advantage in applying rule- as opposed to act-utilitarianism to our sheriff case. The only difference between them is in the method of reckoning utilities, but the resulting value—either
positive or negative—is the same.

We conclude that rule-utilitarianism fares no better than act-utilitarianism in
handling those problems of justice raised by the issue of punishment. Since the one
theory reduces to the other, the difficulties of one are difficulties of both.[12] . . .

[11]Some philosophers have pointed out that we are hardly ever in a position to know what everyone else is
doing. Because of this Kurt Baier argues that if we merely have "reason to suppose" general performance
or non-performance of the act in question, we have a morally good reason to act in one way rather than
another: *The Moral Point of View* (Cornell Univ. Press, 1958), pp. 211–212. Utilitarians, however, disagree
about the validity of this argument. Some argue that one cannot justify an action on the grounds that one
has good reason to believe that since so many people are doing it anyway, one's own abstention would be
useless. For everyone may think the same thing and for the same good reason, but if everyone who thought
this were on that account to do the act in question the results would be bad. See Jonathan Harrison, "Utilitarianism, Universalization, and Our Duty to be Just," *Proceedings of the Aristotelian Society,* LIII (1952–53),
128–129.

Another argument against basing behavior on reasoned beliefs about what others are doing is that "if
part of my special circumstances is my reasoned belief about how others will act in the same circumstances,
then part of *their* special circumstances is their belief about how others, including myself, will act. . . . I must
. . . judge how they believe I will act and they in turn must have a belief about what I believe they believe.
And so on." A. K. Stout, "But Suppose Everyone Did the Same," *Australasian Journal of Philosophy,* XXXII
(May 1954), 18–19.

An answer to both these arguments can be found in David Lyons, *Forms and Limits of Utilitarianism*
(Oxford Univ. Press, 1965), pp. 109–110 and 112–115.

[12]Of course, one may reject this version of rule-utilitarianism on grounds other than its equivalence with
act-utilitarianism. One may reject it, for example, on the grounds that it commits the fallacy of assuming that
because it is wrong for everyone to do *X,* it is wrong for anyone to do *X.*

Let us consider, then, another version of rule-utilitarianism, generally, referred to as "ideal" rule-utilitarianism: An act is right if and only if it conforms to a *set of rules* general acceptance of which would maximize utility.[13] This version rests the morality of an act not on its utility, nor on the subsumption of the act in question under a rule to which conformity would maximize utility, but rather on the utility of having the rule under which if falls as part of the *moral code* which would be ideal for that society.

Now let us consider the merits of adopting an "ideal" form of rule-utilitarianism by returning to the example of our sheriff. The ideal rule-utilitarian is in the same position with respect to our sheriff case as the rule-utilitarian₂: he can offer no relevant advice because his criterion, by definition, excludes consideration of the sheriff's predicament. The reasoning is the same as before. Since the criterion appealed to determines the rightness or wrongness of an act by judging that act's relation to a set of rules whose acceptance proves of maximum utility, it cannot determine the morality of an act which *ex hypothesi* is to be performed in a context of *non*acceptance of the rule which maximizes utility.[14] Once again, then, we have a form of rule-utilitarianism recommended as a viable alternative to the act-utilitarian's inadequate handling of the problem of punishment, which fails to cope with our sheriff case because it is irrelevant to the circumstances in which that problem as well as most other ethical problems arise—viz., circumstances in which there is general disconformity to the rules which maximize utility.

However, it is important to note that this form of rule-utilitarianism, . . . is an alternative: it does not reduce to, but is substantially different from, act-utilitarianism. Once we realize this, it is clear that ideal rule-utilitarianism, . . . fails as a strictly *utilitarian* principle. For unlike act-utilitarianism which determines the rightness or wrongness of acts by applying the criterion of maximization of utility directly to the acts themselves, ideal rule-utilitarianism applies the criterion of maximization of utility only to sets of ideal rules with the result that although

> following Act-Utilitarianism will produce the best consequences in every case, following Ideal Rule-Utilitarianism will not necessarily produce the best consequences in every case. . . . In accepting [Ideal Rule-Utilitarianism] one is committed to regarding as right some acts that do not have as good consequences as every alternative.[15]

Thus, in adopting ideal rule-utilitarianism, which does *not* yield judgments equivalent to those produced by an act-utilitarian evaluation, one adopts a criterion which—because it evaluates an act according to whether it conforms to a set of rules which *if*

---

[13]R. B. Brandt, "Some Merits of One Form of Rule Utilitarianism," *University of Colorado Studies Series in Philosophy,* No. 3, 1966, pp. 39–65.

[14]Brandt takes issue with this. He claims that although "it might be thought . . . than an ideal moral code could take no cognizance . . . of the possibility that many persons are ignoring some prohibitions of the code . . . it is sufficient answer to this suggestion, to point out that our actual moral code appears to contain some such prescriptions. For instance . . . the case in which almost everyone is understating his income." (Brandt, p. 56.) I do not think Brandt is right in thinking that our moral code prescribes for the case where other people are cheating on their taxes. But right or wrong, this is no answer to the objection that the ideal moral code we are discussing cannot take into account nonconformity with the rules of the code. The objection is not just that *a* moral code cannot prescribe for the contingency of other people's non-conformity, but that a moral code *whose justification lies in the utility of adherence to it* cannot. And our code is not one of the latter sort.

[15]Lyons, *op. cit.,* pp. 158–159.

conformed to *would* produce more utility than any other set of rules—disregards the *actual* utility of an act in favor of its evaluation in terms of a hypothesized conformity with certain utilitarian *ideals*. Another way of putting this is that to adopt ideal rule- over act-utilitarianism is to forsake consideration of *actual* utility in favor of consider- ing the utility an act or rule *would have were a certain counter-factual hypothesis true,* viz., general conformity to optimum rules. Endorsement of ideal rule-utilitarianism cannot be sanctioned by a "pure" utilitarian precisely because in appealing to an ideal set of rules, judgments may be generated which conflict with those derived from the evaluation of actual utility. But it is only *actual* utility and not ideal utility which is in strict conformity with the principle of utility as the strict utilitarian sees the matter. To adopt ideal rule-utilitarianism over act-utilitarianism is to hold ". . . not that Ideal Rule- Utilitarianism or some alternative is a better theory of the same kind, but rather that it is a theory of another kind, and that the other is a better kind."[16] . . .

IV

I want now to consider another version of utilitarianism which seems to offer what is needed, one which rests the morality of an action not on the utility of an enlarged number of performances of that act but rather on an enlarged conception of the utility required for its justification. This theory is often referred to as "ideal-utilitarianism" (not to be confused with ideal rule-utilitarianism).

The ideal-utilitarian agrees that the morality of an act depends on its utility, but views the utility of an act as the amount of *intrinsic value* produced, where intrinsic value includes but is not exhausted by the furtherance of the general welfare.[17] Exactly which things are intrinsically good is an open question, to be decided, one writer sug- gests, by asking in each case whether "it would be a good thing that the thing in ques- tion should exist, even if it existed *quite alone,* without any further accompaniments or effects whatever."[18]

Once the ideal-utilitarian enlarges the utilitarian principle to refer not only to the production of happiness but to the production of other intrinsic goods as well, he can then easily justify just punishments and condemn unjust ones. All he has to claim is that justice is intrinsically good and injustice intrinsically bad. One ideal-utilitarian argues that

> the infliction of pain on a person whose state of mind is bad may, if the pain be not too intense, create a state of things that is better *on the whole* than if the evil state of mind had existed unpunished.[19]

By arguing in this way, the ideal utilitarian is relieved of the charge of injustice. In rec- ognizing a variety of intrinsic goods, he can recognize the value of justice itself.

Let us now apply the principle of ideal-utilitarianism to our test case of the sher-

[16]*Ibid.,* p. 160.
[17]At the beginning of this essay, we noted differences of opinion as to what is relevant to the moral assess- ment of human action. The notion that it was pleasure was dropped in favor of the broader concept of happi- ness and welfare of mankind, and the view that it is the intrinsic goodness which an act produces was claimed to reduce to the welfare of mankind if the latter is construed broadly enough. That intrinsic good- ness is translatable into cudaemonistic terms is what is being denied here.
[18]Moore, *Ethics,* p. 42.
[19]Moore, *Principia Ethica,* p. 214.

iff in the racist town. If the sheriff follows the recommendation of the ideal-utilitarian he will consider whether handing over his prisoner will bring about a state of affairs of greater intrinsic worth than would result by turning away the mob. Now, if he hands over his prisoner, then (1) many innocent people will be saved, i.e. the general welfare will be maximized, an intrinsic good, but also (2) an innocent person will be harmed, a state of affairs intrinsically bad. On the other hand, were he to protect his prisoner, then (1) many innocent people will lose their lives, a state of affairs of negative intrinsic value, but (2) justice will be asserted, an intrinsically good result. So what should he do?

Since the act which the sheriff considers leads to effects which are both intrinsically good *and* intrinsically bad, acceptance of the ideal-utilitarian's position leaves undetermined the question of whether the sheriff's act is right or wrong. What is needed is a principle that can adjudicate between competing goods and evils, but the ideal-utilitarian offers us none.

It is interesting that the difficulty with the ideal-utilitarian's position is a difficulty in Ross's position too. For Ross also offers no principle in accordance with which the relative stringencies of competing moral claims may be assessed, with the analogous result that when one *prima facie* duty (to be just, for example) conflicts with another (say, to produce happiness), it is not clear whether one ought to do the just act which is non-utilitarian or the unjust act which serves utilitarian ends.

Furthermore, ideal-utilitarianism and Ross's view suffer from indeterminacy for the same reason: each includes within his theory the moral point of the other's view with the result that each refers the question of our right to act to a plurality of concerns (either—as Ross sees it—concerns reflected by our *prima facie* obligations, or—as the ideal-utilitarian claims—concerns defined by the different goods of intrinsic worth) accompanied by no second-order principles which can help in case of conflict.

Once we note the similarity between Ross's view and ideal-utilitarianism, and remember that the ideal-utilitarian can extend his list of intrinsic values to include any or all the *prima facie* obligations Ross considers relevant to the question of justice, we might wonder whether there is *any difference* between these "opposing" views. The ideal-utilitarian is able to incorporate into his ideals *all* those intuitions that Ross sees as our *prima facie* duties, and the ideal-utilitarian can defend his list of specific intrinsic goods in the same way that Ross claims to know his *prima facie* duties—he "sees" them to be so. Specifically with respect to the issues of justice raised by punishment, both can make a case for considering the desert of the person punished independent of the good that his punishment will do, yet both may allow, though do not require, the overriding of this concern by concern for the general good.

In the end, then, we do have a utilitarian principle which can recognize the demands of justice independent of their eudaemonistic utility—but only at a price. In enlarging the compass of what counts as "utility," the ideal-utilitarian sacrifices the integrity of his principle as a *unitary* standard of right action, and as a result, impairs it as a self-sufficient principle capable of generating *determinate* answers to ethical questions.

It has been suggested that criticism of utilitarian justifications of certain acts, punishment included, fails to recognize that (1) there is a difference between justifying rules and justifying particular acts in accordance with these rules; (2) a successful justification of punishment depends on what *about* punishment is being justified (its harshness, its point, its authority, its usefulness), as well as *to whom;* and (3) what sorts of justification are allowable depends on the office one holds and the role one plays (the types of justification open to a legislator, for example, are not open to a judge though both are concerned with the issue of punishment). Once the proper distinctions are made, utilitarianism will be seen to apply only to the decision whether to have certain practices but has no place in deciding the particular case.

But this attempt to salvage utilitarianism will not do. There is no reason why an entire system of punishment may not be unjust and yet be more useful than its alternative and so justified on utilitarian grounds. Furthermore, the strict utilitarian is committed to the production of the best possible state of affairs, no matter what the issue. Sometimes utility will be maximized by denying exceptions to utilitarian-justified institutions, but sometimes it will not. When it is not, utilitarian reasoning will be appropriate not only at the level of the practice but at the level of the particular case as well.[20]

[20]The final two paragraphs are substituted for the original by the author.

Chapter II

Kantian Deontology

JAMES GAFFNEY

The Golden Rule: Abuses and Uses

Every now and then the Golden Rule encounters a kind of inversion of the legendary philosophers' stone, so that its gold appears transmuted into baser metal. That is one reason why we should, every now and then, take it out, dust it off, polish it up, reassure ourselves that it is the real stuff and prepare for the next round of antialchemy. Attacks of that kind have come from some very notable philosophers, and may come from the most unexpected sources. The most recent one to attract my attention was launched, seemingly with the best of intentions, by a German Catholic moral theologian whose first book in English has just been published.

This writer begins his discussion by recalling how, in the book of Deuteronomy, a law calling for the release of slaves (actually only purchased Hebrew ones are referred to) in their seventh year of servitude is followed by what appears to be a reason or motive for that norm: "You shall remember that you were a slave in the land of Egypt, and the Lord your God redeemed you; therefore I command you this today." The writer paraphrases the text: "Just as you were a slave and were set free, so you must free your slaves." It is then that the trouble begins. For he goes on to say: "It takes no great acumen to recognize in this short sentence an application of the Golden Rule," proposing "as the basic formulation of the Golden Rule the statement: Treat others as you wish others to treat you." Already at this point a serious misunderstanding of the Golden Rule may be suspected. Since the suspicion is fully confirmed by what follows, it may be useful to explore its grounds before going further.

"Treat others as you wish others to treat you" will do well enough as a terse statement of the principle that, variously formulated, has come to be known as the Golden Rule. Even without "great acumen," a critical reader may doubt whether that principle is being applied in the statement "just as you were a slave and were set free, so you must free your slaves." One way to confirm such doubt is simply to take the Golden Rule as stated and apply it directly and with common sense to the matter of slavery.

Does a determination to "treat others as you wish others to treat you" really lead, by any tolerable moral logic, to the conclusion that, after using for six years a slave one has bought, one ought to let him or her go? Is that really how normal people, even 25 centuries ago, could seriously be supposed to "wish others to treat" them? In the 18th and 19th centuries the Golden Rule was, of course, often directly and explicitly applied to the slavery question, but no one, as far as I know, had any doubt that that principle, other considerations apart, had only one conceivable implication for slavery: Not that enslavement should be limited, but that it should be excluded. "Treat others as you wish others to treat you" is an immensely different principle from one that calls upon us to treat others as others have treated us. Israelites might certainly say to themselves, "We were enslaved for a time, but eventually set free." They might certainly find in that recollection a motive for deciding, "We shall enslave others for no more than six years before setting them free." And their response to that motive might certainly contribute to improvements in social morality. Nevertheless, the motive itself is as different from the Golden Rule as are the social improvements it generates from those that would follow from that rule.

That the writer chosen for this illustrative critique did not merely choose an inept illustration but wholly failed to appreciate the moral distinctiveness of the Golden Rule becomes evident when we follow him only a few sentences further. After noting that the Golden Rule presupposes "everyone wants others to treat him or her well," he exhibits unmistakably both the nature and the depth of his misunderstanding of it. He does so by offering us two "reformulations" of the Golden Rule that are, in fact, fundamental distortions of it. "Next," he says, "we can reformulate this Golden Rule in two ways, depending on whether the good treatment by others is something that has already happened or something still be be longed for: 1) Others have done good to you; you should likewise do good to others. 2) Do good to others, and others will do good to you (variant: in order that others may do good to you). It is only a short step to including God (Yahweh, Christ) among the 'others.' "

I shall refrain from comment on that last sentence (it introduces difficulties of another, more theological kind) to concentrate on the central ethical fallacy. In the jargon of moral philosophers, what has occurred here is the confusion of a categorical imperative with a hypothetical one, or, more remarkably still, with two different hypothetical imperatives. The Golden Rule is absolutely unconditional: Treat others as you would have others treat you. But both of the writer's supposed reformulations of it are conditional: Treat others well since they have treated you well; treat others well so that they will treat you well. The Golden Rule is a norm of treating others as one would be treated, whether one has been or expects to be so treated by others; it is a norm of doing so no matter what. It has nothing whatever to do with either one's experience or one's anticipation of being well treated. There is, of course, nothing wrong with treating others well either because they so treated you, or because you hope that they will treat you well. To do so is to behave in the one case gratefully and in the other case prudently. The Golden Rule is not predicated on either gratitude or prudence, and its moral demands greatly exceed the implications of both.

What I have argued to be a particular author's confusions about the Golden Rule are certainly not peculiar to the source from which I have borrowed them. They occur frequently. One of them is to be found in Hobbes, and the other in Bentham, to cite only famous writers on ethics. Whereas Hobbes and Bentham obviously have reductionistic and naturalistic axes to grind, the appearance of the same confusions on the part of a respected Catholic moral theologian suggests a much wider susceptibility.

A discussion, like the one just concluded, of what the Golden Rule is not goes a long way toward reminding us what it is: an unconditional and universal norm of doing as one would be done to by others. That is, of applying the same moral standards in evaluating one's own behavior toward others that one applies in evaluating others' behavior toward oneself. In that sense it expresses the fundamental assumption of equality before the moral law that underlies our most familiar and practical assumptions about strictly universal justice.

There are, nevertheless, aspects of the Golden Rule that raise significant difficulties. The first of them has to do with a potentially misleading incompleteness about the way the rule is commonly formulated. That is, when we affirm that we should treat others as we would be treated by others, that "would" has to be understood as representing not casual whimsy but moral conviction. It is a matter of treating other as we *judge* it would be *right*—not simply as we *feel* it would be *nice*—for them to treat us!

A second difficulty has to do with the fact that our norm of treating others as we would be treated by them must always take realistic account of all relevant differences between "us" and "them." Treating someone who is hungry as one should like to be treated when one has overeaten is obviously not the sort of thing the Golden Rule is driving at! The point is to treat another person as one would consider it right to be treated if one were in that other person's circumstances. That is why the Golden Rule makes practical demands on our capacities for human understanding, for putting ourselves in another's place, for exercising a kind of sympathetic social imagination. All that becomes more difficult the more unfamiliar we are with different kinds of people and circumstances. It is in this connection that both humanistic education and the social sciences render their chief services to morality. A narrow mind trying to abide by the Golden Rule is never a pretty sight, though it often is a funny one.

Another major difficulty about the Golden Rule has to do with what is sometimes referred to as its formal character, its emptiness of concrete prescriptions. It tells us to treat others as we should judge it right for others to treat us, but it does not tell us what we should judge to be the right way for others to treat us. It supposes we already have definite convictions about that and, of course, we have. It does not suppose that those convictions are perfect, that they will not change or that they cannot improve. It only supposes that, at any given moment, our effective insights into the concrete meaning of doing right or wrong will be rooted in our habitual understanding, however acquired, of what it means to be treated right or wrong. The Golden Rule does not furnish us with a supply of values; it tells us what to do, as moral beings, about the values we already possess. The only values it implicitly affirms are its own and that of those to whom it is addressed. In that sense, enlightened self-interest must furnish the data for even the most unselfish morality, which is what the poet Alexander Pope had in mind in that intriguing couplet: "Ev'n mean self-love becomes, by force divine,/The scale to measure others' wants by thine."

No doubt that scale functions much more sensitively in some people than in others, and on certain occasions than on others. The fact remains that in each of us and at any given time it is, and has to be, the final measure. It is for that reason that the biblical norm "Love your neighbor as yourself" *can* be a genuine reformulation of the Golden Rule. Whether it is depends, of course, on whether the term "neighbor" is taken to designate a restricted category—the question that, in the New Testament, provides a conceptual setting for the parable of the Good Samaritan. It is when "neighbors" and "others" become morally synonymous that Christian ethics rise to the level of the Golden Rule.

At this point it becomes clear that the distortions of the Golden Rule, whereby an unconditional norm is "reformulated" as a pair of conditional ones, has the further effect of greatly narrowing the scope of the principle's practical significance. If "treat others as you wish others to treat you" really did mean merely that we should treat others well because they had or in hope that they would treat us well, it would leave out everybody who neither was nor was likely to become our benefactor. There is surely nothing very golden about a rule like that!

One of the most remarkable things about the Golden Rule is the way it seems to have emerged as a fundamental discovery from serious moral reflection carried out in an extraordinary variety of cultures, including cultures historically disconnected and in other respects strikingly dissimilar. The American philosopher Marcus Singer has expressed in very measured terms the widely shared opinion that "the nearly universal acceptance of the Golden Rule and its promulgation by persons of considerable intelligence, though otherwise of divergent outlooks, would therefore seem to provide some evidence for the claim that it is a fundamental ethical truth."

An age when even putatively fundamental ethical truths, actually embraced as such by numerous disparate segments of humanity, seem to be in such great demand and short supply, strikes me as an especially bad time to trivialize the Golden Rule.

Kant and the Golden Rule

In this chapter we will look at a theory rather different from utilitarianism, but one that is also basic to the way we think abut moral issues. Utilitarian ethics, as we have seen, determines the rightness or wrongness of actions by looking at the *consequences* of an action. Utilitarianism is "consequentialist." Yet, this approach does not always square with common-sense ideas about ethics. Often people will argue that certain types of actions (for example, cheating, stealing, or killing) are just plain wrong—regardless of the possibly good consequences such actions sometimes produce. This idea is popularly expressed by the saying that "the end doesn't justify the means." In the study of ethics, theories which hold that certain types of actions are right or wrong regardless of consequences are called *deontological theories*. The term "deontological" comes from Greek literally, and broadly, meaning "the science of duty;" but in contemporary ethics the term refers specifically to theories that are nonconsequentialist. From here on we will use "deontological" as referring to nonconsequentialist theories.

We will not be looking at every deontological theory ever proposed, but concentrate on one such theory deeply rooted in common moral reasoning. Often when we are trying to convince people that they are doing something wrong we say, "What if everyone were to do that?" or "How would you like it if someone did that to you?" The point of these questions is this: If people would not want everyone to act as they do or would not want such a thing done to them, then they should not do it—the action is morally wrong. And, it is comparatively easy to see the root moral idea behind these questions. If we were not willing to allow everyone to act as we do or not willing to be treated as we treat others, we would, in effect, be asking for special treatment. "I'd like to do *x* (lie, cheat, steal), but I don't want *x* done to me and I don't want everyone doing *x*." What's wrong with this attitude? It is unfair to others because it advocates unequal treatment. I want to be allowed to do things that I'm unwilling to let others do. This in unfair.

This sort of moral reasoning is common to us not just because our parents have used it on us any number of times; it is a central doctrine of Judeo-Christian ethical teaching (and the ethical teaching of many other world religions). Both Judaism and Christianity subscribe to versions of the Golden Rule: "Do unto to others as you would have them do unto you." While the author of our lead piece points out that this moral idea is a widely held one, formulating it in such a way that it is free of difficulties is not an easy task. There is a central problem with the Golden Rule as usually stated. It appears to be too subjective to qualify as a moral first principle. We would expect a moral principle to give firm answers about the rightness or wrongness of actions. As such, it is a shortcoming of a proposed moral principle if it gives either the "wrong" judgment about an action or, in the case we are considering, if it gives several, conflicting answers depending upon who is using the principle.

Let's consider a simple example that illustrates this problem. Jim is taking an exam for which he is not well prepared; however, Jane, whom he knows is well prepared, is sitting next to him. Jim is tempted to get answers from Jane's paper, but he considers whether it would be a right thing to do. Jim may well try to apply the Golden Rule. For most of us, applying the Golden Rule in this case would lead us to conclude that we shouldn't steal answers from others since we wouldn't want others to steal from us. Jim may not feel this way, however. He may not much care if other people take answers from him. If he doesn't care, then by applying the Golden Rule he concludes that there's nothing wrong with this kind of cheating on an exam. There are even more extreme examples imaginable. If a certain people really would not mind being enslaved (surely rare), then it seems that their enslaving someone else would not be prohibited by the Golden Rule. Enslavers are only doing to others as they would allow others to do to them, although for almost everyone else applying the rule, slavery would be prohibited. Most of us are unwilling to be enslaved. Thus, in this example, following the Golden Rule gives conflicting answers depending upon who applies it.

To a large measure the theoretical readings that follow attempt to amend the shortcomings of Golden Rule ethics mentioned above. There is a problem concerning how to incorporate into a moral principle the key idea of treating persons in an equal and even-handed way without making the principle so arbitrary and subjective that it gives different (and sometimes unacceptable) results depending upon a person's individual tastes. Undoubtedly the most influential attempt in this direction is that given by the eighteenth-century German philosopher Immanuel Kant. Kant proposed the following as the first principle of ethical conduct: "Act only according to that maxim by which you can at the same time will that it should become a universal law." This principle is what Kant calls the *categorical imperative:* "categorical" in the sense that the principle is not based upon different goals and desires people might happen to have, and "imperative" since it tells people what they ought to do. To cut through Kant's language a bit, he proposes the following test for the morality of actions. An action is morally permissible if you would be willing to have everyone act as you are proposing to act (if you would be willing to have the "maxim" of your action become a universal law). An action is morally wrong if you are not willing to have everyone act as you are proposing to act. To use the example from above, it would be all right to cheat on your exam if you are willing to have everyone else do the same sort of thing; it would be morally wrong to cheat if you are not willing.

On the face of it, Kant's moral principle runs into the same problem as the more familiar Golden Rule. It seems as though there is nothing preventing Jim from saying that he wouldn't mind if everyone cheated on an exam—even if this meant that people would be stealing answers from him. However, Kant wants to argue that there are some sorts of action (the ones that are morally wrong) which none of us, regardless of our specific tastes and interests, can seriously intend to become a universal law. Kant claims that trying to "universalize" (will to be universal law) some actions will involve us in a contradiction. The example about Jim will help illustrate this point. Kant would argue that we cannot intend that cheating on exams become a universal law since the idea of universalized cheating is incoherent. (There is a contradiction in "conception" of universalized cheating.) The point is this: The purpose of giving exams is to evaluate the performance of individual students. However, if cheating were rampant, then this purpose could no longer be served because exams would no longer represent the performance of an individual student. At most, performance on exams would show how clever a person is at cheating. If the purpose of exam giving were subverted, we would expect that exams would no longer be given. As such, Kant would argue, the idea of conception of universal cheating on exams is incoherent. There cannot be such a thing as universal exam cheating since the practice of exam giving would go out of existence far short of universal cheating.

While some actions like cheating on an exam cannot be universalized because the idea of universalizing them is incoherent, Kant argues that other actions cannot be coherently universalized since they conflict with basic goals and desires we all share. To illustrate this point Kant uses the example of not helping the needy—that is, an action of refusing to assist persons in genuine need of help. In Kant's terminology, intending not to help someone in need would involve us in a "contradiction in willing." While there may be nothing contradictory about *conceiving* of a universal practice of not helping the needy, there is something contradictory about *wanting* (or "willing") such a universal practice. Kant assumes that each one of us would want to be helped if we were to become needy. This desire, however, conflicts with a general policy of not helping the needy. A result of such a general policy would be the following. If it so happened that I were in need of help from someone, then I could expect no one to help me. This is contrary, however, to my desire to be helped in such circumstances.

The above is only a thumbnail sketch of Kant's position. Onora O'Neil's article provides a detailed analysis of Kant's "categorical imperative" and specifically the contradiction-in-conception/contradiction-in-willing test. While the details of Kant's theory are complicated, as O'Neil's article shows, we should not lose sight of the reason why Kant goes to such great lengths. He wants to put forward a principle of morality that shares the same root idea as the Golden Rule, but which is not so subjective. In general terms, the way Kant tries to do this is to argue that there are certain kinds of actions that we cannot rationally will to be universal. There is some limit, shared by all rational creatures, to what can and cannot pass the test of the categorical imperative.

Although Onora O'Neil does a good job of defending the plausibility of Kant's categorical imperative as a principle of morality, not everyone finds Kant's solution wholly successful. R. M. Hare, for example, defends only one piece of Kant's position. Hare argues that Kant is right to insist that universalizability (ability to will as a universal law) is central to practical reasoning, but universalizability is not enough to establish a substantive moral principle. First the positive point: Hare argues that the ability to universalize our actions is part and parcel of what is involved in making reasoned moral judgments. Our decision to act in one way or another commits us, on pain of contradiction, to allow anyone else to act in a similar way—of course with the possible consequence that people will act toward us as we do toward them. Hare's point is rather simple. If I say to myself, it's all right for me to cancel classes in order to go to a meeting, then I can't complain if my colleagues do the same thing. I've said that it's all right for me to do this sort of thing, and if I cannot establish some important difference between myself and my colleague, it would be contradictory for me to claim that such an action is not permissible for her. This would be contradictory roughly in the same way that judging the worth of two identical cars (for example, two new Fords) differently would be contradictory. I can't really say that this Ford is a good car, while that one (which is identical to the first in all important respects) is a lousy car. This is incoherent; they are the same kind of car.

Hare agrees with Kant that universalizability is necessary if we are to act morally. But, Hare claims, universalizability is not sufficient to yield a substantive moral principle. To say that universalizability is not sufficient for a moral principle is to say that while universalizability may be part of what makes our actions moral, it is not the whole story. There must be more to morality than universalizability. Universalizability only insures that our actions are consistent, that is, that our doing x to someone entails that it is permissible for someone to do x to me. As Hare sees it, the main lesson of universalizability is that we should seriously consider the effects of our actions on others. A willingness to universalize means a willingness to consider what it would be like if we were the recipients of our own actions. However, our moral reasoning cannot stop here. Once we appreciate how others will be affected by our actions, we must yet make a judgment as to what to do. At this juncture Hare invokes utilitarianism as a supplement to Kantian ethics. The final decision concerning how to act will be a matter of summing up the effects of our actions on the preferences of ourselves and others. In a sense Hare tries to give a moral theory that strikes a middle ground between Kantian deontology and utilitarian consequentialism. He hopes, at least, to incorporate the best elements of both approaches to ethics.

The selection from C. E. Harris, Jr., also attempts to repair the perceived deficiencies with Kant's categorical imperative. We have focused so far on the notion of universalizability as central to Kantian ethics, but it can be argued that there is more to Kant's position than universalizability. Toward the end of the selection from Kant, he claims that acting according to the categorical imperative amounts to treating persons as "ends in themselves," not as mere "means" to our individual ends or purposes. And further, to treat persons as "ends in themselves" is, according to Kant, to respect persons as persons. It is a controversial interpretative point as to whether the doctrine of respect for persons is really the same position as that expressed in the categorical imperative, as Kant wants us to believe, or a new and more substantial position that Kant advances. Regardless of where the truth lies in this interpretative debate, the doctrine of respect for persons is worthwhile to consider on its own merits.

Harris develops the doctrine of "respect for person" by claiming that to respect a person entails three principles: (1) that we give due consideration to persons as "moral agents," (2) that if we fail to treat others this way we "forfeit" our rights for such treatment (for example, deserve punishment), and (3) in rare cases, where any available action results in persons being harmed as moral agents, that the harm be distributed as "equally" as possible. Central to Harris' account is the principle that respect for persons entails treating persons as moral agents. And, further, Harris claims that to treat someone as a moral agent requires us, negatively, not to hamper someone's freedom or well-being and, positively, to actively assist persons in achieving their freedom or well-being. This position seemingly goes beyond the mere claim to universalizability toward a more substantive moral theory. The doctrine of respect for persons does not merely claim that we must allow everyone to act as we propose, but that there are certain values (freedom and well-being) that define the way in which we wish to be treated; then, because of the principle of universalizability, the doctrine extends to the way we ought to treat other persons.

It should be noted that Harris does not claim his account of "respect for persons" to be what Kant intended to claim, although Harris' position is clearly based upon a Kantian idea. The appropriate question for us in this chapter is whether or not Harris' "respect for persons" is an acceptable specification of the root moral idea behind the Golden Rule. And, further, is the idea of respect for persons, as Harris understands it, able to stand as the principle of moral behavior?

Like Hare, John Rawls has a mixed opinion about Kantian ethics. On the one hand, Rawls finds much to recommend the idea of universalizability. The principle, as he sees it, contains the root idea of fair and equal treatment of each individual. If morality obliges us to universalize our actions, then, as we have seen, this means that the same do's and don't's apply across the board to everyone—universalizability disallows any sort of double standard. But, on the other hand, Rawls thinks this aspect is overemphasized in Kant. What is more important, he believes, is that Kantian ethics looks upon moral principles as the result of a "rational choice." We decide what policies to adopt under the fairness constraints imposed by the universalizability requirement. But, this by itself does not say which policies, in particular, to choose—this is Rawls' way of expressing the problem that universalizability may not be enough to generate substantive moral principles. Rawls' solution to the problem, of which we will see more in Chapter 5, is to argue that our choice of moral principles is guided by fairness and a goal to have policies that best secure for persons their basic and commonly shared desires. These are desires for what Rawls calls "primary goods" and include rights and liberties, powers and opportunities, income and wealth. It is the notion of primary goods that puts content into what Rawls and others tend to regard as the empty formalism of Kant's universalizability requirement.

We have so far focused most of our attention upon Kant's categorical imperative and the associated idea of universalizing our actions—bearing in mind that Kant's principle shares the basic idea of the Golden Rule. In the final article of this chapter, we consider the Golden Rule itself and what may be done to make it an acceptable moral principle. Alan Gewirth squarely addresses the problem we have noted with the Golden Rule (and arguably shared by Kant's categorical imperative); namely, if taken at face value, the Golden Rule can be twisted and turned by the merely subjective desires of those who use the rule. Gewirth's way of trying to eliminate the subjectivity in the usual statement of the Golden Rule is to argue for what he calls a *Rational Golden Rule*. The basic idea is this: When applying the Golden Rule, we ought not consider just any desires a person might have (this is what causes the subjectivity problems); but, we should consider only "rational" desires. Gewirth's position shares much in common with Rawls' and goes some distance toward realizing one of Kant's original goals in arguing for the categorical imperative. Like Rawls, Gewirth believes that while persons vary widely in the particular interests and desires they have, there is a hard core of basic desires common to all rational agents (those who know what is in their own best interests). And like Harris, Gewirth claims that we all have desires for freedom and well-being. Each of us needs some amount of freedom and well-being in order to satisfy whatever particular desires we might happen to have. Like Kant, Gewirth attempts to uphold the idea that a version of the Golden Rule can be defended on the grounds that it represents the most "rational" sort of moral principle one can conjure up.

Let us sum up what has been discussed above. In reading the selections that follow, we ought to keep our eyes on the following points. The root moral idea we are concerned with in this chapter is the one expressed in the Golden Rule; namely, the idea that to act properly toward one's fellow human being is to act in a way that we would like to be treated or in a way we would be willing to have everyone act. This expresses the idea of fair and equal treatment that, arguably, lies at the heart of moral conduct. However, there is a serious question whether fair and equal treatment gives enough specificity to qualify as a first principle of morality. It can be argued that both the Golden Rule and Kant's categorical imperative leave too much to the wish and whim of those who use the principles. Each of the readings in this chapter, including O'Neil's defense of Kant, can be seen in part as attempts to fill out the idea behind the Golden Rule in such a way as to make it an acceptable moral first principle.

FIRST SECTION
Transition from the Ordinary Rational Knowledge of Morality to the Philosophical

Immanuel Kant

There is no possibility of thinking of anything at all in the world, or even out of it, which can be regarded as good without qualification, except a *good will*. Intelligence, wit, judgment, and whatever talents of the mind one might want to name are doubtless in many respects good and desirable, as are such qualities of temperament as courage, resolution, perseverance. But they can also become extremely bad and harmful if the will, which is to make use of these gifts of nature and which in its special constitution is called character, is not good. The same holds with gifts of fortune; power, riches, honor, even health, and that complete well-being and contentment with one's condition which is called happiness make for pride and often hereby even arrogance, unless there is a good will to correct their influence on the mind and herewith also to rectify the whole principle of action and make it universally conformable to its end. The sight of being who is not graced by any touch of a pure and good will but who yet enjoys an uninterrupted prosperity can never delight a rational and impartial spectator. Thus a good will seems to constitute the indispensable condition of being even worthy of happiness. . . .

A good will is good not because of what it effects or accomplishes, nor because of its fitness to attain some proposed end; it is good only through its willing, i.e., it is good in itself. When it is considered in itself, then it is to be esteemed very much higher than anything which it might ever bring about merely in order to favor some inclination, or even the sum total of all inclinations. Even if, by some especially unfortunate fate or by the niggardly provision of stepmotherly nature, this will should be wholly lacking in the power to accomplish its purpose; if with the greatest effort it should yet achieve nothing, and only the good will should remain (not, to be sure, as a mere wish but as the summoning of all the means in our power), yet would it, like a jewel, still shine by its own light as something which has its full value in itself. Its usefulness or fruitlessness can neither augment nor diminish this value. Its usefulness would be, as it were, only the setting to enable us to handle it in ordinary dealings or to attract to it the attention of those who are not yet experts, but not to recommend it to real experts or to determine its value. . . .

The concept of a will estimable in itself and good without regard to any further end must now be developed. This concept already dwells in the natural sound understanding and needs not so much to be taught as merely to be elucidated. It always holds first place in estimating the total worth of our actions and constitutes the condition of all the rest. Therefore, we shall take up the concept of *duty,* which includes that of a good will, though with certain subjective restrictions and hindrances, which far from hiding a good will or rendering it unrecognizable, rather bring it out by contrast and make it shine forth more brightly.

From Immanuel Kant, *Grounding for the Metaphysics of Morals,* trans. by James W. Ellington (Indianapolis: Hackett Publishing Co., Inc., 1981). Reprinted by permission. Bracket notes are provided by James W. Ellington.

I here omit all actions already recognized as contrary to duty, even though they may be useful for this or that end; for in the case of these the question does not arise at all as to whether they might be done from duty, since they even conflict with duty. I also set aside those actions which are really in accordance with duty, yet to which men have no immediate inclination, but perform them because they are impelled thereto by some other inclination. For in this [second] case to decide whether the action which is in accord with duty has been done from duty or from some selfish purpose is easy. This difference is far more difficult to note in the [third] case where the action accords with duty and the subject has in addition an immediate inclination to do the action. For example,[1] that a dealer should not overcharge an inexperienced purchaser certainly accords with duty; and where there is much commerce, the prudent merchant does not overcharge but keeps to a fixed price for everyone in general, so that a child may buy from him just as well as everyone else may. Thus customers are honestly served, but this is not nearly enough for making us believe that the merchant has acted this way from duty and from principles of honesty; his own advantage required him to do it. He cannot, however, be assumed to have in addition [as in the third case] an immediate inclination toward his buyers, causing him, as it were, out of love to give no one as far as price is concerned any advantage over another. Hence the action was done neither from duty nor from immediate inclination, but merely for a selfish purpose.

On the other hand,[2] to preserve one's life is a duty; and, furthermore, everyone has also an immediate inclination to do so. But on this account the often anxious care taken by most men for it has no intrinsic worth, and the maxim of their action has no moral content. They preserve their lives, to be sure, in accordance with duty, but not from duty. On the other hand,[3] if adversity and hopeless sorrow have completely taken away the taste for life, if an unfortunate man, strong in soul and more indignant at his fate than despondent or dejected, wishes for death and yet preserves his life without living it—not from inclination or fear, but from duty—then his maxim indeed has a moral content.[4]

---

[1][The ensuing example provides an illustration of the second case.]
[2][This next example illustrates the third case.]
[3][The ensuing example illustrates the fourth case.]
[4][Four different cases have been distinguished in the two foregoing paragraphs. Case 1 involves those actions which are contrary to duty (lying, cheating, stealing, etc.). Case 2 involves those which accord with duty but for which a person perhaps has no immediate inclination, though he does have a mediate inclination thereto (one pays his taxes not because he likes to but in order to avoid the penalties set for delinquents, one treats his fellows well not because he really likes them but because he wants their votes when at some future time he runs for public office, etc.). A vast number of so-called "morally good" actions actually belong to this case 2—they accord with duty because of self-seeking inclinations. Case 3 involves those which accord with duty and for which a person does have an immediate inclination (one does not commit suicide because all is going well with him, one does not commit adultery because he considers his wife to be the most desirable creature in the whole world, etc.). Case 4 involves those actions which accord with duty but are contrary to some immediate inclination (one does not commit suicide even when he is in dire distress, one does not commit adultery even though his wife has turned out to be an impossible shrew, etc.). Now case 4 is the crucial test case of the will's possible goodness—but Kant does not claim that one should lead his life in such a way as to encounter as many such cases as possible in order constantly to test his virtue (deliberately marry a shrew so as to be able to resist the temptation to commit adultery). Life itself forces enough such cases upon a person without his seeking them out. But when there is a conflict between duty and inclination, duty should always be followed. Case 3 makes for the easiest living and the greatest contentment, and anyone would wish that life might present him with far more of these cases than with cases 2 or 4. But yet one should not arrange his life in such a way as to avoid case 4 at all costs and to seek out case 3 as much as possible (become a recluse so as to avoid the possible rough and tumble involved

To be beneficent where one can is a duty; and besides this, there are many persons who are so sympathetically constituted that, without any further motive of vanity or self-interest, they find an inner pleasure in spreading joy around them and can rejoice in the satisfaction of others as their own work. But I maintain that in such a case an action of this kind, however dutiful and amiable it may be, has nevertheless no true moral worth.[5] It is on a level with such actions as arise from other inclinations, e.g., the inclination for honor, which if fortunately directed to what is in fact beneficial and accords with duty and is thus honorable, deserves praise and encouragement, but not esteem; for its maxim lacks the moral content of an action done not from inclination but from duty. Suppose then the mind of this friend of mankind to be clouded over with his own sorrow so that all sympathy with the lot of others is extinguished, and suppose him still to have the power to benefit others in distress, even though he is not touched by their trouble because he is sufficiently absorbed with his own; and now suppose that, even though no inclination moves him any longer, he nevertheless tears himself from this deadly insensibility and performs the action without any inclination at all, but soley from duty—then for the first time his action has genuine moral worth.[6] Further still, if nature has put little sympathy in this or that man's heart, if (while being an honest man in other respects) he is by temperament cold and indifferent to the sufferings of others, perhaps because as regards his own sufferings he is endowed with the special gift of patience and fortitude and expects or even requires that others should have the same; if such a man (who would truly not be nature's worst product) had not been exactly fashioned by her to be a philanthropist, would he not yet find in himself a source from which he might give himself a worth far higher than any that a good-natured temperament might have? By all means, because just here does the worth of the character come out; this worth is moral and incomparably the highest of all, viz., that he is beneficent, not from inclination, but from duty.[7]

To secure one's own happiness is a duty (at least indirectly); for discontent with one's condition under many pressing cares and amid unsatisfied wants might easily become a great temptation to transgress one's duties. But here also do men of themselves already have, irrespective of duty, the strongest and deepest inclination toward happiness, because just in this idea are all inclinations combined into a sum total.[8] But the precept of happiness if often so constituted as greatly to interfere with some inclinations, and yet men cannot form any definite and certain concept of the sum of satisfaction of all inclinations that is called happiness. Hence there is no wonder that a single inclination which is determinate both as to what it promises and as to the time within which it can be satisfied may outweigh a fluctuating idea; and there is no wonder that a man, e.g., a gouty patient, can choose to enjoy what he likes and to suffer what he may, since by his calculation he has here at least not sacrificed the enjoyment of the present moment to some possibly groundless expectations of the good fortune that is supposed to be found in health. But even in this case, if the universal inclination to happiness did not determine his will and if health, at least for him, did not figure as

with frequent association with one's fellows, avoid places where one might encounter the sick and the poor so as to spare oneself the pangs of sympathy and the need to exercise the virtue of benefiting those in distress, etc.). For the purpose of philosophical analysis Kant emphasizes case 4 as being the test case of the will's possible goodness, but he is not thereby advocating puritanism.]

[5][This is an example of case 3.]
[6][This is an example of case 4.]
[7][This is an even more extreme example of case 4.]
[8][This is an example of case 3.]

so necessary an element in his calculations; there still remains here, as in all other cases, a law, viz., that he should promote his happiness not from inclination but from duty, and thereby for the first time does his conduct have real moral worth.[9]

Undoubtedly in this way also are to be understood those passages of Scripture which command us to love our neighbor and even our enemy. For love as an inclination cannot be commanded; but beneficence from duty, when no inclination impels us[10] and even when a natural and unconquerable aversion opposes such beneficence,[11] is practical, and not pathological, love. Such love resides in the will and not in the propensities of feeling, in principles of action and not in tender sympathy; and only this practical love can be commanded.

The second proposition[12] is this: An action done from duty has its moral worth, not in the purpose that is to be attained by it, but in the maxim according to which the action is determined. The moral worth depends, therefore, not on the realization of the object of the action, but merely on the principle of volition according to which, without regard to any objects of the faculty of desire, the action has been done. From what has gone before it is clear that the purposes which we may have in our actions, as well as their effects regarded as ends and incentives of the will, cannot give to actions any unconditioned and moral worth. Where, then, can this worth lie if it is not to be found in the will's relation to the expected effect? Nowhere but in the principle of the will, with no regard to the ends that can be brought about through such action. For the will stands, as it were, at a crossroads between its a priori principle, which is formal, and its a posteriori incentive, which is material; and since it must be determined by something, it must be determined by the formal principle of volition, if the action is done from duty—and in that case every material principle is taken away from it.

The third proposition, which follows from the other two, can be expressed thus: Duty is the necessity of an action done out of respect for the law. I can indeed have an inclination for an object as the effect of my proposed action; but I can never have respect for such an object, just because it is merely an effect and is not an activity of the will. Similarly, I can have no respect for inclination as such, whether my own or that of another. I can at most, if my own inclination, approve it; and, if that of another, even love it, i.e., consider it to be favorable to my own advantage. An object of respect can only be what is connected with my will solely as ground and never as effect—something that does not serve my inclination but, rather, outweighs it, or at least excludes it from consideration when some choice is made—in other words, only the law itself can be an object of respect and hence can be a command. Now an action done from duty must altogether exclude the influence of inclination and therewith every object of the will. Hence there is nothing left which can determine the will except objectively the law and subjectively pure respect for this practical law, i.e., the will can be subjectively determined by the maxim[13] that I should follow such a law even if all my inclinations are thereby thwarted.

[9][This example is a weak form of case 4; the action accords with duty but is not contrary to some immediate inclination.]

[10][This is case 4 in its weak form.]
[11][This is case 4 in its strong form.]

[12][The first proposition or morality says that an action must be done from duty in order to have any moral worth. It is implicit in the preceding examples but was never explicitly stated.]

[13]A maxim is the subjective principle of volition. The objective principle (i.e., one which would serve all rational beings also subjectively as a practical principle if reason had full control over the faculty of desire) is the practical law. [See below Kant's footnote at Ak. 420–21.]

Thus the moral worth of an action does not lie in the effect expected from it nor in any principle of action that needs to borrow its motive from this expected effect. For all these effects (agreeableness of one's condition and even the furtherance of other people's happiness) could have been brought about also through other causes and would not have required the will of a rational being, in which the highest and unconditioned good can alone be found. Therefore, the pre-eminent good which is called moral can consist in nothing but the representation of the law in itself, and such a representation can admittedly be found only in a rational being insofar as this representation, and not some expected effect, is the determining ground of the will. This good is already present in the person who acts according to this representation, and such good need not be awaited merely from the effect.[14]

But what sort of law can that be the thought of which must determine the will without reference to any expected effect, so that the will can be called absolutely good without qualification? Since I have deprived the will of every impulse that might arise for it from obeying any particular law, there is nothing left to serve the will as principle except the universal conformity of its actions to law as such, i.e., I should never act except in such a way that I can also will that my maxim should become a universal law.[15] Here mere conformity to law as such (without having as its basis any law determining particular actions) serves the will as principle and must so serve it if duty is not to be a vain delusion and a chimerical concept. The ordinary reason of mankind in its practical judgments agrees completely with this, and always has in view the aforementioned principle.

For example, take this question. When I am in distress, may I make a promise with the intention of not keeping it? I readily distinguish here the two meanings which the question may have; whether making a false promise conforms with prudence or with duty. Doubtless the former can often be the case. Indeed I clearly see that escape from some present difficulty by means of such a promise is not enough. In addition I must carefully consider whether from this lie there may later arise for greater inconvenience for me than from what I now try to escape. Furthermore, the consequences of my false promise are not easy to forsee, even with all my supposed cunning; loss of confidence in me might prove to be far more disadvantageous than the misfortune which I now try to avoid. The more prudent way might be to act according to a univer-

---

[14]There might be brought against me here an objection that I take refuge behind the word "respect" in an obscure feeling, instead of giving a clear answer to the question by means of a concept of reason. But even though respect is a feeling, it is not one received through any outside influence but is, rather, one that is self-produced by means of a rational concept; hence it is specifically different from all feelings of the first kind, which can all be reduced to inclination or fear. What I recognize immediately as a law for me, I recognize with respect; this means merely the consciousness of the subordination of my will to a law without the mediation of other influences upon my sense. The immediate determination of the will by the law, and the consciousness thereof, is called respect, which is hence regarded as the effect of the law upon the subject and not as the cause of the law. Respect is properly the representation of a worth that thwarts my self-love. Hence respect is something that is regarded as an object of neither inclination nor fear, although it has at the same time something analogous to both. The object of respect is, therefore, nothing but the law—indeed that very law which we impose on ourselves and yet recognize as necessary in itself. As law, we are subject to it without consulting self-love; as imposed on us by ourselves, it is a consequence of our will. In the former aspect, it is analogous to fear: in the latter, to inclination. All respect for a person is properly only respect for the law (of honesty, etc.) of which the person provides an example. Since we regard the development of our talents as a duty, we think of a man of talent as being also a kind of example of the law (the law of becoming like him by practice), and that is what constitutes our respect for him. All so-called moral interest consists solely in respect for the law.

[15][This is the first time in the *Grounding* that the categorical imperative is stated.]

sal maxim and to make it a habit not to promise anything without intending to keep it. But that such a maxim is, nevertheless, always based on nothing but a fear of consequences becomes clear to me at once. To be truthful from duty is, however, quite different from being truthful from fear of disadvantageous consequences; in the first case the concept of the action itself contains a law for me, while in the second I must first look around elsewhere to see what are the results for me that might be connected with the action. For to deviate from the principle of duty is quite certainly bad; but to abandon my maxim of prudence can often be very advantageous for me, though to abide by it is certainly safer. The most direct and infallible way, however, to answer the question as to whether a lying promise accords with duty is to ask myself whether I would really be content if my maxim (of extricating myself from difficulty by means of a false promise) were to hold as a universal law for myself as well as for others, and could I really say to myself that everyone may promise falsely when he finds himself in a difficulty from which he can find no other way to extricate himself. Then I immediately become aware that I can indeed will the lie but can not at all will a universal law to lie. For by such a law there would really be no promises at all, since in vain would my willing future actions be professed to other people who would not believe what I professed, or if they over-hastily did believe, then they would pay me back in like coin. Therefore, my maxim would necessarily destroy itself just as soon as it was made a universal law.[16]

Therefore, I need no far-reaching acuteness to discern what I have to do in order that my will may be morally good. Inexperienced in the course of the world and incapable of being prepared for all its contingencies, I only ask myself whether I can also will that my maxim should become a universal law. If not, then the maxim must be rejected, not because of any disadvantage accruing to me or even to others, but because it cannot be fitting as a principle in a possible legislation of universal law, and reason exacts from me immediate respect for such legislation. Indeed I have as yet no insight into the grounds of such respect (which the philosopher may investigate). But I at least understand that respect is an estimation of a worth that far outweighs any worth of what is recommended by inclination, and that the necessity of acting from pure respect for the practical law is what constitutes duty, to which every other motive must give way because duty is the condition of a will good in itself, whose worth is above all else. . . .

SECOND SECTION
Transition from Popular Moral Philosophy to a Metaphysics of Morals

. . . Everything in nature works according to laws. Only a rational being has the power to act according to his conception of laws, i.e., according to principles, and thereby has he a will. Since the derivation of actions from laws requires reason, the will is nothing but practical reason. If reason infallibly determines the will, then in the case of such a being actions which are recognized to be objectively necessary are also subjectively necessary, i.e., the will is a faculty of choosing only that which reason, independently of inclination, recognizes as being practically necessary, i.e., as good. But if

---

[16][This means that when you tell a lie, you merely take exception to the general rule that says everyone should always tell the truth and believe that what you are saying is true. When you lie, you do not thereby will that everyone else lie and not believe that what you are saying is true, because in such a case your lie would never work to get you what you want.]

reason of itself does not sufficiently determine the will, and if the will submits also to subjective conditions (certain incentives) which do not always agree with objective conditions; in a word, if the will does not in itself completely accord with reason (as is actually the case with men), then actions which are recognized as objectively necessary are subjectively contingent, and the determination of such a will according to objective laws is necessitation. That is to say that the relation of objective laws to a will not thoroughly good is represented as the determination of the will of a rational being by principles of reason which the will does not necessarily follow because of its own nature.

The representation of an objective principle insofar as it necessitates the will is called a command (of reason), and the formula of the command is called an imperative.

All imperatives are expressed by an *ought* and thereby indicate the relation of an objective law of reason to a will that is not necessarily determined by this law because of its subjective constitution (the relation of necessitation). Imperatives say that something would be good to do or to refrain from doing, but they say it to a will that does not always therefore do something simply because it has been represented to the will as something good to do. That is practically good which determines the will by means of representations of reason and hence not by subjective causes, but objectively, i.e., on grounds valid for every rational being as such. It is distinguished from the pleasant as that which influences the will only by means of sensation from merely subjective causes, which hold only for this or that person's senses but do not hold as a principle of reason valid for everyone.[17]

A perfectly good will would thus be quite as much subject to objective laws (of the good), but could not be conceived as thereby necessitated to act in conformity with law, inasmuch as it can of itself, according to its subjective constitution, be determined only by the representation of the good. Therefore no imperatives hold for the divine will, and in general for a holy will; the *ought* is here out of place, because the *would* is already of itself necessarily in agreement with the law. Consequently, imperatives are only formulas for expressing the relation of objective laws of willing in general to the subjective imperfection of the will of this or that rational being, e.g., the human will.

Now all imperatives command either hypothetically or categorically. The former represent the practical necessity of a possible action as a means for attaining something else that one wants (or may possibly want). The categorical imperative would be one which represented an action as objectively necessary in itself, without reference to another end.

Every practical law represents a possible action as good and hence as necessary for a subject who is practically determinable by reason; therefore all imperatives are

---

[17]The dependence of the faculty of desire on sensations is called inclination, which accordingly always indicates a need. The dependence of a contingently determinable will on principles of reason, however, is called interest. Therefore an interest is found only in a dependent will which is not of itself always in accord with reason; in the divine will no interest can be thought. But even the human will can take an interest in something without thereby acting from interest. The former signifies practical interest in the action, while the latter signifies pathological interest in the object of the action. The former indicates only dependence of the will on principles of reason by itself, while the latter indicates the will's dependence on principles of reason for the sake of inclination, i.e., reason merely gives the practical rule for meeting the need of inclination. In the former case the action interests me, while in the latter case what interests me is the object of the action (so far as this object is pleasant for me). In the First Section we have seen that in the case of an action done from duty regard must be given not to the interest in the object, but only to interest in the action itself and in its rational principle (viz., the law).

formulas for determining an action which is necessary according to the principle of a will that is good in some way. Now if the action would be good merely as a means to something else, so is the imperative hypothetical. But if the action is represented as good in itself, and hence as necessary in a will which of itself conforms to reason as the principle of the will, then the imperative is categorical.

An imperative thus says what action possible by me would be good, and it presents the practical rule in relation to a will which does not forthwith perform an action simply becaue it is good, partly because the subject does not always know that the action is good and partly because (even if he does know it is good) his maxims might yet be opposed to the objective principles of practical reason.

A hypothetical imperative thus says only that an action is good for some purpose, either possible or actual. In the first case it is a problematic practical principle; in the second case an assertoric one. A categorical imperative, which declares an action to be of itself objectively necessary without reference to any purpose, i.e., without any other end, holds as an apodeictic practical principle.

Whatever is possible only through the powers of some rational being can be thought of as a possible purpose of some will. Consequently, there are in fact infinitely many principles of action insofar as they are represented as necessary for attaining a possible purpose achievable by them. All sciences have a practical part consisting of problems saying that some end is possible for us and of imperatives telling us how it can be attained. These can, therefore, be called in general imperatives of skill. Here there is no question at all whether the end is reasonable and good, but there is only a question as to what must be done to attain it. The prescriptions needed by a doctor in order to make his patient thoroughly healthy and by a poisoner in order to make sure of killing his victim are of equal value so far as each serves to bring about its purpose perfectly. Since there cannot be known in early youth what ends may be presented to us in the course of life, parents especially seek to have their children learn many different kinds of things, and they provide for skill in the use of means to all sorts of arbitrary ends, among which they cannot determine whether any one of them could in the future become an actual purpose for their ward, though there is always the possibility that he might adopt it. Their concern is so great that they commonly neglect to form and correct their children's judgment regarding the worth of things which might be chosen as ends.

There is, however, one end that can be presupposed as actual for all rational beings (so far as they are dependent beings to whom imperatives apply); and thus there is one purpose which they not merely can have but which can certainly be assumed to be such that they all do have by a natural necessity, and this is happiness. A hypothetical imperative which represents the practical necessity of an action as means for the promotion of happiness is assertoric. It may be expounded not simply as necesssary to an uncertain, merely possible purpose, but as necessary to a purpose which can be presupposed a priori and with certainty as being present in everyone because it belongs to his essence. Now skill in the choice of means to one's own greatest well-being can be called prudence[18] in the narrowest sense. And thus the imperative that refers to the choice of means to one's own happiness, i.e., the precept of prudence, still re-

---

[18]The word "prudence" is used in a double sense: firstly, it can mean worldly wisdom, and, secondly, private wisdom. The former is the skill of someone in influencing others so as to use them for his own purposes. The latter is the sagacity to combine all these purposes for his own lasting advantage. The value of the former is properly reduced to the latter, and it might better be said of one who is prudent in the former sense but not in the latter that he is clever and cunning, but on the whole imprudent.

mains hypothetical; the action is commanded not absolutely but only as a means to a further purpose.

Finally, there is one imperative which immediately commands a certain conduct without having as its condition any other purpose to be attained by it. This imperative is categorical. It is not concerned with the matter of the action and its intended result, but rather with the form of the action and the principle from which it follows; what is essentially good in the action consists in the mental disposition, let the consequences be what they may. This imperative may be called that of morality.

Willing according to these three kinds of principles is also clearly distinguished by dissimilarity in the necessitation of the will. To make this dissimilarity clear I think that they are most suitably named in their order when they are said to be either *rules of skill, counsels of prudence,* or *commands (laws) of morality.* For law alone involves the concept of a necessity that is unconditioned and indeed objective and hence universally valid, and commands are laws which must be obeyed, i.e., must be followed even in opposition to inclination. Counsel does indeed involve necessity, but involves such necessity as is valid only under a subjectively contingent condition, viz., whether this or that man counts this or that as belonging to his happiness. On the other hand, the categorical imperative is limited by no condition, and can quite properly be called a command since it is absolutely, though practically, necessary. The first kind of imperatives might also be called technical (belonging to art), the second kind pragmatic[19] (belonging to welfare), the third kind moral (belonging to free conduct as such, i.e., to morals).

The question now arises: how are all of these imperatives possible?[20] This question does not seek to know how the fulfillment of the action commanded by the imperative can be conceived, but merely how the necessitation of the will expressed by the imperative in setting a task can be conceived. How an imperative of skill is possible requires no special discussion. Whoever wills the end, wills (so far as reason has decisive influence on his actions) also the means that are indispensably necessary to his actions and that lie in his power. This proposition, as far as willing is concerned, is analytic. For in willing an object as my effect there is already thought the causality of myself as an acting cause, i.e., the use of means. The imperative derives the concept of actions necessary to this end from the concept of willing this end. (Synthetic propositions are indeed required for determining the means to a proposed end; but such propositions are concerned not with the ground, i.e., the act of the will, but only with the way to realize the object of the will.) Mathematics teaches by nothing but synthetic propositions that in order to bisect a line according to a sure principle I must from each of its extremities draw arcs such that they intersect. But when I know that the proposed result can come about only by means of such an action, then the proposition (if I fully will the effect, then I also will the action required for it) is analytic. For it is one and the same thing to conceive of something as an effect that is possible in a certain way through me and to conceive of myself as acting in the same way with regard to the aforesaid effect.

[19]It seems to me that the proper meaning of the word "pragmatic" could be defined most accurately in this way. For those sanctions are called pragmatic which properly flow not from the law of states as necessary enactments but from provision for the general welfare. A history is pragmatically written when it teaches prudence, i.e., instructs the world how it can provide for its interests better than, or at least as well as, has been done in former times.

[20][That is, why should one let his actions be determined at various times by one or the other of these three kinds of imperatives?]

If it were only as easy to give a determinate concept of happiness, then the imperatives of prudence would exactly correspond to those of skill and would be likewise analytic. For there could be said in this case just as in the former that whoever wills the end also wills (necessarily according to reason) the sole means thereto which are in his power. But, unfortunately, the concept of happiness is such an indeterminate one that even though everyone wishes to attain happiness, yet he can never say definitely and consistently what it is that he really wishes and wills. The reason for this is that all the elements belonging to the concept of happiness are unexceptionally empirical, i.e., they must be borrowed from experience, while for the idea of happiness there is required an absolute whole, a maximum of well-being in my present and in every future condition. Now it is impossible for the most insightful and at the same time most powerful, but nonetheless finite, being to frame here a determinate concept of what it is that he really wills. Does he want riches? How much anxiety, envy, and intrigue might he not thereby bring down upon his own head! Or knowledge and insight? Perhaps these might only give him an eye that much sharper for revealing that much more dreadfully evils which are at present hidden but are yet unavoidable, or such an eye might burden him with still further needs for the desires which already concern him enough. Or long life? Who guarantees that it would not be a long misery? Or health at least? How often has infirmity of the body kept one from excesses into which perfect health would have allowed him to fall, and so on? In brief, he is not able on any principle to determine with complete certainty what will make him truly happy, because to do so would require omniscience. Therefore, one cannot act according to determinate principles in order to be happy, but only according to empirical counsels, e.g., of diet, frugality, politeness, reserve, etc., which are shown by experience to contribute on the average the most to well-being. There follows from this that imperatives of prudence, strictly speaking, cannot command at all, i.e., present actions objectively as practically necessary. They are to be taken as counsels *(consilia)* rather than as commands *(praecepta)* of reason. The problem of determining certainly and universally what action will promote the happiness of a rational being is completely insoluble. Therefore, regarding such action no imperative that in the strictest sense could command what is to be done to make one happy is possible, inasmuch as happiness is not an ideal of reason but of imagination. Such an ideal rests merely on empirical grounds; in vain can there be expected that such grounds should determine an action whereby the totality of an infinite series of consequences could be attained. This imperative of prudence would, nevertheless, be an analytical practical proposition if one assumes tht the means to happiness could with certainty be assigned; for it differs from the imperative of skill only in that for it the end is given while for the latter the end is merely possible. Since both, however, command only the means to what is assumed to be willed as an end, the imperative commanding him who wills the end to will likewise the means thereto is in both cases analytic. Hence there is also no difficulty regarding the possibility of an imperative of prudence.

On the other hand, the question as to how the imperative of morality is possible is undoubtedly the only one requiring a solution. For it is not at all hypothetical; and hence the objective necessity which it presents cannot be based on any presupposition, as was the case with the hypothetical imperatives. Only there must never here be forgotten that no example can show, i.e., empirically, whether there is any such imperative at all. Rather, care must be taken lest all imperatives which are seemingly categorical may nevertheless be covertly hypothetical. For instance, when it is said that you should not make a false promise, the assumption is that the necessity of this avoidance is no mere advice for escaping some other evil, so that it might be said that you should not make a false promise lest you ruin your credit when the falsity comes to light. But when it is asserted than an action of this kind must be regarded as bad in itself, then the imperative of prohibition is therefore categorical. Nevertheless, it cannot with certainty be shown by means of an example that the will is here determined soley by the law without any other incentive, even though such may seem to be the case. For it is always possible that secretly there is fear of disgrace and perhaps also obscure dread of other dangers; such fear and dread may have influenced the will. Who can prove by experience that a cause is not present? Experience only shows that a cause is not perceived. But in such a case the so-called moral imperative, which as such appears to be categorical and unconditioned, would actually be only a pragmatic precept which makes us pay attention to our own advantage and merely teaches us to take such advantage into consideration.

We shall, therefore, have to investigate the possibility of a categorical imperative entirely a priori, inasmuch as we do not here have the advantage of having its reality given in experience and consequently of thus being obligated merely to explain its possibility rather than to establish it. In the meantime so much can be seen for now: the categorical imperative alone purports to be a practical law, while all the others may be called principles of the will but not laws. The reason for this is that whatever is necessary merely in order to attain some arbitrary purpose can be regarded as in itself contingent, and the precept can always be ignored once the purpose is abandoned. Contrariwise, an unconditioned command does not leave the will free to choose the opposite at its own liking. Consequently, only such a command carries with it that necessity which is demanded from a law.

Secondly, in the case of this categorical imperative, or law of morality, the reason for the difficulty (of discerning it possibility) is quite serious. The categorical imperative is an a priori synthetic practical proposition;[21] and since discerning the possibility of propositions of this sort involves so much difficulty in theoretic knowledge, there may readily be gathered that there will be no less difficulty in practical knowledge.

In solving this problem, we want first to inquire whether perhaps the mere concept of a categorical imperative may not also supply us with the formula containing the proposition that can alone be a categorical imperative. For even when we know the purport of such an absolute command, the question as to how it is possible will still require a special and difficult effort, which we postpone to the last section.

If I think of a hypothetical imperative in general, I do not know beforehand what it will contain until its condition is given. But if I think of a categorical imperative, I know immediately what it contains. For since, besides the law, the imperative contains only the necessity that the maxim[22] should accord with this law, while the law contains no condition to restrict it, there remains nothing but the universality of a law as such

---

[21]I connect a priori, and therefore necessarily, the act with the will without presupposing any condition taken from some inclination (though I make such a connection only objectively, i.e., under the idea of a reason having full power over all subjective motives). Hence this is a practical proposition which does not analytically derive the willing of an action from some other willing already presupposed (for we possess no such perfect will) but which connects the willing of an action immediately with the concept of the will of a rational being as something which is not contained in this concept.

[22]A maxim is the subjective principle of acting and must be distinguished from the objective principle, viz., the practical law. A maxim contains the practical rule which reason determines in accordance with the conditions of the subject (often his ignorance or his inclinations) and is thus the principle according to which the subject does act. But the law is the objective principle valid for every rational being, and it is the principle according to which he ought to act, i.e., an imperative.

with which the maxim of the action should conform. This conformity alone is properly what is represented as necessary by the imperative.

Hence there is only one categorical imperative and it is this: Act only according to that maxim whereby you can at the same time will that it should become a universal law.[23]

Now if all imperatives of duty can be derived from this one imperative as their principle, then there can at least be shown what is understood by the concept of duty and what it means, even though there is left undecided whether what is called duty may not be an empty concept.

The universality of law according to which effects are produced constitutes what is properly called nature in the most general sense (as to form), i.e., the existence of things as far as determined by universal laws. Accordingly, the universal imperative of duty may be expressed thus: Act as if the maxim of your action were to become through your will a universal law of nature.[24]

We shall now enumerate some duties, following the usual division of them into duties to ourselves and to others and into perfect and imperfect duties.[25]

1. A man reduced to despair by a series of misfortunes feels sick of life but is still so far in possession of his reason that he can ask himself whether taking his own life would not be contrary to his duty to himself.[26] Now he asks whether the maxim of his action could become a universal law of nature. But his maxim is this: from self-love I make as my principle to shorten my life when its continued duration threatens more evil than it promises satisfaction. There only remains the question as to whether this principle of self-love can become a universal law of nature. One sees at once a contradiction in a system of nature whose law would destroy life by means of the very same feeling that acts so as to stimulate the furtherance of life, and hence there could be no existence as a system of nature. Therefore, such a maxim cannot possibly hold as a universal law of nature and is, consequently, wholly opposed to the supreme principle of all duty.

2. Another man in need finds himself forced to borrow money. He knows well that he won't be able to repay it, but he sees also that he will not get any loan unless he firmly promises to repay it within a fixed time. He wants to make such a promise, but he still has conscience enough to ask himself whether it is not permissible and is contrary to duty to get out of difficulty in this way. Suppose, however, that he decides to do so. The maxim of his action would then be expressed as follows: when I believe myself to be in need of money, I will borrow money and promise to pay it back, although I know that I can never do so. Now this principle of self-love or personal advantage may perhaps be quite compatible with one's entire future welfare, but the

---

[23][This formulation of the categorical imperative is often referred to as the formula of universal law.]

[24][This is often called the formula of the law of nature.]

[25]There should be noted here that I reserve the division of duties for a future *Metaphysics of Morals* [in Part II of the *Metaphysics of Morals*, entitled *The Metaphysical Principles of Virtue*, Ak. 417–474]. The division presented here stands as merely an arbitrary one (in order to arrange my examples). For the rest, I understand here by a perfect duty one which permits no exception in the interest of inclination. Accordingly, I have perfect duties which are external [to others], while other ones are internal [to oneself]. This classification runs contrary to the accepted usage of the schools, but I do not intend to justify it here, since there is no difference for my purpose whether this classification is accepted or not.

[26][Not committing suicide is an example of a perfect duty to oneself. See *Metaphysical Principles of Virtue*, Ak. 422–24.]

question is now whether it is right.[27] I then transform the requirement of self-love into a universal law and put the question thus: how would things stand if my maxim were to become a universal law? He then sees at once that such a maxim could never hold as a universal law of nature and be consistent with itself, but must necessarily be self-contradictory. For the universality of a law which says that anyone believing himself to be in difficulty could promise whatever he pleases with the intention of not keeping it would make promising itself and the end to be attained thereby quite impossible, inasmuch as no one would believe what was promised him but would merely laugh at all such utterances as being vain pretenses.

3. A third finds in himself a talent whose cultivation could make him a man useful in many respects. But he finds himself in comfortable circumstances and prefers to indulge in pleasure rather than to bother himself about broadening and improving his fortunate natural aptitudes. But he asks himself further whether his maxim of neglecting his natural gifts, besides agreeing of itself with his propensity to indulgence, might agree also with what is called duty.[28] He then sees that a system of nature could indeed always subsist according to such a universal law, even though every man (like South Sea Islanders) should let his talents rust and resolve to devote his life entirely to idleness, indulgence, propagation, and, in a word, to enjoyment. But he cannot possibly will that this should become a universal law of nature or be implanted in us as such law by a natural instinct. For as a rational being he necessarily wills that all his faculties should be developed, inasmuch as they are given him for all sorts of possible purposes.

4. A fourth man finds things going well for himself but sees others (whom he could help) struggling with great hardships; and he thinks; what does it matter to me? Let everybody be as happy as Heaven wills or as he can make himself; I shall take nothing from him nor even envy him; but I have no desire to contribute anything to his well-being or to his assistance when in need. If such a way of thinking were to become a universal law of nature, the human race admittedly could very well subsist and doubtless could subsist even better than when everyone prates about sympathy and benevolence and even on occasion exerts himself to practice them but, on the other hand, also cheats when he can, betrays the rights of man, or otherwise violates them. But even though it is possible that a universal law of nature could subsist in accordance with that maxim, still it is impossible to will that such a principle should hold everywhere as a law of nature.[29] For a will which resolved in this way would contradict itself, inasmuch as cases might often arise in which one would have need of the love and sympathy of others and in which he would deprive himself, by such a law of nature springing from his own will, of all hope of the aid he wants for himself.

These are some of the many actual duties, or at least what are taken to be such, whose derivation from the single principle cited above is clear. We must be able to will that a maxim of our action become a universal law; this is the canon for morally estimating any of our actions. Some actions are so constituted that their maxims cannot without contradiction even be thought as a universal law of nature, much less be willed as what should become one. In the case of others this internal impossibility is indeed not found, but there is still no possibility of willing that their maxim should be

---

[27][Keeping promises is an example of a perfect duty to others. See *ibid.,* Ak. 423–31.]
[28][Cultivating one's talents is an example of an imperfect duty to oneself. See *ibid.,* Ak. 444–46.]
[29][Benefiting others is an example of an imperfect duty to others. See *ibid.,* Ak. 452–54.]

raised to the universality of a law of nature, because such a will would contradict itself. There is no difficulty in seeing that the former kind of action conflicts with strict or narrow [perfect] (irremissible) duty, while the second kind conflicts only with broad [imperfect] (meritorious) duty.[30] By means of these examples there has thus been fully set forth how all duties depend as regards the kind of obligation (not the object of their action) upon the one principle.

If we now attend to ourselves in any transgression of a duty, we find that we actually do not will that our maxim should become a universal law—because this is imposible for us—but rather that the opposite of this maxim should remain a law universally.[31] We only take the liberty of making an exception to the law for ourselves (or just for this one time) to the advantage of our inclination. Consequently, if we weighed up everything from one and the same standpoint, namely, that of reason, we would find a contradiction in our own will, viz., that a certain principle be objectively necessary as a universal law and yet subjectively not hold universally but should admit of exceptions. But since we at one moment regard our action from the standpoint of a will wholly in accord with reason and then at another moment regard the very same action from the standpoint of a will affected by inclination, there is really no contradiction here. Rather, there is an opposition *(antagonismus)* of inclination to the precept of reason, whereby the universality *(univeralitas)* of the principle is changed into a mere generality *(generalitas)* so that the practical principle of reason may meet the maxim halfway. Although this procedure cannot be justified in our own impartial judgment, yet it does show that we actually acknowledge the validity of the categorical imperative and (with all respect for it) merely allow ourselves a few exceptions which, as they seem to us, are unimportant and forced upon us.

We have thus at least shown that if duty is a concept which is to have significance and real legislative authority for our actions, then such duty can be expressed only in categorical imperatives but not at all in hypothetical ones. We have also—and this is already a great deal—exhibited clearly and definitely for every application what is the content of the categorical imperative, which must contain the principle of all duty (if there is such a thing at all). But we have not yet advanced far enough to prove a priori that there actually is an imperative of this kind, that there is a practical law which of itself commands absolutely and without any incentives, and that following this law is duty. . . .

Now I say that man, and in general every rational being, exists as an end in himself and not merely as a means to be arbitrarily used by this or that will. He must in all his actions, whether directed to himself or to other rational beings, always be regarded at the same time as an end. All the objects of inclinations have only a conditioned value; for if there were not these inclinations and the needs founded on them, then their object would be without value. But the inclinations themselves, being sources of needs, are so far from having an absolute value such as to render them desirable for their own sake that the universal wish of every rational being must be, rather, to be wholly free from them. Accordingly, the value of any object obtainable by our action is always conditioned. Beings whose existence depends not on our will but

---

[30][Compare *ibid.,* Ak. 390–94, 410–11, 421–51.]

[31][This is to say, for example, that when you tell a lie, you do so on the condition that others are truthful and believe that what you are saying is true, because otherwise your lie will never work to get you what you want. When you tell a lie, you simply take exception to the general rule that says eveyone should always tell the truth.]

on nature have, nevertheless, if they are not rational beings, only a relative value as means and are therefore called things. On the other hand, rational beings are called persons inasmuch as their nature already marks them out as ends in themselves, i.e., as something which is not to be used merely as means and hence there is imposed thereby a limit on all arbitrary use of such beings, which are thus objects of respect. Persons are, therefore, not merely subjective ends, whose existence as an effect of our actions has a value for us; but such beings are objective ends, i.e., exist as ends in themselves. Such an end is one for which there can be substituted no other end to which such beings should serve merely as means, for otherwise nothing at all of absolute value would be found anywhere. But is all value were conditioned and hence contingent, then no supreme practical principle could be found for reason at all.

If then there is to be a supreme practical principle and, as far as the human will is concerned, a categorical imperative, then it must be such that from the conception of what is necessarily an end for everyone because this end is an end in itself it constitutes an objective principle of the will and can hence serve as a practical law. The ground of such a principle is this: rational nature exists as an end in itself. In this way man necessarily thinks of his own existence; thus far is it a subjective principle of human actions. But in this way also does every other rational being think of his existence on the same rational ground that holds also for me;[32] hence it is at the same time an objective principle, from which, as a supreme practical ground, all laws of the will must be able to be derived. The practical imperative will therefore be the following: Act in such a way that you treat humanity, whether in your own person or in the person of another, always at the same time as an end and never simply as a means.[33] We now want to see whether this can be carried out in practice.

Let us keep to our previous examples.

First, as regards the concept of necessary duty to oneself, the man who contemplates suicide will ask himself whether his action can be consistent with the idea of humanity as an end in itself. If he destroys himself in order to escape from a difficult situation, then he is making use of his person merely as a means so as to maintain a tolerable condition till the end of his life. Man, however, is not a thing and hence is not something to be used merely as a means; he must in all his actions always be regarded as an end in himself. Therefore, I cannot dispose of man in my own person by mutiliating, damaging, or killing him. (A more exact determination of this principle so as to avoid all misunderstanding, e.g., regarding the amputation of limbs in order to save oneself, or the exposure of one's life to danger in order to save it, and so on, must here be omitted; such questions belong to morals proper.)

Second, as concerns necessary or strict duty to others, the man who intends to make a false promise will immediately see that he intends to make use of another man merely as a means to an end which the latter does not likewise hold. For the man whom I want to use for my own purposes by such a promise cannot possibly concur with my way of acting toward him and hence cannot himself hold the end of this action. This conflict with the principle of duty to others becomes even clearer when instances of attacks on the freedom and property of others are considered. For then it becomes clear that a transgressor of the rights of men intends to make use of the persons of others merely as a means, without taking into consideration that, as rational

---

[32]This proposition I here put forward as a postulate. The grounds for it will be found in the last section.

[33][This oft-quoted version of the categorical imperative is usually referred to as the formula of the end in itself.]

beings, they should always be esteemed at the same time as ends, i.e., be esteemed only as beings who must themselves be able to hold the very same action as an end.[34]

Third, with regard to contingent (meritorious) duty to oneself, it is not enough that the action does not conflict with humanity in our own person as an end in itself; the action must also harmonize with this end. Now there are in humanity capacities for greater perfection which belong to the end that nature has in view as regards humanity in our own person. To neglect these capacities might perhaps be consistent with the maintenance of humanity as an end in itself, but would not be consistent with the advancement of this end.

Fourth, concerning meritorious duty to others, the natural end that all men have is their own happiness. Now humanity might indeed subsist if nobody contributed anything to the happiness of others, provided he did not intentionally impair their happiness. But this, after all, would harmonize only negatively and not positively with humanity as an end in itself, if everyone does not also strive, as much as he can, to further the ends of others. For the ends of any subject who is an end in himself must as far as possible be my ends also, if that conception of an end in itself is to have its full effect in me.

This principle of humanity and of every rational nature generally as an end in itself is the supreme limiting condition of every man's freedom of action. This principle is not borrowed from experience, first, because of its universality, inasmuch as it applies to all rational beings generally, and no experience is capable of determining anything about them; and, secondly, because in experience (subjectively) humanity is not thought of as the end of men, i.e., as an object that we of ourselves actually make our end which as a law ought to constitute the supreme limiting condition of all subjective ends (whatever they may be): and hence this principle must arise from pure reason [and not from experience]. That is to say that the ground of all practical legislation lies objectively in the rule and in the form of universality, which (according to the first principle) makes the rule capable of being a law (say, for example, a law of nature). Subjectively, however, the ground of all practical legislation lies in the end; but (according to the second principle) the subject of all ends is every rational being as an end in himself. From this there now follows the third practical principle of the will as the supreme condition of the will's conformity with universal practical reason, viz., the idea of the will of every rational being as a will that legislates universal law.[35]

According to this principle all maxims are rejected which are not consistent with the will's own legislation of universal law. The will is thus not merely subject to the law but is subject to the law in such a way that it must be regarded also as legislating for itself and only on this account as being subject to the law (of which it can regard itself as the author).

In the previous formulations of imperatives, viz., that based on the conception of the conformity of actions to universal law in a way similar to a natural order and that based on the universal prerogative of rational beings as ends in themselves, these im-

---

[34]Let it not be thought that the trivial *quod tibi non vis fieri, etc.* [do not do to others what you do not want done to yourself] can here serve as a standard or principle. For it is merely derived from our principle, although with several limitations. It cannot be a universal law, for it contains the ground neither of duties to oneself nor of duties of love toward others (for many a man would gladly consent that others should not benefit him, if only he might be excused from benefiting them). Nor, finally, does it contain the ground of strict duties toward others, for the criminal would on this ground be able to dispute with the judges who punish him; and so on.

[35][This is usually called the formula of autonomy.]

peratives just because they were thought of as categorical excluded from their legislative authority all admixture of any interest as an incentive. They were, however, only assumed to be categorical because such an assumption had to be made if the concept of duty was to be explained. But that there were practical propositions which commanded categorically could not itself be proved, nor can it be proved anywhere in this section. But one thing could have been done, viz., to indicate that in willing from duty the renunciation of all interest is the specific mark distinguishing a categorical imperative from a hypothetical one and that such renunciation was expressed in the imperative itself by means of some determination contained in it. This is done in the present (third) formulation of the principle, namely, in the idea of the will of every rational being as a will that legislates universal law.

When such a will is thought of, then even though a will which is subject to law may be bound to this law by means of some interest, nevertheless a will that is itself a supreme lawgiver is not able as such to depend on any interest. For a will which is so dependent would itself require yet another law restricting the interest of its self-love to the condition that such interest should itself be valid as a universal law.

Thus the principle that every human will as a will that legislates universal law in all its maxims,[36] provided it is otherwise correct, would be well suited to being a categorical imperative in the following respect: just because of the idea of legislating universal law such as imperative is not based on any interest, and therefore it alone of all possible imperatives can be unconditional. Or still better, the proposition being converted, if there is a categorical imperative (i.e., a law for the will of every rational being), then it can only command that everything be done from the maxim of such a will as could at the same time have as its object only itself regarded as legislating universal law. For only then are the practical principle and the imperative which the will obeys unconditional, inasmuch as the will can be based on no interest at all.

Applying the Categorical Imperative
Onora O'Neil

... The problem faced in trying to devise an acceptable interpretation of the contradiction in conception test is then that of finding a test that selects (at least roughly) those maxims which Kant, and we, would probably think maxims of justice; which does not select (many) false positives, and which in some sense shows that there is an *inner* impossibility in the UTC's[1] of maxims contrary to duties of justice. Clearly the derivation

---

[36]I may here be excused from citing instances to elucidate this principle inasmuch as those which were first used to elucidate the categorical imperative and its formula can all serve the same purpose here.

Onora O'Neil, *Acting on Principle*, copyright © (1975), Columbia University Press. Used by permission.

[1]The term UTC is professor O'Neil's abbreviation for "universalized typified counterpart," which itself is a precise way of describing the universalized version of our proposed actions. For example, assume I wish to test my proposed action of "stealing a car if I need one in order to impress my friends." The UTC of this is "everyone will steal a car if they need to in order to impress their friends."

of a contradiction from the UTC's of maxims that are contrary to duties of justice is not often possible unless additional empirical premises are used. But which other empirical premises is it legitimate to assume?

Consider the wording of Formulas I and Ia of the Categorical Imperative once again. As first stated, they run, respectively,

1. Act only on that maxim through which you can at the same time will that it should become a universal law.

1a. Act as if the maxim of your action were to become through your will a universal law of nature.

Two elements in the first of these formulations should be noted. Maxims which are not contrary to duty must be conceivable as a universal law *through* the maxim and *at the same time as* the maxim is held.[2] Both applications of the Formula of Universal Law are tests which an agent applies to his own intentions as expressed in his maxim; even the contradiction in conception test is a test of a consistent will or set of intentions.

In making the contradiction in conception test, two elements are under consideration: a maxim of action and its UTC. We must see, not whether the UTC alone or in conjunction with arbitrarily selected true empirical premises entails a contradiction, but whether the agent can consistently *simultaneously* hold his maxim and will its UTC. But what is meant by willing a hypothetical law of nature? Clearly it is not a matter of whether the agent wants or wishes that the UTC were an actual law of nature. If the contradiction in conception test made such an appeal to inclinations it could not, according to Kant's views, be a test of the rightness, or more generally of the moral acceptability, of maxims. But though an agent does not have to want that the UTC of his maxim become an actual law of nature, he must be able to *intend* that it do so. Since he is not able to legislate or enforce universal laws (whether practical laws or laws of nature) such an intention cannot be realized by an individual agent. Hence the criteria for ascribing such intentions to agents must be rather unusual.

An attribution of the intention that the UTC of a given maxim be universal law is justified if the agent would have that intention if his will were "a will which by all its maxims enacts unviersal law."[3] This fictitious assumption of a capacity to legislate universally is also indicated in the opening words of Formula Ia, "Act *as if*. . . ." By assuming the fiction that his will is universally legislating, an agent is able to stage a direct confrontation between two intentions: the intention embodied in his maxim and that expressed in its UTC which, *qua* universal legislator, he also intends. If these two intentions are not compatible his maxim is not permissible. . . .

One might, however, wonder whether there can ever be any contradiction between intending to do some act and the intention that everyone similarly situated do

[2]Cf. also the renderings of these formulae at *G.* [Grounding for the Metaphysics of Morals], pp. 434 and 436–37 (twice), *K.P.V.* [Critique of Pure Reason], p. 30 and *M.S.* [Metaphysics of Morals], p. 224. In all these the qualification "at the same time" appears, and in some the qualification that the universal law must be willable "through" the agent's maxim.

[3]*G.*, p. 432 ff. This indicates how close to the Formula of Universal Law the Formula of the Kingdom of Ends is, despite its superficial differences. That formula requires us to act so "that the will can regard itself as at the same time making universal law by means of its maxims," *G.*, p. 434. It is no part of this chapter to vindicate Kant's claim that all formulations of the Categorical Imperative are equivalent. But that claim receives some corroboration from the interpretation here given to the Formula of Universal Law.

the same act. If we consider the two intentions schematically it would seem impossible. For they would be, respectively:

> **(3′) I will — — — — if . . . .**
> **(6) Everyone will — — — — if . . . .**

Rather it seems that (3′) is an instantiation of (6), and that no contradiction would ever be possible. But to draw this conclusion is to take too limited a view of what it is to have an intention. If I intend to, say, rob a bank, I intend also some sufficient set of conditions to realize my ends and the normal, predictable results of the success of my intended action.[4] For instance, I intend the continued existence of the bank I plan to rob, that I be neither discovered nor interrupted during the theft, and that I shall use or enjoy the fruits of the theft. These are not separate intentions which a person who intends to rob a bank may or may not have; they are part and parcel of normal intentions to rob banks. Similarly if I intend *qua* universal legislator that everyone should rob some bank, then I must also intend some conditions sufficient for them to do so and the normal and predictable results of their succeeding in doing so. But I cannot intend that everybody be not interrupted or discovered in their theft from a bank and be able to use or enjoy the fruits of their theft. I must intend the normal and predictable results of the success of any course of action which I intend, and the normal result of everyone's stealing from banks is that banks will take ever greater precautions to impede and discover thieves and to prevent them using or enjoying their loot. Failing successful prevention, banks, as we know them, would close down.

    I cannot intend a system of nature in which everybody does what I do. So if my maxim is to rob a bank I cannot universalize it. In my capacity as universal legislator, I would intend that all theft from banks and, hence, my theft from a bank and the use and enjoyment of its results become increasingly difficult and eventually impossible; yet in my private capacity I intend that my theft from a bank be feasible and successful. If an agent does act on the maxim of robbing a bank, or on any other maxim whose universalization would require him to have self-contradictory intentions, then the outcome will be ". . . no contradiction, but rather an opposition to the precept of reason (antagonismus), whereby the universality of the principle (universalitas) is turned to mere generality (generalitas)."[5]

    In such cases we intend that we should be an exception to the universal law, and that the law be not really universal. In the example given, we intend both that banks continue to exist in their present form, as part of the necessary conditions for the robberies we intend, and that banks do not continue to exist in their present form, as part of the normal and predictable results of the robberies we intend. Rational beings cannot intend a society of bank robbers. . . .

    This interpretation of the contradiction in conception test proposes a far from mechanical method for determining whether acting on a maxim is compatible with

---

[4]Though it is hard to find any objection to either of these amplifications of what is involved in intending to do some act, it is also hard to produce a convincing justification for either. Kant held that the requirement that one intend some sufficient means to an act intended was, at least in a loose sense, analytic of the notion of rationality. Cf. *G.,* p. 417 " 'If I fully will the effect, I also will the action required for it' is analytic," and also L. W. Beck *A Commentary on Kant's Critique of Practical Reason,* pp. 84–88. We can call this the Principle of Hypothetical Imperatives. The requirement that one intend the normal and predictable results of one's acts might equally loosely, but convincingly, be defended as analytic of the notion of rationality.

[5]*G.,* p. 424.

...ıt the method is still relatively clear and definite. It asks whether we can simul-
...ously intend to do *x* (assuming that we must intend some set of conditions suffi-
...ent for the successful carrying out of our intentions and the normal and predictable
results of successful execution) and intend everyone else to do *x* (assuming again that
we must intend some conditions sufficient for the successful execution of their intentions and the normal and predictable results of such execution). No appeal is made in
this interpretation of the test to particular desires or inclinations or to particular empirical situations. Naturally an agent who is working out what his intentions commit
him to must take certain empirical facts into account. But a limit is placed on the sort
of empirical material which may be adduced in testing a maxim by the relevance of
the empirical material to the coherence of the agent's intentions. There are still good
reasons for calling the contradictions which may be derived from applications of this
test "inner impossiblities." They mark an incoherence *within* the intentions of a particular agent.

Only given a certain background of empirical facts can an agent's intention to do
an act be determinate. For only given these can he work out whether there is some
feasible means for executing his intention and what the normal and predictable results of successful execution of the intention would be. But just which sorts of facts
may or must an agent assume to see what exactly his intentions commit him to? . . .

Is it, for instance, permissible for an agent testing the maxim of embezzlement
to assume as an empirical fact that he will not be apprehended? Or is this not part of
the normal and predictable results of successful embezzling? The answer in such cases
is that he may do so only if he assumes also that, if everyone else embezzles, they will
not be apprehended. The only sense in which Kant does rely upon the notion of a system of nature in the statement of the contradiction in conception test is that he requires that we ask "Whether if the action you propose should take place by a law of
nature of which you yourself were a part you could regard it as possible through your
will."[6] Appeal cannot be made to empirical facts such as that not everyone will do likewise or that this act will (or will not) serve as a bad example. For the hypothesis
against which a maxim is tested is precisely that others do the same, whether or not
because of the example given.

But this is not a sufficient restriction on the sorts of empirical circumstance
which a man may assume in determining what his intentions commit him to. He must
assume, not only that he belongs to the same system of nature as others, but, if he is
seeing whether his maxim is a maxim of human duty, he must assume that he belongs
to that system of nature to which men belong. He cannot, for instance, assume that a
duplicate of stolen property is somehow miraculously presented to the owner, who is
therefore not deprived while the thief enjoys the original. If we did live in such a system of nature, precautions against theft would presumably never be taken and the
maxim of thieving could consistently be universalized. But this is no reason for rejecting the interpretation of the test. One would not expect the moral status of theft to be
the same in such a system of nature as it is in our own.

Tests of the capacity of maxims to guide any human moral choices must assume
those natural laws in whose context all human society operates—that men are mortal
and learn from experience; that material goods are not infinitely abundant and are desired, and additional specific laws of this sort. No doubt it is not entirely clear which
generalizations about the human condition are laws of nature, but this is a question

[6]*K.P.V.,* p. 69.

which judgment is not powerless to solve. The fact that agents testing the rightness and moral worth of acts done or proposed have to make judgments of this sort does, however, show once again how far from mechanical this test is. To apply it fairly, agents must assess their intentions and the probable results of their success with complete honesty. This fact may account for the enormous stress which Kant places on duties such as integrity and conscientiousness. . . .

The contradiction in the will test depends on showing that there are certain ends which it is a duty for men to have. But the very notion of an obligatory end has seemed to many incompatible with central parts of Kant's ethical theory. Does not Kant say that ethics must not depend on any human desires? So, before one can turn to any of Kant's arguments that there must be obligatory ends, or to his arguments identifying specific obligatory ends, it is essential to show that the notion of an obligatory end is consistent with the rest of his ethical theory.

Kant defines an end as "an object of the power of choice (of a rational being) through the thought of which choice is determined to an action to produce this object."[7] The evidence that a given state of affairs, *s,* is an end for an agent is that the agent does something or other to achieve *s* (unless no course of action is available to him, and known by him to be available). The act he does can be explained (in part) by showing that *s* is an end for him. The most obvious sort of end is an end which is wanted or desired. The evidence that an agent wants *s* is that he does something to achieve *s* (if this is open to him), and his act can be explained (in part) by pointing out that he wants *s*. But throughout his writings on ethics Kant maintains that the want and desires of particular agents have no bearing on the moral acceptability of their acts. "All practical principles which presuppose an *object* [material] of the faculty of desire as the determining ground of the will are without exception empirical and can furnish no practical laws."[8] Hence his claim that there can be ends that are obligatory, which agents ought to adopt in their "maxims of ends," depends on there being ends that are not the wants and desires of particular agents. There must be at least some "objects of the power of rational choice" which are not also "objects of the faculty of desire" if Kant's doctrine of obligatory ends is to be consistent with the rest of his ethical theory.

A satisfactory interpretation of Kant's ethical theory, and in particular of his *Metaphysik der Sitten,* requires that there be ends other than those desired. Kant assumes that there are, as is shown by the frequency with which he speaks of "adopting ends" or "choosing ends" and of "ends which we ought to have." We do not adopt or choose desires; we have them. And if there are any desires which we ought to have, then we cannot acquire them by any direct process of choice, but only by some sort of education or cultivation of ourselves. Our duties to adopt ends are not duties to have certain desires. A duty of love, for example does not require that we want to treat others in a certain way. Feelings are irrelevant to duty. A duty of love "must rather be taken as a maxim of benevolence (practical love) which has beneficence as its consequence."[9] Similarly the most general duties of virtue cannot be duties to want our own perfection and others' happiness. . . .

In the next chapter I hope to link the doctrine of obligatory ends with the theory that moral worth depends on the motive with which an act is done. In this chapter my aim is more modest. I shall try to give an interpretation of the contradiction in the will

[7]*M.S.,* p. 380; cf. *ibid.,* p. 383.
[8]*K.P.V.,* p. 21; cf. *G.,* p. 400.
[9]*M.S.,* p. 448.

light of the firt principle of ethics, which has textual support as well as prac-
...ications.

...n structure, the test for maxims of virtue is the same as that for maxims of jus-
... This is not surprising since both tests are applications of the Formula of Universal
Law. But the point of application of the two tests is different. Acts violate duties of virtue if their maxim of ends, not their maxim of action, cannot be consistently universalized. So an application of the test for a maxim of virtue begins by considering the
agent's complete maxim of ends, of form

(4) To – – – – if . . . . in order to ———,

and forming it UTC,

(7) Everyone will – – – – if . . . . in order to ———.

Assuming that acts done on such a maxim violate no duty of justice, any contradiction
derivable from (4) and (7) must depend on the introduction of the purposive component "in order to ———." There are two ways in which such a component could lead
to a contradiction. The first case would be where the act described in the composite
act description could not lead to the end mentioned in the purposive component. In
this case an act done on the maxim would be irrational and might yet have a permissible or even obligatory end. Though it is essential to consider which maxims of action
are compatible with which maxims of ends for a complete statement of the contradiction in the will test, such compatibilty in no way guarantees that the end aimed at is
permissible, let alone obligatory. In determining which are maxims of virtue it is essential to establish first which ends—if any—are obligatory. So the contradiction in
the will test must derive contradictions only from the purposive components of maxims of ends; i.e., only from *incomplete* maxims of ends and not from an incompatibility between act and end. We must begin by considering

(4″) To do/omit what is needed in order to ———,

with UTC of form

(7′) Everyone will do/omit what is needed in order to ———.

As in the case of the contradiction in conception test, it seems at first as though
a contradiction could never be derived from a maxim of ends of form (4″) and its UTC
of form (7′) unless the specification of the purposive component, "———," were itself incoherent. But in such a case Kant would have held that the agent did not really
have any maxim of ends to which the test could be applied. The contradiction in the
will test is intended to show certain coherent purposes forbidden, and others either
merely permissible or obligatory. . . .

The actual test procedure can now be examined, beginning as in the discussion
of the test for duties of justice, with the examples Kant gives in the *Grundlegung*. In
his examples of applications of the Formula of Universal Law, Kant discusses the duty
to develop one's talents and the duty to help others in need. If these are to be shown
obligatory ends, then a contradiction should be derivable from an attempt to will as
universal law a maxim of neglecting these ends.

If there is any duty to help others in need, Kant points out, it must be a wide duty. We can quite consistently intend a system of nature in which men do not help one another. It is not contrary to any duty of justice to act on the maxim

1. To neglect everything needed to help the needy.

We can consistently will 1, and its UTC,

2. Everyone will neglect everything needed to help the needy.

For 2 is a possible law of a nature of which I might will to be a part consistently with all those considerations which may be relevantly adduced in a contradiction in conception test. But certain other considerations are relevant in the contradiction in the will test.

One necessary fact about men is, Kant thinks, here relevant. That is that men have ends. This is not a fact that anybody would be inclined to dispute, though the basis for calling it "necessary" may be unclear.[10] I do not propose to investigate that claim of Kant's. But once this fact is taken as a premise, a contradiction may quite readily be deduced from 1 and 2. If men have ends they must, by the Principle of Hypothetical Imperatives (which Kant thinks is analytic), will some sufficient means to those ends. But if I will whatever means are needed to achieve whatever ends I may have, then I must will that, should I be unable to achieve my ends by my unaided efforts, I should be given assistance. I must will to be helped if in need. But if I will this in my private capacity, I cannot also will 2.

The contradiction in the will is a contradiction between a maxim which any human agent must have to be rational, and the UTC of the proposed maxim of neglecting some things needed to help any other in need. It should be noted that this argument shows only that a maxim of giving *no* help to *any* other in need is contrary to duty. The UTC of an intention to neglect everything needed to help the needy commits an agent to the intention that others neglect some things needed to help him in need. Complete lack of beneficence is contrary to duty, but we do not have a duty to help all who need help. Beneficence may be selective without violation of duty. Nor do we have a duty to give all necessary help to any one of those in need. Beneficence may also be partial without violation of duty. Duty requires only the adoption of the contrary of 1, "I will do some of what is needed to help the needy."

The argument, incidentally, also enables Kant to show reciprocity of help a duty without showing that reciprocal acts ought to be reciprocated in the merest details.

The example of developing our own talents has been left till last because it has one peculiarity. Although the argument establishing that it is an obligatory end can fit the very same pattern as the argument showing that it is an obligatory end to help others in need, it also fits into a simpler pattern. It is not essential to make any reference to the UTC of a maxim of neglecting all one's talents to show that this maxim of

---

[10]The contradiction in conception test, of course, also relies on this premise, but for a very different purpose. There certain laws of nature were assumed in order to determine what various intentions would commit an agent to. Should men come to live in a very different system of nature, these premises could not be assumed. But Kant does not think the premise that men have ends could ever be dropped. Indeed the very use of the premise in a test of the moral status of ends assumes that the agent testing his maxim has at least one end.

ends is contrary to duty. A contradiction can be derived from the conjunction of the agent's maxim of neglect and the fact that men have ends. But this anomaly is, in fact, what we might expect of a duty that can be carried out whether or not there are any other agents. Even in a system of nature of which we were the sole human members we would have opportunity to develop our talents, whereas we would have no opportunity to help others.

The derivation of a contradiction proceeds as follows: given a maxim,

3. I will neglect everything needed in order to develop my talents,

with UTC

4. Everyone will neglect everything needed to develop his talents,

Kant points out that there is no contradiction in the idea of a system of nature in which men entirely neglect their talents. But he claims that there is a contradiction in a rational agent's willing to be part of such a system. Rational beings have ends; they also will some sufficient means to these ends, and the development of some talents is a part of the means to ends of any sort. So rational agents must make it an end to develop at least some of their own talents. If they do not have this end, they cannot claim to have any other end. "For as a rational being he necessarily wills that all his powers should be developed, since they serve him and are given him for all sorts of ends."[11] But the conclusion that all rational agents will to develop some talents contradicts both 3 and 4. Hence, neglecting everything needed to develop some talents is impermissible, and so it is obligatory to do what is needed to develop some talents. It is optional from the point of view of duty which talents we develop to what extent. But we may not do nothing. What we do must depend on our situation.[12]

So far I have shown that the contradiction in the will test can be used to substantiate Kant's claim that developing some talents and helping some others in need are obligatory ends. But developing some talents is only part of developing one's perfection. Perfection includes moral perfection. And helping those in need is only part of promoting others' happiness. Respect and sympathy as well as beneficence are said to be duties of virtue. Kant does not try in the *Grundlegung* to establish the two most general duties of virtue, i.e., the two obligatory ends of the *Metaphysik der Sitten,* by applying the Formula of Universal Law. When he comes to applying the Formula of the End in Itself, on the other hand, he does argue that we have a duty to promote our own perfection and others' happiness in general. The arguments used in the *Metaphysik der Sitten* to establish these obligatory ends are also not applications of the contradiction in the will test, but the test can be used for this purpose.

To neglect one's own perfection in general is to neglect both one's moral perfection and the development of one's talents. The latter sort of neglect has already been shown contrary to duty. So it remains to consider neglect of cultivation of moral

---

[11]*G.,* p. 423.

[12]Cf. *M.S.,* p. 391. "Then too, the different situations in which men may find themselves make a man's choice of the sort of occupation for which he should cultivate his talents quite arbitrary. With regard to natural perfection, accordingly, reason gives no law for actions but only a law for the maxims of actions, which runs as follows: 'Cultivate your powers of mind and body so that they are fit to realize any end you can come upon,' for it cannot be said which of these could, at some time, become yours."

perfection. Kant thinks that there is only one "moral perfection" or "moral talent": a strength of will which an agent manifests in his ability to do his duty without any further incentives, simply because it is his duty.[13] This strength of will is manifested whenever an agent acts on a maxim of virtue, and whenever he acts not merely according to but out of duty of, justice. It is the constant formal element in all acts done on a maxim of virtue.[14] The maxim to which the contradiction in conception test must be applied is therefore

5. **I will neglect to do everything needed to develop my moral strength of will.**

If an agent has this maxim, then, since he must will the means to his ends, he cannot will any end for which developing one's strength of will is an essential means. But developing one's strength of will is a necessary means to one end only: that of acting virtuously or doing one's duty not for any further end but for its own sake, and we know from the previous argument that there is at least one duty of virtue. Acquiring a capacity for any sort of act is always an essential means to doing that act unless the capacity is inborn, which moral strength of will is not.

From the premises that there are some duties of virtue and that agents must will some sufficient means to any ends they desire, the conclusion that developing one's capacity for moral action is required by duty easily follows. Whatever other conditions may be needed for virtuous action, the cultivation of a capacity for such action is clearly a part of any sufficient set of conditions. Moral as well as natural perfection must be cultivated if one is to act dutifully. Perfection of oneself in general is a duty.

Universalization

R. M. Hare

. . . It must also be noted that the thesis that moral judgements are universalizable has not yet played a crucial role in the argument. Mentions of it in the preceding chapter were all mere anticipations of what is going to be said in this, except for its use to show that rational moral thinking requires cognizance of the facts; and even that, as we saw, could be dispensed with if we accept the view that all prescriptions, universal and singular, have to be made in cognizance of the facts if they are to be rational. But in . . . what follows universalizability will begin to play a crucial role.

[13]*M.S.*, pp. 391, 446.
[14]*Ibid.*, p. 404.

I wish to stress that there are not, strictly speaking, as Mr. Mackie claims that there are, different *stages* of universalization.[1] Moral judgements are, I claim, universalizable in only one sense, namely that they entail identical judgements about all cases identical in their universal properties. There is, however, as Mackie sees, a progression in the use we make of this single logical property as we develop our theory of moral reasoning. The effect of the argument of the preceding chapter is to facilitate one step in this progression, namely the step from prescriptions which I accept for my own experiences to prescriptions which I must accept for experiences I should have, were I to be in someone else's position with his preferences. In establishing the possibility of this step, we appealed to universalizability only to the limited extent mentioned in the preceding paragraph, and that did not require any special sense of universalizability beyond the one just defined.

It follows form universalizability that if I now say that I ought to do a certain thing to a certain person, I am committed to the view that the very same thing ought to be done to me, were I in exactly his situation, including having the same personal characteristics and in particular the same motivational states. But the motivational states he actually now has may run quite counter to my own present ones. For example, he may very much want not to have done to him what I am saying I ought to do to him (which involves prescribing that I do it). But we have seen that if I fully represent to myself his situation, including his motivations, I shall myself acquire a corresponding motivation, which would be expressed in the prescription that the same thing *not be* done to me, were I to be forthwith in just that situation. But this prescription is inconsistent with my original "ought-statement, if that was, as we have been assuming, prescriptive. For, as we have just seen, the statement that I ought to do it to him commits me to the view that it ought to be done to me, were I in his situation. And this, since "ought" is prescriptive, entails the prescription that the same *be* done to me in that situation. So, if I have this full knowledge of his situation, I am left with two inconsistent prescriptions. I can avoid this "contradiction in the will"[2] only by abandoning my original "ought"-statement, given my present knowledge of my proposed victim's situation.

6.2   A problem arises here, however, about this conflict between my own and my victim's preferences. There is first of all the difficulty, which we shall be dealing with in the next chapter, of comparing his preferences with mine in respect of intensity. How am I to say which is the greater, and by how much? But even if we assume that this difficulty can be overcome, the problem remains of why my preferences, even if they are less intense, should be subordinated to his. And if mine are more intense than his, ought they to be subordinated at all? Suppose, for example, that all I think I ought to do to him is move his bicycle so that I can park my car, and he has a mild aversion to my doing this (not because he dislikes someone else interfering with his property, but simply because he wants it to stay where it is). This problem seems even more pressing in multilateral cases in which the preferences of many people are affected; but it will do no harm to deal with it in this simple bilateral case first.

I can see no reason for not adopting the same solution here as we do in cases where our own preferences conflict with one another. For example, let us change the

[1]Meckie, J. L., Ethics: *Inventing Right and Wrong* (1977) Peguin Press, 83 ff.

[2]Kant, I., *Grundlegung zur Metaphysik der Sitten* (Groundwork to the Metaphysic of Morals) (1785), translated as *The Moral Law* by H. J. Paton (1948) Huntchinson and Barnes and Noble. References are to pages of second edition in margin. See page 58.

case and suppose that it is my own bicycle, and that it is moderately inconvenient to move it, but highly inconvenient not to be able to park my car; I shall then naturally move the bicycle, thinking that that is what, prudentially speaking, I ought to do, or what I most want, all in all, to do. Reverting now to the bilateral case: we have established that, if I have full knowledge of the other person's preferences, I shall myself have acquired preferences equal to his regarding what should be done to me were I in his situation; and these are the preferences which are now conflicting with my original prescription. So we have in effect not an interpersonal conflict of preferences or prescriptons, but an intrapersonal one; both the conflicting preferences are mine. I shall therefore deal with the conflict in exactly the same way as with that between two original preferences of my own.

Multilateral cases now present less difficulty than at first appeared. For in them too the interpersonal conflicts, however complex and however many persons are involved, will reduce themselves, given full knowledge of the preferences of others, to intrapersonal ones. And since we are able, in our everyday life, to deal with quite complex intrapersonal conflicts of preferences, I can see no reason why we should not in the same way deal with conflicts of this special sort, which have arisen through our awareness of the preferences of others combined with the requirement that we universalize our moral prescriptions.

Let us apply this to our simple bilateral car–bicycle case. The other party wants me not to move his bicycle, but I want more to move it in order to park my car. I am fully aware of the strength of his desire, and therefore have a desire of equal strength that, were I in his situation, the bicycle should stay where it is. But I also have my original desire to move it in order to park my car. This latter desire wins by superior strength. On the other hand, if the positions were reversed (the bicycle mine, the car his), and I could somehow prevent the bicycle being moved, the case would be from my individual point of view different (though not different in its universal properties). Suppose that, in this different case, my desire not to have the bicycle moved is far weaker than the other party's desire to park his car; and suppose that I am fully aware of the strength of his desire and therefore have an equal desire that, were I in his position, I should be able to park my car. I shall then, in this different situation, have again two desires: the original desire to leave my bicycle where it is, and my acquired desire that were I the other party I should be able to park my car; and the latter will be the stronger. So in this different situation I shall think that the bicycle ought to be moved.

Note that, although the situations are different, they differ only in what *individuals* occupy the two roles; their *universal* properties are all the same. That is why (and this is interesting and significant) in both cases the conclusion is that the bicycle ought to be moved; this is because in each case its owner's desire to leave it where it is is less than the car-owner's desire to park his car. We see here in miniature how the requirement to universalize our prescriptons generates utilitarianism. And we see also how in principle unanimity can be reached by our method of reasoning, once each fully represents to himself the situation of the other. And there is in principle no difficulty in extending the method to multilateral cases; the difficulties are all practical ones of acquiring the necessary knowledge and correctly performing some very complex thought-processes. In difficult cases it would take an archangel to do it. . . .

The third objection, which I shall deal with in the next section, is the following. We have been assuming that we are constrained to apply our moral principles, because they are universal, to all identical situations, whether actual or hypothetical. Since there are not likely to be any identical actual situations . . . , the application to hypothetical ones is crucial. It might be objected that someone who wanted to escape our argument might just refuse to consider the application of the moral principle, to which his moral judgement about the present case commits him, to any but actual situations. If we allow him to get away with this, we shall be unable to pursue the above argument, because that depended on asking him to prescribe for the hypothetical case in which he occupied the position of his victim—a case which, we may suppose, will never actually arise (*FR* 6.4; H 1978a:78).[3]

6.4   There is implicit in what I have said (5.3) an answers to this objection. I have maintained that in so far as I know what it is like to be the other person, I have already acquired motivations, equal to his, with regard to the hypothetical case in which I should be in his position. So the prescription which is going to conflict with my proposed moral judgement is already there. But the objector might retort that this judgement, in committing me to a universal principle (viz. that the same ought to be done in all identical cases) commits me only to judgements about cases which are or will be actual, not to hypothetical ones. The question which arises, therefore, is whether moral principles, in order to be universal, have to apply to all cases both actual and hypothetical, or only to actual cases. To use the fashionable terminology, do we have to be able to apply our moral principles to all logically possible worlds, or only to the actual world?

We shall certainly become confused here unless we observe carefully the distinction between intuitive and critical thinking. What we are concerned with here is critical thinking; the principle to which the proposed moral judgement will commit its author is a highly specific one, namely that in all cases just like this a certain thing should be done. I have in other places, and elsewhere in this book . . . , insisted that intuitive or prima facie principles have to be selected for their acceptance-utility in the actual world; and that therefore it should not be held against them that in hypothetical cases, *different* in their universal properties from what would be likely to occur in the actual world, they would yield unhappy results, nor should it be held against utilitarianism that in such cases it could conflict with these intuitions. The incautious might therefore expect me to say here too that what results a principle will produce in hypothetical cases is irrelevant to the argument. But actually I am going to say the opposite, and must therefore explain why.

The point is that what we are concerned with in this kind of critical thinking are hypothetical cases *not different* in their universal properties from the actual (*FR* 3.6).[4] It follows from this that any properly universal principle will apply to them too. There is no way of framing a properly universal principle which prescribes for actual cases but does not similarly prescribe for non-actual cases which resemble the actual cases in all their universal properties and differ from them only in the roles played in them by particular individuals. Given two cases differing solely in that in one of them individuals *A* and *B* occupy certain roles, and in the other the roles are reversed, any universal principle must yield the same prescriptions about them both. In order to yield different prescriptions about the two cases, the principle would have to contain the names of the individuals, and would therefore not be universal. . . .

The thesis of universalizability itself was established by arguments of a philo-

[3]Hare, R. M., *Freedom and Reason* (1963) Oxford University Press, 6.4; Hare, R. M. "Predition and Moral Appraisal," Mid-West Studies 3, 78.

[4]Hare, R. M., *Freedom and Reason* (1963) Oxford University Press, 3.6.

sophical-logical sort (1.2, 1.6, 4.7; *FR* 2.2 ff.; *LM* 8.2, 10.3 f.).[5] The most important of these consists in showing that a person who makes different moral judgements about cases which he admits to be identical in their non-moral universal properties encounters the same kind of incomprehension as is encountered by a logical inconsistency (for example a self-contradiction). If any dispute arises about precisely what properties are to count as universal for the purposes of the thesis, the same test can be applied again. For example, it is usually held that spatial and temporal properties do not count (because they cannot be defined without reference to an individual point of origin of the coordinate system); and they can be shown not to count by pointing out that the sort of logical incomprehension just described would arise if somebody treated the date (irrespective of what sorts of things happened on that or on related dates) as morally relevant; and similarly for the grid map reference (irrespective of what was at that or at related locations).

The same move can be made in the present case. If somebody says "I ought to do it to him, but nobody ought to do it to me if I were in precisely his position with his preferences," and gives as his reason, not that he is he, nor that today is today, but that this is the actual case and that merely hypothetical, then, I claim, the same logical incomprehension would arise as if he had said either of those two other things. I am here appealing to our *linguistic* intuitions, being confident of my own, and confident that they are linguistic not moral (because they must be shared by anybody who understands the use of "ought," whatever his moral opinions).

⊭ ⊭⊭

The Ethics of Respect for Persons

C. E. Harris, Jr.

A hypothetical person called John Whiteman is a racist of the old school: he believes that all blacks should be slaves. He would even be willing to be enslaved himself if he were found to have "black blood." Most of us would consider his view to be the very model of immorality, so we are more than a little disturbed to realize that Mr. Whiteman's position passes the test of the universalization principle. His viewpoint is not self-defeating, because everyone's holding this position and acting in accordance with it would not prohibit Mr. Whiteman from holding his views.

The fact that such a patently immoral action can pass the test of the universalization principle points out the inadequacy of this principle as a complete guide to morality. Relatively few actions are self-defeating, although the test is useful when it does

---

[5]See above sections 1.2, 1.6, 4.7; Hare, R. M., *Freedom and Reason* (1963) Oxford University Press, 2.2ff.; and Hare, R. M., *Language of Morals* (1952), Oxford University Press, 8.2, 10.3f.

apply. The universalization principle emphasizes the equality of all human beings, which is an important part of the ethics of respect for persons. It provides a minimal condition for morally acceptable rules. But the condition is not sufficient for a morally acceptable action, as this example shows. For this reason, we must consider another version of the moral standard of the ethics of respect for persons—the *means-ends principle*. The principle can be stated as follows:

> **MS 2: Those actions are right that treat human beings, whether you or another person, as an end and not simply as a means.**

What does it mean to treat someone as an end rather than a means? The answer to this question goes to the heart of the distinction between things and persons. Persons or moral agents have a capacity to formulate and carry out their own goals, whereas things have their purposes determined from the outside. A pencil sharpener, for example, was manufactured to perform a specific function, as was a coffee mug. Human beings, on the other hand, can determine their own purposes. This capacity of persons or moral agents to determine their own purposes is the basis of the means-ends principle. We shall say that "treating a person as an end" means respecting the conditions necessary for his or her effective functioning as a moral agent.

Before examining the conditions for the effective exercise of one's moral agency, however, we should ask what is meant by the reference to treating someone "*simply* as a means." This phrase implies that in some sense it is legitimate to treat a person as a means. In relating to other people in our day-to-day lives, we often do treat them as a means in the sense of being relatively unconcerned with their status as persons. When I go to the post office, I have no special interest in the aspirations of the postal worker who sells me stamps, other than a general positive attitude toward her. In one sense, I do treat her as a means to my end of obtaining stamps. But I do not treat her *simply* or *merely* as a means, because I do nothing to negate her status as a moral being.

Many social relationships involve the element of treating others as a means, but not solely as a means. I may treat my doctor as a means to recover from my illness, but I do not treat him simply as a means, because I do not deny him his status as a person. Students treat their professors as a means to gaining knowledge and getting a degree, but they do not treat them simply as a means, because they do not obstruct the professors' humanity. Social relationships would be impossible if treating a person as a means were not permissible in this limited way.

Preliminary Concepts.   The basic idea of the means-ends principle is simple, but its application is often difficult. In order to help you to apply the principle, we shall discuss three issues: (1) the conditions of moral agency, (2) the principle of forfeiture, and (3) the principle of equality.[1]

1. The Conditions of Moral Agency.   Two fundamental conditions are necessary in order for a person to act as a moral agent. The first of these conditions is *freedom* or *voluntariness,* whereby a person controls or initiates his behavior by his unforced choices. The second condition is *purposiveness* or *well-being,* whereby a

---

[1]The following discussion relies heavily on Alan Gewirth, *Reason and Morality* (Chicago: University of Chicago Press, 1978), especially pp. 199–271, 338–354.

person sets goals for herself and has the abilities necessary for achieving them. Let's consider both of these conditions.

The condition of freedom or voluntariness naturally brings to mind the right to protection from violence and coercion. In acts of violence, such as robbery or rape, a person's freedom is diminished. He or she is acted on with direct physical or psychological compulsion and has no opportunity for consent. In acts of coercion, such as forced prostitution, a person gives his or her consent but has no real free choice in doing so. Deception also limits the freedom of others; in deception the person gives unforced consent, but only as a result of falsehoods or misrepresentations intentionally presented to him or her.

A person's freedom may be interfered with in other ways as well. Physical or mental illness, willful ignorance or self-deception, and obsessive submission to some dominating passion like drugs or alcohol can limit a person's voluntary action. Lack of knowledge is also a major impediment to free decisions.

The other condition necessary for moral agency is what we have called well-being—namely, the goods necessary for carrying out one's freely chosen purposes. If a person can choose goals but has no ability to carry them out, his moral agency is worth very little.

Several categories of goods are necessary for effective moral agency. *Basic goods,* such as life, food, clothing, shelter, physical health, and emotional stability; are prerequisites of our purposive action. *Nonsubtractive goods* are abilities or conditions needed for maintaining undiminished one's level of purpose-fulfillment. These goods include not being lied to, cheated, defamed, or insulted. They alwo include not having one's promises broken or one's privacy invaded. We have already seen that breaking promises not only violates the self-defeating test, but also tends to lower a person's capacity for action. Finally, *additive goods* are abilities and conditions needed for raising the level of purpose-fulfillment. These goods include owning property, having a sense of well-being and self-respect, and being treated in a nondiscriminatory way. Additive goods also include the virtues of character, such as courage, temperance, and prudence, that enable people more effectively to pursue their goals. Other aspects of freedom and well-being also are important for one's being able to act as a moral agent. It is impossible to enumerate all aspects, but they will often be important in making moral decisions.

2. The Principle of Forfeiture.   The means-ends principle requires that I treat everyone, myself and others alike, as ends and not mere means. The universalization principle also implies that everyone should live according to the same rules, which means that one loses the right to be treated as an end if he does not treat others this way. Therefore the ethics of respect for persons requires a principle of forfeiture, much as in natural law. The *principle of forfeiture* says that, if I treat others as mere means, I forfeit my rights to freedom and well-being. I do not necessarily forfeit all my rights, but in general my rights are forfeited in proportion to the rights of others that I trespass.

When the state punishes a criminal by putting him in prison or taking his life, he is deprived of some of the aspects of freedom and well-being necessary for his full functioning as a moral agent. Nevertheless the punishment is justified, because the criminal by his action has treated someone else as a mere means. Whether he has committed theft, fraud, rape, murder, or some other crime, he has done something to deprive others of their freedom or well-being. Punishment is a legitimate response to this action and is not a violation of the means-ends principle.

Criminal action is not the only way in which a person may forfeit some of his rights to be treated as an end and never as a mere means. If I slander or insult you, it might be appropriate for you to hit me or in some other way limit my freedom or well-being. When a businessperson or professional, through negligence, endangers the safety of her client or the general public, it may be appropriate to reprimand her or deprive her of her job, even if nothing worthy of legal action has been done.

A modified version of the principle of forfeiture is applicable when a person either voluntarily or by implication enters into certain kinds of relationships. If you and I are the proprietors of two different stores that are competing for the same business and I eventually run you out of business, I am certainly harming your freedom and well-being. Still, I may be justified in running you out of business, because one implicitly consents to this possibility when entering the competitive business environment.

3. The Principle of Equality.   Another issue that you will frequently encounter in applying the means-ends principle is the problem of conflicting obligations. Recall the story of the two female counterspies who were in Britain during World War II. While they were there, the Allies learned that the Nazis knew their identity. If they were sent back, they would almost certainly be apprehended, tortured, and killed. What should have been done from the standpoint of the ethics of respect for persons?

The problem is that someone's freedom or well-being will be harmed regardless of which alternative is taken. If the counterspies are returned to the continent, they will suffer loss of freedom, physical violence, and death. If they are not returned, the Allied cause will lose a considerable advantage in the war, and probably many additional lives will be lost. Someone's freedom and well-being will be harmed with either alternative.

The idea of equal treatment implicit in the two moral standards again provides the fundamental guideline. The *principle of equality* says that, when someone's freedom or well-being must be violated, people should be treated equally unless reasons exist for them to be treated otherwise. Some additional criteria will be helpful in carrying out this principle. In treating everyone equally as an end, we must consider (1) how important the aspects of freedom and well-being are that are being threatened, (2) how severely these aspects will be limited, and (3) whether the aspects of freedom and well-being involved would be directly or indirectly violated.

If we applied these criteria to the case of the counterspies, we would probably come to the following conclusions: (1) The aspects of freedom and well-being involved are of the highest importance: ability to make a free decision and physical life itself. (2) The values of the women are seriously threatened; that is, they would suffer not simply harm to their freedom or well-being, but loss of life and freedom altogether. Those who would be killed or injured because of the prolongation of the war would also suffer loss of life and freedom. (3) The threat to the women is obviously more direct and immediate than the threat to the Allied soldiers and civilians who would be harmed by the loss of access to the Nazi code.

Applying the principle of equality, we would probably conclude that returning the counterspies to the continent was morally wrong, primarily because their rights are more directly and severely violated. They were being used as mere means. If we are to justify returning them to Germany, we must use utilitarian considerations rather than arguments derived from the ethics of respect for persons.

We can use two tests to determine whether we are treating a person as an end and not as a mere means. The negative test asks whether a person's freedom or well-being is threatened by our actions. (Have we treated the person as a mere means?) The positive test asks whether we have assisted others in achieving their freedom and well-being. (Have we treated them as an end?) The negative test is more stringent than the positive test. We shall consider each of them in turn.

The Negative Test.   Our first inclination might be to argue that we should never override the rights of others, but the preceding considerations have shown us that sometimes we must. In situations that involve criminal activity or a conflict of obligations, someone's freedom or well-being must be overridden. Keeping this point in mind, we shall formulate the question that constitutes the *negative test* of the means-ends principle:

Does the action override my own or others' freedom or well-being?

As discussed in the previous section, this test is not always easy to apply. We must remember that the principle of forfeiture may apply. We must also remember that sometimes obligations can conflict such that someone's right to freedom and well-being must be overridden or neglected to some degree.

Let us apply the negative test to the case of the 37-year-old accountant . . . Elliott has been diagnosed as having a fatal cancer. He has only a few months to live, and he is experiencing excruciating nerve-root pain that drugs can no longer relieve. His illness is depleting his family's modest finances. Furthermore, he perceives that his wife and children have already begun withdrawing emotionally from him in preparation for his inevitable death. Would it be wrong for him to take his own life, according to the negative test of the means-ends principle?

We could formulate the rule Elliott would be using if he took his own life as the following:

A person may end his life when death is inevitable, he is in great pain, and he has no compelling reasons for staying alive.

The means-ends principle requires that Elliott treat both himself and others as an end and not merely as a means. The people affected in this case are the members of his immediate family. First let's consider the application of the negative test to Elliott. The negative test stipulates that Elliott must not override his now freedom or well-being. He is not overriding his own freedom if he genuinely wants to end his life. However he may feel unduly pressured by the fact that his illness is depleting the family's resources. If he were actually ending his life to save his family's financial resources and acting against his own true desires, he would be treating his own life as a mere means and his suicide would be illegitimate. On the other hand, if he sincerely wishes to end his life as a gesture of self-sacrifice for his family, this act could be in accord with the negative test of the means-ends principle.

In Elliott's case, pursuit of freedom and well-being conflict. By committing suicide Elliott may be acting freely, but by doing so he eliminates his life and thereby all other goods as well. Is this decision to accord priority to freedom justifiable? In this case the pursuit of well-being beyond a minimal level is doomed to failure, and Elliott will soon lose his life in any case. Therefore it seems legitimate for him to give freedom priority over well-being. We shall say that, if Elliott's decision to end his life is freely and knowledgeably made, it does not violate the negative test of the means-end principle as far as he is concerned.

Now let us look at the effect of Elliott's suicide on his family. If his family has indeed begun to accept his inevitable death, then he probably is not overriding their freedom or well-being. However, they might be able to accept his natural death but not his voluntary death. Even if they could not accept his voluntary death, though, would Elliott's suicide indicate that he is using his family as a mere means? Two replies can be made here.

First, Elliott's and his family's wishes might conflict, in which case full freedom for both sides is not possible. If Elliott's family achieves the goal of keeping him alive as long as possible (assuming this choice is their goal), then he cannot achieve his goal of ending his own misery. Alternatively, if he achieves his goal of ending his misery, they cannot accomplish their goal. Given that full freedom is not possible, Elliott can argue plausibly that his freedom to control his life takes priority, using the guidelines developed from the principle of equality.

Second, Elliott could also maintain that ending his life does not interfere with the well-being of his family; in fact, he could argue that it enhances their well-being by preserving their economic independence. Therefore we can maintain that the negative test is not violated for Elliott's family. His suicide would then not be a violation of the means-ends principle.

The Positive Test.   The positive test of the means-ends principle requires that we do more than simply refrain from interfering with our rights to freedom and well-being and those of others. In addition, we must positively contribute to others' status as moral agents, as well as our own. However this obligation does not require that we devote our lives slavishly to helping others achieve a fuller state of self-realization. We would then be treating ourselves as a mere means to the good of others, which is forbidden by the means-ends principle itself. Therefore, each individual must determine when, where, and how this moral obligation is to be fulfilled with respect to others. So we will state the question posed by the *positive test* as follows:

> **Does the action assist oneself (or others, in certain circumstances) in achieving one's own (or others') freedom and well-being?**

To see how this test might be applied, let us begin with an example.

Thirteen-year-old Jason Simmons has been diagnosed as having a ruptured appendix. His physician says he needs immediate surgery; however, Jason has been attending Christian Science services and has come to believe in healing through prayer. He does not want surgery, even though his parents do. Disregarding legal questions for the moment, should the physician defend the boy's right not to have surgery or should she go along with his parents' request?

Applying the ethics of respect for persons, the rule presupposed by the position Jason has taken might be formulated as follows:

> **People should be allowed to follow their own convictions, even if the result is their death.**

The self-defeating test is not violated by this rule, since Jason could pursue his course of action even if the rule presupposed by his action is universalized. His action would pass the negative test of the means-end principle, because he is not interfering in an illegitimate way with others' freedom or well-being. Although he would be interfering with his parents' desires to keep him alive, his action does not deny them an equal freedom to determine their own lives. Must we conclude, then, that it is morally impermissible for the physician to oppose Jason's request?

This case involves *paternalism,* which we may define as using coercion to get another person to do or refrain from doing something for his or her own good. In the usual version of paternalism, which we shall call *strong paternalism,* another person determines what is for my own good. Strong paternalism is clearly incompatible with the means-ends principle, since it allows the freedom of other people to be overridden. Another kind of paternalism, called *weak paternalism,* says that paternalistic coercion can be used, but only to the extent necessary to preserve a person's freedom. Several circumstances—such as ignorance, intellectual immaturity, emotional disturbance, and social pressures—can decrease a person's ability to make a free and informed decision. Weak paternalism justifies the use of coercion to keep a person from making a decision under these circumstances or to enable someone else to make a decision for that person. The use of paternalistic coercion, the weak paternalist argues, actually protects the long-term freedom of the individual.

Does the positive test of the means-ends principle apply in any way to weak paternalism? I believe it does. We have already seen that the central idea in the means-end principle is the preservation of people's ability to act as moral agents. The basic thrust of the positive test, then, must be that in certain situations we have an obligation to actively promote the status of others as moral agents. Weak paternalism is simply the use of coercion to preserve that status when it is threatened. Therefore weak paternalism can be justified by the positive test of the means-ends principle.

The key issue in this example for the ethics of respect for persons is whether Jason is making a genuinely free and informed decision. If he is, then living by the principles of Christian Science, even at the risk of losing his own life, represents his true goal. However, if Jason's decision is not genuinely free and informed, that choice does not represent his true goal. Several factors might prevent him from making a free and informed decision. For example, a 13-year-old boy may not be intellectually mature enough to evaluate the religious teachings on which he is basing his decision. Or he might be under undue emotional pressure from his peers or from Christian Scientists whom he has come to respect. Or he may be rebelling against his parents in his decision.

In order to justify disregarding Jason's wishes, the physician must believe that she is actually assisting him in achieving greater long-range freedom. She must also believe that her special relationship as the boy's physician provides the proper occasion for the application of the means-ends principle. Because we can plausibly argue that a boy of Jason's age is not in a position to make a free and informed decision about such a serious issue and that the special patient–physician relationship does justify the obligation to help Jason realize his true goals, paternalistic action by the physician seems permissible.

The positive test for the means-ends principle may be relevant in areas other than paternalism. Special relationships (for example, professional relationships and family relationships) are especially likely to require that we actively promote the opportunity of others to realize their goals. Being in a position to help another person in dire need also produces an obligation in accordance with the positive test of the means-ends principle. Suppose John is fishing in his boat and suddenly becomes aware that someone is struggling in the water several hundred feet away. The person is shouting for help and obviously is in immediate danger of drowning. John could easily rescue him but does not do so and the person drowns. Most people would agree that John ought to have tried to rescue him. But why? John's behavior passes the self-defeating test, so if John's action is immoral by the ethics of respect for persons, it is because it violates the means-ends principle. It does not violate the negative test, but it does violate the positive test. John is in a position to help a person in extreme danger with relatively little cost to himself. John's relationship to the person (his being in a position to help) therefore imposes an obligation to aid the person in distress.

Finally, merely living in a society creates an obligation to help less fortunate members of society, at least within certain limits. Just how far this obligation extends is a matter of considerable controversy, but it seems reasonable to hold that I have an obligation to pay taxes to help those who are unable to provide for themselves. This obligation must, however, have limits; otherwise I will be used as a mere means by the less fortunate. But we must keep in mind that the principle of equality requires that everyone should be treated equally as an end, insofar as is possible.

. . . One further problem in applying the ethics of respect for persons should be mentioned. If both the action and its alternative fail one or more of the tests, either action will ordinarily be considered morally permissible. However, an action that does not violate the tests as seriously as the alternative should be the chosen one. To settle this issue, do not use utilitarian considerations, but determine which tests are most seriously violated by the standards of the tests themselves. The principles of forfeiture and equality will often be useful.

The Kantian Interpretation of Justice as Fairness

John Rawls

For the most part I have considered the content of the principle of equal liberty and the meaning of the priority of the rights that it defines. It seems appropriate at this point to note that there is a Kantian interpretation of the conception of justice from which this principle derives. This interpretation is based upon Kant's notion of autonomy. It is a mistake, I believe, to emphasize the place of generality and universality in Kant's ethics. That moral principles are general and universal is hardly new with him; and as we have seen these conditions do not in any case take us very far. It is impos-

Excerpted by permission of the publisher from John Rawls, *A Theory of Justice* (Cambridge: Harvard University Press). © 1971 by the president and fellows of Harvard College.

sible to construct a moral theory on so slender a basis, and therefore to limit the discussion of Kant's doctrine to these notions is to reduce it to triviality. The real force of his view lies elsewhere.[1]

For one thing, he begins with the idea that moral principles are the object of rational choice. They define the moral law that men can rationally will to govern their conduct in an ethical commonwealth. Moral philosophy becomes the study of the conception and outcome of a suitably defined rational decision. This idea has immediate consequences. For once we think of moral principles as legislation for a kingdom of ends, it is clear that these principles must not only be acceptable to all but public as well. Finally Kant supposes that this moral legislation is to be agreed to under conditions that characterize men as free and equal rational beings. The description of the original position is an attempt to interpret this conception. I do not wish to argue here for this interpretation on the basis of Kant's text. Certainly some will want to read him differently. Perhaps the remarks to follow are best taken as suggestions for relating justice as fairness to the high point of the contractarian tradition in Kant and Rousseau.

Kant held, I believe, that a person is acting autonomously when the principles of his action are chosen by him as the most adequate possible expression of his nature as a free and equal rational being. The principles he acts upon are not adopted because of his social position or natural endowments, or in view of the particular kind of society in which he lives or the specific things that he happens to want. To act on such principles is to act heteronomously. Now the veil of ignorance deprives the persons in the original position of the knowledge that would enable them to choose heteronomous principles. The parties arrive at their choice together a free and equal rational persons knowing only that those circumstances obtain which give rise to the need for principles of justice.

To be sure, the argument for these principles does add in various ways to Kant's conception. For example, it adds the feature that the principles chosen are to apply to the basic structure of society; and premises characterizing this structure are used in deriving the principles of justice. But I believe that this and other additions are natural enough and remain fairly close to Kant's doctrine, at least when all of his ethical writings are viewed together. Assuming, then, that the reasoning in favor of the principles of justice is correct, we can say that when persons act on these principles they are acting in accordance with principles that they would choose as rational and independent persons in an original position of equality. The principles of their actions do not depend upon social or natural contingencies, nor do they reflect the bias of the particulars of their plan of life or the aspirations that motivate them. By acting from these principles persons express their nature as free and equal rational beings subject to the general conditions of human life. For to express one's nature as a being of a particular

---

[1]To be avoided at all costs is the idea that Kant's doctrine simply provides the general, or formal, elements for a utilitarian (or indeed for any other) theory. See, for example, R. M. Hare, *Freedom and Reason* (Oxford, The Clarendon Press, 1963), pp. 123f. One must not lose sight of the full scope of his view, one must take the later works into consideration. Unfortunately, there is no commentary on Kant's moral theory as a whole; perhaps it would prove impossible to write. But the standard works of H. J. Paton, *The Categorical Imperative* (Chicago, University of Chicago Press, 1948), and L. W. Beck, *A Commentary on Kant's Critique of Practical Reason* (Chicago, University of Chicago Press, 1960), and others need to be further complemented by studies of the other writings. See here M. J. Gregor's *Laws of Freedom* (Oxford, Basil Blackwell, 1963), an account of *The Metaphysics of Morals,* and J. G. Murphy's brief *Kant: The Philosophy of Right* (London, Macmillan, 1970). Beyond this, *The Critique of Judgment, Religion within the Limits of Reason,* and the political writings cannot be neglected without distorting his doctrine. For the last, see *Kant's Political Writings,* ed. Hans Reiss and trans. H. B. Nisbet (Cambridge, The University Press, 1970).

kind is to act on the principles that would be chosen if this nature were the decisive determining element. Of coure, the choice of the parties in the original position is subject to the restrictions of that situation. But when we knowingly act on the principles of justice in the ordinary course of events, we deliberately assume the limitations of the original position. One reason for doing this, for persons who can do so and want to, is to give expression to one's nature.

The principles of justice are also categorical imperatives in Kant's sense. For by a categorical imperative Kant understands a principle of conduct that applies to a person in virtue of his nature as a free and equal rational being. The validity of the principle does not presuppose that one has a particular desire or aim. Whereas a hypothetical imperative by contrast does assume this: it directs us to take certain steps as effective means to achieve a specific end. Whether the desire is for a particular thing, or whether it is for something more general, such as certain kinds of agreeable feelings or pleasures, the corresponding imperative is hypothetical. Its applicability depends upon one's having an aim which one need not have as a condition of being a rational human individual. The argument for the two principles of justice does not assume that the parties have particular ends, but only that they desire certain primary goods. These are things that it is rational to want whatever else one wants. Thus given human nature, wanting them is part of being rational; and while each is presumed to have some conception of the good, nothing is known about his final ends. The preference for primary goods is derived, then, from only the most general assumptions about rationality and the conditions of human life. To act from the principles of justice is to act from categorical imperatives in the sense that they apply to us whatever in particular our aims are. This simply reflects the fact that no such contingencies appear as premises in their derivation.

We may note also that the motivational assumption of mutual disinterest accords with Kant's notion of autonomy, and gives another reason for this condition. So far this assumption has been used to characterize the circumstances of justice and to provide a clear conception to guide the reasoning of the parties. We have also seen that the concept of benevolence, being a second-order notion, would not work out well. Now we can add that the assumption of mutual disinterest is to allow for freedom in the choice of a system of final ends.[2] Liberty in adopting a conception of the good is limited only by principles that are deduced from a doctrine which imposes no prior constraints on these conceptions. Presuming mutual disinterest in the original position carries out this idea. We postulate that the parties have opposing claims in a suitably general sense. If their ends were restricted in some specific way, this would appear at the outset as an arbitrary restriction on freedom. Moreover, if the parties were conceived as altruists, or as pursuing certain kinds of pleasures, then the principles chosen would apply, as far as the argument would have shown, only to persons whose freedom was restricted to choices compatible with altruism or hedonism. As the argument now runs, the principles of justice cover all persons with rational plans of life, whatever their content, and these principles represent the appropriate restrictions on freedom. Thus it is possible to say that the constraints on conceptions of the good are the result of an interpretation of the contractual situation that puts no prior limitations on what men may desire. There are a variety of reasons, then, for the motivational premise of mutual disinterest. This premise is not only a matter of realism about the

---

[2]For this point I am indebted to Charles Fried.

circumstances of justice or a way to make the theory manageable. It also connects up with the Kantian idea of autonomy.

There is, however, a difficulty that should be clarified. It is well expressed by Sidgwick.[3] He remarks that nothing in Kant's ethics is more striking than the idea that a man realizes his true self when he acts from the moral law, whereas if he permits his actions to be determined by sensuous desires or contingent aims, he becomes subject to the law of nature. Yet in Sidgwick's opinion this idea comes to naught. It seems to him that on Kant's view the lives of the saint and the scoundrel are equally the outcome of a free choice (on the part of the noumenal self) and equally the subject of causal laws (as a phenomenal self). Kant never explains why the scoundrel does not express in a bad life his characteristic and freely chosen selfhood in the same way that a saint expresses his characteristic and freely chosen selfhood in a good one. Sidgwick's objection is decisive, I think, as long as one assumes, as Kant's exposition may seem to allow, both that the noumenal self can choose any consistent set of principles and that acting from such principles, whatever they are, is sufficient to express one's choice as that of a free and equal rational being. Kant's reply must be that though acting on any consistent set of principles could be the outcome of a decision on the part of the noumenal self, not all such action by the phenomenal self expresses this decision as that of a free and equal rational being. Thus if a person realizes his true self by expressing it in his actions, and if he desires above all else to realize this self, then he will choose to act from principles that manifest his nature as a free and equal rational being. The missing part of the argument concerns the concept of expression. Kant did not show that acting from the moral law expresses our nature in identifiable ways that acting from contrary principles does not.

This defect is made good, I believe, by the conception of the original position. The essential point is that we need an argument showing which principles, if any, free and equal rational persons would choose and these principles must be applicable in practice. A definite answer to this question is required to meet Sidgwick's objection. My suggestion is that we think of the original position as the point of view from which noumenal selves see the world. The parties qua noumenal selves have complete freedom to choose whatever principles they wish; but they also have a desire to express their nature as rational and equal members of the intelligible realm with precisely this liberty to choose, that is, as beings who can look at the world in this way and express this perspective in their life as members of society. They must decide, then, which principles when consciously followed and acted upon in everyday life will best manifest this freedom in their community, most fully reveal their independence from natural contingencies and social accident. Now if the argument of the contract doctrine is correct, these principles are indeed those defining the moral law, or more exactly, the principles of justice for institutions and individuals. The description of the original position interprets the point of view of noumenal selves, of what it means to be a free and equal rational being. Our nature as such beings is displayed when we act from the principles we would choose when this nature is reflected in the conditions determining the choice. Thus men exhibit their freedom, their independence from the contingencies of nature and society, by acting in ways they would acknowledge in the original position.

---

[3]See *The Methods of Ethics,* 7th ed. (London, Macmillan, 1907), Appendix, "The Kantian Conception of Free Will" (reprinted from *Mind,* vol. 13, 1888), pp. 511–516, esp. p. 516.

Properly understood, then, the desire to act justly derives in part from the desire to express most fully what we are or can be, namely free and equal rational beings with a liberty to choose. It is for this reason, I believe, that Kant speaks of the failure of guilt. And this is appropriate, since for him acting unjustly is acting in a manner that fails to express our nature as a free and equal rational being. Such actions therefore strike at our self-respect, our sense of our own worth, and the experience of this loss is shame. . . . We have acted as though we belonged to a lower order, as though we were a creature whose first principles are decided by natural contingencies. Those who think of Kant's moral doctrine as one of law and guilt badly misunderstand him. Kant's main aim is to deepen and to justify Rousseau's idea that liberty is acting in accordance with a law that we give to ourselves. And this leads not to a morality of austere command but to an ethic of mutual respect and self-esteem.[4]

The original position may be viewed, then, as a procedural interpretation of Kant's conception of autonomy and the categorical imperative. The principles regulative of the kingdom of ends are those that would be chosen in this position, and the description of this situation enables us to explain the sense in which acting from these principles expresses our nature as free and equal rational persons. No longer are these notions purely transcendent and lacking explicable connections with human conduct, for the procedural conception of the original position allows us to make these ties. It is true that I have departed from Kant's views in several respects. I sahll not discuss these matters here; but two points should be noted. The person's choice as-a noumenal self I have assumed to be a collective one. The force of the self's being equal is that the principles chosen must be acceptable to other selves. Since all are similarly free and rational, each must have an equal say in adopting the public principles of the ethical commonwealth. This means that as noumenal selves, everyone is to consent to these principles. Unless the scoundrel's principles would be chosen, they cannot express this free choice, however much a single self might be of a mind to opt for them. Later I shall try to define a clear sense in which this unanimous agreement is best expressive of the nature of even a single self. . . . It in no way overrides a person's interests as the collective nature of the choice might seem to imply. But I leave this aside for the present.

Secondly, I have assumed all along that the parties know that they are subject to the conditions of human life. Being in the circumstances of justice, they are situated in the world with other men who likewise face limitations of moderate scarcity and competing claims. Human freedom is to be regulated by principles chosen in the light of these natural restrictions. Thus justice as fairness is a theory of human justice and among its premises are the elementary facts about persons and their place in nature. The freedom of pure intelligences not subject to these constraints, and the freedom of God, are outside the scope of the theory. It might appear that Kant meant his doctrine to apply to all rational beings as such and therefore to God and the angels as well. Men's social situation in the world may seem to have no role in his theory in determining the first principles of justice. I do not believe that Kant held this view, but I cannot discuss this question here. It suffices to say that if I am mistaken, the Kantian interpretation of justice as fairness is less faithful to Kant's intentions than I am presently inclined to suppose.

[4]See B. A. O. Williams, "The Idea of Equality," in *Philosophy, Politics and Society,* Second Series, ed. Peter Laslett and W. G. Runciman (Oxford, Basil Blackwell, 1962), pp. 115f. For confirmation of this interpretation, see Kant's remarks on moral education in *The Critique of Practical Reason,* pt. II. See also Beck, *A Commentary on Kant's Critique of Practical Reason,* pp. 233–236.

The Golden Rule Rationalized

Alan Gewirth

The Golden Rule is the common moral denominator of all the world's major religions.[1] In one of its most famous formulations it says, "Do unto others as you would have them do unto you." The Rule's imperative ("Do . . .") may be interpreted as an "ought," as prescribing how persons morally ought to act toward others or at least how it is morally right for them to act toward others. Thus the Golden Rule sets forth a criterion of the moral rightness of interpersonal actions, or transactions. This criterion consists in the agent's desires or wishes for himself *qua* recipient: what determines the moral rightness of a transaction initiated or controlled by some person is whether he would himself want to undergo such a transaction at the hands of other persons.

I

There are at least two traditional criticisms of the Golden Rule as a moral criterion or principle. First, the agent's wishes for himself *qua* recipient may not be in accord with his recipient's own wishes as to how he is to be treated. As Bernard Shaw put it in a famous quip, "Do not do unto others as you would that they should do unto you. Their tastes may not be the same."[2] Thus, if the agent A treats his recipient B as A himself would want to be treated, this may inflict gratuitous suffering on B, for B may not want to be treated in this way. For example, a person who likes others to quarrel or intrigue with him would be authorized by the Golden Rule to quarrel with others or involve them in networks of intrigue regardless of their own wishes in the matter; a *roué* who would want some young woman to climb into his bed at night would be justified in climbing into her bed at night; a fanatical believer in the sanctity of contracts who would want others to imprison him for defaulting on his debts would be allowed to imprison persons who default on their debts to him, and so forth.

A second criticism of the Golden Rule is that the agent's wishes for himself *qua* recipient may go counter to many justified social rules, legal, economic, and other. Even if the agent's wishes for himself are not opposed to those of his recipient, both sets of wishes may be immoral. As Sidgwick put it, "one might wish for another's cooperation in sin, and be willing to reciprocate it."[3] For example, a law-violator A who bribes a corrupt policeman B may be treating B as A would himself want to be treated.

The point of this criticism can be brought out further if the Golden Rule is given its negative formulation: "Do not do unto others as you would not have them do unto you." On this formulation together with the preceding positive one, accord with the agent's wishes for himself *qua* recipient is both the necessary and the sufficient condition of the moral rightness of tranactions. The difficulty of its being a necessary condi-

From Chapter Four of *Human Rights*, by Alan Gewirth. © 1983 by the University of Chicago Press. Originally published in *Midwest Studies in Philosophy*.

[1]See, *The Eleven Religions and Their Proverbial Lore*, ed. S. G. Champion (London, 1944), pp. xvi–xviii, 18, 44, 84, 90, 104, 129, 153, 160, 161, 194, 215, 218, 265, 302; R. E. Hume, *The World's Living Religions* (New York, 1949), pp. 265–266.

[2]George Bernard Shaw, *Man and Superman*, app., "Maxims for Revolutionists" in *Collected Works of Bernard Shaw* X (New York, 1930):217.

[3]Henry Sidgwick, *The Methods of Ethics*, 7th ed. (London, 1907), p. 380.

tion is frequently illustrated by the case of a criminal before a judge; as Kant put it, "on the basis (of the Golden Rule), the criminal would be able to dispute with the judges who punish him."[4] For on this interpretation of the Golden Rule the judges would be justified in meting out punishment to the criminal only if they would be willing to receive such treatment themselves, so that the criminal could appeal to their own dislike for being punished as a basis for arguing that their sentencing of him is morally wrong. Not only criminal punishment but the collection of money owed by recalcitrant borrowers, the payment of lesser wages for inferior work, the giving of lower grades to poorer students, and the infliction of many similar sorts of hardships would be prohibited by the Golden Rule whenever it could be shown that the respective agents would not themselves want to undergo such adverse treatment. The Rule does not recognize the existence of justified disparities of merit and reward among agents and their recipients, including those which arise in competitive relations. More generally, in making the agent's wishes for himself *qua* recipient the criterion of right actions, the Rule ignores that various institutions may set requirements which are justified without regard to those wishes. . . .

II

I now want to suggest that these difficulties of the Golden Rule are to be resolved not by completely surrendering the Rule's substantive basis in the desires of the agent for himself *qua* recipient, but rather by adding the requirement that the desires in question must be *rational*. Thus the Golden Rule should be amended to read: Do unto others as you would rationally want them to do unto you. I shall call this the *Rational Golden Rule,* and I shall say that the Golden Rule is "rationalized" when its form and content are made to include this reference to rationality. Similarly, the Generic interpretation of the Rule should be amended to read: Act in accord with your recipient's rational desires as well as your own. The difficulties of the Golden Rule noted above have been elicited by noting that its applications may conflict with intuitions most of us have about the morally right ways to act toward other persons. To rationalize the Rule by grounding it in rational desires serves not only to save these intuitions but also to show how they and all other correct moral judgments have a rational basis. . . .

When conceptual analysis is brought to bear on the concepts of action and wanting, a principle is derived which replaces the contingent desires of the traditional interpretations of the Golden Rule by a certain necessary content. This content is one of *rights* to the generic features of action. In this new formulation, the Golden Rule will read as follows: Do unto others as you have a right that they do unto you. Or, to put it in its Generic formulation: Act in accord with the generic rights of your recipients as well as of yourself.

Since I have presented the argument for this in various other places,[5] I shall merely summarize the main points here. We begin from the agent who wants to attain

[4]*Foundations of the Metaphysics of Morals* VI (Akademie ed.): 430 n.; trans., H. J. Paton, *The Moral Law* (London, 1947), p. 97 n. See John Selden, "Equity" in *Table Talk,* xxxvii, s.v., ed. S. H. Reynolds (Oxford, 1892), pp. 61–62.

[5]See my "Categorial Consistency in Ethics," *Philosophical Quarterly* 17 (1967):289–299; "Obligation: Political, Legal, Moral," *Nomos XII: Political and Legal Obligation* (1970), pp. 55–88; "The Normative Structure of Action," *Review of Metaphysics* 25 (1971):238–261; "The Justification of Egalitarian Justice," *American Philosophical Quarterly* 8 (1971):331–341; "Moral Rationality," Lindley Lecture, University of Kansas (1972), "The 'Is-Ought' Problem Resolved," *Proceedings and Addresses of the American Philosophical Association* 47 (1974):34–61. In my Reason and Morality (Chicago, 1978), I present the whole argument more extensively.

various of his purposes. Such wants are necessarily attributable to every agent, for what it means to be an agent is that one controls one's behavior with a view to achieving ends which constitute one's reasons for acting, and which one hence intends to achieve. Since the agent regards his purposes as good according to whatever criteria (not necessarily moral ones) are involved in his reasons for acting, he must hold *a fortiori* that the generic features which characterize all his actions, and which are the proximate necessary conditions of his acting for purposes, are necessary goods. These generic features consist in the freedom or voluntariness whereby he controls or initiates his behavior by his unforced choice, and in the purposiveness or well-being whereby he sets goals for himself and has the abilities required for achieving them. Because freedom and well-being are necessary goods to the agent, he must hold at least implicitly that he has rights to them, in that all other persons ought to refrain from interfering with his having freedom and well-being. I shall call these *generic rights,* since they are rights to the generic features of action. If some agent were to deny that he has these rights, he would contradict himself. For he would then judge both that freedom and well-being are necessary goods which he upholds for himself as the conditions of his acting for any other goods, and also that it is permissible for other persons to interfere with his having these necessary goods.

Every agent must hold that he has the generic rights on the ground or for the sufficient reason that he is a prospective agent who has purposes he wants to fulfill. Suppose some agent were to maintain that he has these rights only for some more restrictive reason R. Since this would entail that in lacking R he would lack the generic rights, A would thereby contradict himself. For since, as we have seen, it is necessarily true of every agent that he holds implicitly that he has the generic right, A would be in the position of holding both that he has the generic rights and that, as lacking R, he does not have these rights. Thus, on pain of self-contradiction, every agent must accept the generalization that all prospective purposive agents have the generic rights because, as we have seen, he must hold that being a prospective purposive agent is a sufficient condition or reason for having the generic rights. This generalization entails that the agent ought to refrain from interfering with the freedom and well-being of all other persons insofar as they are prospective purposive agents; this is the same as to say that he must refrain from coercing and harming them. Since to refrain from such interferences is to act in such a way that one's actions are in accord with the generic rights of all other persons, every agent is logically committed, on pain of inconsistency, to accept the following precept: *Act in accord with the generic rights of your recipients as well as yourself.* I call this the *Principle of Generic Consistency* (PGC), since it combines the formal consideration of consistency with the material consideration of the generic features and right of action. . . .

The PGC also retains the mutualist, egalitarian form of the spirit of the Golden Rule, but again with the substantive difference that the agent is to act toward others not according to his wishes or desires for himself *qua* recipient but rather according to his generic rights as well as those of his recipients. By the above analysis, however, the agent rationally desires to act in this way. He rationally desires to act in accord with his own generic rights because, if his freedom and well-being are interfered with by other persons, he will not be able to act, either at all or at least successfully. The force of "rational" is here in part a matter of means-end calculation and hence of inductive inference, but it is mainly a matter of conceptual analysis whereby the agent becomes aware of the necessary conditions of his action and applies this awareness to his conative concern with achievement of his purposes. Since it is necessarily true of the agent that he wants to achieve his purposes and since his having the generic rights is logically necessary to such achievement, the rational agent, being aware of this logical necessity, wants to have and act in accord with his generic rights.

The agent also rationally desires to act in accord with the generic rights of his recipient. As we have seen, if he violates or denies the PGC he contradicts himself. To incur or accept self-contradiction is to violate the most basic logical canon of rationality. Thus when the requirment of rationality is imposed on the wants or desires of an agent who intends to achieve his purposes, there loically emerges a certain normative moral principle consisting in equality or mutuality of rights to freedom and well-being. Every rational agent, in the sense of "rational" just indicated, necessarily accepts this principle. . . .

Let us examine somewhat more fully how it is that the agent's rational desires for the actions of other persons toward himself have the same general contents or objects as are had by his rational desires for his own actions toward other persons. He rationally wants other persons to act toward himself in accord with his own generic rights, since the objects of these rights are the necesssary conditions of his own actions. Hence, by the Rational Golden Rule, he also ought to act toward other persons in accord with their generic rights. Since the logical consequence of the Rational Golden Rule is rationally derived from the Rule, the agent whose desires are governed by it has rational desires as determined by the Rule. But these desires of his, by this logical consequences of the Rational Golden Rule, now have as their objects his own actions toward other persons: he ought to act in accord with his recipients' generic rights. Thus the Rational Golden Rule, like the PGC, sets for the agent's conduct requirements based on his rational desires as to how he is to act toward other persons, namely, in accord with their generic right.

This result can also be established in another way. The requirement that one act in accord with the generic rights of one's recipients is not only a logical consequence of the Rational Golden Rule; it also logically follows, independently of this Rule, from the agent's rational desire for himself *qua* recipient. For in rationally wanting that other persons act toward himself in accord with his generic rights, he holds (because of the correlativity of rights and "oughts") that other persons ought to refrain from interferring with his freedom and well-being, and he holds this for the sufficient reason that he is a prospective purposive agent. Hence, he must also hold, on pain of self-contradiction, that there ought to be such refraining from interference in the case of all prospective purposive agents: their freedom and well-being too ought to be respected and not interfered with. From this it follows that the agent himself ought to refrain from interfering with the freedom and well-being of other persons insofar as they are prospective purposive agents, so that he ought to act toward them in accord with their generic rights. Moreover, he rationally desires to act in this way, since it logically follows from his rational desire for himself *qua* recipient. But this rational desire of his now has as its object his own actions toward other persons: he rationally wants that he act toward other persons in accord with their generic rights. Since this rational desire is identical in its object with what is required by the Rational Golden Rule, it follows that this Rule, like the PGC, requires that the agent act toward others as he rationally wants himself to act toward them, namely, in accord with their generic rights. . . .

. . . The PGC and the Rational Golden Rule overcome the difficulties of the Golden Rule indicated above. The general reason for this is that whereas the traditional Golden Rule allows the rightness of actions to be determined by the agent's even arbitrary or contingent desires for himself *qua* recipient, the PGC and the Rational

Golden Rule require that the agent's desires for himself *qua* recipient be subjected to rational requirements. As we have seen, these requirements serve both to limit the scope of the agent's determining desires for himself *qua* recipient and to assure that his own recipients are entitled to the same generic emoluments of action as he claims for himself. Thus the mutualist and beneficent intentions of the traditional Golden Rule are fulfilled and its crippling difficulties avoided.

Where the traditional Golden Rule allows the agent to oppress his recipients when his own desires for himself *qua* recipient go counter to his recipient's desires, the PGC prohibits such oppression. For the rightness of a transaction is now determined by the agent's rational desires for himself *qua* recipient, and such rational desires require that he act in accord with his recipients' generic rights as well as his own. Thus the actions of the quarreler, of the *roué,* and of the imprisoner of debtors are prohibited by the Rational Golden Rule, since such actions violate their recipients' rights to freedom or well-being or both. The requirement that the agent's desires for himself *qua* recipient be rational also obviates the difficulty of the Inversion conception of the traditional Golden Rule, whereby the agent must fulfill his recipients' arbitrary desires regardless of the cost to himself. For the Rational Golden Rule and the PGC require that the agent act in accord with his own generic rights as well as those of his recipient.

We saw above that in the Generic interpretation of the traditional Golden Rule, which tells the agent to act in accord with his recipients' desires as well as his own, no provision was made for situations where the agent's desires conflict with the desires of his recipients. The case is otherwise, however, when the desires in question must be rational. For this involves that desires are ruled out from consideration when they require actions which violate the generic rights of their recipients; similarly, the recipients' desires must not intend violation of other persons' generic rights.

There may still be conflicts between the generic rights of the agent and of his recipients. For example, the agent's right to freedom may conflict with his recipients' right to well-being, and indeed the agent's right to freedom may also conflict with his own right to well-being. But in the first place, such conflicts are far fewer than the conflicts among desires taken indiscriminately. And in the second place, the fact that the generic rights are derived from the necessary conditions of agency provides a rational basis for resolving conflicts among specific rights. For, other things being equal, one right takes precedence over another to the degree to which the former is more necessary for action than is the latter. For example, A's right not to be killed takes precedence over B's right to be told the truth when the two are in conflict, and C's right to be saved from drowning takes precedence over D's right to be free from any encumbrances on his leisure.

Where the traditional Golden Rule permits actions which go counter to justified social rules, this is not the case with the Rational Golden Rule or the PGC. For the PGC provides the ultimate basis for the justification of social rules. All such rules, to be justified, must be derivable from the PGC either procedurally or instrumentally, that is, either as deriving from voluntary agreement and hence from the right to freedom, or as deriving from the requirements of well-being. The rules of voluntary associations such as baseball teams are justified in the former way; the rules of the minimum state with its criminal law are justified in the latter way. It is hence not open to any person who participates in such justified groupings to try to evade the requirements of their rules on the ground that he would not want to be treated as the rules require. The arbitrary or contingent desires of the participants, including the law-violator and the corrupt policeman, must here give way to the rational desires which are in conformity with the respective social rules.

Although the PGC as the basis of the Rational Golden Rule deals primarily with the generic rights and hence prescribes strict "oughts" to agents, it can also deal with the myriad moral situations which involve other rights, as well as those which bear on supererogatory rather than strict duties, whether they concern simple amenities or heroic and saintly actions. On the one hand, all other rights, in order to be justified, must derive directly or indirectly from the generic rights. On the other hand, so far as concerns supererogatory actions, their recipients, by definition, do not have rights to them, such that severe censure or even coercion is justified if the conduct in question is not forthcoming. Nevertheless, every person insofar as he is rational must desire that he be the recipient of such supererogatory actions in relevant circumstances; hence, according to the Rational Golden Rule, it is right or fitting that he perform such actions toward others. For although the actions in question are not matters of rights or strict duties, they go in the same direction as do the generic rights, serving to advance the freedom or well-being of their recipients either directly or by promoting a social context in which these necessary goods are furthered. Because of these connections with the generic rights, every rational person must want that he be the recipient of such supererogatory actions in relevant circumstances. Hence, the Rational Golden Rule provides for the rightness of such actions. The Rational Golden Rule and the PGC, like the traditional Golden Rule, require that an agent treat his recipients according to the same rules or principles as the agent wants for his own treatment. But whereas the traditional Golden Rule leaves completely open and indeterminate the contents of the agent's wants for himself and hence of the rules or principles, the PGC focuses on what the agent necessarily wants or values insofar as he is rational, namely that he be acted on in accord with his generic rights. Applications of the PGC and the Rational Golden Rule, unlike those of the traditional Golden Rule, cannot be immoral because they cannot be tailored, in their antecedents, to the agent's variable inclinations or ideals without regard to the generic rights of their recipient. The Rational Golden Rule and the PGC hence provide in their applications an indefeasible guarantee of reciprocal fairness to both agents and recipients.

This normative moral point also has a deeper logical corollary. The traditional Golden Rule leaves open the question of why any person ought to act in accordance with it. Even if the Rule is assimilated to or derived from a principle of universalizability, that what is right for one person must be right for any relevantly similar person in similar circumstances, the criterion of relevant similarity is still left subject to all the variabilities which we saw to attach to the contingent desires or predilections of agents. The Rational Golden Rule, on the other hand, contains within itself both a formal and material necessity which determines quite conclusively why every person ought to obey it. Formally, the Rational Golden Rule, like the PGC, is necessary in that to deny or violate it is to contradict oneself. Materially, this self-contradiction is inescapable because, unlike the traditional Golden Rule, the Rational Golden Rule and the PGC are derived from the necessities of purposive agency. It is not the contingent desires of agents but rather aspects of agency which cannot rationally be varied or evaded by any agent that determine the content of the Rational Golden Rule and the PGC. Thus, when the Golden Rule is rationalized it has a conclusive rational justification which the traditional Golden Rule lacks. Nevertheless, such rationality may be said to be implicit in the traditional Golden Rule because it serves to preserve and elucidate the Rule's mutualist intentions in a logically necessary way.

Chapter III

Ethics of Virtue

JERRY BUCKLEY

Bootstrap Time in a Luckless Land

T he classroom does not look like any that Dennis Carlson knew back at Johns Hopkins University in Baltimore. The room is small, and the walls, a mixture of mud and saplings, are cracking. Backless benches double as both desks and chairs. But the "students" are as eager as any Carlson has ever taught. Indeeed, all 12 are volunteers, and most have walked several hours to attend the monthly meeting of community-health agents and traditional birth assistants in Ethiopia's Qewet district. For months, Carlson has labored to convey the importance of linking pregnancy and birth registrations as a way to monitor child development. Near the end of this meeting, he senses his message has finally gotten through. He's not the cheerleader type, but he can't resist a pep talk. "We have done a great deal of work," he says, "but in the coming months and years, there is much more to be done. You are among the most active. I hope you will lead the way for others."

Job would have liked Dennis Carlson. For 30 years, in hospitals and colleges in the U.S. and Africa, he has been a patient doctor and teacher, dedicated to public health. Now, at 57, he is back in Ethiopia for his fourth tour of duty, this time as coordinator of primary health care for Save the Children Federation/USA (SCF). Ethiopia has long tested do-gooders' mettle—its per capita annual income of $110 makes it the world's poorest country—but doing good in this East African nation is especially difficult these days. Drought, war and the wrongheaded policies of its Marxist government have combined to push much of its population to the brink of starvation.

It was only three years ago that television brought the unprecedented Ethiopian famine to the living rooms of the Western World. The scourge and its diseases killed more than 1 million people and prompted the biggest flow of private charity for foreigners—$250 million—

in U.S. history. Last summer, with the country barely on the road to recovery, the big rains that had to come didn't come. Now, relief officials estimate that at least 6 million of Ethiopia's 46 million people are about to starve.

In SCF's Yifatna Timuga Project area, Field Director Gerry Salole says 217,000 of the 430,000 people will need food from shipments in the next few months. Some villages already are out of food, and Salole has borrowed grain to feed them. The threat of famine is adding urgency to Carlson's work and that of his wife Beulah Downing, 54, who manages SCF's children's programs. As the couple moves from village to village, they see men, women and children beside the road, selling firewood and jewelry to earn money for food, if there is any left to buy.

Victories in the Bush

Drought or no drought, Dennis and Beulah are accustomed to working long days amid frustrations and few comforts. Finding a new set of clothes for an orphan or immunizing a pregnant woman is a small but important victory. Installing a modern pump in a primitive village and helping to build a community-health post are causes for genuine celebration. In all cases, the couple are guided by convictions that individuals can make a difference—and that the only long-term solution for the people of Yifatna Timuga is for them to help themselves. "The biggest mistake outsiders make is in saying, 'We've got the answers if you'll just do what we tell you,' " says Dennis. "We want to work with the people so that when we leave, the Ethiopian capacity is better for us having been here."

Save the Children's Ethiopian project began in 1984 after donations began pouring into its

Westport, Conn., headquarters. It targeted Yifatna Timuga because the region offered not just an opportunity for emergency relief but, more important, a potential for long-term community development. Yifatna Timuga, by car, is 5 hours north of Addis Ababa, the Ethiopian capital, but it is still 150 miles from the worst-hit provinces of Tigray and Eritrea in the far north. In those areas, soil erosion, drought and overpopulation are much more severe, and warfare between government troops and rebels hinders relief efforts. Yifatna Timuga is also better off because it never had the disease-ridden feeding camps so common in other areas during the last famine. "There is no automatic despair here," say Salole. "Our people know they can wait on their land and we will probably get to them. Up north, people will again vote with their feet."

Getting food to those and other Ethiopians isn't easy. The U.S. government recently approved an SCF request for 16,400 metric tons of grain—only part of what's needed—but then, eight days before Christmas, half of the allocation vanished when a grain-laden tanker hit a freighter in the Atlantic and sank.

"The Kids Are Getting Edgy"

Thus, while development is SCF's goal in Yifatna Timuga, relief and emergency work again are becoming much of the reality. For Beulah, this means more-frequent visits to the 12 SCF-sponsored orphan homes. SCF gives the six orphans and a housemother in each home money to buy food. But as food becomes scarcer, prices rise and Beulah has to be sure the allowance is adequate. "It was only three years ago that these kids lost their parents," she explains after visiting a home in Yemlawa. "We've worked with them for just a year. The kids are getting edgy. They're wondering if we're going to be able to take care of them."

Nutrition also is on Dennis Carlson's mind. A good indicator of a community in trouble is the height and weight of its children. Dennis and his 27-member staff have traveled to dozens of villages in recent weeks to weigh and measure the children. The results are recorded for past and future comparisons and, if necessary, to help decide priorities for distributing food. One recent afternoon, Dennis

drove for 2 hours over rugged terrain to visit the remote mountaintop village of Murré, where a five-day nutritional assessment was under way. Several hundred villagers assembled, and he was relieved to learn that the children were still, at least for a while, above the danger zone.

Dennis and Beulah took very different paths to Ethiopia. The Iowa-born son of a Baptist minister and a nurse, he first came in 1958 as part of a Swedish Baptist missionary group. He spent four years as the only doctor for 500,000 people and quickly grasped that his clinical and surgical work, however skillful, would always leave him treating Ethiopia's symptoms and not its underlying problems. He saw that development—in education, agriculture and water—was Ethiopia's only hope for better health care.

After earning a master's degree in public health from Berkeley, Dennis returned to Ethiopia in 1963 and served until 1967 as dean of the School of Public Health at Haile Selassie University in Gondar. It was at Gondar that he taught many of the people who now form the backbone of Ethiopia's national and local public-health service. Their shared past and current camaraderie are a source of great pride for Dennis. In the 1970s, he served as a dean and professor at Johns Hopkins and, in the '80s, practiced public health in Baltimore's inner city.

It was during that time that he met and married Beulah. She, like Dennis, was divorced and the parent of four grown children. As a math teacher turned social worker, she was ready for something different. "I had never been abroad and was fascinated by Dennis's stories," she recalls. "I felt the urge to share some of them." When the '84 famine hit, Dennis knew the time had come for him to return to the place where three of his children were born. The one non-negotiable requirement in their search for a project was that Beulah be hired for a real job. They arrived in Ethiopia two Septembers ago.

Beulah has since expanded her duties beyond the orphan program so that they now include education and sponsorship. The work that she and SCF do with schools is vital. What's learned in the classrooms of poor countries can mean the difference between life and death. It has been shown, for example, that if a mother finishes the third grade, her child has a 50 percent better chance of surviving infancy. Sadly, few Ethiopian children go to school and those who do rarely make it past the early grades. In Yemlawa, where SCF has an orphan home and supplies pencils, paper and books to the school, barely 200 of the 600 children are in school. Most stay away to gather firewood and tend the cattle and sheep. "Surviving here often takes everything a family has," says Dennis. "You can't worry about investing in your kid over 10 years. You have to worry about tomorrow." But Beulah and her staff keep trying to stretch precious supplies and resources so more children can attend school. They used money donated by students in Ridgefield, Conn., for example, to build an addition on the school in the village of Kobbo.

Recruits for the Future

Ironically, the heart of Dennis's work is to teach and train the local people to care for themselves long after tomorrow. "The family and community control health care, not technicians and professionals," he says. "I want them to take responsibility when their child gets sick." To help them do that, he started an ambitious program to recruit and train young Ethiopians to administer basic health care, incuding personal hygiene, nutritional assessments, immunization and sanitation. SCF has taught 203 community-health agents and 66 traditional birth attendants in Yifatna Timuga and plans to train hundreds more. Dennis also is helping the Ethiopians to develop the buildings they need for health care. In the past year, with SCF's help, 52 villages constructed simple four-room health posts, and 125 more are planned in the next few years. The new post in Godachile means that 3,000 residents no longer must walk 10 miles for basic health assistance. A food-for-work program to encourage remote villagers to build access roads is also under way. And in Kobbo, a new $2,500 pump is delivering a steady, relatively clean water supply to villagers who used to rely on a murky stream. It's estimated that half of the 40,000 children who die in the world each day could be saved if they had clean water. During the last

famine, 90 children from Kobbo died of hunger and disease.

Fortunately, Dennis and Beulah are seeing payoffs from their labor. Their SCF teams instructed 60,000 mothers to practice oral rehydration therapy—often a regimen of water and locally grown grain—to restore valuable body fluids in their children. As a result, deaths from diarrhea, the No. 1 killer of children under 5 during the last famine, dropped in one year from 1,400 to 700 in the 34 communities where SCF concentrated its work. Nearly 3 of every 5 people in Yifatna Timuga have now been immunized against an array of diseases, from polio and measles to tuberculosis and tetanus. Its overall death rate, which was 9 percent during the height of the 1985 famine, is now down to 1 percent. As a result, the SCF project is fast becoming a model not just for other relief agencies but also for the Ethiopian government.

Such progress—along with Saturday evenings spent listening to tapes of Garrison Keillor's "Prairie Home Companion"—helps make life in the bush easier for Dennis and Beulah. Their home is a two-bedroom house on SCF's campus in Efeson. They have no phone. Kerosene powers the refrigerator, and the lights go off each night at 10. Beulah has a small battery-powered computer but uses a 1922 typewriter to write letters to her 86-year-old mother back in Baltimore. For Dennis, the mailbag brings valued medical journals plus month-old issues of *Sports Illustrated*.

What they see every day, though, are signs of despair and of hope. There are the children who will never grow old—and the half-grown sorghum stalks that serve as vivid reminders that Ethiopia's recent and tragic history may repeat itself. But the evergreen they transplanted from a field to serve as their Christmas tree represents a brighter future. So, too, do the young men and women who so eagerly look to them for skills and ideas. Dennis Carlson and Beulah Downing have learned to cope with this conflicting landscape. For they know that saving the children—and the parents—requires a balance of urgency and patience. "Time is our most precious resource," says Dennis. "Yet we must be willing to wait for progress. It doesn't come overnight."

Ethics of Virtue

Utilitarianism and Kantianism have been the most influential ethical theories in modern times. It had been thought until recently that a "best" theory would have to be some version of either utilitarianism or Kantianism. Either we must take as basic the idea that actions are to be judged by their consequences for human happiness (utilitarianism) or that actions are to be judged in terms of fairness and equality (Kantianism). However, as we shall see in this chapter, and the ones that follow, there are alternatives to utilitarianism and Kantianism. While few people would question that human welfare or fairness and equality are important values in ethics, there are reasons to believe that a theory based solely on one or the other of these ideas does not accurately or completely represent the moral landscape.

The theory we will study in this chapter is a response to the presumed defects in both utilitarianism and Kantianism. The latter theories, it can be argued, distort our view of ethics. Although they are different from one another, utilitarianism and Kantianism share some common and possibly troublesome premises. Both theories assume that the job of ethics is to provide a single first principle that evaluates our actions in terms of our duties or obligations. Both Kantianism and utilitarianism can be called "duty ethics." To be a bit more specific, both positions assume that an ethical theory must formulate a principle that evaluates actions as falling into one of three categories: (1) morally right actions (ones that are our duty to perform); (2) morally wrong actions (ones that are our duty not to perform); and (3) morally neutral actions (ones that conflict with no duty we have). Killing an innocent person for no good reason is morally wrong (our duty not to do). Keeping a promise to repay a debt is morally right (our duty to do). However, actions like choosing an after-dinner dessert or picking a movie to see are morally neutral actions (no duty one way or the other).

There are at least three assumptions lying behind the common outlook of utilitarianism and Kantianism, each of which is challenged in the readings that follow. (1) It is assumed that the job of an ethical theory is to make evaluations about human *actions*. Perhaps we should not be as much concerned with actions, however, as we should be concerned with evaluation of *persons*. Ethics may be more a matter of evaluating the moral worth of a person, as a whole, than each, individual action. At least this seems often to be true in ordinary discussion. Our lead essay, by Jerry Buckley, praises the personal qualities of relief workers (their conviction and dedication) at least as much as citing their particular accomplishments. (2) Focusing exclusively upon duties and obligations does not seem to tell the whole story of ethics. Again, our lead article gives a good example of this point. There can be little doubt that the relief workers in Africa deserve moral praise. This praise cannot be attributed, however, to the fact that they are merely 'doing their duty" or fulfilling their "obligations to their fellow humans." instead, these people are doing something over and above what we would consider to be one's duty. (The technical term for actions exceeding our duties is *supererogatory actions*.) In the readings that follow, J. O. Urmson and Joel Feinberg bring out an important fact about the way ethical theorizing has been done for at least the last two centuries. Theories have concentrated upon finding a highest principle of duty or obligation. But, if there are people whom we praise because they do things over and above duty, then surely a principle of duty cannot be all there is to morality.

In addition (3), utilitarianism and Kantianism may be mistaken in their search for a *single,* first principle of ethics. Perhaps, as G. J. Warnock argues, there is not just one overarching principle that incorporates all that is of moral value. Instead, there may be several different moral values each competing for our attention. If Warnock is right about this, however, there is a problem. If there is not a single evaluating idea (like the categorical imperative or the principle of utility) but many, then there can be moral dilemmas that are irresolvable. For example, Warnock considers both "non-maleficence" (not harming people) and "non-deception" (truthfulness) to be moral values. Yet, these two values will from time to time come into conflict. Say, for example, my friend buys an expensive, but quite honestly awful, new jacket. Sincerely believing that he's making an important fashion statement, he asks me how I like the new jacket. In this situation I cannot both spare his feeings (non-maleficence) and tell him the truth (non-deception). And, if Warnock is right that there is no overarching principle to decide in cases where moral values like non-maleficence and non-deception conflict, then there can be no way to resolve moral conflicts like the one described. This seems somewhat disappointing since we would have hoped that an ethical theory would be able to tell us what to do in difficult moral situations.

The above represent some, but not all, of the problems philosophers have found with so-called *duty ethics*. The search for an alternative theory, curiously enough, has led back in history to one of the earliest writers on ethics—to the works of Aristotle, an ancient Greek philosopher. Aristotle's approach to ethics differs from that of "duty ethics" in a number of respects. Most importantly, Aristotle is interested in judging the moral value of a person's character, not judging individual actions. Thus, for Aristotle, the fundamental question of ethics is what counts as a "good" or "virtuous" person. Generally, for the set of readings in this chapter, a "virtue" can be defined as a morally good character trait. A character trait can be defined as a disposition to act in a certain sort of way. Thus, the task of a moral theory as understood in this group of readings is to specify the morally good character dispositions a person should have.

This sets the stage for theories grouped under the heading of "Ethics of Virtue." The brief sketch above, however, raises a number of issues that must be resolved in order to have a more complete theory. For example, if we assume that moral evaluation should be an evaluation of character traits (dispositions), then we also need some way of determining which are the moral traits. What are the virtues? Aristotle argues both for a method of determining the virtues and a specific list of what he takes to be the morally important virtues. First, let's consider the method. Aristotle holds that a question such as what is a good "man" (person) is the same kind of question as, for example, what is a good knife. We settle the question of what is a good knife by citing the characteristics a knife must have if it is to perform its *function* well. Since the function of a knife is to cut, it is fairly obvious that in order to perform that function well, a knife must be sharp, strong, and so on.

This method, of course, makes a big assumption about human beings; namely, that they too have a function or purpose and, as such "good" persons are persons who have the character traits (virtues) that well serve their function. Aristotle clearly makes this assumption. He believes that persons have a function and, broadly speaking, it is to develop and exercise their rational abilities. Rationality, argues Aristotle, is a faculty unique to persons, hence defining their essence. Having achieved this much, Aristotle takes a further, and needed, step to fill out his ethical theory. Aristotle must now specify which character traits are needed to perform one's "function" well. The answer to this question is given by Aristotle's so-called *doctrine of the mean*. I shall only sketch the gist of the doctrine here. The basic idea of the doctrine of the mean is that we should use our reason to moderate our emotions or "passions." For example, Aristotle holds that one may have too much or too little "confidence" when facing a difficult challenge. Too much confidence is rash or foolhardy, while too little is cowardly. One should choose the mean between these extremes—courage. Thus, courage is a human virtue. This is not, of course, the only virtue Aristotle identifies. By using the technique of the doctrine of the mean, he goes on to draw up a lengthy list of virtues including temperance, truthfulness, and modesty.

There is one final point that needs to be mentioned about Aristotle's ethics. In the theories that we have already considered, acting morally is fairly naturally contrasted with acting for one's self-interest. To be sure, there will be times when doing the right thing will also further our own interests, but this is not always (or not frequently) the case. Typically it seems as though we must push ourselves to act morally even though we would prefer doing something else. However, Aristotle argues that cultivating moral virtues leads to personal happiness—that morality and self-interest coincide. To see this point we must recall that for Aristotle virtues are character traits that help persons realize their "function" or "goal." And so, it is argued, realizing one's goal leads to happiness. An example will help to clarify here. Suppose that a person has a natural talent or propensity for music. We might well expect that cultivating this native ability will make the person happy, while frustrating the ability will make that person unhappy. If there is an overarching "function" common to all persons, we would similarly expect that acting in accordance with that function would be personally fulfilling, while acting against it would be frustrating.

As we shall see, the various philosophers represented in this section do not subscribe to all of the details of Aristotle's theory, although there is agreement that moral evaluation should be evaluation of character traits. Philippa Foot goes farther than most in her agreement with Aristotle, arguing that the virtues (courage, temperance, widsom, and justice) should be seen as "correctives" to our various temptations or passions. However, she does not use Aristotle's doctine of the mean to sort out exactly how the virtues are to be correctives. Foot also raises some important problems that an ethics of virtue following Aristotle must solve. For example, one must distinguish between moral and nonmoral virtues. There may well be a number of character traits that lead to the smooth functioning of human beings, but surely only a special class of these could be called "moral" traits. Health and physical strength are traits that benefit humans, but we would hardly give *moral* praise to a person possessing them. What this suggests is that while being a trait beneficial to humanity is surely a necessary condition for being a moral virtue, this is not a sufficient condition. We need to specify the definition of moral virtue further.

Foot also raises a different sort of problem that a virtue theory of ethics must solve. While it may be granted that the focus of moral evaluation should be character traits, not actions, surely moral virtues cannot be completely unconnected with the morality of actions. It would be inappropriate to praise a certain character trait as morally good, if that trait were regularly put to a bad end. And, it surely seems as if some of the traits that are standardly cited as moral virtues have this disadvantage. For example, both Aristotle and Foot consider courage as a moral virtue, but it looks as if courage could be put to a bad end. It seems possible to talk about a "courageous criminal" even though we condemn the criminal's actions. Foot attempts to argue that a better understanding of the virtues can avoid this problem since, she claims virtues, understood properly, always lead to good actions. As we shall see, not everyone is satisfied with Foot's solution to this problem.

One of the most influential recent books on ethical virtue is Alasdair MacIntyre's *After Virtue*. Selections from Chapter Fourteen of this book are included here. In the early part of our selection MacIntyre points out that people have proposed different lists of what are considered to be moral virtues. If one wants to develop a normative ethics using the notion of virtue, however, then something must be done about the conflicting accounts of virtue. One must at least make an attempt to argue for some definitive list of the genuine moral virtues. In the selection we shall read, MacIntyre does not specifically give such a list, but rather lays some important groundwork needed to complete such a task. Generally speaking, MacIntyre's selection is of interest since he attempts to tell us where to look for a proper list of moral virtues.

MacIntyre's account of the virtues centers around the notion of "practices." Roughly, his claim is that virtues are human characteristics that help us to achieve the kind of goods that are "internal" to practices. MacIntyre has the following in mind. Like Aristotle, he believes that a virtue is a character trait that benefits humanity (works toward the "good"). But there are two sort of "good" people can pursue. On the one hand, many of us work and struggle for some specific item— fame, success, fortune, or whatever. On the other hand, we sometimes find that a certain sort of activity, just by doing it, is rewarding. Some activities (let's call them "practices") are aimed at a specific and desirable end state—and that's why we bother to do them. Other practices, however, are ones we engage in simply because we find the doing of them worthwhile. Practices can have either external or internal goods (or even both). If the good of a practice is some end-state, then according to MacIntyre's definition, the good is "external," but if good of a practice is in the doing, then the good is called "internal." To use one of MacIntyre's own examples, playing chess can be either an external or internal good. If people play chess to impress their friends, then the good of playing chess is "external." If people find chess rewarding just because playing it is enjoyable, however, then the good of chess is "internal." Similar to Aristotle, MacIntyre argues that the place to look for moral virtues is in the arena of goods internal to practices. Virtues are the set of characteristics needed to enjoy the goods internal to (at least some) practices. It should be noted that MacIntyre's result here can be seen as a specification of Aristotle's root idea of a moral virtue. Aristotle also rejected the idea of human good as some set of things to accumulate in favor of a notion of living a life well—enjoying something for the sake of doing it. Of course, Aristotle further believed that the sole "practice" of interest to humans is the "practice" of rational activity. He may have been wrong about this, however. There may be other practices that are of importance to persons.

It should be noted that the selection included from MacIntyre only goes about half-way toward a complete account of virtues. Even if MacIntyre is right that moral virtues are character traits needed to enjoy the internal goods of practices, surely only some such traits deserve to be called moral virtues. To take the chess example again, we would hardly think that the character traits required to get "internal" enjoyment from chess are moral virtues. Some practices must be more morally important than others. MacIntyre only hints here what a fuller solution to the problem will look like, but in general terms it is this: Like Aristotle, MacIntyre is on the lookout for practices that will contribute to an overall sense of human good. Unlike Aristotle, however, MacIntyre does not think there is one sort of human good for all times and places. Rather, MacIntyre suggests, we must look for a standard of human good in an historical moral tradition. Presumably, with a bit of hard work we can look at our historical experience and identify some broad strands of moral ideas that will allow us to formulate a standard of morality that will be specific to our society.

Even though Foot and MacIntyre deviate considerably from the details of Aristotelian ethics, they share one rather important notion. Moral virtues are character traits needed in our project of seeking our own good—realizing the end or purpose of human life. G. J. Warnock sharply criticizes this approach. Warnock agrees that moral evaluation must be evaluation of character traits and even further agrees that morally good traits are those that help to achieve some goal. However, he disagrees with the Aristotelian idea that the goal must be the good life for individual persons. In fact, Warnock argues, the notion of the "good life" for individuals ought not play a central role in determining moral virtues. His point is fairly easy to understand. We would surely think that a morally good person is one who is disposed, generally speaking, to better the "human predicament" (to use Warnock's language). To be sure, virtues directed toward improving the human predicament are typically included in an Aristotelian scheme (consider Foot's list of courage, temperance, wisdom, and justice), but it should be recalled that in order for a virtue to get on an Aristotelian list it must qualify as the sort of character trait that each of us finds conducive to our own personal happiness. But, Warnock argues that, at best, it is a mere coincidence that acting justly or temperately leads to our own happiness. If we want to find true moral virtues, Warnock argues, we should look directly at those character traits that improve the human predicament, even if such traits do not give us personal happiness. A consequence of Warnock's view is that, contrary to Aristotle, there may yet be a gulf between morality and human happiness.

There is, of course, continuity between Warnock and the Aristotelian tradition. Warnock can agree that ethical virtues are character traits that further some larger goal. However, Warnock departs from the tradition concerning the proper goal of morality. For Aristotelians, virtues are character traits in the service of the "good life" for an individual. For Warnock, the goal ought to be something distinctly altruistic, namely, the welfare of others.

It will be appropriate before closing this introduction to virtue theories of ethics to make a few cautionary comments. It perhaps goes without saying that not everyone who works in ethical theory is convinced that theories like utilitarianism and Kantianism must be rejected in favor of some version of virtue theory. There are a couple of reasons why a utilitarian or Kantian may be unconvinced that the notion of virtue is a good starting point for ethical theory. (1) It is open to the utilitarian or Kantian to argue that there is room within their larger framework for supererogatory actions—thereby undercutting one of the motivations for virtue ethics. Just to take one example, a utilitarian might argue that a certain amount of "utility maximizing" is our duty and anything more is supererogatory. (2) It can be argued that evaluations of actions are more basic to ethics than evaluation of character traits. Character traits are only good insofar as they are dispositions to *act* in a morally good fashion. Thus, actions are more basic to the issue of the morality than character traits. These rejoinders may or may not succeed against the virtue theorists, but they ought to be kept in mind when reading the offerings in this chapter.

Virtue

Aristotle

SUBJECT OF OUR INQUIRY

All human activities aim at some good: some goods subordinate to others

1.   Every art and every inquiry, and similarly every action and pursuit, is thought to aim at some good; and for this reason the good has rightly been declared . . . to be that at which all things aim. But a certain difference is found among ends; some are activities, others are products apart from the activities that produce them. Where there are ends apart from the actions, it is the nature of the products to be better than the activities. Now, as there are many actions, arts, and sciences, their ends also are many; the end of the medical art is health, that of shipbuilding a vessel, that of strategy victory, that of economics wealth. But where such arts fall under a single capacity—as bridle-making and the other arts concerned with the equipment of horses fall under the act of riding, and this and every military action under strategy, in the same way other arts fall under yet others—in all of these the ends of the master arts are to be preferred to all the subordinate ends; for it is for the sake of the former that the latter are pursued. It makes no difference whether the activities themselves are the ends of the actions, or something else apart from the activities, as in the case of the sciences just mentioned.

The science of the good for man is politics

2.   If, then, there is some end of the things we do, which we desire for its own sake (everything else being desired for the sake of this), and if we do not choose everything for the sake of something else (for at that rate the process would go on to infinity, so that our desire would be empty and vain), clearly this must be the good and the chief good. Will not the knowledge of it, then, have a great influence on life? Shall we not, like archers who have a mark to aim at, be more likely to hit upon what is right? If so, we must try, in outline at least, to determine what it is, and of which of the sciences or capacities it is the object. It would seem to belong to the most authoritative art and that which is most truly the master art. And politics appears to be of this nature; for it is this that ordains which of the sciences should be studied in a state, | and which each class of citizens should learn and up to what point they should learn them; and we see even the most highly esteemed of capacities to fall under this, e.g. strategy, economics, rhetoric; now, since politics uses the rest of the sciences, and since, again, it legislates as to what we are to do and what we are to abstain from, the end of this science must include those of the others, so that this end must be the good for man. For even if the end is the same for a single man and for a state, that of the state seems at all events something greater and more complete whether to attain or to preserve; though it is worth while to attain the end merely for one man, it is finer and more godlike to attain

From Book I, "The Good for Man," from *The Nicomachean Ethics of Aristotle* translated by Sir David Ross (the Oxford translation of Aristotle, vol. 9, 1925)

it for a nation or for city-states. These, then, are the ends at which our inquiry aims, since it is political science, in one sense of that term. . . .

4.   Let us resume our inquiry and state, in view of the fact that all knowledge and every pursuit aims at some good, what it is that we say political science aims at and what is the highest of all goods achievable by action. Verbally there is very general agreement; for both the general run of men and people of superior refinement say that it is happiness, and identify living well and doing well with being happy; but with regard to what happiness is they differ, and the many do not give the same account as the wise. For the former think it is some plain and obvious thing, like pleasure, wealth, or honour; they differ, however, from one another—and often even the same man identifies it with different things, with health when he is ill, with wealth when he is poor; but, conscious of their ignorance, they admire those who proclaim some great ideal that is above their comprehension. Now some . . . thought that apart from these many goods there is another which is self-subsistent and causes the goodness of all these as well. To examine all the opinions that have been held were perhaps somewhat fruitless; enough to examine those that are most prevalent or that seem to be arguable.

Let us not fail to notice, however, that there is a difference between arguments from and those to the first principles. For Plato, too, was right in raising this question and asking, as he used to do, "Are we on the way from or to the first principles?" There is a difference, as there is | in a race-course between the course from the judges to the turning-point and the way back. For, while we must begin with what is known, things are objects of knowledge in two senses—some to us, some without qualification. Presumably, then, *we* must begin with things known to *us*. Hence any one who is to listen intelligently to lectures about what is noble and just and, generally, about the subjects of political science must have been brought up in good habits. For the fact is the starting-point, and if this is sufficiently plain to him, he will not at the start need the reason as well; and the man who has been well brought up has or can easily get starting-points. . . .

Presumably, however, to say that happiness is the chief good seems a platitude, and a clearer account of what it is is still desired. This might perhaps be given, if we could first ascertain the function of man. For just as for a flute-player, a sculptor, or any artist, and, in general, for all things that have a function or activity, the good and the "well" is thought to reside in the function, so would it seem to be for man, if he has a function. Have the carpenter, then, and the tanner certain functions or activities, and has man none? Is he born without a function? Or as eye, hand, foot, and in general each of the parts evidently has a function, may one lay it down that man similarly has a function apart from all these? What then can this be? Life seems to belong even to plants, but we are seeking what is peculiar to man. Let us exclude, therefore, the life of nutrition and growth. | Next there would be a life of perception, but *it* also seems to be shared even by the horse, the ox, and every animal. There remains, then, an active life of the element that has a rational principle; of this, one part has such a principle in the sense of being obedient to one, the other in the sense of possessing one and exercising thought. And, as "life of the rational element" also has two meanings, we must state that life in the sense of activity is what we mean; for this seems to be the more proper sense of the term. Now if the function of man is an activity of soul which follows or implies a rational principle, and if we say "a so-and-so" and "a good so-and-so" have a function which is the same in kind, e.g. a lyre-player and a good lyre-player, and so without qualification in all cases, eminence in respect of goodness being added to the name of the function (for the function of a lyre-player is to play the lyre, and that of a good lyre-player is to do so well): if this is the case [and we state the function of man to be a certain kind of life, and this to be an activity or actions of the soul implying a rational principle, and the function of a good man to be the good and noble performance of these, and if any action is well performed when it is performed in accordance with the appropriate excellence: if this is the case], human good turns out to be activity of soul in accordance with virtue, and if there are more than one virtue, in accordance with the best and most complete.

But we must add "in a complete life." For one swallow does not make a summer, nor does one day; and so too one day, or a short time, does not make a man blessed and happy. . . .

Happiness then is the best, noblest, and most pleasant thing in the world, and these attributes are not severed as in the inscription at Delos—

Most noble is that which is justest, and best in health; But most pleasant it is to win what we love.

For all these properties belong to the best activities; and these, or one—the best—of these, we identify with happiness.

Yet evidently, as we said, . . . it needs the external goods as well; for it is impossible, or not easy, to do noble acts without the proper equipment. In may actions | we use friends and riches and political power as instruments; and there are some things the lack of which takes the lustre from happiness—good birth, goodly children, beauty; for the man who is very ugly in appearance or ill-born or solitary and childless is not very likely to be happy, and perhaps a man would be still less likely if he had thoroughly bad children or friends or had lost good children or friends by death. As we said, . . . then, happiness seems to need this sort of prosperity in addition; for which reason some identify happiness with good fortune, though others identify it with virtue. . . .

5.   Next we must consider what virtue is. Since things that are found in the soul are of three kinds—passions, faculties, states of character—virtue must be one of these. By passions I mean appetite, anger, fear, confidence, envy, joy, friendly feeling, hatred, longing, emulation, pity, and in general the feelings that are accompanied by pleasure or pain; by faculties the things in virtue of which we are said to be capable of feeling these, e.g. of becoming angry or being pained or feeling pity; by states of character the things in virtue of which we stand well or badly with reference to the passions, e.g. with reference to anger we stand badly if we feel it violently or too weakly, and will if we feel it moderately; and similarly with reference to the other passions.

Now neither the virtues nor the vices are *passions,* because we are not called good or bad on the ground of our passions, but are so called on the ground of our virtues and our vices, and because we are neither praised nor blamed for our passions (for the man who feels fear or anger is not praised, nor is the man who simply feels anger blamed, but the man who feels it in a certain way), | but for our virtues and our vices we *are* praised or blamed.

Again, we feel anger and fear without choice, but the virtues are modes of choice or involve choice. Further, in respect of the passions we are said to be moved, but in respect of the virtues and the vices we are said not to be moved but to be disposed in a particular way.

For these reasons also they are not *faculties;* for we are neither called good or bad, nor praised or blamed, for the simple capacity of feeling the passions; again, we have the faculties by nature, but we are not made good or bad by nature; we have spoken of this before. . . .

If, then, the virtues are neither passions nor faculties, all that remains is that they should be *states of character*.

Thus we have stated what virtue is in respect of its genus.

The differentia of moral virtue: it is a disposition to choose the mean

6. We must, however, not only describe virtue as a state of character, but also say what sort of state it is. We may remark, then, that every virtue or excellence both brings into good condition the thing of which it is the excellence and makes the work of that thing be done well; e.g. the excellence of the eye makes both the eye and its work good; for it is by the excellence of the eye that we see well. Similarly the excellence of the horse makes a horse both good in itself and good at running and at carrying its rider and at awaiting the attack of the enemy. Therefore, if this is true in every case, the virtue of man also will be the state of character which makes a man good and which makes him do his own work well.

How this is to happen we have stated already, . . . but it will be made plain also by the following consideration of the specific nature of virtue. In everything that is continuous and divisible it is possible to take more, less, or an equal amount, and that either in terms of the thing itself or relatively to us; and the equal is an intermediate between excess and defect. By the intermediate in the object I mean that which is equidistant from each of the extremes, which is one and the same for all men; by the intermediate relatively to us that which is neither too much nor too little—and this is not one, nor the same for all. For instance, if ten is many and two is few, six is the intermediate, taken in terms of the object; for it exceeds and is exceeded by an equal amount; this is intermediate according to arithmetical proportion. But the intermediate relatively to us is not to be taken so; if ten pounds are too much for a particular person to eat and two too little, | it does not follow that the trainer will order six pounds; for this also is perhaps too much for the person who is to take it, or too little—too little for Milo. . . . too much for the beginner in athletic exercises. The same is true of running and wrestling. Thus a master of any art avoids excess and defect, but seeks the intermediate and chooses this—the intermediate not in the object but relatively to us.

If it is thus, then, that every art does its work well—by looking to the intermediate and judging its works by this standard (so that we often say of good works of art that it is not possible either to take away or to add anything, implying that excess and defect destroy the goodness of works of art, while the mean preserves it; and good artists, as we say, look to this in their work), and if, further, virtue is more exact and better than any art, as nature also is, then virtue must have the quality of aiming at the intermediate. I mean moral virtue; for it is this that is concerned with passions and actions, and in these there is excess, defect, and the intermediate. For instance, both fear and confidence and appetite and anger and pity and in general pleasure and pain may be felt both too much and too little, and in both cases not well; but to feel them at the right times, with reference to the right objects, towards the right people, with the right motive, and in the right way, is what is both intermediate and best, and this is characteristic of virtue. Similarly with regard to actions also there is excess, defect, and the intermediate. Now virtue is concerned with passions and actions, in which excess is a form of failure, and so is defect, while the intermediate is praised and is a form of success; and being praised and being successful are both characteristics of virtue. Therefore virtue is a kind of mean, since, as we have seen, it aims at what is intermediate.

Again, it is possible to fail in many ways (for evil belongs to the class of the unlimited, as the Pythagoreans conjectured, and good to that of the limited), while to succeed is possibly only in one way (for which reason also one is easy and the other difficult—to miss the mark easy, to hit it difficult); for these reasons also, then, excess and defect are characteristic of vice, and the mean of virtue;

For men are good in but one way, but bad in many.

Virtue, then, is a state of character concerned with choice, lying in a mean, i.e. the mean relative to us, | this being determined by a rational principle, and by that principle by which the man of practical wisdom would determine it. Now it is a mean between two vices, that which depends on excess and that which depends on defect; and again it is a mean because the vices respectively fall short of or exceed what is right in both passions and actions, while virtue both finds and chooses that which is intermediate. Hence in respect of its substance and the definition which states its essence virtue is a mean, with regard to what is best and right an extreme. . . .

7. We must, however, not only make this general statement, but also apply it to the individual facts. For among statements about conduct those which are general apply more widely, but those which are particular are more genuine, since conduct has to do with individual cases, and our statements must harmonize with the facts in these cases. We may take these cases from our table. With regard to feelings of fear and confidence courage is the mean; | of the people who exceed, he who exceeds in fearlessness has no name (many of the states have no name), while the man who exceeds in confidence is rash, and he who exceeds in fear and falls short in confidence is a coward. With regard to pleasures and pains—not all of them, and not so much with regard to the pains—the mean is temperance, the excess self-indulgence. Persons deficient with regard to the pleasures are not often found; hence such persons also have received no name. But let us call them "insensible."

With regard to giving and taking of money the mean is liberality, the excess and the defect prodigality and meanness. In these actions people exceed and fall short in contrary ways; the prodigal exceeds in spending and falls short in taking, while the mean man exceeds in taking and falls short in spending. (At present we are giving a mere outline or summary, and are satisfied with this; later these states will be more exactly determined.) . . . With regard to money there are also other dispositions—a mean, magnificence (for the magnificent man differs from the liberal man; the former deals with large sums, the latter with small ones), an excess, tastelessness and vulgarity, and a deficiency, niggardliness; these differ from the states opposed to liberality, and the mode of their difference will be stated later. . . .

With regard to honour and dishonour the mean is proper pride, the excess is known as a sort of "empty vanity," and the deficiency is undue humility; and as we said . . . liberality was related to magnificence, differing from it by dealing with small sums, so there is a state similarly related to proper pride, being concerned with small honours while that is concerned with great. For it is possible to desire honour as one ought, and more than one ought, and less, and the man who exceeds in his desires is called ambitious, the man who falls short unambitious, while the intermediate person has no name. The dispositions also are nameless, except that that of the ambitious man is called ambition. Hence the people who are at the extremes lay claim to the middle place; and we ourselves sometimes call the intermediate person ambitious and sometimes unambitious, and sometimes praise the ambitious man and sometimes the unambitious. | The reason of our doing this will be stated in what follows; . . . but now let us speak of the remaining states according to the method which has been indicated.

With regard to anger also there is an excess, a deficiency, and a mean. Although they can scarcely be said to have names, yet since we call the intermediate person good-tempered let us call the mean good temper; of the persons at the extremes let the one who exceeds be called irascible, and his vice irascibility, and the man who falls short an unirascible sort of person, and the deficiency unirascibility.

There are also three other means, which have a certain likeness to one another, but differ from one another: for they are all concerned with intercourse in words and actions, but differ in that one is concerned with truth in this sphere, the other two with pleasantness; and of this one kind is exhibited in giving amusement, the other in all the circumstances of life. We must therefore speak of these too, that we may the better see that in all things the mean is praiseworthy, and the extremes neither praisworthy nor right, but worthy of blame. Now most of these states also have no names, but we must try, as in the other cases, to invent names ourselves so that we may be clear and easy to follow. With regard to truth, then, the intermediate is a truthful sort of person and the mean may be called truthfulness, while the pretence which exaggerates is boastfulness and the person characterized by it a boaster, and that which understates is mock modesty and the person characterized by it mock-modest. With regard to pleasantness in the giving of amusement the intermediate person is ready-witted and the disposition ready wit, the excess is buffoonery and the person characterized by it a buffoon, while the man who falls short is a sort of boor and his state is boorishness. With regard to the remaining kind of pleasantness, that which is exhibited in life in general, the man who is pleasant in the right way is friendly and the mean is friendliness, while the man who exceeds is an obsequious person if he has no end in view, a flatterer if he is aiming at his own advantage, and the man who falls short and is unpleasant in all circumstances is a quarrelsome and surly sort of person.

There are also means in the passions and concerned with the passions; since shame is not a virtue, and yet praise is extended to the modest man. For even in these matters one man is said to be intermediate, and another to exceed, as for instance the bashful man who is ashamed of everything; while he who falls short or is not ashamed of anything at all is shameless, and the intermediate person is modest. Righteous indignation is a mean between envy and spite, | and these states are concerned with the pain and pleasure that are felt at the fortunes of our neighbours; the man who is characterized by righteous indignation is pained at undeserved good fortune, the envious man, going beyond him, is pained at all good fortune, and the spiteful man falls so far short of being pained that he even rejoices. . . .

And first let us speak of courage.

COURAGE

***Courage concerned with the feelings of fear and confidence—
strictly speaking, with the fear of death in battle***

6. That it is a mean with regard to feelings or feat and confidence has already been made evident, . . . and plainly the things we fear are terrible things, and these are, to speak without qualification, evils; for which reason people even define fear as expectation of evil. Now we fear all evils, e.g. disgrace, poverty, disease, friendlessness, death, but the brave man is not thought to be concerned with all; for to fear some things is even right and noble, and it is base not to fear them—e.g. disgrace; he who fears this is good and modest, and he who does not is shameless. He is, however, by some people called brave, by a transference of the word to a new meaning; for he has in him something which is like the brave man, since the brave man also is a fearless person. Poverty and disease we perhaps ought not to fear, nor in general the things that do not proceed from vice and are not due to a man himself. But not even the man who is fearless of these is brave. Yet we apply the word to him also in virtue of a similarity; for some who in the dangers of war are cowards are liberal and are confident in face of the loss of money. Nor is a man a coward if he fears insult to his wife and children or envy or anything of the kind; nor brave if he is confident when he is about to be flogged. With what sort of terrible things, then, is the brave man concerned? Surely with the greatest; for no one is more likely than he to stand his ground against what is awe-inspiring. Now death is the most terrible of all things; for it is the end, and nothing is thought to be any longer either good or bad for the dead. But the brave man would not seem to be concerned even with death in *all* circumstances, e.g. at sea or in disease. In what circumstances, then? Surely in the noblest. Now such deaths are those in battle; for these take place in the greatest and noblest danger. And these are correspondingly honoured in city-states and at the courts of monarchs. Properly, then, he will be called brave who is fearless in face of a noble death, and of all emergencies that involve death; and the emergencies of war are in the highest degree of this kind. Yet at sea also, and in disease, the brave man is fearless, but not in the same way as the seamen; for he has given up hope of safety, and is disliking the thought of death in this shape, while they are hopeful because of their experience. At the same time, we show courage in situations where there is the opportunity of showing prowess or where death is noble; but in these forms of death neither of these conditions is fulfilled.

The motive of courage is the sense of honor; characteristics of the opposite vices, cowardice and rashness

7. What is terrible is not the same for all men; but we say there are things terrible even beyond human strength. These, then, are terrible to every one—at least to every sensible man; but the terrible things that are *not* beyond human strength differ in magnitude and degree, and so too do the things that inspire confidence. Now the brave man is as dauntless as man may be. Therefore, while he will fear even the things that are not beyond human strength, he will face them as he ought and as the rule directs for honour's sake; for this is the end of virtue. But it is possible to fear these more, or less, and again to fear things that are not terrible as if they were. Of the faults that are committed, one consists in fearing what we should not, another in fearing as we should not, another in fearing when we should not, and so on; and so too with respect to the things that inspire confidence. The man, then, who faces and who fears the right things and from the right motive, in the right way and at the right time, and who feels confidence under the corresponding conditions, is brave; for the brave man feels and acts according to the merits of the case and in whatever way the rule directs. Now the end of every activity is conformity to the corresponding state of character.

This is true, therefore, of the brave man as well as of others. But courage is noble. Therefore, the end also is noble; for each thing is defined by its end. Therefore it is for a noble end that the brave man endures and acts as courage directs.

Of those who go to excess he who exceeds in fearlessness has no name (we have said previously that many states of character have no names), but he would be a sort of madman or insensible person if he feared nothing, neither earthquakes nor the waves, as they say the Celts do not; while the man who exceeds in confidence about what really is terrible is rash. The rash man, however, is also thought to be boastful and only a pretender to courage; at all events, as the brave man *is* with regard to what is terrible, so the rash man wishes to *appear;* and so he imitates him in situations where he can. Hence also most of them are a mixture of rashness and cowardice; for, while in these situations they display confidence, they do not hold their ground against what is really terrible. The man who exceeds in fear is a coward; for he fears both what he ought not and as he ought not, and all the similar characterizations attach to him. He is lacking also in confidence; | but he is more concpicuous for his excess of fear in painful situations. The coward, then, is a despairing sort of person; for he fears everything. The brave man, on the other hand, has the opposite disposition; for confidence is the mark of a hopeful disposition. The coward, the rash man, and the brave man, then, are concerned with the same objects but are differently disposed towards them; for the first two exceed and fall short, while the third holds the middle, which is the right, position; and rash men are precipitate, and wish for dangers beforehand but draw back when they are in them, while brave men are excited in the moment of action, but collected beforehand.

As we have said, then, courage is a mean with respect to things that inspire confidence or fear, in the circumstances that have been stated; ... and it chooses or endures things because it is noble to do so, or because it is base not to do so. ... But to die to escape from poverty or love or anything painful is not the mark of a brave man, but rather of a coward; for it is softness to fly from what is troublesome, and such a man endures death not because it is noble but to fly from evil. ...

Though courage is concerned with feelings of confidence and of fear; it is not concerned with both alike, but more with the things that inspire fear; for he who is undisturbed in face of these and bears himself as he should towards these is more truly brave than the man who does so towards the things that inspire confidence. It is for facing what is painful, then, as has been said, ... that men are called brave. Hence also courage involves pain, and is justly praised; for it is harder to face what is painful than to abstain from what is pleasant. Yet the end which courage sets before itself would seem to be pleasant, | but to be concealed by the attending circumstances, as happens also in athletic contests; for the end at which boxers aim is pleasant—the crown and the honours—but the blows they take are distressing to flesh and blood, and painful, and so is their whole exertion; and because the blows and the exertions are many the end, which is but small, appears to have nothing pleasant in it. And so, if the case of courage is similar, death and wounds will be painful to the brave man and against his will, but he will face them because it is noble to do so or because it is base not to do so. And the more he is possessed of virtue in its entirety and the happier he is, the more he will be pained at the thought of death; for life is best worth living for such a man, and he is knowingly losing the greatest goods, and this is painful. But he is none the less brave, and perhaps all the more so, because he chooses noble deeds of war at that cost. It is not the case, then, with all the virtues that the exercise of them is pleasant, except in so far as it reaches its end. But it is quite possible that the best soldiers may be not men of this sort but those who are less brave but have no other good; for these are ready to face danger, and they sell their life for trifling gains. . . .

Since the lawless man was seen . . . to be unjust and the law-abiding man just, evidently all lawful acts are in a sense just acts; for the acts laid down by the legislative art are lawful, and each of these, we say, is just. Now the laws in their enactments on all subjects aim at the common advantage either of all or of the best or of those who hold power, or something of the sort; so that in one sense we call those acts just that tend to produce and preserve happiness and its components for the political society. And the law bids us do both the acts of a brave man (e.g. not to desert our post nor take to flight nor throw away our arms), and those of a temperate man (e.g. not to commit adultery nor to gratify one's lust), and those of a good-tempered man (e.g. not to strike another nor to speak evil), and similarly with regard to the other virtues and forms of wickedness, commanding some acts and forbidding others; and the rightly-framed law does this rightly, and the hastily conceived one less well.

This form of justice, then, is complete virtue, but not absolutely, but in relation to our neighbour. And therefore justice is often thought to be the greatest of virtues, and "neither evening nor morning star" is so wonderful; and proverbially "in justice is every virtue comprehended." And it is complete virtue in its fullest sense because it is the actual exercise of complete virtue. It is complete because he who possesses it can exercise his virtue not only in himself but towards his neighbour also; for many men can exercise virtue in their own affairs, but not in their relations to their neighbour. | This is why the saying of Bias is thought to be true, that "rule will show the man"; for a ruler is necessarily in relation to other men, and a member of a society. For this same reason justice, alone of the virtues, is thought to be "another's good," . . . because it is related to our neighbour; for it does what is advantageous to another, either a ruler or a co-partner. Now the worst man is he who exercises his wickedness both towards himself and towards his friends, and the best man is not he who exercises his virtue towards himself but he who exercises it towards another; for this is a difficult task. Justice in this sense, then, is not part of virtue but virtue entire, nor is the contrary injustice a part of vice but vice entire. What the difference is between virtue and justice in this sense is plain from what we have said; they are the same but their essence is not the same; what, as a relation to one's neighbour, is justice is, as a certain kind of state without qualification, virtue.

The just as the fair and equal: divided into distributive and rectificatory justice

2.   But at all events what we are investigating is the justice which is a *part* of virtue; for there is a justice of this kind, as we maintain. Similarly it is with injustice in the particular sense that we are concerned.

That there is such a thing is indicated by the fact that while the man who exhibits in action the other forms of wickedness acts wrongly indeed, but not graspingly (e.g. the man who throws away his shield through cowardice or speaks harshly through bad temper or fails to help a friend with money through meanness), when a man acts graspingly he often exhibits none of these vices—no, nor all together, but certainly wickedness of some kind (for we blame him) and injustice. There is, then, another kind of injustice which is a part of injustice in the wide sense, and a use of the word "unjust" which answers to a part of what is unjust in the wide sense of "contrary to the law." Again, if one man commits adultery for the sake of gain and makes money by it, while another does so at the bidding of appetite though he loses money and is penalized for it, the latter would be held to be self-indulgent rather than grasping, but the former is unjust, but not self-indulgent; evidently, therefore, he is unjust by reason of his making gain by his act. Again, all other unjust acts are ascribed invariably to some particular kind of wickedness, e.g. adultery to self-indulgence, the desertion of a comrade in battle to cowardice, physical violence to anger; but if a man makes gain, his action is ascribed to no form of wickedness but injustice. Evidently, therefore, there is apart from injustice in the wide sense another, 'particular', injustice which shares the name and nature of the first, because its definition falls within the same genus; | for the significance of both consists in a relation to one's neighbour, but the one is concerned with honour or money or safety—or that which includes all these, if we had a single name for it—and its motive is the pleasure that arises from gain; while the other is concerned with all the objects with which the good man is concerned.

It is clear, then, that there is more than one kind of justice, and that there is one which is distinct from virtue entire; we must try to grasp its genus and differentia.

The unjust has been divided into the unlawful and the unfair, and the just into the lawful and the fair. To the unlawful answers the aforementioned sense of injustice. But since the unfair and the unlawful are not the same, but are different as a part is from its whole (for all that is unfair is unlawful, but not all that is unlawful is unfair), the unjust and injustice in the sense of the unfair are not the same as but different from the former kind, as part from whole; for injustice in this sense is a part of injustice in the wide sense, and similarly justice in the one sense of justice in the other. Therefore we must speak also about particular justice and particular injustice, and similarly about the just and the unjust. The justice, then, which answers to the whole of virtue, and the corresponding injustice, one being the exercise of virtue as a whole, and the other that of vice as a whole, towards one's neighbour, we may leave on one side. And how the meanings of "just" and "unjust" which answer to these are to be distinguished is evident; for practically the majority of the acts commanded by the law are those which are prescribed from the point of view of virtue taken as a whole; for the law bids us practise every virtue and forbids us to practise any vice. And the things that tend to produce virtue taken as a whole are those of the acts prescribed by the law which have been prescribed with a view to education for the common good. But with regard to the education of the individual as such, which makes him without qualification a good *man,* we must determine later . . . whether this is the function of the political art or of another; for perhaps it is not the same to be a good man and a good citizen of any state taken at random.

Of particular justice and that which is just in the corresponding sense, (A) one kind is that which is manifested in distributions of honour or money or the other things that fall to be divided among those who have a share in the constitution (for in these it is possible for one man to have a share either unequal or equal to that of another), and (B) one is that which plays a rectifying part in transactions between man and man. | Of this there are two divisions; of transactions (1) some are voluntary and (2) others involuntary—voluntary such transactions as sale, purchase, loan for consumption, pledging, loan for use, depositing, letting (they are called voluntary because the *origin* of these transactions is voluntary), while of the involuntary *(a)* some are clandestine, such as theft, adultery, poisoning, procuring, enticement of slaves, assassination, false witness, and *(b)* others are violent, such as assault, imprisonment, murder, robbery with violence, mutilation, abuse, insult.

Distributive justice, in accordance with geometrical proportion

3.   (A) We have shown that both the unjust man and the unjust act are unfair or unequal; now it is clear that there is also an intermediate between the two unequals involved in either case. And this is the equal; for in any kind of action in which there is
a more and a less there is also what is equal. If, then, the unjust is unequal, the just
is equal, as all men suppose it to be, even apart from argument. And since the equal is
intermediate, the just will be an intermediate. Now equality implies at least two things.
The just, then, must be both intermediate and equal and relative (i.e. for certain persons). And *qua* intermediate it must be between certain things (which are respectively
greater and less); *qua* equal, it involves *two* things; *qua* just, it is for certain people.
The just, therefore, involves at least four terms; for the persons for whom it is in fact
just are two, and the things in which it is manifested, the objects distributed, are two.
And the same equality will exist between the persons and between the things concerned; for as the latter—the things concerned—are related, so are the former; if they
are not equal, they will not have what is equal, but this is the origin of quarrels and
complaints—when either equals have and are awarded unequal shares, or unequals
equal shares. Further, this is plain from the fact that awards should be "according to
merit"; for all men agree that what is just in distribution must be according to merit in
some sense, though they do not all specify the same sort of merit, but democrats identify it with the status of freeman, supporters of oligarchy with wealth (or with noble
birth), and supporters of aristocracy with excellence.

The just, then, is a species of the proportionate (proportion being not a property
only of the kind of number which consists of abstract units, but of number in general).
For proportion is equality of ratios, and involves four terms at least (that discrete proportion involves four terms is plain, but so does continuous proportion, for it uses
one term as two and mentions it twice; | e.g. "as the line A is to the line B, so is the
line B to the line C"; the line B, then, has been mentioned twice, so that if the line B
be assumed twice, the proportional terms will be four); and the just, too, involves at
least four terms, and the ratio between one pair is the same as that between the other
pair; for there is a similar distinction between the persons and between the things. As
the term A, then, is to B, so will C be to D, and therefore, *alternando,* as A is to C, B
will be to D. Therefore also the whole is in the same ratio to the whole; . . . and this
coupling the distribution effects, and, if the terms are so combined, effects justly. The
conjunction, then, of the term A with C and of B with D is what is just in distribution
. . . and this species of the just is intermediate, and the unjust is what violates the proportion; for the proportional is intermediate, and the just is proportional (Mathemati-
cians call this kind of proportion geometrical; for it is in geometrical proportion that
it follows that the whole is to the whole as either part is to the corresponding part.)
This proportion is not continuous; for we cannot get a single term standing for a person and a thing.

This, then, is what the just is—the proportional; the unjust is what violates the
proportion. Hence one term becomes too great, the other too small, as indeed happens in practice; for the man who acts unjustly has too much, and the man who is unjustly treated too little, of what is good. In the case of evil the reverse is true; for the
lesser evil is reckoned a good in comparison with the greater evil, since the lesser evil
is rather to be chosen than the greater, and what is worthy of choice is good, and what
is worthier of choice a greater good.

This, then, is one species of the just.

Rectifactory justice, in accordance with arithmetical progression

4. (B) The remaining one is the rectificatory, which arises in connexion with transactions both voluntary and involuntary. This form of the just has a different specific character from the former. For the justice which distributes common possessions is always in accordance with the kind of proportion mentioned above . . . (for in the case also in which the distribution is made from the common funds of a partnership it will be according to the same ratio which the funds put into the business by the partners bear to one another); and the injustice opposed to this kind of justice is that which violates the proportion. But the justice in transactions between man and man is a sort of equality indeed, and the injustice a sort of inequality; | not according to that kind of proportion, however, but according to arithmetical proportion. For it makes no difference whether a good man has defrauded a bad man or a bad man a good one, nor whether it is a good or a bad man that has committed adultery; the law looks only to the distinctive character of the injury, and treats the parties as equal, if one is in the wrong and the other is being wronged, and if one inflicted injury and the other has received it . . .

10.   Our next subject is equity and the equitable (τὸἐπιεικές), and their respective relations to justice and the just. For on examination they appear to be neither absolutely the same nor generically different; and while we sometimes praise what is equitable and the equitable man (so that we apply the name by way of praise even to instances of the other virtues, instead of "good," meaning by ἐπιεικέστερον that a thing is better), at other times, when we reason it out, it seems strange if the equitable, being something different from the just, is yet praiseworthy; for either the just or the equitable is not good, if they are different; or, if both are good, they are the same.

These, then, are pretty much the considerations that give rise to the problem about the equitable; they are all in a sense correct and not opposed to one another; for the equitable, though it is better than one kind of justice, yet is just, and it is not as being a different class of thing that it is better than the just. The same thing, then, is just and equitable, and while both are good the equitable is superior. What creates the problem is that the equitable is just, but not the legally just but a correction of legal justice. The reason is that all law is universal but about some things it is not possible to make a universal statement which shall be correct. In those cases, then, in which it is necessary to speak universally, but not possible to do so correctly, the law takes the usual case, though it is not ignorant of the possibility of error. And it is none the less correct; for the error is not in the law nor in the legislator but in the nature of the thing, since the matter of practical affairs is of this kind from the start. When the law speaks universally, then, and a case arises on it which is not covered by the universal statement, then it is right, where the legislator fails us and has erred by over-simplicity, to correct the omission—to say what the legislator himself would have said had he been present, and would have put into his law if he had known. Hence the equitable is just, and better than one kind of justice—not better than absolute justice, but better than the error that arises from the absoluteness of the statement. And this is the nature of the equitable, a correction of law where it is defective owing to its universality. . . .

We divided the virtues of the soul and said that some are virtues of character and others of intellect. . . . Now we have discussed in detail the moral virtues; . . . with regard to the others let us express our view as follows, beginning with some remarks about the soul. We said before . . . that there are two parts of the soul—that which grasps a rule or rational principle, and the irrational; let us now draw a similar distinction within the part which grasps a rational principle. And let it be assumed that there are two parts which grasp a rational principle—one by which we contemplate the kind of things whose originative causes are invariable, and one by which we contemplate variable things; for where objects differ in kind the part of the soul answering to each of the two is different in kind, since it is in virtue of a certain likeness and kinship with their objects that they have the knowledge they have. Let one of these parts be called the scientific and the other the calculative; for to deliberate and to calculate are the same thing, but no one deliberates about the invariable. Therefore the calculative is one part of the faculty which grasps a rational principle. We must, then, learn what is the best state of each of these two parts; for this is the virtue of each.

Saints and Heroes

J. O. Urmson

Moral philosophers tend to discriminate, explicitly or implicitly, three types of action from the point of view of moral worth. First, they recognize actions that are a duty, or obligatory, or that we ought to perform, treating these terms as approximately synonymous; second, they recognize actions that are right in so far as they are permissible from a moral standpoint and not ruled out by moral considerations, but that are not morally required of us, like the lead of this or that card at bridge; third, they recognize actions that are wrong, that we ought not to do. Some moral philosophers, indeed, could hardly discriminate even these three types of action consistently with the rest of their philosophy. Moore, for example, could hardly recognize a class of morally indifferent actions, permissible but not enjoined, since it is to be presumed that good or ill of some sort will result from the most trivial of our actions. But most moral philosophers recognize these three types of action and attempt to provide a moral theory that will make intelligible such a threefold classification.

To my mind this threefold classification, or any classification that is merely a variation on or elaboration of it, is totally inadequate to the facts of morality; any moral theory that leaves room only for such a classification will in consequence also be inadequate. My main task in this paper will be to show the inadequacy of such a classification by drawing attention to two of the types of action that most conspicuously lie outside such a classification; I shall go on to hazard some views on what sort of theory will most easily cope with the facts to which I draw attention, but the facts are here the primary interest.

We sometimes call a person a saint, or an action saintly, using the word "saintly"

Excerpted from *Essays in Moral Philosophy,* ed. by A. I. Meldon, 1958. © 1958, University of Washington Press. By permission of the University of Washington Press.

in a purely moral sense with no religious implications; also we sometimes call a person a hero or an action heroic. It is too clear to need argument that the words "saint" and "hero" are at least normally used in such a way as to be favorably evaluative; it would be impossible to claim that this evaluation is always moral, for clearly we sometimes call a person a saint when evaluating him religiously rather than morally and may call a person the hero of a game or athletic contest in which no moral qualities were displayed, but I shall take it that no formal argument is necessary to show that at least sometimes we use both words for moral evaluation.

If "hero" and "saint" can be words of moral evaluation, we may proceed to the attempt to make explicit the criteria that we implicitly employ for their use in moral contexts. It appears that we so use them in more than one type of situation, and that there is a close parallel between the ways in which the two terms "hero" and "saint" are used; we shall here notice three types of situation in which they are used which seem to be sufficiently different to merit distinction. As the first two types of situation to be noticed are ones that can be readily subsumed under the threefold classification mentioned above, it will be sufficient here to note them and pass on to the third type of situation, which, since it cannot be subsumed under that classification, is for the purposes of this paper the most interesting.

A person may be called a saint (1) if he does his duty regularly in contexts in which inclination, desire, or self-interest would lead most people not to do it, and does so as a result of exercising abnormal self-control; parallel to this a person may be called a hero (1) if he does his duty in contexts in which terror, fear, or a drive to self-preservation would lead most men not to do it, and does so by exercising abnormal self-control. Similarly for actions: an action may be called saintly (1) if it is a case of duty done by virtue of self-control in a context in which most men would be led astray by inclination or self-interest, and an action may be called heroic (1) if it is a case of duty done by virtue of self-control in a context in which most men would be led astray by fear or a drive for self-preservation. The only difference between the saintly and the heroic in this sort of situation is that the one involves resistance to desire and self-interest; the other, resistance to fear and self-preservation. This is quite a clear difference, though there may be marginal cases, or cases in which motives were mixed, in which it would be equally appropriate to call an action indifferently saintly or heroic. It is easy to give examples of both the heroic and the saintly as distinguished above; the unmarried daughter does the saintly deed of staying at home to tend her ailing and widowed father; the terrified doctor heroically stays by his patients in a plague-ridden city.

A person may be called a saint (2) if he does his duty in contexts in which inclination or self-interest would lead most men not to do it, not, as in the previous paragraph, by abnormal self-control, without effort; parallel to this a person may be called a hero (2) if he does his duty in contexts in which fear would lead most men not to do it, and does so without effort. The corresponding accounts of a saintly (2) or heroic (2) action can easily be derived. Here we have the conspicuously virtuous deed, in the Aristotelian sense, as opposed to the conspicuously self-controlled, encratic deed of the previous paragraph. People thus purged of temptation or disciplined against fear may be rare, but Aristotle thought there could be such; there is a tendency today to think of such people as merely lucky or unimaginative, but Aristotle thought more highly of them than of people who need to exercise self-control.

It is clear that, in the two types of situation so far considered, we are dealing with actions that fall under the concept of duty. Roughly, we are calling a person saintly or heroic because he does his duty in such difficult contexts that most men would fail in them. Since for the purposes of this paper I am merely conceding that we do use the terms "saintly" and "heroic" in these ways, it is unnecessary here to spend time arguing that we do so use them or in illustrating such uses. So used, the threefold classification of actions whose adequacy I wish to deny can clearly embrace them. I shall therefore pass immediately to a third use of the terms "heroic" and "saintly," which I am not merely willing to concede but obliged to establish.

I contend, then, that we may also call a person a saint (3) if he does actions that are far beyond the limits of his duty, whether by control of contrary inclination and interest or without effort; parallel to this we may call a person a hero (3) if he does actions that are far beyond the bounds of his duty, whether by control of natural fear or without effort. Such actions are saintly (3) or heroic (3). Here, as it seems to me, we have the hero or saint, heroic or saintly deed, par excellence; until now we have been considering but minor saints and heroes. We have considered the, certainly, heroic action of the doctor who does his duty by sticking to his patients in a plague-stricken city; we have now to consider the case of the doctor, who, no differently situated from countless other doctors in other places, volunteers to join the depleted medical forces in that city. Previously we were considering the soldier who heroically does his duty in the face of such dangers as would cause most to shirk—the sort of man who is rightly awarded the Military Medal in the British Army; we have now to consider the case of the soldier who does more than his superior officers would ever ask him to do—the man to whom, often posthumously, the Victoria Cross is awarded. Similarly, we have to turn from saintly self-discipline in the way of duty to the dedicated, self-effacing life in the service of others which is not even contemplated by the majority of upright, kind, and honest men, let alone expected of them.

Let us be clear that we are not now considering cases of natural affection, such as the sacrifice made by a mother for her child; such cases may be said with some justice not to fall under the concept of morality but to be admirable in some different way. Such cases as are here under consideration may be taken to be as little bound up with such emotions as affection as any moral action may be. We may consider an example of what is meant by "heroism" (3) in more detail to bring this out.

We may imagine a squad of soldiers to be practicing the throwing of live hand grenades; a grenade slips from the hand of one of them and rolls on the ground near the squad; one of the sacrifices his life by throwing himself on the grenade and protecting his comrades with his own body. It is quite unreasonable to suppose that such a man must be impelled by the sort of emotion that he might be impelled by if his best friend were in the squad; he might only just have joined the squad; it is clearly an action having moral status. But if the soldier had not thrown himself on the grenade would he have failed in his duty? Though clearly he is superior in some way to his comrades, can we possibly say that they failed in their duty by not trying to be the one who sacrificed himself? If he had not done so, could anyone have said to him, "You ought to have thrown yourself on that grenade"? Could a superior have decently ordered him to do it? The answer to all these questions is plainly negative. We clearly have here a case of a moral action, a heroic action, which cannot be subsumed under the classification whose inadequacy we are exposing.

But someone may not be happy with this conclusion, and for more respectable reasons than a desire to save the traditional doctrine. He may reason as follows: in so far as the soldier had time to feel or think at all, he presumably felt that he ought to do that deed; he considered it the proper thing to do; he, if no one else, might have reproached himself for failing to do his duty if he had shirked the deed. So, it may be argued, if an act presents itself to us in the way this act may be supposed to have presented itself to this soldier, then it is our duty to do it; we have no option. This objection to my thesis clearly has some substance, but it involves a misconception of what is at issue. I have no desire to present the act of heroism as one that is naturally regarded as optional by the hero, as something he might or might not do; I concede that he might regard himself as being obliged to act as he does. But if he were to survive the action only a modesty so excessive as to appear false could make him say, "I only did my duty," for we know, and he knows, that he has done more than duty requires. Further, though he might say to himself that so to act was a duty, he could not say so even beforehand to anyone else, and no one else could ever say it. Subjectively, we may say, at the time of action, the deed presented itself as a duty, but it was not a duty.

Another illustration, this time of saintliness, may help. It is recorded by Bonaventura that after Francis of Assisi had finished preaching to the birds on a celebrated occasion his companions gathered around him to praise and admire. But Francis himself was not a bit pleased; he was full of self-reproach that he had hitherto failed in what he now considered to be his duty to preach to the feathered world. There is indeed no degree of saintliness that a suitable person may not come to consider it to be his duty to achieve. Yet there is a world of difference between this failure to have preached hitherto to the birds and a case of straightforward breach of duty, however venial. First, Francis could without absurdity reproach himself for his failure to do his duty, but it would be quite ridiculous for anyone else to do so, as one could have done if he had failed to keep his vows, for example. Second, it is not recorded that Francis ever reproached anyone else for failure to preach to the birds as a breach of duty. He could claim this action for himself as a duty and could perhaps have exhorted others to preach to the birds; but there could be no question of reproaches for not so acting.

To sum up on this point, then, it seems clear that there is no action, however quixotic, heroic, or saintly, which the agent may not regard himself as obliged to perform, as much as he may feel himself obliged to tell the truth and to keep his promises. Such actions do not present themselves as optional to the agent when he is deliberating; but, since he alone can call such an action of his a duty, and then only from the deliberative viewpoint, only for himself and not for others, and not even for himself as a piece of objective reporting, and since nobody else can call on him to tell the truth and to keep his promises, there is here a most important difference from the rock-bottom duties which are duties for all and from every point of view, and to which anyone may draw attention. Thus we need not deny the points made by our imaginary objector in order to substantiate the point that some acts of heroism and saintliness cannot be adequately subsumed under the concept of duty.

Let us then take it as established that we have to deal in ethics not with a simple trichotomy of duties, permissible actions, and wrong actions, or any substantially similar conceptual scheme, but with something more complicated. We have to add at least the complication of actions that are certainly of moral worth but that fall outside the notion of a duty and seem to go beyond it, actions worthy of being called heroic or saintly. It should indeed be noted that heroic or saintly actions are not the sole, but merely conspicuous, cases of actions that exceed the basic demands of duty; there can be cases of disinterested kindness and generosity, for example, that are clearly more than basic duty requires and yet hardly ask for the high titles, "saintly" and "heroic." Indeed, every case of "going the second mile" is a case in point, for it cannot be one's duty to go the second mile in the same basic sense as it is to go the first—otherwise it could be argued first that it is one's duty to go two miles and therefore that the spirit of the rule of the second mile requires that one go altogether four miles, and by repetition one could establish the need to go every time on an infinite journey. It is possible to go just beyond one's duty by being a little more generous, forbearing, helpful, or forgiving than fair dealing demands, or to go a very long way beyond the basic code of duties with the saint or the hero. When I here draw attention to the heroic and saintly deed, I do so merely in order to have conspicuous cases of a whole realm of actions that lie outside the trichotomy I have criticized and therefore, as I believe, outside the purview of most ethical theories.

Before considering the implications for ethics for the facts we have up to now been concerned to note, it might be of value to draw attention to a less exalted parallel to these facts. If we belong to a club there will be rules of the club, written or unwritten, calling upon us to fulfill certain basic requirements that are a condition of membership, and that may be said to be the duties of membership. It may perhaps be such a basic requirement that we pay a subscription. It will probably be indifferent whether we pay this subscription by check or in cash—both procedures will be "right"—and almost certainly it will be quite indifferent what sort of hat we wear at the meetings. Here, then, we have conformity to rule which is the analogue of doing one's duty, breach of rule which is the analogue of wrongdoing, and a host of indifferent actions, in accordance with the traditional trichotomy. But among the rule-abiding members of such a club what differences there can be! It is very likely that there will be one, or perhaps two or three, to whose devotion and loyal service the success of the club is due far more than to the activities of all the other members together, there are the saints and the heroes of the clubs, who do more for them by far than any member could possibly be asked to do, whose many services could not possibly be demanded in the rules. Behind them come a motley selection, varying from the keen to the lukewarm, whose contributions vary in value and descend sometimes to almost nothing beyond what the rules demand. The moral contribution of people to society can vary in value in the same way.

So much, then, for the simple facts to which I have wished to draw attention. They are simple facts and, unless I have misrepresented them, they are facts of which we are all, in a way, perfectly well aware. It would be absurd to suggest that moral philosophers have hitherto been unaware of the existence of saints and heroes and have never even alluded to them in their works. But it does seem that these facts have been neglected in their general, systematic accounts of morality. It is indeed easy to see that on some of the best-known theories there is no room for such facts. If for Moore, and for most utilitarians, any action is a duty that will produce the greatest possible good in the circumstances, for them the most heroic self-sacrifice or saintly self-forgetfulness will be duties on all fours with truth-telling and promise-keeping. For Kant, beyond the counsels of prudence and the rules of skill, there is only the categorical imperative of duty, and every duty is equally and utterly binding on all men; it is true that he recognizes the limiting case of the holy will, but the holy will is not a will that goes beyond duty but a will that is beyond morality through being incapable of acting except in accordance with the imperative. The nearest to an equivalent to a holy will in the cases we have been noting is the saintly will in the second sense we distinguished—the will that effortlessly does its duty when most would fail—but this is not a true parallel and in any case does not fall within the class of moral actions that go beyond duty to which our attention is primarily given. It is also true that Kant recognized virtues and talents as having conditional value, but not moral value, whereas the acts of heroism and saintliness we have considered have full moral worth, and their value is as unconditional as anyone could wish. Without committing ourselves to a scholarly examination of Kant's ethical works, it is surely evident that Kant could not consistently do justice to the facts before us. Intuitionism seems to me so obscurantist that I should not wish to prophesy what an intuitionist might feel himself entitled to say; but those intuitionists with whose works I am acquainted found their theories on an intuition of the fitting, the prima facie duty or the claim; the act that has this character to the highest degree at any time is a duty. While they recognize greater and lesser, stronger and weaker, claims, this is only in order to be able to deal with the problem of the conflict of duties; they assign no place to the act that, while not a duty, is of high moral importance.

Simple utilitarianism, Kantianism, and intuitionism, then, have no obvious theoretical niche for the saint and the hero. It is possible, no doubt, to revise these theories to accommodate the facts, but until so modified successfully they must surely be treated as unacceptable, and the modifications required might well detract from their plausibility. The intuitionists, for example, might lay claim to the intuition of a nonnatural characteristic of saintliness, of heroism, of deceny, of sportingness, and so on, but this would give to their theory still more the appearance of utilizing the advantages of theft over honest toil.

Thus as moral theorists we need to discover some theory that will allow for both absolute duties, which, in Mill's phrase, can be exacted from a man like a debt, to omit which is to do wrong and to deserve censure, and which may be embodied in formal rules or principles, and also for a range of actions which are of moral value and which an agent may feel called upon to perform, but which cannot be demanded and whose omission cannot be called wrongdoing. Traditional moral theories, I have suggested, fail to do this. It would be well beyond the scope of this paper and probably beyond my capacity, to produce here and now a full moral theory designed to accommodate all these facts, including the facts of saintliness and heroism. But I do think that of all traditional theories utilitarianism can be most easily modified to accommodate the facts, and would like before ending this paper to bring forward some considerations tending to support this point of view.

Moore went to great pains to determine exactly the nature of the intrinsically good, and Mill to discover the *summum bonum,* Moore's aim being to explain thereby directly the rightness and wrongness of particular actions and Mill's to justify a set of moral principles in the light of which the rightness or wrongness of particular actions can be decided. But, though there can be very tricky problems of duty, they do not naturally present themselves as problems whose solution depends upon an exact determination of an ultimate end; while the moral principles that come most readily to mind—truth-telling; promise-keeping; abstinence from murder, theft, and violence; and the like—make a nice discrimination of the supreme good seem irrelevant. We do not need to debate whether it is Moore's string of intrinsic goods or Mill's happiness that is achieved by conformity to such principles; it is enough to see that without them social life would be impossible and any life would indeed be solitary, poor, nasty, brutish, and short. Even self-interest (which some have seen as the sole foundation of morality) is sufficient ground to render it wise to preach, if not to practice, such principles. Such considerations as these, which are not novel, have led some utilitarians to treat avoidance of the *summum malum* rather than the achievement of the *summum bonum* as the foundation of morality. Yet to others this has seemed, with some justification, to assign to morality too ignoble a place.

But the facts we have been considering earlier in this paper are surely relevant at this point. It is absurd to ask just what ideal is being served by abstinence from murder; but on the other hand nobody could see in acts of heroism such as we have been considering a mere avoidance of antisocial behavior. Here we have something more gracious, actions that need to be inspired by a positive ideal. If duty can, as Mill said, be exacted from persons as a debt, it is because duty is a minimum requirement for living together; the positive contribution of actions that go beyond duty could not be so exacted.

It may, however, be objected that this is a glorification of the higher flights of morality at the expense of duty, toward which an unduly cynical attitude is being taken. In so far as the suggestion is that we are forgetting how hard the way of duty may be and that doing one's duty can at times deserve to be called heroic and saintly, the answer is that we have mentioned this and acknowledge it; it is not forgotten but irrelevant to the point at issue, which is the place of duty in a moral classification of actions, not the problem of the worth of moral agents. But I may be taken to be acquiescing in a low and circumscribed view of duty which I may be advised to enlarge. We should, it may be said, hitch our wagons to the stars and not be content to say: you must do this and that as duties, and it would be very nice if you were to do these other things but we do not expect them of you. Is it perhaps only an imperfect conception of duty which finds it not to comprise the whole of morality? I want to examine this difficulty quite frankly, and to explain why I think that we properly recognize morality that goes beyond duty; for it seems to me incontestable that property or improperly we do so.

No intelligent person will claim infallibility for his moral views. But allowing for this one must claim that one's moral code is ideal so far as one can see; for to say, "I recognize moral code A but see clearly that moral code B is superior to it," is but a way of saying that one recognizes moral code B but is only prepared to live up to moral code A. In some sense, then, everybody must be prepared to justify his moral code as ideal; but some philosophers have misunderstood this sense. Many philosophers have thought it necessary, if they were to defend their moral code as ideal, to try to show that it had a superhuman, a priori validity. Kant, for example, tried to show that the moral principles he accepted were such as any rational being, whether man or angel, must inevitably accept; the reputedly empiricist Locke thought that it must be possible to work out a deductive justification of moral laws. In making such claims such philosophers have unintentionally done morality a disservice; for their failure to show that the moral code was ideal in the sense of being a rationally justifiable system independent of time, place, circumstance, and human nature has led many to conclude that there can be no justification of a moral code, that moral codes are a matter of taste or convention.

But morality, I take it, is something that should serve human needs, not something that incidentally sweeps man up with itself, and to show that a morality was ideal would be to show that it best served man—man as he is and as he can be expected to become, not man as he would be if he were perfectly rational or an incorporeal angel. Just as it would be fatuous to build our machines so that they would give the best results according to an abstract conception of mechanical principles, and is much more desirable to design them to withstand to some extent our hamfistedness, ignorance, and carelessness, so our morality must be one that will work. In the only sense of "ideal" that is of importance in action, it is part of the ideal that a moral code should actually help to contribute to human well-being, and a moral code that would work only for angels (for whom it would in any case be unnecessary) would be a far from ideal moral code for human beings. There is, indeed, a place for ideals that are practically unworkable in human affairs, as there is a place for the blueprint of a machine that will never go into production; but it is not the place of such ideals to serve as a basic code of duties.

If, then, we are aiming at a moral code that will best serve human needs, a code that is ideal in the sense that a world in which such a code is acknowledged will be a better place than a world in which some other sort of moral code is acknowledged, it seems that there are ample grounds why our code should distinguish between basic rules, summarily set forth in simple rules and binding on all, and the higher flights of morality of which saintliness and heroism are outstanding examples. These grounds I shall enumerate at once.

1. It is important to give a special status of urgency, and to exert exceptional pressure, in those matters in which compliance with the demands of morality by all is indispensable. An army without men of heroic valor would be impoverished, but without general attention to the duties laid down in military law it would become a mere rabble. Similarly, while life in a world without its saints and heroes would be impoverished, it would only be poor and not necessarily brutish or short as when basic duties are neglected.

2. If we are to exact basic duties like debts, and censure failure, such duties must be, in ordinary circumstances, within the capacity of the ordinary man. It would be silly for us to say to ourselves, our children, and our fellow men, "This and that you and everyone else must do," if the acts in question are such that manifestly but few could bring themselves to do them, though we may ourselves resolve to try to be of that few. To take a parallel from positive law, the prohibition laws asked too much of the American people and were consequently broken systematically; and as people got used to breaking the law a general lowering of respect for the law naturally followed; it no longer seemed that a law was something that everybody could be expected to obey. Similarly in Britian the gambling laws, some of which are utterly unpractical, have fallen into contempt as a body. So, if we were to represent the heroic act of sacrificing one's life for one's comrades as a basic duty, the effect would be to lower the degree of urgency and stringency that the notion of duty does in fact possess. The basic moral code must not be in part too far beyond the capacity of the ordinary men or ordinary occasions, or a general breakdown of compliance with the moral code would be an inevitable consequence; duty would seem to be something high and unattainable, and not for "the likes of us." Admirers of the Sermon on the Mount do not in practice, and could not, treat failure to turn the other cheek and to give one's cloak also as being on all fours with breaches of the Ten Commandments, however earnestly they themselves try to live a Christian life.

3. A moral code, if it is to be a code, must be formulable, and if it is to be a code to be observed it must be formulable in rules of manageable complexity. The ordinary man has to apply and interpret this code without recourse to a Supreme Court or House of Lords. But one can have such rules only in cases in which a type of action that is reasonably easy to reconize is almost invariably desirable or undesirable, as killing is almost invariably undesirable and promise-keeping almost invariably desirable. Where no definite rule of manageable complexity can be justified, we cannot work on that moral plane on which types of action can be enjoined or condemned as duty or crime. It has no doubt often been the case that a person who has gone off to distant parts to nurse lepers has thereby done a deed of great moral worth. But such an action is not merely too far beyond average human capacity to be regarded as a duty, as was insisted in (2) above; it would be quite ridiculous for everyone, however circumstanced, to be expected to go off and nurse lepers. But it would be absurd to try to formulate complicated rules to determine in just what circumstances such an action is a duty. This same point can readily be applied to such less spectacular matters as excusing legitimate debts or nursing sick neighbors.

4. It is part of the notion of a duty that we have a right to demand compliance from others even when we are interested parties. I may demand that you keep your promises to me, tell me the truth, and do me no violence, and I may reproach you if you transgress. But however admirable the tending of strangers in sickness may be it is not a basic duty, and we are not entitled to reproach those to whom we are strangers if they do not tend us in sickness; nor can I tell you, if you fail to give me a cigarette when I have run out, that you have failed in your duty to me, however much you may subsequently reproach yourself for your meanness if you do so fail. A line must be drawn between what we can expect and demand from others and what we can merely hope for and receive with gratitude when we get it; duty falls on one side of this line, and other acts with moral value on the other, and rightly so.

5. In the case of basic moral duties we act to some extent under constraint. We have no choice but to apply pressure on each other to conform in these fundamental matters; here moral principles are like public laws rather than like private ideas. But free choice of the better course of action is always preferable to action under pressure, even when the pressure is but moral. When possible, therefore, it is better that pressure should not be applied and that there should be encouragement and commendation for performance rather than outright demands and censure in the event of nonperformance. There are no doubt degrees in this matter. Some pressure may reasonably be brought to persuade a person to go some way beyond basic duty in the direction of kindliness and forbearance, to be not merely a just man but also not too hard a man. But, while there is nothing whatever objectionable in the idea of someone's being pressed to carry out such a basic duty as promise-keeping, there is something horrifying in the thought of pressure being brought on him to perform an act of heroism. Though the man might feel himself morally called upon to do the deed, it would be a moral outrage to apply pressure on him to do such a deed as sacrificing his life for others.

These five points make it clear why I do not think that the distinction of basic duty from other acts of moral worth, which I claim to detect in ordinary moral thought, is a sign of the inferiority of our everyday moral thinking to that of the general run of moral theorists. It in no way involves anyone in acquiescing in a second best. No doubt from the agent's point of view it is imperative that he should endeavor to live up to the highest ideals of behavior that he can think of, and if an action falls within the ideal it is for him irrelevant whether or not it is a duty or some more supererogatory act. But it simply does not follow that the distinction is in every way unimportant, for it is important that we should not demand ideal conduct from others in the way in which we must demand basic morality from them, or blame them equally for failures in all fields. It is not cynicism to make the minimum positive demands upon one's fellow men; but to characterize an act as a duty is so to demand it.

Thus we may regard the imperatives of duty as prohibiting behavior that is intolerable if men are to live together in society and demanding the minimum of cooperation toward the same end; that is why we have to treat compliance as compulsory and dereliction as liable to public censure. We do not need to ask with Bentham whether pushpin is as good as poetry, with Mill whether it is better to be Socrates dissatisfied or a fool satisfied, or with Moore whether a beautiful world with no one to see it would have intrinsic worth; what is and what is not tolerable in society depends on no such nice discrimination. Utilitarians, when attempting to justify the main rules of duty in terms of a *summum bonum,* have surely invoked many different types of utilitarian justification, ranging from the avoidance of the intolerable to the fulfillment of the last detail of a most rarefied ideal.

Thus I wish to suggest that utilitarianism can best accommodate the facts to which I have drawn attention; but I have not wished to support any particular view about the supreme good or the importance of pleasure. By utilitarianism I mean only a theory that moral justification of actions must be in terms of results. We can be content to say that duty is mainly concerned with the avoidance of intolerable results, while other forms of moral behavior have more positive aims.

To summarize, I have suggested that the trichotomy of duties, indifferent actions, and wrongdoing is inadequate. There are many kinds of action that involve going beyond duty proper, saintly and heroic actions being conspicuous examples of such kinds of action. It has been my main concern to note this point and to ask moral philosophers to theorize in a way that does not tacitly deny it, as most traditional theories have. But I have also been so rash as to suggest that we may look upon our duties as basic requirements to be universally demanded as providing the only tolerable basis of social life. The higher flights of morality can then be regarded as more positive contributions that go beyond what is universally to be exacted; but while not exacted publicly they are clearly equally pressing *in foro interno* on those who are not content merely to avoid the intolerable. Whether this should be called a version of utilitarianism, as I suggest, is a matter of small moment.

Supererogation and Rules

Joel Feinberg

> *Moral philosophers tend to discriminate, explicitly or implicitly, three types of actions from the point of view of moral worth. First, they recognize actions that are a duty, or obligatory, or that we ought to perform, treating these terms as approximately synonymous; second they recognize actions that are . . . permissible . . . but not morally required of us . . . ; third . . . actions that are wrong, that we ought not to do.*

Thus writes J. O. Urmson in his article "Saints and Heroes."[1] He then argues convincingly that this traditional classification of actions is "totally inadequate to the facts of morality" because it is unable to accommodate acts of supererogatory saintliness and heroism. I shall argue in this essay that the unnamed philosophers criticized by Urmson have committed more mistakes than he notices, that these mistakes fall into a pattern, and that merely enlarging the classification of actions to include actions "in excess of duty" will not correct them.

The fundamental error committed by the philosophers criticized by Urmson is the uncritical acceptance of jural laws and institutional "house rules" as models for the understanding of all counsels of wisdom and all forms of human worth. Many institutions have rules which allow persons to accumulate extra points of credit by oversubscribing their assigned quotas of cash or work. Merely acknowledging the existence of saintly and heroic actions which go beyond duty will not help if they are understood on the model of these institutional oversubscriptions. To so understand them is to commit the same sort of mistake as that committed by philosophers who take the prohibitory rules of jural law and other institutions as a model for understanding all so-called moral rules which contain the word "ought" and thus commit themselves to identifying all meritorious actions with the performance of "duties." The fundamental error in both cases is to treat what are essentially *non*institutional facts as if they were some kind of *special* institutional facts. This is the same sort of trick as that performed by those who treat unselfish acts as a special species of selfish ones or unreal things as a special, spooky kind of real thing. In all these cases, concepts normally understood as contrasting are related as genus and species because of some superficial likeness between them. As a result, we are led into paradoxes or are arbitrarily deprived of the tools for saying what we wish to say.

I shall consider in this essay some paradoxical consequences of interpreting counsels of wisdom and the word "ought" on the model of prohibitory rules and the word "duty," and of treating nonduties such as simple favors and heroic self-denials on the model of institutional oversubscriptions.

I

First, consider how the word "ought" differs from the word "duty." Suppose a stranger approaches me on a street corner and politely asks me for a match. Ought I to give him one? I think most people would agree that I should, and that any reasonable man of good will would, offer the stranger a match. Perhaps a truly virtuous man would do more than that. He would be friendly, reply with a cheerful smile, and might even volunteer to light the stranger's cigarette.

Now suppose that Jones is on the street corner and another stranger politely requests a light from him. Jones is in a sour mood this morning, and even normally he does not enjoy encounters with strangers. He brusquely refuses to give the stranger a match. I think we can agree that Jones's behavior on the street corner does not constitute an ideal for human conduct under such circumstances; that it is not what a perfectly virtuous man would have done; that it was not what Jones ought to have done.

If we reproach Jones, however, for his uncivil treatment of the stranger, he may present us with a vigorous self-defense. "Perhaps I was not civil," he might admit, "but surely I was under no *obligation* to give a match to that man. Who is he to me? He had

---

[1] In A. I. Melden (ed.), *Essays in Moral Philosophy* (Seattle: University of Washington Press, 1958), 198.

no *claim* on me; he has no authority to *command* any performance from me; I don't *owe* him anything. It may be nice to do favors for people; but a favor, by definition, is nothing that we are legally or morally *required* to do. I am an honorable man. In this instance I did not fail to honor a commitment; neither did I fail to discharge an obligation, moral or legal; nor did I break any rule, of man or God.[2] You have, therefore, no right to reproach me."

Jones's defense makes me think no better of him. Still, from a certain legal-like point of view, it appears perfectly cogent. Everything Jones said in his own defense was true. The moral I draw from this tale is that there are some actions which it would be desirable for a person to do and which, indeed, he *ought* to do, even though they are actions he is under no *obligation* and has no *duty* to do. It follows logically that to say that someone has a duty or an obligation to do X is not simply another way of saying that he ought to do X.[3]

We speak of duties and obligations in three different connections. First, there are actions required by laws and by authoritative command. These can be called "duties of obedience." Second, there are the assigned tasks which "attach" to stations, offices, jobs, and roles, which for some reason seem better named by the word "duty" than by the word "obligation." Third, there are those actions to which we voluntarily commit ourselves by making promises, borrowing money, making appointments, and so on. When we commit ourselves, we put ourselves "under an obligation" ("duty" seems to fit less comfortably here) to some assignable person or persons to behave in the agreed-upon way; and we do this by utilizing certain social contrivances or techniques designed for just this purpose. When a person invokes these procedures, he creates his own "artificial chains," dons them, and hands the key to the other. This act "binds" or "ties" him to the agreed-upon behavior and give the other the authority to require it of him. The other can, if he chooses, release him from his chains, or he can, in Mill's much quoted words, exact performance from him "as one exacts a debt."[4]

All duties and obligations, whether imposed by authoritative injunctions and prohibitions, acquired through accepting or inheriting an office, job, or role, or voluntarily incurred through promises and other contractual agreements, share the common character of being *required;* and this in turn, while it may involve more than coercion or pressure, rarely involves less. In the legal sense, to have a duty or an obligation is to be subject to civil liability or criminal punishment for nonperformance. In general, the law requries citizens to discharge their legal duties *or else* face up to the unpleasant legal consequences.[5] Similarly, it follows from the rules of nonjural institu-

---

[2]One could argue that God commands us to do favors for one another. But that would be to regard such actions as *obligatory,* and it is logically contradictory for one and the same act to be both required and freely given, both a duty and a favor.

[3]Cf. C. H. Whiteley's very important article "On Duties," *Proceedings of the Aristotelian Society,* 53 (1952/53); and also H. L. A. Hart's "Legal and Moral Obligation," in Melden (ed.), *op. cit.,* 82–108.

[4]John Stuart Mill, *Utilitarianism* (Indianapolis: The Bobbs-Merrill Co., 1948), 60.

[5]An interesting logical consequence of the point that obligations are liabilities is that one can have a (real) obligation even though one is incapable of discharing it. Certain disabilities which make it impossible for a person to discharge his obligation do not prevent others from exacting payment from him for his omission. So, for example, in civil law an insane person can be held liable for his torts. Thomas M. Cooley, in his *A Treatise on the Law of Torts,* ed. D. Avery Haggard, 4th edn. (Chicago: Callaghan & Co., 1932), 188, writes that this rule "imposes upon [insane persons] an *obligation* to observe the same care and precautions respecting the rights of others that the law demands of one in the full possession of his faculties" (my italics). This may be morally absurd, as Cooley argues, but it is not *logically absurd.*

tions (house rules) that a member who does not pay his dues can be dropped; an employee who fails to perform the duties of his job is liable to be fired; a negligent bureaucrat is liable to demotion, a wayward student to flunking, a disobedient soldier to court-martial.

That liability for failure to perform is an essential part of what we mean by "duty," when we talk of the duties of stations and positions, is suggested by our willingness to substitute in many contexts the word "responsibility" for the word "duty." To be assigned a task or a job in some organization is to be made responsible (answerable, accountable) for its performance. Without this associated accountability, I submit, we should be unwilling to speak of "the job" as involving any *duties* at all.

The point holds also for obligations of commitment. Reneging on a promise, without valid excuse, is understood by all parties to involve forfeiture of trust. It is impossible to conceive of promises being "binding" in a world in which continued failure to keep them did nothing at all to weaken confidence and where the reneger is trusted over and over again to make new agreements. Thus commitments, as the metaphor of the binding chains suggests, also involve, in an essential way, a coercive element.

It is clear that, if all duties are acts which are required, then there are meritorious acts, such as favors, which are not the performance of duty, for not all good deeds are requitals or repayments or fulfillments of bargains. Neither are the remainder all acts of obedience and performances of one's job. The man who has been stationed on the street corner by a match company and assigned the task of distributing free samples of its product has a duty to give the stranger a match. Jones and I do not. . . .

II

What is it to go "beyond the limits of one's duty?" Urmson uses this and a like expression in his definition of both saintly and heroic actions, and elsewhere he speaks of actions which "exceed the demands of duty." There are at least two distinct ways of interpreting such phrases as "above," "beyond," "more than," and "in excess of" duty. First of all, there is a straightforwardly quantitative interpretation. A janitor has a duty to spend eight hours cleaning his employer's floors. He works ten hours for eight hours' pay. Duty required eight hours; he did his duty and then some and thus, in a perfectly intelligible sense, did "more than" his duty. Furthermore, in respect to this and similar oversubscriptions, we can specify exactly by *how much,* as measured in additive units, the performance exceeded duty. If the state taxes a patriotic citizen one hundred dollars and he pays two hundred dollars, intending the balance as a gift, then the citizen has exceeded his duty by exactly one hundred dollars. This is not a controversial judgment of moral philosophy. It is simply a truth of arithmetic.

Doing a favor is not similarly commensurable with duty. If I had given the stranger two matches, I would not have been going "beyond duty" in the present sense, for I had no duty to give him one match. If giving him no matches would not be to fall one match "below" what duty requires, then giving him two matches would not be to go one match "beyond" the demands of duty. Neither am I behaving supererogatorily when I give the stranger one match, for I have no duty to give him any number of matches, one or zero. A favor, then, is neither a duty nor (in the present sense) more than a duty. Rather, it is simply *other* than a duty and properly located on an altogether different scale than that occupied jointly by duties, derelictions, and oversubscriptions. A favor can be, but is not *always*, the performance of a duty plus more of the same; often it is an action where *none* is required, rather than a contribution of more than is required.

There are some favors, however, which are not only *other* than duty but, in some sense, *more* than duty. It would be an exaggeration to describe my act of offering the stranger a match as "above and beyond the call of duty," but if I spend three long hard days away from my own work helping a friend paint his house, it would seem an understatement to describe that performance as a mere favor. Still other actions in the service of others are, like favors, meritorious and not required by duty, and yet so profoundly different from the mere offering of a match that we would not call them favors at all, and for roughly the same kind of reason that we would not call a giant redwood a sapling. Urmson's example of "the doctor who, no differently situated from countless other doctors in other places, volunteers to join the depleted medical forces in [a plague-stricken] city" seems to demand a different interpretation of the phrase "more than duty." Unlike the hard-working janitor and the patriotic taxpayer, Urmson's heroic doctor is not simply doing his "duty plus more of the same." He does not travel a definite number of miles more than the total required by duty; neither does he treat a definite number of patients more than duty requires, nor a definite number of hours more than is necessary, at the loss of a definite number of dollars in excess of what is obligatory. The point is, he has no duty to travel one step toward the plague-stricken city or to treat one single victim in it. The whole of his duty as a doctor is to continue treating the patients who constitute his own comfortable and remunerative practice. Still, if he gives all of this up and, at great inconvenience and danger, volunteers to help the suffering in a distant city, his action surely exceeds, in some sense, the requirements of duty.

In what way does the doctor's act "exceed" duty? It seems clear that the "excessive" element in his action is *sacrifice*.[6] His action cost him something, or at any rate it appeared likely to cost him something at the time he undertook it. In volunteering to help the unfortunate in a distant city, he made himself liable to great inconvenience and hardship, and he incurred the risk of loss of health and even life. But if probable sacrifice is the "excessive" element, what does it exceed? Certainly not the sacrifice involved in every actual duty. Consider Urmson's other doctor whose residence and practice are in the stricken city and who stands by his post working round the clock to help the sick, exposing himself to the contagion at every turn. He is making precisely the same sacrifice as his heroic colleague from the distant city, yet he is only doing his duty.

The sacrificial element in supererogatory actions, then, does not necessarily exceed that in the performance of a duty; rather, what it exceeds is the sacrifice *normally* involved in the doing of a duty. A point frequently overlooked by philosophers who have been influenced by Kant is that performances of duties are more often than not routine or habitual, even pleasant, activities. Many a debt is repaid cheerfully, and often enough vocational requirements are performed by men who whistle while they work. Of course, if a man's inclinations *always and necessarily* corresponded with the actions demanded of him, then, as Kant pointed out, the concept of duty would not apply to him. It would be absurd to say of such a person: "It is impossible for him not to do it, but he had better do it or else." Human beings are not "holy wills," and consequently they do have duties; but it does not follow that duty is always or even often

---

[6]In the case of saintly and other supererogatory actions, the excessive element may be will-power or self-denial. See Urmson, *op.cit.,* 200–204. I shall restrict my attention here to actions of a "heroic" character.

onerous, or that it is engaged in a perpetual internal cold war with inclination. An undertaking that is "beyond duty" in this second sense, then, is one which has at least the following two characteristics: (1) it is not itself a duty; and (2) it exceeds, in the sacrifice it seems likely to require, that normally involved in the performance of duties.

That these two necessary conditions are not sufficient, however, can be shown by examples of actions which satisfy them but which nevertheless we should be extremely reluctant to label "above and beyond the call of duty." The greedy adventurer who sets off on an arduous journey into the heart of the jungle, determined to brave all dangers in order to find a buried treasure, is certainly not merely doing his duty or even his "duty plus"; nor is he even likely to believe he is. The dedicated crackpot who nearly freezes to death trying to convert the indifferent Eskimos to Caribbean voodooism may believe he is only doing his duty, but we know better. The embittered misanthrope who sacrifices his own life to the police in the process of machine-gunning as many passersby as he can is surely not discharging a duty thereby. In each of these examples, the agent does something other than his duty and does it at a much greater cost than duty normally involves; and yet we should be loath to say of any of the three that he did "more than duty required." The reason, I think, is plain. We do not regard either of the first two actions as particularly meritorious, and the third action, while brave and self-sacrificing, is actually reprehensible. We praise an act when we call it "more than a duty," and none of these examples seems praiseworthy. The third necessary condition of an action that exceeds duty in the second sense, then, is praiseworthiness or, in Urmson's phrase, "moral worth"; and a supererogatory act in this sense is, therefore, a *meritorious, abnormally risky nonduty*.

When we come, as we naturally must at this point, to the question of what makes an action meritorious, we encounter straight off a difficulty for Urmson's assumption that, in distinguishing duties and "more than duties," he is classifying actions according to their "moral worth." Urmson's final view seems to be as follows: There are several distinct ways in which an action can acquire moral worth, positive or negative. If it does what is wrong or prohibited, it has negative worth; if it does what is obligatory or required, it achieves positive merit; and if it goes "beyond duty," in the manner of saintly and heroic actions, for example, then also it acquires moral worth, though not necessarily more merit than some obligatory actions, which can be very demanding indeed. But when we get around to examining Urmson's examples of actions in excess of duty, such as the heroic doctor's, we find that, instead of acquiring worth by being saintly or heroic, they are not correctly called "saintly" or "heroic" at all unless they are already worthy or meritorious on some other ground. And of course that other ground cannot be their requiredness, because *ex hypothesi* they are nonduties. It follows that Urmson's addition of actions in excess of duty to the traditional classification of prohibited, permissible, and obligatory actions does very little, if anything, to make it more adequate as a classification of actions "from the point of view of moral worth."

The point suggested by our examples, however, is a more radical one, namely, that moral worth has no necessary connection with any of the categories in Urmson's expanded classificaiton. Performances of duties can proceed from evil motives; "forbidden" actions can be prompted by the highest motives. And if supererogatory actions are understood on the "duty plus" model, a whole range of meritorious conduct finds no place in the classification. Meritorious, abnormally risky nonduties, if they are to be classified on such a scale, have only one proper pigeonhole. They are not duties; they are not derelictions; they are not oversubscriptions. They are simply "permitted."

When we compare them with other actions in that drab category, it becomes clear that it is not their character *qua* "permitted" that makes them morally worthy.[7]

III

Each of the two kinds of supererogation—namely, "oversubscription," or "duty plus," and "meritorious nonduty"—fits into its own distinctive complex of concepts, including a distinct way of conceiving personal merit and a special kind of moral rule. One complex, that in which "oversubscription" is at home, I shall call institutional or legal-like and the other (to avoid begging any questions) simply noninstitutional or non-legal-like. Which, if either, of these is "distinctively moral" is a question to be considered (but not very seriously) in the final section of the essay.

The "institutional complex" consists of (1) essentially jural or institutionally connected rules which enjoin, permit, and prohibit, and thus impose duties and obligations, and (2) other rules which prescribe procedures for determining merits and demerits. In such institutions as schools, military units, corporations, and the like, in which behavior is in part governed by such rules and regulations, a soldier, or a student, or a janitor can acquire merit in two ways: by consistent performance of duty and by accumulating extra "bonus-points" by doing "duty plus." Similarly, he can incur demerits not only by complete disobedience of the regulations (that is, by nonperformance of duty) but also by failing by some measurable amount to come up to the requirements of duty. The latter failures, or partial derelictions, can be placed on the same scale as dutiful performance and "duty plus." Gross derelictions of duty render ān employee liable to sacking; partial derelictions subject him to demerits on his work record analogous to the liabilities or debits on his bank account when it is overdrawn. Similarly, under some rules, employees and other officeholders can store up assets on their accounts to guard against unexpected expenditures of credit. A truly worthy officeholder never goes into the red; he keeps a meritorious work record. The most deserving of all, through the diligent accumulations of "surplus" credits, become qualified for rewards and promotions.

On the other hand, in the nonlegal-like, noninstitutional complex, there is a quite different conception of personal merit and a quite distinct sort of rule. Often we are concerned with a person's merit or worth, not merely in respect to this or that job or office, skill, or function, but "in the last analysis," *all things considered*. A man may have a very small balance in his bank account, a smaller balance of good will in his place of employment, and through absentmindedness an unenviable driver's record; but, for all of that, in the final appraisal he may be deemed an unusually worthy man, even a paragon of human excellence. Overall worth as a man is not simply some computable function of one's various records and accounts. Nor is final human worth to be identified completely with the virtues of trustworthiness and obedience. A "good man all things considered" is not simply the man who is *good at* doing his duties and accumulating points, as a good ballplayer is good at making hits and avoiding errors. He will also be a man with a hearty and subtle sense of humor, tact and social sensitivity, warmth, hardiness, and perhaps a redeeming sense of his own absurdity.

In making a final appraisal of a man, we must compare not only his mutually

---

[7]For suggestive discussions of moral worth, see W. D. Ross, *The Right and the Good* (Oxford: Clarendon Press, 1930), 4–7, 155–175, and *Foundations of Ethics* (Oxford: Clarendon Press, 1939), 290–311.

comparable talents and records but also parts of his character and history which are mutually incommensurable. Needless to say, there can be no magical formula for doing this. There can be no simple answer, for example, to the question of whether Green's benevolent infidelity ranks above or below Brown's faithful malevolence. And we can no more tote up a man's final score in respect to excellence than we can calculate his overall "quantitativeness" by multiplying his age by his weight by his pulse beat by the number of his blood relations.

Final worth is not wholly determined, then, by the rules that confer duties and prescribe ways of accumulating debits and credits; but it is related, in an indirect way, to rules of a quite different sort. We have seen that the word "ought" can be used to prescribe or give advice in particular cases. Singular pieces of advice, such as "You ought to keep your promise in this case," are often generalized into such principles as "you ought to keep your promises (generally)," "You ought to be kind," and "You ought to do favors." There is no harm in calling statements of generalized advice "rules"; indeed, it is consonant with usage to do so. But it is important to notice that these rules do not enjoin, prohibit, or confer obligations and duties. They are rules in a quite different sense, better named "maxims" or "precepts" than "injunctions" or "commands." Perhaps "counsels of wisdom" or "rules of advice" would be the most appropriate designations, since these names suggest, quite correctly, that these are rules of thumb rather than "laws" on some jural or institutional model.

Counsels of wisdom guide the wise man's conduct and sometimes, also, that of the fool; for to have the right precepts without knowing how to apply them in puzzling circumstances or where they come into conflict is to be merely sententious, not wise. The better part of wisdom is a kind of knack or flair which cannot be bottled up in simple formulas. A man is on his own when he must decide whether to stick safely by his station or do the "meritorious, abnormally risky nonduty," or whether to honor his duty or an opposing commitment of a different order—whether to stay with Mother or join the Free French forces. There are, unfortunately, no strict superrules for applying counsels of wisdom in such situations and no simple commands to obey. If it is a matter of being conscientious or not, then by all means be conscientious. But of what use is this good advice if it is your conscience itself which is confused?

In the noninstitutional setting in which we must make final, overall appraisals and final, all-things-considered decisions and prescriptions, rules are at best only a rough guide. There are no very reliable rules either for comparing incommensurable virtues and vices or for getting from sound counsels of wisdom to a wise piece of singular advice or a wise decision. In the institutional realm these appraisals and decisions, or rather their analogues, have been made artificially simple. A man's worth as a ballplayer is determined by the averages in his record; his worth as a politician by the tally at the polls; his worth as a bureaucrat, or executive officeholder, by his balance of credits and debits, merits and demerits, oversubscriptions and derelictions, as determined by the rules of his institution. And while the janitor's problem of knowing what in the final analysis, all things considered, he *ought* to do, can on occasion be as difficult as anyone else's, he need rarely have any doubt about what his duties and obligations are. For to know his duties, he need not consider "all things," but only the orders of his boss, the conditions of his employment, his voluntary commitment, his social roles, and the civil law. These are things he can look up. But if they conflict, and he wishes to know what he *ought* to do, he may not be able to look that up quite as easily.

IV

Which facts are the "facts of morality?" Some writers identify the moral realm with what I have called the nonjural, noninstitutional complex. For these writers, a man's worth, all things considered, is by definition his *moral worth;* and what he ought to do in the last analysis, all things considered, is what he *morally* ought to do; and *all* relevant counsels of wisdom, not merely those concerned with duties and obligations, are *moral rules.* On the other hand, many writers adopt the very opposite procedure, reserving the moral label for the realm of duties, commands, and prohibitory rules. Thus Santayana, to pick just one of many possible examples, *identifies* the moral with the legal-like, especially with the concept of duty, and then distinguishes it from the wider genus of "values."[8] Still a third way of making the distinction is to treat morality as a genus with legal-like and nonlegal-like species. H. L. A. Hart, for example, speaks alternatively to two "sectors," "scales," or "segments" within the "field" of morality.[9]

I have no intention of deciding which of these three ways of marking the distinction between the two complexes is the "correct" one. Indeed, that seems to me to be a verbal problem and one which, in any case, is hopelessly tangled. The word "moral," reflecting a variety of disparate and contrary uses in the technical literature of law, theology, and philosophy, is not simply ambiguous, but ambiguous in such an extraordinary way that some of its senses are antonyms.[10]

I wish here only to insist that the two realms I have distinguished be kept distinct, whichever, if either, is to be called the distinctively "moral" realm. There is a widespread tendency, which I think even Urmson has not altogether avoided, to mark the distinction by blowing up the institutional side to incorporate the other. A main task of moral philosophy, according to many philosophers, is to catalogue the duties of men. Since this is much too simple a task if we confine our attention to duties in the ordinary practice- and institution-connected sense, and since, moreover, moral philosophers wish to concern themselves with other important matters, such as what to do when duties conflict, and whether and when we should perform favors and difficult, meritorious nonduties, they expand the sense of "duty" to incude all that is normally contrasted with it. Thus, in addition to the duties of fathers, citizens, club members, janitors, and promisers, there are said to be duties of man *qua* man, which on examination turn out to be those acts of beneficence, service, and gratitude which come to have the meaning they do by being contrasted with duty. Similarly, since janitors and fathers derive their own peculiar merits from doing their respective jobs well, and since these merits are not to be identified with their overall human worth, it is thought that there must be some special job of a man as such, so that being good at that job confers final, overall worth.

---

[8]George Santayana, "The Philosophy of Bertrand Russell," *Winds of Doctrine* (London: J. M. Dent & Sons, 1940), 138. The "unregenerate naturalist," he writes, is "propitiated" by Russell's kind of intuitionism because it implies that "ethics is concerned with the economy of all values and not with 'moral' goods only, or with duty...."

[9]*Op.cit.,* 83.

[10]On the one hand, for example, "moral" has the ring of supreme authority, and on the other, it still carries its original sense of informal "customs" or "ways." Aristotle *contrasted* the moral with the intellectual; Kant *identified* it with the *rational.* Lawyers use it to refer, on the one hand, to loose and informal agreements and arrangements beneath the official attention of the law and, on the other hand, to an ultimate standard for appraising the law.

Furthermore, in each case the noninstitutional is reinterpreted as the special institutional. Hence those counsels of wisdom which could serve a man even in an institutionless state of nature, and in some respects even if he were the last man on earth, are treated as if they were the company rules of some shadowy moral corporation or the statutes of a ghostly moral State. For example, counsels of wisdom, which as nonbinding rules of thumb are distinct in kind from jural laws and house rules, are called "moral laws" and regarded simply as a special eccentric species of jural law, or as a kind of moral house rule; and the counsels to do meritorious acts which are not duties are said by these philosophers to impose special duties, which, since they seem to differ in all essential respects from garden-variety duties, are called "duties of imperfect obligation." These philosophical inventions are devices for blurring the distinction they were meant to explicate.

The concept of supererogation too can contribute in this way to conceptual confusion. It remains only to illustrate how this can happen. Probably the most familiar kind of supererogation is that which I have already called "oversubscription." Institutional rules of various kinds allow persons to accumulate credit surpluses to guard against future deficiencies and also to oversubscribe assigned quotas to make up for earlier undersubscriptions of one's own or, in some cases, undersubscriptions of other persons. Those philosophers deserve our gratitude who call our attention to these rules and especially to the inability of the traditional threefold classification to do full justice to their complexity. But the ever present danger of taking the institutional model too seriously lurks here as well. The trap is set. First, the unsuspecting philosopher takes the familiar as a model for understanding the relatively unfamiliar, the institutional for the noninstitutional, the janitor or the taxpayer for the heroic doctor. Then he allows the institutional model to become inflated to the point where it absorbs its noninstitutional opposite as an eccentric subspecies of itself. Thus the philosopher's natural partiality for the familiar leads to a distinctive sort of conceptual aggression. As a consequence of his failure to observe conceptual boundary lines, a contrast essential to both distinguished concepts disappears. The effects here as elsewhere are misleading and bizarre.

The unwary philosopher posits a special moral account or record corresponding to a person's bank account or work record. Procedures are assumed whereby moral agents can accumulate moral debits and credits through undersubscribing and oversubscribing their assigned moral "quotas" or duties. Then, having made this tidy Proscrustean bed, the philosopher is obliged to try to jam into it the unsolicited services, gifts, and favors, the saintly and heroic feats, the meritorious, abnormally risky nonduties.

Virtues and Vices

Philippa Foot

I

For many years the subject of the virtues and vices was strangely neglected by moralists working within the school of analytic philosophy. The tacitly accepted opinion was that a study of the topic would form no part of the fundamental work of ethics; and since this opinion was apparently shared by philosophers such as Hume, Kant, Mill, G. E. Moore, W. D. Ross, and H. A. Prichard, from whom contemporary moral philosophy has mostly been derived, perhaps the neglect was not so surprising after all. However that may be, things have recently been changing. During the past ten or fifteen years several philosophers have turned their attention to the subject; notably G. H. von Wright and Peter Geach. Von Wright devoted a not at all perfunctory chapter to the virtues in his book *The Varieties of Goodness*[1] published in 1963, and Peter Geach's book called *The Virtues*[2] appeared in 1977. Meanwhile a number of interesting articles on the topic have come out in the journals.

In spite of this recent work, it is best when considering the virtues and vices to go back to Aristotle and Aquinas. I myself have found Plato less helpful, because the individual virtues and vices are not so clearly or consistently distinguished in his work. It is certain, in any case, that the most systematic account is found in Aristotle, and in the blending of Aristotelian and Christian philosophy found in St. Thomas. By and large Aquinas followed Aristotle—sometimes even heroically—where Aristotle gave an opinion, and where St. Thomas is on his own, as in developing the doctrine of the theological virtues of faith, hope and charity, and in his theocentric doctrine of happiness, he still uses an Aristotelian framework where he can: as for instance in speaking of happiness as man's last end. However, there are different emphases and new elements in Aquina's ethics: often he works things out in far more detail than Aristotle did, and it is possible to learn a great deal from Aquinas that one could not have got from Aristotle. It is my opinion that the *Summa Theologica* is one of the best sources we have for moral philosophy, and moreover that St. Thomas's ethical writings are as useful to the atheist as to the Catholic or other Christian believer.

There is, however, one minor obstacle to be overcome when one goes back to Aristotle and Aquinas for help in constructing a theory of virtues, namely a lack of coincidence between their terminology and our own. For when we talk about the virtues we are not taking as our subject everything to which Aristotle gave the name *aretē* or Aquinas *virtus,* and consequently not everything called a virtue in translations of these authors. "The virtues" to us are the moral virtues whereas *aretē* and *virtus* refer also to arts, and even to excellences of the speculative intellect whose domain is theory rather than practice. And to make things more confusing we find some dispositions called moral virtues in translations from the Greek and Latin, although the class of virtues that Aristotle calls *aretē ēthikai* and Aquinas *virtutes morales* does not exactly cor-

[1]G. H. von Wright, *The Varieties of Goodness* (London, 1963).
[2]Peter Geach, *The Virtues* (Cambridge, 1977).

respond with our class of moral virtues. For us there are four cardinal moral virtues: courage, temperance, wisdom and justice. But Aristotle and Aquinas call only three of these virtues moral virtues; practical wisdom (Aristotle's *phronēsis* and Aquinas's *prudentia*) they class with the intellectual virtues, though they point out the close connexions between practical wisdom and what they call moral virtues; and sometimes they even use *aretē* and *virtus* very much as we use "virtue".

I will come back to Aristotle and Aquinas, and shall indeed refer to them frequently in this paper. But I want to start by making some remarks, admittedly fragmentary, about the concept of a moral virtue as we understand the idea.

First of all it seems clear that virtues are, in some general way, beneficial. Human beings do not get on well without them. Nobody can get on well if he lacks courage, and does not have some measure of temperance and wisdom, while communities where justice and charity are lacking are apt to be wretched places to live, as Russia was under the Stalinist terror, or Sicily under the Mafia. But now we must ask to whom the benefit goes, whether to the man who has the virtue or rather to those who have to do with him? In the case of some of the virtues the answer seems clear. Courage, temperance and wisdom benefit both the man who has these dispositions and other people as well; and moral failings such as pride, vanity, worldliness, and avarice harm both their possessor and others, though chiefly perhaps the former. But what about the virtues of charity and justice? These are directly concerned with the welfare of others, and with what is owed to them; and since each may require sacrifice of interest on the part of the virtuous man both may seem to be deleterious to their possessor and beneficial to others. Whether in fact it is so has, of course, been a matter of controversy since Plato's time or earlier. It is a reasonable opinion that on the whole a man is better off for being charitable and just, but this is not to say that circumstances may not arise in which he will have to sacrifice everything for charity or justice.

Nor is this the only problem about the relation between virtue and human good. For one very difficult question concerns the relation between justice and the common good. Justice, in the wide sense in which it is understood in discussions of the cardinal virtues, and in this paper, has to do with that to which someone has a right—that which he is owed in respect of non-interference and positive service—and rights may stand in the way of the pursuit of the common good. Or so at least it seems to those who reject utilitarian doctrines. This dispute cannot be settled here, but I shall treat justice as a virtue independent of charity, and standing as a possible limit on the scope of that virtue.

Let us say then, leaving unsolved problems behind us, that virtues are in general beneficial characteristics, and indeed ones that a human being needs to have, for his own sake and that of his fellows. This will not, however, take us far towards a definition of a virtue, since there are many other qualities of a man that may be similarly beneficial, as for instance bodily characteristics such as health and physical strength, and mental powers such as those of memory and concentration. What is it, we must ask, that differentiates virtues from such things?

As a first approximation to an answer we might say that while health and strength are excellences of the body, and memory and concentration of the mind, it is the will that is good in a man of virtue. But this suggestion is worth only as much as the explanation that follows it. What might we mean by saying that virtue belongs to the will?

In the first place we observe that it is primarily by his intentions that a man's moral dispositions are judged. If he does something unintentionally this is usually irrelevant to our estimate of his virtue. But of course this thesis must be qualified, because failures in performance rather than intention may show a lack of virtue. This will be so when, for instance, one man brings harm to another without realising he is doing it, but where his ignorance is itself culpable. Sometimes in such cases there will be a previous act or omission to which we can point as the source of the ignorance. Charity requires that we take care to find out how to render assistance where we are likely to be called on to do so, and thus, for example, it is contrary to charity to fail to find out about elementary first aid. But in an interesting class of cases in which it seems again to be performance rather than intention that counts in judging a man's virtue there is no possibility of shifting the judgement to previous intentions. For sometimes one man succeeds where another fails not because there is some specific difference in their previous conduct but rather because his heart lies in a different place; and the disposition of the heart is part of virtue.

Thus it seems right to attribute a kind of moral failing to some deeply discouraging and debilitating people who say, without lying, that they mean to be helpful; and on the other side to see virtue *par excellence* in one who is prompt and resourceful in doing good. In his novel *A Single Pebble* John Hersey describes such a man, speaking of a rescue in a swift flowing river:

> It was the head tracker's marvellous swift response that captured my admiration at first, his split second solicitousness when he heard a cry of pain, his finding in mid-air, as it were, the only way to save the injured boy. But there was more to it than that. His action, which could not have been mulled over in his mind, showed a deep, instinctive love of life, a compassion, an optimism, which made me feel very good . . .

What this suggests is that a man's virtue may be judged by his innermost desires as well as by his intentions; and this fits with our idea that a virtue such as generosity lies as much in someone's attitudes as in his actions. Pleasure in the good fortune of others is, one thinks, the sign of a generous spirit; and small reactions of pleasure and displeasure often the surest signs of a man's moral disposition.

None of this shows that it is wrong to think of virtues as belonging to the will; what it does show is that "will" must here be understood in its widest sense, to cover what is wished for as well as what is sought.

A different set of considerations will, however, force us to give up any simple statement about the relation between virtue and will, and these considerations have to do with the virtue of wisdom. Practical wisdom, we said, was counted by Aristotle among the intellectual virtues, and while our *wisdom* is not quite the same as *phronēsis* or *prudentia* it too might seem to belong to the intellect rather than the will. Is not wisdom a matter of knowledge, and how can knowledge be a matter of intention or desire? The answer is that it isn't, so that there is good reason for thinking of wisdom as an intellectual virtue. But on the other hand wisdom has special connexions with the will, meeting it at more than one point.

In order to get this rather complex picture in focus we must pause for a little and ask what it is that we ourselves understand by wisdom: what the wise man knows and what he does. Wisdom, as I see it, has two parts. In the first place the wise man knows the means to certain good ends; and secondly he knows how much particular ends are worth. Wisdom in its first part is relatively easy to understand. It seems that there are some ends belonging to human life in general rather than to particular skills such as medicine or boatbuilding, ends having to do with such matters as friendship, marriage, the bringing up of children, or the choice of ways of life; and it seems that knowledge of how to act well in these matters belongs to some people but not to others. We call those who have this knowledge wise, while those who do not have it are seen as lacking wisdom. So, as both Aristotle and Aquinas insisted, wisdom is to be contrasted with cleverness because cleverness is the ability to take the right steps to any end, whereas wisdom is related only to good ends, and to human life in general rather than to the ends of particular arts.

Moreover, we should add, there belongs to wisdom only that part of knowledge which is within the reach of any ordinary adult human being: knowledge that can be acquired only by someone who is clever or who has access to special training is not counted as part of wisdom, and would not be so counted even if it could serve the ends that wisdom serves. It is therefore quite wrong to suggest that wisdom cannot be a moral virtue because virtue must be within the reach of anyone who really wants it and some people are too stupid to be anything but ignorant even about the most fundamental matters of human life. Some people are wise without being at all clever or well informed: they make good decisions and they know, as we say, "what's what."

In short wisdom, in what we called its first part, is connected with the will in the following ways. To begin with it presupposes good ends: the man who is wise does not merely know *how* to do good things such as looking after his children well, or strengthening someone in trouble, but must also want to do them. And then wisdom, in so far as it consists of knowledge which anyone can gain in the course of an ordinary life, is available to anyone who really wants it. As Aquinas put it, it belongs "to a power under the direction of the will."[3]

The second part of wisdom, which has to do with values, is much harder to describe, because here we meet ideas which are curiously elusive, such as the thought that some pursuits are more worthwhile than others, and some matters trivial and some important in human life. Since it makes good sense to say that most men waste a lot of their lives in ardent pursuit of what is trivial and unimportant it is not possible to explain the important and the trivial in terms of the amount of attention given to different subjects by the average man. But I have never seen, or been able to think out, a true account of this matter, and I believe that a complete account of wisdom, and of certain other virtues and vices must wait until this gap can be filled. What we can see is that one of the things a wise man knows and a foolish man does not is that such things as social position, and wealth, and the good opinion of the world, are too dearly bought at the cost of health or friendship or family ties. So we may say that a man who lacks wisdom "has false values," and that vices such as vanity and worldliness and avarice are contrary to wisdom in a special way. There is always an element of false judgement about these vices, since the man who is vain for instance sees admiration as more important than it is, while the worldly man is apt to see the good life as one of wealth and power. Adapting Aristotle's distinction between the weak-willed man (the akratēs) who follows pleasure though he knows, in some sense, that he should not, and the licentious man (the akolastos) who sees the life of pleasure as the good life,[4]

---

[3] Aquinas, *Summa Theologica,* 1a2ae Q.56 a.3.
[4] Aristotle, *Nicomachean Ethics,* especially bk. VII.

we may say that moral failings such as these are never purely "akratic". It is true that a man may criticise himself for his worldliness or vanity or love of money, but then it is his values that are the subject of his criticism.

Wisdom in this second part is, therefore, partly to be described in terms of apprehension, and even judgement, but since it has to do with a man's attachments it also characterises his will.

The idea that virtues belong to the will, and that this helps to distinguish them from such things as bodily strength or intellectual ability has, then, survived the consideration of the virtue of wisdom, albeit in a fairly complex and slightly attenuated form. And we shall find this idea useful again if we turn to another important distinction that must be made, namely that between virtues and other practical excellences such as arts and skills.

Aristotle has sometimes been accused, for instance by von Wright, of failing to see how different virtues are from arts or skills;[5] but in fact one finds, among the many things that Aristotle and Aquinas say about this difference, the observation that seems to go the heart of the matter. In the matter of arts and skills, they say, voluntary error is preferable to involuntary error, while in the matter of virtues (what we call virtues) it is the reverse.[6] The last part of the thesis is actually rather hard to interpret, because it is not clear what is meant by the idea of involuntary viciousness. But we can leave this aside and still have all we need in order to distinguish arts or skills from virtues. If we think, for instance, of someone who deliberately makes a spelling mistake (perhaps when writing on the blackboard in order to explain this particular point) we see that this does not in any way count against his skill as a speller: "I did it deliberately" rebuts an accusation of this kind. And what we can say without running into any difficulties is that there is no comparable rebuttal in the case of an accusation relating to lack of virtue. If a man acts unjustly or uncharitably, or in a cowardly or intemperate manner, "I did it deliberately" cannot on any interpretation lead to exculpation. So, we may say, a virtue is not, like a skill or an art, a mere capacity: it must actually engage the will.

II

I shall now turn to another thesis about the virtues, which I might express by saying that they are *corrective,* each one standing at a point at which there is some temptation to be resisted or deficiency of motivation to be made good. As Aristotle put it, virtues are about what is difficult for men, and I want to see in what sense this is true, and then to consider a problem in Kant's moral philosophy in the light of what has been said.

Let us first think about courage and temperance.

Aquinas contrasted these virtues with justice in the following respect. Justice was concerned with operations, and courage and temperance with passions.[7] What he meant by this seems to have been, primarily, that the man of courage does not fear immoderately nor the man of temperance have immoderate desires for pleasure, and that there was no corresponding moderation of a passion implied in the idea of justice. This particular account of courage and temperance might be disputed on the ground that a man's courage is measured by his action and not by anything as uncon-

[5]von Wright, op. cit. chapter VIII.
[6]Aristotle, op.cit. 1140 b 22–25. Aquinas op. cit. 1a2ae Q.57 a.4.
[7]Rightly or wrongly Aquinas attributed this doctrine to Aristotle. See op. cit. 1a2ae q.60 a.2.

trollable as fear; and similarly that the temperate man who must on occasion refuse pleasures need not *desire* them any less than the intemperate man. Be that as it may (and something will be said about it later) it is obviously true that courage and temperance have to do with particular springs of action as justice does not. Almost any desire can lead a man to act unjustly, not even excluding the desire to help a friend or to save a life, whereas a cowardly act must be motivated by fear or a desire for safety, and an act of intemperance by a desire for pleasure, perhaps even for a particular range of pleasures such as those of eating or drinking or sex. And now, going back to the idea of virtues as correctives, one may say that it is only because fear and the desire for pleasure often operate as temptations that courage and temperance exist as virtues at all. As things are we often want to run away not only where that is the right thing to do but also where we should stand firm; and we want pleasure not only where we should seek pleasure but also where we should not. If human nature had been different there would have been no need of a corrective disposition in either place, as fear and pleasure would have been good guides to conduct throughout life. So Aquinas says, about the passions

> They may incite us to something against reason, and so we need a curb, which we name *temperance*. Or they may make us shirk a course of action dictated by reason, through fear of dangers or hardships. Then a person needs to be steadfast and not run away from what is right; and for this *courage* is named.[8]

As with courage and temperance so with many other virtues: there is, for instance, a virtue of industriousness only because idleness is a temptation; and of humility only because men tend to think too well of themselves. Hope is a virtue because despair too is a temptation; it might have been that no one cried that all was lost except where he could really see it to be so, and in this case there would have been no virtue of hope.

With virtues such as justice and charity it is a little different, because they correspond not to any particular desire or tendency that has to be kept in check but rather to a deficiency of motivaton; and it is this that they must make good. If people were as much attached to the good of others as they are to their own good there would no more be a general virtue of benevolence than there is a general virtue of self-love. And if people cared about the rights of others as they care about their own rights no virtue of justice would be needed to look after the matter, and rules about such things as contracts and promises would only need to be made public, like the rules of a game that everyone was eager to play.

On this view of the virtues and vices everything is seen to depend on what human nature is like, and the traditional catalogue of the two kinds of dispositions is not hard to understand. Nevertheless it may be defective, and anyone who accepts the thesis that I am putting forward will feel free to ask himself where the temptations and deficiencies that need correcting are really to be found. It is possible, for example, that the theory of human nature lying behind the traditional list of the virtues and vices puts too much emphasis on hedonistic and sensual impulses, and does not sufficiently take account of less straightforward inclinations such as the desire to be put upon and dissatisfied, or the unwillingness to accept good things as they come along.

It should now be clear why I said that virtues should be seen as correctives; and

---

[8]Aquinas op. cit. 1a2ae Q.61 a.3.

part of what is meant by saying that virtue is about things that are difficult for men should also have appeared. The further application of this idea is, however, controversial, and the following difficulty presents itself: that we both are and are not inclined to think that the harder a man finds it to act virtuously the more virtue he shows if he does act well. For on the one hand great virtue is needed where it is particularly hard to act virtuously; yet on the other it could be argued that difficulty in acting virtuously shows that the agent is imperfect in virtue: according to Aristotle, to take pleasure in virtuous action is the mark of true virtue, with the self-mastery of the one who finds virtue difficult only a second best. How then is this conflict to be decided? Who shows most courage, the one who wants to run away but does not, or the one who does not even want to run away? Who shows most charity, the one who finds it easy to make the good of others his object, or the one who finds it hard?

What is certain is that the thought that virtues are corrective does not constrain us to relate virtue to difficulty in each individual man. Since men in general find it hard to face great dangers or evils, and even small ones, we may count as courageous those few who without blindness or indifference are nevertheless fearless even in terrible circumstances. And when someone has a natural charity or generosity it is at least part of the virtue that he has; if natural virtue cannot be the whole of virtue this is because a kindly or fearless disposition could be disastrous without justice and wisdom, and because these virtues have to be learned, not because natural virtue is too easily acquired. I have argued that the virtues can be seen as correctives in relation to human nature in general but not that each virtue must present a difficulty to each and every man.

Nevertheless many people feel strongly inclined to say that it is for moral effort that moral praise is to be bestowed, and that in proportion as a man finds it easy to be virtuous so much the less is he to be morally admired for his good actions. The dilemma can be resolved only when we stop talking about difficulties standing in the way of virtuous action as if they were of only one kind. The fact is that some kinds of difficulties do indeed provide an occasion for much virtue, but that others rather show that virtue is incomplete.

To illustrate this point I shall first consider an example of honest action. We may suppose for instance that a man has an opportunity to steal, in circumstances where stealing is not morally permissible, but that he refrains. And now let us ask our old question. For one man it is hard to refrain from stealing and for another man it is not: which shows the greater virtue in acting as he should? It is not difficult to see in this case that it makes all the difference whether the difficulty comes from circumstances, as that a man is poor, or that his theft is unlikely to be detected, or whether it comes from something that belongs to his own character. The fact that a man is *tempted* to steal is something about him that shows a certain lack of honesty: of the thoroughly honest man we say that it "never entered his head," meaning that it was never a real possibility for him. But the fact that he is poor is something that makes the occasion more *tempting,* and difficulties of this kind make honest action all the more virtuous.

A similar distinction can be made between different obstacles standing in the way of charitable action. Some circumstances, as that great sacrifice is needed, or that the one to be helped is a rival, give an occasion on which a man's charity is severely tested. Yet in given circumstances of this kind it is the man who acts easily rather than the one who finds it hard who shows the most charity. Charity is a virtue of attachment, and that sympathy for others which makes it easier to help them is part of the virtue itself.

These are fairly simple cases, but I am not supposing that it is always easy to say where the relevant distinction is to be drawn. What, for instance, should we say about the emotion of fear as an obstacle to action? Is a man more courageous if he fears much and nevertheless acts, or if he is relatively fearless? Several things must be said about this. In the first place it seems that the emotion of fear is not a necessary condition for the display of courage; in face of a great evil such as death or injury a man may show courage even if he does not tremble. On the other hand even irrational fears may give an occasion for courage: if someone suffers from claustrophobia or a dread of heights he may require courage to do that which would not be a courageous action for others. But not all fears belong from this point of view to the circumstances rather than to a man's character. For while we do not think of claustrophobia or a dread of heights as features of character, a general timorousness may be. Thus, although pathological fears are not the result of a man's choices and values some fears may be. The fears that count against a man's courage are those that we think he could overcome, and among them, in a special class, those that reflect the fact that he values safety too much.

In spite of problems such as these, which have certainly not all been solved, both the distinction between different kinds of obstacles to virtuous action and the general idea that virtues are correctives will be useful in resolving a difficulty in Kant's moral philosophy closely related to the issues discussed in the preceding paragraphs. In a passage in the first section of the *Groundwork of the Metaphysics of Morals* Kant notoriously tied himself into a knot in trying to give an account of those actions which have as he put it "positive moral worth." Arguing that only actions done out of a sense of duty have this worth he contrasts a philanthropist who "takes pleasure in spreading happiness around him" with one who acts out of respect for duty, saying that the actions of the latter but not the former have moral worth. Much scorn has been poured on Kant for this curious doctrine, and indeed it does seem that something has gone wrong, but perhaps we are not in a position to scoff unless we can give our own account of the idea on which Kant is working. After all it does seem that he is right in saying that some actions are in accordance with duty, and even required by duty, without being the subjects of moral praise, like those of the honest trader who deals honestly in a situation in which it is in his interest to do so.

It was this kind of example that drove Kant to his strange conclusion. He added another example, however, in discussing acts of self-preservation; these he said, while they normally have no positive moral worth, may have it when a man preserves his life not from inclination but without inclination and from a sense of duty. Is he not right in saying that acts of self-preservation normally have no moral significance but that they may have it, and how do we ourselves explain this fact?

To anyone who approaches this topic from a consideration of the virtues the solution readily suggests itself. Some actions are in accordance with virtue without requiring virtue for their performance, whereas others are both in accordance with virtue and such as to show possession of a virtue. So Kant's trader was dealing honestly in a situation in which the virtue of honesty is not required for honest dealing, and it is for this reason that his action did not have "positive moral worth." Similarly, the care that one ordinarily takes for one's life, as for instance on some ordinary morning in eating one's breakfast and keeping out of the way of a car on the road, is something for which no virtue is required. As we said earlier there is no general virtue of self-love as there is a virtue of benevolence or charity, because men are generally attached sufficiently to their own good. Nevertheless in special circumstances virtues such as temperance, courage, fortitude, and hope may be needed if someone is to preserve his life. Are these circumstances in which the preservaton of one's own life is a duty? Sometimes it is so, for sometimes it is what is owed to others that should keep a man from destroying himself, and then he may act out of a sense of duty. But not all cases in which acts of self-preservation show virtue are like this. For a man may display each of the virtues just listed even where he does not do any harm to others if he kills himself or fails to preserve his life. And it is this that explains why there may be a moral aspect to suicide which does not depend on possible injury to other people. It is not that suicide is "always wrong," whatever that would mean, but that suicide is *sometimes* contrary to virtues such as courage and hope.

Let us now return to Kant's philanthropists, with the thought that it is action that is in accordance with virtue and also displays a virtue that has moral worth. We see at once that Kant's difficulties are avoided, and the happy philanthropist reinstated in the position which belongs to him. For charity is, as we said, a virtue of attachment as well as action, and the sympathy that makes it easier to act with charity is part of the virtue. The man who acts charitably out of a sense of duty is not to be undervalued, but it is the other who most shows virtue and therefore to the other that most moral worth is attributed. Only a detail of Kant's presentation of the case of the dutiful philanthropist tells on the other side. For what he actually said was that this man felt no sympathy and took no pleasure in the good of others because "his mind was clouded by some sorrow of his own," and this is the kind of circumstance that increases the virtue that is needed if a man is to act well.

III

It was suggested above that an action with "positive moral worth," or as we might say a positively good action, was to be seen as one which was in accordance with virtue, by which I mean contrary to no virtue, and moreover one for which a virtue was required. Nothing has so far been said about another case, excluded by the formula, in which it might seem that an act displaying one virtue was nevertheless contrary to another. In giving this last description I am thinking not of two virtues with competing claims, as if what were required by justice could nevertheless be demanded by charity, or something of that kind, but rather of the possibility that a virtue such as courage or temperance or industry which overcomes a special temptation, might be displayed in an act of folly or villainy. Is this something that we must allow for, or is it only good or innocent actions which can be acts of these virtues? Aquinas, in his definition of virtue, said that virtues can produce only good actions, and that they are dispositions "of which no one can make bad use,"[9] except when they are treated as objects, as in being the subject of hatred or pride. The common opinion nowadays is, however, quite different. With the notable exception of Peter Geach hardly anyone sees any difficulty in the thought that virtues may sometimes be displayed in bad actions. Von Wright, for instance, speaks of the courage of the villain as if this were a quite unproblematic idea, and most people take it for granted that the virtues of courage and temperance may aid a bad man in his evil work. It is also supposed that charity may lead a man to act badly, as when someone does what he has no right to do, but does it for the sake of a friend.

There are, however, reasons for thinking that the matter is not so simple as this.

[9]Aquinas op. cit. 1a2ae Q.56 a.5.

If a man who is willing to do an act of injustice to help a friend, or for the common good, is supposed to act out of charity, and he so acts where a just man will not, it should be said that the unjust man has more charity than the just man. But do we not think that someone not ready to act unjustly may yet be perfect in charity, the virtue having done its whole work in prompting him to do the acts that are permissible? And is there not more difficulty than might appear in the idea of an act of injustice which is nevertheless an act of courage? Suppose for instance that a sordid murder were in question, say a murder done for gain or to get an inconvenient person out of the way, but that this murder had to be done in alarming circumstances or in the face of real danger; should we be happy to say that such an action was an act of courage or a courageous act? Did the murderer, who certainly acted boldly, or with intrepidity, if he did the murder, also act courageously? Some people insist that they are ready to say this, but I have noticed that they like to move over to a murder for the sake of conscience, or to some other act done in the course of a villainous enterprise but whose immediate end is innocent or positively good. On their hypothesis, which is that bad acts can easily be seen as courageous acts or acts of courage, my original example should be just as good.

What are we to say about this difficult matter? There is no doubt that the murderer who murdered for gain was *not a coward:* he did not have a second moral defect which another villain might have had. There is no difficulty about this because it is clear that one defect may neutralise another. As Aquinas remarked, it is better for a blind horse if it is slow.[10] It does not follow, however, that an act of villainy can be courageous; we are inclined to say that it "took courage," and yet it seems wrong to think of courage as equally connected with good actions and bad.

One way out of this difficulty might be to say that the man who is ready to pursue bad ends does indeed have courage, and shows courage in his action, but that in him courage is not a virtue. Later I shall consider some cases in which this might be the right thing to say, but in this instance it does not seem to be. For unless the murderer consistently pursues bad ends his courage will often result in good; it may enable him to do many innocent or positively good things for himself or for his family and friends. On the strength of an individual bad action we can hardly say that in him courage is not a virtue. Nevertheless there is something to be said even about the individual action to distinguish it from one that would readily be called an act of courage or a courageous act. Perhaps the following analogy may help us to see what it is. We might think of words such as "courage" as naming characteristics of human beings in respect of a certain power, as words such as "poison" and "solvent" and "corrosive" so name the properties of physical things. The power to which virtue-words are so related is the power of producing good action, and good desires. But just as poisons, solvents and corrosives do not always operate characteristically, so it could be with virtues. If P (say arsenic) is a poison it does not follow that P acts as a poison wherever it is found. It is quite natural to say on occasion "P does not act as a poison here" though P is a poison and it is P that is acting here. Similarly courage is not operatng as a virtue when the murderer turns his courage, which is a virtue, to bad ends. Not surprisingly the resistance that some of us registered was not to the expression "the courage of the murderer" or to the assertion that what he did "took courage" but rather to the description of that action as an act of courage or a courageous act. It is not that the ac-

---

[10]Aquinas op. cit. 1a2ae Q.58 a.4.

tion *could* not be so decribed, but that the fact that courage does not here have its characteristic operation is a reason for finding the description strange.

In this example we were considering an action in which courage was not operating as a virtue, without suggesting that in that agent it generally failed to do so. But the latter is also a possibility. If someone is both wicked and foolhardy this may be the case with courage, and it is even easier to find examples of a general connexion with evil rather than good in the case of some other virtues. Suppose, for instance, that we think of someone who is over-industrious, or too ready to refuse pleasure, and this is characteristic of him rather than something we find on one particular occasion. In this case the virtue of industry, or the virtue of temperance, has a systematic connexion with defective action rather than good action; and it might be said in either case that the virtue did not operate as a virtue in this man. Just as we might say in a certain setting "P is not a poison here" though P is a poison and P is here, so we might say that industriousness, or temperance, is not a virtue in some. Similarly in a man habitually given to wishful thinking, who clings to false hopes, hope does not operate as a virtue and we may say that it is not a virtue in him.

The thought developed in the last paragraph, to the effect that not every man who has a virtue has something that is a virtue in him, may help to explain a certain discomfort that one may feel when discussing the virtues. It is not easy to put one's finger on what is wrong, but it has something to do with a disparity between the moral ideals that may seem to be implied in our talk about the virtues, and the moral judgement that we actually make. Someone reading the foregoing pages might, for instance, think that the author of this paper always admired most those people who had all the virtues, being wise and temperate as well as courageous, charitable, and just. And indeed it is sometimes so. There are some people who do possess all these virtues and who are loved and admired by all the world, as Pope John XXIII was loved and admired. Yet the fact is that many of us look up to some people whose chaotic lives contain rather little of wisdom or temperance, rather than to some others who possess these virtues. And while it may be that this is just romantic nonsense I suspect that it is not. For while wisdom always operates as a virtue, its close relation prudence does not, and it is prudence rather than wisdom that inspires many a careful life. Prudence is not a virtue in everyone, any more than industriousness is, for in some it is rather an over-anxious concern for safety and propriety, and a determination to keep away from people or situations which are apt to bring trouble with them; and by such defensiveness much good is lost. It is the same with temperance. Intemperance can be an appalling thing, as it was with Henry VIII of whom Wolsey remarked that

> rather than he will either miss or want any part of his will or appetite, he will put the loss of one half of his realm in danger.

Nevertheless in some people temperance is not a virtue, but is rather connected with timidity or with a grudging attitude to the acceptance of good things. Of course what is best is to live boldly yet without imprudence or intemperance, but the fact is that rather few can manage that.

The Nature of the Virtues

Alasdair MacIntyre

One response to the history which I have narrated so far might well be to suggest that even within the relatively coherent tradition of thought which I have sketched there are just too many different and incompatible conceptions of a virtue for there to be any real unity to the concept or indeed to the history. Homer, Sophocles, Aristotle, the New Testament and medieval thinkers differ from each other in too many ways. They offer us different and incompatible lists of the virtues; they give a different rank order of importance to different virtues; and they have different and incompatible theories of the virtues. If we were to consider later Western writers on the virtues, the list of differences and incompatibilities would be enlarged still further; and if we extended our enquiry to Japanese, say, or American Indian cultures, the differences would become greater still. It would be all too easy to conclude that there are a number of rival and alternative conceptions of the virtues, but, even within the tradition which I have been delineating, no single core conception.

The case for such a conclusion could not be better constructed than by beginning from a consideration of the very different lists of items which different authors in different times and places have included in their catalogues of virtues. Some of these catalogues—Homer's, Aristotle's and the New Testament's—I have already noticed at greater or lesser length. Let me at the risk of some repetition recall some of their key features and then introduce for further comparison the catalogues of two later Western writers, Benjamin Franklin and Jane Austin.

The first example is that of Homer. At least some of the items in a Homeric list of the *aretai* would clearly not be counted by most of us nowadays a virtues at all, physical strength being the most obvious example. To this it might be replied that perhaps we ought not to translate the word *aretê* in Homer by our word "virtue," but instead by our word "excellence"; and perhaps, if we were so to translate it, the apparently surprising difference between Homer and ourselves would at first sight have been removed. For we could allow without any kind of oddity that the possession of physical strength is the possession of an excellence. But in fact we would not have removed, but instead would merely have relocated, the difference between Homer and ourselves. For we would now seem to be saying that Homer's concept of an *aretê,* and excellence, is one thing and that our concept of a virtue is quite another since a particular quality can be an excellence in Homer's eyes, but not a virtue in ours and *vice versa*.

But of course it is not that Homer's list of virtues differs only from our own; it also notably differs from Aristotle's. And Aristotle's of course also differs from our own. For one thing, as I noticed earlier, some Greek virtue-words are not easily translatable into English or rather out of Greek. Moreover consider the importance of friendship as a virtue in Aristotle's list—how different from us! Or the place of *phronêsis*—how different from Homer and from us! The mind receives from Aristotle the kind of tribute which the body receives from Homer. But it is not just the case that the

Chapter 14 from Alasdair MacIntyre, *After Virtue: A Study in Moral Theory,* © 1982 by the University of Notre Dame Press, Norte Dame, IN 46556. Reprinted by permission.

difference between Aristotle and Homer lies in the inclusion of some items and the omission of others in their respective catalogues. It turns out also in the way in which those catalogues are ordered, in which items are ranked as relatively central to human excellence and which marginal.

Moreover the relationship of virtues to the social order has changed. For Homer the paradigm of human excellence is the warrior; for Aristotle it is the Athenian gentleman. Indeed according to Aristotle certain virtues are only available to those of great riches and of high social status; there are virtues which are unavailable to the poor man, even if he is a free man. And those virtues are on Aristotle's view ones central to human life; magnanimity—and once again, any translation of *megalopsuchia* is unsatisfactory—and munificence are not just virtues, but important virtues within the Aristotelian scheme.

At once it is impossible to delay the remark that the most striking contrast with Aristotle's catalogue is to be found neither in Homer's nor in our own, but in the New Testament's. For the New Testament not only praises virtues of which Aristotle knows nothing—faith, hope and love—and says nothing about virtues such a *phronêsis* which are crucial for Aristotle, but it praises at least one quality as a virtue which Aristotle seems to count as one of the vices relative to magnanimity, namely humility. Moreover since the New Testament quite clearly sees the rich as destined for the pains of Hell, it is clear that the key virtues cannot be available to them; yet they *are* available to slaves. And the New Testament of course differs from both Homer and Aristotle not only in the items included in its catalogue, but once again in its rank ordering of the virtues.

Turn now to compare all three lists of virtues considered so far—the Homeric, the Aristotelian, and the New Testament's—with two much later lists, one which can be compiled from Jane Austen's novels and the other which Benjamin Franklin constructed for himself. Two features stand out in Jane Austin's list. The first is the importance that she allots to the virtue which she calls "constancy," a virtue about which I shall say more in a later chapter. In some ways constancy plays a role in Jane Austen analogous to that of *phronêsis* in Aristotle; it is a virtue the possession of which is a prerequisite for the possession of other virtues. The second is the fact that what Aristotle treats as the virtue of agreeableness (a virtue for which he says there is no name) she treats as only the simulacrum of a genuine virtue—the genuine virtue in question is the one she calls amiability. For the man who practices agreeableness does so from considerations of honour and expediency, according to Aristotle; whereas Jane Austen thought it possible and necessary for the possessor of that virtue to have a certain real affection for people as such. (It matters here that Jane Austen is a Christian.) Remember that Aristotle himself had treated military courage as a simulacrum of true courage. Thus we find here yet another type of disagreement over the virtues; namely, one as to which human qualities are genuine virtues and which mere simulacra.

In Benjamin Franklin's list we find almost all the types of difference from at least one of the other catalogues we have considered and one more. Franklin includes virtues which are new to our consideration such as cleanliness, silence and industry; he clearly considers the drive to acquire itself a part of virtue, whereas for most ancient Greeks this is the vice of *pleonexia;* he treats some virtues which earlier ages had considered minor as major; but he also redefines some familiar virtues. In the list of thirteen virtues which Franklin compiled as part of his system of private moral accounting, he elucidates each virtue by citing a maxim obedience to which *is* the virtue in question. In the case of chastity the maxim is "Rarely use venery but for health or offspring—never to dullness, weakness or the injury of your own or another's peace or reputation." This is clearly not what earlier writers had meant by "chastity."

We have therefore accumulated a startling number of differences and incompatibilities in the five stated and implied accounts of the virtues. So the question which I raised at the outset becomes more urgent. If different writers in different times and places, but all within the history of Western culture, include such different sets and types of items in their lists, what grounds have we for supposing that they do indeed aspire to list items of one and the same kind, that there is any shared concept at all? A second kind of consideration reinforces the presumption of a negative answer to this question. It is not just that each of these five writers lists different and differing kinds of items; it is also that each of these lists embodies, is the expression of a different theory about what a virtue is.

In the Homeric poems a virtue is a quality the manifestation of which enables someone to do exactly what their well-defined social role requires. The primary role is that of the warrior king and that Homer lists those virtues which he does becomes intelligible at once when we recognise that the key virtues therefore must be those which enable a man to excel in combat and in the games. It follows that we cannot identify the Homeric virtues until we have first identified the key social roles in Homeric society and the requirements of each of them. The concept of *what anyone filling such-and-such a role ought to do* is prior to the concept of a virtue; the latter concept has application only via the former.

On Aristotle's account matters are very different. Even though some virtues are available only to certain types of people, none the less virtues attach not to men as inhabiting social roles, but to man as such. It is the *telos* of man as a species which determines what human qualities are virtues. We need to remember however that although Aristotle treats the acquisition and exercise of the virtues as means to an end, the relationship of means to end is internal and not external. I call a means internal to a given end when the end cannot be adequately characterised independently of a characterisation of the means. So it is with the virtues and the *telos* which is the good life for man on Aristotle's account. The exercise of the virtues is itself a crucial component of the good life for man. This dinstinction between internal and external means to an end is not drawn by Aristotle himself in the *Nicomachean Ethics,* as I noticed earlier, but it is an essential distinction to be drawn if we are to understand what Aristotle intended. The dinstinction *is* drawn explicitly by Aquinas in the course of his defense of St. Augustine's definition of a virtue, and it is clear that Aquinas understood that in drawing it he was maintaining an Aritotelian point of view.

The New Testament's account of the virtues, even if it differs as much as it does in content from Aristotle's—Aristotle would certainly not have admired Jesus Christ and he would have been horrified by St. Paul—does have the same logical and conceptual structure as Aristotle's account. A virtue is, as with Aristotle, a quality the exercise of which leads to the achievement of the human telos. *The* good for man is of course a supernatural and not only a natural good, but supernature redeems and completes nature. Moreover the relationship of virtues as means to the end which is human incorporation in the divine kingdom of the age to come is internal and not external, just as it is in Aristotle. It is of course this parallelism which allows Aquinas to synthesise Aristotle and the New Testament. A key feature of this parallelism is the way in which the concept of *the good life for man* is prior to the concept of a virtue in just the way in which on the Homeric account the concept of a social role was prior. Once again it is the way in which the former concept is applied which determines how the latter is to be applied. In both cases the concept of a virtue is a secondary concept.

The intent of Jane Austen's theory of the virtues is of another kind. C. S. Lewis has rightly emphasised how profoundly Christian her moral vision is and Gilbert Ryle has equally rightly emphasised her inheritance from Shaftesbury and from Aristotle. In fact her views combine elements from Homer as well, since she is concerned with social roles in a way that neither the New Testament nor Aristotle are. She is therefore important for the way in which she finds it possible to combine what are at first sight disparate theoretical accounts of the virtues. But for the moment any attempt to assess the significance of Jane Austen's systhesis must be delayed. Instead we must notice the quite different style of theory articulated in Benjamin Franklin's account of the virtues.

Franklin's account, like Aristotle's, is teleological; but unlike Aristotle's, it is utilitarian. According to Franklin in his *Autobiography* the virtues are means to an end, but he envisages the means-ends relationship as external rather than internal. The end to which the cultivation of the virtues ministers is happiness, but happiness understood as success, prosperity in Philadelphia and ultimately in heaven. The virtues are to be useful and Franklin's account continuously stresses utility as a criterion in individual cases: "Make no expence but to do good to others or yourself; i.e. waste nothing," "Speak not but what may benefit others or yourself. Avoid trifling conversation" and, as we have already seen, "Rarely use venery but for health or offspring ..." When Franklin was in Paris he was horrified by Parisian architecture: "Marble, porcelain and gilt are squandered without utility."

We thus have at least three very different conceptions of a virtue to confront: a virtue is a quality which enables an individual to discharge his or her social role (Homer); a virtue is a quality which enables an individual to move towards the achievement of the specifically human *telos,* whether natural or supernatural (Aristotle, the New Testament and Aquinas); a virtue is a quality which has utility in achieving earthly and heavenly success (Franklin). Are we to take these as three rival accounts of the same thing? Or are they instead accounts of three different things? Perhaps the moral structures in archaic Greece, in fourth-century Greece, and in eighteenth-century Pennsylvania were so different from each other that we should treat them as embodying quite different concepts, whose difference is initially disguised from us by the historical accident of an inherited vocabulary which misleads us by linguistic resemblance long after conceptual identity and similarity have failed. Our initial question has come back to us with redoubled force.

Yet although I have dwelt upon the *prima facie* case for holding that the differences and incompatibilities between different accounts at least suggest that there is no single, central, core conception of the virtues which might make a claim for universal allegiance, I ought also to point out that each of the five moral accounts which I have sketched so summarily does embody just such a claim. It is indeed just this feature of those accounts that makes them of more than sociological or antiquarian interest. Every one of these accounts claims not only theoretical, but also an institutional hegemony. For Odysseus the Cyclopes stand condemned because they lack agriculture, on *agora* and *themis*. For Aristotle the barbarians stand condemned because they lack the *polis* and are therefore incapable of politics. For New Testament Christians there is no salvation outside the apostolic church. And we know that Benjamin Franklin found the virtues more at home in Philadelphia than in Paris and that for Jane Austen the touchstone of the virtues is a certain kind of marriage and indeed a certain kind of naval officer (that is, a certain kind of *English* naval officer).

The question can therefore now be posed directly: are we or are we not able to disentangle from these rival and various claims a unitary core concept of the virtues of which we can give a more compelling account than any of the other accounts so far? I am going to argue that we can in fact discover such a core concept and that it turns out to provide the tradition of which I have written the history with its conceptual unity. It will indeed enable us to distinguish in a clear way those beliefs about the virtues which genuinely belong to the tradition from those which do not. Unsurprisingly perhaps it is a complex concept, different parts of which derive from different stages in the development of the tradition. Thus the concept itself in some sense embodies the history of which it is the outcome.

One of the features of the concept of a virtue which has emerged with some clarity from the argument so far is that it always requires for its application the acceptance of some prior account of certain features of social and moral life in terms of which it has to be defined and explained. So in the Homeric account the concept of a virtue is secondary to that of *a social role,* in Aristotle's account it is secondary to that of *the good life for man* conceived as the *telos* of human action and in Franklin's much later account it is secondary to that of utility. What is it in the account which I am about to give which provides in a similar way the necessary background against which the concept of a virtue has to be made intelligible? It is in answering this question that the complex, historical, multilayered character of the core concept of virtue becomes clear. For there are no less than three stages in the logical development of the concept which have to be identified in order, if the core conception of a virtue is to be understood, and each of these stages has its own conceptual background. The first stage requires a background account of what I shall call a practice, the second an account of what I have already characterised as the narrative order of a single human life and the third an account a good deal fuller than I have given up to now of what constitutes a moral tradition. Each later stage presupposes the earlier, but not *vice versa*. Each earlier stage is both modified by and reinterpreted in the light of, but also provides an essential constituent of each later stage. The progress in the development of the concept is closely related to, although it does not recapitulate in any straightforward way, the history of the tradition of which it forms the core.

In the Homeric account of the virtues—and in heroic societies more generally—the exercise of a virtue exhibits qualities which are required for sustaining a social role and for exhibiting excellence in some well-marked area of social practice: to excel is to excel at war or in the games, as Achilles does, in sustaining a household, as Penelope does, in giving counsel in the assembly, as Nestor does, in the telling of a tale, as Homer himself does. When Aristotle speaks of excellence in human activity, he sometimes though not always, refers to some well-defined type of human practice: flute-playing, or war, or geometry. I am going to suggest that this notion of a particular type of practice as providing the arena in which the virtues are exhibited and in terms of which they are to receive their primary, if incomplete, definition is crucial to the whole enterprise of identifying a core concept of the virtues. I hasten to add two *caveats* however.

The first is to point out that my argument will not in any way imply that virtues are *only* exercised in the course of what I am calling practices. The second is to warn that I shall be using the word "practice" in a specially defined way which does not completely agree with current ordinary usage, including my own previous use of that word. What am I going to mean by it?

By a "practice" I am going to mean any coherent and complex form of socially established cooperative human activity through which goods internal to that form of activity are realised in the course of trying to achieve those standards of excellence which are appropriate to, and partially definitive of, that form of activity, with the result that human powers to achieve excellence, and human conceptions of the ends and goods involved, are systematically extended. Tic-tac-toe is not an example of a practice in this sense, nor is throwing a football with skill; but the game of football is, so is chess. Bricklaying is not a practice; architecture is. Planting turnips is not a practice; farming is. So are the enquiries of physics, chemistry and biology, and so is the work of the historian, and so are painting and music. In the ancient and medieval worlds the creation and sustaining of human communities—of households, cities, nations—is generally taken to be a practice in the sense of which I have defined it. Thus the range of practices is wide: arts, sciences, games, politics in the Aristotelian sense, the making and sustaining of family life, all fall under the concept. But the question of the precise range of practices is not at this stage of the first importance. Instead let me explain some of the key terms involved in my definition, beginning with the option of goods internal to a practice.

Consider the example of a highly intelligent seven-year-old child whom I wish to teach to play chess, although the child has no particular desire to learn the game. The child does however have a very strong desire for candy and little chance of obtaining it. I therefore tell the child that if the child will play chess with me once a week I will give the child 50¢ worth of candy; moreover I tell the child that I will always play in such a way that it will be difficult, but not impossible, for the child to win and that, if the child wins, the child will receive an extra 50¢ worth of candy. Thus motivated the child plays and plays to win. Notice however that, so long as it is the candy alone which provides the child with a good reason for playing chess, the child has no reason not to cheat and every reason to cheat, provided he or she can do so successfully. But, so we may hope, there will come a time when the child will find in those goods specific to chess, in the achievement of a certain highly particular kind of analytical skill, strategic imagination and competitive intensity, a new set of reasons, reasons now not just for winning on a particular occasion, but for trying to excel in whatever way the game of chess demands. Now if the child cheats, he or she will be defeating not me, but himself or herself.

There are thus two kinds of good possibly to be gained by playing chess. On the one hand there are those goods externally and contingently attached to chess-playing and to other practices by the accidents of social circumstance—in the case of the imaginary child candy, in the case of real adults such goods as prestige, status and money. There are always alternative ways for achieving such goods, and their achievement is never to be had *only* by engaging in some particular kind of practice. On the other hand there are the goods internal to the practice of chess which cannot be had in any way but by playing chess or some other game of that specific kind. We call them internal for two reasons: first, as I have already suggested, because we can only specify them in terms of chess or some other game of that specific kind and by means of examples from such games (otherwise the meagerness of our vocabulary for speaking of such good forces us into such devices as my own resort to writing of "a certain highly particular kind of"); and secondly because they can only be identified and recognised by the experience of participating in the practice in question. Those who lack the relevant experience are incompetent thereby as judges of internal goods.

This is clearly the case with all the major examples of practices: consider for example—even if briefly and inadequately—the practice of portrait painting as it developed in Western Europe from the late middle ages to the eighteenth century. The successful portrait painter is able to achieve many goods which are in the sense just defined external to the practice of portrait painting—fame, wealth, social status, even a measure of power and influence at courts upon occasion. But those external goods are not to be confused with the goods which are internal to the practice. The internal goods are those which result from an extended attempt to show how Wittgenstein's dictum "The human body is the best picture of the human soul" (*Investigations,* p. 178e) might be made to become true by teaching us "to regard . . . the picture on our wall as the object itself (the men, landscape and so on) depicted there" (p. 205e) in a quite new way. What is misleading about Wittgenstein's dictum as it stands is its neglect of the truth in George Orwell's thesis "At 50 everyone has the face he deserves." What painters from Giotto to Rembrandt learnt to show was how the face at any age may be revealed as the face that the subject of a portrait deserves. . . .

A practice involves standards of excellence and obedience to rules as well as the achievement of goods. To enter into a practice is to accept the authority of those standards and the inadequacy of my own performance as judged by them. It is to subject my own attitudes, choices, preferences and tastes to the standards which currently and partially define the practice. Practices of course, as I have just noticed, have a history: games, sciences and arts all have histories. Thus the standards are not themselves immune from criticism, but none the less we cannot be initiated into a practice without accepting the authority of the best standards realised so far. If, on starting to listen to music, I do not accept my own incapacity to judge correctly, I will never learn to hear, let alone to appreciate, Bartok's last quartets. If, on starting to play baseball, I do not accept that others know better than I when to throw a fast ball and when not, I will never learn to appreciate good pitching let alone to pitch. In the realm of practice the authority of both goods and standards operates in such a way as to rule out all subjectivist and emotivist analyses of judgment. De gustibus *et* disputandum.

We are now in a position to notice an important difference between what I have called internal and what I have called external goods. It is characteristic of what I have called external goods that when achieved they are always some individual's property and possession. Moreover characteristically they are such that the more someone has of them, the less there is for other people. This is sometimes necessarily the case, as with power and fame, and sometimes the case by reason of contingent circumstance as with money. External goods are therefore characteristically objects of competition in which there must be losers as well as winners. Internal goods are indeed the outcome of competition to excel, but it is characteristic of them that their achievement is a good for the whole community who participate in the practice. So when Turner transformed the seascape in painting or W. G. Grace advanced the art of batting in cricket in a quite new way their achievement enriched the whole relevant community.

But what does all or any of this have to do with the concept of the virtues? It turns out that we are now in a position to formulate a first, even if partial and tentative definition of a virtue: *A virtue is an acquired human quality the possession and exercise of which tends to enable us to achieve those goods which are internal to practices and the lack of which effectively prevents us from achieving any such goods.* Later this definition will need amplification and amendment. But as a first approximation to an adequate definition it already illuminates the place of the virtues in human life. For it is not difficult to show for a whole range of key virtues that without them the goods internal to practices are barred to us, but not just barred to us generally, barred in a very particular way.

It belongs to the concept of a practice as I have outlined it—and as we are all familiar with it already in our actual lives, whether we are painters or physicists or quarterbacks or indeed just lovers of good painting or first-rate experiments or a well-thrown pass—that its goods can only be achieved by subordinating ourselves to the best standard so far achieved, and that entails subordinating ourselves within the practice in our relationship to other practitioners. We have to learn to recognise what is due to whom; we have to be prepared to take whatever self-endangering risks are demanded along the way; and we have to listen carefully to what we are told about our own inadequacies and to reply with the same carefulness for the facts. In other words we have to accept as necessary components of any practice with internal goods and standards of excellence the virtues of justice, courage, and honesty. For not to accept these, to be willing to cheat as our imagined child was willing to cheat in his or her early days at chess, so far bars us from achieving the standards of excellence or the goods internal to that practice that it renders the practice pointless except as a device for achieving external goods.

We can put the same point in another way. Every practice requires a certain kind of relationship between those who participate in it. Now the virtues are those goods by reference to which, whether we like it or not, we define our relationships to those other people with whom we share the kind of purposes and standards which inform practices. Consider an example of how reference to the virtues has to be made in certain kinds of human relationship.

A, B, C, and D are friends in that sense of friendship which Aristotle takes to be primary: they share in the pursuit of certain goods. In my terms they share in a practice. D dies in obscure circumstances, A discovers how D died and tells the truth about it to B while lying to C. C discovers the lie. What A cannot then intelligibly claim is that he stands in the same relationship of friendship to both B and C. By telling the truth to one and lying to the other he has partially defined a difference in the relationship. Of course it is open to A to explain this difference in a number of ways; perhaps he was trying to spare C pain or perhaps he is simply cheating C. But some difference in the relationship now exists as a result of the lie. For their allegiance to each other in the pursuit of common goods has been put in question.

Just as, so long as we share the standards and purposes characteristic of practices, we define our relationships to each other, whether we acknowledge it or not, by reference to standards of truthfulness and trust, so we define them too by reference to standards of justice and of courage. If A, a professor, gives B and C the grades that their papers deserve, but grades D because he is attracted by D's blue eyes or is repelled by D's dandruff, he has defined his relationship to D differently from his relationship to the other members of the class, whether he wishes it or not. Justice requires that we treat others in respect of merit or desert according to uniform and impersonal standards; to depart from the standards of justice in some particular instance defines our relationship with the relevant person as in some way special or distinctive.

The case with courage is a little different. We hold courage to be a virtue because the care and concern for individuals, communities and causes which is so crucial to so much in practices requires the existence of such a virtue. If someone says that he cares for some individual, community or cause, but is unwilling to risk harm or danger on his, her or its own behalf, he puts in question the genuineness of his care and concern. Courage, the capacity to risk harm or danger to oneself, has its role in human life because of this connection with care and concern. This is not to say that a man cannot genuinely care and also be a coward. It is in part to say that a man who genuinely cares and has not the capacity for risking harm or danger has to define himself, both to himself and to others, as a coward. . . .

To situate the virtues any further within practices it is necessary now to clarify a little further the nature of a practice by drawing two important contrasts. The discussion so far I hope makes it clear that a practice, in the sense intended, is never just a set of technical skills, even when directed towards some unified purpose and even if the exercise of those skills can on occasion be valued or enjoyed for their own sake. What is distinctive of a practice is in part the way in which conceptions of the relevant goods and ends which the technical skills serve—and every practice does require the exercise of technical skills—are transformed and enriched by these extensions of human powers and by that regard for its own internal goods which are partially definitive of each particular practice or type of practice. Practices never have a goal or goals fixed for all time—painting has no such goal nor has physics—but the goals themselves are transmuted by the history of the activity. It therefore turns out not to be accidental that every practice has its own history and a history which is more and other than that of the improvement of the relevant technical skills. This historical dimension is crucial in relation to the virtues.

To enter into a practice is to enter into a relationship not only with its contemporary practitioners, but also with those who have preceded us in the practice, particularly those whose achievements extended the reach of the practice to its present point. It is thus the achievement, and *a fortiori* the authority, of a tradition which I then confront and from which I have to learn. And for this learning and the relationship to the past which it embodies the virtues of justice, courage and truthfulness are prerequisite in precisely the same way and for precisely the same reasons as they are in sustaining present relationships within practices. . . .

Virtues then stand in a different relationship to external and to internal goods. The possession of the virtues—and not only of their semblance and simulacra—is necessary to achieve the latter; yet the possession of the virtues may perfectly well hinder us in achieving external goods. I need to emphasise at this point that external goods genuinely are goods. Not only are they characteristic objects of human desire, whose allocation is what gives point to the virtues of justice and of generosity, but no one can despise them altogether without a certain hypocrisy. Yet notoriously the cultivation of truthfulness, justice and courage will often, the world being what it contingently is, bar us from being rich or famous or powerful. Thus although we may hope that we can not only achieve the standards of excellence and the internal goods of certain practices by possessing the virtues *and* become rich, famous and powerful, the virtues are always a potential stumbling block to this comfortable ambition. We should therefore expect that, if in a particular society the pursuit of external goods were to become dominant, the concept of the virtues might suffer first attrition and then perhaps something near total effacement, although simulacra might abound.

The time has come to ask the question of how far this partial account of a core conception of the virtues—and I need to emphasise that all that I have offered so far is the first stage of such an account—is faithful to the tradition which I delineated. How far, for example, and in what ways is it Aristotelian? It is—happily—not Aristotelian in two ways in which a good deal of the rest of the tradition also dissents from Aristotle. First, although this account of the virtues is teleological, it does not require the identification of any teleology in nature, and hence it does not require any allegiance to Aristotle's metaphysical biology. And secondly, just because of the multiplicity of human practices and the consequent multiplicity of goods in the pursuit of which the virtues may be exercised—goods which will often be contingently incompatible and which will therefore make rival claims upon our allegiance—conflict will not spring solely from flaws in individual character. But it was just on these two matters that Aristotle's account of the virtues seemed most vulnerable; hence if it turns out to be the case that this socially teleological account can support Aristotle's general account of the virtues as well as does his own biologically teleological account, these differences from Aristotle himself may well be regarded as strengthening rather than weakening the case for a generally Aristotelian standpoint.

There are at least three ways in which the account that I have given *is* clearly Aristotelian. First it requires for its completion a cogent elaboration of just those distinctions and concepts which Aristotle's account requires: voluntariness, the distinction between the intellectual virtues and the virtues of character, the relationship of both to natural abilities and to the passions and the structure of practical reasoning. On every one of these topics something very like Aristotle's view has to be defended, if my own account is to be plausible.

Secondly my account can accommodate an Aristotelian view of pleasure and enjoyment, whereas it is interestingly irreconcilable with any utilitarian view and more particularly with Franklin's account of the virtues. We can approach these questions by considering how to reply to someone who, having considered my account of the differences between goods internal to and goods external to a practice required into which class, if either, does pleasure or enjoyment fall? The answer is, "Some types of pleasure into one, some into the other."

Someone who achieves excellence in a practice, who plays chess or football well or who carries through an enquiry in physics or an experimental mode in painting with success, characteristically enjoys his achievement and his activity in achieving. So does someone who, although not breaking the limit of achievement, plays or thinks or acts in a way that leads towards such a breaking of limit. As Aristotle says, the enjoyment of the activity and the enjoyment of achievement are not the ends at which the agent aims, but the enjoyment supervenes upon the successful activity in such a way that the activity achieved and the activity enjoyed are one and the same state. Hence to aim at the one is to aim at the other; and hence also it is easy to confuse the pursuit of excellence with the pursuit of enjoyment *in this specific sense*. This particular confusion is harmless enough; what is not harmless is the confusion of enjoyment *in this specific sense* with other forms of pleasure.

For certain kinds of pleasure are of course external goods along with prestige, status, power and money. Not all pleasure is the enjoyment supervening upon achieved activity; some is the pleasure of pyschological or physical states independent of all activity. Such states—for example that produced on a normal palate by the closely successive and thereby blended sensations of Colchester oyster, cayenne pepper and Veuve Cliquot—may be sought as external goods, as external rewards which may be purchased by money or received in virtue of prestige. Hence the pleasures are categorised neatly and appropriately by the classification into internal and external goods.

It is just this classification which can find no place within Franklin's account of the virtues which is formed entirely in terms of external relationships and external goods. Thus although by this stage of the argument it is possible to claim that my account does capture a conception of the virtues which is at the core of the particular ancient and medieval tradition which I have delineated, it is equally clear that there is more than one possible conception of the virtues and that Franklin's standpoint and indeed any utilitarian standpoint is such that to accept it will entail rejecting the tradition and *vice versa*.

One crucial point of incompatibility was noted long ago by D. H. Lawrence. When Franklin asserts, "Rarely use venery but for health or offspring . . . ," Lawrence replies, 'Never *use* venery.' It is of the character of a virtue that in order that it be effective in producing the internal goods which are the rewards of the virtues it should be exercised without regard to consequences. For it turns out to be the case that—and this is in part at least one more empirical factual claim—although the virtues are just those qualities which tend to lead to the achievement of a certain class of goods, none the less unless we practice them irrespective of whether in any particular set of contingent circumstances they will produce those goods or not, we cannot possess them at all. We cannot be genuinely courageous or truthful and be so only on occasion. Moreover, as we have seen, cultivation of the virtues always may and often does hinder the achievement of those external goods which are the mark of worldly success. The road to success in Philadelphia and the road to heaven may not coincide after all.

Furthermore we are now able to specify one crucial difficulty for *any* version of utilitarianism—in addition to those which I noticed earlier. Utilitarianism cannot accommodate the distinction between goods internal to and goods external to a practice. Not only is that distinction marked by none of the classical utilitarians—it cannot be found in Bentham's writings nor in those of either of the Mills or of Sidgwick—but internal goods and external goods are not commensurable with each other. Hence the notion of summing goods—and *a fortiori* in the light of what I have said about kinds of pleasure and enjoyment the notion of summing happiness—in terms of one single formula or conception of utility, whether it is Franklin's or Bentham's or Mill's, makes no sense. None the less we ought to note that although *this* distinction is alien to J. S. Mill's thought, it is plausible and in no way patronising to suppose that something like this is the distinction which he was trying to make in *Utilitarianism* when he distinguished between "higher" and "lower" pleasures. At the most we can say "something like this"; for J. S. Mill's upbringing had given him a limited view of human life and powers, had unfitted him, for example, for appreciating games just because of the way it had fitten him for appreciating philosophy. None the less the notion that the pursuit of excellence in a way that extends human powers is at the heart of human life is instantly recognisable as at home in not only J. S. Mill's political and social thought, but also in his and Mrs. Taylor's life. Were I to choose human exemplars of certain of the virtues as I understand them, there would of course be many names to name, those of St. Benedict and St. Francis of Assisi and St. Theresa *and* those of Frederick Engels and Eleanor Marx and Leon Trotsky among them. But that of John Stuart Mill would have to be there as certainly as any other.

Thirdly my account is Aristotelian in that it links evaluation and explanation in a characteristically Aristotelian way. From an Aristotelian standpoint to identify certain actions as manifesting or failing to manifest a virtue or virtues is never only to evaluate; it is also to take the first step towards explaining why those actions rather than some others were performed. Hence for an Aristotelian quite as much as for a Platonist the fate of a city or an individual can be explained by citing the injustice of a tyrant or the courage of its defenders. Indeed without allusion to the place that justice and injustice, courage and cowardice play in human life very little will be genuinely explicable. It follows that many of the explanatory projects of the modern social sciences, a methodological canon of which is the separation of "the facts" . . . from all evaluation, are bound to fail. For the fact that someone was or failed to be courageous or just cannot be recognised as "a fact" by those who accept the methodological canon. The account of the virtues which I have given is completely at one with Aristotle's on this point. But now the question may be raised: your account may be in many respects Aristotelian, but is it not in some respects false? Consider the following important objection.

I have defined the virtues partly in terms of their place in practices. But surely, it may be suggested, some practices—that is, some coherent human activities which answer to the description of what I have called a practice—are evil. So in discussions by some moral philosophers of this type of account of the virtues it has been suggested that torture and sado-masochistic sexual activities might be examples of practices. But how can a disposition be a virtue if it is the kind of disposition which sustains practices and some practices issue in evil? My answer to this objection falls into two parts.

First I want to allow that there *may* be practices—in the sense in which I understand the concept—which simply *are* evil. I am far from convinced that there are, and I do not in fact believe that either torture or sado-masochistic sexuality answer to the description of a practice which my account of the virtue employs. But I do not want to rest my case on this lack of conviction, especially since it is plain that as a matter of contingent fact many types of practice may on particular occasions be productive of evil. For the range of practices includes the arts, the sciences and certain types of intellectual and athletic game. And it is at once obvious that any of these may under certain conditions be a source of evil: the desire to excel and to win can corrupt, a man may be so engrossed by his painting that he neglects his family, what was initially an honourable resort to war can issue in savage cruelty. But what follows from this?

It certainly is not the case that my account entails *either* that we ought to excuse or condone such evils *or* that whatever flows from a virtue is right. I do have to allow that courage sometimes sustains injustice, that loyalty has been known to strengthen a murderous aggressor and that generosity has sometimes weakened the capacity to do good. But to deny this would be to fly in the face of just those empirical facts which I invoked in criticising Aquinas' account of the unity of the virtues. That the virtues need initially to be defined and explained with reference to the notion of a practice thus in no way entails approval of all practices in all circumstances. That the virtues—as the objection itself presupposed—*are* defined not in terms of good and right practices, but of practices, does not entail or imply that practices as actually carried through at particular times and places do not stand in need of moral criticism. And the resources for such criticism are not lacking. There is in the first place no inconsistency in appealing to the requirements of a virtue to criticise a practice. Justice may be initially defined as a disposition which in its particular way is necessary to sustain practices; it does not follow that in pursuing the requirements of a practice violations of justice are not to be condemned. I have already pointed out . . . that a morality of virtues requires as its counterpart a conception of moral law. Its requirements too have to be met by practices. But, it may be asked, does not all this imply that more needs to be said about the place of practices in some larger moral context? Does not this at least suggest that there is more to the core concept of a virtue than can be spelled out in terms of practice? I have after all emphasised that the scope of any virtue in human life extends beyond the practices in terms of which it is initially defined. What then is the place of the virtues in the larger arena of human life?

I stressed earlier that any account of the virtues in terms of practices could only be a partial and first account. What is required to complement it? The most notable difference so far between my account and any account that could be called Aristotelian is that although I have in no way restricted the exercise of the virtues to the context of practices, it is in terms of practices that I have located their point and function. Whereas Aristotle locates that point and function in terms of the notion of a type of whole human life which can be called good. And it does seem that the question "What would a human being lack who lacked the virtues?" must be given a kind of answer which goes beyond anything which I have said so far. For such an individual would not merely fail *in a variety of particular ways* in respect of the kind of excellence which can be achieved through participation in practices and in respect of the kind of human relationship required to sustain such excellence. His own life *viewed as a whole* would perhaps be defective; it would not be the kind of life which someone would describe in trying to answer the question "What is the best kind of life for this kind of man or woman to live?" And that question cannot be answered without at least raising Aristotle's own question, "What is the good life for man?" Consider three ways in which a human life informed only by the conception of the virtues sketched so far would be defective.

It would be pervaded, first of all, by *too many* conflicts and *too much* arbitrariness. I argued earlier that it is a merit of an account of the virtues in terms of a multiplicy of goods that it allows for the possibility of tragic conflict in a way in which Aristotle's does not. But it may also produce even in the life of someone who is virtuous and disciplined too many occasions when one allegiance points in one direction, another in another. The claims of one practice may be incompatible with another in such a way that one may find oneself oscillating in an arbitrary way, rather than making rational choices. So it seems to have been with T. E. Lawrence. Commitment to sustaining the kind of community in which the virtues can flourish may be incompatible with the devotion which a particular practice—of the arts, for example—requires. So there may be tensions between the claims of family life and those of the arts—the problem that Gauguin solved or failed to solve by fleeing to Polynesia, or between the claims of politics and those of the arts—the problem that Lenin solved or failed to solve by refusing to listen to Beethoven.

If the life of the virtues is continuously fractured by choices in which one allegiance entails the apparently arbitrary renunciation of another, it may seem that the goods internal to practices do after all derive their authority from our individual choices; for when different goods summon in different and in incompatible directions, "I" have to choose between their rival claims. The modern self with its criterionless choices apparently reappears in the alien context of what was claimed to be an Aristotelian world. This accusation might be rebutted in part by returning to the question of why both goods and virtues do have authority in our lives and repeating what was said earlier in this chapter. But this reply would only be partly successful; the distinctively modern notion of choice would indeed have reappeared, even if with a more limited scope for its exercise than it has usually claimed.

Secondly without an overriding conception of the *telos* of a whole human life, conceived as a unity, our conception of certain individual virtues has to remain partial and incomplete. Consider two examples. Justice, on an Aristotelian view, is defined in terms of giving each person his or her due or desert. To deserve well is to have contributed in some substantial way to the achievement of those goods, the sharing of which and the common pursuit of which provide foundations for human community. But the goods internal to practices, including the goods internal to the practice of making and sustaining forms of community, need to be ordered and evaluated in some way if we are to assess relative desert. Thus only substantive application of an Aristotelian concept of justice requires an understanding of goods and of the good that goes beyond the multiplicity of goods which inform practices. As with justice, so also with patience. Patience is the virtue of waiting attentively without complaint, but not of waiting thus for anything at all. To treat patience as a virtue presupposes some adequate answer to the question: waiting for what? Within the context of practices a partial, although for many purposes adequate, answer can be given: the patience of a craftsman with refractory material, of a teacher with a slow pupil, of a politician in negotiations, are all species of patience. But what if the material is just too refractory, the pupil too slow, the negotiations too frustrating? Ought we always at a certain point just to give up in the interests of the practice itself? The medieval exponents of the virtue of patience claimed that there are certain types of situation in which the virtue of patience requires that I do not ever give up on some person or task, situations in which, as they would have put it, I am required to embody in my attitude to that person or task something of the patient attitude of God towards his creation. But this could only be so if patience served some overriding good, some *telos* which warranted putting other goods in a subordinate place. Thus is turns out that the content of the virtue of patience depends upon how we order various goods in a hierarchy and *a fortiori* on whether we are able rationally so to order these particular goods.

I have suggested so far that unless there is a *telos* which transcends the limited goods of practices by constituting the good of a whole human life, the good of a human life conceived as a unity, it will *both* be the case that a certain subversive arbitrariness will invade the moral life *and* that we shall be unable to specify the context of certain virtues adequately. These two considerations are reinforced by a third: that there is at least one virtue recognised by the tradition which cannot be specified at all except with reference to the wholeness of a human life—the virtue of integrity or constancy. "Purity of heart," said Kierkegaard, "is to will one thing." This notion of singleness of purpose in a whole life can have no application unless that of a whole life does.

It is clear therefore that my preliminary account of the virtues in terms of practices captures much, but very far from all, of what the Aristotelian tradition taught about the virtues. It is also clear that to give an account that is at once more fully adequate to the tradition and rationally defensible, it is necessary to raise a question to which the Aristotelian tradition presupposed an answer, an answer so widely shared in the pre-modern world that it never had to be formulated explicitly in any detailed way. This question is: is it rationally justifiable to conceive of each human life as a unity, so that we may try to specify each such life as having its good and so that we may understand the virtues as having their function in enabling an individual to make of his or her life one kind of unity rather than another?

Moral Virtues

G. J. Warnock

In the second chapter of this book I raised the question: what is the apparatus of moral evaluation *for*? What is it supposed to do? If one were asked why it was worth going in for, what should be one's answer? I ventured there the very vague and general proposition (difficult, I believe, but doubtless by no means impossible, to disagree with) that the general object of the exercise—of moral evaluation of oneself or of others, of one's own acts or other people's, of past, present, future, or merely hypothetical acts—must be "to contribute in some respects, by way of the actions of rational beings, to the amelioration of the human predicament"; and I went on to sketch out, in that same chapter, some of the "limitations" inherent in the human predicament in virtue of which things are liable to go rather badly, and consequently to stand in need of amelioration. It is to this topic that, in search of illumination of the notion of "moral reasons," I now want to return. For it seems evident that what, from the moral point of view, can be reasons to commend or condemn, to do or to abstain from doing, for both judgement and action, must be some function of what moral evaluation is supposed to achieve, of the end in view, and of the *way* in which it is supposed to achieve it; and this is an issue on which we have not yet found much to say that seemed at all satisfactory. We have rejected the idea that morality is supposed to work by proposing, in opposition to the native egoism of the unregenerate human, the single, simple injunction of universal beneficence; and we have rejected also the idea that it is supposed to work by requiring compliance with an—itself supposedly beneficent—system of rules. So now we need, in a sense, to re-open the question. There are certain very general facts about the human predicament, including certain very general facts about human beings, which seem to be reasonably regarded as setting up, in ways already briefly sketched, an inherent liability for things to go rather badly; what then, let us ask, is required, if things are to go better—or rather if, as by and large is the case, they are not actually to go quite so badly as they seem inherently liable to do? And where, among such requirements, might morality be seen as fitting in?

One might begin by saying that, if things are to go better in the sense in question—if, that is, people's needs and interests, and some at least of their wants, are to be more fully satisfied than they otherwise might be—one very basic *desideratum* would surely be greater resources from which to satisfy them. . . .

Continuing at the same level of monstrous generality, one might mention next the obvious need for organization. It is perfectly obvious that very little of any sort would ever be done, if every individual attempted to do everything on his own, or merely in such more or less fortuitous groups as might be formed *ad hoc* from time to time by individual initiative. For vastly many purposes, the long-run co-operation of many individuals is absolutely necessary; and if such co-operation is to be effective, it must be somehow directed—there must be some way of determining objectives, and of regulating more or less closely what the roles of individuals are to be in the co-operative undertaking. It is of course largely at any rate from this necessity that there

Chapter 6 from *The Object of Morality* © 1971 by G. J. Warnock. By permission of the author (G. J. Warnock, formerly Principal of Hertford College, Oxford).

come to exist what may generally be called "institutions"—tribes, national states, federations of states, clubs, associations and parties of all kinds, firms, trade unions, armies, universities, the Mafia, and so on. It need not be maintained that the formation and character of such more or less co-operative institutions is fully determined by strictly practical ends; some may be in part just "natural," like the family perhaps in its more general aspects, though not in details, and some may be wholly or in part, as one might say, for fun, for the sake of the pleasures of association in itself. But that there *is* a practical necessity here is indisputable; there are countless things that we want and need that we could not possibly get, even it if were known how they could be got, without the organized, institutionalized co-operation of many individuals, and for that matter also of institutions with other institutions.

That, then, which is of course a very great deal, is obviously part of what is required if amelioration of the human predicament, or perhaps merely the avoidance of its excessive deterioration, is to be practically possible; if we have the requisite information and technical skills, and if there are institutional forms for bringing about the application of knowledge and skills in directed co-operative undertakings, then many things towards human betterment *can* be done. But this of course does not ensure that they will be. That is a problem of a totally different kind.

Well, at least one idea for its solution comes readily to mind. If, as has been suggested, humans have, placed as they are, a certain inherent propensity to act to the disadvantage or detriment of other humans, and even of themselves, then, if they are not to do so, they can be *made* not to do so. If, for instance, they are prone to be a good deal less concerned with the wants, needs, and interests of others than with their own, then, if they are to act in some other or in the general interest rather than purely in their own, they can be made so to act. What is required, one may reason, for the suitable modification of the patterns of behaviour towards which people are "naturally" prone, may thus be some suitably designed system of coercion. People must be given an interest, which they do not just naturally have, in doing things which they are not just naturally inclined towards doing; and this is exactly what a system of coercion can supply.

Now there is every reason to think that this is part of the answer; but there is also every reason to think that it is not and could not be, as perhaps Hobbes thought it was, the sole and whole answer. Part of the answer, certainly: taking things as they are and have been and are likely to continue to be, it is not deniable that there are people who are deflected from acting damagingly to others, or even to themselves, solely or mainly by the anticipation of consequences disagreeable to themselves if they so act— consequences liable to be deliberately imposed on them by others, by whom to that extent they can be said to be coerced. No doubt the most conspicuous example here is law. A community without laws is not absolutely inconceivable; and in fact rather small-scale examples actually exist. It is not inconceivable that a system of law should be non-coercive, that is, should make no provision for the actual punishment of law-breakers; and on a small and rather informal scale, in some clubs for example, something like this is sometimes actually the case. Again, the prevention of diminution by coercive means of damaging conduct is by no means, of course, the only object, not even the only avowed or ostensible object, of legal systems. But it clearly is part of the ostensible object, and probably always of the actual object too; and though some would argue that ideally such systems of coercion would be dispensable, it is pretty clear that they are in fact a practical necessity in nearly all circumstances. If society at large suddenly resolved, in the manner of what used to be regarded as progressive schools, completely to dismantle all machinery of coercion, there is plenty of reason to apprehend that things on the whole would go rather worse as a result than they actually do.

However, it is not true, and scarcely could be true, that people are brought to abstain from acting damagingly to others, or even to themselves, solely by coercion or by coercive deterrence. There is a practical point here, and also, I think, a kind of logical point. In the first place, if nothing but coercion kept people in order, then the machinery of coercion would have to be very vast—police, say, might have to equal in number the rest of the population, or at any rate somehow be ubiquitous and powerful enough for their surveillance to be pretty continuous and continuously effective. In practice this seems, in most societies, not in fact to be necessary for the purpose. (Though vast coercive systems are not unknown, it is more than doubtful whether it is for *this* purpose that they are maintained.) But it seems a point of no less importance that coercion is itself something that people do; such a system is directed and executed, after all, by people. If it is to do any good, or to do good rather than harm, then it must be directed and executed (let us say vaguely) properly; and it seems that it could not solely be coercion that brought this about. If coercion is ever to operate, except by pure chance, in any general interest, it seems reasonable to hold that there must be some persons, indeed many persons, prepared to act in that general interest without themselves being coerced into doing so. . . .

We thus come to what seems clearly most important in the present connection. If any of those things towards the amelioration of the human predicament which can be done are to be done in fact, then not only must people sometimes be *made* to do things which they are not just naturally disposed to do anyway; they must also sometimes voluntarily, without coercion, act otherwise than people are just naturally disposed to do. It is necessary that people should acquire, and should seek to ensure that others acquire, what may be called *good dispositions*—that is, some readiness on occasion voluntarily to do desirable things which not all human beings are just naturally disposed to do anyway, and similarly not to do damaging things.

We may say, then, speaking still in quite monstrously general terms, that, if things are not actually to go quite so badly as, given the nature of the human predicament, they are inherently liable to do, there are conspicuously four sorts of general *desiderata*—knowledge, so that what is in fact amelioratively practicable is brought within the scope of feasibility by human action; organization, so that the doings of many people and of groups of people can be brought into directed, co-operative, non-conflicting channels; coercion, so that at least to some extent people may be made to behave in desirable ways, and stopped from behaving otherwise; and "good dispositions," that is, some degree of readiness voluntarily to act desirably, and to abstain from behaving otherwise. . . . All these things, one might say, have to do with our capacity to influence the way things go; they do not determine how that capacity is to be used, or whether it is to be used to our or anyone's detriment or benefit. What matters most is what, of the things we can do, we choose to do; if this goes wrong, then everything goes wrong, and only more wrong, the more efficiently it goes.

There comes into view, then, among very general *desiderata* for the betterment of the human predicament, a distinction which seems to be of great and (I hope) of obvious importance—a distinction, namely, between what makes betterment possible, and what tends to bring it about that it actually occurs; roughly, between means available to people for the improvement of their lot, and the disposition to make beneficial use of those means. Moreover, if we now look again at this topic of human dispositions, it seems possible to discern here also a similar distinction—between, as one may put it, those dispositions whose tendency is to increae the effectiveness, or capacity, of a person, and those which tend to determine to what uses his capacities will be put. . . .

Now as to these I offer the suggestion—which I take not to be just arbitrary, though I have also no doubt at all that it will not be universally accepted—that, while there is clear and good reason to regard these dispositions as virtues, it would not be unreasonable to hold that they are not *moral* virtues. They may be, indeed in some degree they certainly are, necessary conditions of the effective exercise of moral virtues, as indeed of effective action of any kind; but one may still wish to say that they *are* not moral virtues. Whether this suggestion is acceptable or not, let me at any rate offer forthwith my reasons for making it. It seems to me that there would be two good reasons for wishing to say this, or perhaps one reason put in two rather different ways. In the first place these virtues, while of course they are not necessarily, yet they may be exclusively and entirely, what might be called self-profiting. That is, the acquisition and exercise of these virtues is not only typically essential to, but could in principle be wholly directed to, the attainment of an agent's personal interest or ends—possibly, indeed, of ends of his to the gross damage or neglect of the interests of others. If, for instance, the dominant object of my life is to maintain, by fair means or foul, my personal power and ascendancy over some group, or party, or gang, or country, or empire, I may well display, and need to display, exceptional industry in maintaining and defending my system of despotism, great courage in resisting the pressures and machinations of my opponents and enemies, and marked self-control in adhering, perhaps sometimes in the teeth of great temptation and difficulty, to the sagacious promotion of my long-run interests, undistracted by impulse, self-indulgence, passion, or pleasure. Courage, asceticism, iron self-control, resolution in the face of hardship or danger or difficulty—these are almost standard equipment for the really major destroyers, whether military, political, or criminal, or all three at once. Thus, while the dispositions here in question are undoubted virtues, they are virtues all of which a very bad man might have; and while probably such qualities are admirable even in a bad man, he is not, it seems to me quite reasonable to maintain, *morally* the better for his possession of those admirable qualities.

Second, while these dispositions certainly do tend to countervail, as it were, something in the human predicament which contributes importantly to its natural tendency to turn out rather badly, they do not tend quite directly to countervail that in the predicament which there seems reason to regard, both in fact and moral theory, as really central. For these dispositions tend to countervail, and are genuinely admirable in so far as they do so, what might be called natural human *weaknesses*—varieties, that is, of the natural inclination to evade or avoid, in its various forms, the burdensome or disagreeable. But they have in themselves no tendency at all to counteract the limitation of human sympathies; and this is really just another way of saying that, as I mentioned a moment ago, they may be wholly self-profiting, and even very damaging to others than the agent himself.

This, then, invites the suggestion, which I am perfectly ready to make, that the paradigmatic *moral* virtues may be, not these, but rather those good dispositions whose tendency is directly to countervail the limitation of human sympathies, and whose exercise accordingly is essentially—though indeed not, by itself, necessarily effectively—good *for* persons other than the agent himself. Let us see what profit we can extract from this proposition.

What questions are they, then, that can appropriately be put to the hypothesis that we now have in view? We are operating with the idea that, "good dispositions" being crucially important to abatement of the ills inherent in the human predicament, one might with reason regard as specifically *moral virtues* those which, not being essentially, or even potentially, exclusively self-profiting, would tend to countervail those particular ills liability to which is to be laid at the door of the limitedness of human sympathies. So, if we seek further light on what these good dispositions would be, we need now to consider in a little more detail what those particular ills are—that is, in what ways, in consequence of the limitedness of human sympathies, people are typically *liable* to act so as to worsen, or not to act so as to ameliorate, the predicament.

The first step on this path, at any rate, seems an easy one to take. If I am exclusively, or even predominantly, concerned with the satisfaction of my own wants, interests, or needs, or of those of some limited group such as my family, or friends, or tribe, or country, or class, with whose interests and ends I am naturally disposed to sympathize, then I, other members of that group, or the group as a whole, may be naturally prone to act directly to the detriment of other persons, non-members of the group, or of other groups. I may be inclined, from competitiveness or mere indifference or even active malevolence, to do positive harm to others, whether in the form of actual injury to them, or of frustration and obstruction of the satisfaction of their wants, interests, and needs. There is here, that is to say, a liability to act simply *maleficently*— harmfully, damagingly—to others, quite directly, either out of sheer unconcern with the damage so inflicted, or even out of a positive taste for the infliction of damage on persons or groups outside the circle of one's sympathies. That being so, it can scarcely seem controversial to say that *one* of the "good dispositions" we are in search of will be the disposition to abstain from (deliberate, unjustified) maleficence. Of course, if we nominate this disposition as one of the moral virtues, it may reasonably be remarked that it is not, in a sense, very much of a virtue; a disposition, that is to say, not to act deliberately maleficently towards other persons, from sheer unconcern for or active malevolence towards them, is, one may hopefully suppose, just normally to be expected in normal persons, who accordingly come up from commendation on this account only if their nonmaleficence is exceptional in degree, or maintained in the face of exceptional temptation, or provocation, or difficulty. However, the propensity *not* to act injuriously towards others whenever one has, or might have, some "natural" inclination to do so, while perhaps not specially creditable in ordinary circumstances, is still very clearly of fundamental importance; for it is obvious what a gangster's world we should find ourselves in without it—and indeed do find ourselves in, when and so far as this disposition is absent.

The next step seems also, in general terms, scarcely more problematic. If we need, and if humans in general do not just naturally, regularly, and reliably have, the disposition of nonmaleficence, just the same can plainly be said of the disposition towards positive beneficence. The limitedness of sympathies tends often to make it not just natural to interest oneself directly in another's good; there is need, then, for cultivation of the disposition to do so, which will very often take the particular form of readiness to give *help* to others in their activities. It seems reasonable to hold, and indeed practically impossible not to hold, that responsibility for pursuit of an individual's good is primarily his own—partly for the reason that it is primarily for him to say (though of course he cannot say infallibly) what that good is, and partly for the plain, practical reason that, in normal circumstances, if everyone embroils himself persistently, however well-meaningly, in other people's concerns rather than his own, a considerable measure of chaos and cross-purposes is likely to ensue. There are, however, many ends a person may have which cannot be secured by his own effects alone. There are common ends, to be secured only by the co-operation of many. There are some persons who have particular claims upon the beneficence of particular other persons. And there are some persons who, though perhaps without any special claims, should be helped because their need of help is exceptionally great, or their ability to help themselves exceptionally restricted. Not much more than this could be said in quite general terms. People and societies clearly differ a good deal, for a variety of reasons, in their assessment of the proportion of time, talents, efforts, and resources that an individual should devote to ends and interests other than his own; moreover, what is required in this way, what there is scope for, depends very much on the organization and institutions of particular societies. How far, for instance, there is need and room for private charity will depend on the extent to which public provision is made for the relief of indigence. But it is worth remarking, I think, that disagreement on this issue is often disagreement on the facts, at least in part. It was once held, notoriously, that it is *in fact* most advantageous for everybody that each, by and large, should pursue and promote his own interests single-mindedly; and though this thesis no doubt was often disingenuously asserted by those who fancied their chances in the envisaged free-for-all, and indeed is certainly not true without qualification, it is still, I suppose, a question of fact, and an unsettled question, in what ways and to what extent it needs to be qualified. In any case we are not attempting to settle here exactly what, in one case or another, the proper exercise of this virtue would actually consist in; what here matters, and what in general terms seems scarcely disputable, is that, along with nonmaleficence, it *is* a virtue.

What else? Well, so far we have laid at the door of "limited sympathies," and accordingly have affirmed the need to countervail, the inclination to act damagingly to others towards whom one is not "naturally" sympathetic, and not to act beneficently when such action is needed or claimed. I believe that we should now add, as an independent requirement, the disposition not to *discriminate,* as surely most humans have some natural propensity to do, to the disadvantage of those outside the limited circle of one's natural concern. If, for instance, twenty people have a claim upon, or are substantially in need of, some service or benefit that I can provide, it seems not enough merely to say that I should not refuse it; it must be added that I should not help or benefit some of them *less* merely because, for instance, I may happen to like them less, or be less well-disposed towards them. The general name for this good disposition is, I take it, fairness. Of course it is commonly supposed, and indeed it would be unrealistically inhuman not to suppose, that actual sympathies and natural ties quite often justify discriminatory treatment; nevertheless, it must be observed that these should issue in discriminatory treatment only when, as is not always the case, they do actually justify it. . . .

Then one more thing. If we consider the situation of a person, somewhat prone by nature to an exclusive concern with his own, or with some limited range of, interests and needs and wants, living among other persons more or less similarly constituted, we see that there is one device in particular, very often remarkably easy to employ, by which he may be naturally more or less inclined to, so to speak, carve out his egoistical way to his own, and if necessary at the expense of other, ends; and that is *deception*. It is possible for a person, and often very easy, by doing things, and especially in the form of saying things, to lead other persons to the belief that this or that is

the case; and one of the simplest and most seductive ways of manipulating and ma-
nœuvring other persons for the sake of one's own ends is that of thus operating self-
interestedly upon their beliefs. Clearly this is not, necessarily, directly damaging. We
all hold from time to time an immense range and variety of false beliefs, and very often
are none the worse for doing so; we are the worse for it only if, as is often not the case,
our false belief leads or partly leads us actually to act to our detriment in some way.
Thus, I do not necessarily do you any harm at all if, by deed or word, I induce you to
believe what is not in fact the case; I may even do you good, possibly by way, for example, of consolation or flattery. Nevertheless, though deception is thus not necessarily
directly damaging, it is easy to see how crucially important it is that the natural inclination to have recourse to it should be counteracted. It is, one might say, not the im-
planting of false beliefs that is damaging, but rather the generation of the suspicion
that they may be being implanted. For this undermines trust; and, to the extent that
trust is undermined, all co-operative undertakings, in which what one person can do
or has reason to do is dependent on what others have done, are doing, or are going
to do, must tend to break down. . . .

  We suggest, then, that, in the general context of the human predicament, there
are these four (at least) distinguishable damaging, or non-ameliorative, types of propensity which tend naturally to emanate directly from "limited sympathies"—those of
maleficence, non-beneficence, unfairness, and deception. If now we apply the supposition that the "object" of morality is to make the predicament less grim than, in a
quasi-Hobbesian state of nature, it seems inherently liable to be, and to do so specifically by seeking to countervail the deleterious liabilities inherent in "limited sympathies," we seem to be led to four (at least) general types of good disposition as those
needed to countervail the above-mentioned four types of propensity; and these dispositions will be, somewhat crudely named, those of non-maleficence, fairness, beneficence, and non-deception. We venture the hypothesis that these (at least) are
fundamental *moral virtues*.

  But we can now manipulate this conclusion a little. If it were agreed that we have
here, in these "good dispositions," four moral virtues, it could scarcely be contentious
to derive from this the proposition that we have here, by the same token, four fundamental moral *standards,* or moral *principles*. To have and to display, say, the moral virtue of non-deception could be said to be to regulate one's conduct in conformity to a
principle of non-deception, or to refer to that as to a *standard* in one's practical decisions. But such a principle would be a principle of judgement as well as of decision.
That is, if I accept a principle of non-deception, I may judge others to be morally condemnable in so far as (without excuse) their acts constitute breaches of it, or morally
praiseworthy in so far as they (laudably) comply with it in practice. And thus we can
say what a "moral reason" is. Namely, it is a consideration, about some person, or
some person's character, or some specimen of actual or possible conduct, which
tends to establish in the subject concerned conformity or conflict with a moral principle. That your act would inflict wanton damage on some other person would be a
"moral reason" for judging that—at least "from the moral point of view"—you ought
not so to act, since it tends to establish that your act would be in conflict with the
moral principle of non-maleficence, or, to put just the same point in a different way,
would be inconsistent with exercise of the moral virtue of non-maleficence. Moral
"pros and cons"—an expression that cropped up in an earlier chapter—will be those
considerations, perhaps very complex and very numerous, concerning some particu-

lar case that comes up for judgement, which indicate respectively conformity to or conflict with some one or more moral principles.

I will end this chapter by offering two observations which, while both comparatively obvious, are of some importance. First, it seems to me that the "principles" we have sketchily elicited, and as to which we offer the hypothesis that they are basic *moral* principles, have to be accepted as independent principles, not reducible either to one another or to anything else. There is indeed, if I am right, some bond of union between them, as well as a very manifest *rationale* behind them—something, that is, that makes it possible coherently to explain why it is that they are grouped together as *moral* principles, and why compliance with them should constitute moral *virtue;* the suggestion is, namely, that they are alike in the respect that their voluntary recognition would tend to counteract the maleficent liabilities of limited sympathies, and in *that* way to work towards amelioration of the human predicament. However, though alike in this, they remain independent. For there is not *one* way in which beings of limited sympathies are inherently liable to act to each other's detriment, but *several* ways, and thus several independent "good dispositions" to be desiderated. This emerges, I think, reasonably clearly from what has been said. It would be just possible, I suppose, though extremely artificial, to class non-maleficence as a sub-species of beneficence; but it seems to me both more natural and more explicit to regard the principle of abstaining from avoidable and unjustified damage as *different* from that of doing solicited or unsolicited good. Abstaining from theft is not a special kind of philanthropy. Fairness, again, is a *different* requirement from that of non-maleficence, or of beneficence; it may often be the case that a maleficent act is unfair, but that is to say about it two things, not one thing; and even if, as may not always be the case, some act of fairness is also an act of beneficence, still the reason for judging it to be the first will not be the same as that for judging it to be the second. An act of deception, as we said before, is not necessarily maleficent; and again, if I benefit you in acting non-deceptively, to show that I do benefit you is a quite different matter from showing that I do not deceive you—even when these go together, they are not the same. To tell you the truth to the best of my ability is not at all the same thing as to tell you what I judge it would be of benefit to you to be told. It has been held that deception is always a breach of the principle of justice, but this again seems to me, though just possible, undesirably artificial; deception, I would think, is appropriately classed as unjust only if the victim has some sort of *special* claim, not merely that which any person has on any other person whatever, not to be deceived. It is perhaps specifically unfair for me to lie to you when you have trustingly favoured me with your confidence; but it is not in the same way *unfair* of me to deceive a total stranger.

There are two major reasons, I believe, why recognition of this fact of independence is of considerable importance. The first is theoretical. Philosophers, professionally in pursuit of systematic unity, and feeling (rightly in my view) that behind morality there is to be discerned an—in some sense—single *rationale,* seem often to have been taken with the idea that perhaps there is really just *one* fundamental moral principle. This seems to be an error. It may be that there is one, very general, end in view; but there is not, as one might put it, just one means to that end. And the second point is practical, or anyway less purely theoretical; it is that what I take to be the plurality and independence of moral principles implies that "moral reasons" may conflict. We are inveterately liable in any case to be perplexed in practice by conflicting considerations; even if, for instance, we are charged with the single requirement of selecting for an appointment the best instructor in philosophy. the circumstance of some applicant's exceptional philosophical ability may conflict with his obvious lack of interest in teaching, or inability to express himself comprehensibly to the student mind. Or again, an arbitrator's decision that would do justice to the claims of one party may sometimes, by exactly the same standard, imply injustice to the claims of another. But if, in morality, there are anyway independent principles, there is the obvious possibility that what conformity with one would require would involve conflict with another; there may, that is, be clear moral pros *and* cons in the very same case; and if that is so, it seems to me quite impossible to exclude the possibility that predicaments may arise which are, literally, morally insoluble. One would indeed wish to avoid this conclusion if possible, but I do not myself see how this possibility of genuine insolubility is to be excluded. It is clear that moral principles *may* point in opposite directions; and I can discern no ground on which one could pronounce *in general* which, in such a case, is to predominate over another. This may indeed be possible in special cases. . . .

My second comment is this. It is obvious but important that morality, seen from the angle that we have here adopted, does not offer an answer to the question "how one should live," in at any rate some important senses of that queer, obscure phrase. But here there are obscurities that call for a little untangling.

What is one to make, anyway, of the question "how one should live," given honourable mention by Plato and by many of his successors? It may look, from one angle at least, a pretty senseless question. Where we have some reasonably well-defined, determinate task or performance, it makes clear sense to ask how that task or performance should be done; one understands the question how one should set about catching trout, reducing consumer demand, seeking an interview with the Prime Minister, or trying perhaps to become Prime Minister oneself. But what is "living"? Presumably it consists in doing things, doing anything whatever, in thinking this or that, having dreams and feelings and moods of some sort, and so on; and what sense does it make to enquire how *that* should be done? In this sense, the question how one ought to live looks in no better case than the question how one ought to cook—not how one ought to cook carrots, or cabbage, or kippers, or anything in particular, but *simply* how one ought to *cook*. A senseless question, one is tempted to say, has no sensible answer.

Presumably, however, there are other ways in which the words can be taken, in which they can be seen to pose a decently intelligible question, though not, indeed, always a question that has a reasonable answer. First, the question "how one should live" might be taken to mean: what goals should one seek to achieve in the course of one's life? Two comments on this. First, while this is, I think, a decently intelligible question, there seems to me every reason to suppose that there is not, quite in general, any sensible answer to it. For is there any goal in life at all of which one could say, quite in general, that "one"—that is, anyone and everyone—should aim at achieving it? The goals, I suppose, that there is reason, at any rate *ceteris paribus,* for me to try to achieve are those that I might be expected to find satisfactory, if I should achieve them. But what those would be, is a function of what sort of person I am, am capable of becoming, or likely to become; and not everyone, both obviously and fortunately, is the same sort of person. The goals appropriate to a "man of action" are not, surely, to be recommended to the contemplative scholar, the dedicated artist, the religious recluse. Such people will pursue, and properly pursue, quite different goals; there is no way in which, in that sense, they *all* should live.

Second, it is clear that "morality," as here envisaged, does not pronounce, in this sense of the question, on how one ought to live—fortunately, indeed, for morality, if I am right in suggesting that the question so taken is not one that can be reasonably answered anyway. For morality, as I see it, does not as such set definite goals before us, or nominate specific ends as those at which we should aim; it should rather be seen, I suggest, as propounding principles to which by and large our conduct should conform in the pursuit of our ends, *whatever* those ends may be. . . .

But one may take "how one ought to live" in a rather different way again. Perhaps what one is to aim at can be regarded, like Aristotle's *eudaimonia,* not so much as a goal to be achieved at some stage of one's life, but rather as a predominant *character* to be realized in one's life as a whole. But here again the two comments just made seem once more appropriate. Is there any real reason to suppose that, for everyone, there is any one general character that his life should have? Are there not, as they say, "life-styles" of many different varieties, each in its own way appropriate to certain sorts of people? And again, does morality as such require a particular "life-style"? There seems no reason to think so. Compliance, once again, with what morality requires seems, while no doubt not compatible with some kinds of life, yet compatible with lives of many very different kinds. There is, it may be, a particular kind of life whose outstanding character is that of concern with the requirements of morality itself—in which living a *moral* life is the predominant concern of living. But it is not at all clear to me that one must suppose that morality itself requires that this should be so. One might think that to be *predominantly* concerned in one's life with, above all else, exact fulfilment of the requirement of morality is to exhibit a kind of moral extremism, or fanaticism, which it is not morally required of everyone that they should do.

Of course, if "how should one live?" means "in conformity with what principles?", then morality as we envisage it does offer an answer; for, precisely, it proposes principles for us to live by. But it does not, I think, even in this sense, offer a *complete* answer; for there are, of course, principles of conduct, of many different sorts, which are not *moral* principles, to which nevertheless it is proper that attention should be paid in considering by what principles one's life ought to be lived.

I can sum up, I think, what I am suggesting here by saying that, so far as I can see, the topic of morality is not at all the same as that of what used to be called "the Good Life." I doubt, for reasons indicated, whether the latter venerable topic is really a very useful one to discuss; for, since it is evident that there are people of very different kinds, with widely different tastes and talents, inclinations and abilities, it seems only reasonable to suppose that there are many *different* ways in which human lives may be satisfactorily, successfully, and admirably lived. But in any case morality, in my view, is only part of this topic. Morality, with the end of ameliorating the human predicament, essentially prescribes what might be called conditions *within which* lives are to be lived and ends to be pursued; but many different lives can be accommodated within those conditions; and for the "good life"—*any* good life—much more is required than simply that those limiting conditions should not be transgressed. One might live, come to that, a very poor life indeed—unsuccessful, unhappy, incoherent, frustrated, unproductive—without necessarily going *morally* astray at any point at all. The possession and exercise of moral virtues may be its own reward; but it is by no means the *only* reward that a reasonable man would hope for.

Chapter IV

Rights Theories

JEANE J. KIRKPATRICK

Establishing a Viable Human Rights Policy

Rights and Goals

In our times, "rights" proliferate at the rhetorical level, with extraordinary speed. To the rights to life, liberty, and security of person have been added the rights to nationality, to privacy, to equal rights in marriage, to education, to culture, to the full development of personality, to self-determination, to self-government, to adequate standards of living.

The United Nations Universal Declaration of Human Rights claims as a universal every political, economic, social right yet conceived.

The Declaration consists of a Preamble and thirty articles, setting forth the human rights and fundamental freedoms to which all men and women, everywhere in the world, are entitled, without any discrimination. Article 1, which lays down the philosophy upon which the Declaration is based, reads: "All human beings are born free and equal in dignity and rights. They are endowed with reason and conscience and should act towards one another in a spirit of brotherhood." Article 2, which sets out the basic principle of equality and nondiscrimination as regards the enjoyment of human rights and fundamental freedoms, forbids "distinction of any kind, such as race, color, sect, language, religion, political or other opinion, national or social origin, property, birth, or other status."

Article 3, a cornerstone of the Declaration, proclaims the right to life, liberty, and security of person: rights which are essential to the enjoyment of all other rights. It introduces the series of articles (4 to 21) in which the human rights of every individual are elaborated further.

The civil and political rights recognized in Articles 4 to 21 of the Declaration include: the right to life, liberty, and security of person; freedom from slavery and servitude; freedom from torture or cruel, inhuman, or degrading treatment or punishment; the right to recognition everywhere as a person before the law; the right to an effective judicial remedy; freedom from arbitrary arrest, detention, or exile; the right to a fair and public hearing by an independent and impartial tribunal; the right to be presumed innocent until proved guilty; freedom from arbitrary interference with privacy, family, home, or correspondence; freedom of movement and residence; the right of asylum; the right to a nationality; the right to marry and to found a family; the right to own property; freedom of thought, conscience, and religion; freedom of opinion and expression; the right to peaceful assembly and association; the right of everyone to take part in the government of his country; and the right of everyone to equal access to public service in his country.

Article 22, the second cornerstone of the Declaration, introduces Articles 23 to 27, in which economic, social, and cultural rights— the rights to which everyone is entitled "as a member of society"—are set out. Article 22 reads: "Everyone, as a member of society, has the right to social security and is entitled to realization, through national effort and international cooperation and in accordance with the organization and resources of each state, of the economic, social, and cultural rights indispensable for his dignity and the full development of his personality."

The economic, social, and cultural rights recognized in Articles 23 to 27 include the right to social security, the right to work, the right to equal pay for equal work, the right to leisure, the right to a standard of living adequate

Reprinted from *World Affairs*, vol. 143, Spring 1981, pp. 323–334.

for health and well-being, the right of education, and the right to participate in the cultural life of the community.

The concluding articles, Articles 28 to 30, stress that everyone "is entitled to a social and international order in which the rights and freedoms set forth in this Declaration can be fully realized" (Article 28); that "everyone has duties to the community in which alone the free and full development of his personality is possible" (Article 29.1); and that "nothing in this Declaration may be interpreted as implying for any State, group or person any right to engage in any activity aimed at the destruction of any of the rights and freedoms set forth herein."

Recently, in Geneva, the United Nations Commission on Human Rights affirmed a "right to development" which carries its own concomitant list of "rights" including the right to a new economic order, peace, and an end to the arms race.

Such declarations of human "rights" take on the character of "a letter to Santa Claus"—as [Orwin and Prangle] noted. They can multiply indefinitely because "no clear standard informs them, and no great reflection produced them." For every goal toward which human beings have worked, there is in our time a "right." Neither nature, experience, nor probability informs these lists of "entitlements," which are subject to no constraints except those of the mind and appetite of their authors. The fact that such "entitlements" may be without possibility of realization does not mean they are without consequences.

The consequence of treating goals as rights is grossly misleading about how goals are achieved in real life. "Rights" are vested in persons; "goals" are achieved by the efforts of persons. The language of rights subtly vests the responsibility in some other. When the belief that one has a right to development coincides with facts of primitive technology, hierarchy, and dictatorship, the tendency to blame someone is almost overwhelming. If the people of the world do not fully enjoy their economic rights it must be because some *one*— some monopoly capitalist, some Zionist, some man—is depriving them of their rightful due.

Utopian expectations concerning the human condition are compounded then by a vague sense that Utopia is one's due; that citizenship in a perfect society is a reasonable expectation for real persons in real societies.

Rights Theories

238

Beginning with this chapter, we will blur a philosophical distinction between ethics and political philosophy. Ethics, as we have seen, is concerned with issues of right and wrong generally, yet one aspect of political philosophy or political theory is concerned with pretty much the same thing. A central project of political philosophy is to determine what sort of rules (laws) a good government may justifiably impose upon its citizens. A broadly correct answer to this question seems to be that the proper laws (particularly criminal laws) are the morally good ones. To put the matter another way, a good government would require citizens to act in a morally proper fashion toward one another. For example, a good government would enforce laws against murder, theft, fraud, contract violation, and so on. Furthermore, the reason for having these laws is that the sort of actions mentioned are ones that are morally wrong. Accordingly, a proper political theory must be concerned with ethical issues.

The projects, then, of ethics and political philosophy intersect at a point. Both are interested in a criterion of ethical conduct. However, there is still a distinction between the two projects. Ethics is interested in finding a criterion for conduct generally speaking. Political theory, as represented above, need only find a criterion for that portion of ethical conduct for which it is appropriate to have legislation. This is to admit that there may be actions that are morally wrong but are not important enough to outlaw. Or, to use an example from the last chapter, if there are "supererogatory" actions, it would not be appropriate to have laws requiring such actions. As we have seen, supererogatory actions, by definition, are not the sort of thing that we can require people to do. And, as we shall see in Chapter 6, there are further limits on the extent to which legislation can be used to enforce morality.

Even granting the above, however, political philosophy may be an appropriate domain in which to look for the central criteria of ethics. Arguably, the moral notions that are incorporated into law are likely to be the fundamental ones. They are the ones we believe are important enough that we are willing to punish people for their transgressions. In this chapter we will look at a central moral idea that is often used in political contexts—the notion of "rights." Perhaps, unlike the moral ideas we have considered so far, the idea of "rights" will seem commonplace. It seems nowadays, as Jeane Kirkpatrick argues, that talk about rights is not only familiar, but has mushroomed out of control. There are not only claims to the more familiar rights to life, free speech, and property but nonsmokers' rights, welfare rights, animal rights—the list seems endless. Kirkpatrick's criticism is not only that the list of rights is getting longer, but that it includes items that really ought not count as rights. We obviously need some way of determining what should count as a right.

One of the central tasks of the essays in this chapter will be to give a careful analysis of "rights." The need for such an analysis is clear and pressing. Only if we understand the nature of rights do we have a chance of sorting out legitimate from illegitimate rights to solve the sort of problem Kirkpatrick poses. Furthermore, as we shall see, until we are satisfied that we have at least come close to a proper analysis, it will be difficult to assess the importance of rights in our moral thinking. We need to decide if rights are all that matter in morality or if there is more to the story.

Even though nearly all the readings that follow aim at a proper analysis of rights, it will be helpful here to do a small amount of analytical work to set the stage. The broad category of rights we will be considering goes by the name, largely due to John Locke, of *natural rights*. Locke's claim, which is echoed in the American Constitution, is that all persons have some rights by nature. These rights are also sometimes called *moral rights* or *human rights*. The idea is this: All persons, in virtue of being persons, have certain rights. Locke, for example, holds that all persons in a "state of nature," that is, before any special social arrangements, have rights to life, liberty, and property. Now, there can be other sorts of rights, for example, rights generated by agreements or contracts. An airline passenger has a right to safe air travel, and a bank has a right to get back the money it lends. These rights are not "natural" rights but rather rights stemming from special agreements.

While this tells us something about who has natural rights, it does not say much about the character of these rights. The predominant view is that natural rights are *claim-rights* or *entitlements*. The core idea of having a claim-right to life, for example, is that we are entitled to a certain sort of consideration from other people, specifically, they ought not do anything that threatens my life. A right to life is a kind of claim we can make against all other persons. We claim as our due that people not threaten our lives and, correlatively, it is our duty not to threaten the lives of others. Another way of putting the last point is to say that natural rights imply duties for other people. If I have a property right to my car, then other people have a duty not to steal it, damage it, or use it without my permission.

Natural rights are not just any kind of claim-rights, however. We can distinguish two sorts of claim-rights, only one of which natural-rights theorists are willing to defend. Claim-rights can either be "positive" or "negative." Let's use the example of a right to life to illustrate this distinction. To have a negative claim-right to life implies that others ought not try to take your life away. To respect people's negative claim rights, it is enough simply to leave them alone in the prescribed ways. However, a positive claim-right to life would mean something much stronger. If someone had a positive claim-right to life, then the rest of us would have a duty to provide the means to sustain that person's life. We would have to provide food, shelter, medicines, and whatever else the person may need to stay alive. We might even be obliged to keep people alive, on sophisticated medical devices, against their will.

Having made the distinction between positive and negative claim-rights, the typical view is that natural rights are only negative claim-rights. This is not to say, however, that there cannot be some positive claim-rights that are generated in special circumstances. The airline passenger has a positive claim-right to the assistance of the crew in cases of emergency. This is a right in virtue of having paid for the services of the airline, however, not simply in virtue of being a human being. The reason most rights theorists are only willing to defend negative claim-rights is fairly easy to see. Let's assume the contrary position for the state of argument and see where it leads; specifically, let's assume that a positive claim-right to life is one of our natural rights. If I have a positive, natural claim-right to life, then everyone else has a duty to provide me with the materials needed for sustaining my life. For example, if I need food and shelter or even an enormously costly medical operation to continue living, others have a duty to provide me with these things. Furthermore, if we think that it is appropriate to defend natural rights by the coercive force of the law, then others had better give me the aid I need or else be subject to punishment.

There is a problem here, however. Asserting a positive claim-right to life rather quickly runs afoul of what Locke and others consider a basic negative, natural claim-right—a right to property. Roughly, Locke and subsequently Robert Nozick, argue that we have a right to any amount of wealth we can earn by the fruits of our labor. We deserve any and all the wealth we have worked to produce, subject to a provision that other people also have the opportunity to acquire wealth by their efforts (this is what Nozick calls the *"Lockean Proviso"*). Note that this is a negative claim-right. On the grounds of a right to property, we cannot demand material goods from others. A right to property, according to Locke and Nozick, only means that we are entitled to property (wealth) that we have earned by our efforts. (Locke and Nozick also allow wealth to be legitimately acquired by gifts and inheritance.) Once we have earned our property, no one is permitted to take it away from us without our permission. If this strikes us as a correct account of what entitles us to property (wealth), then we cannot assert that there are any natural, positive claim-rights. As we have seen, a positive claim-right asserts that a person is entitled to the resources of others. This position sharply conflicts with the idea behind a property right, namely, that persons are entitled only to the fruits of their own labor—not someone else's. Taken to the extreme (as, for example, Nozick does), if anyone tries to enforce a positive claim-right by taking some of your wealth to help someone else, then you could claim theft. Wealth that you deserve has been taken away from you without your consent.

The above begins to explain why natural rights are typically restricted to negative claim-rights. It also explains why property rights in particular have played a fairly sizable role in rights theorist's discussion. The selections from John Locke, Robert Nozick, and Judith Jarvis Thomson are weighted to the topic of property rights. It should be noted that I am using the category "rights theorists" in a restrictive way. In a broad sense, anyone who insists upon the importance of rights (positive, negative, natural, legal, and so on) could be counted as a rights theorist. However, by the purposes of this chapter, we will specify the notion of a rights theorist more narrowly. Roughly, a rights theorist, in the sense we will be using, is one who holds that rights (negative claim-rights) define either the total extent to our moral obligations or at least the most important part of our moral obligations. Rights are either all important or most important. Notice that these are rather different claims. The most rigid version of rights theory is that if we respect other people's negative claim-rights, we have no other moral obligations to them (unless we freely consent to impose obligations on ourselves by making promises or signing contracts). A less rigid view about rights is that while there may be moral considerations over and above a person's rights, the principle of nonviolation of rights is the only one that should be enforced in a society. For example, it may be morally good (but not enforceable) to be charitable to the needy even though it is not our (enforceable) duty to give since the needy have no right to our assistance.

While we have discussed the nature of natural rights generally, there are two further issues that need to be addressed. We need to entertain arguments as to the proper list of natural rights. (What are our natural rights?) We also need to consider the importance of rights. (Why do we think respecting rights is so morally important?) Let's consider the latter question first. What a right gives people is a specifiable piece of liberty. To have a right (a negative claim-right) gives people freedom to make a life for themselves, without the interference of others. Both Richard Wasserstrom and Joel Feinberg argue that natural rights insure respect for human dignity in the sense that rights allow people to take responsibility for the course of their lives. For example, having a right to religious belief allows persons to make up their own minds about which religion, if any, to follow in their lives. Or, differently, the guarantee that we are entitled to property we have earned makes each of us responsible for the material comforts we choose to have.

Rights, then, are valued because they ensure some elbow room for people to shape their lives. It is important to contrast this conception of value with a utilitarian approach. On the face of it the theories may look similar. While it is fair to say that both utilitarianism and rights theory are concerned with people achieving a good life for themselves, there is an important difference. Utilitarianism, as we have seen, is interested in maximizing human happiness—in adopting policies that will tend to help people satisfy the wants and desires they have. Rights theories, however, want to ensure that people are given the room to make decisions about which desires to have, and an opportunity to satisfy those desires. The goals of the two theories will tend to conflict. For example, it could be argued that allowing people the freedom to make their own choices about how they live their lives—say, their own choices about religion—will not be the best thing to do according to utilitariansim. It is arguably the case that people often make bad choices about religion. As such, people might be happier if choices about religion were made for them. Even if this were true, however, a proponent of rights may still insist that people be allowed to make their own decisions. Even if allowing people to make their own decisions nets less utility, there is still a value in having this sort of freedom. Freedom to make one's own decisions, a rights theorist may argue, respects "human dignity."

If we now have a rough idea of the importance of natural rights, we have yet to give a list of people's natural rights. I will not attempt to argue for a specific list in this introduction, but we can get an idea what a general answer would look like. If it is the case that rights are important because they guarantee us the freedom to shape our own lives, then a proper list of natural rights should include those freedoms needed for this purpose. Accordingly, a good reason for claiming there is a specific right is that the freedom which the right protects is one important to the business of making a life for oneself. In this regard it is not surprising that a typical list of natural rights includes rights to life, privacy, free expression, and property. It can be argued that each of these areas needs to be protected because they are important to developing and pursuing life plans.

If it can be agreed that there are some rights, then it is reasonable to ask how much moral weight rights carry. We can separate two distinct issues here. First, we would like to know if there are any restrictions upon the sort of liberty protected by rights. For example, may people do anything they wish in the name of religious belief? And, second, we would like to know, in Ronald Dworkin's language, how seriously rights ought to be taken. Are rights the only thing of moral value or are there other, possibly overriding, moral considerations? If we respect other persons' rights, then have we done anything we ought morally to do for people? Or does morality require more of us than simply respecting rights?

There is a reasonably safe answer to the first question. Most rights theorists will agree that to claim a specific bit of freedom, say, for example, the right to religious belief, does not give a person the liberty to do just anything in the name of religious freedom. There are some limitations. A rule of thumb is that we can exercise our rights in whatever way we choose so long as we do not violate another person's rights. For example, on the grounds of religious freedom, I cannot practice human sacrifice since this, obviously, would violate another's right to life. I cannot steal money from the collection plate since this would violate another's right to property. A full specification of the rule of not violating another's rights depends upon an exact list of the rights in question.

Beyond this relatively obvious reply, it can yet be asked whether a person's rights can be limited for any other reason. On this score the readings by Ronald Dworkin, Robert Nozick, and Judith Jarvis Thomson are relevant; each gives a rather different answer to the question. Nozick adopts the strongest position on rights. He holds that rights cannot be overridden or limited for any reason but the nonviolation of other person's rights. In the selection for our reading, the issue is property rights, and Nozick argues, specifically, that the property that people are genuinely entitled to cannot be taken away from them without their consent; nor can the use of their property be restricted for any reason other than the nonviolation of another's rights. Nozick, like Locke before him, is willing to allow a government to take money from its citizens (by taxation) for the purposes of defending the rights we have, but he disallows taxation for any other reasons. The result of this position is rather harsh. It means that no one, including a government, can take money away from people to give positive, material assistance to even the most needy. If Nozick is correct, then we have no enforceable obligations to help the needy. Of course, it may be a charitable good deed to offer help, but it is not required.

Nozick holds that natural rights are absolute. There can be no limitations on a person's rights except the nonviolation of another's rights. That is to say, not only does Nozick hold that respecting a person's natural, negative claim-rights is morally important, but he holds that respecting natural rights is our only legally enforceable moral obligation. We are under no (enforceable) moral obligation to do anything for our fellow human beings other than leave them alone in the ways specified by the list of natural rights. However, it is consistent with Nozick's position to hold that it would be morally good (although not required as an obligation) to provide positive assistance to others.

Not everyone in our readings agrees with Nozick's extreme views on natural rights. While rights are morally important, rights alone may not tell the whole story of morality. A simple example will illustrate the problem with an absolutist version of rights theory. Suppose I go to the beach one day for a little sun. While sunbathing, I notice a person floundering in the surf and no one else is around. With no risk to myself I could save the person. On a strict version of rights theory, it can be argued that I have no moral obligation to do so. After all, my only moral duties are to respect other's natural rights. Natural rights are negative claim-rights, and negative claim-rights do not require me to assist anyone in any way. I respect the person's natural rights by allowing her to drown, and respecting rights is all I'm obliged to do. This surely doesn't seem like the moral thing to do in the circumstances, however. Rather, we are tempted to say that even if the person has no "right" to my help, it would nonetheless be immoral to deny her help.

Examples such as the one above lead people to think that the moral value of respecting natural rights must be "balanced" against other moral values, for example, utilitarian considerations of welfare However, Ronald Dworkin argues against at least one version of this "balancing" idea. It might be held, on the strength of our drowning example, that a person's right can be overridden whenever doing so promises greater utility than respecting rights. As Dworkin argues, however, this position has its own problems. For example, one could argue that the right to free speech must be limited to speech that does not irritate people. Some kinds of speech cause more harm than good. If we allowed this sort of restriction, it would defeat the whole idea of having a right.

Although Dworkin is a strong advocate of rights, he is not an absolutist. He recognizes that there will be cases (perhaps the drowning person case is one) where a slight intrusion on rights will have a large utilitarian benefit. In these cases it may be legitimate to either limit the extent of rights or demand from a person more than the simple respect for others' rights. Dworkin is at pains, however, to argue the model cannot be a mere balancing, if we are to "take rights seriously."

Judith Jarvis Thomson attacks directly Nozick's absolutist position on property rights. She considers a case, like our drowning person example, where we could "steal" some medicine to save a dying child. In an absolutist view of property rights, such an action cannot be justified—rights cannot be bridged for any reasons other than the nonviolation of other people's rights. And, again, we assume that the child does not have a "right" (negative claim-right) to someone else's property (the medicine) just because it is in need. Thus, in an absolutist view we are morally prohibited from taking the medicine even if it is the only way to save the child. Thompson finds this result unacceptable. It would be morally "indecent" to stand on one's property rights in cases like this. Thompson argues that although natural rights are important, respecting rights is not the only sort of moral duty we have. We may also have some (enforceable) duties to giving positive assistance to people in need. If this is so, then there may even be a good moral argument for taxing people to provide welfare assistance—contrary to Nozick's claim. Taxing for welfare assistance can be considered a way of enforcing our nonrights duty to help the needy.

To sum up, there are three major questions to keep in mind when reading the selections for this chapter. What exactly is a natural right? We need a close analysis of the concept to know what a rights holder is entitled to. Why are natural rights important? An adequate answer to this question will help to identify natural rights by uncovering the root moral idea behind rights. And finally, how important are rights? We need to know whether respecting natural rights is the only kind of moral obligation we need to obey.

Natural Rights

John Locke

OF THE STATE OF NATURE

§ **4.** To understand political power right, and derive it from its original, we must consider, what state all men are naturally in, and that is, a *state of perfect freedom* to order their actions, and dispose of their possessions and persons, as they think fit, within the bounds of the law of nature, without asking leave, or depending upon the will of any other man.

A *state* also *of equality,* wherein all the power and jurisdiction is reciprocal, no one having more than another; there being nothing more evident, than that creatures of the same species and rank, promiscuously born to all the same advantages of nature, and the use of the same faculties, should also be equal one amongst another without subordination or subjection, unless the lord and master of them all should, by any manifest declaration of his will, set one above another, and confer on him, by an evident and clear appointment, an undoubted right to dominion and sovereignty. . . .

§ **6.** But though this be a *state of liberty,* yet *it is not a state of license:* though man in that state have an uncontrollable liberty to dispose of his person or possessions, yet he has not liberty to destroy himself, or so much as any creature in his possession, but where some nobler use than its bare preservation calls for it. The *state of nature* has a law of nature to govern it, which obliges every one: and reason, which is that law, teaches all mankind, who will but consult it, that being all *equal and independent,* no one ought to harm another in his life, health, liberty, or possessions: for men being all the workmanship of one omnipotent, and infinitely wise maker; all the servants of one sovereign master, sent into the world by his order, and about his business; they are his property, whose workmanship they are, made to last during his, one another's pleasure: and being furnished with like faculties, sharing all in one community of nature, there cannot be supposed any such *subordination* among us, that many authorize us to destroy one another, as if we were made for one another's uses, as the inferior ranks of creatures are for our's. Every one, as he is *bound to preserve himself*, and not to quit his station willfuly, so by the like reason, when his own preservation comes not in competition, ought he, as much as he can, *to preserve the rest of mankind,* and may not, unless it be to do justice on an offender, take away, or impair the life, or what tends to the preservation of the life, the liberty, health, limb, or goods of another.

§ **7.** And that all men may be restrained from invading others rights, and from doing hurt to one another, and the law of nature be observed, which willeth the peace and *preservation of all mankind,* the *execution* of the law of nature is, in that state, put into every man's hands, whereby every one has a right to punish the transgressors of that law to such a degree, as may hinder its violation: for the *law of nature* would, as all other laws that concern men in this world, be in vain, if there were no body that in the state of nature had a *power to execute* that law, and thereby preserve the innocent

Excerpted from Chapters II, V, and IX of John Locke, *Two Treatises of Government* (first edition 1690, selections from the 1764 edition).

and restrain offenders. And if any one in the state of nature may punish another for any evil he has done, every one may do so; for in that *state of perfect equality,* where naturally there is no superiority or jurisdiction of one over another, what any may do in prosecution of that law, every one must needs have a right to do.

§ **8.** And, thus, in the state of nature, *one man comes by a power over another;* but yet no absolute or arbitrary power, to use a criminal, when he has got him in his hands, according to the passionate heats, or boundless extravagancy of his own will; but only to retribute to him, so far as calm reason and conscience dictate, what is proportionate to his transgression, which is so much as may serve for *reparation,* and *restraint,* for these two are the only reasons, why one man may lawfully do harm to another, which is that we call *punishment.* In transgressing the law of nature, the offender declares himself to live by another rule than that of reason and common equity, which is that measure God has set to the actions of men, for their mutual security; and so he becomes dangerous to mankind, the tye, which is to secure them from injury and violence, being slighted and broken by him. Which being a trespass against the whole species, and the peace and safety of it, provided for by the law of nature, every man upon this score, by the right he hath to preserve mankind in general, may restrain, or where it is necessary, destroy things noxious to them, and so may bring such evil on any one, who hath transgressed that law, as may make him repent the doing of it, and thereby deter him, and by his example others, from doing the like mischief. And in the case, and upon this ground, *every man hath a right to punish the offender, and be executioner of the law of nature....*

§ **10.** Besides the crime which consists in violating law, and varying from the right rule of reason, whereby a man so far becomes degenerate, and declares himself to quit the principles of human nature, and to be a noxious creature, there is commonly *injury* done to some person or other, and some other man receives damage by his transgression: in which case he who hath received any damage has, besides the right of punishment common to him with other men, a particular right to seek *reparation* from him that has done it: and any other person, who finds it just, may also join with him that is injured, and assist him in recovering from the offender so much as may make satisfaction for the harm he has sufferred.

§ **11.** From these *two distinct rights,* the one of *punishing* the crime *for restraint,* and preventing the like offense, which right of punishing is in every body; the other of taking *reparation,* which belongs only to the injured party, comes it to pass that the magistrate, who by being magistrate hath the common right of punishing put into his hands, can often, where the public good demands not the execution of the law, *remit* the punishment of criminal offences by his own authority, but yet cannot *remit* the satisfaction due to any private man for the damage he has received. That, he who has suffered the damage has a right to demand in his own name, and he alone can remit; the damnified person has this power of appropriating to himself the goods or service of the offender, *by right of self-preservation,* as every man has a power to punish the crime, to prevent its being committed again, *by the right he has of preserving all mankind,* and doing all reasonable things he can in order to that end: and thus it is, that every man, in the state of nature, has a power to kill a murderer, both *to deter* others from doing the like injury, which no reparation can compensate, by the example of the punishment that attends it from every body, and also to secure men from the attempts of a criminal, who having renounced reason, the common rule and measure God hath given to mankind, hath, by the unjust violence and slaughter he hath committed upon one, declared war against all mankind, and therefore may be destroyed as a *lion* or a *tyger,* one of those wild savage beasts, with whom men can have no society nor security: and upon this is grounded that great law of nature, *Whoso sheddeth man's blood, by man shall his blood be shed.* And *Cain* was so fully convinced, that every one had a right to destroy such a criminal, that after the murder of his brother, he cries out, *Every one that findeth me, shall slay me;* so plain was it writ in the hearts of all mankind.

§ **12.** By the same reason may a man in the state of nature *punish the lesser breaches* of that law. It will perhaps be demanded, with death? I answer, each transgression may be *punished* to that *degree,* and with so much *severity,* as will suffice to make it an ill bargain to the offender, give him cause to repent, and terrify others from doing the like. Every offence, that can be committed in the state of nature, may in the state of nature be also punished equally, and as far forth as it may in a common-wealth: for though it would be besides may present purpose, to enter here into the particulars of the law of nature, or its *measures of punishment;* yet, it is certain there is such a law, and that too, as intelligible and plain to a rational creature, and a studier of that law, as the positive laws of common-wealths; nay, possibly plainer; as much as reason is easier to be understood, than the fancies and intricate contrivances of men, following contrary and hidden interests put into words; for so truly are a great part of the *municipal laws* of the countries, which are only so far right, as they are founded on the law of nature, by which they are to be regulated and interpreted.

§ **13.** To this strange doctrine, *viz.* That *in the state of nature every one has the executive power* of the law of nature, I doubt not but it will be objected, that it is unreasonable for men to be judges in their own cases, that self-love will make men partial to themselves and their friends: and on the other side, that ill nature, passion and revenge will carry them too far in punishing others; and hence nothing but confusion and disorder will follow, and that therefore God hath certainly appointed government to restrain the partiality and violence of men. I easily grant, that *civil government* is the proper remedy for the inconveniences of the state of nature, which must certainly be great, where men may be judges in their own case, since it is easy to be imagined, that he who was so unjust as to do his brother an injury, will scarce be so just as to condemn himself for it: but I shall desire those who make this objection, to remember, that *absolute monarchs* are but men; and if government is to be the remedy of those evils, which necessarily follow from men's being judges in their own cases, and the state of nature is therefore not to be endured, I desire to know what kind of government that is, and how much better it is than the state of nature, where one man, commanding a multitude, has the liberty to be judge in his own case, and may do to all his subjects whatever he pleases, without the least liberty to any one to question or controul those who execute his pleasure? and in whatsoever he doth, whether led by reason, mistake or passion, must be submitted to? much better it is in the state of nature, wherein men are not bound to submit to the unjust will of another; and if he that judges amiss in his own, or any other case, he is answerable for it to the rest of mankind. . . .

OF PROPERTY

§ **25.** Whether we consider natural *reason,* which tells us, that men, being once born, have a right to their preservation, and consequently to meat and drink, and such other things as nature affords for their subsistence: or *revelation,* which gives us an account of those grants God made of the world to *Adam,* and to *Noah,* and his sons, it is very clear, that God, as king *David* says, *Psal,* cxv. 16. *has given the earth to the children of men;* given it to mankind in common. But this being supposed, it seems to some a very great difficulty, how any one should ever come to have a *property* in any thing: I will not content myself to answer, that if it be difficult to make out *property,* upon a supposition that God gave the world to *Adam,* and his posterity in common, it is impossible that any man, but one universal monarch, should have any *property* upon a supposition, that God gave the world to *Adam,* and his heirs in succession, exclusive of all the rest of his posterity. But I shall endeavour to shew, how men might come to have a *property* in several parts of that which God gave to mankind in common, and that without any express compact of all the commoners.

§ 26. God, who hath given the world to men in common, hath also given them reason to make use of it to the best advantage of life, and convenience. The earth, and all that is therein, is given to men for the support and comfort of their being. And tho' all the fruits it naturally produces, and beasts it feeds, belong to mankind in common, as they are produced by the spontaneous hand of nature; and no body has originally a private dominion, exclusive of the rest of mankind, in any of them, as they are thus in their natural state: yet being given for the use of men, there must of necessity be *a means to appropriate* them some way or other, before they can be of any use, or at all beneficial to any particular man. The fruit, or venison, which nourishes the wild *Indian,* who knows no inclosure, and is still a tenant in common, must be his, and so his, *i.e.* a part of him, that another can no longer have any right to it, before it can do him any good for the support of his life.

§ 27. Though the earth, and all inferior creatures, be common to all men, yet every man has a *property* in his own *person:* this no body has any right to but himself. The *labour* of his body, and the *work* of his hands, we may say, are properly his. Whatsoever then he removes out of the state that nature hath provided, and left it in, he hath mixed his *labour* with, and joined to it something that is his own, and thereby makes it his *property.* It being by him removed from the common state nature hath placed it in, it hath by this *labour* something annexed to it, that excludes the common right of other men: for this *labour* being the unquestionable property of the labourer, no man but he can have a right to what that is once joined to, at least where there is enough, and as good, left in common for others.

§ 28. He that is nourished by the acorns he picked up under an oak, or the apples he gathered from the trees in the wood, has certainly appropriated them to himself. No body can deny but the nourishment is his. I ask then, when did they begin to be his? when he digested? or when he eat? or when he boiled? or when he brought them home? or when he picked them up? and it is plain, if the first gathering made them not his, nothing else could. That *labour* put a distinction between them and common: that added something to them more than nature, the common mother of all, had done; and so they became his private right. And will any one say, he had no right to those acorns or apples, he thus appropriated, because he had not the consent of all mankind to make them his? Was it a robbery thus to assume to himself what belonged to all in common? If such a consent as that was necessary, man had starved, notwithstanding the plenty God had given him. We see in *commons,* which remain so by compact, that it is the taking any part of what is common, and removing it out of the state nature leaves it in, which *begins the property;* without which the common is of no use. And the taking of this or that part, does not depend on the express consent of all the commoners. Thus the grass my horse has bit; the turfs my servant has cut; and the ore I have digged in any place, where I have a right to them in common with others, become my *property*, without the assignation or consent of any body. The *labour* that was mine, removing them out of that common state they were in, hath *fixed* my *property* in them.

§ **29.** By making an explicit consent of every commoner, necessary to any one's appropriating to himself any part of what is given in common, children or servants could not cut the meat, which their father or master had provided for them in common, without assigning to every one his peculiar part. Though the water running in the fountain be every one's, yet who can doubt, but that in the pitcher is his only who drew it out? His *labour* hath taken it out of the hands of nature, where it was common, and belonged equally to all her children, and *hath* thereby *appropriated* it to himself.

§ **30.** Thus this law of reason makes the deer that *Indian's* who hath killed it; it is allowed to be his goods, who hath bestowed his labour upon it, though therefore it was the common right of every one. And amongst those who are counted the civilized part of mankind, who have made and multiplied positive laws to determine *property*, this original law of nature, for the *beginning of property*, in what was before common, still takes place; and by virtue thereof, what fish any one catches in the ocean, that great and still remaining common of mankind; or what ambergrise any one takes up here, is by the *labour* that removes it out of that common state nature left it in, *made his property*, who takes that pains about it. And even amongst us, the hare that any one is hunting, is thought his who pursues her during the chase: for being a beast that is still looked upon as common, and no man's private possession; whoever has employed so much *labour* about any of that kind, as to find and pursue her, as thereby removed her from the state of nature, wherein she was common, and hath *begun a property*.

§ **31.** It will perhaps be objected to this, that if gathering the acorns, or other fruits of the earth, &c. makes a right to them, then any one may *ingross* as much as he will. To which I answer, Not so. The same law of nature, that does by this means give us property, does also *bound* that *property* too. *God has given us all things richly.* 1 Tim. vi. 12. is the voice of reason confirmed by inspiration. But how far has he given it us? *To enjoy.* As much as any one can make use of to any advantage of life before it spoils, so much he may by his labour fix a property in: whatever is beyond this, is more than his share, and belongs to others. Nothing was made by God for man to spoil or destroy. And thus, considering the plenty of natural provisions there was a long time in the world, and the few spenders; and to how small a part of that provision the industry of one man could extend itself, and ingross it to the prejudice of others; especially keeping within the *bounds,* set by reason, of what might serve for his *use;* there could be then little room for quarrels or contentions about property so established.

§ **32.** But the *chief matter of property* being now not the fruits of the earth, and the beasts that subsist on it, but *the earth itself;* as that which makes in and carries with it all the rest; I think it is plain, that *property* in that too is acquired as the former. *As much land* as a man tills, plants, improves, cultivates, and can use the product of, so much is his *property.* He by his labour does, as it were, inclose it from the common. Nor will it invalidate his right, to say every body else has an equal title to it; and therefore he cannot appropriate, he cannot inclose, without the consent of all his fellow-commoners, all mankind. God, when he gave the world in common to all mankind, commanded man also to labour, and the penury of his condition required it of him. God and his reason commanded him to subdue the earth, *i.e.* improve it for the benefit of life, and therein lay out something upon it that was his own, his labour. He that in obedience to this command of God, subdued, tilled and sowed any part of it, thereby annexed to it something that was his *property,* which another had no title to, nor could without injury take from him.

§ **33.** Nor was this *appropriation* of any parcel of *land,* by improving it, any prejudice to any other man, since there was still enough, and as good left; and more than the yet unprovided could use. So that, in effect, there was never the less left for others because of his inclosure for himself: for he that leaves as much as another can make use of, does as good as take nothing at all. No body could think himself injured by the drinking of another man, though he took a good draught, who had a whole river of the same water left him to quench his thirst: and the case of land and water, where there is enough of both, is perfectly the same.

§ **34.** God gave the world to men in common; but since he gave it them for their benefit, and the greatest conveniences of life they were capable to draw from it, it cannot be supposed he meant it should always remain common and uncultivated. He gave it to the use of the industrious and rational (and *labour* was to be *his title* to it); not to the fancy or covetousness of the quarrelsome and contentious. He that had as good left for his improvement, as was already taken up, needed not complain, ought not to meddle with what was already improved by another's labour: if he did, it is plain he desired the benefit of another's pains, which he had no right to, and not the ground which God had given him in common with others to labour on, and whereof there was as good left, as that already possessed, and more than he knew what to do with, or his industry could reach to. . . .

§ **36.** The *measure of property* nature has well set by the extent of men's *labour and the conveniences of life:* no man's labour could subdue, or appropriate all; nor could his enjoyment consume more than a small part; so that it was impossible for any man, this way, to intrench upon the right of another, or acquire to himself a property, to the prejudice of his neighbour, who would still have room for as good, and as large a possession (after the other had taken out his) as before it was appropriated. This *measure* did confine every man's *possession* to a very moderate proportion, and such as he might appropriate to himself, without injury to any body, in the first ages of the world, when men were more in danger to be lost, by wandering from their company, in the then vast wilderness of the earth, than to be straitened for want of room to plant in. And the same *measure* may be allowed still without prejudice to any body, as full as the world seems: for supposing a man, or family, in the state they were at first peopling of the world by the children of *Adam,* or *Noah;* let him plant in some in-land, vacant places of *America,* we shall find that the *possessions* he could make himself, upon the *measures* we have given, would not be very large, nor, even to this day, prejudice the rest of mankind, or give them reason to complain, or think themselves injured by this man's incroachment, though the race of men have now spread themselves to all the corners of the world, and do infinitely exceed the small number was at the beginning. Nay, the extent of *ground* is of so little value, *without labour,* that I have heard it affirmed, that in *Spain* itself a man may be permitted to plough, sow and reap, without being disturbed, upon land he has no other title to, but only his making use of it. But, on the contrary, the inhabitants think themselves beholden to him, who, by his industry on neglected, and consequently waste land, has increased the stock of corn, which they wanted. But be this as it will, which I lay no stress on; this I dare boldly affirm, that the same *rule of propriety, (viz.)* that every man should have as much as he could make use of, would hold still in the world, without straitening any body; since there is land enough in the world to suffice double the inhabitants, had not the *invention of money*, and the tacit agreement of men to put a value on it, introduced (by consent) larger possessions, and a right to them; which, how it has done, I shall by and by shew more at large.

§ **37.** This is certain, that in the beginning, before the desire of having more than man needed had altered the intrinsic value of things, which depends only on their usefulness to the life of man; or had *agreed, that a little piece of yellow metal*, which would keep without wasting or decay, should be worth a great piece of flesh, or a whole heap of corn; though men had a right to appropriate, by their labour, each one of himself, as much of the things of nature, as he could use: yet this could not be much, nor to the prejudice of others, where the same plenty was still left to those who would use the same industry. To which let me add, that he who appropriates land to himself by his labour, does not lessen, but increase the common stock of mankind: for the provisions serving to the support of human life, produced by one acre of inclosed and cultivated land, are) to speak much within compass) ten times more than those which are yielded by an acre of land of an equal richness lying waste in common. And therefore he that incloses land, and has a greater plenty of the conveniences of life from ten acres, than he could have from an hundred left to nature, may truly be said to give ninety acres to mankind: for his labour now supplies him with provisions out of ten acres, which were but the product of an hundred lying in common. I have here rated the improved land very low, in making its product but as ten to one, when it is much nearer an hundred to one: for I ask, whether in the wild woods and uncultivated waste of *America,* left to nature, without any improvement, tillage or husbandry, a thousand acres yield the needy and wretched inhabitants as many conveniences of life, as ten acres of equally fertile land do in *Devonshire,* where they are well cultivated?

Before the appropriation of land, he who gathered as much of the wild fruit, killed, caught, or tamed, as many of the beasts, as he could; he that so imployed his pains about any of the spontaneous products of nature, as any way to alter them from the state which nature put them in, *by* placing any of his *labour* on them, did thereby *acquire a property in them:* but if they perished, in his possession, without their due use; if the fruits rotted, or the venison putrified, before he could spend it, he offended against the common law of nature, and was liable to be punished; he invaded his neighbour's share, for he had *no right, farther than his use* called for any of them, and they might serve to afford him conveniences of life. . . .

§ **40.** Nor is it so strange, as perhaps before consideration it may appear, that the *property of labour* should be able to over-balance the community of land: for it is *labour* indeed that *puts the difference of value* on every thing; and let any one consider what the difference is between an acre of land planted with tobacco or sugar, sown with wheat or barley, and an acre of the same land lying in common, without any husbandry upon it, and he will find, that the improvement of *labour makes* the far greater part of the value. I think it will be but a very modest computation to say, that of the *products* of the earth useful to the life of man nine tenths are the *effects of labour:* nay, if we will rightly estimate things as they come to our use, and cast up the several expences about them, what in them is purely owing to *nature,* and what to *la-*

bour, we shall find, that in most of them ninety-nine hundredths are wholly to be put on the account of *labour.*

§ **41.** There cannot be a clearer demonstration of any thing, than several nations of the *Americans* are of this, who are rich in land, and poor in all the comforts of life; whom nature having furnished as liberally as any other people, with the materials of plenty, *i.e.* a fruitful soil, apt to produce in abundance, what might serve for food, raiment, and delight, yet for want of improving it by labour, have not one hundredth part of the conveniences we enjoy: and a king of a large and fruitful territory there, feeds, lodges, and is clad worse than a day-labourer in *England.*

§ **42.** To make this a little clearer, let us but trace some of the ordinary provisions of life, through their several progresses, before they come to our use, and see how much they receive of their *value from human industry.* Bread, wine and cloth, are things of daily use, and great plenty; yet notwithstanding, acorns, water and leaves, or skins, must be our bread, drink and clothing, did not *labour* furnish us with these more useful commodities: for whatever *bread* is more worth than acorns, wine than water, and *cloth* or *silk,* than leaves, skins or moss, that is wholly *owing to labour* and *industry*; the one of these being the food and raiment which unassisted nature furnishes us with; the other, provisions which our industry and pains prepare for us, which how much they exceed the other in value, when any one hath computed, he will then see how much *labour makes the far greatest part of the value* of things we enjoy in this world: and the ground which produces the materials, is scarce to be reckoned in, as any, or at most, but a very small part of it; so little, that even amongst us, land that is left wholly to nature, that hath no improvement of pasturage, tillage, or planting, is called, as indeed it is, *waste;* and we shall find the benefit of it amount to little more than nothing.

This shows how much numbers of men are to be preferred to largeness of dominions; and that the increase of lands, and the right employing of them, is the great art of government: and that prince, who shall be so wise and godlike, as by established laws of liberty to secure protection and encouragement to the honest industry of mankind, against the oppression of power and narrowness of party, will quickly be too hard for his neighbours: but this by the by. To return to the argument in hand,

§ **43.** An acre of land, that bears here twenty bushels of wheat, and another in *America,* which, with the same husbandry, would do the like, are, without doubt, of the same natural intrinsic value: but yet the benefit mankind receives from the one in a year, is worth 5*l.* and from the other possibly not worth a penny, if all the profit an *Indian* received from it were to be valued, and sold here; at least, I may truly say, not one thousandth. It is *labour* then which *puts the greatest part of value upon land,* without which it would scarcely be worth any thing: it is to that we owe the greatest part of all its useful products; for all that the straw, bran, bread, of that acre of wheat, is more worth than the product of an acre of as good land, which lies waste, is all the effect of labour: for it is not barely the plough-man's pains, the reaper's and thresher's toil, and the baker's sweat, is to be counted into the *bread* we eat; the labour of those who broke the oxen, who digged and wrought the iron and stones, who felled and framed the timber employed about the plough, mill, oven, or any other utensils, which are a vast number, requisite to this corn, from its being feed to be sown to its being made bread, must all be *charged on* the account of labour, and received as an effect of that: nature and the earth furnished only the almost worthless materials, as in themselves. It would be a strange *catalogue of things, that industry provided and made use of, about every loaf of bread,* before it came to our use, if we could trace them; iron, wood, leather, bark, timber, stone, bricks, coals, lime, cloth, dying drugs, pitch, tar, masts, ropes, and all the materials made use of in the ship, that brought any of the commodities made use of by any of the workmen, to any part of the work; all which it would be almost impossible, at least too long, to reckon up.

§ **44.** From all which it is evident, that though the things of nature are given in common, yet man, by being master of himself, and *proprietor of his own person, and the actions or labour of it, had still in himself the great foundation of property;* and that, which made up the great part of what he applied to the support or comfort of his being, when invention and arts had improved the conveniences of life, was perfectly his own, and did not belong in common to others.

§ **45.** Thus *labour,* in the beginning, *gave a right of property,* wherever any one was pleased to employ it upon what was common, which remained as long while the far greater part, and is yet more than mankind makes use of. Men, at first, for the most part, contented themselves with what unassisted nature offered to their necessities: and though afterwards, in some parts of the world, (where the increase of people and stock, with the *use of money,* had made land scarce, and so of some value) the several *communities* settled the bounds of their distinct territories, and by laws within themselves regulated the properties of the private men of their society, and so, *by compact* and agreement, *settled the property* which labour and industry began; and the leagues that have been made between several states and kingdoms, either expressly or tacitly disowning all claim and right to the land in the others possession, have, by common consent, given up their pretences to their natural common right, which originally they had to those countries, and so have, by *positive agreement, settled a property* amongst themselves, indistinct parts and parcels of the earth; yet there are still *great tracts of ground* to be found, which (the inhabitants thereof not having joined with the rest of mankind, in the consent of the use of their common money) *lie waste,* and are more than the people who dwell on it do, or can make use of, and so still lie in common; tho' this can scarce happen amongst that part of mankind that have consented to the use of money.

§ **46.** The greatest part of *things really useful* to the life of man, and such as the necessity of subsisting made the first commoners of the world look after, as it doth the *Americans* now, *are* generally things of *short duration;* such as, if they are not consumed by use, will decay and perish of themselves: gold, silver and diamonds, are things that fancy or agreement hath put the value on, more than real use, and the necessary support of life. Now of those good things which nature hath provided in common, every one had a right (as hath been said) to as much as he could use, and *property* in all that he could effect with his labour; all that his *industry* could extend to, to alter from the state nature had put it in, was his. He that *gathered* a hundred bushels of acorns or apples, had thereby a *property* in them, they were his goods as soon as gathered. He was only to look, that he used them before they spoiled, else he took more than his share, and robbed others. And indeed it was a foolish thing, as well as dishonest, to hoard up more than he could make use of. If he gave away a part to any body else, so that it perished not uselesly in his possession, these he also made use of. And if he also bartered away plums, that would have rotted in a week, for nuts that would last good for his eating a whole year, he did no injury; he wasted not the common stock; destroyed no part of the portion of goods that belonged to others, so long as nothing perished uselessly in his hands. Again, if he would give his nuts for a piece of metal, pleased with its colour; or exchange his sheep for shells, or wool for a sparkling pebble or a diamond, and keep those by him all his life, he invaded not the right of others, he might heap up as much of these durable things as he pleased; the *exceeding of the bounds of his just property* not lying in the largeness of his possession, but the perishing of any thing uselessly in it.

§ **47.** And thus *came in the use of money,* some lasting thing that men might keep without spoiling, and that by mutual consent men would take in exchange for the truly useful, but perishable supports of life.

§ **48.** And as different degrees of industry were apt to give men possessions in different proportions, so this *invention of money* gave them the opportunity to continue and enlarge them; for supposing an island, separate from all possible commerce with the rest of the world, wherein there were but an hundred families, but there were sheep, horses and cows, with other useful animals, wholesome fruits, and land enough for corn for a hundred thousand times as many, but nothing in the island, either because of its commonness, or perishableness, fit to supply the place of *money;* what reason could any one have there to enlarge his possessions beyond the use of his family, and a plentiful supply to its *consumption,* either in what their own industry produced, or they could barter for like perishable, useful commodities, with others? Where there is not some thing, both lasting and scarce, and so valuable to be hoarded up, there men will not be apt to enlarge their *possessions of land,* were it never so rich, never so free for them to take; for I ask, what would a man value ten thousand, or an hundred thousand acres of excellent *land,* ready cultivated, and well stocked too with cattle, in the middle of the inland parts of *America,* where he had no hopes of commerce with other parts of the world, to draw *money* to him by the sale of the product? It would not be worth the inclosing, and we should see him give up again to the wild common of nature, whatever was more than would supply the conveniences of life to be had there for him and his family. . . .

§ **50.** But since gold and silver, being little useful to the life of man in proportion to food, raiment, and carriage, has its *value* only from the consent of men, whereof *labour* yet *makes,* in great part, *the measure,* it is plain, that men have agreed to a disproportionate and unequal *possession of the earth,* they having, by a tacit and voluntary consent, found out a way how a man may fairly possess more land than he himself can use the product of, by receiving in exchange for the overplus gold and silver, which may be hoarded up without injury to any one; these metals not spoiling or decaying in the hands of the possessor. This partage of things in an inequality of private possessions, men have made practicable out of the bounds of society, and without compact, only by putting a value on gold and silver, and tacitly agreeing in the use of money: for in governments, the laws regulate the right of property, and the possession of land is determined by positive constitutions.

§ **51.** And thus, I think, it is very easy to conceive, without any difficulty, *how labour could at first begin a title of property* in the common things of nature, and how the spending it upon our uses bounded it. So that there could then be no reason of quarrelling about title, nor any doubt about the largeness of possession it gave. Right and conveniency went together; for as a man had a right to all he could employ his labour upon, so he had no temptation to labour for more than he could make use of.

This left no room for controversy about the title, nor for incroachment on the right of others; what portion a man carved to himself, was easily seen; and it was useless, as well as dishonest, to carve himself too much, or take more than he needed. . . .

OF THE ENDS OF POLITICAL SOCIETY AND GOVERNMENT

§ **123.** If man in the state of nature be so free, as has been said; if he be absolute lord of his own person and possessions, equal to the greatest, and subject to no body, why will he part with his freedom? why will he give up this empire, and subject himself to the dominion and controul of any other power? To which it is obvious to answer, that though in the state of nature he hath such a right, yet the enjoyment of it is very uncertain, and constantly exposed to the invasion of others: for all being kings as much as he, every man his equal, and the greater part no strict observers of equity and justice, the enjoyment of the property he has in this state is very unsafe, very unsecure. This makes him willing to quit a condition, which, however free, is full of fears and continual dangers: and it is not without reason, that he seeks out, and is willing to join in society with others, who are already united, or have a mind to unite, for the mutual *preservation* of their lives, liberties and estates, which I call by the general name, *property*.

§ **124.** The great and *chief end,* therefore, of men's uniting into commonwealths, and putting themselves under government, *is the preservation of their property*. To which in the state of nature there are many things wanting.

First, There wants an *established,* settled, known *law,* received and allowed by common consent to be the standard of right and wrong, and the common measure to decide all controversies between them: for though the law of nature be plain and intelligible to all rational creatures; yet men being biassed by their interest, as well as ignorant for want of study of it, are not apt to allow of it as a law binding to them in the application of it to their particular cases.

§ **125.** *Secondly,* In the state of nature there wants *a known and indifferent judge,* with authority to determine all differences according to the established law: for every one in that state being both judge and executioner of the law of nature, men being partial to themselves, passion and revenge is very apt to carry them too far, and with too much heat, in their own cases; as well as negligence, and unconcernedness, to make them too remiss in other men's.

§ **126.** *Thirdly.* In the state of nature there often wants *power to* back and support the sentence when right, and to give it due *execution*. They who by any injustice offended, will seldom fail, where they are able, by force to make good their injustice; such resistance many times makes the punishment dangerous, and frequently destructive, to those who attempt it.

§ **127.** Thus mankind, notwithstanding all the privileges of the state of nature, being but in an ill condition, while they remain in it, are quickly driven into society. Hence it comes to pass, that we seldom find any number of men live any time together in this state. The inconveniencies that they are therein exposed to, by the irregular and uncertain exercise of the power every man has of punishing the transgressions of others, make them take sanctuary under the established laws of government, and therein seek *the preservation of their property*. It is this makes them so willingly give up every one his single power of punishing, to be exercised by such alone, as shall be appointed to it amongst them; and by such rules as the community, or those authorized by them to that purpose, shall agree on. And in this we have the original *right and rise of both the legislative and executive power,* as well as of the governments and societies themselves.

§ **128.** For in the state of nature, to omit the liberty he has of innocent delights, a man has two powers.

The first is to do whatsoever he thinks fit for the preservation of himself, and others within the permission of the *law of nature:* by, which law, common to them all, he and all the rest of *mankind* are *one community,* make up one society, distinct from all other creatures. And were it not for the corruption and vitiousness of degenerate men, there would be no need of any other; no necessity that men should separate from this great and natural community, and by positive agreements combine into smaller and divided associations.

The other power a man has in the state of nature, is the *power to punish the crimes* committed against the law. Both these he gives up, when he joins in a private, if I may so call it, or particular politic society, and incorporates into any common-wealth, separate from the rest of mankind.

§ **129.** The first *power,* viz. *of doing whatsoever he thought for the preservation of himself,* and the rest of mankind, *he gives up to* be regulated by laws made by the society, so far forth as the preservation of himself, and the rest of that society shall require; which laws of the society in many things confine the liberty he had by the law of nature.

§ **130.** *Secondly,* The *power of punishing he wholly gives up,* and engages his natural force (which he might before employ in the execution of the law of nature, by his own single authority, as he thought fit) to assist the executive power of the society, as the law thereof shall require: for being now in a new state, wherein he is to enjoy many conveniences, from the labour, assistance, and society of others in the same community, as well as protection from its whole strength; he is to part also with as much of his natural liberty, in providing for himself, as the good, prosperity, and safety of the society shall require; which is not only necessary, but just, since the other members of the society do the like.

§ **131.** But though men, when they enter into society, give up the equality, liberty, and executive power they had in the state of nature, into the hands of the society, to be so far disposed of by the legislative, as the good of the society shall require; yet it being only with an intention in every one the better to preserve himself, his liberty and property; (for no rational creature can be supposed to change his condition with an intention to be worse) the power of the society, or *legislative* constituted by them, can *never be supposed to extend farther, than the common good;* but is obliged to secure every one's property, by providing against those three defects above mentioned, that made the state of nature so unsafe and uneasy. And so whoever has the legislative or supreme power of any common-wealth, is bound to govern by established *standing laws,* promulgated and known to the people, and not by extemporary decrees; by *indifferent* and upright *judges,* who are to decide controversies by those laws; and to employ the force of the community at home, *only in the execution of such laws,* or abroad to prevent or redress foreign injuries, and secure the community from inroads and invasion. And all this to be directed to no other *end,* but the *peace, safety,* and *public good* of the people.

Rights, Human Rights, and Racial Discrimination

Richard Wasserstrom

The subject of natural, or human, rights is one that has recently come to enjoy a new-found intellectual and philosophical respectability. This has come about in part, I think, because of a change in philosophical mood—in philosophical attitudes and opinions toward topics in moral and political theory. And this change in mood has been reflected in a renewed interest in the whole subject of rights and duties. In addition, though, this renaissance has been influenced, I believe, by certain events of recent history—notably the horrors of Nazi Germany and the increasingly obvious injustices of racial discrimination in both the United States and Africa. For in each case one of the things that was or is involved is a denial of certain human rights.

This concern over the subject of natural rights, whatever the causes may be, is, however, in the nature of a reinstatement. Certainly there was, just a relatively few years ago, fairly general agreement that the doctrine of natural rights had been thoroughly and irretrievably discredited. Indeed, this was sometimes looked upon as the paradigm case of the manner in which a moral and political doctrine could be both rhetorically influential and intellectually inadequate and unacceptable. A number of objections, each deemed absolutely dispositive, had been put forward: the vagueness of almost every formulation of a set of natural rights, the failure of persons to agree upon what one's natural rights are, the ease with which almost everyone would acknowledge the desirability of overriding or disregarding any proffered natural rights in any one of a variety of readily familiar circumstances, the lack of any ground or argument for any doctrine of natural rights.

Typical is the following statement from J. B. Mabbott's little book, *The State and the Citizens.*[1]

> [T]he niceties of the theory [of natural rights] need not detain us if we can attack it at its roots, and there it is most clearly vulnerable. Natural rights must be self-evident and they must be absolute if they are to be rights at all. For if a right is derivative from a more fundamental right, then it is not natural in the sense intended; and if a right is to be explained or defended by reference to the good of the community or of the individual concerned, then these "goods" are the ultimate values in the case, and their pursuit may obviously infringe or destroy the "right" in question. Now the only way in which to demonstrate the absurdity of a theory which claims self-evidence for every article of its creed is to make a list of the articles. . . .
>
> Not only are the lists indeterminate and apricious in extent, they are also confused in content. . . . [T]here is no single "natural right" which is, in fact, re-

Reprinted from the *Journal of Philosophy,* vol. LVI, no. 20 (Oct. 29, 1964). © 1964 Journal of Philosophy. By permission of Journal of Philosophy and Richard Wasserstrom.

[1]London: Arrow, 1958.

garded even by its own supporters as sacrosanct. Every one of them is constantly invaded in the public interest with universal approval (57–58).

Mabbott's approach to the problem is instructive both as an example of the ease with which the subject has been taken up and dismissed, and more importantly, as a reminder of the fact that the theory of natural rights has not been a single coherent doctrine. Instead, it has served, and doubtless may still serve, as a quite indiscriminate collection of a number of logically independent propositions. It is, therefore, at least as necessary here as in many other situations that we achieve considerable precision in defining and describing the specific subject of inquiry.

This paper is an attempt to delineate schematically the form of one set of arguments for natural, or human rights.[2] I do this in the following fashion. First, I consider several important and distinctive features and functions of rights in general. Next, I describe and define certain characteristics of human rights and certain specific functions and attributes that they have. Then, I delineate and evaluate one kind of argument for human rights, as so described and defined. And finally, I analyze one particular case of a denial of human rights—that produced by the system of racial discrimination as it exists in the South today.

1

If there are any such things as human rights, they have certain important characteristics and functions just because rights themselves are valuable and distinctive moral "commodities." This is, I think, a point that is all too often overlooked whenever the concept of a right is treated as a largely uninteresting, derivative notion—one that can be taken into account in wholly satisfactory fashion through an explication of the concepts of duty and obligation.[3]

Now, it is not my intention to argue that there can be rights for which there are no correlative duties, nor that there can be duties for which there are no correlative rights—although I think that there are, e.g., the duty to be kind to animals or the duty to be charitable. Instead, what I want to show is that there are important differences between rights and duties, and, in particular, that rights fulfill certain functions that neither duties (even correlative duties) nor any other moral or legal concepts can fulfill.

Perhaps the most obvious thing to be said about rights is that they are constitutive of the domain of entitlements. They help to define and serve to protect those things concerning which one can make a very special kind of claim—a claim of right. To claim or to acquire anything as a matter of right is crucially different from seeking or obtaining it as through the grant of a privilege, the receipt of a favor, or the presence of a permission. To have a right to something is, typically, to be entitled to re-

---

[2]Because the phrase "natural rights" is so encrusted with certain special meanings, I shall often use the more neutral phrase "human rights." For my purposes there are no differences in meaning between the two expressions.

[3]See, for example, S. I. Benn and R. S. Peters, *Social Principles and the Democratic State,* p. 89: "Right and duty are different names for the same normative relation, according to the point of view from which it is regarded."

ceive or possess or enjoy it now,[4] and to do so without securing the consent of another. As long as one has a right to anything, it is beyond the reach of another properly to withhold or deny it. In addition, to have a right is to be absolved from the obligation to weigh a variety of what would in other contexts be relevant considerations; it is to be entitled to the object of the right—at least *prima facie*—without any more ado. To have a right to anything is, in short, to have a very strong moral or legal claim upon it. It is the strongest kind of claim that there is.

Because this is so, it is apparent, as well, that the things to which one is entitled as a matter of right are not usually trivial or insignificant. The objects of rights are things that matter.

Another way to make what are perhaps some of the same points is to observe that rights provide special kinds of grounds or reasons for making moral judgments of at least two kinds. First, if a person has a right to something, he can properly cite that right as the *justification* for having acted in accordance with or in the exercise of that right. If a person has acted so as to exercise his right, he has, without more ado, acted rightly—at least *prima facie*. To exercise one's right is to act in a way that gives appreciable assurance of immunity from criticism. Such immunity is far less assured when one leaves the areas of rights and goes, say, to the realm of the permitted or the non-prohibited.

And second, just as exercising or standing upon one's rights by itself needs no defense, so invading or interfering with or denying another's rights is by itself appropriate ground for serious censure and rebuke. Here there is a difference in emphasis and import between the breach or neglect of a duty and the invasion of or interference with a right. For to focus upon duties and their breaches is to concentrate necessarily upon the person who has the duty; it is to invoke criteria by which to make moral assessments of his conduct. Rights, on the other hand, call attention to the injury inflicted; to the fact that the possessor of the right was adversely affected by the action. Furthermore, the invasion of a right constitutes, as such, a special and independent injury, whereas this is not the case with less stringent claims.

Finally, just because rights are those moral commodities which delineate the areas of entitlement, they have an additional important function: that of defining the respects in which one can reasonably entertain certain kinds of expectations. To live in a society in which there are rights and in which rights are generally respected is to live in a society in which the social environment has been made appreciably more predictable and secure. It is to be able to count on receiving and enjoying objects of value. Rights have, therefore, an obvious psychological, as well as moral, dimension and significance.

2

If the above are some of the characteristics and characteristic functions of rights in general, what then can we say about human rights? More specifically, what is it for a right to be a human right, and what special role might human rights play?

Probably the simplest thing that might be said of a human right is that it is a right possessed by human beings. To talk about human rights would be to distinguish those

---

[4]There are some rights as to which the possession of the object of the right can be claimed only at a future time, e.g., the right (founded upon a promise) to be repaid next week.

rights which humans have from those which nonhuman entities, e.g., animals or corporations, might have.

It is certain that this is not what is generally meant by human rights. Rather than constituting the genus of all particular rights that humans have, human rights have almost always been deemed to be one species of these rights. If nothing else about the subject is clear, it is evident that one's particular legal rights, as well as some of one's moral rights, are not among one's human rights. If any right is a *human* right, it must, I believe, have at least four very general characteristics. First, it must be possessed by all human beings, as well as only by human beings. Second, because it is the same right that all human beings possess, it must be possessed equally by all human beings. Third, because human rights are possessed by all human beings, we can rule out as possible candidates any of those rights which one might have in virtue of occupying any particular status or relationship, such as that of parent, president, or promisee. And fourth, if there are any human rights, they have the additional characteristic of being assertable, in a manner of speaking, "against the whole world." That is to say, because they are rights that are not possessed in virtue of any contingent status or relationship, they are rights that can be claimed equally against any and every other human being.

Furthermore, to repeat, if there are any human *rights,* they also have certain characteristics as rights. Thus, if there are any human rights, these constitute the strongest of all moral claims that all men can assert. They serve to define and protect those things which all men are entitled to have and enjoy. They indicate those objects toward which and those areas within which every human being is entitled to act without securing further permission or assent. They function so as to put certain matters beyond the power of anyone else to grant or to deny. They provide every human being with a ready justification for acting in certain ways, and they provide each person with ready grounds upon which to condemn any interference or invasion. And they operate, as well, to induce well-founded confidence that the values or objects protected by them will be readily and predictably obtainable. If there are any human rights, they are powerful moral commodities.

Finally, it is, perhaps, desirable to observe that there are certain characteristics I have not ascribed to these rights. In particular, I have not said that human rights need have either of two features: absoluteness and self-evidence, which Mabbott found to be most suspect. I have not said that human rights are absolute in the sense that there are no conditions under which they can properly be overriden, although I have asserted—what is quite different—that they are absolute in the sense that they are possessed equally without any special, additional qualification by all human beings.[5]

Neither have I said (nor do I want to assert) that human rights are self-evident in any sense. Indeed, I want explicitly to deny that a special manner of knowing or a specific epistemology is needed for the development of a theory of human rights. I want to assert that there is much that can be said in defense or support of the claim that a particular right is a human right. And I want to insist, as well, that to adduce reasons for human rights is consistent with their character as human, or natural, rights. Nothing that I have said about human rights entails a contrary conclusion.

[5]For the purposes of this paper and the points I wish here to make, I am not concerned with whether human rights are *prima facie* or absolute. I do not think that anything I say depends significantly upon this distinction. Without analyzing the notion, I will assume, though, that they are *prima facie* rights in the sense that there may be cases in which overriding a human right woud be less undesirable than protecting it.

3

To ask whether there are any human, or natural, rights is to pose a potentially misleading question. Rights of any kind, and particularly natural rights, are not like chairs or trees. One cannot simply look and see whether they are there. There are, though, at least two senses in which rights of all kinds can be said to exist. There is first the sense in which we can ask and answer the empirical question of whether in a given society there is intellectual or conceptual acknowledgment of the fact that persons or other entities have rights at all. We can ask, that is, whether the persons in that society "have" the concept of a right (or a human right), and whether they regard that concept as meaningfully applicable to persons or other entities in that society. And there is, secondly, the sense in which we can ask the question, to what extent, in a society that acknowledges the existence of rights, is there general respect for, protection of, or noninterference with the exercise of those rights.[6]

These are not, though, the only two questions that can be asked. For we can also seek to establish whether any rights, and particularly human rights, ought to be both acknowledged and respected. I want now to begin to do this by considering the way in which an argument for human rights might be developed.

It is evident, I think, that almost any argument for the acknowledgment of any rights as human rights starts with the factual assertion that there are certain respects in which all persons are alike or equal. The argument moves typically from that assertion to the conclusion that there are certain human rights. What often remains unclear, however, is the precise way in which the truth of any proposition about the respects in which persons are alike advances an argument for the acknowledgment of human rights. And what must be supplied, therefore, are the plausible intermediate premises that connect the initial premise with the conclusion.

One of the most careful and complete illustrations of an argument that does indicate some of these intermediate steps is that provided by Gregory Vlastos in an article entitled, "Justice and Equality."[7] Our morality, he says, puts an equal intrinsic value on each person's well-being and freedom. In detail, the argument goes like this:

There is, Vlastos asserts, a wide variety of cases in which all persons are capable of experiencing the same values:

> Thus, to take a perfectly clear case, no matter how A and B might differ in taste and style of life, they would both crave relief from acute physical pain. In that case we would put the same value on giving this to either of them, regardless of the fact that A might be a talented, brilliantly successful person, B "a mere nobody." . . . [I]n all cases where human beings are capable of enjoying the same goods, we feel that the intrinsic value of their enjoyment is the same. In just this sense we hold that (1) *one man's well-being is as valuable as any other's* . . . [Similarly] we feel that choosing for oneself what one will do, believe, approve, say, read, worship, has its own intrinsic value, the same for all persons, and quite independently of the value of the things they happen to choose. Naturally we

---

[6]This is an important distinction. Incontinence in respect to rights is a fairly common occurrence. In the South, for example, many persons might acknowledge that Negroes have certain rights while at the same time neglecting or refusing (out of timidity, cowardice, or general self-interest) to do what is necessary to permit these rights to be exercised.

[7]In Richard B. Brandt, ed., *Social Justice* (Englewood Cliffs, N.J.: Prentice-Hall, 1962), pp. 31–72.

hope that all of them will make the best possible use of their freedom of choice. But we value their exercise of the freedom, regardless of the outcome and we value it equally for all. For us (2) *one man's freedom is as valuable as any other's....* [Thus], since we do believe in equal value as to human well-being and freedom, we should also believe in the *prima facie* equality of men's *right* to well-being and to freedom (51–52).

As it is stated, I am not certain that this argument answers certain kinds of attack. In particular, there are three questions that merit further attention. First, why should anyone have a right to the enjoyment of any goods at all, and, more specifically, well-being and freedom? Second, for what reasons might we be warranted in believing that the intrinsic value of the enjoyment of such goods is the same for all persons? And third, even if someone ought to have a right to well-being and freedom and even if the intrinsic value of each person's enjoyment of these things is equal, why should all men have the equal right—and hence the human right—to secure, obtain, or enjoy these goods?

I think that the third question is the simplest of the three to answer. If anyone has a right to well-being and freedom and if the intrinsic value of any person's enjoyment of these goods is equal to that of any other's, then all men do have an equal right—and hence a human right—to secure, obtain, or enjoy these goods, just because it would be irrational to distinguish among persons as to the possession of these rights. That is to say, the principle that no person should be treated differently from any or all other persons unless there is some general and relevant reason that justifies this difference in treatment is a fundamental principle of morality, if not of rationality itself. Indeed, although I am not certain how one might argue for this, I think it could well be said that all men do have a "second-order" human right—that is, an absolute right—to expect all persons to adhere to this principle.

This principle, or this right, does not by itself establish that there are any specific human rights. But either the principle or the right does seem to establish that well-being and freedom are human rights if they are rights at all and if the intrinsic value of each person's enjoyment is the same. For, given these premises, it does appear to follow that there is no relevant and general reason to differentiate among persons as to the possession of this right.

I say "seem to" and "appear to" because this general principle of morality may not be strong enough. What has been said so far does not in any obvious fashion rule out the possibility that there is some general and relevant principle of differentiation. It only, apparently, rules out possible variations in intrinsic value as a reason for making differentiations.

The requirement of *relevance* does, I think, seem to make the argument secure. For, if *the reason* for acknowledging in a person a right to freedom and well-being is the intrinsic value of his enjoyment of these goods, then the nature of the intrinsic value of any other person's enjoyment is the only relevant reason for making exceptions or for differentiating among persons as to the possession of these rights.[8]

---

[8]See, e.g., Bernard Williams, "The Idea of Equality," in P. Laslett and W. C. Runciman, eds., *Philosophy, Politics and Society*, II (Oxford: Basil Blackwell, 1962), pp. 111–113).

Professor Vlatos imposes a somewhat different requirement which, I think, comes to about the same thing: "An equalitarian concept of justice may admit just inequalities without inconsistency if, and only if, it provides grounds for equal human rights *which are also grounds for unequal rights of other sorts*" (Vlastos, op. cit. p. 40; italics in text).

As to the first question, that of whether a person has a right to well-being and freedom, I am not certain what kind of answer is most satisfactory. If Vlastos is correct in asserting that these enjoyments are *values,* then that is, perhaps, answer enough. That is to say, if enjoying well-being is something *valuable*—and especially if it is intrinsically valuable—then it seems to follow that this is the kind of thing to which one ought to have a right. For if anything ought to be given the kind of protection afforded by a right, it ought surely be that which is valuable. Perhaps, too, there is nothing more that need to be said than to point out that we simply do properly value well-being and freedom.

I think that another, more general answer is also possible. Here I would revert more specifically to my earlier discussion of some of the characteristics and functions of rights. There are two points to be made. First, if we are asked, why ought anyone have a right to anything? or why not have a system in which there are not rights at all? the answer is that such a system would be a morally impoverished one. It would prevent persons from asserting those kinds of claims, it would preclude persons from having those types of expectations, and it would prohibit persons from making those kinds of judgments which a system of rights makes possible.

Thus, if we can answer the question of why have rights at all, we can then ask and answer the question of what things—among others—ought to be protected by *rights.* And the answer, I take it, is that one ought to be able to claim as entitlements those minimal things without which it is impossible to develop one's capabilities and to live a life as a human being. Hence, to take one thing that is a precondition of well-being, the relief from acute physical pain, this is the kind of enjoyment that ought to be protected as a right of some kind just because without such relief there is precious little that one can effectively do or become. And similarly for the opportunity to make choices, examine beliefs, and the like.

To recapitulate. The discussion so far has indicated two things: (1) the conditions under which any specific right would be a human right, and (2) some possible grounds for arguing that certain values or enjoyments ought to be regarded as matters of right. The final question that remains is whether there are many specific rights that satisfy the conditions necessary to make them human rights. Or, more specifically, whether it is plausible to believe that there are no general and relevant principles that justify making distinctions among persons in respect to their rights to well-being and freedom.

Vlastos has it that the rights to well-being and freedom do satisfy these conditions, since he asserts that we, at least, do regard each person's well-being and freedom as having equal intrinsic value. If this is correct, if each person's well-being and freedom does have *equal* intrinsic value, then there is no general and relevant principle for differentiating among persons as to these values and, hence, as to their rights to secure these values. But this does not seem wholly satisfactory. It does not give us any reason for supposing that it is plausible to ascribe equal intrinsic value to each person's well-being and freedom.

The crucial question, then, is the plausibility of ascribing intrinsic value to each person's well-being and freedom. There are, I think, at least three different answers that might be given.

First, it might be asserted that this ascription simply constitutes another feature of our morality. The only things that can be done are to point out that this is an assumption that we do make and to ask persons whether they would not prefer to live in a society in which such an assumption is made.

While perhaps correct and persuasive, this does not seem to me to be all that can be done. In particular, there are, I think, two further arguments that may be made.

The first is that there are cases in which all human beings *equally* are capable of enjoying the same goods, e.g., relief from acute physical pain,[9] or that they are capable of deriving equal enjoyment from the same goods. If this is true, then if anyone has a right to this enjoyment, that right is a human right just because there is no rational ground for preferring one man's enjoyment to another's. For, if all persons do have equal capacities of these sorts and if the existence of these capacities is the reason for ascribing these rights to anyone, then all persons ought to have the right to claim equality of treatment in respect to the possession and exercise of these rights.

The difficulty inherent in this assignment is at the same time the strength of the next one. The difficulty is simply that it does seem extraordinarily difficult to know how one would show that all men are equally capable of enjoying any of the same goods, or even how one might attempt to gather or evaluate relevant evidence in this matter. In a real sense, interpersonal comparisons of such a thing as the ability to bear pain seems to be logically as well as empirically unobtainable. Even more unobtainable, no doubt, is a measure of the comparative enjoyments derivable from choosing for oneself.[10] These are simply enjoyments the comparative worths of which, as different persons, there is no way to assess. If this is so, then this fact gives rise to an alternative argument.

We do know, through inspection of human history as well as of our own lives, that the denial of the opportunity to experience the enjoyment of these goods makes it impossible to live either a full or a satisfying life. In a real sense, the enjoyment of these goods differentiates human from nonhuman entities. And therefore, even if we have no meaningful or reliable criteria for comparing and weighing capabilities for enjoyment or for measuring their quantity or quality, we probably know all we need to know to justify our refusal to attempt to grade the value of the enjoyment of these goods. Hence, the dual grounds for treating their intrinsic values as equal for all persons: either these values are equal for all persons, or, if there are differences, they are not in principle discoverable or measurable. Hence, the argument, or an argument, for the human rights to well-being and freedom.

Because the foregoing discussion has been quite general and abstract, I want finally to consider briefly one illustration of a denial of human rights and to delineate both the several ways in which such a denial can occur and some of the different consequences of that denial. My example is that of the way in which Negro persons are regarded and treated by many whites in the South.

The first thing that is obvious is that many white Southerners would or might be willing to accept all that has been said so far and yet seek to justify their attitudes and behavior toward Negroes.

They might agree, for example, that all persons do have a right to be accorded equal treatment unless there is a general and relevant principle of differentiation.

[9]See, Williams, op. cit. p. 112: "These respects [in which men are alike] are notably the capacity to feel pain, both from immediate physical causes and from various situations represented in perception and in thought; and the capacity to feel affection for others, and the consequences of this, connected with the frustration of this affection, loss of its objects, etc."

[10]At times, Vlastos seems to adopt this view as well as the preceding one. See, e.g., Vlastos, op. cit., p. 49: "So understood, a person's well being and freedom are aspects of his individual existence as unique and unrepeatable as is that existence itself. . . ."

They would also surely acknowledge that some persons do have rights to many different things, including most certainly well-being and freedom. But they would insist, nonetheless, that there exists a general and relevant principle of differentiation, namely, that some persons are Negroes and others are not.

Now, those who do bother to concern themselves with arguments and with the need to give reasons would not, typically, assert that the mere fact of color difference does constitute a general and relevant reason. Rather, they would argue that this color difference is correlated with certain other characteristics and attitudes that are relevent.[11] In so doing, they invariably commit certain logical and moral mistakes.

First, the purported differentiating characteristic is usually not relevant to the differentiation sought to be made; e.g., none of the characteristics that supposedly differentiate Negroes from whites has any relevance to the capacity to bear acute physical pain or to the strength of the desire to be free from it. Indeed, almost all arguments neglect the fact that the capacities to enjoy those things which are constitutive of well-being and freedom are either incommensurable among persons or alike in all persons.

Second, the invocation of these differentiating characteristics always violates the requirement of relevance in another sense. For, given the typical definition of a Negro (in Alabama the legal definition is any person with "a drop of Negro blood"), it is apparent that there could not—under any plausible scientific theory—be good grounds for making any differentiations between Negroes and whites.[12]

Third, and related to the above, any argument that makes distinctions as to the possession of human rights in virtue of the truth of certain empirical generalizations invariably produces some unjust denials of those rights. That is to say, even if some of the generalizations about Negroes are correct, they are correct only in the sense that the distinguishing characteristics ascribed to Negroes are possessed by some or many Negroes but not by all Negroes. Yet, before any reason for differentiating among persons as to the possession of human rights can be a relevant reason, that reason must be relevant in respect to *each person* so affected or distinguished. To argue otherwise is to neglect the fact, among other things, that human rights are personal and of at least *prima facie* equal importance to each possessor of those rights.

A different reaction or argument of white Southerners in respect to recent events in the South is bewilderment. Rather than (or in addition to) arguing for the existence of principles of differentiation, the white Southerner will say that he simply cannot understand the Negro's dissatisfaction with his lot. This is so because he, the white Southerner, has always treated his Negroes very well. With appreciable sincerity, he will assert that he has real affection for many Negroes. He would never needlessly inflict pain or suffering upon them. Indeed, he has often assumed special obligations to make certain that their lives were free from hunger, pain, and disease.

Now of course, this description of the facts is seldom accurate at all. Negroes have almost always been made to endure needless and extremely severe suffering in all too many obvious ways for all too many obviously wrong reasons. But I want to assume for my purposes the accuracy of the white Southerner's assertions. For these as-

---

[11]See, Williams, op. cit., p. 13.

[12]This is to say nothing, of course, of the speciousness of any principle of differentiation that builds upon inequalities that are themselves produced by the unequal and unjust distribution of *opportunities*.

sertions are instructive just because they reveal some of the less obvious effects of a denial of human rights.

What is wholly missing from this description of the situation is the ability and inclination to conceptualize the Negro—any Negro—as the possible possessor of rights of any kind, and *a fortiori* of any human rights. And this has certain especially obnoxious consequences.

In the first place, the white Southerner's moral universe illustrates both the fact that it is possible to conceive of duties without conceiving of their correlative rights and the fact that the mistakes thereby committed are not chiefly mistakes of logic and definition. The mistakes matter morally. For what this way of conceiving most denies to any Negro is the opportunity to assert claims as a matter of right. It denies him the standing to protest against the way he is treated. If the white Southerner fails to do his duty, that is simply a matter between him and his conscience.

In the second place, it requires of any Negro that *he* make out his case for the enjoyment of any goods. It reduces all of *his* claims to the level of requests, privileges, and favors. But there are simply certain things, certain goods, that nobody ought to have to request of another. There are certain things that no one else ought to have the power to decide to refuse or to grant. To observe what happens to any person who is required to adopt habits of obsequious, deferential behavior in order to minimize the likelihood of physical abuse, arbitrary treatment, or economic destitution is to see most graphically how important human rights are and what their denial can mean. To witness what happens to a person's own attitudes, aspirations, and conceptions of himself[13] when he must request or petition for the opportunity to voice an opinion, to consult with a public official, or to secure the protection of the law is to be given dramatic and convincing assurance of the moral necessity of a conception of human rights.

And there is one final point. In a real sense, a society that simply lacks any conception of human rights is less offensive than one which has such a conception but denies that some persons have these rights. This is so not just because of the inequality and unfairness involved in differentiating for the wrong reasons among persons. Rather, a society based on such denial is especially offensive because it implicitly, if not explicitly, entails that there are some persons who do not and would not desire or need or enjoy those minimal goods which all men do need and desire and enjoy. It is to read certain persons, all of whom are most certainly human beings, out of the human race. This is surely among the greatest of all moral wrongs.

I know of no better example of the magnitude of this evil than that provided by a lengthy account in a Southern newspaper about the high school band program in a certain city. The article described fully the magnificence of the program and emphasized especially the fact that it was a program in which *all high school students* in the city participated.

Negro children neither were nor could be participants in the program. The article, however, saw no need to point this out. I submit that it neglected to do so not because everyone knew the fact, but because in a real sense the writer and the news-

---

[13]Vlastos puts what I take to be the same point this way: "Any practice which tends to so weaken and confuse the personal esteem of a group of persons—slavery, serfdom or, in our own time racial segregation—may be morally condemned on this one ground, even if there were no other for indicting it" (Vlastos, op. cit., p. 71).

paper do not regard Negro high school students as children—persons, human beings—at all.

What is the Negro parent who reads this article to say to his children? What are
his children supposed to think? How does a Negro parent even begin to demonstrate
to the world that his children are really children, too? These are burdens no civilized
society ought ever to impose. These are among the burdens that an established and
acknowledged system of human rights helps to eliminate.

The Nature and Value of Rights[1]

Joel Feinberg

1

I would like to begin by conducting a thought experiment. Try to imagine Nowheresville—a world very much like our own except that no one, or hardly anyone (the
qualification is not important), has *rights*. If this flaw makes Nowheresville too ugly to
hold very long in contemplation, we can make it as pretty as we wish in other moral
aspects. We can, for example, make the human beings in it as attractive and virtuous as
possible without taxing our conceptions of the limits of human nature. In particular,
let the virtues of moral sensibility flourish. Fill this imagined world with as much benevolence, compassion, sympathy, and pity as it will conveniently hold without strain.
Now we can imagine men helping one another from compassionate motives merely,
quite as much or even more than they do in our actual world from a variety of more
complicated motives.

This picture, pleasant as it is in some respects, would hardly have satisfied Immanuel Kant. Benevolently motivated actions do good, Kant admitted, and therefore
are better, *ceteris paribus,* than malevolently motivated actions; but no action can have
supreme kind of worth—what Kant called "moral worth"—unless its whole motivating power derives from the thought that it is *required by duty*. Accordingly, let us try
to make Nowheresville more appealing to Kant by introducing the idea of duty into it,
and letting the sense of duty be a sufficient motive for many beneficent and honorable
actions. But doesn't this bring our original thought experiment to an abortive conclu-

From *The Journal of Value Inquiry,* vol. 4 (1970). © 1970 by Marinus Nijhoff Publishers. Reprinted by permission Kluwer Academic Publishers.

[1]This article was first given as an Isenberg Memorial Lecture at Michigan State University, Winter Series,
1969. Presented to the Conference on Political and Moral Philosophy held at Ripon College, Wisconsin, Sept.
18 and 19, 1969, and to AMINATAPHIL, Nov. 1969.

sion? If duties are permitted entry into Nowheresville, are not rights necessarily smuggled in along with them?

The question is well-asked, and requires here a brief digression so that we might consider the so-called "doctrine of the logical correlativity of rights and duties." This is the doctrine that (i) all duties entail other people's rights and (ii) all rights entail other people's duties. Only the first part of the doctrine, the alleged entailment from duties to rights, need concern us here. Is this part of the doctrine correct? It should not be surprising that my answer is: "In a sense yes and in a sense no." Etymologically, the word "duty" is associated with actions that are *due* someone else, the payments of debts *to* creditors, the keeping of agreements with promisees, the payment of club dues, or legal fees, or tariff levies to appropriate authorities or their representatives. In this original sense of "duty," all duties are correlated with the rights of those *to* whom the duty is owed. On the other hand, there seem to be numerous classes of duties, both of a legal and non-legal kind, that are *not* logically correlated with the rights of other persons. This seems to be a consequence of the fact that the word "duty" has come to be used for *any* action understood to be *required,* whether by the rights of others, or by law, or by higher authority, or by conscience, or whatever. When the notion of requirement is in clear focus it is likely to seem the only element in the idea of duty that is essential, and the other component notion—that a duty is something *due* someone else—drops off. Thus, in this widespread but derivative usage, "duty" tends to be used for any action we feel we *must* (for whatever reason) do. It comes, in short, to be a term of moral modality merely; and it is no wonder that the first thesis of the logical correlativity doctrine often fails.

Let us then introduce duties into Nowheresville; but only in the sense of actions that are, or are believed to be, morally mandatory, but not in the older sense of actions that are due others and can be claimed by others as their right. Nowheresville now can have duties of the sort imposed by positive law. A legal duty is not something we are implored or advised to do merely; it is something the law, or an authority under the law, *requires* us to do whether we want to or not, under pain of penalty. When traffic lights turn red, however, there is no determinate person who can plausibly be said to claim our stopping as his due, so that the motorist owes it to *him* to stop, in the way a debtor owes it to his creditor to pay. In our own actual world, of course, we sometimes owe it to our *fellow motorists* to stop; but that kind of right-correlated duty does not exist in Nowheresville. There, motorists "owe" obedience to the Law, but they owe nothing to one another. When they collide, no matter who is at fault, no one is morally accountable to anyone else, and no one has any sound grievance or "right to complain."

When we leave legal contexts to consider moral obligations and other extra-legal duties, a greater variety of duties-without-correlative-rights present themselves. Duties of charity, for example, require us to contribute to one or another of a large number of eligible recipients, no one of whom can claim our contribution from us as his due. Charitable contributions are more like gratuitous services, favors, and gifts than like repayments of debts or reparations; and yet we do have duties to be charitable. Many persons, moreover, in our actual world believe that they are required by their own consciences to do more than that "duty" that *can* be demanded of them by their prospective beneficiaries. I have quoted elsewhere the citation from H. B. Acton of a character in a Malraux novel who "gave all his supply of poison to his fellow prisoners to enable them by suicide to escape the burning alive which was to be their fate and his." This man, Acton adds, "probably did not think that [the others] had more of a right to the poison than he had, though he thought it his duty to give it to them."[2] I am sure that there are many actual examples, less dramatically heroic than this fictitious one, of persons who believe, rightly or wrongly, that they *must do* something (hence the word "duty") for another person in excess of what that person can appropriately demand of him (hence the absence of "right").

Now the digression is over and we can return to Nowheresville and summarize what we have put in it thus far. We now find spontaneous benevolence in somewhat larger degree than in our actual world, and also the acknowledged existence of duties of obedience, duties of charity, and duties imposed by exacting private consciences, and also, let us suppose, a degree of conscientiousness in respect to those duties somewhat in excess of what is to be found in our actual world. I doubt that Kant would be fully satisfied with Nowheresville even now that duty and respect for law and authority have been added to it; but I feel certain that he would regard their addition at least as an improvement. I will now introduce two further moral practices into Nowheresville that will make that world very little more appealing to Kant, but will make it appear more familiar to us. These are the practices connected with the notions of *personal desert* and what I call a *sovereign monopoly of rights*.

When a person is said to deserve something good from us what is meant in part is that there would be a certain propriety in our giving that good thing to him in virtue of the kind of person he is, perhaps, or more likely, in virtue of some specific thing he has done. The propriety involved here is a much weaker kind than that which derives from our having promised him the good thing or from his having qualified for it by satisfying the well-advertised conditions of some public rule. In the latter case he could be said not merely to deserve the good thing but also to have a *right* to it, that is to be in a position to demand it as his due; and of course we will not have that sort of thing in Nowheresville. That weaker kind of propriety which is mere desert is simply a kind of *fittingness* between one party's character or action and another party's favorable response, much like that between humor and laughter, or good performance and applause.

The following seems to be the origin of the idea of deserving good or bad treatment from others: A master or lord was under no obligation to reward his servant for especially good service; still a master might naturally feel that there would be a special fittingness in giving a gratuitous reward as a grateful response to the good service (or conversely imposing a penalty for bad service). Such an act while surely fitting and proper was entirely supererogatory. The fitting response in turn from the rewarded servant should be gratitude. If the deserved reward had not been given him he should have had no complaint, since he only *deserved* the reward, as opposed to having a *right* to it, or a ground for claiming it as his due.

The idea of desert has evolved a good bit away from its beginnings by now, but nevertheless, it seems clearly to be one of those words J. L. Austin said "never entirely forget their pasts."[3] Today servants qualify for their wages by doing their agreed upon chores, no more and no less. If their wages are not forthcoming, their contractual rights have been violated and they can make legal claim to the money that is their due.

---

[2]H. B. Acton, "Symposium on 'Rights'," *Proceedings of the Aristotelian Society,* Supplementary Volume 24 (1950), pp. 107–8.

[3]J. L. Austin, "A Plea for Excuses," *Proceedings of the Aristotelian Society,* Vol. 57 (1956–57).

If they do less than they agreed to do, however, their employers may "dock" them, by paying them proportionately less than the agreed upon fee. This is all a matter of right. But if the servant does a splendid job, above and beyond his minimal contractual duties, the employer is under no further obligation to reward him, for this was not agreed upon, even tacitly, in advance. The additional service was all the servant's idea and done entirely on his own. Nevertheless, the morally sensitive employer may feel that it would be exceptionally appropriate for him to respond, freely on *his* own, to the servant's meritorious service, with a reward. The employee cannot demand it as his due, but he will happily accept it, with gratitude, as a fitting response to his desert.

In our age of organized labor, even this picture is now archaic; for almost every kind of exchange of service is governed by hard bargained contracts so that even bonuses can sometimes be demanded as a matter of right, and nothing is given for nothing on either side of the bargaining table. And perhaps that is a good thing; for consider an anachronistic instance of the earlier kind of practice that survives, at least as a matter of form, in the quaint old practice of "tipping." The tip was originally conceived as a reward that has to be earned by "zealous service." It is not something to be taken for granted as a standard response to *any* service. That is to say that its payment is a *"gratuity,"* not a discharge of obligation, but something given apart from, or in addition to, anything the recipient can expect as a matter of right. That is what tipping originally meant at any rate, and tips are still referred to as "gratuities" in the tax forms. But try to explain all that to a New York cab driver! If he has *earned* his gratuity, by God, he has it coming, and there had better be sufficient acknowledgement of his desert or he'll give you a piece of his mind! I'm not generally prone to defend New York cab drivers, but they do have a point here. There is the making of a paradox in the queerly unstable concept of an "earned gratuity." One can understand how "desert" in the weak sense of "propriety" or "mere fittingness" tends to generate a stronger sense in which desert is itself the ground for a claim of right.

In Nowheresville, nevertheless, we will have only the original weak kind of desert. Indeed, it will be impossible to keep this idea out if we allow such practices as teachers grading students, judges awarding prizes, and servants serving benevolent but class-conscious masters. Nowheresville is a reasonably good world in many ways, and its teachers, judges, and masters will generally try to give students, contestants, and servants the grades, prizes, and rewards they deserve. For this the recipients will be grateful; but they will never think to complain, or even feel aggrieved, when expected responses to desert fail. The masters, judges, and teachers don't *have* to do good things, after all, for *anyone*. One should be happy that they *ever* treat us well, and not grumble over their occasional lapses. Their hoped for responses, after all, are *gratuities,* and there is no wrong in the omission of what is merely gratuitous. Such is the response of persons who have no concept of *rights*, even persons who are proud of their own deserts.[4]

Surely, one might ask, rights have to come in somewhere, if we are to have even moderately complex forms of social organization. Without rules that confer rights and impose obligations, how can we have ownership of property, bargains and deals, promises and contracts, appointments and loans, marriages and partnerships? Very well, let us introduce all of these social and economic practices into Nowheresville,

---

[4]For a fuller discussion of the concept of personal desert see my "Justice and Personal Desert," *Nomos VI, Justice,* ed. by C. J. Friedrich and J. Chapman (New York: Atherton Press, 1963), pp. 69–97.

but *with one big twist*. With them I should like to introduce the curious notion of a "sovereign right-monopoly." You will recall that the subjects in Hobbes's *Leviathan* had no rights whatever against their sovereign. He could do as he liked with them, even gratuitously harm them, but this gave them no valid grievance against him. The sovereign, to be sure, had a certain duty to treat his subjects well, but this duty was owed not to the subjects directly, but to God, just as we might have a duty to a person to treat his property well, but of course no duty to the property itself but only to its owner. Thus, while the sovereign was quite capable of *harming* his subjects, he could commit no wrong against them that they could complain about, since they had no prior claims against his conduct. The only party *wronged* by the sovereign's mistreatment of his subjects was God, the supreme lawmaker. Thus, in repenting cruelty to his subjects, the sovereign might say to God, as David did after killing Uriah, "to Thee only have I sinned."[5]

Even in the *Leviathan,* however, ordinary people had ordinary rights *against one another*. They played roles, occupied offices, made agreements, and signed contracts. In a genuine "sovereign right-monopoly," as I shall be using that phrase, they will do all those things too, and thus incur genuine obligations toward one another; but the obligations (here is the twist) will not be owed directly *to* promises, creditors, parents, and the like, but rather to God alone, or to the members of some elite, or to a single sovereign under God. Hence, the rights correlative to the obligations that derive from these transactions are all owned by some "outside" authority.

As far as I know, no philosopher has ever suggested that even our role and contract obligations (in this, our actual world) are all owed directly to a divine intermediary; but some theologians have approached such extreme moral occasionalism. I have in mind the familiar phrase in certain widely distributed religious tracts that "it takes three to marry," which suggests that marital vows are not made between bride and groom directly but between each spouse and God, so that if one breaks his vow, the other cannot rightly complain of being wronged, since only God could have claimed performance of the marital duties as his *own* due; and hence God alone had a claim-right violated by nonperformance. If John breaks his vow to God, he might then properly repent in the words of David: "To Thee only have I sinned."

In our actual world, very few spouses conceive of their mutual obligations in this way; but their small children, at a certain stage in their moral upbringing, are likely to feel precisely this way toward *their* mutual obligations. If Billy kicks Bobby and is punished by Daddy, he may come to feel contrition for his naughtiness induced by his painful estrangement from the loved parent. He may then be happy to make amends and sincere apology *to Daddy;* but when Daddy insists that he apologize to his wronged brother, that is another story. A direct apology to Billy would be a tacit recognition of Billy's status as a right-holder against him, someone he can wrong as well as harm, and someone to whom he is directly accountable for his wrongs. This is a status Bobby will happily accord Daddy; but it would imply a respect for Billy that he does not presently feel, so he bitterly resents according it to him. On the "three-to-marry" model, the relations between each spouse and God would be like those between Bobby and Daddy; respect for the other spouse as an independent claimant would not even be necessary; and where present, of course, never sufficient.

The advocates of the "three to marry" model who conceive it either as a descrip-

---

[5]II Sam. 11. Cited with approval by Thomas Hobbes in *The Leviathan,* Part II, Chap. 21.

tion of our actual institution of marriage or a recommendation of what marriage ought to be, may wish to escape this embarrassment by granting rights to spouses in capacities other than as promisees. They may wish to say, for example, that when John promises God that he will be faithful to Mary, a right is thus conferred not only on God as promisee but also on Mary herself as third-party beneficiary, just as when John contracts with an insurance company and names Mary as his intended beneficiary, she has a right to the accumulated funds after John's death, even though the insurance company made no promise to her. But this seems to be an unnecessarily cumbersome complication contributing nothing to our understanding of the marriage bond. The life insurance transaction is necessarily a three-party relation, involving occupants of three distinct offices, no two of whom alone could do the whole job. The transaction, after all, is defined as the purchase by the customer (first office) from the vendor (second office) of protection for a beneficiary (third office) against the customer's untimely death. Marriage, on the other hand, in this our actual world, appears to be a binary relation between a husband and wife, and even though third parties such as children, neighbors, psychiatrists, and priests may sometimes be helpful and even causally necessary for the survival of the relation, they are not logically necessary to our *conception* of the relation, and indeed many married couples do quite well without them. Still, I am not now purporting to describe our actual world, but rather trying to contrast it with a counterpart world of the imagination. In that world, it takes three to make almost *any* moral relation and all rights are owned by God or some sovereign under God.

There will, of course, be delegated authorities in the imaginary world, empowered to give commands to their underlings and to punish them for their disobedience. But the commands are all given in the name of the right-monopoly who in turn are the only persons to whom obligations are owed. Hence, even intermediate superiors do not have claim-rights against their subordinates but only legal *powers* to create obligations in the subordinates *to* the monopolistic right-holders, and also the legal *privilege* to impose penalties in the name of that monopoly.

2

So much for the imaginary "world without rights." If some of the moral concepts and practices I have allowed into that world do not sit well with one another, no matter. Imagine Nowheresville with all of these practices if you can, or with any harmonious subset of them, if you prefer. The important thing is not what I've let into it, but what I have kept out. The remainder of this paper will be devoted to an analysis of what precisely a world is missing when it does not contain rights and why that absence is morally important.

The most conspicuous difference, I think, between the Nowheresvillians and ourselves has something to do with the activity of *claiming*. Nowheresvillians, even when they are discriminated against invidiously, or left without the things they need, or otherwise badly treated, do not think to leap to their feet and make righteous demands against one another, though they may not hesitate to resort to force and trickery to get what they want. They have no notion of rights, so they do not have a notion of what is their due: hence they do not claim before they take. The conceptual linkage between personal rights and claiming has long been noticed by legal writers and is reflected in the standard usage in wnich "claim-rights" are distinguished from the mere liberties, immunities, and powers, also sometimes called "rights," with which they are easily confused. When a person has a legal claim-right to *X,* it must be the case (i) that he is at liberty in respect to *X,* i.e., that he has no duty to refrain from or relinquish *X* and also (ii) that his liberty is the ground of other people's *duties* to grant him *X* or not to interfere with him in respect to *X*. Thus, in the sense of claim-rights, it is true by definition that rights logically entail other people's duties. The paradigmatic examples of such rights are the creditor's right to be paid a debt by his debtor, and the land-owner's right not to be interfered with by anyone in the exclusive occupancy of his land. The creditor's right against his debtor, for example, and the debtor's duty to his creditor, are precisely the same relation seen from two different vantage points, as inextricably linked as the two sides of the same coin.

And yet, this is not quite an accurate account of the matter, for it fails to do justice to the way claim-rights are somehow prior to, or more basic than, the duties with which they are necessarily correlated. If Nip has a claim-right against Tuck, it is because of this fact that Tuck has a duty to Nip. It is only because something from Tuck is *due* Nip (directional element) that there is something Tuck *must do* (modal element). This is a relation, moreover, in which Tuck is bound and Nip is free. Nip not only *has* a right, but he can choose whether or not to exercise it, whether to claim it, whether to register complaints upon its infringement, even whether to release Tuck from his duty, and forget the whole thing. If the personal claim-right is also backed up by criminal sanctions, however, Tuck may yet have a duty of obedience to the law from which no one, not even Nip, may release him. He would even have such duties if he lived in Nowheresville, but duties subject to acts of claiming, duties derivative from and contingent upon the personal rights of others, are unknown and undreamed of in Nowheresville.

Many philosophical writers have simply identified rights with claims. The dictionaries tend to define "claims," in turn, as "assertions of right," a dizzying piece of circularity that led one philosopher to complain—"We go in search of rights and are directed to claims, and then back again to rights in bureaucratic futility."[6] What then is the relation between a claim and a right?

As we shall see, a right *is* a kind of claim, and a claim is "an assertion of right," so that a formal definition of either notion in terms of the other will not get us very far. Thus if a "formal defintion" of the usual philosophical sort is what we are after, the game is over before it has begun, and we can say that the concept of a right is a "simple, undefinable, unanalysable primitive." Here as elsewhere in philosophy this will have the effect of making the commonplace seem unnecessarily mysterious. We would be better advised, I think, not to attempt a formal definition of either "right" or "claim," but rather to use the idea of a claim in informal elucidation of the idea of a right. This is made possible by the fact that *claiming* is an elaborate sort of rule-governed *activity*. A claim is that which is claimed, the object of the act of claiming. There is, after all, a verb "to claim," but no verb "to right." If we concentrate on the whole activity of claiming, which is public, familiar, and open to our observation, rather than on its upshot alone, we may learn more about the generic nature of rights than we could ever hope to learn from a formal definition, even if one were possible. Moreover, certain facts about rights more easily, if not solely, expressible in the language of claims and claiming are essential to a full understanding not only of what rights are, but also why they are so vitally important.

[6]H. B.Acton. *Op. cit.*

Let us begin then by distinguishing between (i) making claim to..., and (ii) claiming that...., and (iii) having a claim. One sort of thing we may be doing when we claim is to *make claim to something*. This is "to petition or seek by virtue of supposed right; to demand as due." Sometimes this is done by an acknowledged right-holder when he serves notice that he now wants turned over to him that which has already been acknowledged to be his, something borrowed, say, or improperly taken from him. This is often done by turning in a chit, a receipt, an I.O.U., a check, an insurance policy, or a deed, that is, a *title* to something currently in the possession of someone else. On other occasions, making claim is making application for titles or rights themselves, as when a mining prospector stakes a claim to mineral rights, or a householder to a tract of land in the public domain, or an inventor to his patent rights. In the one kind of case, to make claim is to exercise rights one already has by presenting title; in the other kind of case it is to apply for the title itself, by showing that one has satisfied the conditions specified by a rule for the ownership of title and therefore that one can demand it as one's due.

Generally speaking, only the person who has a title or who has qualified for it, or someone speaking in his name, can make claim to something as a matter of right. It is an important fact about rights (or claims), then, that they can be claimed only by those who have them. Anyone can claim, of course, *that* this umbrella is yours, but only you or your representative can actually claim the umbrella. If Smith owes Jones five dollars, only Jones can claim the five dollars as his own, though any bystander can *claim that* it belongs to Jones. One important difference then between *making legal claim to* and *claiming that* is that the former is a legal performance with direct legal consequences whereas the latter is often a mere piece of descriptive commentary with no legal force. Legally speaking, *making claim to* can itself make things happen. This sense of "claiming," then, might well be called "the performative sense." The legal power to claim (performatively) one's right or the things to which one has a right seems to be essential to the very notion of a right. A right to which one could not make claim (i.e., not even for recognition) would be a very "imperfect" right indeed!

Claiming that one has a right (what we can call "propositional claiming" as opposed to "performative claiming") is another sort of thing one can do with language, but it is not the sort of doing that characteristically has legal consequences. To claim that one has rights is to make an assertion that one has them, and to make it in such a manner as to demand or insist that they be recognized. In the sense of "claim" many things in addition to rights can be claimed, that is, many other kinds of proposition can be asserted in the claiming way. I can claim, for example, that you, he, or she has certain rights, or that Julius Caesar once had certain rights; or I can claim that certain statements are true, or that I have certain skills, or accomplishments, or virtually anything at all. I can claim that the earth is flat. What is essential to *claiming that* is the manner of assertion. One can assert without even caring very much whether anyone is listening, but part of the point of propositional claiming is to *make sure* people listen. When I claim to others that I know something, for example, I am not merely asserting it, but rather "obtruding my putative knowledge upon their attention, demanding that it be recognized, that appropriate notice be taken of it by those concerned...."[7] Not every truth is properly assertable, much less claimable, in every con-

---

[7]G. J. Warnock, "Claims to Knowledge," *Proceedings of the Aristotelian Society,* Supplementary Volume 36 (1962), p. 21.

text. To claim that something is the case in circumstances that justify no more than calm assertion is to behave like a boor. (This kind of boorishness, I might add, is probably less common in Nowheresville.) But not to claim in the appropriate circumstances that one has a right is to be spiritless or foolish. A list of "appropriate circumstances" would include occasions when one is challenged, when one's possession is denied, or seems insufficiently acknowledged or appreciated; and of course even in these circumstances, the claiming should be done only with an appropriate degree of vehemence.

Even if there are conceivable circumstances in which one would admit rights differently, there is no doubt that their characteristic use and that for which they are distinctively well suited, is to be claimed, demanded, affirmed, insisted upon. They are especially sturdy objects to "stand upon," a most useful sort of moral furniture. Having rights, of course, makes claiming possible; but it is claiming that gives rights their special moral significance. This feature of rights is connected in a way with the customary rhetoric about what it is to be a human being. Having rights enables us to "stand up like men," to look others in the eye, and to feel in some fundamental way the equal of anyone. To think of oneself as the holder of rights is not to be unduly but properly proud, to have that minimal self-respect that is necessary to be worthy of the love and esteem of others. Indeed, respect for persons (this is an intriguing idea) may simply be respect for their rights, so that there cannot be the one without the other, and what is called "human dignity" may simply be the recognizable capacity to assert claims. To respect a person then, or to think of him as possessed of human dignity, simply *is* to think of him as a potential maker of claims. Not all of this can be packed into a definition of "rights"; but these are *facts* about the possession of rights that argue well their supreme moral importance. More than anything else I am going to say, these facts explain what is wrong with Nowheresville.

We come now to the third interesting employment of the claiming vocabulary, that involving not the verb "to claim" but the substantive "a claim." What is it to *have a claim* and how is this related to rights? I would like to suggest that *having a claim consists in being in a position to claim, that is, to make claim to or claim that*. If this suggestion is correct it shows the primacy of the verbal over the nominative forms. It links claims to a kind of activity and obviates the temptation to think of claims as *things,* on the model of coins, pencils, and other material possessions which we can carry in our hip pockets. To be sure, we often make or establish our claims by presenting titles, and these typically have the form of receipts, tickets, certificates, and other pieces of paper or parchment. The title, however, is not the same thing as the claim; rather it is the evidence that establishes the claim as valid. On this analysis, one might have a claim without ever claiming that to which one is entitled, or without even knowing that one has the claim; for one might simply be ignorant of the fact that one is in a position to claim; or one might be unwilling to exploit that position for one reason or another, including fear that the legal machinery is broken down or corrupt and will not enforce one's claim despite its validity.

Nearly all writers maintain that there is some intimate connection between having a claim and having a right. Some identify right and claim without qualification; some define "right" as justified or justifiable claim, others as recognized claim, still others as valid claim. My own preference is for the latter definition. Some writers, however, reject the identification of rights and valid claims on the ground that all claims as such are valid, so that the expression "valid claim" is redundant. These writers, therefore, would identify rights with claims *simpliciter*. But this is a very simple confusion. All claims, to be sure, are *put forward* as justified, whether they are justified in fact or not. A claim conceded even by its maker to have no validity is not a claim at all, but a mere demand. The highwayman, for example, *demands* his victim's money; but he hardly makes claim to it as rightfully his own.

But it does not follow from this sound point that it is redundant to qualify claims as justified (or as I prefer, valid) in the definition of a right; for it remains true that not all claims put forward as valid really are valid; and only the valid ones can be acknowledged as rights.

If having a valid claim is not redundant, i.e., if it is not redundant to pronounce *another's* claim valid, there must be such a thing as having a claim that is not valid. What would this be like? One might accumulate just enough evidence to argue with relevance and cogency that one has a right (or ought to be granted a right), although one's case might not be overwhelmingly conclusive. In such a case, one might have strong enough argument to be entitled to a hearing and given fair consideration. When one is in this position, it might be said that one "has a claim" that deserves to be weighed carefully. Nevertheless, the balance of reasons may turn out to militate against recognition of the claim, so that the claim, which one admittedly had, and perhaps still does, is not a valid claim or right. "Having a claim" in this sense is an expression very much like the legal phrase "having a *prima facie* case." A plaintiff establishes a *prima facie* case for the defendant's liability when he establishes grounds that will be sufficient for liability unless outweighed by reasons of a different sort that may be offered by the defendant. Similarly, in the criminal law, a grand jury returns an indictment when it thinks that the prosecution has sufficient evidence to be taken seriously and given a fair hearing, whatever countervailing reasons may eventually be offered on the other side. That initial evidence, serious but not conclusive, is also sometimes called a *prima facie* case. In a parallel *"prima facie* sense" of "claim," having a claim to X is not (yet) the same as having a right to X, but is rather having a case of at least minimal plausibility that one has a right to X, a case that does establish a right, not to X, but to a fair hearing and consideration. Claims, so conceived, differ in degree: some are stronger than others. Rights, on the other hand, do not differ in degree; no one right is more of a right than another.[8]

Another reason for not identifying rights with claims *simply* is that there is a well-established usage in international law that makes a theoretically interesting distinction between claims and rights. Statesmen are sometimes led to speak of "claims" when they are concerned with the natural needs of deprived human beings in conditions of scarcity. Young orphans *need* good upbringings, balanced diets, education, and technical training everywhere in the world; but unfortunately there are many places where these goods are in such short supply that it is impossible to provision all who need them. If we persist, nevertheless, in speaking of these needs as constituting rights and not merely claims, we are committed to the conception of a right which is an entitlement *to* some good, but not a valid claim *against* any particular individual, for in con-

---

[8]This is the important difference between rights and mere claims. It is analogous to the difference between *evidence* of guilt (subject to degrees of cogency) and conviction of guilt (which is all or nothing). One can "have evidence" that is not conclusive just as one can "have a claim" that is not valid. "Prima-facieness" is built into the sense of "claim," but the notion of a "prima facie right" makes little sense. On the latter point see A. I. Melden, *Rights and Right Conduct* (Oxford: Basil Blackwell, 1959), pp. 18–20, and Herbert Morris, "Persons and Punishment," *The Monist,* Vol. 52 (1868), pp. 498–9.

ditions of scarcity there may be no determinate individuals who can plausibly be said to have a duty to provide the missing goods to those in need. J. E. S. Fawcett therefore prefers to keep the distinction between claims and rights firmly in mind. "Claims," he writes, "are needs and demands in movement, and there is a continuous transformation, as a society advances [toward greater abundance] of economic and social claims into civil and political rights . . . and not all countries or all claims are by any means at the same stage in the process."[9] The manifesto writers on the other side who seem to identify needs, or at least basic needs, with what they call "human rights," are more properly described, I think, as urging upon the world community the moral principle that *all* basic human needs ought to be recognized as *claims* (in the customary *prima facie* sense) worthy of sympathy and serious consideration right now, even though, in many cases, they cannot yet plausibly be treated as *valid* claims, that is, as grounds of any other people's duties. This way of talking avoids the anomaly of ascribing to all human beings now, even those in pre-industrial societies, such "economic and social rights" as "periodic holidays with pay."[10]

Still, for all of that, I have a certain sympathy with the manifesto writers and I am, even willing to speak of a special "manifesto sense" of "right," in which a right need not be correlated with another's duty. Natural needs are real claims if only upon hypothetical future beings not yet in existence. I accept the moral principle that to have an unfulfilled need is to have a kind of claim against the world, even if against no one in particular. A natural need for some good as such, like a natural desert, is always a reason in support of a claim to that good. A person in need, then, is always "in a position" to make a claim, even when there is no one in the corresponding position to do anything about it. Such claims, based on need alone, are "permanent possibilities of rights," the natural seed from which rights grow. When manifesto writers speak of them as if already actual rights, they are easily forgiven, for this is but a powerful way of expressing the conviction that they ought to be recognized by states here and now as potential rights and consequently as determinants of *present* aspirations and guides to *present* policies. That usage, I think, is a valid exercise of rhetorical license.

I prefer to characterize rights as valid claims rather than justified ones, because I suspect that justification is rather too broad a qualification. "Validity," as I understand it, is justification of a peculiar and narrow kind, namely justification within a system of rules. A man has a legal right when the official recognition of his claim (as valid) is called for by the governing rules. This definition, of course, hardly applies to moral rights, but that is not because the genus of which moral rights are a species is something other than *claims*. A man has a moral right when he has a claim the recognition of which is called for—not (necessarily) by legal rules—but by moral principles, or the principles of an enlightened conscience.

There is one final kind of attack on the generic identification of rights with claims, and it has been launched with great spirit in a recent article by H. J. McCloskey, who holds that rights are not essentially claims at all, but rather entitlements. The springboard of his argument is his insistence that rights in their essential character are always *rights to,* not *rights against*:

[9]J. E. S. Fawcett. "The International Protection of Human Rights," in *Political Theory and the Rights of Man,* ed. by D. D. Raphael (Bloomington: Indiana University Press, 1967), pp. 125 and 128.

[10]As declared in Article 24 of *The Universal Declaration of Human Rights* adopted on December 10, 1948, by the General Assembly of the United Nations.

My right to life is not a right against anyone. It is my right and by virtue of it, it is normally permissible for me to sustain my life in the face of obstacles. It does give rise to rights against others in the sense that others have or may come to have duties to refrain from killing me, but it is essentially a right of mine, not an infinite list of claims, hypothetical and actual, against an infinite number of actual, potential, and as yet nonexistent human beings. . . . Similarly, the right of the tennis club member to play on the club courts is a right to play, not a right against some vague group of potential or possible obstructors.[11]

The argument seems to be that since rights are essentially rights *to,* whereas claims are essentially claims *against,* rights cannot be claims, though they can be grounds for claims. The argument is doubly defective though. First of all, contrary to McCloskey, rights (at least legal claim-rights) *are* held *against* others. McCloskey admits this in the case of *in personam* rights (what he calls "special rights") but denies it in the case of *in rem* rights (which he calls "general rights"):

Special rights are sometimes against specific individuals or institutions—e.g. rights created by promises, contracts, etc. . . . but these differ from . . . characteristic . . . general rights where the right is simply a right to. . . .[12]

As far as I can tell, the only reason McCloskey gives for denying that *in rem* rights are against others is that those against whom they would have to hold make up an enormously multitudinous and "vague" group, including hypothetical people not yet even in existence. Many others have found this a paradoxical consequence of the notion of *in rem* rights, but I see nothing troublesome in it. If a general rule gives me a right of noninterference in a certain respect against everybody, then there are literally hundreds of millions of people who have a duty toward me in that respect; and if the same general rule gives the same right to everyone else, then it imposes on me literally hundreds of millions of duties—or duties towards hundreds of millions of people. I see nothing paradoxical about this, however. The duties, after all, are negative; and I can discharge all of them at a stroke simply by minding my own business. And if all human beings make up one moral community and there are hundreds of millions of human beings, we should expect there to be hundreds of millions of moral relations holding between them.

McCloskey's other premise is even more obviously defective. There is no good reason to think that all *claims* are "essentially" *against,* rather than *to.* Indeed most of the discussion of claims above has been of claims *to,* and as we have seen, the law finds it useful to recognize claims *to* (or "mere claims") that are not yet qualified to be claims *against,* or rights (except in a "manifesto sense" of "rights").

Whether we are speaking of claims or rights, however, we must notice that they seem to have two dimensions, as indicated by the prepositions "to" and "against," and it is quite natural to wonder whether either of these dimensions is somehow more fundamental or essential than the other. All rights seem to merge *entitlements to* do have, omit, or be something with *claims against* others to act or refrain from acting in certain ways. In some statements of rights the entitlement is perfectly determinate

[11]H. J. McCloskey, "Rights," *Philosophical Quarterly,* Vol. 15 (1965), p. 118.
[12]*Loc. cit.*

(e.g., *to* play tennis) and the claim vague (e.g., *against* "some vague group of potential or possible obstructors"); but in other cases the object of the claim is clear and determinate (e.g., *against* one's parents), and the entitlement general and indeterminate (e.g., to be given a proper upbringing). If we mean by "entitlement" that *to* which one has a right and by "claim" something directed at those *against* whom the right holds (as McCloskey apparently does), then we can say that all claim-rights necessarily involve both, though in individual cases the one element or the other may be in sharper focus.

In brief conclusion: To have a right is to have a claim against someone whose recognition as valid is called for by some set of governing rules or moral principles. To have a *claim* in turn, is to have a case meriting consideration, that is, to have reasons or grounds that put one in a position to engage in performative and propositional claiming. The activity of claiming, finally, as much as any other thing, makes for self-respect and respect for others, gives a sense to the notion of personal dignity, and distinguishes the otherwise morally flawed world from the even worse world of Nowheresville.

Taking Rights Seriously

Ronald Dworkin

1. THE RIGHTS OF CITIZENS

The language of rights now dominates political debate in the United States. Does the Government respect the moral and political rights of its citizens? Or does the Government's foreign policy, or its race policy, fly in the face of these rights? Do the minorities whose rights have been violated have the right to violate the law in return? Or does the silent majority itself have rights, including the right that those who break the law be punished? It is not surprising that these questions are now prominent. The concept of rights, and particularly the concept of rights against the Government, has its most natural use when a political society is divided, and appeals to co-operation or a common goal are pointless.

The debate does not include the issue of whether citizens have *some* moral rights against their Government. It seems accepted on all sides that they do. Conventional lawyers and politicians take it as a point of pride that our legal system recognizes, for example, individual rights of free speech, equality, and due process. They base their claim that our law deserves respect, at least in part, on that fact, for they would not claim that totalitarian systems deserve the same loyalty.

Some philosophers, of course, reject the idea that citizens have rights apart, from

Reprinted by permission of the publishers from Chapter 7, *Taking Rights Seriously* by Ronald Dworkin (Cambridge: Harvard University Press © 1970, 1977, 1978).

what the law happens to give them. Bentham thought that the idea of moral rights was "nonsense on stilts." But that view has never been part of our orthodox political theory, and politicians of both parties appeal to the rights of the people to justify a great part of what they want to do. I shall not be concerned, in this essay, to defend the thesis that citizens have moral rights against their governments; I want instead to explore the implications of that thesis for those, including the present United States Government, who profess to accept it.

It is much in disputee, of course, what *particular* rights citizens have. Does the acknowledged right to free speech, for example, include the right to participate in nuisance demonstrations? In practice the Government will have the last word on what an individual's rights are, because its police will do what its officials and courts say. But that does not mean that the Government's view is necessarily the correct view; anyone who thinks it does must believe that men and women have only such moral rights as Government chooses to grant, which means that they have no moral rights at all.

All this is sometimes obscured in the United States by the constitutional system. The American Constitution provides a set of individual *legal* rights in the First Amendment, and in the due process, equal protection, and similar clauses. Under present legal practice the Supreme Court has the power to declare an act of Congress or of a state legislature void if the Court finds that the act offends these provisions. This practice has led some commentators to suppose that individual moral rights are fully protected by this system, but that is hardly so, nor could it be so.

The Constitution fuses legal and moral issues, by making the validity of a law depend on the answer to complex moral problems, like the problem of whether a particular statute respects the inherent equality of all men. This fusion has important consequences for the debates about civil disobedience; I have described these elsewhere . . . and I shall refer to them later. But it leaves open two prominent questions. It does not tell us whether the Constitution, even properly interpreted, recognizes all the moral rights that citizens have, and it does not tell us whether, as many suppose, citizens would have a duty to obey the law even if it did invade their moral rights.

But questions become crucial when some minority claims moral rights which the law denies, like the right to run its local school system, and which lawyers agree are not protected by the Constitution. The second question becomes crucial when, as now, the majority is sufficiently aroused so that Constitutional amendments to eliminate rights, like the right against self-incrimination, are seriously proposed. It is also crucial in nations, like the United Kingdom, that have no constitution of a comparable nature.

Even if the Constitution were perfect, of course, and the majority left it alone, it would not follow that the Supreme Court could guarantee the individual rights of citizens. A Supreme Court decision is still a legal decision, and it must take into account precedent and institutional considerations like relations between the Court and Congress, as well as morality. And no judicial decision is necessarily the right decision. Judges stand for different positions on controversial issues of law and morals and, as the fights over Nixon's Supreme Court nominations showed, a President is entitled to appoint judges of his own persuasion, provided that they are honest and capable.

So, though the constitutional system adds something to the protection of moral rights against the Government, it falls far short of guaranteeing these rights, or even establishing what they are. It means that, on some occasions, a department other than the legislature has the last word on these issues, which can hardly satisfy someone who thinks such a department profoundly wrong.

It is of course inevitable that some department of government will have the final say on what law will be enforced. When men disagree about moral rights, there will be no way for either side to prove its case, and some decision must stand if there is not to be anarchy. But that piece of orthodox wisdom must be the beinning and not the end of a philosophy of legislation and enforcement. If we cannot insist that the Government reach the right answers about the rights of its citizens, we can insist at least that it try. We can insist that it take rights seriously, follow a coherent theory of what these rights are, and act consistently with its own professions. I shall try to show what that means. and how it bears on the present political debates.

2. RIGHTS AND THE RIGHT TO BREAK THE LAW

I shall start with the most violently argued issue. Does an American ever have the moral right to break a law? Suppose someone admits a law is valid; does he therefore have a duty to obey it? Those who try to give an answer seem to fall into two camps. The conservatives, as I shall call them, seem to disapprove of any act of disobedience; they appear satisfied when such acts are prosecuted, and disappointed when convictions are reversed. The other group, the liberals, are much more sympathetic to at least some cases of disobedience; they sometimes disapprove of prosecutions and celebrate acquittals. If we look beyond these emotional reactions, however, and pay attention to the arguments the two parties use, we discover an astounding fact. Both groups give essentially the same answer to the question of principle that supposedly divides them.

The answer that both parties give is this. In a democracy, or at least a democracy that in principle respects individual rights, each citizen has a general moral duty to obey all the laws, even though he would like some of them changed. He owes that duty to his fellow citizens, who obey laws that they do not like, to his benefit. But this general duty cannot be an absolute duty, because even a society that is in principle just may produce unjust laws and policies, and a man has duties other than his duties to the State. A man must honour his duties to his God and to his conscience, and if these conflict with his duty to the State, then he is entitled, in the end, to do what he judges to be right. If he decides that he must break the law, however, then he must submit to the judgment and punishment that the State imposes, in recognition of the fact that his duty to his fellow citizens was overwhelmed but not extinguished by his religious or moral obligation.

Of course this common answer can be elaborated in very different ways. Some would describe the duty to the State as fundamental, and picture the dissenter as a religious or moral fanatic. Others would describe the duty to the State in grudging terms, and picture those who oppose it as moral heroes. But these are differences in tone, and the position I described represents, I think, the view of most of those who find themselves arguing either for or against civil disobedience in particular cases.

I do not claim that it is everyone's view. There must be some who put the duty to the State so high that they do not grant that it can ever be overcome. There are certainly some who would deny that a man ever has a moral duty to obey the law, at least in the United States today. But these two extreme positions are the slender tails of a bell curve, and all those who fall in between hold the orthodox position I described—that men have a duty to obey the law but have the right to follow their consciences when it conflicts with that duty.

But if that is so, then we have a paradox in the fact that men who give the same answer to a question of principle should seem to disagree so much, and to divide so fiercely, in particular cases. The paradox goes even deeper, for each party, in at least some cases, takes a position that seems flatly inconsistent with the theoretical position they both accept. This position was tested, for example, when someone evaded the draft on grounds of conscience, or encouraged others to commit this crime. Conservatives argued that such men must be prosecuted, even though they are sincere. Why must they be prosecuted? Because society cannot tolerate the decline in respect for the law that their act constitutes and encourages. They must be prosecuted, in short, to discourage them and others like them from doing what they have done.

But there seems to be a monstrous contradiction here. If a man has a right to do what his conscience tells him he must, then how can the State be justified in discouraging him from doing it? Is it not wicked for a state to forbid and punish what it acknowledges that men have a right to do?

Moreover, it is not just conservatives who argue that those who break the law out of moral conviction should be prosecuted. The liberal is notoriously opposed to allowing racist school officials to go slow on desegregation, even though he acknowledges that these school officials think they have a moral right to do what the law forbids. The liberal does not often argue, it is true, that the desegregation laws must be enforced to encourage general respect for law. He argues instead that the desegregation laws must be enforced because they are right. But his position also seems inconsistent: can it be right to prosecute men for doing what their conscience requires, when we acknowledge their right to follow their conscience?

We are therefore left with two puzzles. How can two parties to an issue of principle, each of which thinks it is in profound disagreement with the other, embrace the same position on that issue? How can it be that each side urges solutions to particular problems which seem flatly to contradict the position of principle that both accept? One possible answer is that some or all of those who accept the common position are hypocrites, play lip service to rights of conscience which in fact they do not grant.

There is some plausibility in this charge. A sort of hypocrisy must have been involved when public officials who claim to respect conscience denied Muhammad Ali the right to box in their states. If Ali, in spite of his religious scruples, had joined the Army, he would have been allowed to box even though, on the principles these officials say they honour, he would have been a worse human being for having done so. But there are few cases that seem so straightforward as this one, and even here the officials did not seem to recognize the contradiction between their acts and their principles. So we must search for some explanation beyond the truth that men often do not mean what they say.

The deeper explanation lies in a set of confusions that often embarrass arguments about rights. These confusions have clouded all the issues I mentioned at the outset and have crippled attempts to develop a coherent theory of how a government that respects rights must behave.

In order to explain this, I must call attention to the fact, familiar to philosophers, but often ignored in political debate, that the word "right" has different force in different contexts. In most cases when we say that someone has "right" to do something, we imply that it would be wrong to interfere with his doing it, or at least that some special grounds are needed for justifying any interference. I use this strong sense of right when I say that you have the right to spend your money gambling, if you wish, though you ought to spend it in a more worthwhile way. I mean that it would be wrong for anyone to interfere with you even though you propose to spend your money in a way that I think is wrong.

There is a clear difference between saying that someone has a right to do something in this sense and saying that it is the "right" thing for him to do, or that he does no "wrong" in doing it. Someone may have the right to do something that is the wrong thing for him to do, as might be the case with gambling. Conversely, something may be the right thing for him to do and yet he may have no right to do it, in the sense that it would not be wrong for someone to interfere with his trying. If our army captures an enemy soldier, we might say that the right thing for him to do is to try to escape, but it would not follow that it is wrong for us to try to stop him. We might admire him for trying to escape, and perhaps even think less of him if he did not. But there is no suggestion here that it is wrong of us to stand in his way; on the contrary, if we think our cause is just, we think it right for us to do all we can to stop him.

Ordinarily this distinction, between the issues of whether a man has a right to do something and whether it is the right thing for him to do, causes no trouble. But sometimes it does, because sometimes we say that a man has a right to do something when we mean only to deny that it is the wrong thing for him to do. Thus we say that the captured soldier has a "right" to try to escape when we mean, not that we do wrong to stop him, but that he has no duty not to make the attempt. We use 'right' this way when we speak of someone having the "right" to act on his own principles, or the 'right' to follow his own conscience. We mean that he does no wrong to proceed on his honest convictions, even though we disagree with these convictions, and even though, for policy or other reasons, we must force him to act contrary to them.

Suppose a man believes that welfare payments to the poor are profoundly wrong, because they sap enterprise, and so declares his full income-tax each year but declines to pay half of it. We might say that he has a right to refuse to pay, if he wishes, but that the Government has a right to proceed against him for the full tax, and to fine or jail him for late payment if that is necessary to keep the collection system working efficiently. We do not take this line in most cases; we do not say that the ordinary thief has a right to steal, if he wishes, so long as he pays the penalty. We say a man has the right to break the law, even though the State has a right to punish him, only when we think that, because of his convictions, he does no wrong in doing so.[1]

These distinctions enable us to see an ambiguity in the orthodox question: Does a man ever have a right to break the law? Does that question mean to ask whether he ever has a right to break the law in the strong sense, so that the Government would do wrong to stop him, by arresting and prosecuting him? Or does it mean to ask whether he ever does the right thing to break the law, so that we should all respect him even though the Government should jail him?

If we take the orthodox position to be an answer to the first—and most impor-

---

[1] It is not surprising that we sometimes use the concept of having a right to say that others must not interfere with an act and sometimes to say that the act is not the wrong thing to do. Often, when someone has *no* right to do something, like attacking another man physically, it is true *both* that it is the wrong thing to do and that others are entitled to stop it, by demand, if not by force. It is therefore natural to say that someone has a right when we mean to deny *either* of these consequences, as well as when we mean to deny both.

tant—question, then the paradoxes I described arise. But if we take it as an answer to the second, they do not. Conservatives and liberals do agree that sometimes a man does not do the wrong thing to break a law, when his conscience so requires. They disagree, when they do, over the different issue of what the State's response should be. Both parties do think that sometimes the State should prosecute. But this is not inconsistent with the proposition that the man prosecuted did the right thing in breaking the law.

The paradoxes seem genuine because the two questions are not usually distinguished, and the orthodox position is presented as a general solution to the problem of civil disobedience. But once the distinction is made, it is apparent that the position has been so widely accepted only because, when it is applied, it is treated as an answer to the second question but not the first. The crucial distinction is obscured by the troublesome idea of a right to conscience; this idea has been at the centre of most recent discussions of political obligation, but it is a red herring drawing us away from the crucial political questions. The state of a man's conscience may be decisive, or central, when the issue is whether he does something morally wrong in breaking the law; but it need not be decisive or even central when the issue is whether he has a right, in the strong sense of that term, to do so. A man does not have the right, in that sense, to do whatever his conscience demands, but he may have the right, in that sense, to do something even though his conscience does not demand it.

If that is true, then there has been almost no serious attempt to answer the questions that almost everyone means to ask. We can make a fresh start by stating these questions more clearly. Does an American ever have the right in a strong sense, to do something which is against the law? If so, when? In order to answer these questions put in that way, we must try to become clearer about the implications of the idea, mentioned earlier, that citizens have at least some rights against their government.

I said that in the United States citizens are supposed to have certain fundamental rights against their Government, certain moral rights made into legal rights by the Constitution. If this idea is significant, and worth bragging about, then these rights must be rights in the strong sense I just described. The claim that citizens have a right to free speech must imply that it would be wrong for the Government to stop them from speaking, even when the Government believes that what they will say will cause more harm than good. The claim cannot mean, on the prisoner-of-war analogy, only that citizens do no wrong in speaking their minds, though the Government reserves the right to prevent them from doing so.

This is a crucial point, and I want to labour it. Of course a responsible government must be ready to justify anything it does, particularly when it limits the liberty of its citizens. But normally it is a sufficient justification, even for an act that limits liberty, that the act is calculated to increase what the philosophers call general utility—that it is calculated to produce more over-all benefit than harm. So, though the New York City government needs a justification for forbidding motorists to drive up Lexington Avenue, it is sufficient justification if the proper officials believe, on sound evidence, that the gain to the many will outweigh the inconvenience to the few. When individual citizens are said to have rights against the Government, however, like the right of free speech, that must mean that this sort of justification is not enough. Otherwise the claim would not argue that individuals have special protection against the law when their rights are in play, and that is just the point of the claim.

Not all legal rights, or even Constitutional rights, represent moral rights against the Government. I now have the legal right to drive either way on Fifty-seventh Street, but the Government would do no wrong to make that street one-way if it thought it in the general interest to do so. I have a Constitutional right to vote for a congressman every two years, but the national and state governments would do no wrong if, following the amendment procedure, they made a congressman's term four years instead of two, again on the basis of a judgment that this would be for the general good.

But those Constitutional rights that we call fundamental like the right of free speech, are supposed to represent rights against the Government in the strong sense; that is the point of the boast that our legal system respects the fundamental rights of the citizen. If citizens have a moral right of free speech, then governments would do wrong to repeal the First Amendment that guarantees it, even if they were persuaded that the majority would be better off if speech were curtailed.

I must not overstate the point. Someone who claims that citizens have a right against the Government need not go so far as to say that the State is *never* justified in overriding that right. He might say, for example, that although citizens have a right to free speech, the Government may override that right when necessary to protect the rights of others, or to prevent a catastrophe, or even to obtain a clear and major public benefit (though if he acknowledged this last as a possible justification he would be treating the right in question as not among the most important or fundamental). What he cannot do is to say that the Government is justified in overrding a right on the minimal grounds that would be sufficient if no such right existed. He cannot say that the Government is entitled to act on nor more than a judgment that its act is likely to produce, overall, a benefit to the community. That admission would make his claim of a right pointless, and would show him to be using some sense of "right" other than the strong sense necessary to give his claim the political importance it is normally taken to have.

But then the answers to our two questions about disobedience seem plain, if unorthodox. In our society a man does sometimes have the right, in the strong sense, to disobey a law. He has that right whenever that law wrongly invades his rights against the Government. If he has a moral right to free speech, that is, then he has a moral right to break any law that the Government, by virtue of his right, had no right to adopt. The right to disobey the law is not a separate right, having something to do with conscience, additional to other rights against the Government. It is simply a feature of these rights against the Government, and it cannot be denied in principle without denying that any such rights exist.

These answers seem obvious once we take rights against the Government to be rights in the strong sense I described. If I have a right to speak my mind on political issues, then the Government does wrong to make it illegal for me to do so, even if it thinks this is in the general interest. If, nevertheless, the Government does make my act illegal, then it does a further wrong to enforce that law against me. My right against the Government means that it is wrong for the Government to stop me from speaking; the Government cannot make it right to stop me just by taking the first step.

This does not, of course, tell us exactly what rights men do have against the Government. It does not tell us whether the right of free speech includes the right of demonstration. But it does mean that passing a law cannot affect such rights as men do have, and that is of crucial importance, because it dictates the attitude that an individual is entitled to take toward his personal decision when civil disobedience is in question.

Both conservatives and liberals suppose that in a society which is generally decent everyone has a duty to obey the law, whatever it is. That is the source of the" general duty" clause in the orthodox position, and though liberals believe that this duty can sometimes be "overridden," even they suppose, as the orthodox position maintains, that the duty of obedience remains in some submerged form, so that a man does well to accept punishment in recognition of that duty. But this general duty is almost incoherent in a society that recognizes rights. If a man believes he has a right to demonstrate, then he must believe that it would be wrong for the Government to stop him, with or without benefit of a law. If he is entitled to believe that, then it is silly to speak of a duty to obey the law as such, or of a duty to accept the punishment that the State has no right to give.

Conservatives will object to the short work I have made of their point. They will argue that even if the Government was wrong to adopt some law, like a law limiting speech, there are independent reasons why the Government is justified in enforcing the law once adopted. When the law forbids demonstration, then, so they argue, some principle more important than the individual's right to speak is brought into play, namely the principle of respect for law. If a law, even a bad law, is left unenforced, then respect for law is weakened, and society as a whole suffers. So an individual loses his moral right to speak when speech is made criminal, and the Government must, for the common good and for the general benefit, enforce the law against him.

But this argument, though popular, is plausible only if we forget what it means to say that an individual has a right against the State. It is far from plain that civil disobedience lowers respect for law, but even if we suppose that it does, this fact is irrelevant. The prospect of utilitarian gains cannot justify preventing a man from doing what he has a right to do, and the supposed gains in respect for law are simply utilitarian gains. There would be no point in the boast that we respect individual rights unless that involved some sacrifice, and the sacrifice in question must be that we give up whatever marginal benefits our country would receive from overriding these rights when they prove inconvenient. So the general benefit cannot be a good ground for abridging rights, even when the benefit in question is a heightened respect for law.

But perhaps I do wrong to assume that the argument about respect for law is only an appeal to general utility. I said that a state may be justified in overriding or limiting rights on other grounds, and we must ask, before rejecting the conservative position, whether any of these apply. The most important—and least well understood— of these other grounds invokes the notion of *competing rights* that would be jeopardized if the right in question were not limited. Citizens have personal rights to the State's protection as well as personal rights to be free from the State's interference, and it may be necessary for the Government to choose between these two sorts of rights. The law of defamation, for example, limits the personal right of any man to say what he thinks, because it requires him to have good grounds for what he says. But this law is justified, even for those who think that it does invade a personal right, by the fact that it protects the right of others not to have their reputations ruined by a careless statement.

The individual rights that our society acknowledges often conflict in this way, and when they do it is the job of government to discriminate. If the Government makes the right choice, and protects the more important at the cost of the less, then it has not weakened or cheapened the notion of a right; on the contrary it would have done so had it failed to protect the more important of the two. So we must acknowledge that the Government has a reason for limiting rights if it plausibly believes that a competing right is more important.

May the conservative seize on this fact? He might argue that I did wrong to characterize his argument as one that appeals to the general benefit, because it appeals instead to competing rights, namely the moral right of the majority to have its laws enforced, or the right of society to maintain the degree of order and security it wishes. These are the rights, he woud say, that must be weighed against the individual's right to do what the wrongful law prohibits.

But this new argument is confused, because it depends on yet another ambiguity in the language of rights. It is true that we speak of the "right" of society to do what it wants, but this cannot be a "competing right" of the sort that may justify the invasion of a right against the Government. The existence of rights against the Government would be jeopardized if the Government were able to defeat such a right by appealing to the right of a democratic majority to work its will. A right against the Government must be a right to do something even when the majority thinks it would be wrong to do it, and even when the majority would be worse off for having it done. If we now say that society has a right to do whatever is in the general benefit, or the right to preserve whatever sort of environment the majority wishes to live in, and we mean that these are the sort of rights that provide justification for overruling any rights against the Government that may conflict, then we have annihilated the latter rights.

In order to save them, we must recognize as competing rights only the rights of other members of the society as individuals. We must distinguish the "rights" of the majority as such, which cannot count as a justification for overruling individual rights, and the personal rights of members of a majority, which might well count. The test we must use is this. Someone has a competing right to protection, which must be weighed against an individual right to act, if that person would be entitled to demand that protection from his government on his own title, as an individual, without regard to whether a majority of his fellow citizens joined in the demand.

It cannot be true, on this test, that anyone has a right to have all the laws of the nation enforced. He has a right to have enforced only those criminal laws, for example, that he would have a right to have enacted if they were not already law. The laws against personal assault may well fall into that class. If the physically vulnerable members of the community—those who need police protection against personal violence—were only a small minority, it would still seem plausible to say that they were entitled to that protection. But the laws that provide a certain level of quiet in public places, or that authorize and finance a foreign war, cannot be thought to rest on individual rights. The timid lady on the streets of Chicago is not entitled to just the degree of quiet that now obtains, nor is she entitled to have boys drafted to fight in wars she approves. There are laws—perhaps desirable laws—that provide these advantages for her, but the justification for these laws, if they can be justified at all, is the common desire of a large majority, not her personal right. If, therefore, these laws do abridge someone else's moral right to protest, or his right to personal security, she cannot urge a competing right to justify the abridgement. She has no personal right to have such laws passed, and she has no competing right to have them enforced either.

So the conservative cannot advance his argument much on the ground of competing rights, but he may want to use another ground. A government, he may argue, may be justified in abridging the personal rights of its citizens in an emergency, or when a very great loss may be prevented, or perhaps, when some major benefit can clearly be secured. If the nation is at war, a policy of censorship may be justified even though it invades the right to say what one thinks on matters of political controversy. But the emergency must be genuine. There must be what Oliver Wendell Holmes described as a clear and present danger, and the danger must be one of magnitude.

Can the conservative argue that when any law is passed, even a wrongful law, this sort of justification is available for enforcing it? His argument might be something of this sort. If the Government once acknowledges that it may be wrong—that the legislature might have adopted, the executive approved, and the courts left standing, a law that in fact abridges important rights—then this admission will lead not simply to a marginal decline in respect for law, but to a crisis of order. Citizens may decide to obey only those laws they personally approve, and that is anarchy. So the Government must insist that whatever a citizen's rights may be before a law is passed and upheld by the courts, his rights therefore are determined by that law.

But this argument ignores the primitive distinction between what may happen and what will happen. If we allow speculation to support the justification of emergency or decisive benefit, then, again, we have annihilated rights. We must, as Learned Hand said, discount the gravity of the evil threatened by the likelihood of reaching that evil. I know of no genuine evidence to the effect that tolerating some civil disobedience, out of respect for the moral position of its authors, will increase such disobedience, let alone crime in general. The case that it will must be based on vague assumptions about the contagion of ordinary crimes, assumptions that are themselves unproved, and that are in any event largely irrelevant. It seems at least as plausible to argue that tolerance will increase respect for officials and for the bulk of the laws they promulgate, or at least retard the rate of growing disrespect.

If the issue were simply the question whether the community would be marginally better off under strict law enforcement, then the Government would have to decide on the evidence we have, and it might not be unreasonable to decide, on balance, that it would. But since rights are at stake, the issue is the very difficult one of whether tolerance would destroy the community or threaten it with great harm, and it seems to me simply mindless to suppose that the evidence makes that probable or even conceivable.

The argument from emergency is confused in another way as well. It assumes that the Government must take the position either that a man never has the right to break the law, or that he always does. I said that any society that claims to recognize rights at all must abandon the notion of a general duty to obey the law that holds in all cases. This is important, because it shows that there are no short cuts to meeting a citizen's claim to right. If a citizen argues that he has a moral right not to serve in the Army, or to protest in a way he finds effective, then an official who wants to answer him, and not simply bludgeon him into obedience, must respond to the particular point he makes, and cannot point to the draft law or a Supreme Court decision as having even special, let alone decisive, weight. Sometimes an official who considers the citizen's moral arguments in good faith will be persuaded that the citizen's claim is plausible, or even right. It does not follow, however, that he will always be persuaded or that he always should be.

I must emphasize that all these propositions concern the strong sense of right, and they therefore leave open important questions about the right thing to do. If a man believes he has the right to break the law, he must then ask whether he does the right thing to exercise that right. He must remember that reasonable men can differ about whether he has a right against the Government, and therefore the right to break the law, that he thinks he has; and therefore that reasonable men can oppose him in good faith. He must take into account the various consequences his acts will have, whether they involve violence, and such other considerations as the context makes relevant; he must not go beyond the rights he can in good faith claim, to acts that violate the rights of others.

On the other hand, if some official, like a prosecutor, believes that the citizen does *not* have the right to break the law, then *he* must ask whether he does the right thing to enforce it. In Chapter 8 I argue that certain features of our legal system, and in particular the fusion of legal and moral issues in our Constitution, mean that citizens often do the right thing in exercising what they take to be moral rights to break the law, and that prosecutors often do the right thing in failing to prosecute them for it. I will not anticipate those arguments here; instead I want to ask whether the requirement that Government take its citizens' rights seriously has anything to do with the crucial question of what these rights are.

3. CONTROVERSIAL RIGHTS

The argument so far has been hypothetical: if a man has a particular moral right against the Government, that right survives contrary legislation or adjudication. But this does not tell us what rights he has, and it is notorious that reasonable men disagree about that. There is wide agreement on certain clearcut cases; almost everyone who believes in rights at all would admit, for example, that a man has a moral right to speak his mind in a non-provocative way on matters of political concern, and that this is an important right that the State must go to great pains to protect. But there is great controversy as to the limits of such paradigm rights, and the so-called "anti-riot" law involved in the famous Chicago Seven trial of the last decade is a case in point.

The defendants were accused of conspiring to cross state lines with the intention of causing a riot. This charge is vague—perhaps unconstitutionally vague—but the law apparently defines as criminal emotional speeches which argue that violence is justified in order to secure political equality. Does the right of free speech protect this sort of speech? That, of course, is a legal issue, because it invokes the free-speech clause of the First Amendment of the Constitution. But it is also a moral issue, because, as I said, we must treat the First Amendment as an attempt to protect a moral right. It is part of the job of governing to "define" moral rights through statutes and judicial decisions, that is, to declare officially the extent that moral rights will be taken to have in law. Congress faced this task in voting on the anti-riot bill, and the Supreme Court has faced it in countless cases. How should the different departments of government go about defining moral rights?

They should begin with a sense that whatever they decide might be wrong. History and their descendants may judge that they acted unjustly when they thought they were right. If they take their duty seriously, they must try to limit their mistakes, and they must therefore try to discover where the dangers of mistake lie.

They might choose one of two very different models for this purpose. The first model recommends striking a balance between the rights of the individual and the demands of society at large. If the Government *infringes* on a moral right (for example, by defining the right of free speech more narrowly than justice requires), then it has done the individual a wrong. On the other hand, if the Government *inflates* a right (by defining it more broadly than justice requires) then it cheats society of some general benefit, like safe streets, that there is no reason it should not have. So a mistake on one side is as serious as a mistake on the other. The course of government is to steer to the middle, to balance the general good and personal rights, giving to each its due.

When the Government, or any of its branches, defines a right, it must bear in mind, according to the first model, the social cost of different proposals and make the necessary adjustments. It must not grant the same freedom to noisy demonstrations as it grants to calm political discussion, for example, because the former causes much more trouble than the latter. Once it decides how much of a right to recognize, it must enforce its decision to the full. That means permitting an individual to act within his rights, as the Government has defined them, but not beyond, so that if anyone breaks the law, even on grounds of conscience, he must be punished. No doubt any government will make mistakes, and will regret decisions once taken. That is inevitable. But this middle policy will ensure that errors on one side will balance out errors on the other over the long run.

The first model, described in this way, has great plausibility, and most laymen and lawyers, I think, would respond to it warmly. The metaphor of balancing the public interest against personal claims is established in our political and judicial rhetoric, and this metaphor gives the model both familiarity and appeal. Nevertheless, the first model is a false one, certainly the case of rights generally regarded as important, and the metaphor is the heart of its error.

The institution of rights against the Government is not a gift of God, or an ancient ritual, or a national sport. It is a complex and troublesome practice that makes the Government's job of securing the general benefit more difficult and more expensive, and it would be a frivolous and wrongful practice unless it served some point. Anyone who professes to take rights seriously, and who praises our Government for respecting them, must have some sense of what that point is. He must accept, at the minimum, one or both of two important ideas. The first is the vague but powerful idea of human dignity. This idea, associated with Kant, but defended by philosophers of different schools, supposes that there are ways of treating a man that are inconsistent with recognizing him as a full member of the human community, and holds that such treatment is profoundly unjust.

The second is the more familiar idea of political equality. This supposes that the weaker members of a political community are entitled to the same concern and respect of their government as the more powerful members have secured for themselves, so that if some men have freedom of decision whatever the effect on the general good, then all men must have the same freedom. I do not want to defend or elaborate these ideas here, but only to insist that anyone who claims that citizens have rights must accept ideas very close to these.[2]

It makes sense to say that a man has a fundamental right against the Government, in the strong sense, like free speech, if that right is necessary to protect his dignity, or

---

[2]He need not consider these ideas to be axiomatic. He may, that is, have reasons for insisting that dignity or equality are important values, and these reasons may be utilitarian. He may believe, for example, that the general good will be advanced, *in the long run,* only if we treat indignity or inequality as very great injustices, and never allow our *opinions* about the general good to justify them. I do not know of any good arguments for or against this sort of "institutional" utilitarianism, but it is consistent with my point, because it argues that we must treat violations of dignity and equality as special moral crimes, beyond the reach of ordinary utilitarian justification.

his standing as equally entitled to concern and respect, or some other personal value of like consequence. It does not make sense otherwise.

So if rights make sense at all, then the invasion of a relatively important right must be a very serious matter. It means treating a man as less than a man, or as less worthy of concern than other men. The institution of rights rests on the conviction that this is a grave injustice, and that it is worth paying the incremental cost in social policy or efficiency that is necessary to prevent it. But then it must be wrong to say that inflating rights is as serious as invading them. If the Government errs on the side of the individual, then it simply pays a little more in social efficiency than it has to pay; it pays a little more, that is, of the same coin that it has already decided must be spent. But if it errs against the individual it inflicts an insult upon him that, on its own reckoning, it is worth a great deal of that coin to avoid.

So the first model is indefensible. It rests, in fact, on a mistake I discussed earlier, namely the confusion of society's rights with the rights of members of society. "Balancing" is appropriate when the Government must choose between competing claims of right—between the Southerner's claim to freedom of association, for example, and the black man's claim to an equal education. Then the Government can do nothing but estimate the merits of the competing claims, and act on its estimate. The first model assumes that the "right" of the majority is a competing right that must be balanced in this way; but that, as I argued before, is a confusion that threatens to destroy the concept of individual rights. It is worth noticing that the community rejects the first model in that area where the stakes for the individual are highest, the criminal process. We say that it is better that a great many guilty men go free than that one innocent man be punished, and that homily rests on the choice of the second model for government.

The second model treats abridging a right as much more serious than inflating one, and its recommendations follow from that judgment. It stipulates that once a right is reconized in clear-cut cases, then the Government should act to cutt off that right only when some compelling reason is presented, some reason that is consistent with the suppositions on which the original right must be based. It cannot be an argument for curtailing a right, once granted, simply that society would pay a further price for extending it. There must be something special about that further cost, or there must be some other feature of the case, that makes it sensible to say that although great social cost is warranted to protect the original right, this particular cost is not necessary. Otherwise, the Government's failure to extend the right will show that its recognition of the right in the original case is a sham, a promise that it intends to keep only until that becomes inconvenient.

How can we show that a particular cost is not worth paying without taking back the initial recognition of a right? I can think of only three sorts of grounds that can consistently be used to limit the definition of a particular right. First, the Government might show that the values protected by the original right are not really at stake in the marginal case, or are at stake only in some attenuated form. Second, it might show that if the right is defined to include the marginal case, then some competing right, in the strong sense I described earlier, would be abridged. Third, it might show that if the right were so defined, then the cost to society would not be simply incremental, but would be of a degree far beyond the cost paid to grant the original right, a degree great enough to justify whatever assault on dignity or equality might be involved.

It is fairly easy to apply these grounds to one group of problems the Supreme

Court faced, imbedded in constitutional issues. The draft law provided an exemption for conscientious objectors, but this exemption, as interpreted by the draft boards, has been limited to those who object to *all* wars on *religious* grounds. If we suppose that the exemption is justified on the ground that an individual has a moral right not to kill in violation of his own principles, then the question is raised whether it is proper to exclude those whose morality is not based on religion, or whose morality is sufficiently complex to distinguish among wars. The Court held, as a matter of Constitutional law, that the draft boards were wrong to exclude the former, but competent to exclude the latter.

None of the three grounds I listed can justify either of these exclusions as a matter of political morality. The invasion of personality in forcing men to kill when they believe killing immoral is just as great when these beliefs are based on secular grounds, or take account of the fact that wars differ in morally relevant ways, and there is no pertinent difference in competing rights or in national emergency. There are differences among the cases, of course, but they are insufficient to justify the distinction. A government that is secular on principle cannot prefer a religious to a nonreligious morality as such. There are utilitarian arguments in favour of limting the exception to religious or universal grounds—an exemption so limited may be less expensive to administer, and may allow easier discrimination between sincere and insincere applicants. But those utilitarian reasons are irrelevant, because they cannot count as grounds for limiting a right.

What about the anti-riot law, as applied in the Chicago trial? Does the law represent an improper limitation of the right to free speech, supposedly protected by the First Amendment? If we were to apply the first model for government to this issue, the argument for the anti-riot law would look strong. But if we set aside talk of balancing as inappropriate, and turn to the proper grounds for limiting a right, then the argument becomes a great deal weaker. The original right of free speech must suppose that it is an assault on human personality to stop a man from expressing what he honestly believes, particularly on issues affecting how he is governed. Surely the assault is greater, and not less, when he is stopped from expressing those principles of political morality that he holds most passionately, in the face of what he takes to be outrageous violations to these principles.

It may be said that the anti-riot law leaves him free to express these principles in a non-provocative way. But that misses the point of the connection between expression and dignity. A man cannot express himself freely when he cannot match his rhetoric to his outrage, or when he must trim his sails to protect values he counts as nothing next to those he is trying to vindicate. It is true that some political dissenters speak in ways that shock the majority, but it is arrogant for the majority to suppose that the orthodox methods of expression are the proper ways to speak, for this is a denial of equal concern and respect. If the point of the right is to protect the dignity of dissenters, then we must make judgments about appropriate speech with the personalities of the dissenters in mind, not the personality of the 'silent' majority for whom the anti-riot law is no restraint at all.

So the argument fails, that the personal values protected by the original right are less at stake in this marginal case. We must consider whether competing rights, or some grave threat to society, nevertheless justify the anti-riot law. We can consider these two grounds together, because the only plausible competing rights are rights to be free from violence, and violence is the only plausible threat to society that the context provides.

I have no right to burn your house, or stone you or your car, or swing a bicycle chain against your skull, even if I find these to be natural means of expression. But the defendants in the Chicago trial were not accused of direct violence; the argument runs that the acts of speech they planned made it likely that others would do acts of violence, either in support of or out of hostility to what they said. Does this provide a justification?

The question would be different if we could say with any confidence how much and what sort of violence the anti-riot law might be expected to prevent. Will it save two lives a year, or two hundred, or two thousand? Two thousand dollars of property, or two hundred thousand, or two million? No one can say, not simply because prediction is next to impossible, but because we have no firm understanding of the process by which demonstration disintegrates into riot, and in particular of the part played by inflammatory speech, as distinct from poverty, police brutality, blood lust, and all the rest of the human and economic failure. The Government must try, of course, to reduce the violent waste of lives and property, but it must recognize that any attempt to locate and remove a cause of riot, short of a reorganization of society, must be an exercise in speculation, trial, and error. It must make its decisions under conditions of high uncertainty, and the institution of rights, taken seriously, limits its freedom to experiment under such conditions.

It forces the Government to bear in mind that preventing a man from speaking or demonstrating offers him a certain and profound insult, in return for a speculative benefit that may in any event be achieved in other if more expensive ways. When lawyers say that rights may be limited to protect other rights, or to prevent catastrophe, they have in mind cases in which cause and effect are relatively clear, like the familiar example of a man falsely crying "Fire!" in a crowded theater.

But the Chicago story shows how obscure the causal connections can become. Were the speeches of Hoffman or Rubin necessary conditions of the riot? Or had thousands of people come to Chicago for the purposes of rioting anyway, as the Government also argues? Were they in any case sufficient conditions? Or could the police have contained the violence if they had not been so busy contributing to it, as the staff of the President's Commission on Violence said they were?

These are not easy questions, but if rights mean anything, then the Government cannot simply assume answers that justify its conduct. If a man has a right to speak, if the reasons that support that right extend to provocative political speech, and if the effects of such speech on violence are unclear, then the Government is not entitled to make its first attack on that problem by denying that right. It may be that abridging the right to speak is the least expensive course, or the least damaging to police morale, or the most popular politically. But these are utilitarian arguments in favor of starting one place rather than another, and such arguments are ruled out by the concept of rights.

This point may be obscured by the popular belief that political activists look forward to violence and "ask for trouble" in what they say. They can hardly complain, in the general view, if they are taken to be the authors of the violence they expect, and treated accordingly. But this repeats the confusion I tried to explain earlier between having a right and doing the right thing. The speaker's motives may be relevant in deciding whether he does the right thing in speaking passionately about issues that may inflame or enrage the audience. But if he has a right to speak, because the danger in allowing him to speak is speculative, his motives cannot count as independent evidence in the argument that justifies stopping him.

But what of the individual rights of those who will be destroyed by a riot, of the passer-by who will be killed by a sniper's bullet or the shopkeeper who will be ruined by looting? To put the issue in this way, as a question of competing rights, suggests a principle that would undercut the effect of uncertainty. Shall we say that some rights to protection are so important that the Government is justified in doing all it can to maintain them? Shall we therefore say that the Government may abridge the rights of others to act when their acts might simply increase the risk, by however slight or speculative a margin, that some person's right to life or property will be violated?

Some such principle is relied on by those who oppose the Supreme Court's recent liberal rulings on police procedure. These rulings increase the chance that a guilty man will go free, and therefore marginally increase the risk that any particular member of the community will be murdered, raped, or robbed. Some critics believe that the Court's decisions must therefore be wrong.

But no society that purports to recognize a variety of rights, on the ground that a man's dignity or equality may be invaded in a variety of ways, can accept such a principle. If forcing a man to testify against himself, or forbidding him to speak, does the damage that the rights against self-incrimination and the right of free speech assume, then it would be contemptuous for the State to tell a man that he must suffer this damage against the possibility that other men's risk of loss may be marginally reduced. If rights make sense, then the degrees of their importance cannot be so different that some count not at all when others are mentioned.

Of course the Government may discriminate and may stop a man from exercising his right to speak when there is a clear and substantial risk that his speech will do great damage to the person or property of others, and no other means of preventing this are at hand, as in the case of the man shouting "Fire!" in a theater. But we must reject the suggested principle that the Government can simply ignore rights to speak when life and property are in question. So long as the impact of speech on these other rights remains speculative and marginal, it must look elsewhere for levers to pull.

4. WHY TAKE RIGHTS SERIOUSLY?

I said at the beginning of this essay that I wanted to show what a government must do that professes to recognize individual rights. It must dispense with the claim that citizens never have a right to break its law, and it must not define citizens' rights so that these are cut off for supposed reasons of the general good. Any Government's harsh treatment of civil disobedience, or campaign against vocal protest, may therefore be thought to count against its sincerity.

One might well ask, however, whether it is wise to take rights all that seriously after all. America's genius, at least in her own legend, lies in not taking any abstract doctrine to its logical extreme. It may be time to ignore abstractions, and concentrate instead on giving the majority of our citizens a new sense of their Government's concern for their welfare, and of their title to rule.

That, in any event, is what former Vice-President Agnew seemed to believe. In a policy statement on the issue of "weirdos" and social misfits, he said that the liberals' concern for individual rights was a headwind blowing in the face of the ship of state. That is a poor metaphor, but the philosophical point it expresses is very well taken. He recognized, as many liberals do not, that the majority cannot travel as fast or as far as it would like if it recognizes the rights of individuals to do what, in the majority's terms, is the wrong thing to do.

Spiro Agnew supposed that rights are divisive, and that national unity and a new respect for law may be developed by taking them more skeptically. But he is wrong. America will continue to be divided by its social and foreign policy, and if the economy grows weaker again the divisions will become more bitter. If we want our laws and our legal institutions to provide the ground rules within which these issues will be contested then these ground rules must not be the conqueror's law that the dominant class imposes on the weaker, as Marx supposed the law of a capitalist society must be. The bulk of the law—that part which defines and implements social, economic, and foreign policy—cannot be neutral. It must state, in its greatest part, the majority's view of the common good. The institution of rights is therefore crucial, because it represents the majority's promise to the minorities that their dignity and equality will be respected. When the divisions among the groups are most violent, then this gesture, if law is to work, must be most sincere.

The institution requires an act of faith on the part of the minorities, because the scope of their rights will be controversial whenever they are important, and because the officers of the majority will act on their own notions of what these rights really are. Of course these officials will disagree with many of the claims that a minority makes. That makes it all the more important that they take their decisions gravely. They must show that they understand what rights are, and they must not cheat on the full implications of the doctrine. The Government will not re-establish respect for law without giving the law some claim to respect. It cannot do that if it neglects the one feature that distinguishes law from ordered brutality. If the Government does not take rights seriously, then it does not take law seriously either.

The Entitlement Theory

Robert Nozick

The subject of justice in holdings consists of three major topics. The first is the *original acquisition of holdings,* the appropriation of unheld things. This includes the issues of how unheld things may come to be held, the process, or processes, by which unheld things may come to be held, the things that may come to be held by these processes, the extent of what comes to be held by a particular process, and so on. We shall refer to the complicated truth about the topic, which we shall not formulate here, as the principle of justice in acquisition. The second topic concerns the *transfer of holdings* from one person to another. By what processes may a person transfer holdings to another? How may a person acquire a holding from another who holds it? Under this topic come general descriptions of voluntary exchange, and gift and (on the other hand) fraud, as well as reference to particular conventional details fixed upon in a given society. The complicated truth about this subject (with placeholders for conven-

Reprinted from *Anarchy, State, and Utopia* by Robert Nozick, © 1974 by Basic Books, Inc. Reprinted by Basic Books, Inc., Publishers.

tional details) we shall call the principle of justice in transfer. (And we shall suppose it also includes principles governing how a person may divest himself of a holding, passing it into an unheld state.)

If the world were wholly just, the following inductive definition would exhaustively cover the subject of justice in holdings.

1. A person who acquires a holding in accordance with the principle of justice in acquisition is entitled to that holding.
2. A person who acquires a holding in accordance with the principle of justice in transfer, from someone else entitled to the holding, is entitled to the holding.
3. No one is entitled to a holding except by (repeated) applications of 1 and 2.

The complete principle of distributive justice would say simply that a distribution is just if everyone is entitled to the holdings they possess under the distribution.

A distribution is just if it arises from another just distribution by legitimate means. The legitimate means of moving from one distribution to another are specified by the principle of justice in transfer. The legitimate first "moves" are specified by the principle of justice in acquisition.[1] Whatever arises from a just situation by just steps is itself just. The means of change specified by the principle of justice in transfer preserve justice. As correct rules of inference are truth-preserving, and any conclusion deduced via repeated application of such rules from only true premises is itself true, so the means of transition from one situation to another specified by the principle of justice in transfer are justice-preserving, and any situation actually arising from repeated transitions in accordance with the principle from a just situation is itself just. The parallel between justice-preserving transformations and truth-preserving transformations illuminates where it fails as well as where it holds. That a conclusion could have been deduced by truth-preserving means from premises that are true suffices to show its truth. That from a just situation a situation *could* have arisen via justice-preserving means does *not* suffice to show its justice. The fact that a thief's victims voluntarily *could* have presented him with gifts does not entitle the thief to his ill-gotten gains. Justice in holdings is historical; it depends upon what actually has happened. We shall return to this point later.

Not all actual situations are generated in accordance with the two principles of justice in holdings: the principle of justice in acquisition and the principle of justice in transfer. Some people steal from others, or defraud them, or enslave them, seizing their product and preventing them from living as they choose, or forcibly exclude others from competing in exchanges. None of these are permissible modes of transition from one situation to another. And some persons acquire holdings by means not sanctioned by the principle of justice in acquisition. The existence of past injustice (previous violations of the first two principles of justice in holdings) raises the third major topic under justice in holdings: the rectification of injustice in holdings. If past injustice has shaped present holdings in various ways, some identifiable and some not, what now, if anything, ought to be done to rectify these injustices? What obligations do the performers of injustice have toward those whose position is worse than it would have been had the injustice not been done? Or, than it would have been had compen-

---

[1] Applications of the principle of justice in acquisition may also occur as part of the move from one distribution to another. You may find an unheld thing now and appropriate it. Acquisitions also are to be understood as included when, so simply, I speak only of transitions by transfers.

sation been paid promptly? How, if at all, do things change if the beneficiaries and those made worse off are not the direct parties in the act of injustice, but, for example, their descendants? Is an injustice done to someone whose holding was itself based upon an unrectified injustice? How far back must one go in wiping clean the historical slate of injustices? What may victims of injustice permissibly do in order to rectify the injustices being done to them, including the many injustices done by persons acting through their government? I do not know of a thorough or theoretically sophisticated treatment of such issues.[2] Idealizing greatly, let us suppose theoretical investigation will produce a principle of rectification. This principle uses historical information about previous situations and injustices done in them (as defined by the first two principles of justice and rights against interference), and information about the actual course of events that flowed from these injustices, until the present, and it yields a description (or descriptions) of holdings in the society. The principle of rectification presumably will make use of its best estimate of subjunctive information about what would have occurred (or a probability distribution over what might have occurred, using the expected value) if the injustice had not taken place. If the actual description of holdings turns out not to be one of the descriptions yielded by the principle, then one of the descriptions yielded must be realized.[3]

The general outlines of the theory of justice in holdings are that the holdings of a person are just if he is entitled to them by the principles of justice in acquisition and transfer, or by the principle of rectification of injustice (as specified by the first two principles). If each person's holdings are just, then the total set (distribution) of holdings is just. To turn these general outlines into a specific theory we would have to specify the details of each of the three principles of justice in holdings: the principle of acquisition of holdings, the principle of transfer of holdings, and the principle of rectification of violations of the first two principles. I shall not attempt the task here. (Locke's principle of justice in acquisition is discussed below.)

HISTORICAL PRINCIPLES AND END-RESULT PRINCIPLES

The general outlines of the entitlement theory illuminate the nature and defects of other conceptions of distributive justice. The entitlement theory of justice in distribution is *historical;* whether a distribution is just depends upon how it came about. In contrast, *current time-slice principles* of justice hold that the justice of a distribution is determined by how things are distributed (who has what) as judged by some *structural* principle(s) of just distribution. A utilitarian who judges between any two distributions by seeing which has the greater sum of utility and, if the sums tie, applies some fixed equality criterion to choose the more equal distribution, would hold a current time-slice principle of justice. As would someone who had a fixed schedule of trade-offs between the sum of happiness and equality. According to a current time-slice principle, all that needs to be looked at, in judging the justice of a distribution, is

[2]See, however, the useful book by Boris Bircker, *The Case for Black Reparations* (New York: Random House, 1973).

[3]If the principle of rectification of violations of the first two principles yield more than one description of holdings, then some choice must be made as to which of these is to be realized. Perhaps the sort of considerations about distributive justice and equality that I argue against play a legitimate role in *this* subsidiary choice. Similarly, there may be room for such considerations in deciding which otherwise arbitrary features a statute will embody, when such features are unavoidable because other considerations do not specify a precise line; yet a line must be drawn.

who ends up with what; in comparing any two distributions one need look only at the matrix presenting the distributions. No further information need be fed into a principle of justice. It is a consequence of such principles of justice that any two structurally identical distributions are equally just. (Two distributions are structurally identical if they present the same profile, but perhaps have different persons occupying the particular slots. My having ten and your having five, and my having five and your having ten are structurally identical distributions.) Welfare economics is the theory of current time-slice principles of justice. The subject is conceived as operating on matrices representing only current information about distribution. This, as well as some of the usual conditions (for example, the choice of distribution is invariant under relabeling of columns), guarantees that welfare economics will be a current time-slice theory, with all of its inadequacies.

Most persons do not accept current time-slice principles as constituting the whole story about distributive shares. They think it relevant in assessing the justice of a situation to consider not only the distribution it embodies, but also how that distribution came about. If some persons are in prison for murder or war crimes, we do not say that to assess the justice of the distribution in the society we must look only at what this person has, and that person has, and that person has, . . . at the current time. We think it relevant to ask whether someone did something so that he *deserved* to be punished, deserved to have a lower share. Most will agree to the relevance of further information with regard to punishments and penalties. Consider also desired things. One traditional socialist view is that workers are entitled to the product and full fruits of their labor; they have earned it; a distribution is unjust if it does not give the workers what they are entitled to. Such entitlements are based upon some past history. No socialist holding this view would find it comforting to be told that because the actual distribution A happens to coincide structurally with the one he desires D, A therefore is no less just than D; it differs only in that the "parasitic" owners of capital receive under A what the workers are entitled to under D, and the workers receive under A what the owners are entitled to under D, namely very little. This socialist rightly, in my view, holds onto the notions of earning, producing, entitlement, desert, and so forth, and he rejects current time-slice principles that look only to the structure of the resulting set of holdings. (The set of holdings from what? Isn't it implausible that how holdings are produced and come to exist has no effect at all on who should hold what?) His mistake lies in his view of what entitlements airse our of what sorts of productive processes.

We construe the position we discuss too narrowly by speaking of *current* time-slice principles. Nothing is changed if structural principles operate upon a time sequence of current time-slice profiles and, for example, give someone more now to counterbalance the less he has had earlier. A utilitarian or an egalitarian or any mixture of the two over time will inherit the difficulties of his more myopic comrades. He is not helped by the fact that *some* of the information others consider relevant in assessing a distribution is reflected, unrecoverably, in past matrices. Henceforth, we shall refer to such unhistorical principles of distributive justice, including the current time-slice principles, as *end-result principles* or *end-state principles*.

In contrast to end-result principles of justice, *historical principles* of justice hold that past circumstances or actions of people can create differential entitlements or differential deserts to things. An injustice can be worked by moving from one distribution to another structurally identical one, for the second, in profile the same, may violate people's entitlements or deserts; it may not fit the actual history.

PATTERNING

The entitlement principles of justice in holdings that we have sketched are historical principles of justice. To better understand their precise character, we shall distinguish them from another subclass of the historical principles. Consider, as an example, the principle of distribution according to moral merit. This principle requires that total distributive shares vary directly with moral merit; no person should have a greater share than anyone whose moral merit is greater. (If moral merit could be not merely ordered but measured on an interval or ratio scale, stronger principles could be formulated.) Or consider the principe that results by substituting "usefulness to society" for "moral merit" in the previous principle. Or instead of "distribute according to moral merit," or "distribute according to usefulness to society," we might consider "distribute according to the weighted sum of moral merit, usefulness to society, and need," with the weights of the different dimensions equal. Let us call a principle of distribution *patterned* if it specifies that a distribution is to vary along with some natural dimension, weighted sum of natural dimensions, or lexicographic ordering of natural dimensions. And let us say a distribution is patterned if it accords with some patterned principle. (I speak of natural dimensions, admittedly without a general criterion for them, because for any set of holdings some artificial dimensions can be gimmicked up to vary along with the distribution of the set.) The principle of distribution in accordance with moral merit is a patterned historical principle, which specifies a patterned distribution. "Distribute according to I.Q." is a patterned principle that looks to information not contained in distributional matrices. It is not historical, however, in that it does not look to any past actions creating differential entitlements to evaluate a distribution; it requires only distributional matrices whose columns are labeled by I.Q. scores. The distribution in a society, however, may be composed of such simple patterned distributions, without itself being simply patterned. Different sectors may operate different patterns, or some combination of patterns may operate in different proportions across a society. A distribution composed in this manner, from a small number of patterned distributions, we also shall term "patterned." And we extend the use of "pattern" to include the overall designs put forth by combinations of end-state principles.

Almost every suggested principle of distributive justice is patterned: to each according to his moral merit, or needs, or marginal product, or how hard he tries, or the weighted sum of the foregoing, and so on. The principle of entitlement we have sketched is *not* patterned.[3] There is no one natural dimension or weighted sum or combination of a small number of natural dimensions that yields the distributions generated in accordance with the principle of entitlement. The set of holdings that re-

---

[3] One might try to squeeze a patterned conception of distributive justice into the framework of the entitlement conception, by formulating a gimmicky obligatory "principle of transfer" that would lead to the pattern. For example, the principle that if one has more than the mean income one must transfer everything one holds above the mean to persons below the mean so as to bring them up to (but not over) the mean. We can formulate a criterion for a "principle of transfer" to rule out such obligatory transfers, or we can say that no correct principle of transfer, no principle of transfer in a free society will be like this. The former is probably the better course, though the latter also is true.

   Alternatively, one might think to make the entitlement conception instantiate a pattern, by using matrix entries that express the relative strength of a person's entitlements as measured by some real-valued function. But even if the limitation to natural dimensions failed to exclude this function, the resulting edifice would *not* capture our system of entitlements to *particular* things.

sults when some persons receive their marginal products, others win at gambling, others receive a share of their mate's income, others receive gifts from foundations, others receive interest on loans, others receive gifts from admirers, others receive returns on investment, others make for themselves much of what they have, others find things, and so on, will not be patterned. Heavy strands of patterns will run through it; significant portions of the variance in holdings will be accounted for by pattern-variables. If most people most of the time choose to transfer some of their entitlements to others only in exchange for something from them, then a large part of what many people hold will vary with what they held that others wanted. More details are provided by the theory of marginal productivity. But gifts to relatives, charitable donations, bequests to children, and the like, are not best conceived, in the first instance, in this manner. Ignoring the strands of pattern, let us suppose for the moment that a distribution actually arrived at by the operation of the principle of entitlement is random with respect to any pattern. Though the resulting set of holdings will be unpatterned, it will not be incomprehensible, for it can be seen as arising from the operation of a small number of principles. These principles specify how an initial distribution may arise (the principle of acquisition of holdings) and how distributions may be transformed into others (the principle of transfer of holdings). The process whereby the set of holdings is generated will be intelligible, though the set of holdings itself that results from this process will be unpatterned. . . .

To think that the task of a theory of distributive justice is to fill in the blank in "to each according to his _____ " is to be predisposed to search for a pattern; and the separate treatment of "from each according to his _____" treats production and distribution as two separate and independent issues. On an entitlement view these are *not* two separate questions. Whoever makes something, having bought or contracted for all other held resources used in the process (transferring some of his holdings for these cooperating factors), is entitled to it. The situation is *not* one of something's getting made, and there being an open question of who is to get it. Things come into the world already attached to people having entitlements over them. From the point of view of the historical entitlement conception of justice in holdings, those who start afresh to complete "to each according to his _____ " treat objects as if they appeared from nowhere, out of nothing. A complete theory of justice might cover this limit case as well; perhaps here is a use for the usual conceptions of distributive justice.[4]

So entrenched are maxims of the usual form that perhaps we should present the entitlement conception as a competitor. Ignoring acquisition and rectification, we might say:

> From each according to what he chooses to do, to each according to what he makes for himself (perhaps with the contracted aid of others) and what others choose to do for him and choose to give him of what they've been given previously (under this maxim) and haven't yet expended or transferred.

---

[4]Varying situations continuously from that limit situation to our own would force us to make explicit the underlying rationale of entitlements and to consider whether entitlement considerations lexicographically precede the considerations of the usual theories of distributive justice, so that the *slightest* strand of entitlement outweighs the considerations of the usual theories of distributive justice.

This, the discerning reader will have noticed, has its defects as a slogan. So as a summary and great simplification (and not as a maxim with any independent meaning) we have:

From each as they choose, to each as they are chosen.

HOW LIBERTY UPSETS PATTERNS

It is not clear how those holding alternative conceptions of distributive justice can reject the entitlement conception of justice in holdings. For suppose a distribution favored by one of these nonentitlement conceptions is realized. Let us suppose it is your favorite one and let us call this distribution D_1; perhaps everyone has an equal share, perhaps shares vary in accordance with some dimension you treasure. Now suppose that Wilt Chamberlain is greatly in demand by basketball teams, being a great gate attraction. (Also suppose contracts run only for a year, with players being free agents.) He signs the following sort of contract with a team: In each home game, twenty-five cents from the price of each ticket of admission goes to him. (We ignore the question of whether he is "gouging" the owners, letting them look out for themselves.) The season starts, and people cheerfully attend his team's games; they buy their tickets, each time dropping a separate twenty-five cents of their admission price into a special box with Chamberlain's name on it. They are excited about seeing him play; it is worth the total admission price to them. Let us suppose that in one season one million persons attend his home games, and Wilt Chamberlain winds up with \$250,000, a much larger sum than the average income and larger even than anyone else has. Is he entitled to this income? Is this new distribution D_2, unjust? If so, why? There is *no* question about whether each of the people was entitled to the control over the resources they held in D_1; because that was the distribution (your favorite) that (for the purposes of argument) we assumed was acceptable. Each of these persons *chose* to give twenty-five cents of their money to Chamberlain. They could have spent it on going to the movies, or on candy bars, or on copies of *Dissent* magazine, or of *Monthly Review*. But they all, at least one million of them, converged on giving it to Wilt Chamberlain in exchange for watching him play basketball. If D_1 was a just distribution, and people voluntarily moved from it to D_2, transferring parts of their shares they were given under D_1 (what was it for if not to do something with?), isn't D_2 also just? If the people were entitled to dispose of the resources to which they were entitled (under D_1), didn't this include their being entitled to give it to, or exchange it with, Wilt Chamberlain? Can anyone else complain on grounds of justice? Each other person already has his legitimate share under D_1. Under D_1, there is nothing that anyone has that anyone else has a claim of justice against. After someone transfers something to Wilt Chamberlain, third parties *still* have their legitimate shares; *their* shares are not changed. By what process could such a transfer among two persons give rise to a legitimate claim of distributive justice on a portion of what was transferred, by a third party who had no claim of justice on any holding of the others *before* the transfer?[5] To cut off objections irrelevant

---

[5]Might not a transfer have instrumental effects on a third party, changing his feasible options? (But what if the two parties to the transfer independently had used their holdings in this fashion?) I discuss this question below, but note here that this question concedes the point for distributions of ultimate intrinsic noninstrumental goods (pure utility experiences, so to speak) that are transferrable. It also might be objected that the

here, we might imagine the exchanges occurring in a socialist society, after hours. After playing whatever basketball he does in his daily work, or doing whatever other daily work he does, Wilt Chamberlain decides to put in *overtime* to earn additional money. (First his work quota is set; he works time over that.) Or imagine it is a skilled juggler people like to see, who puts on shows after hours.

Why might someone work overtime in a society in which it is assumed their needs are satisfied? Perhaps because they care about things other than needs. I like to write in books that I read, and to have easy access to books for browsing at odd hours. It would be very pleasant and convenient to have the resources of Widener Library in my back yard. No society, I assume, will provide such resources close to each person who would like them as part of his regular allotment (under D_1). Thus, persons either must do without some extra things that they want, or be allowed to do something extra to get some of these things. On what basis could the inequalities that would eventuate be forbidden?[5] Notice also that small factories would spring up in a socialist society, unless forbidden. I melt down some of my personal possessions (under D_1) and build a machine out of the material. I offer you, and others, a philosophy lecture once a week in exchange for your cranking the handle on my machine, whose products I exchange for yet other things, and so on. (The raw materials used by the machine are given to me by others who possess them under D_1, in exchange for hearing lectures.) Each person might participate to gain things over and above their allotment under D_1. Some persons even might want to leave their job in socialist industry and work full time in this private sector. I shall say something more about these issues in the next chapter. Here I wish merely to note how private property even in means of production would occur in a socialist society that did not forbid people to use as they wished some of the resources they are given under the socialist distribution D_1.[6] The

---

transfer might make a third party more envious because it worsens his position relative to someone else. I find it incomprehensible how this can be thought to involve a claim of justice....

Here and elsewhere in this chapter, a theory which incorporates elements of pure procedural justice might find what I say acceptable, *if* kept in its proper place; that is, if background institutions exist to ensure the satisfaction of certain conditions on distributive shares. But if these institutions are not themselves the sum or invisible-hand result of people's voluntary (nonaggressive) actions, the constraints they impose require justification. At no point does *our* argument assume any background institutions more extensive than those of the minimal night-watchman state, a state limited to protecting persons against murder, assault, theft, fraud, and so forth.

[6]See the selection from John Henry MacKay's novel, *The Anarchists,* reprinted in Leonard Krimmerman and Lewis Perry, eds., *Patterns of Anarchy* (New York: Doubleday Anchor Books, 1966), in which an individualist anarchist presses upon a communist anarchist the following question: "Would you, in the system of society which you call "free Communism" prevent individuals from exchanging their labor among themselves by means of their own medium of exchange? And further: Would you prevent them from occupying land for the purpose of personal use?" The novel continues: "[the] question was not to be escaped. If he answered 'Yes!' he admitted that society had the right of control over the individual and threw overboard the autonomy of the individual which he had always zealously defended; if on the other hand, he answered 'No!' he admitted the right of private property which he had just denied so emphatically.... Then he answered 'In Anarchy any number of men must have the right of forming a voluntary association, and so realizing their ideas in practice. Nor can I understand how any one could justly be driven from the land and house which he uses and occupies ... every serious man must declare himself: for Socialism, and thereby for force and against liberty, or for Anarchism, and thereby for liberty and against force.' " In contrast, we find Noam Chomsky writing, "Any consistent anarchist must oppose private ownership of the means of production," "the consistent anarchist then ... will be a socialist ... of a particular sort." Introduction to Daniel Guerin, *Anarchism: From Theory to Practice* (New York: Monthly Review Press, 1970), pages xiii, xv.

socialist society would have to forbid capitalist acts between consenting adults.

The general point illustrated by the Wilt Chamberlain example and the example of the entrepreneur in a socialist society is that no end-state principle or distributional patterned principle of justice can be continuously realized without continuous interference with people's lives. Any favored pattern would be transformed into one unfavored by the principle, by people choosing to act in various ways; for example, by people exchanging goods and services with other people, or giving things to other people, things the transferrers are entitled to under the favored distributional pattern. To maintain a pattern one must either continually interfere to stop people from transferring resources as they wish to, or continually (or periodically) interfere to take from some persons resources that others for some reason chose to transfer to them. (But if some time limit is to be set on how long people may keep resources others voluntarily transfer to them, why let them keep these resources for *any* period of time? Why not have immediate confiscation?) It might be objected that all persons voluntarily will choose to refrain from actions which would upset the pattern. This presupposes unrealistically (1) that all will most want to maintain the pattern (are those who don't, to be "reeducated" or forced to undergo "self-criticism"?), (2) that each can gather enough information about his own actions and the ongoing activities of others to discover which of his actions will upset the pattern, and (3) that diverse and far-flung persons can coordinate their actions to dovetail into the pattern. Compare the manner in which the market is neutral among persons' desires, and it reflects and transmits widely scattered information via prices, and coordinates person's activities.

It puts things perhaps a bit too strongly to say that every patterned (or end-state) principle is liable to be thwarted by the voluntary actions of the individual parties transferring some of their shares they receive under the principle. For perhaps some *very* weak patterns are not so thwarted.[7] Any distributional pattern with any egalitarian component is overturnable by the voluntary actions of individual persons over time; as is every patterned condition with sufficient content so as actually to have been proposed as presenting the central core of distributive justice. Still, given the possibility that some weak conditions or patterns may not be unstable in this way, it would be better to formulate an explicit description of the kind of interesting and contentful patterns under discussion, and to prove a theorem about their instability. Since the weaker the patterning, the more likely it is that the entitlement system itself satisfies it, a plausible conjecture is that any patterning either is unstable or is satisfied by the entitlement system. . . .

[7]Is the patterned principle stable that requires merely that a distribution be Pareto-optimal? One person might give another a gift or bequest that the second could exchange with a third to their mutual belief. Before the second makes this exchange, there is not Pareto-optimality. In a stable pattern presented by a principle choosing that among the Pareto-optimal positions that satisfies some further condition *C*? It may seem that there cannot be a counterexample, for won't any voluntary exchange made away from a situation show that the first situation wasn't Pareto-optimal? (Ignore the implausibility of this last claim for the case of bequests.) But principles are to be satisfied over time, during which new possibilities arise. A distribution that at one time satisfies the criterion of Pareto-optimality might do so when some new possibilities arise (Wilt Chamberlain grows up and starts playing basketball); and though people's activities will tend to move then to a new Pareto-optimal position, *this* new one need not satisfy the contentful condition *C*. Continual interference will be needed to insure the continual satisfaction of *C*. (The theoretical possibility of a pattern's being maintained by some invisible-hand process that brings it back to an equilibrium that fits the pattern when deviations occur should be investigated.)

REDISTRIBUTION AND PROPERTY RIGHTS

Apparently, patterned principles allow people to choose to expend upon themselves, but not upon others, those resources they are entitled to (or rather, receive) under some favored distributional pattern D_1. For if each of several persons chooses to expend some of his D_1 resources upon one other person, then that other person will receive more than his D_1 share, disturbing the favored distributional pattern. Maintaining a distributional pattern is individualism with a vengeance! Patterned distributional principles do not give people what entitlement principles do, only better distributed. For they do not give the right to choose what to do with what one has; they do not give the right to choose to pursue an end involving (intrinsically, or as a means) the enhancement of another's position. To such views, families are disturbing; for within a family occur transfers that upset the favored distributional pattern. Either families themselves become units to which distribution takes place, the column occupiers (on what rationale?), or loving behavior is forbidden. We should note in passing the ambivalent position of radicals toward the family. Its loving relationships are seen as a model to be emulated and extended across the whole society, at the same time that it is denounced as a suffocating institution to be broken and condemned as a focus of parochial concerns that interfere with achieving radical goals. Need we say that it is not appropriate to enforce across the wider society the relationships of love and care appropriate within a family, relationships which are voluntarily undertaken?[8] Incidentally, love is an interesting instance of another relationship that is historical, in that (like justice) it depends upon what actually occurred. An adult may come to love another because of the other's characteristics; but it is the other person, and not the characteristics, that is loved. The love is not transferrable to someone else with the same characteristics, even to one who "scores" higher for these characteristics. And the love endures through changes of the characteristics that gave rise to it. One loves the particular person one actually encountered. Why love is historical, attaching to persons in this way and not to characteristics, is an interesting and puzzling question.

Proponents of patterned principles of distributive justice focus upon criteria for determining who is to receive holdings; they consider the reasons for which someone should have something, and also the total picture of holdings. Whether or not it is better to give than to receive, proponents of patterned principles ignore giving altogether. In considering the distribution of goods, income, and so forth, their theories are theories of recipient justice; they completely ignore any right a person might have to give something to someone. Even in exchanges where each party is simultaneously giver and recipient, patterned principles of justice focus only upon the recipient role and its supposed rights. Thus discussions tend to focus on whether people (should) have a right to inherit, rather than on whether people (should) have a right to be-

---

[8]One indication of the stringency of Rawls' difference principle, which we attend to in the second part of this chapter, is its inappropriateness as a governing principle even within a family of individuals who love one another. Should a family devote its resources to maximizing the position of its least well off and least talented child, holding back the other children or using resources for their education and development only if they will follow a policy through their lifetimes of maximizing the position of their least fortunate sibling? Surely not. How then can this even be considered as the appropriate policy for enforcement in the wider society? (I discuss below what I think would be Rawls' reply: that some principles apply at the macro level which do not apply to micro-situations.)

queath or on whether persons who have a right to hold also have a right to choose that others hold in their place. I lack a good explanation of why the usual theories of distributive justice are so recipient oriented; ignoring givers and transferrers and their rights is of a piece with ignoring producers and their entitlements. But why is it *all* ignored?

Patterned principles of distributive justice necessitate *re*distributive activities. The likelihood is small that any actual freely-arrived-at set of holdings fits a given pattern; and the likelihood is nil that it will continue to fit the pattern as people exchange and give. From the point of view of an entitlement theory, redistribution is a serious matter indeed, involving, as it does, the violation of people's rights. (An exception is those takings that fall under the principle of the rectification of injustices.) From other points of view, also, it is serious.

Taxation of earnings from labor is on a par with forced labor.[9] Some persons find this claim obviously true: taking the earnings of *n* hours labor is like taking *n* hours from the person; it is like forcing the person to work *n* hours for another's purpose. Others find the claim absurd. But even these, *if* they object to forced labor, would oppose forcing unemployed hippies to work for the benefit of the needy.[10] And they would also object to forcing each person to work five extra hours each week for the benefit of the needy. But a system that takes five hours' wages in taxes does not seem to them like one that forces someone to work five hours, since it offers the person forced a wider range of choice in activities than does taxation in kind with the particular labor specified. (But we can imagine a gradation of systems of forced labor, from one that specifies a particular activity, to one that gives a choice among two activities, to. . . ; and so on up.) Furthermore, people envisage a system with something like a proportional tax on everything above the amount necessary for basic needs. Some think this does not force someone to work extra hours, since there is no fixed number of extra hours he is forced to work, and since he can avoid the tax entirely by earning only enough to cover his basic needs. This is a very uncharacteristic view of forcing for those who *also* think people are forced to do something *whenever* the alternatives they face are considerably worse. However, *neither* view is correct. The fact that others intentionally intervene, in violation of a side constraint against aggression, to threaten force to limit the alternatives, in this case to paying taxes or (presumably the worse alternative) bare subsistence, makes the taxation system one of forced labor and distinguishes it from other cases of limited choices which are not forcings.[11]

The man who chooses to work longer to gain an income more than sufficient for his basic needs prefers some extra goods or services to the leisure and activities he could perform during the possible nonworking hours; whereas the man who chooses

[9]I am unsure as to whether the arguments I present below show that such taxation merely *is* forced labor; so that "is on a par with" means "is one kind of." Or alternatively, whether the arguments emphasize the great similarities between such taxation and forced labor, to show it is plausible and illuminating to view such taxation in the light of forced labor. This latter approach would remind one of how John Wisdom conceives of the claims of metaphysicians.

[10]Nothing hangs on the fact that here and elsewhere I speak loosely of *needs,* since I go on, each time, to reject the criterion of justice which includes it. If, however, something did depend upon the notion, one would want to examine it more carefully. For a skeptical view, see Kenneth Minogue, *The Liberal Mind,* (New York: Random House, 1963), pp. 103–112.

[11]*Further details which this statement should include are contained in my essay "Coercion," in *Philosophy, Science, and Method,* ed. S. Morgenbesser, P. Suppes, and M. White (New York: St. Martin, 1969).

not to work the extra time prefers the leisure activities to the extra goods or services he could acquire by working more. Given this, if it would be illegitimate for a tax system to seize some of a man's leisure (forced labor) for the purpose of serving the needy, how can it be legitimate for a tax system to seize some of a man's goods for that purpose? Why should we treat the man whose happiness requires certain material goods or services differently from the man whose preferences and desires make such goods unnecessary for his happiness? Why should the man who prefers seeing a movie (and who has to earn money for a ticket) be open to the required call to aid the needy, while the person who prefers looking at a sunset (and hence need earn no extra money) is not? Indeed, isn't it surprising that redistributionists choose to ignore the man whose pleasures are so easily attainable without extra labor, while adding yet another burden to the poor unfortunate who must work for his pleasures? If anything, one would have expected the reverse. Why is the person with the nonmaterial or non-consumption desire allowed to proceed unimpeded to his most favored feasible alternative, whereas the man whose pleasures or desires involve material things and who must work for extra money (thereby serving whomever considers his activities valuable enough to pay him) is constrained in what he can realize? Perhaps there is no difference in principle. And perhaps some think the answer concerns merely administrative convenience. (These questions and issues will not disturb those who think that forced labor to serve the needy or to realize some favored end-state pattern is acceptable.) In a fuller discussion we would have (and want) to extend our argument to include interest, entrepreneurial profits, and so on. Those who doubt that this extension can be carried through, and who draw the line here at taxation of income from labor, will have to state rather complicated patterned *historical* principles of distributive justice, since end-state principles would not distinguish *sources* of income in any way. It is enough for now to get away from end-state principles and to make clear how various patterned principles are dependent upon particular views about the sources or the illegitimacy or the lesser legitimacy of profits, interest, and so on; which particular views may well be mistaken.

What sort of right over others does a legally institutionalized end-state pattern give one? The central core of the notion of a property right in X, relative to which other parts of the notion are to be explained, it is the right to determine what shall be done with X; the right to choose which of the constrained set of options concerning X shall be realized or attempted.[12] The constraints are set by other principles or laws operating in the society; in our theory, by the Lockean rights people possess (under the minimal state). My property rights in my knife allow me to leave it where I will, but not in your chest. I may choose which of the acceptable options involving the knife is to be realized. The notion of property helps us to understand why earlier theorists spoke of people as having property in themselves and their labor. They viewed each person as having a right to decide what would become of himself and what he would do, and as having a right to reap the benefits of what he did.

This right of selecting the alternative to be realized from the constrained set of alternatives may be held by an *individual* or by a *group* with some procedure for reaching a joint decision; or the right may be passed back and forth, so that one year I decide what's to become of X, and the next year you do (with the alternative of de-

---

[12]On the themes in this and the next paragraph, see the writings of Armen Alchian.

struction, perhaps, being excluded). Or, during the same time period, some types of decisions about *X* may be made by me, and others by you. And so on. We lack an adequate, fruitful, analytical apparatus for classifying the *types* of constraints on the set of options among which choices are to be made, and the *types* of ways decision powers can be held, divided, and amalgamated. A *theory* of property would, among other things, contain such a classification of constraints and decision modes, and from a small number of principles would follow a host of interesting statements about the *consequences* and effects of certain combinations of constraints and modes of decision.

When end-result principles of distributive justice are built into the legal structure of a society, they (as do most patterned principles) give each citizen an enforceable claim to some portion of the total social product; that is, to some portion of the sum total of the individually and jointly made products. This total product is produced by individuals laboring, using means of production others have saved to bring into existence, by people organizing production or creating means to produce new things or things in a new way. It is on this batch of individual activities that patterned distributional principles give each individual an enforceable claim. Each person has a claim to the activities and the products of other persons, independently of whether the other persons enter into particular relationships that give rise to these claims, and independently of whether they voluntarily take these claims upon themselves, in charity or in exchange for something.

Whether it is done through taxation or wages or on wages over a certain amount, or through seizure of profits, or through there being a big *social pot* so that it's not clear what's coming from where and what's going where, patterned principles of distributive justice involve appropriating the actions of other persons. Seizing the results of someone's labor is equivalent to seizing hours from him and directing him to carry on various activities. If people force you to do certain work, or unrewarded work, for a certain period of time, they decide what you are to do and what purposes your work is to serve apart from your decisions. This process whereby they take this decision from you makes them a *part-owner* of you; it gives them a property right in you. Just as having such partial control and power of decisions, by right, over an animal or inanimate object would be to have a property right in it.

End-state and most patterned principles of distributive justice institute (partial) ownership by others of people and their actions and labor. These principles involve a shift from the classical liberals' notion of self-ownership to a notion of (partial) property rights in *other* people.

Considerations such as these confront end-state and other patterned conceptions of justice with the question of whether the actions necessary to achieve the selected pattern don't themselves violate moral side constraints. Any view holding that there are moral side constraints on actions, that not all moral considerations can be built into end states that are to be achieved . . . must face the possibility that some of its goals are not achievable by any morally permissible available means. An entitlement theorist will face such conflicts in a society that deviates from the principles of justice for the generation of holdings, if and only if the only actions available to realize the principles themselves violate some moral constraints. Since deviation from the first two principles of justice (in acquisition and transfer) will involve other persons' direct and aggressive intervention to violate rights, and since moral constraints will not exclude defensive or retributive action in such cases, the entitlement theorist's problem rarely will be pressing. And whatever difficulties he has in applying the principle of rectification to persons who did not themselves violate the first two principles are difficulties in balancing the conflicting considerations so as correctly to formulate the complex principle of rectification itself; he will not violate moral side constraints by applying the principle. Proponents of patterned conceptions of justice, however, often will face head-on clashes (and poignant ones if they cherish each party to the clash) between moral side constraints on how individuals may be treated and their patterned conception of justice that presents an end state or other pattern that *must* be realized.

May a person emigrate from a nation that has institutionalized some end-state or patterned distributional principle? For some principles (for example, Hayek's) emigration presents no theoretical problem. But for others it is a tricky manner. Consider a nation having a compulsory scheme of minimal social provision to aid the neediest (for one organized so as to maximize the position of the worst-off group); no one may opt out of participating in it. (None may say, "Don't compel me to contribute to others and don't provide for me via this compulsory mechanism if I am in need.") Everyone above a certain level is forced to contribute to aid the needy. But if emigration from the country were allowed, anyone could choose to move to another country that did not have compulsory social provision but otherwise was (as much as possible) identical. In such a case, the person's *only* motive for leaving would be to avoid participating in the compulsory scheme of social provision. And if he does leave, the needy in his initial country will receive no (compelled) help from him. What rationale yields the result that the person be permitted to emigrate, yet forbidden to stay and opt out of the compulsory scheme of social provision? If providing for the needy is of overriding importance, this does militate against allowing internal opting out; but it also speaks against allowing external emigration. (Would it also support, to some extent, the kidnapping of persons living in a place without compulsory social provision, who could be forced to make a contributin to the needy in your community?) Perhaps the crucial component of the position that allows emigration solely to avoid certain arrangements, while not allowing anyone internally to opt out of them, is a concern for fraternal feelings within the country. "We don't want anyone here who doesn't contribute, who doesn't care enough about the others to contribute." That concern, in this case, would have to be tied to the view that forced aiding tends to produce fraternal feelings between the aided and the aider (or perhaps merely to the view that the knowledge that someone or other voluntarily is not aiding produces unfraternal feelings).

LOCKE'S THEORY OF ACQUISITION

Before we turn to consider other theories of justice in detail, we must introduce an additional bit of complexity into the structure of the entitlement theory. This is best approached by considering Locke's attempt to specify a principle of justice in acquisition. Locke views property rights in an unowned object as originating through someone's mixing his labor with it. This gives rise to many questions. What are the boundaries of what labor is mixed with? If a private astronaut clears a place on Mars, has he mixed his labor with (so that he comes to own) the whole planet, the whole uninhabited universe, or just a particular plot? Which plot does an act bring under ownership? The minimal (possibly disconnected) area such that an act decreases entropy in the area, and not elsewhere? Can virgin land (for the purposes of ecological investigation by high-flying airplane) come under ownership by a Lockean process? Building a fence around a territory presumably would make one the owner of only the fence (and the land immediately underneath it).

Why does mixing one's labor with something make one the owner of it? Perhaps because one owns one's labor, and so one comes to own a previously unowned thing that becomes permeated with what one owns. Ownership seeps over into the rest. But why isn't mixing what I own with what I don't own a way of losing what I own rather than a way of gaining what I don't? If I own a can of tomato juice and spill it in the sea so that its molecules (made radioactive, so I can check this) mingle evenly throughout the sea, do I thereby come to own the sea, or have I foolishly dissipated my tomato juice? Perhaps the idea, instead, is that laboring on something improves it and makes it more valuable; and anyone is entitled to own a thing whose value he has created. (Reinforcing this, perhaps, is the view that laboring is unpleasant. If some people made things effortlessly, as the cartoon characters in *The Yellow Submarine* trail flowers in their wake, would they have lesser claim to their own products whose making didn't *cost* them anything?) Ignore the fact that laboring on something may make it less valuable (spraying pink enamel paint on a piece of driftwood that you have found). Why should one's entitlement extend to the whole object rather than just to the *added value* one's labor has produced? (Such reference to value might also serve to delimit the extent of ownership; for example, substitute "increases the value of" for "decreases entropy in" in the above entropy criterion.) No workable or coherent value-added property scheme has yet been devised, and any such scheme presumably would fall to objections (similar to those) that fell the theory of Henry George.

It will be implausible to view improving an object as giving full ownership to it, if the stock of unowned objects that might be improved is limited. For an object's coming under one person's ownership changes the situation of all others. Whereas previously they were at liberty (in Hohfeld's sense) to use the object, they now no longer are. This change in the situation of others (by removing their liberty to act on a previously unowned object) need not worsen their situation. If I appropriate a grain of sand from Coney Island, no one else may now do as they will with *that* grain of sand. But there are plenty of other grains of sand left for them to do the same with. Or if not grains of sand, then other things. Alternatively, the things I do with the grain of sand I appropriate might improve the position of others, counterbalancing their loss of the liberty to use that grain. The crucial point is whether appropriation of an unowned object worsens the situation of others.

Locke's proviso that there be "enough and as good left in common for others" (sect. 27) is meant to ensure that the situation of others is not worsened. (If this proviso is met is there any motivation for his further condition of nonwaste?) It is often said that this proviso once held but now no longer does. But there appears to be an argument for the conclusion that if the proviso no longer holds, then it cannot ever have held so as to yield permanent and inheritable property rights. Consider the first person Z for whom there is not enough as a good left to appropriate. The last person Y to appropriate left Z without his previous liberty to act on an object, and so worsened Z's situation. So Y's appropriation is not allowed under Locke's proviso. Therefore the next to last person X to appropriate left Y in a worse position, for X's act ended permissible appropriation. Therefore X's appropriation wasn't permissible. But then the appropriate two from last, W, ended permissible appropriation and so, since it worsened *X*'s position, *W*'s appropriation wasn't permissible. And so on back to the first person *A* to appropriate a permanent property right.

This argument, however, proceeds too quickly. Someone may be made worse off by another's appropriation in two ways: first, by losing the opportunity to improve his situation by a particular appropriation or any one; and second, by no longer being able to use freely (without appropriation) what he previously could. A *stringent* requirement that another not be made worse off by an appropriation would exclude the first way if nothing else counterbalances the diminution in opportunity, as well as the second. A *weaker* requirement would exclude the second way, though not the first. With the weaker requirement, we cannot zip back so quickly from *Z* to *A,* as in the above argument; for though person *Z,* can no longer *appropriate,* there may remain some for him to *use* as before. In this case *Y*'s appropriation would not violate the weaker Lockean condition. (With less remaining the people are at liberty to use, users might face more inconvenience, crowding, and so on; in that way the situation of others might be worsened, unless appropriation stopped far short of such a point.) It is arguable that no one legitimately can complain if the weaker provision is satisfied. However, since this is less clear than in the case of the more stringent proviso, Locke may have intended this stringent proviso by "enough and good" remaining, and perhaps he meant the nonwaste condition to delay the end point from which the argument zips back.

Is the situation of persons who are unable to appropriate (there being no more accessible and useful unowned objects) worsened by a system allowing appropriation and permanent property? Here enter the various familiar social considerations favoring private property: it increases the social product by putting means of production in the hands of those who can use them most efficiently (profitably); experimentation is encouraged, because with separate persons controlling resources, there is no one person or small group whom someone with a new idea must convince to try it out; private property enables people to decide on the pattern and types of risks they wish to bear, leading to specialized types of risk bearing; private property protects future persons by leading some to hold back resources from current consumption for future markets; it provides alternate sources of employment for unpopular persons who don't have to convince any one person or small group to hire them, and so on. These considerations enter a Lockean theory to support the claim that appropriation of private property satisfies the intent behind the "enough and as good left over" proviso, *not* as a utilitarian justification of property. They enter to rebut the claim that because the proviso is violated no natural right to private property can arise by a Lockean process. The difficulty in working such an argument to show that the proviso is satsified is in fixing the appropriate base line for comparison. Lockean appropriation makes people no worse off than they would be *how?*[13] The question of fixing the baseline needs more detailed investigation than we are able to give it here. It would be desirable to have an estimate of the general economic importance of original appropriation in order to see how much leeway there is for differing theories of appropriation and of the location of the baseline. Perhaps this importance can be measured by the percentage

---

[13] I have not seen a precise estimate. David Friedman, *The Machinery of Freedom* (N.Y.: Harper & Row, 1973), pp. xiv, xv, discusses the issue and suggests 5 percent of U.S. national income as an upper limit for the first two factors mentioned. However he does not attempt to estimate the percentage of current wealth which is based upon such income in the past. (The vague notion of "based upon" merely indicates a topic needing investigation.)

of all income that is based upon untransformed raw materials and given resources (rather than upon human actions), mainly rental income representing the unimproved value of land, and the price of raw material *in situ,* and by the percentage of current wealth which represents such income in the past.[14]

We should note that it is not only persons favoring *private* property who need a theory of how property rights legitimately originate. Those believing in collective property, for example those believing that a group of persons living in an area jointly own the territory, or its mineral resources, also must provide a theory of how such property rights arise; they must show why the persons living there have rights to determine what is done with the land and resources there that persons living elsewhere don't have (with regard to the same land and resources).

THE PROVISO

Whether or not Locke's particular theory of appropriation can be spelled out so as to handle various difficulties, I assume that any adequate theory of justice in acquisition will contain a proviso similar to the weaker of the ones we have attributed to Locke. A process normally giving rise to a permanent bequeathable property right in a previously unowned thing will not do so if the position of others no longer at liberty to use the thing is thereby worsened. It is important to specify *this* particular mode of worsening the situation of others, for the proviso does not encompass other modes. It does not include the worsening due to more limited opportunities to appropriate (the first way above, corresponding to the more stringent condition), and it does not include how I "worsen" a seller's position if I appropriate materials to make some of what he is selling, and then enter into competition with him. Someone whose appropriation otherwise would violate the proviso still may appropriate provided he compensates the others so that their situation is not thereby worsened; unless he does compensate these others, his appropriation will violate the proviso of the principle of justice in acquisition and will be an illegitimate one.[15] A theory of appropriation incorporating this Lockean proviso will handle correctly the cases (objections to the theory lacking the proviso) where someone appropriates the total supply of something necessary for life.[16]

---

[14]Compare this with Robert Paul Wolff's "A Refutation of Rawls' Theorem on Justice," *Journal of Philosophy,* March 31, 1966, sect. 2. Wolff's criticism does not apply to Rawl's conception under which the baseline is fixed by the difference principle.

[15]Fourier held that since the process of civilization had deprived the members of society of certain liberties (to gather, pasture, engage in the chase), a socially guaranteed minimum provision for persons was justified as compensation for the loss (Alexander Gray, *The Socialist Tradition* (New York: Harper & Row, 1968), p. 188). But this puts the point too strongly. This compensation would be due to those persons, if any, for whom the process of civilization was a *net loss,* for whom the benefits of civilization did not counterbalance being deprived of these particular liberties.

[16]For example, Rashdall's case of someone who comes upon the only water in the desert several miles ahead of others who also will come to it and appropriate it all. Hastings Rashdall, "The Philosophical Theory of Property," in *Property, its Duties and Rights* (London: MacMillan, 1915).

We should note Ayn Rand's theory of property rights ("Man's Rights" in *The Virtue of Selfishness* (New York: New American Library, 1964), p. 94), wherein these follow from the right to life, since people need physical things to live. But a right to life is not a right to whatever one needs to live; other people may have rights over these other things . . . At most, a right to life would be a right to have or strive for whatever one needs to live, provided that having it does not violate anyone else's rights. With regard to material things, the question is whether having it does violate any right of others. (Would appropriateness of all unknown

A theory which includes this proviso in its principle of justice in acquisition must also contain a more complex principle of justice in transfer. Some reflection of the proviso about appropriation constrains later actions. If my appropriating all of a certain substance violates the Lockean proviso, then so does my appropriating some and purchasing all the rest from others who obtained it without otherwise violating the Lockean proviso. If the proviso excludes someone's appropriating all the drinkable water in the world, it also excludes his purchasing it all. (More weakly, and messily, it may exclude his charging certain prices for some of his supply.) This proviso (almost?) never will come into effect; the more someone acquires of a scarce substance which others want, the higher the price of the rest will go, and the more difficult it will become for him to acquire it all. But still, we can imagine, at least, that something like this occurs: someone makes simultaneous secret bids to the separate owners of a substance, each of whom sells assuming he can easily purchase more from the other owners; or some natural catastophe destroys all of the supply of something except that in one person's possession. The total supply could not be permissibly appropriated by one person at the beginning. His later acquisition of it all does not show that the original appropriation violated the proviso (even by a reverse argument similar to the one above that tried to zip back from Z to A). Rather, it is the combination of the original appropriation *plus* all the later transfers and actions that violates the Lockean proviso.

Each owner's title to his holding includes the historical shadow of the Lockean proviso on appropriation. This excludes his transferring it into an agglomeration that does violate the Lockean proviso and excludes his using it in a way, in coordination with others or independently of them, so as to violate the proviso by making the situation of others worse than their baseline situation. Once it is known that someone's ownership runs afoul of the Lockean proviso, there are stringent limits on what he may do with (what it is difficult any longer unreservedly to call) "his property." Thus a person may not appropriate the only water hole in a desert and charge what he will. Nor may he charge what he will if he possesses one, and unfortunately it happens that all the water holes in the desert dry up, except for his. This unfortunate circumstance, admittedly no fault of his, brings into operation the Lockean proviso and limits his property rights.[17] Similarly, an owner's property right in the only island in an area does not allow him to order a castaway from a shipwreck off his island as a trespasser, for this would violate the Lockean proviso.

Notice that the theory does not say that owners do have these rights, but that the rights are overridden to avoid some catastrophe. (Overridden rights do not disappear; they leave a trace of a sort absent in the cases under discussion.)[18] There is no such external (and *ad hoc?*) overriding. Considerations internal to the theory of property itself, to its theory of acquisition and appropriation, provide the means for handling

---

things do so? Would appropriating the water hole in Rashdall's example?) Since special considerations (such as the Lockean proviso) may enter with regard to material property, one *first* needs a theory of property rights before one can apply any supposed right to life (as amended above). Therefore the right to life cannot provide the foundation for a theory of property rights.

[17]The situation would be different if his water hole didn't dry up, due to special precautions he took to prevent this. Compare our discussion of the case in the text with Hayek, *The Constitution of Liberty,* p. 136; and also with Ronald Hamowy, "Hayek's Concept of Freedom; A Critique," *New Individualist Review,* April 1961, pp. 28–31.

[18]I discuss overriding and its moral traces in "Moral Complications and Moral Structures," *Natural Law Forum,* 1968, pp. 1–50.

such cases. The results, however, may be coextensive with some condition about catastrophe, since the baseline for comparison is so low as compared to the productiveness of a society with private appropriation that the question of the Lockean proviso being violated arises only in the case of catastrophe (or a desert-island situation).

The fact that someone owns the total supply of something necessary for others to stay alive does *not* entail that his (or anyone's) appropriation of anything left some people (immediately or later) in a situation worse than the baseline one. A medical researcher who synthesizes a new substance that effectively treats a certain disease and who refuses to sell except on his terms does not worsen the situation of others by depriving them of whatever he has appropriated. The others easily can possess the same materials he appropriated; the researcher's appropriation or purchase of chemicals didn't make those chemicals scarce in a way so as to violate the Lockean proviso. Nor would someone else's purchasing the total supply of the synthesized substance from the medical researcher. The fact that the medical researcher uses easily available chemicals to synthesize the drug no more violates the Lockean proviso than does the fact that the only surgeon able to perform a particular operation eats easily obtainable food in order to stay alive and to have the energy to work. This shows that the Lockean proviso is not an "end state principle"; it focuses on a particular way that appropriate actions affect others, and not on the structure of the situation that results.[19]

Intermediate between someone who takes all of the public supply and someone who makes the total supply out of easily obtainable substances is someone who appropriates the total supply of something in a way that does not deprive the others of it. For example, someone finds a new substance in an out-of-the-way place. He discovers that it effectively treats a certain disease and appropriates the total supply. He does not worsen the situation of others; if he did not stumble upon the substance no one else could have, and the others would remain without it. However, as time passes, the likelihood increases that others would have come across the substance; upon this fact might be based a limit to his property right in the substance so that orders are not below their baseline position; for example, its bequest might be limited. The theme of someone worsening another's situation by depriving him of something he otherwise would possess may also illuminate the example of patents. An inventor's patent does not deprive others of an object which would not exist if not for the inventor. Yet patents would have this effect on others who independently invent the object. Therefore, these independent inventors, upon whom the burden of proving independent discovery may rest, should not be excluded from utilizing their own invention as they wish (including selling it to others). Furthermore, a known inventor drastically lessens the chances of actual independent invention. For persons who know of an invention usually will not try to reinvent it, and the notion of independent discovery here would be murky at best. Yet we may assume that in the absence of the original invention, sometime later someone else would have come up with it. This suggests placing a time limit on patents, as a rough rule of thumb to approximate how long it would have taken, in the absence of knowledge of the invention, for independent discovery.

---

[19]Does the principle of compensation (Chapter 4) introduce patterning considerations? Though it requires compensation for the disadvantages imposed by those seeking security from risks, it is not a patterned principle. For it seeks to remove only those disadvantages which prohibitions inflict on those who might present risks to others, not all disadvantages. It specifies an obligation on those who impose the prohibition, which stems from their own particular acts, to remove a particular complaint those prohibited may make against them.

I believe that the free operation of a market system will not actually run afoul of the Lockean proviso. If this is correct, the proviso will not play a very important role in the activities of protective agencies and will not provide a significant opportunity for future state action. Indeed, were it not for the effects of previous *illegitimate* state action, people would not think the possibility of the proviso's being violated as of more interest than any other logical possibility. (Here I make an empirical historical claim; as does someone who disagrees with this.) This completes our indication of the complication in the entitlement theory introduced by the Lockean proviso.

Some Ruminations on Rights

Judith Jarvis Thomson

In *Anarchy, State, and Utopia,* Robert Nozick says that a government which imposes taxes for the purpose of redistribution violates the rights of its citizens.[1] The word "imposes" perhaps needs no stress: Nozick could hardly object to a government's withholding a percentage of income for this purpose if its citizens had unanimously requested it to do so. What he objects to—on the ground of its constituting a violation of rights—is forcing payment for this purpose on those who do not wish to pay. What we might expect Nozick to give us, then, is a theory of rights, or at least a clear picture of why this should be so. In fact, we get neither.

Nozick makes two quite general points about rights, both of them important. He says, first, that the fact that if we bring about that such and such is the case there will be more good in the world than there otherwise would be does not by itself justify our bringing about that it is the case, and this on the ground that to bring it about may be to violate a right. This seems to me to be wholly right. Suppose, for example, that if we bring about that Alfred takes a certain aspirin tablet there will be more good in the world than there otherwise would be. This does not by itself justify our bringing about that Alfred takes it, for it might be that to do so would be to violate a right. For example, it might be that Bert owns that aspirin tablet and does not wish Alfred to take it; in that case, to bring about that Alfred takes it would be to violate a right of Bert's. Indeed, it might be that Alfred himself owns it but does not wish to take it; in that case, to bring about that he does would be to violate, paternalistically, a right of Alfred's.

This point, though important, is familiar enough. What is perhaps less familiar in Nozick's second point: That the fact that if we bring about that such and such is the case there will be more good in the world than there otherwise would be does not by itself justify our bringing about that it is the case—even if we require that, in assessing

Reprinted from Chapter 4, *The University of Arizona Law Review,* vol. 19 (1977). © 1977, Arizona Board of Regents. Reprinted by permission.

[1]Robert Nozick, *Anarchy, State, and Utopia* (New York: Basic Books, 1974), pp. 171–174.

how much good there will be in the world, account be taken of which rights, if any, will be infringed and of how stringent those rights are. This point too seems to me to be wholly right. If we do opt for this requirement on an assessment of how much good there will be in the world, then it seems to me we may suppose that if we bring about that Alfred takes a certain aspirin tablet there will *not* be more good in the world than there otherwise would be, however bad Alfred's headache may be: for there would have to be considered in arriving at the assessment, not merely the fact that if we bring about that Alfred takes the aspirin his headache will go away, but also (as it might be) the fact that a right of Bert's will be infringed, or (as it might be) the fact that a right of Alfred's will be infringed. If so, this is not really a case in which, even though there will be more good in the world if we act than there otherwise would be, it is not morally permissible for us to act. But there are other cases. Suppose that a villain threatens to kill five people if you will not kill Charles. Even prima facie it seems that if you act, there will be more good in the world than there otherwise would be since five lives are four more than one life. And now let us include in our assessment infringements of rights. If you act, fewer rights will be infringed than if you do not, for five violations of the right to not be killed are four more than one violation of the right to not be killed. Therefore, if we require that in assessing how much good there will be in the world account be taken of which rights, if any, will be infringed and of how stringent those rights are, *this* is a case in which there will be more good in the world if you act than if you do not. Yet you surely cannot act, since you surely cannot kill in response to such a threat.

This kind of case has been appearing fairly often in recent literature.[2] The kind of case I mean is this: For the agent to act would acquire him to infringe a right, but he is under threat that if he does not act, others will infringe more, equally stringent rights. Most people agree that the agent in such a case cannot act. What is particularly good in Nozick's treatment of these matters is the connection he makes between cases of this kind on the one hand, and the case of Alfred on the other hand. Nozick's discussion brings out that if a utilitarian saves this theory in face of putative countercases such as that of Alfred by claiming that right infringements themselves have disvalue, which disvalue must be counted in assessing how much good there will be in the world if the agent acts, he thereby ensures that cases where the agent must infringe a right to avoid greater right infringement on the part of others *will* be countercases.

As I say, I think these points are wholly correct. Nozick does not argue for them; nor shall I. But to have arrived here is to be miles away from Nozick's thesis about government and taxation for the purpose of redistribution. What we have so far is that the fact that if we bring about that such and such is the case there will be more good in the world than there otherwise would be does not by itself justify our bringing about that it is the case. Thus suppose redistribution is, in one way or another, a good, and that if we make a certain redistributive move there will in fact be more good in the world than there otherwise would be. What we have is that fact does not by itself justify our making that redistributive move. However, this leaves it wide open that something which includes—or even something entirely other than—that fact *does* justify our making it.

Let us begin with a point of terminology. Suppose that someone has a right that

[2]A typical example is the following: You are a sheriff in a small southern town. A murder has been committed, and you do not have the least idea who committed it, but a lynch mob will hang five others if you do not fasten the crime on one individual.

such and such shall not be the case. I shall say that we infringe a right of his if and only if we bring about that it is the case.[3] I shall say that we violate a right of his if and only if *both* we bring about that it is the case *and* we act wrongly in so doing. The difference I have in mind comes out in the following case, which I shall call A:

> (A) There is a child who wil die if he is not given some drug in the near future. The only bit of that drug which can be obtained for him in the near future is yours. You are out of town, and hence cannot be asked for consent within the available time. You keep your supply of the drug in a locked box on your back porch.

In this case the box is yours, you have a right that it not be broken into without your consent; since the drug is yours, you have a right that it shall not be removed and given to someone without your consent. So if we break into the box, remove the drug, and feed it to the child, we thereby infringe a number of rights of yours. But I take it that a child's life being at stake, we do not act wrongly if we go ahead; that is, though we infringe a number of your rights, we violate none of them.

It might be said that we do violate one or more of our rights if we go ahead, but that our act, though wrongful, is excusable. In other words, although we act wrongly if we go ahead, we are not to be blamed for doing so. It is true that for clarity about rights we need, and do not have, a general account of when one should say "a non-wrongful infringement of a right" and when one should instead say "a wrongful, but excusable, infringement of a right." I think (but without great confidence) that the difference lies in this: The former may not be said where, and the latter may only be said where the agent ought not to act or ought not have acted. If so, then the proposal we are considering is false: For it surely is plain that a third party would not speak truly if he said to us, given we are in (A): "You ought not go ahead."

In any case, the proposal in a certain sense hangs in midair. What I have in mind is this. It is presumably agreed universally that if we go ahead in (A), we are not to be blamed, punished, scolded, or the like, for doing so. Now the question is: Why? One possible answer is: if we go ahead in (A) we do not act wrongly, and that is why we are not to be blamed for doing so. That this is my answer shows itself in the paragraph in which I first set out (A). But how is proponent of the proposal we are now considering to answer? On his view, we act wrongly if we go ahead; what, on his view, is the reason why we are not to be blamed for doing so? There are cases in which there is an answer to an analogous question. Thus if I break your box in a rage which you provoked, then I acted wrongly, but perhaps excusably, and the reason why I am not to be blamed (if I am not) is at hand: you yourself provoked the rage out of which I acted. Again, a reason why I am not to be blamed in another case might be: I was not fully aware of what I was doing; or I was so frantic with worry I could not think clearly; or I was so frantic with worry, nothing else seemed to matter. If (A) had read: "*Our* child will die if he is not given. . . ," then there might have been a toehold for an answer of the kind just

---

[3]This is a simplified account of what I mean by "infringe a right." For example, someone might have a right that such and such shall be the case, and we might bring about that it is not the case, but our act might at one and the same time bring about both that it is not the case and that he no longer has a right that it is the case. It is possible that in some cases (that is, those in which we infringe no other right of his in bringing about that he no longer has that right), no right of his is "infringed," in the sense I mean this word to have. But the difficulties I point to here are of no interest for present purposes, so I ignore them.

pointed to. But (A) says: "There is a child who will die if he is not given. . . ," and it is possible to suppose that we go ahead in (A)—break the box, and give the drug to the child—calmly, coolly, carefully weighing all the relevant considerations. If so, just what is a proponent of the proposal we are now considering to give as an answer to the question of why we are not to be blamed for doing so?

So I shall simply assume that this proposal is false, and I shall take it, then, that while we infringe some of your rights if we go ahead, we do not violate them.[4]

A second way of responding to what I said of our act if we go ahead in (A) is this: True, we violate no rights if we go ahead, but we also infringe no rights if we go ahead. What I have in mind is the possibility of saying that you do not have either of the rights it might have been thought you had—that you do not have a right that your box not be broken into without your consent, and that you do not have a right that your drug not be removed and given to someone without your consent—on the ground that it is morally permissible for us to go ahead in (A). What rights do you have over your box and drug on this view? Well, I suppose it would be said that what you have is at most a right that your-box-not-be-broken-into-and-your-drug-not-taken-without-your-consent-when-there-is-no-child-who-needs-that-drug-for-life. The inclinations to take, everywhere, either the view discussed just above, or the view indicated here, is the inclination to regard all rights as "absolute." That is, it is the inclination to take it that if a man has a right that such and such shall not be the case, then if we bring about that it is the case, we act wrongly in so doing. As the point might be put, every infringing of a right is a violation of a right. So if a man really does have a right that such and such shall not be the case (as it might be, that his drug not be removed from his box), then we act at best excusably if we bring about that it is the case—as in the view discussed just above. If we do not act wrongly in bringing it about, then he did not really have a right that it not come about, but at most right that it-not-come-about-when-the-circumstances-are-so-and-so, as in the view indicated here.

It seems to me, however, that you do have a right that your box not be broken into without your consent and a right that your drug not be removed and given to someone without your consent, and that what shows this is the fact that if we go ahead in (A)—break into your box and give some of the drug to the child—we shall have later to pay you some, if not all, of the cost we imposed on you by doing so. We shall have to pay some, if not all, of the cost of repairing or replacing the box and of replacing the drug we removed.[5] You may reject payment you may say, on your return, that, the circumstances having been what they were, all is well, and that you do not mind bearing the costs yourself. But we must at least offer. If you had no right that we not do these things without your consent, why would we have to pay you some of the costs we imposed on you by doing them?

It is sometimes said (see Essay 3) that if we go ahead in (A) we shall have to *compensate* you for the costs we imposed on you by doing so, and that *that* is what shows that we infringed some of your rights by going ahead—for compensation is repay-

---

[4]It is worth noticing, in passing, that for present purposes it would not matter if I were wrong to make this assumption. There are acts which Nozick says are violation of rights. I shall say that some of them, anyway, are unwrongful infringements of rights. Suppose I am mistaken in this way. That what I should have said is that they are wrongful, though excusable, infringements of rights. Since Nozick plainly thinks those acts are not merely wrongful, but excusable, what I shall say would still conflict with what he thinks.

[5]It is of the greatest interest whether or not we have to pay *all* this back, a question to which I shall return later.

ment for a wrong. But I think that this is not a good way to put the point, and will bring out my reason for thinking so later.

In any case, it seems to me we do well to agree that rights are not all absolute: There are rights which can be infringed without being violated. In particular, it seems to me that if we go ahead in (A), we infringe some of your property rights, but do not violate any of them.

What people who would agree with me on this matter would say is this: If we go ahead in (A), we will infringe your property rights, but we would not violate them, since those rights are "overridden" by the fact that the child will die if we do not go ahead.

A more stringent right than your property rights over your box and drug might not have been overridden by this fact. For example, if it had been necessary for the saving of the child's life that we kill you, then it would not have been morally permissible that we go ahead. Your right to not be killed is considerable more stringent than any of your property rights, and would not have been overridden by the child's need.

The question just how stringent our several rights are is obviously a difficult one. It does not even seem to be obvious that there is any such thing as *the* degree of stringency of any given right. Perhaps a right may be more or less stringent, as a rightholder's circumstances vary, and also, in the case of special rights, as the means by which he acquired the right vary. One thing only is plain: Only an absolute right is infinitely stringent. For only an absolute right is such that every possible infringement of it is a violation of it. Indeed, we may re-express the thesis that all rights are absolute as follows: all rights are infinitely stringent.

There are passages in *Anarchy, State, and Utopia* which suggest that Nozick thinks all rights are infinitely stringent. He say: "[O]ne might place [rights] as side consraints upon the actions to be done: don't violate constraints C. The rights of others determine the constraints upon your actions. . . . The side-constraint view forbids you to violate these moral constraints in the pursuit of your goals,"[6] If you use "violate" in the way I suggested we should use it, this "side-constraint view" does not amount to much—under that reading of the term, all Nozick says is that we may not wrongly infringe a right. Of course we may not. But I think he does not mean to use the term "violate," in this passage at any rate. I think that in this passage all he means by it is "infringe." Thus I think that we are to take this "side-constraint view" to say that we may not ever infringe a right. Accordingly, every infringing of a right is wrong. Compare what Nozick says a few pages on:

> A specific side constraint upon action toward others expresses the fact that others may not be used in the specific ways the side constraint excludes. Side constraints express the inviolability of others, in the ways they specify. These modes of inviolability of others, in the ways they specify. These modes of inviolability are expressed by the following injunction: "Don't use people in specified ways."[7]

Now Nozick does not in fact say that his view is the "side-constraint view," so interpreted, but he implies that it is. Certainly this thesis about redistribution suggests it: for according to that thesis it is not morally permissible to tax people for the purpose

[6]Nozick, *Anarchy, State, and Utopia*, p. 29.
[7]Ibid., p. 32.

of redistribution, however dire the human need which makes redistribution seem called for, and if dire human need does not override a right, what on earth would?

There are also passages which suggest that Nozick thinks that rights *may* be overrideable, and thus not infinitely stringent, though *very* stringent all the same. He says that it is an open question "whether these side constraints are absolute, or whether they may be violated in order to avoid catastrophic moral horror."[8] Catastrophic moral horror is pretty horrible moral horror; so even if rights are overrideable, as the passage suggests is possible; it is likely to be a rare occasion on which they are overridden. Unfortunately, Nozick leaves the question unanswered; he says it "is one I hope largely to avoid."[9]

There are also passages which suggest that Nozick thinks that some rights at least are overrideable even where catastrophic moral horror is not in the offing. In the course of a discussion of what may be done to animals, he asks: "Can't one save 10,000 animals from excruciating suffering by inflicting some slight discomfort on a person who did not cause the animals' suffering?"[10] And he adds: "One may feel the side constraint is not absolute when it is *people* who can be saved from excruciating suffering. So perhaps the side constraint also relaxes, though not as much, when animals' suffering is at stake."[11] Of course Nozick does not *say* the side constraint relaxes when animals' suffering is at stake, but he seems to think so, and it would surely be mad to think it did not. Well, perhaps 10,000 animals suffering excruciating pain counts as catastrophic moral horror. But does it require 10,000 of them, in excruciating pain, to override your right to not be caused some slight discomfort? I take it you have a right to not be pinched without your consent. But surely we can pinch you without your consent, if doing so is required to save even one cow from excruciating suffering. Indeed I should have thought we could do so if doing so is required to save just one cow from suffering which is considerably less than excruciating.

This wobbling about the degree of stringency of rights makes a reader feel nervous. It also makes it very unclear just how Nozick is to get from his starting point, which is that we have rights, to his thesis that a government which imposes taxes for the purpose of redistribution violates the rights of its citizens. I am inclined to think that what happens is this: At the outset, he is unclear what degree of stringency should be assigned to rights (and hopes to avoid having to take a stand on the matter); but by the time he gets to government, all is forgotten, and rights—at any rate, property rights—are infinitely stringent. It is my impression on his argument for his thesis rests entirely on the supposition that they are.

But surely it is plain as day that property rights are not infinitely stringent. It hardly needs argument to show they are not. In any case, the fact that it is morally permissible for us to go ahead in (A) would show—if it needed showing—that they are not.

Consider now case (B), which is in an interesting way different from (A):

(B) There is a child who will die if he is not given some drugs in the future. The only bit of that drug which can be obtained for him in the near future is

---

[8]Ibid., p. 30n.
[9]Ibid.
[10]Ibid., p. 41.
[11]Ibid. (emphasis in original).

yours. You are out of town, so we telephone you to ask. You refuse consent. You keep your supply of the drug in a locked box on your back porch.

"They did it without Jones' consent" covers two interestingly different kinds of cases: In the one kind, they were unable to get Jones' consent because he was not available to be asked for his consent; in the other kind, they were unable to get Jones' consent because he refused to give it. In the latter kind of case they acted, not merely without Jones' consent, but against his wishes. (A) is a case of the first kind; we cannot reach you to ask for consent. (B) is a case of the second kind; if we go ahead in (B) we act, not merely without your consent, but against your wishes. I said it is morally permissible for us to go ahead in (A); is it morally permissible for us to go ahead in (B)?

The fact is that our going ahead in (B)—our breaking into the box and removing the drug to give it to the child—seems morally suspect in a way in which our going ahead in (A) does not. Why? And should it?

Anyone who thinks that it is morally permissible for us to go ahead in (A) but not in (B) must think that there is at least a good chance that in (A), you would give consent if we were able to reach you to ask for consent. Surely if it were known that if we were to ask for consent in (A) you would refuse to give it, then it would be no better to go ahead in (A) than it is to go ahead in (B). For then (A) too would be a case in which going ahead would be acting against your wishes—though not against any wish that was in fact given expression.

Anyone who thinks that it is not morally permissible for us to go ahead in (B) must think that the box and the drug in it are in some way very important to you— that you place a very high value on the box not being broken into, and on the drug not being taken away from you. Suppose, however, that there is a toothpick on your desk, and it is in no way special to you. By virtue of some peculiarity in nature, we can save a life if we snap it in two. We ask if we can, but you are feeling refractory and say "No." Can we not go ahead and snap it in two, despite your expressed wish that we not do so? By contrast, suppose what is on your desk is the last remaining photograph of your dead mother, and what we need to do to save the life is to burn it. Well, some people would say we can go ahead all the same. Suppose that what we need to do is to destroy *all* the now existing beautiful works of art, and that their owners (individuals, museums, governments) say, "Alas no, we are very sorry, but no." Could we go ahead all the same?

If (X), "The box and drug are, at most, of little value to you," is true, then we may surely go ahead in both (A) and (B). If (X) is true and we are in (A), then in the absence of information to the contrary, we shall rightly assume you would consent if we were able to ask. But even if we have information to the effect that you would not consent—even if we were in (B) instead of (A)—it is morally permissible for us to go ahead all the same. Why? Because if (X) is true, then it would be indecent for you to refuse consent in (A), and it is indecent for you to refuse consent in (B). I said you might be feeling refractory; alternatively, you might think: "What is that child to me?" There are other possible sources of refusal, but none of them bears looking at.

What if, instead, (Y), "The box and drug are of immense value to you," is true? Some would say we can go ahead all the same. If feel considerable sympathy of this view, but I do not hold it myself. It seems to me that if (Y) is true, we may not go ahead in (B), and in the absence of reason to think you would consent despite the truth of

(Y), we may not go ahead in (A) either. I hope that when I first produced (A) above, your intuition agreed with mine; if so, I think that was because you were assuming that nothing so strong as (Y) was true. Why may we not go ahead if (Y) is true? It is not morally splendid to value bits of property more than human lives; but if there are some which you do—and this for no morally suspect reason—then it seems to me that there are cases, and that this is one of them, in which we must withdraw.

There are all manner of possibilities between (X) and (Y), but it is not necessary for our purposes that we attend to them. . . .

I said that it is my impression that Nozick's argument for this thesis rests entirely on the supposition that property rights are infinitely stringent, and I said also that it is plain as day that they are not. Well, setting aside Nozick's argument for the thesis, what about the thesis itself?

The rights which Nozick thinks would be violated by a redistributive move are property rights. I shall make no criticism here of his account of the source and content of those rights. However, it is perhaps worth just drawing attention to the fact that Nozick allows that title to property is clouded in existing states: He grants that injustices lie behind their current property distributions.[12] This means, then, that a redistributive move in an existing state may very well not really conflict with property rights, and in fact there is no practical moral lesson about redistributive moves in existing states to be learned from Nozick's book.

In light of that fact we had better take Nozick to be speaking only of governments in "ideal" states—states in which property rights are not clouded; more precisely, states in which the distribution of property satisfies Nozick's principles of distributive justice.

One thing we know is that there are circumstances in which it is morally permissible, and hence no violation of any right, to take from Smith—even against his wishes—to give to Jones. Any case in which Jones needs something, and he needs it for *life,* and the only way of providing him with it is by taking it from Smith, and Smith places at most little value on it, is such a case. Suppose we live in an ideal state. Then there are circumstances in which agents of government can arrange this redistribution. Would that count as imposing a tax for the purpose of redistribution? It is hard to see why not.

Something of great interest comes out if we consider, now, a second kind of case. Suppose there is an "ideal" state of only eleven people. One person will die if he is not provided with a certain amount of a particular drug. Eight of the remaining ten people would very much like for him to get that amount of the drug. (I make it a large majority, though I have no very clear idea how its being a majority matters. I also made the sick one be a citizen of the state, though I have no very clear idea how his being so matters.) The eight can scrape together the needed amount of the drug from among their own supplies, but to do so would require each of them to deplete his supply drastically—not to the point at which any of their lives is at risk, but to the point at which they would have a bare sufficiency. By contrast, the remaining two people have ample supplies; each of them could, himself, easily supply the needed amount. But these two individuals refuse to contribute.

This case is different from (A) and (B): In this case, by contrast with those we

---

[12]See Nozick, *Anarchy, State, and Utopia,* pp. 152–153.

have been looking at, the agents do not have to take anything from anyone else in order to meet the need of the eleventh. They can meet his need themselves. Does this mean that they must meet it themselves? On Nozick's view they must. On Nozick's view, the meeting of human needs is a consumer good like any other. Or rather, it is like any other expensive consumer good.[13] If you want a color television set, and buying one will deplete your assets to the point at which you have a bare sufficiency to live on, well, so be it, it is up to you whether or not a color television is worth that much to you. You certainly cannot take from anyone else in order to be able to buy one without having to deplete your assets! Similarly for the meeting of human needs.

It is plain enough, however, that the meeting of human needs is not a consumer good like any other. I hasten to say I have no account of what marks needs off from mere wants. But certainly if a man will die unless he gets something, then that thing is something he needs. And we know that if we cannot provide him with that thing which he needs for life without taking it from Smith, then—at least in such cases as Smith places at most little value on it—it is permissible for us to take it from Smith. This marks a difference. For even if you cannot get a color television at all unless you take from someone else, then all the same you cannot take from him in order to buy one, even if he has plenty of money.

But is this difference relevant to the case at hand? Suppose Nozick were to grant it, and say: "Very well, the meeting of human needs is not a consumer good like any other—it differs from color televisions in the way you indicate. [He would thus acknowledge that property rights arenot infinitely stringent.] Still, if the eight *can* meet the need of the eleventh by themselves, how can they presume to take from the two who do not care if the need is met?"

Nozick might go on: "In those cases you have been describing in which Jones needs something for life, and it is permissible to take it from Smith and give it to Jones, what overrides Smith's right that the thing not be taken from him is not the mere fact that Jones needs it for life, but the complex fact that Jones needs it for life *and* we can provide it in no other way than by taking it from Smith. Suppose what Jones needs for life is a drug which you have ample supplies of and Smith has only a little of; surely you cannot say. 'How nice! The fact that Jones needs that drug for life overrides Smith's right that his drug not be taken away from him, so I do not have to provide for Jones myself—I can take from Smith to provide for Jones.' Surely you cannot take from Smith if you have plenty yourself! But if it is the complex fact I pointed to which is doing the real work in the cases you describe—if it is that fact which really does the overriding—then those cases have no bearing at all on the case now at hand. So I repeat: Given the eight can meet the need of the eleventh by themselves, how can they presume to take from the two who do not care if the need is met?"

Nozick might go on: "And wouldn't it be like that in ideal states generally? In other words, that those who refuse to contribute would be few enough so that those willing to contribute could, by themselves, meet such needs as they wanted met?[14] If so, nothing so far said counts against my thesis that a government of an ideal state which imposes taxes for the purposes of redistribution violates the rights of its citizens."

It is hard to know what to say about people who would live in "ideal" states if

[13]Ibid., pp. 160–164, 168–172.
[14]Ibid., pp. 182, 265–268.

there were any. What would they be like? But I join the many other readers of *Anarchy, State, and Utopia* who have doubts about their generosity.[15]

Moreover, the instability of the situation I invited you to imagine is obvious. Suppose that if only one of the eight ceased to be willing to contribute, then the remaining seven could no longer meet the need of the eleventh by themselves, so that the case would then collapse into a case of the kind we were looking at earlier. Would it not pay them to draw straws to choose one among them to volunteer to say he has changed his mind? Then, instead of the eight having to deplete their own supplies of the drug, the remaining seven could take from the two who are rich in it. Would they even need to draw straws to choose a liar? If the eight were given the information that if there were only seven, the seven could take from the two, would there not be at least one who would *really* change his mind? It would be an odd moral theory that yielded either the conclusion that the eight must not be given that information, or the conclusion that the eight must meet the need of the eleventh by themselves unless they are lucky enough to get that information, in which case they do not have to.

All the same, the question my hypothetical Nozick raises is a hard one. If the eight can meet the need of the eleventh by themselves, how can they presume to take from the two who do not care if the need is met? I am sure that the instability I pointed to should figure in the answer, but I do not see clearly how.

One's intuition, I think, is that it just is not *fair* that the eight should have to deplete their supplies so drastically in order to meet the need of the eleventh. The source of that intuition is, I think, this: One thinks of the needs as *having* to be met by the citizens of that state, and therefore thinks that the burden of meeting it should be shared, as in the case of any other project which the citizens have to carry out.

Why does the need *have* to be met by the citizens of the state? By hypothesis, the need is one which can be met by them at little cost to any of them, for each of the two with ample supplies could easily meet the need by himself. But if a need can be met at little cost—remembering that it is a need for something to sustain life itself—then it is indecent that the need not be met. (I here say something of a community which would be true of an individual.) So it has to be met. So, as in the case of any other project which the citizens of a state have to carry out, it is only fair that the burden of doing so be shared. But if the two with ample supplies give nothing at all, the entire burden falls on the remaining eight, who can least afford to share it. Hence it is not fair that it should fall on them alone.

If the two with ample supplies can each meet the need at very little cost, then it makes little difference whether or not one takes the whole amount needed from one, or takes half the needed amount from each, or imposes a proportional tax on all ten of them, under which the two pay the lion's share, and the remaining eight pay a grain or two each. Another possibility is that each of the two might be ordered to provide half, and the remaining eight suffer a comparable loss by having to pay the two, or the community at large, in some commodity other than the drug.

There are cases, however, in which it will make a difference. Let us look back again at case (A). I said that if we go ahead, and break into the box and give the drug to the child, we shall have later to pay you some, if not all, the cost we imposed on you

[15]Thomas Nagel, in his review of Nozicks' book, makes the interesting suggestion that insisting that contributions be voluntary is "an excessively demanding moral position" and that "excessive demands on the will . . . you bemore irksome than automatic demands on the purse." Nagel, Book Reivew, *Yale Law Journal* 85 (November 975), pp. 136, 145–146.

by doing so. Kindhearted students sometimes look askance at this proposal—for if we go ahead, we do so to save the life of a child, after all. But the idea that the burdens must be fairly shared cuts both ways. If we go ahead, we must share, with you, the burden of meeting that child's need: We must impose the entire burden of meeting its need on you. If I am right, it follows that we need not reimburse you for the entire cost of repairing or replacing the box and replacing the drug, but only such part of that cost as leaves you to pay the same amount as each of the rest of us. It is for this reason that I preferred not to speak of that payment as *compensation:* its point is not so much to compensate for a loss as to reduce that loss to the point at which it is no greater than ours.

I should stress, however, that the cases I have drawn attention to are all cases in which the redistribution aimed at is aimed at in order to meet the human needs. None of them is a case in which the redistribution aimed at is aimed at simply in order that there is less inequality. Taxation for redistribution for that purpose is a wholly different matter.

Chapter V

Social Contract Theories

Article I of the United Nations Charter

Article 1

The Purposes of the United Nations are:
1. To maintain international peace and security, and to that end: to take effective collective measures for the prevention and removal of threats to the peace, and for the suppression of acts of aggression or other breaches of the peace, and to bring about by peaceful means, and in conformity with the principles of justice and international law, adjustment or settlement of international disputes or situations which might lead to a breach of the peace;

2. To develop friendly relations among nations based on respect for the principle of equal rights and self-determination of peoples, and to take other appropriate measures to strengthen universal peace;

3. To achieve international cooperation in solving international problems of an economic, social, cultural, or humanitarian character, and in promoting and encouraging respect for human rights and for fundamental freedoms for all without distinction as to race, sex, language, or religion; and

4. To be a center for harmonizing the actions of nations in the attainment of these common ends. . . .

Commentary

During World War I, the concept of self-determination was given explicit formulation by Woodrow Wilson in his Fourteen Points as a principle governing the determination of territorial boundaries in the peace treaties to be signed at the end of the war. Yet, this principle found no place in the Covenant of the League of Nations and its application was confined to Central and Eastern Europe.

On colonial matters Wilson demanded "[a] free, open-minded, and absolutely impartial adjustment of all colonial claims, based upon a strict observance of the principle that in determining all such questions of sovereignty the interests of the populations concerned *must* have equal weight with the equitable claims of the government whose title is to be determined."

In the interwar period, criticism of colonialism began to gather momentum and the outbreak of World War II greatly strengthened the belief that colonialism was dying. This was brought home to many, particularly in the United States, by the slight resistance with which the colonial peoples of South East Asia, with the exception of the Filipinos who had been promised independence, opposed the Japanese invaders. Thus, the United States, in its wartime planning for the future international organization, gave considerable attention to proposals providing for a system of international supervision over all dependent peoples. The Atlantic Charter proclaimed the "right of all peoples to choose the form of government under which they will live"; . . . however, Prime Minister Churchill did not consider this statement applicable to colonial peoples.

The principle of equal rights and self-determination received no mention in the Dumbarton Oaks Proposals. The addition of the phrase "based on respect for the principle of equal rights and self-determination of peoples" to the second paragraph of Chapter 1 (Purposes) was proposed at the San Francisco Conference by

Commentary reprinted by permission of Leland M. Goodrich; Edward Hambro, and Patricia Simons, 1969.

the Sponsoring Governments at the suggestion of the Soviet Union. When the amendment was discussed in Committee I/1, two different viewpoints developed. On the one hand, "it was strongly emphasized . . . that this principle corresponded closely to the will and desires of peoples everywhere and should be clearly enunciated." On the other hand, "it was stated that the principle conformed to the purposes of the Charter only in so far as it implied the right of self-government of peoples and not the right of secession." . . . Controversy focused also on the use of the words "nations" and "peoples" rather than "the more usual reference throughout the Charter to relations among 'states.'" . . . In recommending the draft, the technical committee indicated its understanding that:

> the principle of equal rights of peoples and that of self-determination are two complementary parts of one standard of conduct: that the respect of that principle is a basis for the development of friendly relations and is one of the measures to strengthen universal peace; that an essential element of the principle in question is a free and genuine expression of the will of the people. . . .

The text of the Sponsors' draft was ultimately approved. However, questions regarding the difference—if any—between the terms "nations," "peoples," and "states," the meaning of "self-determination," and whether one or two principles were involved, were left unresolved. . . .

Despite the opposition of some members, the General Assembly in 1950 recognized that the right of peoples and nations to self-determination is a fundamental human right. . . . Subsequently it decided to include in the covenants on human rights an article on the right of self-determination. . . . In 1955, the following text was accepted in the Third Committee, over the opposition of many Western European countries, for inclusion in both draft covenants on human rights:

> All peoples have the right of self-determination. By virtue of this right they freely determine their political status and freely pursue their economic, social and cultural development.
>
> The peoples may, for their own ends, freely dispose of their natural wealth and resources without prejudice to any obligations arising out of international economic cooperation, based upon the principle of mutual benefit, and international law. In no case may a people be deprived of its own means of subsistence. . . .

In 1954, the General Assembly requested the Commission on Human Rights to make recommendations concerning the permanent sovereignty of peoples over their "natural wealth and resources, having due regard to the rights and duties of states under international law and to the importance of encouraging international cooperation in the economic development of underdeveloped countries." . . . Subsequently, in 1958, the General Assembly after "noting" that the right of peoples and nations to self-determination includes permanent sovereignty over their natural wealth and resources, decided to establish a Commission "to conduct a full survey of the status of this basic constituent element of the right of self-determination." . . . Based on the report of this Commission, the General Assembly in 1962 adopted a resolution in which it referred to the "inalienable right" of all states "freely to dispose of their natural wealth and resources. . . ."

The principle of self-determination has played a key role in the concerted effort to end colonialism. On December 14, 1960, the General Assembly unanimously adopted the Declaration on the Granting of Independence to Colonial Countries and Peoples sponsored by forty-three Asian and African members. The General Assembly "[s]olemnly" proclaimed therein "the necessity of bringing to a speedy and unconditional end colonialism in all its forms and manifestations"; declared that "all peoples have the right to self-determination" and that immediate steps should be taken to transfer all powers to the peoples of all territories not yet independent without any conditions or reservations; and denied that inadequacy of preparation should ever be a pretext for delaying the exercise of the right of self-determination. . . .

At the following session, the Assembly established a special committee to examine the application of the Declaration and make suggestions and recommendations on the progress of its implementation. Subsequently, the Assembly invited the committee to propose specific measures for the speedy application of the Declaration and authorized it to bring to the attention of the Security Council any developments in the colonial sphere which might threaten international peace and security. . . .

The Declaration on the Granting of Independence to Colonial Countries and Peoples and the practice of the General Assembly and the special committee all suggest the following conclusions with respect to the principle of self-determination, status compatible with it, and groups to which it applies:

1. The principle has been applied to situations involving colonial rule of noncontiguous territories inhabited by people of a predominantly different culture.

2. There has been a very strong inclination on the part of a sizable majority of members to insist that independence is the only status compatible with the principle of self-determination, although there has been a growing awareness of the need for some flexibility in the case of dependencies which, because of the smallness of their territory and population, are hardly viable entities;

3. The principle of "self-determination of peoples" has been interpreted to mean that the inhabitants of a territory treated as an administrative unit by the colonial power should determine its political status on the basis of universal adult suffrage and by majority vote. Once the choice has been made, attempts at secession by disaffected minority groups have been held to be incompatible with the Charter. . . .

Social Contract Theories

As a broad characterization we can say that ethics proposes a set of rules that constrains people's action toward one another. In previous chapters we have considered several attempts to say what these rules are—even one theory (virtue ethics) which holds that character traits, not rules, are most important to ethics. However, a person might not be satisfied that we have used a truly reasonable procedure for discovering such principles. We have searched around trying to square our clear case moral judgments with various theoretical proposals. One of the advantages of the social contract approach to ethics is that it gives a plausible procedure concerning how we should decide upon just and fair rules by which to live in a society. As it was in the last chapter, social contract theory is often discussed in political philosophy, but recently it has gained interest as a way to approach ethics more generally. The root idea behind the theory is that any set of rules, or any institution using rules, will be fair and just if persons agree (contract) to abide by these rules. After all, it can be argued, it is only right that people are obliged to abide by rules and institutions to which they willingly consent. To discover the precise nature of ethical principles we need only discover which principles people will choose to impose upon themselves.

The basic idea behind a social contract theory—that it is only fair that people be obliged to obey rules to which they have consented—is a principle often found in everyday contexts. For example, our lead essay, which gives the first article of the United Nations charter along with a commentary, depends upon a principle much like this to decide issues in foreign affairs. As the authors (Goodrich, Hambro, and Simons) of the commentary point out, a long-standing idea in foreign affairs is the *principle of national self-determination*—sometimes called the *principle of popular will* or the *principle of autonomy*. According to this principle, every group of people has the right to decide what kind of government it wishes to have imposed upon itself. Stated differently, a group of people has no basis to complain against the rules a government imposes upon them if they have agreed to or consented to that government and those rules. The idea of self-determination is not peculiar to politics or ethics. It comes up in some everyday contexts as well. Consider what goes on when a group of persons decides to form some club or organization, for example, a bird-watching club. To form such a club requires making decisions about rules and regulations that will be imposed upon the members: payment of fees, meeting times, election of officers, and so on. There may well be no obviously "right" set of rules for such a club, but it can be argued there is a "right" way to decide what the rules should be. A fair way of setting up a club is to propose a set of rules to which all founding members will agree. (Future members will express their agreement by the simple act of joining the club.) Ideally, all founding members will agree to some kind of organization and promise to abide by the terms specified. There is a good reason why the birdwatchers are willing to impose constraints upon themselves that they otherwise would not need to worry about: By banding together in an organization they all hope to further their interest in bird-watching.

There is a typical story told by social contract theorists that draws a close parallel between setting up principles for a society and adopting rules for a bird-watching club. Imagine a time before people lived in societies governed by rules. Social contract theorists call this presocial stage a *state of nature*. Living in a state of nature would not be altogether bad: At least in a state of nature we would not be burdened by all the rules and regulations that we find in modern society. With variations among the different theorists we will read, a state of nature is characterized as a situation where people have a considerable amount of freedom to do as they want. However, while life in a state of nature would be considerably freer than life in society, there are major disadvantages to living in a nonsocial setting. Without a common authority we would have no protection against people acting badly toward us. Nothing, it would seem, could prevent people from stealing, murdering, or harming us in any number of ways.

A typical argument made by the writers in this chapter is the following: Given a choice between living in a state of nature and living in a society governed by rules designed to protect us from harm, it is reasonable to choose to be in society. The term *reasonable* is important here. We assume that people want to live as well as they possibly can. Everyone wants to maximize his or her personal benefit. As with forming a club for the mutual benefit of bird-watching, it is supposed that people form a society for mutual benefit. The benefits of society, however, are quite broad. People contract into society for the overarching purpose of better living their version of the good life. The task of a social contract theorist is to convince us that consent to (or contracting into) a society is the best thing for us to do, given that we all want to live as well as possible. A social contract is often regarded as a kind of trade—a good trade at that. By contracting into a society we give up some of our freedom, but, in return, we enhance our chances of living a better life.

A social contract theory, like the political idea of self-determination, appeals to the idea that a social system is a fair one because people consent to it. But there is an important difference here. To see this difference, let's consider a problem that the principle of self-determination faces. Although it may seem right to say that it is only fair to force people to abide by a social system of their own choosing, the usual understanding of self-determination posits that a social system can be enforced when a *majority* of people choose that system. This idea may not sit well, however, with people who find themselves in the minority. If we allow a majority of people to call the tune for everyone, it can turn out that the majority will treat the rest of the people in society horribly. For example, if we used the principle that a social system is just when a majority of a society's members consent to it, then it would seem that Nazi Germany was a just society. Most people's best guess is that Hitler's dictatorship was approved of by the majority of German citizens, in spite of the fact that it committed unspeakable atrocities against a minority of its citizens. Examples such as these—and surely there are more—cast doubt on the political principle of self-determination. We would not want to say that any social system is just simply because a majority of citizens consents to it.

It seems as though nothing less than unanimous consent justifies our obligation to a social system. If a social system is going to impose rules and regulations on its citizens and we hold to the idea that such an imposition is fair only if consented to, then everyone must give their consent. If even one person does not consent, then he or she has been treated unfairly because rules have been forced on that person against his or her will. It is this sort of reasoning that leads each of the writers we will study to require unanimous consent to a social contract.

However, if unanimous consent is needed to justify a social system, then there is another problem. It would seem that no such system could ever be justified. After all, the chances of getting everyone to agree to any social system seems slim. For example, we may feel that the laws imposed upon Americans by their government are by and large good ones. If we had to justify these laws by appeal to the unanimous consent of the American citizenry, however, we would be in trouble. There is little doubt that there will be some people who object to one law or another, and perhaps even some who will object to the system as a whole. Consent of every person in a society is an overly stiff requirement—and one that is likely never met.

There is a theoretical remedy here, but one that puts distance between contract theory and cases like national self-determination or the formation of bird-watching clubs. Recent social contract theories advocates such as John Rawls and David Gauthier are clear that a social contract should be thought of as a *hypothetical* agreement between fully *rational* persons. The claim is that we can specify morally binding social principles by requiring that the principles are ones to which all reasonable persons would consent, if given the chance. By relying upon the presumably harmless fictions of "hypothetical consent" and "reasonable persons," the problem of obtaining unanimity from a group of real, not always reasonable persons, can be avoided. However, the picture of what justifies social rules changes with the introduction of rational, hypothetical consent. It can no longer be said that a set of rules ought to be followed by a group of persons because they have actually agreed to these rules. Rather, it is argued that certain institutions or rules are just and fair because they are the ones to which we would consent, if we thought about the matter clearly and carefully.

Now that we have set the stage by describing the shared viewpoint of social contract theories, it is appropriate to consider some differences between the writers we will consider. There is a distinction we can make between social contract theories that will divide them into two camps. The most ambitious version of the social contract theory, as represented by Thomas Hobbes, attempts to support the full scope of social ethics using only the idea of a social contract. In its most extreme form, a social contract theory holds that there are no moral duties except those we impose on ourselves by consent (with one possible exception, which will be considered shortly). Consider again the analogy with a bird-watching club.

Before deciding to be a member of the club a person has no obligation to pay money for the preservation of endangered species of birds, for example. However, if one of the rules agreed to by all parties forming the club is that each member is required to contribute 20 dollars per year to endangered species, then each member is morally obliged to contribute. After all, by agreeing to join the club a person has, in effect, promised to abide by the rules. Promising to abide gives moral force to practices that are otherwise morally neutral. Hobbes makes the same sort of point about forming a society: In Hobbes' state of nature no one has moral obligations to anyone. It is neither right nor wrong to cheat, steal, murder, and so on in the state of nature. However, the simple act of agreeing, promising, or contracting into a particular form of social organization imposes moral obligations upon the agreeing parties. Social rules by themselves may be neither right nor wrong. Once we have consented to them (promised to obey them), however, we are morally bound to conform since we are morally bound to abide by our promises. In fact, in its most extreme form, social contract theorists need only convince us that people ought to keep the promises they make—all other social obligations can be derived from an obligation to keep promises. Perhaps, as Gauthier suggests, we need not merely assume that we ought to keep promises.

However, Hobbes' strong version of the social contract is not the only version. Locke offers a less ambitious account of the social contract. We have already run across Locke in the last chapter, where we categorized him as a natural rights theorist since he holds that all of us have a basic moral obligation to respect the rights of others. For Locke we have these moral obligations even outside the bounds of society. To this extent Locke differs from Hobbes. Unlike Hobbes, Locke holds that there are some moral obligations in the state of nature. Locke, however, also has a role for a social contract: While we are morally obliged to respect rights, Locke is aware that enforcement of such moral obligations in a state of nature would be impossible. Accordingly, he argues that we should agree to form a society with laws, courts, and so on for the purpose of protecting those rights we all have prior to agreeing to society. This still gives society considerable moral authority. For example, it allows society to judge what counts as a rights violation (in terms of legislation and adjudication) and allows it to affix penalties for such infringement. Locke's position is that when entering a society we give to society the rights to "judge and punish." Our consent obliges us to respect social decisions in these important areas.

One way we can distinguish the various positions on a social contract approach to ethics is to see whether they tend to have Hobbes' extreme view that all moral obligations are generated agreement or Locke's more restricted view that a social contract agreement only adds to our moral scheme. On this score Jean-Jacques Rousseau is closer to Hobbes than to Locke. Rousseau tends to think that people have no moral obligations until they agree to a social arrangement. In fact, Rousseau goes so far as to claim that socialization transforms a person from a nonmoral creature into a moral agent. Alternatively, John Rawls, at least as understood by David Lyons, is perhaps closer to Locke than to Hobbes. Rawls argues that a hypothetical social contract is the best way to argue for ethical principles. However, Lyons points out, Rawls does not make his argument in a moral vacuum. Put briefly, Rawls holds that the proper set of moral principles for a society are those that a rational person would agree to under constraints of absolute fairness. To ensure fairness Rawls asks us to imagine choosing principles under a *veil of ignorance*. He argues that to choose social principles fairly we should pretend as though we know nothing about our personal interests and abilities. Choosing principles under such conditions of "ignorance" prevents us from trying to pick principles that are partial to us at the expense of others. The veil of ignorance is intended to insure fairness by requiring impartiality. Thus, Rawls seems to assume that we have at least one moral obligation prior to a social contract: Namely, we ought to treat people fairly and impartially. After all, fairness is a condition that must be met before we choose principles to impose upon ourselves.

David Gauthier pursues a stronger version of social contract much in the spirit of Thomas Hobbes. Gauthier's aim is to show how we can be obliged to follow a set of social rules and regulations—ones that place limits on pursuing our self-interested "preferences." In the brief article included in our readings, Gauthier works out only one example of his social contract theory. He wants to justify a principle of *distributive justice* (i.e., a just principle for distributing wealth in society) using a social contract method. Like Hobbes, Gauthier wants to show that we are obliged to a principle of justice on the basis of rational consent alone. To be more specific, Gauthier will argue that rational persons would agree to distribute wealth in society according to the rule that everyone make "equal concessions" (concessions from the maximum benefits they could obtain from a social economy). Without going into the details of Gauthier's position, it is important to note the kind of social contract theory he offers. Gauthier assumes only that people are self-interested. However, he hopes to show that certain moral duties (such as duties concerning distributive justice) arise once we think about what kind of agreement rationally self-interested persons would make.

There is another way we can distinguish different versions of the social contract theory. So far we have considered the extent to which a social contract agreement can support moral obligations. For example, Locke argues that a social contract supports some of our obligations, while Hobbes seems to claim that all of our obligations stem from a social contract. Theories also differ, however, with respect to the kinds of principles or institutions that we should promise to obey. More specifically, social contract theories differ concerning which rules or institutions they claim would be agreed to by rational persons. Recall that social contract theorists make the same basic claim. Moral obligations to a set of social rules can be justified by showing that they are the ones to which a rational person would consent. However, as we shall see in the readings, there is room for debate as to precisely which set of rules or institutions demands our rational consent.

Hobbes argues that the only reasonable kind of social organization is authoritarian—one that gives a sovereign the absolute authority to make and enforce laws. Hobbes thinks that only a strong authoritarian institution can hold society together and thus keep us out of a state of nature. If we grant that any kind of social order is preferable to the anarchy of a state of nature and, further, that only an authoritarian society can avoid such anarchy, then it seems rational to consent to authoritarianism. Locke, however, argues differently. Since Locke has an antecedent notion of natural rights, his position is that rational people would only agree to a social organization that best protects their rights. After all, for Locke protecting rights is the chief reason for consenting to a political authority in the first place. As such, Locke sharply disagrees with Hobbes' argument for an absolute sovereign. Plausibly enough, Locke argues that an authoritarian society would not guarantee our natural rights.

Rousseau's position differs from those of Hobbes and Locke. Rousseau argues in the following fashion: If we think that consent is a good basis for forming a society, then consent is an equally good process for deciding upon specific rules and regulations within society. Accordingly, Rousseau does not argue that a specific set of rules is the rational one to choose but instead argues that a certain procedure is the proper way to decide upon rules. The procedure he recommends is democracy: Social rules ought to be subject to majoritarian, democratic approval. While this makes Rousseau sound as though he endorses a system much like ours, we should not be so hasty. Rousseau places considerable restraints on democracy. In Rousseau's view people should vote for a piece of legislation if and only if the law promotes the *general will*. The "general will" is Rousseau's term for that which benefits society "generally" or as a whole. Unfortunately, Rousseau isn't terribly clear about its content. However, it is often thought that Rousseau's concern for the benefit of society as a whole puts the interests of the individual at risk. It may well be that Rousseau is willing to sacrifice the interests of some individuals for the sake of the greater good.

Rawls gives us the most detailed account of what he thinks should be the substance of the social contract—the terms to which we should agree. As stated above, Rawls is careful to set up the parameters under which we should choose the principles for our society. They should be chosen with an eye to our own rational self-interest but under the fairness constraints represented by the "veil of ignorance." As odd as it may seem, Rawls wants us to consider social institutions that would most benefit us individually; however, we are not allowed to know much about ourselves. We cannot know what sort of skills we have, what our particular interests and preferences are, and so on. However, even given such restrictions, Rawls argues that we will all agree that the best principles to choose are broadly the following: We should (1) provide for the most extensive range of liberties compatible with the same amount of liberty for everyone; and (2) allow inequalities in wealth and social privilege, but only if these inequalities benefit everyone in society and only if anyone is allowed to compete for society's top spots.

Rawls' theory can be criticized at two levels. First, one could argue that Rawls is mistaken about the principles that would be chosen under the "veil of ignorance." Perhaps it is more reasonable to choose principles different from Rawls' favored two. This is surely an issue we should consider when reading this theorist. Second, however, is a deeper level at which we can worry about Rawls. David Lyons is not altogether convinced that Rawls' method will yield any kind of ethical principles. While we might grant the original idea of a social contract, namely, that we are morally bound to abide by principles to which we have consented (as in our bird-watching club), it is much less clear that we are morally bound to abide by principles that hypothetical rational persons would agree to under a veil of ignorance. After all, one could argue, in Rawls' theory no real people actually consent to his two principles.

Gauthier gives a social contract argument that is more streamlined and, we would hope, less objectionable than Rawls'. As we have seen, Gauthier wants to justify social rules based solely on the idea of rational, self-interested consent—with no need for Rawls' additional assumption of a veil of ignorance. To be a bit more specific, Gauthier argues that his principle of distributive justice is one that would be chosen by rationally self-interested persons who know what their interests and abilities are. Simply put, Gauthier's argument is that our long-range interests require the mutual cooperation of others in society, and that limiting our self-interested pursuits out of consideration for others is the price we must pay to obtain such cooperation. This sort of reasoning presumably lays the foundation for our agreeing to social rules protecting everyone's interests in society.

The recent work of Rawls, Gauthier, and others has rekindled interest in the social contract theory, whose heyday was in the seventeenth and eighteenth centuries. At the heart of the recent attempts is contemporary work on the notion of rational, self-interested decision theory—worked out largely in the context of current economic theory. Perhaps, with the aid of these modern tools, one of the original goals of social contract theory can be met. It may be that we can find a convincing argument of the following kind: If we considered the matter carefully, then we would find that it is in our self-interest to constrain our activities in a way that respects the interests of others. This is the root idea of morality. We will leave as an open question whether any of the versions of social contract have achieved this goal as yet. At the very least, as Gauthier points out, social contract theories, if successful, have a distinct advantage over other theories we have considered. We can convince persons of the importance of subscribing to some set of "moral" restrictions by making only a few assumptions about people. Minimally, as with Gauthier, we need only assume that people are self-interested or, in Rawls' case, that people are self-interested and have a basic sense of fair play.

Leviathan

Thomas Hobbes

OF THE FIRST AND SECOND NATURAL LAWS,
AND OF CONTRACTS

THE RIGHT OF NATURE, which writers commonly call *jus naturale,* is the liberty each man hath, to use his own power, as he will himself, for the preservation of his own nature; that is to say, of his own life; and consequently, of doing any thing, which in his own judgment, and reason, he shall conceive to be the aptest means thereunto.

By LIBERTY, is understood, according to the proper signification of the word, the absence of external impediments: which impediments, may oft take away part of a man's power to do what he would; but cannot hinder him from using the power left him, according as his judgment, and reason shall dictate to him.

A LAW OF NATURE, *lex naturalis,* is a precept or general rule, found out by reason, by which a man is forbidden to do that, which is destructive of his life, or taketh away the means of preserving the same; and to omit that, by which he thinketh it may be best preserved. For though they that speak of this subject, use to confound *jus,* and *lex, right* and *law:* yet they ought to be distinguished; because RIGHT, consisteth in liberty to do, or to forbear; whereas LAW, determineth, and bindeth to one of them: so that law, and right, differ as much, as obligation, and liberty; which in one and the same matter are inconsistent.

And because the condition of man, as hath been declared in the precedent chapter, is a condition of war of every one against every one: in which case every one is governed by his own reason; and there is nothing he can make use of, that may not be a help unto him, in preserving his life against his enemies; it followeth, that in such a condition, every man has a right to every thing; even to one another's body. And therefore, as long as this natural right of every man to every thing endureth, there can be no security to any man, how strong or wise soever he be, of living out the time, which nature ordinarily alloweth men to live. And consequently it is a precept, or general rule of reason, *that every man, ought to endeavour peace, as far as he has hope of obtaining it; and when he cannot obtain it, that he may seek, and use, all helps, and advantages of war.* The first branch of which rule, containeth the first, and fundamental law of nature; which is, *to seek peace, and follow it.* The second, the sum of the right of nature; which is, *by all means we can, to defend ourselves.*

From this fundamental law of nature, by which men are commanded to endeavour peace, is derived this second law; *that a man be willing, when others are so too, as far-forth, as for peace, and defence of himself he shall think it necessary, to lay down this right to all things; and be contented with so much liberty against other men, as he would allow other men against himself.* For as long as every man holdeth this right, of doing any thing he liketh; so long are all men in the condition of war. But if other men will not lay down their right, as well as he; then there is no reason for any one, to divest himself of his: for that were to expose himself to prey, which no man is bound to,

Excerpted from Thomas Hobbes, *Leviathan* (London, 1651), Chapters XIV, XV, and XVII.

rather than to dispose himself to peace. This is that law of the Gospel; *whatsoever you require that others should do to you, that du ye to them*. And that law of all men, *quod tibi fieri non vis, alteri ne feceris*.

To *lay down* a man's *right* to any thing, is to *divest* himself of the *liberty,* of hindering another of the benefit of his own right to the same. For he that renounceth, or passeth away his right, giveth not to any other man a right which he had not before; because there is nothing to which every man had not right by nature: but only standeth out of his way, that he may enjoy his own original right, without hindrance from him; not without hindrance from another. So that the effect which redoundeth to one man, by another man's defect of right, is but so much diminution of impediments to the use of his own right original.

Right is laid aside, either by simply renouncing it; or by transferring it to another. By *simply* RENOUNCING; when he cares not to whom the benefit thereof redoundeth. By TRANSFERRING; when he intendeth the benefit thereof to some certain person, or persons. And when a man hath in either manner abandoned, or granted away his right; then is he said to be OBLIGED, or BOUND, not to hinder those, to whom such right is granted, or abandoned, from the benefit of it: and that he *ought,* and it is his DUTY, not to make void that voluntary act of his own: and that such hindrance is INJUSTICE, and INJURY, as being *sine jure;* the right being before renounced, or transferred. So that *injury,* or *injustice,* in the controversies of the world, is somewhat like to that, which in the disputations of scholars is called *absurdity*. For as it is there called an absurdity, to contradict what one maintained in the beginning: so in the world, it is called injustice, and injury, voluntarily to undo that, which from the beginning he had voluntarily done. The way by which a man either simply renounceth, or transferreth his right, is a declaration, or signification, by some voluntary and sufficient sign, or signs, that he doth so renounce, or transfer; or hath so renounced, or transferred the same, to him that accepteth it. And these signs are either words only, or actions only; or, as it happeneth most often, both words, and actions. And the same are the BONDS, by which men are bound, and obliged: bonds, that have their strength, not from their own nature, for nothing is more easily broken than a man's word, but from fear of some evil consequence upon the rupture.

Whensoever a man transferreth his right, or renounceth it; it is either in consideration of some right reciprocally transferred to himself; or for some other good he hopeth for thereby. For it is a voluntary act: and of the voluntary acts of every man, the object is some *good to himself*. And therefore there be some rights, which no man can be understood by any words, or other signs, to have abandoned, or transferred. As first a man cannot lay down the right of resisting them, that assault him by force, to take away his life; because he cannot be understood to aim thereby, at any good to himself. The same may be said of wounds, and chains, and imprisonment; both because there is no benefit consequent to such patience; as there is to the patience of suffering another to be wounded, or imprisoned: as also because a man cannot tell, when he seeth men proceed against him by violence, whether they intend his death or not. And lastly the motive, and end for which this renouncing, and transferring of right is introduced, is nothing else but the security of a man's person, in his life, and in the means of so preserving life, as not to be weary of it. And therefore if a man by words, or other signs, seem to despoil himself of the end, for which those signs were intended; he is not to be understood as if he meant it, or that it was his will; but that he was ignorant of how such words and actions were to be interpreted.

The mutual transferring of right, is that which men call CONTRACT.

There is difference between transferring of right to the thing; and transferring, or tradition, that is delivery of the thing itself. For the thing may be delivered together with the translation of the right; as in buying and selling with ready-money; or exchange of goods, or lands: and it may be delivered some time after.

Again, one of the contractors, may deliver the thing contracted for on his part, and leave the other to perform his part at some determinate time after, and in the mean time be trusted; and then the contract on his part, is called PACT, or COVENANT: or both parts may contract now, to perform hereafter: in which cases, he that is to perform in time to come, being trusted, his performance is called *keeping of promise,* or faith; and the failing of performance, if it be voluntary, *violation of faith.*

When the transferring of right, is not mutual: but one of the parties transferreth, in hope to gain thereby friendship, or service from another, or from his friends; or in hope to gain the reputation of charity, or magnanimity; or to deliver his mind from the pain of compassion; or in hope of reward in heaven; this is not contract, but GIFT, FREE-GIFT, GRACE: which words signify one and the same thing.

Signs of contract, are either *express,* or *by inference.* Express, are words spoken with understanding of what they signify: and such words are either of the time *present,* or *past;* as, *I give, I grant, I have given, I have granted, I will that this be yours:* or of the future; as, *I will give, I will grant:* which words of the future are called PROMISE.

Signs by inference, are sometimes the consequence of words: sometimes the consequence of silence; sometimes the consequence of actions; sometimes the consequence of forbearing an action: and generally a sign by inference, of any contract, is whatsoever sufficiently argues the will of the contractor.

Words alone, if they be of the time to come, and contain a bare promise, are an insufficient sign of a free-gift, and therefore not obligatory. For if they be of the time to come, as *to-morrow I will give,* they are a sign I have not given yet, and consequently that my right is not transferred, but remaineth till I transfer it by some other act. But if the words be of the time present, or past, as, *I have given,* or, *do give to be delivered to-morrow,* then is my to-morrow's right given away to day; and that by the virtue of the words, though there were no other argument of my will. And there is a great difference in the signification of these words, *volo hoc tuum esse cras,* and *cras dabo;* that is, between *I will that this be thine to-morrow,* and, *I will give it thee to-morrow:* for the word *I will,* in the former manner of speech, signifies an act of the will present; but in the latter, it signifies a promise of an act of the will to come: and therefore the former words, being of the present, transfer a future right; the latter, that be of the future, transfer nothing. But if there be other signs of the will to transfer a right, besides words; then, though the gift be free, yet may the right be understood to pass by words of the future: as if a man propound a prize to him that comes first to the end of a race, the gift is free; and though the words be of the future, yet the right passeth: for if he would not have his words so be understood, he should not have let them run.

In contracts, the right passeth, not only where the words are of the time present, or past, but also where they are of the future: because all contract is mutual translation, or change of right; and therefore he that promiseth only, because he hath already received the benefit for which he promiseth, is to be understood as if he intended the right should pass: for unless he had been content to have his words so understood, the other would not have performed his part first. And for that cause, in buying, and selling, and other acts of contract, a promise is equivalent to a convenant; and therefore obligatory.

He that performeth first in the case of a contract, is said to MERIT that which he is to receive by the performance of the other; and he hath it as *due*. Also when a prize is propounded to many, which is to be given to him only that winneth; or money is thrown amongst many, to be enjoyed by them that catch it; though this be a free gift; yet so to win, or so to catch, is to *merit,* and to have it as DUE. For the right is transferred in the propounding of the prize, and in throwing down the money; though it be not determined to whom, but by the event of the contention. But there is between these two sorts of merit, this difference, that in contract, I merit by virtue of my own power, and the contractor's need; but in this case of free gift, I am enabled to merit only by the benignity of the giver: in contract, I merit at the contractor's hand that he should depart with his right; in this case of gift, I merit not that the giver should part with his right; but that when he has parted with it, it should be mine, rather than another's. And this I think to be the meaning of that distinction of the Schools, between *meritum congrui,* and *meritum condigni.* For God Almighty, having promised Paradise to those men, hoodwinked with carnal desires, that can walk through this world according to the precepts, and limits prescribed by him; they say, he that shall so walk, shall merit Paradise *ex congruo.* But because no man can demand a right to it, by his own righteousness, or any other power in himself, but by the free grace of God only; they say, no man can merit Paradise *ex condigno.* This I say, I think is the meaning of that distinction; but because disputers do not agree upon the signification of their own terms of art, longer than it serves their turn; I will not affirm any thing of their meaning: only this I say; when a gift is given indefinitely, as a prize to be contended for, he that winneth meriteth, and may claim the prize as due.

If a covenant be made, wherein neither of the parties perform presently, but trust one another; in the condition of mere nature, which is a condition of war of every man against every man, upon any reasonable suspicion, it is void: but if there be a common power set over them both, with right and force sufficient to compel performance, it is not void. For he that performeth first, has no assurance the other will perform after; because the bonds of words are too weak to bridle men's ambition, avarice, anger, and other passions, without the fear of some coercive power; which in the condition of mere nature, where all men are equal, and judges of the justness of their own fears, cannot possibly be supposed. And therefore he which performeth first, does but betray himself to his enemy; contrary to the right, he can never abandon, of defending his life, and means of living.

But in a civil estate, where there is a power set up to constrain those that would otherwise violate their faith, that fear is no more reasonable; and for that cause, he which by the covenant is to perform first, is obliged so to do.

The cause of fear, which maketh such a covenant invalid, must be always something arising after the convenant made; as some new fact, or other sign of the will not to perform: else it cannot make the covenant void. For that which could not hinder a man from promising, ought not to be admitted as a hindrance of performing.

He that transferreth any right, transferreth the means of enjoying it, as far as lieth in his power. As he that selleth land, is understood to transfer the herbage, and whatsoever grows upon it: nor can he that sells a mill turn away the stream that drives it. And they that give to a man the right of government in sovereignty, are understood to give him the right of levying money to maintain soldiers; and of appointing magistrates for the administration of justice. . . .

OF OTHER LAWS OF NATURE

From that law of nature, by which we are obliged to transfer to another, such rights, as being retained, hinder the peace of mankind, there followeth a third; which is this, *that men perform their covenants made:* without which, covenants are in vain, and but empty words; and the right of all men to all things remaining, we are still in the condition of war.

And in this law of nature, consisteth the fountain and original of JUSTICE. For where no covenant hath preceded, there hath no right been transferred, and every man has right to every thing; and consequently, no action can be unjust. But when a covenant is made, then to break it is *unjust:* and the definition of INJUSTICE, is no other than *the not performance of covenant.* And whatsoever is not unjust, is *just.*

But because covenants of mutual trust, where there is a fear of not performance on either part, as hath been said in the former chapter, are invalid; though the original of justice be the making of covenants; yet injustice actually there can be none, till the cause of such fear be taken away; which while men are in the natural condition of war, cannot be done. Therefore before the names of just, and unjust can have place, there must be some coercive power, to compel men equally to the performance of their covenants, by the terror of some punishment, greater than the benefit they expect by the breach of their covenant; and to make good that propriety, which by mutual contract men acquire, in recompense of the universal right they abandon: and such power there is none before the erection of a commonwealth. And this is also to be gathered out of the ordinary definition of justice in the Schools: for they say, that *justice is the constant will of giving to every man his own.* And therefore where there is no *own,* that is no propriety, there is no injustice; and where there is no coercive power erected, that is, where there is no commonwealth, there is no propriety; all men having right to all things: therefore where there is no commonwealth, there nothing is unjust. So that the nature of justice, consisteth in keeping of valid covenants: but the validity of covenants begins not but with the constitution of a civil power, sufficient to compel men to keep them: and then it is also that propriety begins.

The fool hath said in his heart, there is no such thing as justice; and sometimes also with his tongue; seriously alleging, that every man's conservation, and contentment, being committed to his own care, there could be no reason, why every man might not do what he thought conduced thereunto: and therefore also to make, or not make; keep, or not keep convenants, was not against reason, when it conduced to one's benefit. He does not therein deny, that there be covenants; and that they are sometimes broken, sometimes kept; and that such breach of them may be called injustice, and the observance of them justice: but the questioneth, whether injustice, taking away the fear of God, for the same fool hath said in his heart there is no God, may not sometimes stand with that reason, which dictateth to every man his own good; and particularly then, when it conduceth to such a benefit, as shall put a man in a condition, to neglect not only the dispraise, and revilings, but also the power of other men. The kingdom of God is gotten by violence: but what if it could be gotten by unjust violence? were it against reason so to get it, when it is impossible to receive hurt by it? and if it be not against reason, it is not against justice; or else justice is not to be approved for good. From such reasoning as this, successful wickedness hath obtained the name of virtue: and some that in all other things have disallowed the violation of faith; yet have allowed it, when it is for the getting of a kingdom. And the heathen that believed, that Saturn was deposed by his son Jupiter, believed nevertheless the same Jupiter to be the avenger of injustice: somewhat like to a piece of law in Coke's *Commentaries on Littleton;* where he says, if the right heir of the crown to be attainted of treason; yet the crown shall descend to him, and *eo instante* the attainder be void: from which instances a man will be very prone to infer; that when the heir apparent of a kingdom, shall kill him that is in possession, though his father; you may call it injustice, or by what other name you will; yet it can never be against reason, seeing all the voluntary actions of men tend to the benefit of themselves; and those actions are most reasonable, that conduce most to their ends. This specious reasoning is nevertheless false.

For the question is not of promise mutual, where there is no security of performance on either side; as when there is no civil power erected over the parties promising; for such promises are no covenants: but either where one of the parties has performed already; or where there is a power to make him perform; there is the question whether it be against reason, that is, against the benefit of the other to perform, or not. And I say it is not against reason. For the manifestation whereof, we are to consider; first, that when a man doth a thing, which notwithstanding any thing can be foreseen, and reckoned on, tendeth to his own destruction, howsoever some accident which he could not expect, arriving may turn it to his benefit; yet such events do not make it reasonably or wisely done. Secondly, that in a condition of war, wherein every man to every man, for want of a common power to keep them all in awe, is an enemy, there is no man who can hope by his own strength, or wit, to defend himself from destruction, without the help of confederates; where every one expects the same defence by the confederation, that any one else does: and therefore he which declares he thinks it reason to deceive those that help him, can in reason expect no other means of safety, than what can be had from his own single power. He therefore that breaketh his covenant, and consequently declareth that he thinks he may with reason do so, cannot be received into any society, that unite themselves for peace and defence, but by the error of them that receive him; nor when he is received, be retained in it, without seeing the danger of their error; which errors a man cannot reasonably reckon upon as the means of his security: and therefore if he be left, or cast out of society, he perisheth; and if he live in society, it is by the errors of other men, which he could not foresee, nor reckon upon; and consequently against the reason of his preservation; and so, as all men that contribute not to his destruction, forbear him only out of ignorance of what is good for themselves.

As for the instance of gaining the secure and perpetual felicity of heaven, by any way; it is frivolous: there being but one way imaginable; and that is not breaking, but keeping of covenant.

And for the other instance of attaining sovereignty by rebellion; it is manifest, that though the event follow, yet because it cannot reasonably be expected, but rather the contrary; and because by gaining it so, others are taught to gain the same in like manner, the attempt thereof is against reason. Justice therefore, that is to say, keeping of covenant, is a rule of reason, by which we are forbidden to do any thing destructive to our life; and consequently a law of nature.

There be some that proceed further; and will not have the law of nature, to be those rules which conduce to the preservation of man's life on earth; but to the attaining of an eternal felicity after death; to which they think the breach of covenant may conduce; and consequently be just and reasonable; such are they that think it a work of merit to kill, or depose, or rebel against, the sovereign power constituted over them by their own consent. But because there is no natural knowledge of man's estate after death; much less of the reward that is then to be given to breach of faith; but only a belief grounded upon other men's saying, that they know it supernaturally, or that they know those, that knew them, that knew others, that knew it supernaturally; breach of faith cannot be called a precept of reason, or nature. . . .

OF THE CAUSES, GENERATION, AND DEFINITION OF A COMMONWEALTH

The final cause, end, or design of men, who naturally love liberty, and dominion over others, in the introduction of that restraint upon themselves, in which we see them live in commonwealths, is the foresight of their own preservation, and of a more contented life thereby; that is to say, of getting themselves out from that miserable condition of war, which is necessarily consequent, as hath been shown in chapter XIII, to the natural passions of men, when there is no visible power to keep them in awe, and tie them by fear of punishment to the performance of their covenants, and observation of those laws of nature set down in the fourteenth and fifteenth chapters.

For the laws of nature, as *justice, equality, modesty, mercy,* and, in sum, *doing to others, as we would be done to,* of themselves, without the terror of some power, to cause them to be observed, are contrary to our natural passions, that carry us to partiality, pride, revenge, and the like. And covenants, without the sword, are but words, and of no strength to secure a man at all. Therefore notwithstanding the laws of nature, which every one hath then kept, when he has the will to keep them, when he can do it safely, if there be no power erected, or not great enough for our security; every man will, and may lawfully rely on his own strength and art, for caution against all other men. And in all places, where men have lived by small families, to rob and spoil one another, has been a trade, and so far from being reputed against the law of nature, that the greater spoils they gained, the greater was their honour; and men observed no other laws therein, but the laws of honour; that is, to abstain from cruelty, leaving to men their lives, and instruments of husbandry. And as small families did then; so now do cities and kingdoms which are but greater families, for their own security, enlarge their dominions, upon all pretences of danger, and fear of invasion, or assistance that may be given to invaders, and endeavour as much as they can, to subdue, or weaken their neighbours, by open force, and secret arts, for want of other caution, justly; and are remembered for it in after ages with honour.

Nor is it the joining together of a small number of men, that gives them this security; because in small numbers, small additions on the one side or the other, make the advantage of strength so great, as is sufficient to carry the victory; and therefore gives encouragement to an invasion. The multitude sufficient to confide in for our security, is not determined by any certain number, but by comparison with the enemy we fear; and is then sufficient, when the odds of the enemy is not of so visible and conspicuous moment, to determine the event of war, as to move him to attempt.

And be there never so great a multitude; yet if their actions be directed according to their particular judgments, and particular appetites, they can expect thereby no defence, nor protection, neither against a common enemy, nor against the injuries of one another. For being distracted in opinions concerning the best use and application of their strength, they do not help but hinder one another; and reduce their strength by mutual opposition to nothing: whereby they are easily, not only subdued by a very few that agree together; but also when there is no common enemy, they make war upon each other, for their particular interests. For if we could suppose a great multitude of men to consent in the observation of justice, and other laws of nature, without a common power to keep them all in awe; we might as well suppose all mankind to do the same; and then there neither would be, nor need to be any civil government, or commonwealth at all; because there would be peace without subjection.

Nor is it enough for the security, which men desire should last all the time of their life, that they be governed, and directed by one judgment, for a limited time; as in one battle, or one war. For though they obtain a victory by their unanimous endeavour against a foreign enemy; yet afterwards, when either they have no common enemy, or he that by one part is held for an enemy, is by another part held for a friend, they must needs by the difference of their interests dissolve, and fall again into a war amongst themselves. . . .

The only way to erect such a common power, as may be able to defend them from the invasion of foreigners, and the injuries of one another, and thereby to secure them in such sort, as that by their own industry, and by the fruits of the earth, they may nourish themselves and live contentedly; is, to confer all their power and strength upon one man, or upon one assembly of men, that may reduce all their wills, by plurality of voices, unto one will: which is as much as to say, to appoint one man, or assembly of men, to bear their person; and every one to own, and acknowledge himself to be author of whatsoever he that so beareth their person, shall act, or cause to be acted, in those things which concern the common peace and safety; and therein to submit their wills, every one to his will, and their judgments, to his judgment. This is more than consent, or concord; it is a real unity of them all, in one and the same person, made by covenant of every man with every man, in such manner, as if every man should say to every man, *I authorise and give up my right of governing myself, to this man, or to this assembly of men, on this condition, that thou give up thy right to him, and authorize all his actions in like manner.* This done, the multitude so united in one person, is called a COMMONWEALTH, in Latin CIVITAS. This is the generation of that great LEVIATHAN, or rather, to speak more reverently, of that *mortal god,* to which we owe under the *immortal God,* our peace and defence. For by this authority, given him by every particular man in the commonwealth, he hath the use of so much power and strength conferred on him, that by terror thereof, he is enabled to perform the wills of them all, to peace at home, and mutual aid against their enemies abroad. And in him consisteth the essence of the commonwealth; which, to define it, is *one person, of whose acts a great multitude, by mutual covenants one with another, have made themselves every one the author, to the end he may use the strength and means of them all, as he shall think expedient, for their peace and common defence.*

And he that carrieth this person, is called SOVEREIGN, and said to have *sovereign power;* and every one besides, his SUBJECT.

The attaining to this sovereign power, is by two ways. One, by natural force; as when a man maketh his children, to submit themselves, and their children to his government, as being able to destroy them if they refuse; or by war subdueth his enemies to his will, giving them their lives on that condition. The other, is when men agree amongst themselves, to submit to some man, or assembly of men, voluntarily, on confidence to be protected by him against all others. This latter, may be called a political commonwealth, or commonwealth by *institution;* and the former, a commonwealth by *acquisition*. At first, I shall speak of a commonwealth by institution.

OF THE RIGHTS OF SOVEREIGNS BY INSTITUTION

A *commonwealth* is said to be *instituted*, when a *multitude* of men do agree, and *covenant, every one, with every one,* that to whatsoever *man,* or *assembly of men,* shall be given by the major part, the *right to present* the person of them all, that is to say, to be their *representative;* every one, as well he that *voted for it,* as he that *voted against it,* shall *authorize* all the actions and judgments, of that man, or assembly of men, in the same manner, as if they were his own, to the end, to live peaceably amongst themselves, and be protected against other men.

From this institution of a commonwealth are derived all the *rights,* and *faculties* of him, or them, on whom sovereign power is conferred by the consent of the people assembled.

First, because they covenant, it is to be understood, they are not obliged by former covenant to anything repugnant hereunto. And consequently they that have already instituted a commonwealth, being thereby bound by covenant, to own the actions, and judgments of one, cannot lawfully make a new covenant, amongst themselves, to be obedient to any other, in any thing whatsoever, without his permission. And therefore, they that are subjects to a monarch, cannot without his leave cast off monarchy, and return to the confusion of a disunited multitude; nor transfer their person from him that beareth it, to another man, or other assembly of men: for they are bound, every man to every man, to own, and be reputed author of all, that he that already is their sovereign, shall do, and judge fit to be done: so that any one man dissenting, all the rest should break their covenant made to that man, which is injustice: and they have also every man given the sovereignty to him that beareth their person; and therefore if they depose him, they take from him that which is his own, and so again it is injustice. Besides, if he that attempteth to depose his sovereign, be killed, or punished by him for such attempt, he is author of his own punishment, as being by the institution, author of all his sovereign shall do: and because it is injustice for a man to do anything, for which he may be punished by his own authority, he is also upon that title, unjust. And whereas some men have pretended for their disobedience to their sovereign, a new covenant, made, not with men, but with God; this also is unjust: for there is no covenant with God, but by meditation of somebody that representeth God's person; which none doth but God's lieutenant, who hath the sovereignty under God. But this pretence of covenant with God, is so evident a lie, even in the pretenders' own consciences, that it is not only an act of an unjust, but also of a vile, and unmanly disposition.

Secondly, because the right of bearing the person of them all, is given to him they make sovereign, by covenant only of one to another, and not of him to any of them; there can happen no breach of covenant on the part of the sovereign; and consequently none of his subjects, by any pretence of forfeiture, can be freed from his subjection. That he which is made sovereign maketh no covenant with his subjects beforehand, is manifest; because either he must make it with the whole multitude, as one party to the covenant; or he must make a several covenant with every man. With the whole, as one party, it is impossible; because as yet they are not one person: and if he make so many several covenants as there be men, those covenants after he hath the sovereignty are void; because what act soever can be pretended by any one of them for breach thereof, is the act both of himself, and of all the rest, because done in the person, and by the right of every one of them in particular. Besides, if any one, or more of them, pretend a breach of the covenant made by the sovereign at his institution; and others, or one other of his subjects, or himself alone, pretend there was no such breach, there is in this case, no judge to decide the controversy; it returns therefore to the sword again; and every man recovereth the right of protecting himself by his own strength, contrary to the design they had in the institution. It is therefore in vain to grant sovereignty by way of precedent covenant. The opinion that any monarch receiveth his power by covenant, that is to say, on condition, proceedeth from want of understanding this easy truth, that covenants being but words and breath, have no force to oblige, contain, constrain, or protect any man, but what it has from the public sword; that is, from the untied hands of that man, or assembly of men that hath the sovereignty, and whose actions are avouched by them all, and performed by the strength of them all, in him united. But when an assembly of men is made sovereign; then no man imagineth any such covenant to have passed in the institution; for no man is so dull as to say, for example, the people of Rome made a covenant with the Romans, to hold the sovereignty on such or such conditions; which not performed, the Romans might lawfully depose the Roman people. That men see not the reason to be alike in a monarchy, and in a popular government, proceedeth from the ambition of some, that are kinder to the government of an assembly, whereof they may hope to participate, than of monarchy, which they despair to enjoy.

Thirdly, because the major part hath by consenting voices declared a sovereign; he that dissented must now consent with the rest; that is, be contented to avow all the actions he shall do, or else justly be destroyed by the rest. For if he voluntarily entered into the congregation of them that were assembled, he sufficiently declared thereby his will, and therefore tacitly covenanted, to stand to what the major part should ordain: and therefore if he refuse to stand thereto, or make protestation against any of their decrees, he does contrary to his covenant, and therefore unjustly. And whether he be of the congregation, or not; and whether his consent be asked, or not, he must either submit to their decrees, or be left in the condition of war he was in before; wherein he might without injustice be destroyed by any man whatsoever.

Fourthly, because every subject is by this institution author of all the actions, and judgements of the sovereign instituted; it follows, that whatsoever he doth, it can be no injury to any of his subjects; nor ought he to be by any of them accused of injustice. For he that doth anything by authority from another, doth therein no injury to him by whose authority he acteth: but by this institution of a commonwealth, every particular man is author of all the sovereign doth: and consequently he that complaineth of injury from his sovereign, complaineth of that whereof he himself is author; and therefore ought not to accuse any man but himself; no nor himself of injury; because to do injury to one's self, is impossible. It is true that they that have sovereign power may commit iniquity; but not injustice, or injury in the proper signification.

Fifthly, and consequently to that which was said last, no man that hath sovereign power can justly be put to death, or otherwise in any manner by his subjects punished. For seeing every subject is author of the actions of his sovereign; he punisheth another for the actions committed by himself.

And because the end of this institution, is the peace and defence of them all; and whosoever has right to the end, has right to the means; it belongeth of right, to whatsoever man, or assembly that hath the sovereignty, to be judge both of the means of peace and defence, and also of the hindrances, and disturbances of the same; and to do whatsoever he shall think necessary to be done, both beforehand, for the preserving of peace and security, by prevention of discord at home, and hostility from abroad; and, when peace and security are lost, for the recovery of the same. And therefore,

Sixthly, it is annexed to the sovereignty, to be judge of what opinions and doctrines are averse, and what conducing to peace; and subsequently, on what occasions, how far, and what men are to be trusted withal, in speaking to multitudes of people; and who shall examine the doctrines of all books before they be published. For the actions of men proceed from their opinions; and in the well-governing of opinions, consisteth the well-governing of men's actions, in order to their peace, and concord. And though in matter of doctrine, nothing ought to be regarded but the truth; yet this is not repugnant to regulating the same by peace. For doctrine repugnant to peace, can no more be true, than peace and concord can be against the law of nature. It is true, that in a commonwealth, where by the negligence, or unskilfulness of governors, and teachers, false doctrines are by time generally received; the contrary truths may be generally offensive. Yet the most sudden, and rough bursting in of a new truth, that can be, does never break the peace, but only sometimes awake the war. For those men that are so remissly governed, that they dare take up arms to defend, or introduce an opinion, are still in war; and their condition not peace, but only a cessation of arms for fear of one another; and they live, as it were, in the precincts of battle continually. It belongeth therefore to him that hath the sovereign power, to be judge, or constitute all judges of opinions and doctrines, as a thing necessary to peace; thereby to prevent discord and civil war.

Seventhly, is annexed to the sovereignty, the whole power of prescribing the rules, whereby every man may know, what goods he may enjoy, and what actions he may do, without being molested by any of his fellow-subjects; and this is it men call *propriety*. For before constitution of sovereign power, as hath already been shown, all men had right to all things; which necessarily causeth war: and therefore this propriety, being necessary to peace, and depending on sovereign power, is the act of that power, in order to the public peace. These rules of propriety, or *meum* and *tuum,* and of *good, evil, lawful,* and *unlawful* in the actions of subjects, are the civil laws; that is to say, the laws of each commonwealth in particular; though the name of civil law be now restrained to the ancient civil laws of the city of Rome; which being the head of a great part of the world, her laws at that time were in these parts the civil law.

Eighthly, is annexed to the sovereignty, the right of judicature: that is to say, of hearing and deciding all controversies, which may arise concerning law, either civil, or natural; or concerning fact. For without the decision of controversies, there is no protection of one subject, against the injuries of another; the laws concerning *meum* and *tuum* are in vain; and to every man remaineth, from the natural and necessary appetite of his own conservation, the right of protecting himself by his private strength, which is the condition of war, and contrary to the end for which every commonwealth is instituted. . . .

State of Nature

John Locke

OF CIVIL-GOVERNMENT

Chap. I. § **1.** It having been shewn in the foregoing discourse,

1. That *Adam* had not, either by natural right of fatherhood, or by positive donation from God, any such authority over his children, or dominion over the world, as is pretended:

2. That if he had, his heirs, yet, had no right to it:

3. That if his heirs had, there being no law of nature nor positive law of God that determines which is the right heir in all cases that may arise, the right of succession, and consequently of bearing rule, could not have been certainly determined:

4. That if even that had been determined, yet the knowledge of which is the eldest line of *Adam's* posterity, being so long since utterly lost, that in the races of mankind and families of the world, there remains not to one above another, the least pretence to be the eldest house, and to have the right of inheritance:

All these premises having, as I think, been clearly made out, it is impossible that the rulers now on earth should make any benefit, or derive any the least shadow of authority from that, which is held to be the fountain of all power, *Adam's private dominion and paternal jurisdiction;* so that he that will not give just occasion to think that all government in the world is the product only of force and violence, and that men live together by no other rules but that of beasts, where the strongest carries it, and so lay a foundation for perpetual disorder and mischief, tumult, sedition and rebellion, (things that the followers of that hypothesis so loudly cry out against) must of necessity find out another rise of government, another original of political power, and another way of designing and knowing the persons that have it, than what Sir *Robert Filmer* hath taught us.

§ **2.** To this purpose, I think it may not be amiss, to set down what I take to be political power; that the power of a *magistrate* over a subject may be distinguished from that of a *father* over his children, a *master* over his servant, a *husband* over his wife, and a *lord* over his slave. All which distinct powers happening sometimes together in the same man, if he be considered under these different relations, it may help us to distinguish these powers one from another, and shew the difference betwixt a ruler of a commonwealth, a father of a family, and a captain of a galley.

§ **3.** *Political power,* then, I take to be a *right* of making laws with penalties of death, and consequently all less penalties, for the regulating and preserving of property, and of employing the force of the community, in the execution of such laws, and in the defence of the common-wealth from the foreign injury; and all this only for the public good.

Excerpted from John Locke, *Two Treatises of Government* (first edition 1690, selections from the 1764 edition), Book II, Chapters I, II, III, IV, VII, and IX.

Of the State of Nature

§ **4.** To understand political power right, and derive it from its original, we must consider, what state all men are naturally in, and that is, a *state of perfect freedom* to order their actions, and dispose of their possessions and persons, as they think fit, within the bounds of the law of nature, without asking leave, or depending upon the will of any other man.

A *state* also *of equality,* wherein all the power and jurisdiction is reciprocal, no one having more than another; there being nothing more evident, than that creatures of the same species and rank, promiscuously born to all the same advantages of nature, and the use of the same faculties, should also be equal one amongst another without subordination or subjection, unless the lord and master of them all should, by any manifest declaration of his will, set one above another, and confer on him, by an evident and clear appointment, an undoubted right to dominion and sovereignty. . . .

§ **6.** But though this be a *state of liberty,* yet *it is not a state of licence:* though man in that state have an uncontroulable liberty to dispose of his person or possessions, yet he has not liberty to destroy himself, or so much as any creature in his possession, but where some nobler use than its bare preservation calls for it. The *state of nature* has a law of nature to govern it, which obliges every one: and reason, which is that law, teaches all mankind, who will but consult it, that being all *equal and independent,* no one ought to harm another in his life, health, liberty, or possessions: for men being all the workmanship of one omnipotent, and infinitely wise maker; all the servants of one sovereign master, sent into the world by his order, and about his business; they are his property, whose worksmanship they are, made to last during his, not one another's pleasure: and being furnished with like faculties, sharing all in one community of nature, there cannot be supposed any such *subordination* among us, that may authorize us to destroy one another, as if we were made for one another's uses, as the inferior ranks of creatures are for our's. Every one, as he is *bound to preserve himself,* and not to quit his station wilfully, so by the like reason, when his own preservation comes not in competition, ought he, as much as he can, *to preserve the rest of mankind,* and may not, unless it be to do justice on an offender, take away, or impair the life, or what tends to the preservation of the life, the liberty, health, limb, or goods of another.

§ **7.** And that all men be restrained from invading others rights, and from doing hurt to one another, and the law of nature be observed, which willeth the peace and *preservation of all mankind,* the *execution* of the law of nature is, in that state, put into every man's hands, whereby every one has a right to punish the transgressors of that law to such a degree, as may hinder its violation: for the *law of nature* would, as all other laws that concern men in this world, be in vain, if there were no body that in the state of nature had a *power to execute* that law, and thereby preserve the innocent and restrain offenders. And if any one in the state of nature may punish another for any evil he has done, every one may do so: for in that *state of perfect equality,* where naturally there is no superiority or jurisdiction of one over another, what any may do in prosecution of that law, every one must needs have a right to do.

§ **8.** And thus, in the state of nature, *one man comes by a power over another;* but yet no absolute or arbitrary power, to use a criminal, when he has got him in his hands, according to the passionate heats, or boundless extravagancy of his own will; but only to retribute to him, so far as calm reason and conscience dictate, what is proportionate to his transgression, which is so much as may serve for *reparation* and *re-straint:* for these two are the only reasons, why one man may lawfully do harm to another, which is that we call *punishment.* In transgressing the law of nature, the offender declares himself to live by another rule than that of reason and common equity, which is that measure God has set to the actions of men, for their mutual security; and so he becomes dangerous to mankind, the tye, which is to secure them from injury and violence, being slighted and broken by him. Which being a trespass against the whole species, and the peace and safety of it, provided for by the law of nature, every man upon this score, by the right he hath to preserve mankind in general, may restrain, or where it is necessary, destroy things noxious to them, and so may bring such evil on any one, who hath transgressed that law, as may make him repent the doing of it, and thereby deter him, and by his example others, from doing the like mischief. And in the case, and upon this ground, *every man hath a right to punish the offender, and be executioner of the law of nature.*

   § **9.** I doubt not but this will seem a very strange doctrine to some men: but before they condemn it, I desire them to resolve me, by what right any prince or state can put to death, or *punish an alien,* for any crime he commits in their country. It is certain their laws, by virtue of any sanction they receive from the promulgated will of the legislative, reach not a stranger: they speak not to him, nor, if they did, is he bound to hearken to them. The legislative authority, by which they are in force over the subjects of that common-wealth, hath no power over him. Those who have the supreme power of making laws in *England, France* or *Holland,* are to an *Indian,* but like the rest of the world, men without authority: and therefore, if by the law of nature every man hath not a power to punish offences against it, as he soberly judges the case to require, I see not how the magistrates of any community can *punish an alien* of another country; since, in reference to him, they can have no more power than what every man naturally may have over another. . . .

   § **14.** It is often asked as a mighty objection, *where are,* or ever were there any *men in such a state of nature?* To which it may suffice as an answer at present, that since all princes and rulers of *independent* governments all through the world, are in a state of nature, it is plain the world never was, nor ever will be, without numbers of men in that state. I have named all governors of *independent communities,* whether they are, or are not, in league with others: for it is not every compact that puts an end to the state of nature between men, but only this one of agreeing together mutually to enter into one community, and make one body politic; other promises, and compacts, men may make one with another, and yet still be in the state of nature. The promises and bargains for truck, *&c.* between the two men in the desert island, mentioned by *Garcilasso de la Vega,* in his history of *Peru;* or between a *Swiss* and an *Indian,* in the woods of *America,* are binding to them, though they are perfectly in a state of nature, in reference to one another: for truth and keeping of faith belongs to men, as men, and not as members of society.

   § **15.** To those that say, there were never any men in the state of nature, I will not only oppose the authority of the judicious *Hooker, Eccl. Pol. lib.* i. *sect.* 10. where he says, *The laws which have been hitherto mentioned,* i.e. the laws of nature, *do bind men absolutely, even as they are men, although they have never any settled fellowship, never any solemn agreement amongst themselves what to do, or not to do: but forasmuch as we are not by ourselves sufficient to furnish ourselves with competent store of things, needful for such a life as our nature doth desire, a life fit for the dignity of man;*

therefore to supply those defects and imperfections which are in us, as living single and solely by ourselves, we are naturally induced to seek communion and fellowship with others: this was the cause of men's uniting themselves at first in politic societies. But I moreover affirm, that all men are naturally in that state, and remain so, till by their own consents they make themselves members of some politic society; and I doubt not in the sequel of this discourse, to make it very clear.

Of the State of War

§ **16.** The *state of war* is a state of *enmity* and *destruction:* and therefore declaring by word or action, not a passionate and hasty, but a sedate settled design upon another man's life, *puts him in a state of war* with him against whom he has declared such an intention, and so has exposed his life to the other's power to be taken away by him, or any one that joins with him in his defence, and espouses his quarrel; it being reasonable and just, I should have a right to destroy that which threatens me with destruction: for, *by the fundamental law of nature, man being to be preserved* as much as possible, when all cannot be preserved, the safety of the innocent is to be preferred: and one may destroy a man who makes war upon him, or has discovered an enmity to his being, for the same reason that he may kill a *wolf* or a *lion;* because such men are not under the ties of the commonlaw of reason, have no other rule, but that of force and violence, and so may be treated as beasts of prey, those dangerous and noxious creatures, that will be sure to destroy him whenever he falls into their power.

§ **17.** And hence it is, that he who attempts to get another man into his absolute power, does thereby *put himself into a state of war* with him; it being to be understood as a declaration of a design upon his life: for I have reason to conclude, that he who would get me into his power without my consent, would use me as he pleased when he had got me there, and destroy me too when he had a fancy to it; for no body can desire to *have me in his absolute power,* unless it be to compel me by force to that which is against the right of my freedom, *i.e.* make me a slave. To be free from such force is the only security of my preservation; and reason bids me look on him, as an enemy to my preservation, who would take away that *freedom* which is the fence to it; so that he who makes an *attempt to enslave* me, thereby puts himself into a state of war with me. He that, in the state of nature, *would take away the freedom* that belongs to any one in that state, must necessarily be supposed to have a design to take away every thing else, that *freedom* being the foundation of all the rest; as he that, in the state of society, would take away the *freedom* belonging to those of that society or commonwealth, must be supposed to design to take away from them everything else, and so be looked on as *in a state of war*.

§ **18.** This makes it lawful for a man to *kill a thief,* who has not in the least hurt him, nor declared any design upon his life, any farther than, by the use of force, so to get him in his power, as to take away his money, or what he pleases, from him; because using force, where he has no right, to get me into his power, let his pretence be what it will, I have no reason to suppose, that he, who would *take away my liberty,* would not, when he had me in his power, take away everything else. And therefore it is lawful for me to treat him as one who has *put himself into a state of war* with me, *i.e.* kill him if I can; for to that hazard does he justly expose himself, whoever introduces a state of war, and is aggressor in it.

§ **19.** And here we have the plain *difference between the state of nature and the* *state of war,* which however some men have confounded, are as far distant, as a state of peace, good will, mutual assistance and preservation, and a state of enmity, malice, violence and mutual destruction, are one from another. Men living together according to reason, without a common superior on earth, with authority to judge between them, is *properly the state of nature.* But force, or a declared design of force, upon the person of another, where there is no common superior on earth to appeal to for relief, *is the state of war:* and it is the want of such an appeal gives a man the right of war even against an *aggressor,* tho' he be in society and a fellow subject. Thus a *thief,* whom I cannot harm, but by appeal to the law, for having stolen all that I am worth, I may kill, when he sets on me to rob me but of my horse or coat; because the law, which was made for my preservation, where it cannot interpose to secure my life from present force, which, if lost, is capable of no reparation, permits me my own defence, and the right of war, a liberty to kill the aggressor, because the aggressor allows not time to appeal to our common judge, nor the decision of the law, for remedy in a case where the mischief may be irreparable. Want of a common judge with authority, puts all men in a state of nature: force without right, upon a man's person, makes a state of war, both where there is, and is not, a common judge.

§ 20. But when the actual force is over, the *state of war ceases* between those that are in society, and are equally on both sides subjected to the fair determination of the law; because then there lies open the remedy of appeal for the past injury, and to prevent future harm: but where no such appeal is, as in the state of nature, for want of positive laws, and judges with authority to appeal to, the state of war once begun, continues, with a right to the innocent party to destroy the other whenever he can, until the aggressor offers peace, and desires reconciliation on such terms as may repair any wrongs he has already done, and secure the innocent for the future; nay, where an appeal to the law, and constituted judges, lies open, but the remedy is denied by a manifest perverting of justice, and a barefaced wresting of the laws to protect or indemnify the violence or injuries of some men, or party of men, *there* it is hard to imagine any thing but *a state of war:* for where-ever violence is used, and injury done, though by hands appointed to administer justice, it is still violence and injury, however coloured with the name, pretences, or forms of law, the end whereof being to protect and redress the innocent, by an unbiassed application of it, to all who are under it; where-ever that is not *bona fide* done, *war is made* upon the sufferers, who having no appeal on earth to right them, they are left to the only remedy in such cases, an appeal to heaven.

§ 21. To avoid this *state of war* (wherein there is no appeal but to heaven, and wherein every the least difference to apt to end, where there is no authority to decide between the contenders) is one great reason of men's putting themselves into society, and quitting the state of nature: for where there is an authority, a power on earth, from which relief can be had by *appeal,* there the continuance of the *state of war* is excluded, and the controversy is decided by that power. Had there been any such court, any superior jurisdiction on earth, to determine the right between *Jephtha* and the *Ammonites,* they had never come to a *state of war:* but we see he was forced to appeal to heaven. *The Lord the Judge* (says he) *be judge this day between the children of* Israel *and the children of* Ammon, *Judg. xi. 27.* and then prosecuting, and relying on his *appeal,* he leads out his army to battle: and therefore in such controversies, where the question is put, *who shall be judge?* It cannot be meant, who shall decide the controversy; every one knows what *Jephtha* here tells us, that *the Lord the Judge* shall judge.

Where there is no judge on earth, the appeal lies to God in heaven. That question then cannot mean, who shall judge, whether another hath put himself in a *state of war* with me, and whether I may, as *Jephtha* did, *appeal to heaven* in it? of that I myself can only be judge in my own conscience, as I will answer it, at the great day, to the supreme judge of all men.

Of Slavery

§ **22.** The *natural liberty* of man is to be free from any superior power on earth, and not to be under the will or legislative authority of man, but to have only the law of nature for his rule. The *liberty of man,* in society, is to be under no other legislative power, but that established, by consent, in the common-wealth; nor under the dominion of any will, or restraint of any law, but what that legislative shall enact, according to the trust put in it. Freedom then is not what Sir *Robert Filmer* tells us, *Observation A. 55. a liberty for every one to do what he lists, to live as he pleases, and not to be tied by any laws:* but *freedom of men under government* is, to have a standing rule to live by, common to every‚one of that society, and made by the legislative power erected in it; a liberty to follow my own will in all things, where the rule prescribes not; and not to be subject to the inconstant, uncertain, unknown, arbitrary will of another man: as *freedom of nature* is, to be under no other restraint but the law of nature.

§ **23.** This *freedom* from absolute, arbitrary power, is so necessary to, and closely joined with a man's preservation, that he cannot part with it, but by what forfeits his preservation and life together: for a man, not having the power of his own life, *cannot,* by compact, or his own consent, *enslave himself* to any one, nor put himself under the absolute, arbitrary power of another, to take away his life, when he pleases. No body can give more power than he has himself; and he that cannot take away his own life, cannot give another power over it. Indeed, having by his fault forfeited his own life, by some act that deserves death; he, to whom he has forfeited it, may (when he has him in his power) delay to take it, and make use of him to his own service, and he does him no injury by it: for, whenever he finds the hardship of his slavery outweigh the value of his life, it is in his power, by resisting the will of his master, to draw on himself the death he desires.

§ **24.** This is the perfect condition of *slavery,* which is nothing else, but *the state of war continued, between a lawful conqueror and a captive:* for, if once *compact* enter between them, and make an agreement for a limited power on the one side, and obedience on the other, the *state of war and slavery* ceases, as long as the compact endures: for, as has been said, no man can, by agreement, pass over to another that which he hath not in himself, a power over his own life.

I confess, we find among the *Jews,* as well as other nations, that men did sell themselves; but, it is plain, this was only to *drudgery, not to slavery:* for, it is evident, the person sold was not under an absolute, arbitrary, despotical power: for the master could not have power to kill him, at any time, whom, at a certain time, he was obliged to let go free out of his service; and the master of such a servant was so far from having an arbitrary power over his life, that he could not, at pleasure, so much as maim him, but the loss of an eye, or tooth, set him free, *Exod.* xxi. . . .

§ **87.** Man being born, as has been proved, with a title to perfect freedom, and an uncontrouled enjoyment of all the rights and privileges of the law of nature, equally with any other man, or number of men in the world, hath by nature a power, not only to preserve his property, that is, his life, liberty and estate, against the injuries and attempts of other men; but to judge of, and punish the breaches of that law in others, as he is persuaded the offence deserves, even with death itself, in crimes where the heinousness of the fact, in his opinion, requires it. But because no *political society* can be, nor subsist, without having in itself the power to preserve the property, and in order thereunto, punish the offences of all those of that society; there, and there only is *political society,* where every one of the members hath quitted this natural power, resigned it up into the hands of the community in all cases that exclude him not from appealing for protection to the law established by it. And thus all private judgment of every particular member being excluded, the community comes to be umpire, by settled standing rules, indifferent, and the same to all parties; and by men having authority from the community, for the execution of those rules, decides all the differences that may happen between any members of that society concerning any matter of right; and punishes those offences which any member hath committed against the society, with such penalties as the law has established: whereby it is easy to discern, who are, and who are not, in *political society* together. Those who are united into one body, and have a common established law and judicature to appeal to, with authority to decide controversies between them, and punish offenders, are in *civil society* one with another: but those who have no such common appeal, I mean on earth, are still in the state of nature, each being, where there is no other, judge for himself, and executioner; which is, as I have before shewed it, the perfect *state of nature*.

§ **88.** And thus the common-wealth comes by a power to set down what punishment shall belong to the several transgressions which they think worthy of it, committed amongst the members of that society (which is the *power of making laws*) as well as it has the power to punish any injury done unto any of its members, by any one that is not of it (which is the *power of war and peace;*) and all this for the preservation of the property of all the members of that society, as far as is possible. But though every man who has entered into civil society, and is become a member of any commonwealth, has thereby quitted his power to punish offences, against the law of *nature,* in prosecution of his own private judgment, yet with the judgment of offences, which he has given up to the legislative in all cases, where he can appeal to the magistrate, he has given a right to the common-wealth to employ his force, for the execution of the judgments of the common-wealth, whenever he shall be called to it; which indeed are his own judgments, they being made by himself, or his representative. And herein we have the original of the *legislative* and *executive power* of civil society, which is to judge by standing laws, how far offences are to be punished, when committed within the common-wealth; and also to determine, by occasional judgments founded on the present circumstances of the fact, how far injuries from without are to be vindicated; and in both these to employ all the force of all the members, when there shall be need. . . .

Of the Ends of Political Society and Government

§ **123.** If man in the state of nature be so free, as has been said; if he be absolute lord of his own person and possessions, equal to the greatest, and subject to no body, why will he part with his freedom? why will he give up this empire, and subject himself to the dominion and controul of any other power? To which it is obvious to answer, that though in the state of nature he hath such a right, yet the enjoyment of it is very uncertain, and constantly exposed to the invasion of others: for all being kings as much as he, every man his equal, and the greater part no strict observers of equity and justice, the enjoyment of the property he has in this state is very unsafe, very unsecure. This makes him willing to quit a condition, which, however free, is full of fears and continual dangers: and it is not without reason, that he seeks out, and is willing to join in society with others, who are already united, or have a mind to unite, for the mutual *preservation* of their lives, liberties and estates, which I call by the general name, *property*.

§ **124.** The great and *chief end,* therefore, of men's uniting into commonwealths, and putting themselves under government, *is the preservation of their property.* To which in the state of nature there are many things wanting.

First, There wants an *established,* settled, known *law,* received and allowed by common consent to be the standard of right and wrong, and the common measure to decide all controversies between them: for though the law of nature be plain and intelligible to all rational cratures; yet men being biassed by their interest, as well as ignorant for want of study of it, are not apt to allow of it as a law binding to them in the application of it to their particular cases.

§ **125.** *Secondly,* In the state of nature there wants *a known and indifferent judge,* with authority to determine all differences according to the established law: for every one in that state being both judge and executioner of the law of nature, men being partial to themselves, passion and revenge is very apt to carry them too far, and with too much heat, in their own cases; as well as negligence, and unconcernedness, to make them too remiss in other men's.

§ **126.** *Thirdly,* In the state of nature there often wants *power* to back and support the sentence when right, and to *give* it due *execution.* They who by any injustice offended, will seldom fail, where they are able, by force to make good their injustice; such resistance many times makes the punishment dangerous, and frequently destructive, to those who attempt it.

§ **127.** Thus mankind, notwithstanding all the privileges of the state of nature, being but in an ill condition, while they remain in it, are quickly driven into society. Hence it comes to pass, that we seldom find any number of men live any time together in this state. The inconveniences that they are therein exposed to, by the irregular and uncertain exercise of the power every man has of punishing the transgressions of others, make them take sanctuary under the established laws of government, and therein seek *the preservation of their property.* It is this makes them so willingly give up every one his single power of punishing, to be exercised by such alone, as shall be appointed to it amongst them; and by such rules as the community, or those authorized by them to that purpose, shall agree on. And in this we have the original *right and rise of both the legislative and executive power,* as well as of the governments and societies themselves.

§ **128.** For in the state of nature, to omit the liberty he has of innocent delights, a man has two powers.

The first is to do whatsoever he thinks fit for the preservation of himself, and others within the permission of the *law of nature:* by which law, common to them all, he and all the rest of *mankind are one community,* make up one society, distinct from all other creatures. And were it not for the corruption and vitiousness of degenerate men, there would be no need of any other; no necessity that men should separate from this great and natural community, and by positive agreements combine into smaller and divided associations.

The other power a man has in the state of nature, is the *power to punish the crimes* committed against that law. Both these he gives up, when he joins in a private, if I may so call it, or particular politic society, and incorporates into any commonwealth, separate from the rest of mankind.

§ **129.** The first *power,* viz. *of doing whatsoever he thought for the preservation of himself,* and the rest of mankind, *he gives up* to be regulated by laws made by the society, so far forth as the preservation of himself, and the rest of that society shall require; which laws of the society in many things confine the liberty he had by the law of nature.

§ **130.** *Secondly,* The *power of punishing he wholly gives up,* and engages his natural force, (which he might before employ in the execution of the law of nature, by his own single authority, as he thought fit) to assist the executive power of the society, as the law thereof shall require: for being now in a new state, wherein he is to enjoy many conveniencies, from the labour, assistance, and society of others in the same community, as well as protection from its whole strength; he is to part also with as much of his natural liberty, in providing for himself, as the good, prosperity, and safety of the society shall require; which is not only necessary, but just, since the other members of the society do the like.

§ **131.** But though men, when they enter into society, give up the equality, liberty, and executive power they had in the state of nature, into the hands of the society, to be so far disposed of by the legislative, as the good of the society shall require; yet it being only with an intention in every one the better to preserve himself, his liberty and property (for no rational creature can be supposed to change his condition with an intention to be worse); thepower of the society, or *legislative* constituted by them, can *never be supposed to extend farther, than the common good;* but is obliged to secure every one's property, by providing against those three defects above mentioned, that made the state of nature so unsafe and uneasy. And so whoever has the legislative or supreme power of any common-wealth, is bound to govern by established *standing laws,* promulgated and known to the people, and not by extemporary decrees; by *indifferent* and upright *judges,* who are to decide controversies by those laws; and to employ the force of the community at home, *only in the execution of such laws,* or abroad to prevent or redress foreign injuries, and secure the community from inroads and invasion. And all this to be directed to no other *end,* but the *peace, safety,* and *public good* of the people.

On the Social Contract

Jean-Jacques Rousseau

Foreword

This short treatise is taken from a more extensive work, which I undertook in the past without considering my strength, and have long since abandoned. Of the various segments that could be taken from what had been done, this is the most considerable, and seemed to me the least unworthy of being offered to the public. The rest no longer exists.[1]

BOOK I

I want to inquire whether there can be a legitimate and reliable rule of administration in the civil order, taking men as they are and laws as they can be. I shall try always to

---

[1]Rousseau's description of the origin of this project is worth citing at length: "Of the different works I had in progress [in 1756, when Rousseau left Paris to live in the country house of Mme d'Epinay], the one which I had been thinking about for the longest, which occupied me with the greatest pleasure, on which I wanted to work all my life, and which I thought would put the seal on my reputation was my *Institutions Politiques*. I had conceived the first idea for it thirteen or fourteen years earlier, when—being in Venice [as Secretary to the Comte de Montaigu, French Ambassador, in 1743–1744]—I had some occasion to note the defects of that so highly praised Government. Since then, my perspective had been greatly extended by the historical study of morality. I had seen that everything is basically tied to politics, and that, however one tried, no people would ever be anything except what the nature of its Government would make it be. Thus this noble question of the best possible Government seemed to me to boil down to this: What is the nature of the Government suited to form a people that is the most virtuous, the most enlightened, the wisest, and finally the best, to take this word in its noblest sense. I thought I saw that this question was closely tied to the following one, if indeed it was different from it: What is the Government which by its nature always stays the closest to the law? From that, What is the law? and a series of questions of this importance. I saw that all this led me to great truths, useful to the happiness of the human race, but above all to that of my country." *Confessions,* VIII (Pléiade, I, 404–405). Rousseau goes on to say that "although I had already been working on this project for five or six years, it had hardly gotten ahead" (Ibid.) This corresponds well with Rousseau's letter to Moultou of January 18, 1762: "I should tell you that I am having printed in Holland a small work that is entitled *Du Contrat social* or *Principes du droit politique,* which is extracted from a larger work, entitled *Institutions Politiques,* started ten years ago and abandoned as I cease writing, and in any event an enterprise that was certainly beyond my strength" (cited Pléiade, III, 1431). Rousseau thus started serious work on his *Political Institutions* around 1751, but only made major headway with it after 1756. Despite Rousseau's "Foreword," some fragments presumably from his original project have survived, notably *État de Guerre* ("That the State of War is born from the Social State"—Vaughan I, 293–307 or Pléiade, III, 601–616), "A Comparison between Rome and Sparta" (Vaughan, I, 314–320 or Pléiade, III, 538–543), "On Luxury, Commerce, and the Arts" (Vaughan, I, 341–349 or Pléiade, III, 516–524), "On Laws" (Vaughan, I, 330–334, 355–356 or Pléiade, III, 491–500), and other materials including what appear to have been a list of chapters and a Preface (Vaughan, I, 339, 350–351 or Pléiade, III, 473–474). Some passages from these fragments are translated into English in editorial notes 21, 26, 46, 58, 66, 89. In the account of the *Confessions* cited earlier in this note, the "historical study of morality" may well refer in part to the fragmentary "History of Morals" (Vaughan, I, 334–339 or Pléiade, III, 554–560).

reconcile in this research what right permits with what interest prescribes, so that justice and utility are not at variance.[2]

I start in without proving the importance of my subject. It will be asked if I am a prince or a legislator to write about politics. I reply that I am neither, and that is why I write about politics. If I were a prince or a legislator, I would not waste my time saying what has to be done. I would do it, or keep silent.[3]

Born a citizen of a free State, and a member of the sovereign, the right to vote there is enough to impose on me the duty of learning about public affairs, no matter how feeble the influence of my voice may be. And I am happy every time I meditate about governments, always to find in my research new reasons to love that of my country![4]

Chapter I: Subject of This First Book

Man was/is born free, and everywhere he is in chains.[5] One who believes himself the master of others is nonetheless a greater slave than they. How did this change occur? I do not know. What can make it *legitimate?* I believe I can answer this question.

If I were to consider only force and the effect it produces, I would say that as long as a people is constrained to obey and does so, it does well; as soon as it can shake off the yoke and does so, it does even better. For in recovering its freedom by means of the same right used to steal it, either the people is justified in taking it back, or those who took it away were not justified in doing so. But the social order is a sacred right that serves as a basis for all the others. However, this right does not come from nature; it is therefore based on conventions. The problem is to know what these conventions are. Before coming to that, I should establish what I have just asserted.

[2]The duality of Rousseau's perception of the problem of political theory deserves emphasis: "men as they are" have concerns of "interest" or "utility" which "prescribe" limits to a solution, whereas "laws as they can be" depend on considerations of "right" and "justice" which "permit"—but only *permit*—of legitimacy. In other words, Rousseau will try to adjust "right" and "justice" to the *necessary* demands of self-interest. Compare *Geneva Manuscript,* I, ii.

[3]This passage is probably a veiled criticism of King Frederick the Great of Prussia, who had published a book entitled *Anti-Machiavel:* see Masters, *Political Philosophy of Rousseau,* pp. 306–309.

[4]Compare *Political Economy,* p. 228. Despite this praise, Rousseau's ambivalent attitude toward his native Geneva has been noted (Introduction, note 27 and references there cited). This ambivalence is not, however, merely a logical contradiction. Since Geneva's republican regime is superior to monarchies, it deserves to be a model for French readers whereas, for Genevan readers, the issue is the extent to which one can slow down the inevitable decline of all governments toward despotism. Compare *Letter to d'Alembert* (ed. Bloom, pp. 17–18, 58–65, 92–123) and *Lettre à Philopolis* (Pléiade, III, 230–236) with *Social Contract,* III, x.

[5]This chapter is a revised version of the first two paragraphs of *Geneva Manuscript,* I, iii (p. 163). For an explanation of the apparently awkward translation of this famous sentence, see Introduction, pp. 10–11. The next sentence deserves particular attention, since it denounces all forms of personal power and authority. As Rousseau says elsewhere: "Freedom *(la liberté)* does not consist as much in acting according to one's own will as in not being subjected to the will of anyone else; it also consists in not subjecting the will of another to our own. Whoever is master cannot be free, and to rule is to obey." *Lettres Écrites de la Montagne,* VIII (Pléiade, III, 841 and 1434). Cf. Hegel's striking analysis of "Lordship and Bondage" in *Phenomenology of Mind* (ed. Baillie [London: George Allen & Unwin, 1931], pp. 229–240). According to one of Rousseau's fragments, in "the relation of master and slave" both participants are "always in a state of war" (Vaughan, I, 310 or Pléiade, III, 615). On the remainder of this paragraph, see also editorial note 15 to the *Geneva Manuscript.*

Chapter II: On the First Societies

The most ancient of all societies, and the only natural one, is that of the family.[6] Yet children remain bound to the father only as long as they need him for self-preservation. As soon as this need ceases, the natural bond dissolves. The children, exempt from the obedience they owed the father, and the father, exempt from the care he owed the children, all return equally to independence. If they continue to remain united, it is no longer naturally but voluntarily, and the family itself is maintained only by convention.[7]

This common freedom is a consequence of man's nature. His first law is to attend to his own preservation, his first cares are those he owes himself; and as soon as he has reached the age of reason, as he alone is the judge of the proper means of preserving himself, he thus becomes his own master.

The family is therefore, so to speak, the prototype of political societies. The leader is like the father, the people are like the children; and since all are born equal and free, they only alienate their freedom for their utility. The entire difference is that in the family, the father's love for his children rewards him for the care he provides; whereas in the State, the pleasure of commanding substitutes for this love, which the leader does not have for his people.

Grotius denies that all human power is established for the benefit of those who are governed. He cites slavery as an example.[8] His most persistent mode of reasoning is always to establish right by fact.[9] One could use a more rational method, but not one more favorable to tyrants.

---

[6]This chapter was added when Rousseau reorganized Book 1, putting his rejection of alternative definitions of the "social bond" *before* his own principles (whereas in the *Geneva Manuscript* most of this material was in I, v—*after* the presentation of the "general will" in I, iii–v). Since the passage of the *Geneva Manuscript*, I, v, which rejects paternal authority as the source of political power had been used in *Political Economy*, presumably Rousseau decided to write a new discussion. The first sentence appears to reflect a shift from the argument of the *Second Discourse*, which treats "the establishment of the family" as the result of a "first revolution" changing man's isolation in the pure state of nature: see Part 1 (ed. Masters, pp. 134–137), Part 2 (pp. 146–147), and note *l* (pp. 213–220). Compare, however, the *Essay on the Origin of Languages*, chap. ix: "In primitive times the sparse human population had no more social structure than the family, no laws but those of nature, no language but that of gesture and some inarticulate sounds. They were not bound by any idea of common brotherhood and, having no rule but that of force, they believed themselves each other's enemies" (ed. Moran and Gode, pp. 31–32). On the status of the family in the state of nature, see Masters, *Political Philosophy of Rousseau*, pp. 125–136.

[7]In the margin of his copy of the *Social Contract*, Voltaire wrote: "But it has to be agreed that this convention is indicated by nature" (ed. Jouvenel, p. 175). Rousseau follows Locke's argument in the *Second Treatise of Civil Government*, chap. vi, especially paragraphs 55, 61–71 (ed. Laslett [Cambridge, Eng.: University Press, 1963], pp. 322–323, 326–332). See also *Second Discourse*, Part 2 (ed. Masters, pp. 165–166) and *Geneva Manuscript*, I, v (pp. 169–171)—used with revisions in *Political Economy* (pp. 209–211). On the relationship between paternal and political authority, compare Plato, *Statesman*, 258e–259c, 276c–e, 287c–291c; Aristotle, *Politics*, I.i.1252a (ed. Barker [Oxford, Clarendon Press, 1952], p. 1); and Jean Bodin, *Six livres de la République*, I, ii (cited Pléiade, III, 1434).

[8]"It is not true, generally and without restriction, that all power is established in favor of those who are governed. There are powers which, by themselves, are established in favor of the one who governs, such as the power of a master over his slave." Grotius, *Droit de la Guerre et de la Paix*, I, iii, § 8 (trad. Barbeyrac—cited in Pléiade, III, 1435). Compare the dialogue between Thrasymachus and Socrates in Plato's *Republic*, I.338a–354c (ed. Bloom [New York: Basic Books, 1968], pp. 15–34).

[9]"Learned research on public right is often merely the history of ancient abuses, and people have gone to a lot of trouble for nothing when they have bothered to study it too much." *Treatise on the Interests of France in Relation to her Neighbors, by M. le Marquis d'Argenson* (printed by Rey in Amsterdam).[10] This is exactly what Grotius has done.

It is therefore doubtful, according to Grotius, whether the human race belongs to a hundred men, or whether these hundred men belong to the human race; and throughout his book he appears to lean toward the former view. This is Hobbes's sentiment as well. Thus the human species is divided into herds of livestock, each with its leader, who tends it in order to devour it.[11]

As a herdsman's nature is superior to that of his herd, so the shepherds of men, who are their leaders, are also superior in nature to their peoples. The emperor Caligula reasoned thus, according to Philo, concluding rather logically from this analogy that the kings were Gods or that people were beasts.

Caligula's reasoning amounts to the same thing as that of Hobbes and Grotius. Before any of them, Aristotle too had said that men are not naturally equal, but that some are born for slavery and others for domination.[12]

Aristotle was right, but he mistook the effect for the cause. Every man born in slavery is born for slavery; nothing could be more certain. Slaves lose everything in their chains, even the desire to be rid of them. They love their servitude as the companions of Ulysses loved their brutishness.[13] If there are slaves by nature, therefore, it is because there have been slaves contrary to nature. Force made the first slaves; their cowardice perpetuated them.

I have said nothing about king Adam or emperor Noah, father of three great monarchs who divided up the universe among themselves, as did the children of Saturn who have been identified with them. I hope this moderation will be appreciated, for as I am a direct descendant of one of these princes, and perhaps of the eldest

[10]In the first edition, the author was indicated only by the initials "M.L.M. d'A." This treatise, which Rousseau cited in 1762 from a manuscript, was subsequently published by Rey in 1764 under the title *Considérations sur le Gouvernement Ancien et Présent de la France;* in the 1782 edition of the *Social Contract,* based on Rousseau's emendations, d'Argenson's name is spelled out. On the possible significance of this work, see Rousseau's fifth note to Book IV, chap. viii and Masters, *Political Philosophy of Rousseau,* pp. 307–309. Note that whereas Grotius supposedly tries to "establish right by fact," for Rousseau the necessary procedure is to "test facts by right": *Second Discourse,* Part 2 (ed. Masters, p. 166). "Let the reader remember that here it is less a question of history and facts than of right and justice." *Etat de Guerre* (Pléiade, III, 603).

[11]Rousseau seems to refer to Hobbes's argument that "whatsoever he [the sovereign] doth, it can be no injury to any of his subjects; nor ought he to be by any of them accused of injustice." Thomas Hobbes, *Leviathan,* Part 2, chap. 18 (ed. Oakeshott [Oxford: Blackwell, 1960], p. 115). For the origin of the comparison between a leader and a shepherd, see Thrasymachus' speech in Plato's *Republic,* I, 343a–344c (ed. Bloom, pp. 21–22).

[12]For the source of Rousseau's reference to Philo *(De Legatione ad Caium),* see Pléiade, III, 1435. Aristotle, in *Politics,* I.ii.1252a, argues that "the element which is able, by virtue of its intelligence, to exercise forethought, is naturally a ruling and master element; the element which is able, by virtue of its bodily power, to do what the other element plans, is a ruled element, which is naturally in a state of slavery." (ed. Barker, p. 3). Note, however, that Aristotle—unlike Thrasymachus or Grotius—immediately adds: "and master and slave have accordingly a common interest" (Ibid.) See also *Politics* I.v–vi. 1254a–1255b (ed. Barker, pp. 11–17).

[13]See a short treatise by Plutarch entitled *That Animals Reason.*[14]

[14]This short dialogue in Plutarch's *Moralia* is worth reading: in reply to Ulysses' request that the Greeks turned into animals be released in human form, Circe asks him to persuade one of them, named Gryllus, that this would be desirable. Gryllus then explains why "man is the most miserable and most calamitous animal in the world" whereas "the soul of animals is better disposed and more perfected for producing virtue, since without being forced, or commanded, or taught, . . . it produces and nourishes the virtue which, according to nature, suits each one." Hence, instead of proving that slavery is unnatural—as the text leads one to expect—Plutarch's dialogue suggests that human *civilization* is unnatural and corrupt; indirectly, the citation thus echoes the central theme of the *Second Discourse* (see ed. Masters, editorial note 26). Rousseau probably consulted the French translation by Jacques Amyot: *Oeuvres Morales et Meslées de Plutarque* (Geneva: Jacob Stoer, 1627), pp. 273–276.

branch, how am I to know whether, through the verification of titles, I would not discover that I am the legitimate king of the human race? However that may be, it cannot be denied that Adam was sovereign of the world, like Crusoe of his island, as long as he was its only inhabitant. And what was convenient in that empire was that the monarch, secure on his throne, had neither rebellions, nor wars, nor conspirators to fear.[15]

Chapter III: On the Right of the Strongest

The strongest is never strong enough to be the master forever unless he transforms his force into right and obedience into duty.[16] This leads to the right of the strongest, a right that is in appearance taken ironically and in principle really established. But won't anyone ever explain this word to us? Force is a physical power. I do not see what morality can result from its effects. Yielding to force is an act of necessity, not of will. At most, it is an act of prudence. In what sense could it be a duty?

Let us suppose this alleged right for a moment. I say that what comes of it is nothing but inexplicable confusion. For as soon as force makes right, the effect changes along with the cause. Any force that overcomes the first one succeeds to its right. As soon as one can disobey without punishment, one can do so legitimately, and since the strongest is always right, the only thing to do is to make oneself the strongest. But what is a right that perishes when force ceases? If it is necessary to obey by force, one need not obey by duty, and if one is no longer forced to obey, one is no longer obligated to do so. It is apparent, then, that this word right adds nothing to force. It is meaningless here.

Obey those in power.[17] If that means yield to force, the precept is good, but superfluous; I reply that it will never be violated. All power comes from God, I admit, but so does all illness. Does this mean it is forbidden to call the doctor? If a brigand takes me by surprise at the edge of a woods, must I not only give up my purse by force; am I obligated by conscience to give it even if I could keep it away? After all, the pistol he holds is also a power.

Let us agree, therefore, [that might does not make right, and that one is only obligated to obey legitimate powers.] Thus my original question still remains.

[15]Rousseau thus rejects with irony Filmer's argument for "the natural power of kings"; compare Locke, *First Treatise of Government,* especially chap. xi, paragraph 111 (ed. Laslett, pp. 239–240).

[16]Like the preceding chapter, this one was newly written for the final version. Rousseau's insistence that "might does not make right" deserves more emphasis than it is usually given, since it means that "legitimate authority" must be freely accepted *"in conscience"* even by those who are being punished for violating the rrules. See editorial note 37. The second sentence contains an untranslatable play on words: when Rousseau speaks of the "right of the strongest" as a right that is *"réellement établi en principe"* he could mean either that this right is "in principle really established" in the works of political theorists like Grotius or Hobbes, or that this right was "really established *in the beginning"* (i.e., that human history was originally based only on the right of the strongest). Compare *Geneva Manuscript,* I, ii; *Essay on the Origin of Language,* chap. ix (ed. Moran and Gode, pp. 33–37); *Second Discourse,* Part 1 (ed. Masters, p. 139), Part 2 (p. 177), and Note *o* (p. 222).

[17]Compare St. Paul's *Letter to the Romans,* xiii, 1–2: "You must all obey the governing authorities. Since all government comes from God, the civil authorities were appointed by God, and so anyone who resists authority is rebelling against God's decision, and such an act is bound to be punished." *Jerusalem Bible* (Garden City, N.Y.: Doubleday, 1971), p. 209.

Chapter IV: On Slavery

Since no man has any natural authority over his fellow man, and since force produces no right, there remain only conventions as the basis of all legitimate authority among men.[18]

If a private individual, says Grotius, can alienate his freedom and enslave himself to a master, why can't a whole people alienate its freedom and subject itself to a king?[19] There are many equivocal words in this that need explaining, but let us limit ourselves to the word *alienate*. To alienate is to give or sell. Now a man who makes himself another's slave does not give himself, he sells himself, at the least for his subsistence. But why does a people sell itself? Far from furnishing the subsistence of his subjects, a king derives his own only from them, and according to Rabelais a king does not live cheaply. Do the subjects give their persons, then, on condition that their goods will be taken too? I do not see what remains for them to preserve.

It will be said that the despot guarantees civil tranquillity to his subjects. Perhaps so, but what have they gained if the wars that his ambition brings on them, if his insatiable greed, if the harassment of his ministers are a greater torment than their dissensions would be? What have they gained, if this tranquillity is one of their miseries? Life is tranquil in jail cells, too. Is that reason enough to like them? The Greeks lived tranquilly shut up in the Cyclop's cave as they awaited their turn to be devoured.[20]

To say that a man gives himself gratuitously is to say something absurd and inconceivable. Such an act is illegitimate and null, if only because he who does so is not in his right mind. To say the same thing about an entire people is to suppose a people of madmen. Madness does not make right.

Even if everyone could alienate himself, he could not alienate his children. They are born men and free. Their freedom belongs to them; no one but themselves has a right to dispose of it. Before they have reached the age of reason, their father can, in

---

[18]With the exception of the sixth paragraph (largely from *Geneva Manuscript,* I, v), this chapter was also written anew for the final version. See the fifth fragment at the end of the *Geneva Manuscript,* used in the eleventh paragraph. The argument of the chapter as a whole, however, echoes the fragment originally titled "That the State of War is born from the Social State"—usually called *État de Guerre* (Pléiade, III, 601–612). This fragment is of interest because it is an attack on the "horrible system of Hobbes" (Pléiade, III, 610), whereas the final version of the *Social Contract* criticizes "Grotius and others." Although the shift may be related to Rousseau's qualified praise of Hobbes in Book IV, chap. viii, the central thrust remains hostile to the Hobbesian version of the social compact.

[19]Rousseau paraphrases Grotius, *Droit de la Guerre et de la Paix,* I, iii. § 8 (trans. Barbeyrac), cited in Pléiade, III, 1438.

[20]Homer, *Odyssey,* IX. 216–436. Compare *État de Guerre,* where Rousseau first uses this example: "I open the books on right and morality, I listen to the scholars and jurists and, touched by their insinuating discourses, I admire the peace and justice established by the civil order, I bless the wisdom of public institutions, and I console myself for being a man by seeing myself as a citizen. Well taught concerning my duties and my happiness, I close the book, leave the classroom, and look around me. I see unfortunate peoples groaning under an iron yoke, the human race crushed by a handful of oppressors, a starving crowd worn out by difficulty and hunger whose blood and tears the rich drink in peace, and everywhere the strong armed against the weak with the fearsome power of the laws. All that is done peacefully and without resistance; it is the tranquillity of Ulysses' companions trapped in the Cyclop's cave, waiting to be devoured." (Pléiade, III, 608–609). Rousseau emphatically denies Hobbes's argument that it is rational to abandon one's natural freedom to enter any society as long as it is peaceful and quiet. Compare *Leviathan,* Part 2, chap 18 (ed. Oakeshott, p. 120) and Locke, *Second Treatise,* chap. xix, paragraph 228 (ed. Laslett, p. 434–435).

their name, stipulate conditions for their preservation, for their well-being; but he cannot give them irrevocably and unconditionally, because such a gift is contrary to the ends of nature and exceeds the rights of paternity. For an arbitrary government to be legitimate, it would therefore be necessary for the people in each generation to be master of its acceptance or rejection. But then this government would no longer be arbitrary.

To renounce one's freedom is to renounce one's status as a man, the rights of humanity and even its duties.[21] There is no possible compensation for anyone who renounces everything. Such a renunciation is incompatible with the nature of man, and taking away all his freedom of will is taking away all morality from his actions. Finally, it is a vain and contradictory convention to stipulate absolute authority on one side and on the other unlimited obedience. Isn't it clear that one is in no way engaged toward a person from whom one has the right to demand everything, and doesn't this condition alone—without equivalent and without exchange—entail the nullification of the act? For what right would my slave have against me, since all he has belongs to me, and his right being mine, my right against myself is a meaningless word?

Grotius and others derive from war another origin of the alleged right of slavery.[22] As the victor has the right to kill the vanquished, according to them, the latter can buy back his life at the cost of his freedom—a convention all the more legitimate in that it is profitable for both of them.

But it is clear that this alleged right to kill the vanquished in no way results from the state of war. Men are not naturally enemies, if only because when living in their original independence, they do not have sufficiently stable relationships among themselves to constitute either the state of peace or the state of war. It is the relationship between things, not between men, that constitutes war; and as the state of war cannot arise from simple, personal relations, but only from proprietary relations, private war between one man and another can exist neither in the state of nature, where there is no stable property, nor in the social state, where everything is under the authority of the laws.

Individual combats, duels, encounters are not acts that constitute a state.[23] And with regard to private wars, authorized by the establishments of King Louis IX of France and suspended by the peace of God, they are abuses of feudal government, an absurd system if there ever was one, contrary to the principles of natural right and to every good polity.

War is not, therefore, a relation between man and man, but between State and State, in which private individuals are enemies only by accident, not as men, nor even

---

[21]Compare *Second Discourse,* Part 2 (ed. Masters, pp. 165–168). The remainder of this paragraph is taken from *Geneva Manuscript,* I, v, paragraph ten.

[22]For the relevant passages, see Grotius, *Droit de la Guerre et de la Paix,* II, v, § 27, and Pufendorf, *Droit de la nature et des gens* VI, iii, § 5 (cited in Pléiade, III, 1438–1439). See also Hobbes's notion of a "commonwealth by acquisition," *Leviathan,* Part 2, chap. 20 (ed. Oakeshott, especially pp. 132–133).

[23]For the original draft of this paragraph, see *État de Guerre* (Pléiade, III, 602–603). The technical point, as this fragment had stressed, is that a state of war in any juridical or "rational" sense can only exist between "the moral beings" known as States, and not between individuals (as in Hobbes's state of nature). As Rousseau puts it in *Geneva Manuscript,* I, v, the "state of war" presupposes a "free and voluntary convention."

as citizens,[24] but as soldiers; not as members of the homeland but as its defenders. Finally, each State can have only other States, and not men, as enemies, since no true relationship can be established between things of differing natures.

This principle even conforms with the established maxims of all ages and with the constant practice of all civilized peoples. Declarations of war are not so much warnings to those in power as to their subjects. The foreigner—whether he be king, private individual, or people—who robs, kills, or imprisons subjects without declaring war on the prince, is not an enemy, but a brigand.[25] Even in the midst of war, a just prince may well seize everything in an enemy country that belongs to the public, but he respects the person and goods of private individuals. He respects rights on which his own are based. The end of war being the destruction of the enemy State, one has the right to kill its defenders as long as they are armed. But as soon as they lay down their arms and surrender, since they cease to be enemies or instruments of the enemy, they become simply men once again, and one no longer has a right to their lives. Sometimes it is possible to kill the State without killing a single one of its members. War confers no right that is not necessary to its end. These principles are not those of Grotius; they are not based on the authority of poets, but are derived from the nature of things, and are based on reason.

With regard to the right of conquest, it has no basis other than the law of the strongest. If war does not give the victor the right to massacre the vanquished peoples, this right he does not have cannot establish the right to enslave them. One only has the right to kill the enemy when he cannot be made a slave. The right to make him a slave does not come, then, from the right to kill him. It is therefore an iniquitous exchange to make him buy his life, over which one has no right, at the cost of his freedom. By establishing the right of life and death on the right of slavery, and the right of slavery on the right of life and death, isn't it clear that one falls into a vicious circle?

Even assuming this terrible right to kill everyone, I say that a man enslaved in

---

[24]The Romans, who understood and respected the right of war better than any nation in the world, were so scrupulous in this respect that a citizen was not allowed to serve as a volunteer unless he had expressly engaged himself against the enemy, and against the particular enemy by name. When a legion in which Cato the Younger was serving for the first time under Popilius had been reorganized, Cato the Elder wrote to Popolius that if he wanted his son to continue to serve under him, Popilius would have to have him take the military oath again, because the first oath being annulled, he could no longer bear arms against the enemy. And the same Cato wrote his son to be careful not to appear in combat without swearing this new oath. I know that the siege of Clusium and other specific events can be raised in contradiction to this, but I cite laws and practices. The Romans were the people who least often transgressed their laws, and they are the only people who had such fine ones.[26]

[25]For the rest of this paragraph up to the last sentence, see the fifth fragment at the end of the *Geneva Manuscript*. Rousseau's argument rests on what he called "fundamental distinctions" in *État de Guerre*: "If things are only considered according to the strict interpretation of the social pact, the land, money, men, and all that is comprised within the boundaries of the state belong to it without reserve. But since the rights of society, founded on those of nature, cannot annihilate them, all these objects should be considered in a double relationship: namely the soil as public territory and as individuals' patrimony, goods as belonging in one sense to the sovereign and in another to the property owners, the inhabitants as citizens and as men. At bottom, since the body politic is only a moral person, it is only a being of reason. Remove the public convention, at that instant the State is destroyed without the slightest alteration in everything that composes it; and all the conventions of men could never change anything in the nature of things" (Pléiade, III, 608). Compare Montesquieu, *Esprit des Lois*, X, iii and XV, ii.

[26]This note was added by Rousseau and first published in the edition of 1782.

war or a conquered people is in no way obligated toward his master, except to obey for as long as he is forced to do so. In taking the equivalent of his life, the victor has not spared it; rather than to kill him purposelessly, he has killed him usefully. Therefore, far from the victor having acquired any authority over him in addition to force, the state of war subsists between them as before; their relation itself is its effect, and the customs of the right of war suppose that there has not been a peace treaty. They made a convention, true; but that convention, far from destroying the state of war, assumes its continuation.

Thus, from every vantage point, the right of slavery is null, not merely because it is illegitimate, but because it is absurd and meaningless. These words *slavery* and *right* are contradictory; they are mutually exclusive. Whether it is said by one man to another or by a man to a people, the following speech will always be equally senseless: *I make a convention with you that is entirely at your expense and entirely for my benefit; that I shall observe for as long as I want, and that you shall observe for as long as I want.*

Chapter V: That It Is Always Necessary to Go Back to a First Convention

Even if I were to grant everything I have thus far refuted, the proponents of despotism would be no better off.[27] There will always be a great difference between subjugating a multitude and governing a society. If scattered men, however many there may be, are successively enslaved by one individual, I see only a master and slaves; I do not see a people and its leader. It is an aggregation, if you wish, but not an association. It has neither public good nor body politic. That man, even if he had enslaved half the world, is nothing but a private individual. His interest, separate from that of the others, is still nothing but a private interest. If this same man dies, thereafter his empire is left scattered and without bonds, just as an oak tree disintegrates and falls into a heap of ashes after fire has consumed it.

A people, says Grotius, can give itself to a king. According to Grotius, a people is therefore a people before it gives itself to a king. This gift itself is a civil act; it presupposes a public deliberation. Therefore, before examining the act by which a people elects a king, it would be well to examine the act by which a people becomes a people. For this act, being necessarily prior to the other, is the true basis of society.

Indeed, if there were no prior convention, what would become of the obligation for the minority to submit to the choice of the majority, unless the election were unanimous; and where do one hundred who want a master get the right to vote for ten who do not? The law of majority rule is itself an established convention, and presupposes unanimity at least once.[28]

---

[27]Again, this chapter was newly written for the final version; however, compare *Geneva Manuscript,* I, v.

[28]In addition to Grotius (see editorial note 20 above), this passage criticizes Hobbes, who admits that each individual has "tacitly covenanted" to accept a majority vote *before* the assembly "hath by consenting voices declared a sovereign"; *Leviathan,* Part 2, chap. 18 (ed. Oakeshott, p. 115). Rousseau insists that the "true basis of society" is Hobbes's "tacit convenant," whereas Hobbes had treated the subsequent election of the sovereign or ruler as the social contract. In other words, Rousseau's definition of the social contract can be treated as the logic which leads any assembly to accept the principle of majority rule.

Chapter VI: On the Social Compact

I assume that men have reached the point where obstacles to their self-preservation in the state of nature prevail by their resistance over the forces each individual can use to maintain himself in that state.[29] Then that primitive state can no longer subsist and the human race would perish if it did not change its way of life.

Now since men cannot engender new forces, but merely unite and direct existing ones, they have no other means of self-preservation except to form, by aggregation, a sum of forces that can prevail over the resistance; set them to work by a single motivation; and make them act in concert.

This sum of forces can arise only from the cooperation of many. But since each man's force and freedom are the primary instruments of his self-preservation, how is he to engage them without harming himself and without neglecting the cares he owes to himself? In the context of my subject, this difficulty can be stated in these terms.

"Find a form of association that defends and protects the person and goods of each associate with all the common force, and by means of which each one, uniting with all, nevertheless obeys only himself and remains as free as before." This is the fundamental problem which is solved by the social contract.

The clauses of this contract are so completely determined by the nature of the act that the slightest modification would render them null and void. So that although they may never have been formally pronounced, they are everywhere the same, everywhere tacitly accepted and recognized, until the social compact is violated, at which point each man recovers his original rights and resumes his natural freedom, thereby losing the conventional freedom for which he renounced it.[30]

Properly understood, all of these clauses come down to a single one, namely the total alienation of each associate, with all his rights, to the whole community. For first of all, since each one gives his entire self, the condition is equal for everyone, and since the condition is equal for everyone, no one has an interest in making it burdensome for the others.

Furthermore, as the alienation is made without reservation, the union is as perfect as it can be, and no associate has anything further to claim. For if some rights were left to private individuals, there would be no common superior who could judge between them and the public. Each man being his own judge on some point would soon claim to be so on all; the state of nature would subsist and the association would necessarily become tyrannical or ineffectual.

---

[29]This chapter is revised from paragraphs two to four of *Geneva Manuscript,* I, iii, which became the first two and last two paragraphs of the final version. Note that from the outset, Rousseau treats the problem of social obligations in the terms of Newtonian mechanics ("forces," "resistance," "obstacles," etc.). Compare the image of the "general will" as a "frictionless surface" in *Geneva Manuscript,* I, iv, and Introduction, p. 20, as well as the repeated references to "springs," "levers," and other mechanistic analogies in the final text.

[30]This paragraph, added in the final version, implies that Rousseau's definition of the social contract is analogous to the law of gravity. "Everywhere the same" even if "never" stated, like Newton's law, Rousseau's principle is also self-enforcing: if "the social contract is violated," it follows immediately that "each man recovers his original rights and resumes his natural freedom." Compare the passage of *État de Guerre* cited in editorial note 26: since the social contract establishes a psychological or rational commitment to live as a community, the sovereign is only a "moral" body and can be destroyed without touching the phsyical or natural existence of the men and objects comprising it. See also the "important proposition" in the first paragraph of *Geneva Manuscript,* I, iv., and *Social Contract,* editorial notes 35 and 36.

Finally, as each gives himself to all, he gives himself to no one; and since there is no associate over whom one does not acquire the same right one grants him over oneself, one gains the equivalent of everything one loses, and more force to preserve what one has.[31]

If, then, everything that is not of the essence of the social compact is set aside, one will find that it can be reduced to the following terms. *Each of us puts his person and all his power in common under the supreme direction of the general will; and in a body we receive each member as an indivisible part of the whole.*

Instantly, in place of the private person of each contracting party, this act of association produces a moral and collective body, composed of as many members as there are voices in the assembly, which receives from this same act its unity, its common *self,* its life, and its will. This public person, formed thus by the union of all the others, formerly took the name *City,*[32] and now takes that of *Republic* or *body politic,* which its members call *State* when it is passive, *Sovereign* when active, *Power* when comparing it to similar bodies. As for the associates, they collectively take the name *people;* and individually are called *Citizens* as participants in the sovereign authority, and *Subjects* as subject to the laws of the State. But these terms are often mixed up and mistaken for one another. It is enough to know how to distinguish them when they are used with complete precision.

[31]These additions to the first draft emphasize the importance of avoiding any form of *personal* dependence. As Rousseau says in *Émile,* II: "There are two kinds of dependence. That on things is from nature; that on men is from society. Since dependence on things has no morality, it neither hinders freedom nor engenders vice. Since the dependence on men is disordered, it engenders them all, and this is how the master and slave mutually deprave each other. If there is some way to remedy this evil within society, it is to substitute law for men, and to arm the general wills with a real force greater than the activity of any private will. If the laws of nations could have an inflexibility like those of nature, so that no human force could ever overcome them, the dependence on men would then become like that on things, one would unite in the Republic all the advantages of the natural state with those of the civil state, one would combine freedom, which keeps man free from vices, with morality, which raises him to virtue" (Pléiade, IV, 311). That this passage relates to the *Social Contract* is proven by a note appended at the word "disordered": "In my *Principles of Political Right,* it is demonstrated that no private will can be well-ordered in the social system" (Ibid.) For a particularly insightful study of the attitudes which led Rousseau to detest dependence on other individuals, see Judith N. Shklar, "Rousseau's Images of Authority." *in Hobbes and Rousseau,* ed. Maurice Cranston and Ricard S. Peters (Garden City, N.Y.: Anchor Books, 1972), pp. 333–365.

[32]The true meaning of this word has been almost entirely lost among modern men. Most of them mistake a town for a City, and a bourgeois for a citizen. They do not know that houses make the town, but that citizens make the City. This same error was very costly to the Carthaginians long ago. I have not read that the title *cives* has ever been given to the subjects of any prince—even in ancient times to the Macedonians or currently to the English, although they are closer to freedom than all others. Only the French use the name *citizens* with complete familiarity, because they have no true idea of its meaning, as can be seen from their dictionaries. If this were not the case, in usurping it they would be guilty of the crime of high treason. For the French, this name expresses a virtue and not a right. When Bodin wanted to talk about our citizens and bourgeois, he made a gross blunder in taking one for the other. M. d'Alembert did not confuse them, and in his article *Geneva* carefully distinguished the four orders of men (even five counting simple foreigners) who are in our town, and of whom only two compose the Republic. No other French author, to my knowledge, has understood the true meaning of the word *citizen.*[33]

[33]Rousseau refers to the early editions of Bodin's *Les six livres de la République,* I, vi, and to d'Alembert's *Geneva* in Volume VII of the *Encyclopédie* (both cited in Pléiade, III, 1446, 1448). Note that Rousseau's terminology takes the ancient *polis* ("city-state") as the norm. The resulting rehabilitation of the word "citizen" was to have profound effects during the French Revolution. Compare *Émile,* IV: "As if there were citizens who were not members of the City, and as such did not have a part in the sovereign authority. But the French, having judged it appropriate to usurp this respectable name of Citizens, formerly due to members of the cities of the Gauls, have denatured the idea to the point where one cannot understand anything" (Pléiade, IV, 667, note). Although the word "bourgeois" has taken on a Marxist class connotation not intended by Rousseau, it will be used to translate the French *"bourgeois."*

Chapter VII: On the Sovereign

This formula shows that the act of association includes a reciprocal engagement between the public and private individuals, and that each individual, contracting with himself so to speak, finds that he is doubly engaged, namely toward private individuals as a member of the sovereign and toward the sovereign as a member of the State.[34] But the maxim of civil right that no one can be held responsible for engagements toward himself cannot be applied here, because there is a great difference between being obligated to oneself, or to a whole of which one is a part.

It must further be noted that the public deliberation that can obligate all of the subjects to the sovereign—due to the two different relationships in which each of them is considered—cannot for the opposite reason obligate the sovereign toward itself; and that consequently it is contrary to the nature of the body politic for the sovereign to impose on itself a law it cannot break. Since the sovereign can only be considered in a single relationship, it is then in the situation of a private individual contracting with himself. It is apparent from this that there is not, nor can there be, any kind of fundamental law that is obligatory for the body of the people, not even the social contract. This does not mean that this body cannot perfectly well enter an engagement toward another with respect to things that do not violate this contract. For with reference to the foreigner, it becomes a simple being or individual.

But the body politic or the sovereign, deriving its being solely from the sanctity of the contract, can never obligate itself, even toward another, to do anything that violates that original act, such as to alienate some part of itself or to subject itself to another sovereign. To violate the act by which it exists would be to destroy itself, and whatever is nothing, produces nothing.[35]

As soon as this multitude is thus united in a body, one cannot harm one of the members without attacking the body, and it is even less possible to harm the body without the members feeling the effects. Thus duty and interest equally obligate the two contracting parties to mutual assistance, and the same men should seek to combine in this double relationship all the advantages that are dependent on it.

Now the sovereign, formed solely by the private individuals composing it, does not and cannot have any interest contrary to theirs. Consequently, the sovereign power has no need of a guarantee toward the subjects, because it is impossible for the body ever to want to harm all its members, and we shall see later that it cannot harm any one of them as an individual. The sovereign, by the sole fact of being, is always what it ought to be.[36]

But the same is not true of the subjects in relation to the sovereign, which, despite the common interest, would have no guarantee of the subjects' engagements if it did not find ways to be assured of their fidelity.

Indeed, each individual can, as a man, have a private will contrary to or differing from the general will he has as a citizen. His private interest can speak to him quite differently from the common interest. His absolute and naturally independent exis-

[34]This chapter is taken over, with some additions and deletions, from *Geneva Manuscript*, I, iii, paragraphs five to seven.

[35]This paragraph, an addition to the first draft, could be read as an assertion of the territorial and social inviolability of the modern nation-state. Compare Alfred Cobban, *Rousseau and the Modern State* (London: George Allen & Unwin, 1934).

[36]These two sentences, added to the first draft, emphasize the extent to which the "body politic" is a "moral person" or "being of reason." See Introduction, pp. 18–20 and *Social Contract,* editorial note 26.

tence can bring him to view what he owes the common cause as a free contribution, the loss of which will harm others less than its payment burdens him. And considering the moral person of the State as an imaginary being because it is not a man, he might wish to enjoy the rights of the citizen without wanting to fulfill the duties of a subject, an injustice whose spread would cause the ruin of the body politic.[37]

Therefore, in order for the social compact not to be an ineffectual formula, it tacitly includes the following engagement, which alone can give force to the others: that whoever refuses to obey the general will shall be constrained to do so by the entire body; which means only that he will be forced to be free.[38] For this is the condition that, by giving each citizen to the homeland, guarantees him against all personal dependence; a condition that creates the ingenuity and functioning of the political machine, and alone gives legitimacy to civil engagements which without it would be absurd, tyrannical, and subject to the most enormous abuses.

Chapter VIII: On the Civil State

This passage from the state of nature to the civil state produces a remarkable change in man, by substituting justice for instinct in his behavior and giving his actions the morality they previously lacked.[39] Only then, when the voice of duty replaces physical impulse and right replaces appetite, does man, who until that time only considered himself, find himself forced to act upon other principles and to consult his reason before heeding his inclinations. Although in this state he deprives himself of several advantages given him by nature, he gains such great ones, his faculties are exercised and developed, his ideas broadened, his feelings ennobled, and his whole soul elevated to such a point that if the abuses of this new condition did not often degrade him be-

---

[37]Note that since the State *is* a "moral person" and thus, in a sense, "an imaginary being," Rousseau's principles of political right could increase injustice if they are taught to selfish or corrupted men. "The democratic constitution is certainly the masterpiece of political art: but the more admirable its artifice, the less it belongs to all eyes to penetrate it." *Lettres Écrites de la Montagne,* VIII (Pléiade, III, 838). Compare *First Discourse,* Part 2 (ed. Masters, pp. 49–50).

[38]The last phrase seems a puzzling contradiction in terms, and has led some to call Rousseau a "totalitarian": for example, J. L. Talmon, *The Origins of Totalitarian Democracy* (New York: Praeger, 1960), pp. 38–49; Lester G. Crocker, "Rousseau et la voi du totalitarisme," *Rousseau et la Philosophie Politique* (Paris: Presses Universitaires, 1965), pp. 99–136. In context, however, the sentence concerns the means by which each individual can have an obligation, in *conscience,* to obey the laws he has previously enacted. Rousseau applied precisely this reasoning in defending his works against the charges brought by the Magistrates of Geneva: "an accuser must convince the accused before the judge. To be treated as a wrongdoer, it is necessary that I be convinced of being one." *Lettres Écrites de la Montagne,* I (Pléiade, III, 693). For a brilliant psychological analysis of the phrase "forced to be free," see John Plamenatz, "Ce qui ne signifie autre chose sinon qu'on le forcera d'étre libre," in *Hobbes and Rousseau,* ed. Cranston and Peters, pp. 318–332. That the passage concerns the conscience of the individual was made clear by the deleted sentence concerning "the oath" and each man's "inner maxims," which comes after the words "vain formula" in *Geneva Manuscript,* I, iii. See also the third paragraph of *Geneva Manuscript,* I, vii, which reappears in *Political Economy* (p. 214). On Rousseau's definition of freedom, see *Social Contract,* editorial note 8.

[39]The first two paragraphs of this chapter come from *Geneva Manuscript,* I, iii, paragraphs eight and nine. Although Rousseau praises civil society, his pessimistic view of history leads to a strong qualification: "if the abuses of this new condition did not often degrade him beneath the condition from which he emerged."Compare *Second Discourse,* especially note *i* (ed. Masters, pp. 192–203); *Émile,* II (cited in *Social Contract,* editorial note 31), and Introduction, above pp. 7–12. The last paragraph of this chapter, an addition to the first draft, clearly refers to *Émile* as the work in which Rousseau "said too much" about the "philosophic meaning of the word *freedom.*"

neath the condition he left, he ought ceaselessly to bless the happy moment that tore him away from it forever, and that changed him from a stupid, limited animal into an intelligent being and a man.

Let us reduce the pros and cons to easily compared terms. What man loses by the social contract is his natural freedom and an unlimited right to everything that tempts him and that he can get; what he gains is civil freedom and the proprietorship of everything he possesses. In order not to be mistaken about these compensations, one must distinguish carefully between natural freedom, which is limited only by the force of the individual, and civil freedom, which is limited by the general will; and between possession, which is only the effect of force or the right of the first occupant, and property, which can only be based on a positive title.

To the foregoing acquisitions of the civil state could be added moral freedom, which alone makes man truly the master of himself. For the impulse of appetite alone is slavery, and obedience to the law one has prescribed for oneself is freedom. But I have already said too much about this topic, and the philosophic meaning of the word *freedom* is not my subject here. . . .

BOOK II

Chapter I: That Sovereignty Is Inalienable

The first and most important consequence of the principles established above is that the general will alone can guide the forces of the State according to the end for which it was instituted, which is the common good.[40] For if the opposition of private interests made the establishment of societes necessary, it is the agreement of these same interests that made it possible. It is what these different interests have in common that forms the social bond, and if there were not some point at which all the interests are in agreement, no society could exist. Now it is uniquely on the basis of this common interest that society ought to be governed.

I say, therefore, that sovereignty, being only the exercise of the general will, can never be alienated, and that the sovereign, which is only a collective being, can only be represented by itself. Power can perfectly well be transferred, but not will.

Indeed, though it is not impossible for a private will to agree with the general will on a given point, it is impossible, at least, for this agreement to be lasting and unchanging. For the private will tends by its nature toward preferences, and the general will toward equality. It is even more impossible for there to be a guarantee of this agreement even should it always exist. It would not be the result of art, but of chance. The sovereign may well say, "I currently want what a particular man wants, or at least what he says he wants." But it cannot say, "What that man will want tomorrow, I shall still want,"since it is absurd for the will to tie itself down for the future and since no will can consent to anything that is contrary to the good of the being that wills. Therefore, if the people promises simply to obey, it dissolves itself by that act; it loses the status of a people. The moment there is a master, there is no longer a sovereign, and from then on the body politic is destroyed.

---

[40]The original draft of this chapter—*Geneva Manuscript,* I, iv—was heavily revised when Rousseau reworked it. This sentence shows clearly, however, that the concept of the "general will" was from the first a voluntaristic equivalent of the traditional concept of the "common good." Compare *Geneva Manuscript,* editorial note 22.

This is not to say that the commands of leaders cannot pass for expressions of the general will, as long as the sovereign, being free to oppose them, does not do so. In such a case, one ought to presume the consent of the people from universal silence. This will be explained at greater length.

Chapter II: That Sovereignty Is Indivisible

For the same reason that sovereignty is inalienable, it is indivisible.[41] Because either the will is general[42] or it is not. It is the will of the people as a body, or of only a part. In the first case, this declared will is an act of sovereignty and constitutes law. In the second case, it is merely a private will or an act of magistracy; it is at most a decree.

But our political theorists, unable to divide the principle of sovereignty, divide it in its object. They divide it into force and will; into legislative power and executive power; into rights of taxation, justice, and war; into internal administration and power to negotiate with foreigners. Sometimes they mix all these parts together, sometimes they separate them. They turn the sovereign into a fantastic body formed of bits and pieces. It is as though they constructed a man out of several bodies, one of which would have eyes, another arms, another feet, and nothing more. Japanese charlatans are said to cut up a child right in front of the audience; then, tossing all the parts into the air one after another, they make the child come back down alive and in one piece. The juggling acts of our political theorists are about like that. After they have taken the social body apart by a trick worthy of a carnival, they put the pieces back together in some unknown way.

This error comes from not having developed precise concepts of sovereign authority, and from having mistaken for parts of that authority what were merely emanations from it. Thus, for example, the acts of declaring war and making peace have been regarded as acts of sovereignty, which they are not, since each of these acts is not a law but merely an application of the law, a particular act which determines the legal situation, as will be clearly seen when the idea attached to the word *law* is established.[43]

By examining the other divisions in the same way, it would be found that every time it is thought that sovereignty is divided, a mistake has been made, and that the rights that are mistaken for parts of that sovereignty are always subordinate to it and always presuppose supreme wills which these rights merely execute.

It is hard to overestimate how much this lack of precision has obscured the decisions of those who have written on the subject of political right when they wanted to judge the respective rights of kings and peoples on the basis of the principles they had established. In chapters III and IV of the first book of Grotius, anyone can see how this learned man and his translator Barbeyrac get entangled and trapped in their sophisms,

---

[41]This chapter and the next were added when Rousseau revised the *Geneva Manuscript*. Many commentators have assumed that Rousseau criticizes Montesquieu when arguing that sovereignty is "indivisible," but Derathé suggests that the chapter is a refutation of Hobbes, Pufendorf, Burlamaqui, and other theorists of "political right" (Pléiade, III, 1453). The last sentence of this chapter is a variant of *État de Guerre* (Pléiade, III, 609).

[42]In order for a will to be general, it is not always necessary for it to be unanimous, but it is necessary that all votes be counted. Any formal exclusion destroys the generality.

[43]See *Social Contract,* II, vi. It follows, for Rousseau, that concerns of foreign affairs or "national security" cannot justify violation of the laws. Compare Locke, *Second Treatise,* chap. xii, para. 145–148 and chap. xiv, especially para. 160 (ed. Laslett, pp. 383–384, 393).

for fear of saying too much or not enough according to their viewpoints, and of offending the interests they needed to reconcile. Grotius—taking refuge in France, discontent with his homeland, and wanting to pay court to Louis XIII to whom his book is dedicated—spares nothing to divest the people of all their rights and to endow kings with them as artfully as possible. This would certainly have been the preference of Barbeyrac, too, who dedicated his translation to King George I of England. But unfortunately the expulsion of James II, which he calls abdication, forced him to be cautious, evasive, and equivocal so as not to make William appear to be a usurper. If these two writers had adopted the true principles, all their difficulties would have been avoided and they would always have been consistent. But they would have told the truth with regret and paid court only to the people. For truth does not lead to fortune, and the people does not confer embassies, professorships, or pensions.

Chapter III: Whether the General Will Can Err

From the foregoing it follows that the general will is always right and always tends toward the public utility. But it does not follow that the people's deliberations always have the same rectitude. One always wants what is good for oneself, but one does not always see it. The people is never corrupted, but it is often fooled, and only then does it appear to want what is bad.

There is often a great difference between the will of all and the general will. The latter considers only the common interest; the former considers private interest, and is only a sum of private wills. But take away from these same wills the pluses and minuses that cancel each other out,[44] and the remaining sum of the differences is the general will.

If, when an adequately informed people deliberates, the citizens were to have no communication among themselves, the general will would always result from the large number of small differences, and the deliberation would always be good. But when factions, partial associations at the expense of the whole, are formed, the will of

---

[44]*Each interest,* says the Marquis d'Argenson, *has different principles. The agreement of two private interests is formed in opposition to the interest of a third.*[45] He could have added that the agreement of all interests is formed in opposition to the interest of each. If there were no different interests, the common interest, which would never encounter any obstacle, would scarcely be felt. Everything would run smoothly by itself and politics would cease to be an art.

[45]*Vera cosa è,* says Machiavelli, *che alcune divisioni nuocono alle Republiche, a alcune giovano: quelle nuocono che sono dalle sette e da partigiani accompagnate: quelle giovano che senza sette, senza partigiani si mantengono. Non potendo adunque provedere un fondatore d'una Republica che non siano nimicizie in quella, hà da proveder almeno che non vi siano sette.* History of Florence, Book VII.[46]

[45]Marquis d'Argenson, *Considérations sur le Gouvernement Ancien et Présent de la France,* chap. ii, pp. 26–27 (see editorial note 12). In Rev's edition, d'Argenson's text reads "by *a reason opposed* to the interest" *(par une raison opposée)* whereas Rousseau's citation says "in opposition to the interest" *(par opposition):* Masters, *Political Philosophy of Rousseau,* p. 308, n. 28. The sentence to which this note is appended presumes that in any society, private interests necessarily conflict: "in the social state, the good of one man necessarily produces the ill of another. This relation is in the nature of the thing, and nothing could possibly change it." *Émile,* II (Pléiade, IV, 340, note). In terms of contemporary game theory, Rousseau asserts that private interests represent a "zero-sum" game. Since the "will of all" appears as a synonym for the "general will" in *Geneva Manuscript,* I, vii (p. 178)—a passage which reappears in *Political Economy* (p. 214)—Rousseau's distinction between these terms may date from his final revision of the manuscript (compare Masters, *Political Philosophy of Rousseau,* pp. 325–327; *Geneva Manuscript,* I, iv [p. 168]; and *Political Economy,* pp. 213, 216, 217).

each of these associations becomes general with reference to its members and particular with reference to the State. One can say, then, that there are no longer as many voters as there are men, but merely as many as there are associations. The differences become less numerous and produce a result that is less general. Finally, when one of these associations is so big that it prevails over all the others, the result is no longer a sum of small differences, but a single difference. Then there is no longer a general will, and the opinion that prevails is merely a private opinion.

In order for the general will to be well expressed, it is therefore important that there be no partial society in the State, and that each citizen give only his own opinion.[46] Such was the unique and sublime system instituted by the great Lycurgus. If there are partial societies, their number must be multiplied and their inequality prevented, as was done by Solon, Numa, and Servius. These precautions are the only valid means of ensuring that the general will is always enlightened and that the people is not deceived.[47]

Chapter IV: On the Limits of the Sovereign Power

If the State or the City is only a moral person whose life consists in the union of its members, and if the most important of its concerns is that of its own preservation, it must have a universal, compulsory force to move and arrange each part in the manner best suited to the whole.[48] Just as nature gives each man absolute power over all his

[46]"True it is, that some divisions injure republics, while others are beneficial to them. When accompanied by factions and parties are injurious; but when maintained without them they contribute to their prosperity. The legislator of a republic, since it is impossible to prevent existence of dissensions, must at least take care to prevent the growth of faction." Machiavelli, *History of Florence,* VII, i (New York: Harper Torchbooks, 1960), p. 310. For Rousseau's generally favorable attitude toward Machiavelli, see *Social Contract,* III, vi, especially the first note. Rousseau's citation reinforces the interpretation of the "general will" as an ideal which cannot be perfectly realized in practice; as Machiavelli says in the sentence preceding the quotation: "those who think a republic may be kept in perfect unity of purpose are greatly deceived." It must be added that Machiavelli's text apparently makes a subtle distinction between "sette" (perhaps best translated as "sects") and *"partigiani"* ("parties"): whereas "sects" are always harmful, "parties" are harmful if accompanied by "sects," but apparently need not themselves be forbidden by the "legislator of a republic."Compare Machiavelli's *Discourses on Titus Livy,* I, 4 (ed. Crick [Baltimore: Penguin, 1970], pp. 113–115)—according to which the Roman Republic was based on the rivalry between plebs and patricians—with the next editorial note.

[47]This criticism of "partial societies" has often been cited as an indication of Rousseau's hostility to pluralist democracy and political practice; some even speak of "totalitarianism" in this regard (ed. Watkins, p. xxx; Vaughan, I, 60). But in reading this passage, one must take into account Rousseau's definition of a "partial society" as a group with a "corporate will": see the group theory of politics spelled out in *Political Economy,* pp. 212–213 and discussed in the Introduction, pp. 21–23. The right to vote in secet, without others watching how the ballot is marked, is based on reasoning like that of Rousseau; expecting "partial societies" in every community, Rousseau's principles are particularly opposed to a single-party system—and oriented to a multiplicity of groups and/or parties, none of which can claim to rule in its own name. Note that while Sparta was "unique and sublime," it was Rome—whose laws were formed by Numa and revised by Servius—which Rousseau calls "the best government that ever existed." *Lettres Écrites de la Montagne,* VII (Pléiade, III, 809). Indeed, in a fragment comparing Sparta and Rome, Rousseau remarks that the founders of both republics established "many electoral divisions *(Colleges)* and private societies in order to create and excite among the citizens those sweet habits and that innocent and disinterested commerce which forms and nourishes patriotism." *Parallèle entre Sparte et Rome,* Frag. 2 (Pléiade, III, 542).

[48]For the first draft, see *Geneva Manuscript,* I, vi, entitled "On the Respective Rights of the Sovereign and the Citizen." Since this chapter was carried over to the final version with relatively few changes, it would seem to reflect an important statement of Rousseau's principles. For that very reason, the modifications of the text are of exceptional importance.

members, the social compact gives the body politic absolute power over all its members, and it is this same power, directed by the general will, which as I have said bears the name sovereignty.

But in addition to the public person, we have to consider the private persons who compose it and whose life and freedom are naturally independent of it. It is a matter, then, of making a clear distinction between the respective rights of the citizens and the sovereign,[49] and between the duties that the former have to fulfill as subjects and the natural rights to which they are entitled as men.

It is agreed that each person alienates through the social compact only that part of his power, goods, and freedom whose use matters to the community; but it must also be agreed that the sovereign alone is the judge of what matters.[51]

A citizen owes the State all the services he can render it as soon as the sovereign requests them. But the sovereign, for its part, cannot impose on the subjects any burden that is useless to the community. It cannot even will to do so, for under the law of reason nothing is done without a cause, any more than under the law of nature.

The engagements that bind us to the social body are obligatory only because they are mutual, and their nature is such that in fulfilling them one cannot work for someone else without also working for oneself. Why is the general will always right and why do all constantly want the happiness of each, if not because there is no one who does not apply this word *each* to himself, and does not think of himself as he votes for all? Which proves that the equality of right, and the concept of justice it produces, are derived from each man's preference for himself and consequently from the nature of man; that the general will, to be truly such, should be general in its object as well as in its essence; that it should come from all to apply to all; and that it loses its natural rectitude when it is directed toward any individual, determinate object. Because then, judging what is foreign to us, we have no true principle of equity to guide us.

Indeed, as soon as it is a matter of fact or a particular right concerning a point that has not been regulated by a prior, general convention, the affair is in dispute. It is a lawsuit where the interested private individuals constitute one party and the public the other, but in which I see neither what law must be followed nor what judge should decide. In this case it would be ridiculous to want to turn to an express decision of the

[49]Attentive readers, please do not be in a hurry to accuse me of inconsistency here. I have been unable to avoid it in my terminology, given the poverty of the language. But wait.[50]

[50]"I have thought a hundred times when writing that it is impossible in a long work to give the same meanings always to the same words. There is no language rich enough to give as many terms, nuances and phrases as our ideas have changes. . . . In spite of that, I am persuaded that one can be clear, even in the poverty of our language; not in always giving the same meaning to the same words, but in so doing that each time that every word is used, the meaning one gives it be sufficiently determined by the ideas related to it. . . ." *Émile,* II (Pléiade, IV, 345 note). Compare *First and Second Discourses* (ed. Masters, pp. 25–26).

[51]The last clause was added to the final version. While it appears to be "collectivist" in tone, Rousseau was concerned by the danger of an individual who sought the protection and benefits of civil society without paying his share of the costs. As he put it in *Geneva Manuscript,* I, ii: "private interest and the general good . . . are mutually exclusive in the natural order of things, and social laws are a yoke that each wants to impose on the other without having to bear himself." In the first draft, Rousseau wrote that the "life and *existence*" of citizens as "private persons" are "naturally independent" of the "public person" (p. 175); in the final version, he changed the phrase to read "life and *freedom*"of "private persons," thus emphasizing "the natural rights to which they are entitled as men." Rousseau constantly tries to *balance* the claims of the individual and of society. Compare Rousseau's "fundamental distinctions," cited in *Social Contract,* editorial note 26.

general will, which can only be the conclusion of one of the parties and which, for the other party, is consequently only a foreign, private will, showing injustice on the occasion and subject to error. Thus just as a private will cannot represent the general will, the general will in turn changes its nature when it has a particular object; and as a general will it cannot pass judgment on either a man or a fact. When the people of Athens, for example, appointed or dismissed its leaders, awarded honors to one or imposed penalties on another, and by means of a multitude of particular decrees performed indistinguishably all the acts of government, the people then no longer had a general will properly speaking. It no longer acted as sovereign, but as magistrate. This will appear contrary to commonly held ideas, but you must give me time to present my own.

It should be understood from this that what generalizes the will is not so much the number of votes as the common interest that unites them, because in this institution everyone necessarily subjects himself to the conditions he imposes on others, an admirable agreement between interest and justice which confers on common deliberations a quality of equity that vanishes in the discussion of private matters, for want of a common interest that unites and identifies the rule of the judge with that of the party.

However one traces the principle, one always reaches the same conclusion, namely that the social compact established an equality between the citizens such that they all engage themselves under the same conditions and should all benefit from the same rights. Thus by the very nature of the compact, every act of sovereignty, which is to say every authentic act of the general will, obligates or favors all citizens equally, so that the sovereign knows only the nation as a body and makes no distinctions between any of those who compose it. What really is an act of sovereignty then? It is not a convention between a superior and an inferior, but a convention between the body and each of its members. A convention that is legitimate because it has the social contract as a basis; equitable, because it is common to all; useful, because it can have no other object than the general good; and solid, because it has the public force and the supreme power as guarantee. As long as subjects are subordinated only to such conventions, they do not obey anyone, but solely their own will; and to ask how far the respective rights of the sovereign and of citizens is to ask how far the latter can engage themselves to one another, each to all and all to each.

It is apparent from this that the sovereign power, albeit entirely absolute, entirely sacred, and entirely inviolable, does not and cannot exceed the limits of the general conventions, and that every man can fully dispose of the part of his goods and freedom that has been left to him by these conventions. So that the sovereign never has the right to burden one subject more than another, because then the matter becomes individual, and its power is no longer competent.

Once these distinctions are acknowledged, it is so false that the social contract involves any true renunciation on the part of private individuals that their situation, by the effect of this contract, is actually preferable to what it was beforehand; and instead of an alienation, they have only exchanged to their advantage an uncertain, precarious mode of existence for another that is better and safer; natural independence for freedom; the power to harm others for their personal safety; and their force, which others could overcome, for a right which the social union makes invincible. Their life itself, which they have dedicated to the State, is constantly protected by it; and when they risk it for the State's defense, what are they then doing except to give back to the State what they have received from it? What are they doing that they did not do more often and with greater danger in the state of nature, when waging inevitable fights they defend at the risk of their life that which preserves it for them? It is true that everyone has to fight, if need be, for the homeland, but also no one ever has to fight for himself. Don't we still gain by risking, for something that gives us security, a part of what we would have to risk for ourselves as soon as our security is taken away? . . .

A Theory of Justice

John Rawls

THE MAIN IDEA OF THE THEORY OF JUSTICE

My aim is to present a conception of justice which generalizes and carries to a higher level of abstraction the familiar theory of the social contract as found, say, in Locke, Rousseau, and Kant.[1] In order to do this we are not to think of the original contract as one to enter a particular society or to set up a particular form of government. Rather, the guiding idea is that the principles of justice for the basic structure of society are the object of the original agreement. They are the principles that free and rational persons concerned to further their own interests would accept in an initial position of equality as defining the fundamental terms of their association. These principles are to regulate all further agreements; they specify the kinds of social cooperation that can be entered into and the forms of government that can be established. This way of regarding the principles of justice I shall call justice as fairness.

Thus we are to imagine that those who engage in social cooperation choose together, in one joint act, the principles which are to assign basic rights and duties and to determine the division of social benefits. Men are to decide in advance how they are to regulate their claims against one another and what is to be the foundation charter of their society. Just as each person must decide by rational reflection what constitutes

---

[1]As the text suggests, I shall regard Locke's *Second Treatise of Government,* Rousseau's *The Social Contract,* and Kant's ethical works beginning with *The Foundations of the Metaphysics of Morals* as definitive of the contract tradition. For all of its greatness, Hobbes's *Leviathan* raises special problems. A general historical survey is provided by J. W. Gough, *The Social Contract,* 2nd ed. (Oxford, The Clarendon Press, 1957), and Otto Gierke, *Natural Law and the Theory of Society,* trans. with an introduction by Ernest Barker (Cambridge, The University Press, 1934). A presentation of the contract view as primarily an ethical theory is to be found in G. R. Grice, *The Grounds of Moral Judgment* (Cambridge, The University Press, 1967). See also §19, note 30.

his good, that is, the system of ends which it is rational for him to pursue, so a group of persons must decide once and for all what is to count among them as just and unjust. The choice which rational men would make in this hypothetical situation of equal liberty, assuming for the present that this choice problem has a solution, determines the principles of justice.

In justice as fairness the original position of equality corresponds to the state of nature in the traditional theory of the social contract. This original position is not, of course, thought of as an actual historical state of affairs, much less as a primitive condition of culture. It is understood as a purely hypothetical situation characterized so as to lead to a certain conception of justice.[2] Among the essential features of this situation is that no one knows his place in society, his class position or social status, nor does any one know his fortune in the distribution of natural assets and abilities, his intelligence, strength, and the like. I shall even assume that the parties do not know their conceptions of the good or their social psychological propensities. The principles of justice are chosen behind a veil of ignorance. This ensures that no one is advantaged or disadvantaged in the choice of principles by the outcome of natural chance or the contingency of social circumstances. Since all are similarly situated and no one is able to design principles to favor his particular condition, the principles of justice are the result of a fair agreement or bargain. For given the circumstances of the original position, the symmetry of everyone's relations to each other, this initial situation is fair between individuals as moral persons, that is, as rational beings with their ends and capable, I shall assume, of a sense of justice. The original position is, one might say, the appropriate initial status quo, and thus the fundamental agreements reached in it are fair. This explains the propriety of the name "justice as fairness": it conveys the idea that the principles of justice are agreed to in an initial situation that is fair. The name does not mean that the concepts of justice and fairness are the same, any more than the phrase "poetry as metaphor" means that the concepts of poetry and metaphor are the same.

Justice as fairness begins, as I have said, with one of the most general of all choices which persons might make together, namely, with the choice of the first principles of a conception of justice which is to regulate all subsequent criticism and reform of institutions. Then, having chosen a conception of justice, we can suppose that they are to choose a constitution and a legislature to enact laws, and so on, all in accordance with the principles of justice initially agreed upon. Our social situation is just if it is such that by this sequence of hypothetical agreements we would have contracted into the general system of rules which defines it. Moreover, assuming that the original position does determine a set of principles (that is, that a particular conception of justice would be chosen), it will then be true that whenever social institutions satisfy these principles those engaged in them can say to one another that they are cooperating on terms to which they would agree if they were free and equal persons whose relations with respect to one another were fair. They could all view their arrangements as meeting the stipulations which they would acknowledge in an initial situa-

[2]Kant is clear that the original agreement is hypothetical. See *The Metaphysics of Morals,* pt. I *(Rechtslehre),* especially §§47, 52; and pt. II of the essay "Concerning the Common Saying: This May Be True in Theory but It Does Not Apply in Practice," in *Kant's Political Writings,* ed. Hans Reiss and trans. by H. B Nisbet (Cambridge, The University Press, 1970), pp. 73–87. See Georges Vlachos, *La Pensée politique de Kant* (Paris, Presses Universitaires de France, 1962), pp. 326–335; and J. G. Murphy, *Kant: The Philosophy of Right* (London, Macmillan, 1970), pp. 109–112, 133–136, for a further discussion

tion that embodies widely accepted and reasonable constraints on the choice of principles. The general recognition of this fact would provide the basis for a public acceptance of the corresponding principles of justice. No society can, of course, be a scheme of cooperation which men enter voluntarily in a literal sense; each person finds himself placed at birth in some particular position in some particular society, and the nature of this position materially affects his life prospects. Yet a society satisfying the principles of justice as fairness comes as close as a society can to being a voluntary scheme, for it meets the principles which free and equal persons would assent to under circumstances that are fair. In this sense its members are autonomous and the obligations they recognize self-imposed.

One feature of justice as fairness is to think of the parties in the initial situation as rational and mutually disinterested. This does not mean that the parties are egoists, that is, individuals with only certain kinds of interests, say in wealth, prestige, and domination. But they are conceived as not taking an interest in one another's interests. They are to presume that even their spiritual aims may be opposed, in the way that the aims of those of different religions may be opposed. Moreover, the concept of rationality must be interpreted as far as possible in the narrow sense, standard in economic theory, of taking the most effective means to given ends. I shall modify this concept to some extent, as explained later (§25), but one must try to avoid introducing into it any controversial ethical elements. The initial situation must be characterized by stipulations that are widely accepted.

In working out the conception of justice as fairness one main task clearly is to determine which principles of justice would be chosen in the original position. To do this we must describe this situation in some detail and formulate with care the problem of choice which it presents. These matters I shall take up in the immediately succeeding chapters. It may be observed, however, that once the principles of justice are thought of as arising from an original agreement in a situation of equality, it is an open question whether the principle of utility would be acknowledged. Offhand it hardly seems likely that persons who view themselves as equals, entitled to press their claims upon one another, would agree to a principle which may require lesser like prospects for some simply for the sake of a greater sum of advantages enjoyed by others. Since each desires to protect his interests, his capacity to advance his conception of the good, no one has a reason to acquiesce in an enduring loss for himself in order to bring about a greater net balance of satisfaction. In the absence of strong and lasting benevolent impulses, a rational man would not accept a basic structure merely because it maximized the algebraic sum of advantages irrespective of its permanent effects on his own basic rights and interests. Thus it seems that the principle of utility is incompatible with the conception of social cooperation among equals for mutual advantage. It appears to be inconsistent with the idea of reciprocity implicit in the notion of a well-ordered society. Or, at any rate, so I shall argue.

I shall maintain instead that the persons in the initial situation would choose two rather different principles: the first requires equality in the assignment of basic rights and duties, while the second holds that social and economic inequalities, for example inequalities of wealth and authority, are just only if they result in compensating benefits for everyone, and in particular for the least advantaged members of society. These principles rule out justifying institutions on the grounds that the hardships of some are offset by a greater good in the aggregate. It may be expedient but it is not just that some should have less in order that others may prosper. But there is no injustice in the greater benefits earned by a few provided that the situation of persons not so fortunate is thereby improved. The intuitive idea is that since everyone's well-being depends upon a scheme of cooperation without which no one could have a satisfactory life, the division of advantages should be such as to draw forth the willing cooperation of everyone taking part in it, including those less well situated. Yet this can be expected only if reasonable terms are proposed. The two principles mentioned seem to be a fair agreement on the basis of which those better endowed, or more fortunate in their social position, neither of which we can be said to deserve, could expect the willing cooperation of others when some workable scheme is a necessary condition of the welfare of all.[3] Once we decide to look for a conception of justice that nullifies the accidents of natural endowment and the contingencies of social circumstance as counters in quest for political and economic advantage, we are led to these principles. They express the result of leaving aside those aspects of the social world that seem arbitrary from a moral point of view.

The problem of the choice of principles, however, is extremely difficult. I do not expect the answer I shall suggest to be convincing to everyone. It is, therefore, worth noting from the outset that justice as fairness, like other contract views, consists of two parts: (1) an interpretation of the initial situation and of the problem of choice posed there, and (2) a set of principles which, it is argued, would be agreed to. One may accept the first part of the theory (or some variant thereof), but not the other, and conversely. The concept of the initial contractual situation may seem reasonable although the particular principles proposed are rejected. To be sure, I want to maintain that the most appropriate conception of this situation does lead to principles of justice contrary to utilitarianism and perfectionism, and therefore that the contract doctrine provides an alternative to these views. Still, one may dispute this contention even though one grants that the contractarian method is a useful way of studying ethical theories and of setting forth their underlying assumptions.

Justice as fairness is an example of what I have called a contract theory. Now there may be an objection to the term "contract" and related expressions, but I think it will serve reasonably well. Many words have misleading connotations which at first are likely to confuse. The terms "utility" and "utilitarianism" are surely no exception. They too have unfortunate suggestions which hostile critics have been willing to exploit; yet they are clear enough for those prepared to study utilitarian doctrine. The same should be true of the term "contract" applied to moral theories. As I have mentioned, to understand it one has to keep in mind that it implies a certain level of abstraction. In particular, the content of the relevant agreement is not to enter a given society or to adopt a given form of government, but to accept certain moral principles. Moreover, the undertakings referred to are purely hypothetical: a contract view holds that certain principles would be accepted in a well-defined initial situation.

The merit of the contract terminology is that it conveys the idea that principles of justice may be conceived as principles that would be chosen by rational persons, and that in this way conceptions of justice may be explained and justified. The theory of justice is a part, perhaps the most significant part, of the theory of rational choice. Furthermore, principles of justice deal with conflicting claims upon the advantages won by social cooperation; they apply to the relations among several persons or groups. The word "contract" suggests this plurality as well as the condition that the ap-

---

[3]For the formulation of the intuitive idea I am indebted to Allan Gibbard.

propriate division of advantages must be in accordance with principles acceptable to all parties. The condition of publicity for principles of justice is also connoted by the contract phraseology. Thus, if these principles are the outcome of an agreement, citizens have a knowledge of the principles that others follow. It is characteristic of contract theories to stress the public nature of political principles. Finally there is the long tradition of the contract doctrine. Expressing the tie with this line of thought helps to define ideas and accords with natural piety. There are then several advantages in the use of the term "contract." With due precautions taken, it should not be misleading.

A final remark. Justice as fairness is not a complete contract theory. For it is clear that the contractarian idea can be extended to the choice of more or less an entire ethical system, that is, to a system including principles for all the virtues and not only for justice. Now for the most part I shall consider only principles of justice and others closely related to them; I make no attempt to discuss the virtues in a systematic way. Obviously if justice as fairness succeeds reasonably well, a next step would be to study the more general view suggested by the name "rightness as fairness." But even this wider theory fails to embrace all moral relationships, since it would seem to include only our relations with other persons and to leave out of account how we are to conduct ourselves toward animals and the rest of nature. I do not contend that the contract notion offers a way to approach these questions which are certainly of the first importance; and I shall have to put them aside. We must recognize the limited scope of justice as fairness and of the general type of view that it exemplifies. How far its conclusions must be revised once those other matters are understood cannot be decided in advance.

THE ORIGINAL POSITION AND JUSTIFICATION

I have said that the original position is the appropriate initial status quo which insures that the fundamental agreements reached in it are fair. This fact yields the name "justice as fairness." It is clear, then, that I want to say that one conception of justice is more reasonable than another, or justifiable with respect to it, if rational persons in the initial situation would choose its principles over those of the other for the role of justice. Conceptions of justice are to be ranked by their acceptability to persons so circumstanced. Understood in this way the question of justification is settled by working out a problem of deliberation: we have to ascertain which principles it would be rational to adopt given the contractual situation. This connects the theory of justice with the theory of rational choice.

If this view of the problem of justification is to succeed, we must, of course, describe in some detail the nature of this choice problem. A problem of rational decision has a definite answer only if we know the beliefs and interests of the parties, their relations with respect to one another, the alternatives between which they are to choose, the procedure whereby they make up their minds, and so on. As the circumstances are presented in different ways, correspondingly different principles are accepted. The concept of the original position, as I shall refer to it, is that of the most philosophically favored interpretation of this initial choice situation for the purposes of a theory of justice.

But how are we to decide what is the most favored interpretation? I assume, for one thing, that there is a broad measure of agreement that principles of justice should be chosen under certain conditions. To justify a particular description of the initial situation one shows that it incorporates these commonly shared presumptions. One argues from widely accepted but weak premises to more specific conclusions. Each of the presumptions should by itself be natural and plausible; some of them may seem innocuous or even trivial. The aim of the contract approach is to establish that taken together they impose significant bounds on acceptable principles of justice. The ideal outcome would be that these conditions determine a unique set of principles; but I shall be satisfied if they suffice to rank the main traditional conceptions of social justice.

One should not be misled, then, by the somewhat unusual conditions which characterize the original position. The idea here is simply to make vivid to ourselves the restrictions that it seems reasonable to impose on arguments for principles of justice, and therefore on these principles themselves. Thus it seems reasonable and generally acceptable that no one should be advantaged or disadvantaged by natural fortune or social circumstances in the choice of principles. It also seems widely agreed that it should be impossible to tailor principles to the circumstances of one's own case. We should insure further that particular inclinations and aspirations, and persons' conceptions of their good do not affect the principles adopted. The aim is to rule out those principles that it would be rational to propose for acceptance, however little the chance of success, only if one knew certain things that are irrelevant from the standpoint of justice. For example, if a man knew that he was wealthy, he might find it rational to advance the principle that various taxes for welfare measures be counted unjust; if he knew that he was poor, he would most likely propose the contrary principle. To represent the desired restrictions one imagines a situation in which everyone is deprived of this sort of information. One excludes the knowledge of those contingencies which sets men at odds and allows them to be guided by their prejudices. In this manner the veil of ignorance is arrived at in a natural way. This concept should cause no difficulty if we keep in mind the constraints on arguments that it is meant to express. At any time we can enter the original position, so to speak, simply by following a certain procedure, namely, by arguing for principles of justice in accordance with these restrictions.

It seems reasonable to suppose that the parties in the original position are equal. That is, all have the same rights in the procedure for choosing principles; each can make proposals, submit reasons for their acceptance, and so on. Obviously the purpose of these conditions is to represent equality between human beings as moral persons, as creatures having a conception of their good and capable of a sense of justice. The basis of equality is taken to be similarity in these two respects. Systems of ends are not ranked in value; and each man is presumed to have the requisite abiity to understand and to act upon whatever principles are adopted. Together with the veil of ignorance, these conditions define the principles of justice as those which rational persons concerned to advance their interests would consent to as equals when none are known to be advantaged or disadvantaged by social and natural contingencies.

There is, however, another side to justifying a particular description of the original position. This is to see if the principles which would be chosen match our considered convictions of justice or extend them in an acceptable way. We can note whether applying these principles would lead us to make the same judgments about the basic structure of society which we now make intuitively and in which we have the greatest confidence; or whether, in cases where our present judgments are in doubt and given with hesitation, these principles offer a resolution which we can affirm on reflection.

There are questions which we feel sure must be answered in a certain way. For example, we are confident that religious intolerance and racial discrimination are unjust. We think that we have examined these things with care and have reached what we believe is an impartial judgment not likely to be distorted by an excessive attention to our own interests. These convictions are provisional fixed points which we presume any conception of justice must fit. But we have much less assurance as to what is the correct distribution of wealth and authority. Here we may be looking for a way to remove our doubts. We can check an interpretation of the initial situation, then, by the capacity of its principles to accommodate our firmest convictions and to provide guidance where guidance is needed.

In searching for the most favored description of this situation we work from both ends. We begin by describing it so that it represents generally shared and preferably weak conditions. We then see if these conditions are strong enough to yield a significant set of principles. If not, we look for further premises equally reasonable. But if so, and these principles match our considered convictions of justice, then so far well and good. But presumably there will be discrepancies. In this case we have a choice. We can either modify the account of the initial situation or we can revise our existing judgments, for even the judgments we take provisionally as fixed points are liable to revision. By going back and forth, sometimes altering the conditions of the contractual circumstances, at others withdrawing our judgments and conforming them to principle, I assume that eventually we shall find a description of the initial situation that both expresses reasonable conditions and yields principles which match our considered judgments duly pruned and adjusted. This state of affairs I refer to as reflective equilibrium.[4] It is an equilibrium because at last our principles and judgments coincide; and it is reflective since we know to what principles our judgments conform and the premises of their derivation. At the moment everything is in order. But this equilibrium is not necessarily stable. It is liable to be upset by further examination of the conditions which should be imposed on the contractual situation and by particular cases which may lead us to revise our judgments. Yet for the time being we have done what we can to render coherent and to justify our convictions of social justice. We have reached a conception of the original position.

I shall not, of course, actually work through this process. Still, we may think of the interpretation of the original position that I shall present as the result of such a hypothetical course of reflection. It represents the attempt to accommodate within one scheme both reasonable philosophical conditions on principles as well as our considered judgments of justice. In arriving at the favored interpretation of the initial situation there is no point at which an appeal is made to self-evidence in the traditional sense either of general conceptions or particular convictions. I do not claim for the principles of justice proposed that they are necessary truths or derivable from such truths. A conception of justice cannot be deducted from self-evident premises or conditions on principles; instead, its justification is a matter of the mutual support of many considerations, of everything fitting together into one coherent view.

A final comment. We shall want to say that certain principles of justice are justified because they would be agreed to in an initial situation of equality. I have empha-

[4]The process of mutual adjustment of principles and considered judgments is not peculiar to moral philosophy. See Nelson Goodman, *Fact, Fiction, and Forecast* (Cambridge, Mass., Harvard University Press, 1955), pp. 65–68, for parallel remarks concerning the justification of the principles of deductive and inductive inference.

sized that this original position is purely hypothetical. It is natural to ask why, if this agreement is never actually entered into, we should take any interest in these principles, moral or otherwise. The answer is that the conditions embodied in the description of the original position are ones that we do in fact accept. Or if we do not, then perhaps we can be persuaded to do so by philosophical reflection. Each aspect of the contractual situation can be given supporting grounds. Thus what we shall do is to collect together into one conception a number of conditions on principles that we are ready upon due consideration to recognize as reasonable. These constraints express what we are prepared to regard as limits on fair terms of social cooperation. One way to look at the idea of the original position, therefore, is to see it as an expository device which sums up the meaning of these conditions and helps us to extract their consequences. On the other hand, this conception is also an intuitive notion that suggests its own elaboration, so that led on by it we are drawn to define more clearly the standpoint from which we can best interpret moral relationships. We need a conception that enables us to envision our objective from afar: the intuitive notion of the original position is to do this for us[5]. . . .

TWO PRINCIPLES OF JUSTICE

I shall now state in a provisional form the two principles of justice that I believe would be chosen in the original position. In this section I wish to make only the most general comments, and therefore the first formulation of these principles is tentative. As we go on I shall run through several formulations and approximate step by step the final statement to be given much later. I believe that doing this allows the exposition to proceed in a natural way.

The first statement of the two principles reads as follows:

> First: each person is to have an equal right to the most extensive basic liberty compatible with a similar liberty for others.
> Second: social and economic inequalities are to be arranged so that they are both (a) reasonably expected to be to everyone's advantage, and (b) attached to positions and offices open to all.

There are two ambiguous phrases in the second principle, namely "everyone's advantage" and "open to all." Determining their sense more exactly will lead to a second formulation of the principle in §13. The final version of the two principles is given in §46; §39 considers the rendering of the first principle.

By way of general comment, these principles primarily apply, as I have said, to the basic structure of society. They are to govern the assignment of rights and duties and to regulate the distribution of social and economic advantages. As their formulation suggests, these principles presuppose that the social structure can be divided into two more or less distinct parts, the first principle applying to the one, the second to the other. They distinguish between those aspects of the social system that define and secure the equal liberties of citizenship and those that specify and establish social and economic inequalities. The basic liberties of citizens are, roughly speaking, politi-

---

[5]Henri Poincaré remarks: "Il nous faut une faculté qui nous fasse voir le but de loin, et, cette faculté, c'est l'intuition." *La Valeur de la science* (Paris, Flammarion, 1909), p. 27.

cal liberty (the right to vote and to be eligible for public office) together with freedom of speech and assembly; liberty of conscience and freedom of thought; freedom of the person along with the right to hold (personal) property; and freedom from arbitrary arrest and seizure as defined by the concept of the rule of law. These liberties are all required to be equal by the first principle, since citizens of a just society are to have the same basic rights.

The second principle applies, in the first approximation, to the distribution of income and wealth and to the design of organizations that make use of differences in authority and responsibility, or chains of command. While the distribution of wealth and income need not be equal, it must be to everyone's advantage, and at the same time, positions of authority and offices of command must be accessible to all. One applies the second principle by holding positions open, and then, subject to this constraint, arranges social and economic inequalities so that everyone benefits.

These principles are to be arranged in a serial order with the first principle prior to the second. This ordering means that a departure from the institutions of equal liberty required by the first principle cannot be justified by, or compensated for, by greater social and economic advantages. The distribution of wealth and income, and the hierarchies of authority, must be consistent with both the liberties of equal citizenship and equality of opportunity.

It is clear that these principles are rather specific in their content, and their acceptance rests on certain assumptions that I must eventually try to explain and justify. A theory of justice depends upon a theory of society in ways that will become evident as we proceed. For the present, it should be observed that the two principles (and this holds for all formulations) are a special case of a more general conception of justice that can be expressed as follows.

> All social values—liberty and opportunity, income and wealth, and the bases of self-respect—are to be distributed equally unless an unequal distribution of any, or all, of these values is to everyone's advantage.

Injustice, then, is simply inequalities that are not to the benefit of all. Of course, this conception is extremely vague and requires interpretation.

As a first step, suppose that the basic structure of society distributes certain primary goods, that is, things that every rational man is presumed to want. These goods normally have a use whatever a person's rational plan of life. For simplicity, assume that the chief primary goods at the disposition of society are rights and liberties, powers and opportunities, income and wealth.... These are the social primary goods. Other primary goods such as health and vigor, intelligence and imagination, are natural goods; although their possession is influenced by the basic structure, they are not so directly under its control. Imagine, then, a hypothetical initial arrangement in which all the social primary goods are equally distributed: everyone has similar rights and duties, and income and wealth are evenly shared. This state of affairs provides a benchmark for judging improvements. If certain inequalities of wealth and organizational powers would make everyone better off than in this hypothetical starting situation, then they accord with the general conception.

Now it is possible, at least theoretically, that by giving up some of their fundamental liberties men are sufficiently compensated by the resulting social and economic gains. The general conception of justice imposes no restrictions on what sort of inequalities are permissible; it only requires that everyone's position be improved. We need not suppose anything so drastic as consenting to a condition of slavery. Imagine instead that men forego certain political rights when the economic returns are significant and their capacity to influence the course of policy by the exercise of these rights would be marginal in any case. It is this kind of exchange which the two principles as stated rule out; being arranged in serial order they do not permit exchanges between basic liberties and economic and social gains. The serial ordering of principles expresses an underlying preference among primary social goods. When this preference is rational so likewise is the choice of these principles in this order.

In developing justice as fairness I shall, for the most part, leave aside the general conception of justice and examine instead the special case of the two principles in serial order. The advantage of this procedure is that from the first the matter of priorities is recognized and an effort made to find principles to deal with it. One is led to attend throughout to the conditions under which the acknowledgement of the absolute weight of liberty with respect to social and economic advantages, as defined by the lexical order of the two principles, would be reasonable. Offhand, this ranking appears extreme and too special a case to be of much interest; but there is more justification for it than would appear at first sight. Or at any rate, so I shall maintain (§82). Furthermore, the distinction between fundamental rights and liberties and economic and social benefits marks a difference among primary social goods that one should try to exploit. It suggests an important division in the social system. Of course, the distinctions drawn and the ordering proposed are bound to be at best only approximations. There are surely circumstances in which they fail. But it is essential to depict clearly the main lines of a reasonable conception of justice; and under many conditions anyway, the two principles in serial order may serve well enough. When necessary we can fall back on the more general conception.

The fact that the two principles apply to institutions has certain consequences. Several points illustrate this. First of all, the rights and liberties referred to by these principles are those which are defined by the public rules of the basic structure. Whether men are free is determined by the rights and duties established by the major institutions of society. Liberty is a certain pattern of social forms. The first principle simply requires that cetain sorts of rules, those defining basic liberties, apply to everyone equally and that they allow the most extensive liberty compatible with a like liberty for all. The only reason for circumscribing the rights defining liberty and making men's freedom less extensive than it might otherwise be is that these equal rights as institutionally defined would intereferre with one another.

Another thing to bear in mind is that when principles mention persons, or require that everyone gain from an inequality, the reference is to representative persons holding the various social positions, or offices, or whatever, established by the basic structures. Thus in applying the second principle I assume that it is possible to assign an expectation of well-being to representative individuals holding these positions. This expectation indicates their life prospects as viewed from their social station. In general, the expectations of representative persons depend upon the distribution of rights and duties throughout the basic structure. When this changes, expectations change. I assume, then, that expectations are connected: by raising the prospects of the representative man in one position we presumably increase or decrease the prospects of representative men in other positions. Since it applies to institutional forms, the second principle (or rather the first part of it) refers to the expectations of representative individuals. As I shall discuss below, neither principle applies to distributions of particular goods to particular individuals who may be identified by their proper names. The situation where someone is considering how to allocate certain commodities to needy persons who are known to him is not within the scope of the principles. They are meant to regulate basic institutional arrangements. We must not assume that there is much similarity from the standpoint of justice between an administrative allotment of goods to specific persons and the appropriate design of society. Our common sense institutions for the former may be a poor guide to the latter.

Now the second principle insists that each person benefit from permissible inequalities in the basic structure. This means that it must be reasonable for each relevant representative man defined by this structure, when he views it as a going concern, to prefer his prospects with the inequality to his prospects without it. One is not allowed to justify differences in income or organizational powers on the ground that the disadvantages of those in one position are outweighed by the greater advantages of those in another. Much less can infringements of liberty be counterbalanced in this way. Applied to the basic structure, the principle of utility would have us maximize the sum of expectations of representative men (weighted by the number of persons they represent, on the classical view); and this would permit us to compensate for the losses of some by the gains of others. Instead, the two principles require that everyone benefit from economic and social inequalities. It is obvious, however, that there are indefinitely many ways in which all may be advantaged when the initial arrangement of equality is taken as a benchmark. How then are we to choose among these possibilities? The principles must be specified so that they yield a determinate conclusion. . . .

THE NATURE OF THE ARGUMENT FOR CONCEPTIONS OF JUSTICE

The intuitive idea of justice as fairness is to think of the first principles of justice as themselves the object of an original agreement in a suitably defined initial situation. These principles are those which rational persons concerned to advance their interests would accept in this position of equality to settle the basic terms of their association. It must be known, then, that the two principles of justice are the solution for the problem of choice presented by the original position. In order to do this, one must establish that, given the circumstances of the parties, and their knowledge, beliefs, and interests, an agreement on these principles is the best way for each person to secure his ends in view of the alternatives available.

Now obviously no one can obtain everything he wants; the mere existence of other persons prevents this. The absolutely best for any man is that everyone else should join with him in furthering his conception of the good whatever it turns out to be. Or failing this, that all others are required to act justly but that he is authorized to exempt himself as he pleases. Since other persons will never agree to such terms of association these forms of egoism would be rejected. The two principles of justice, however, seem to be a reasonable proposal. In fact, I should like to show that these principles are everyone's best reply, so to speak, to the corresponding demands of the others. In this sense, the choice of this conception of justice is the unique solution to the problem set by the original position.

By arguing in this way one follows a procedure familiar in social theory. That is, a simplified situation is described in which rational individuals with certain ends and related to each other in certain ways are to choose among various courses of action in view of their knowledge of the circumstances. What these individuals will do is then derived by strictly deductive reasoning from these assumptions about their beliefs and interests, their situation and the options open to them. Their conduct is, in the phrase of Pareto, the resultant of tastes and obstacles.[6] In the theory of price, for example, the equilibrium of competitive markets is thought of as arising when many individuals each advancing his own interests give way to each other what they can best part with in return for what they most desire. Equilibrium is the result of agreements freely struck between willing traders. For each person it is the best situation that he can reach by free exchange consistent with the right and freedom of others to further their interests in the same way. It is for this reason that this state of affairs is an equilibrium, one that will persist in the absence of further changes in the circumstances. No one has any incentive to alter it. If a departure from this situation sets in motion tendencies which restore it, the equilibrium is stable.

Of course, the fact that a situation is one of equilibrium, even a stable one, does not entail that it is right or just. It only means that given men's estimate of their position, they act effectively to preserve it. Clearly a balance of hatred and hostility may be a stable equilibrium; each may think that any feasible change will be worse. The best that each can do for himself may be a condition of lesser injustice rather than of greater good. The moral assessment of equilibrium situations depends upon the background circumstances which determine them. It is at this point that the conception of the original position embodies features peculiar to moral theory. For while the theory of price, say, tries to account for the movements of the market by assumptions about the actual tendencies at work, the philosophically favored interpretation of the initial situation incorporates conditions which it is thought reasonable to impose on the choice of principles. By contrast with social theory, the aim is to characterize the situation so that the principles that would be chosen, whatever they turn out to be, are acceptable from a moral point of view. The original position is defined in such a way that it is a status quo in which any agreements reached are fair. It is a state of affairs in which the parties are equally represented as moral persons and the outcome is not conditioned by arbitrary contingencies or the relative balance of social forces. Thus justice as fairness is able to use the idea of pure procedural justice from the beginning.

It is clear, then, that the original position is a purely hypothetical situation. Nothing resembling it need ever take place, although we can by deliberately following the constraints it expresses simulate the reflections of the parties. The conception of the original position is not intended to explain human conduct except insofar as it tries to account for our moral judgments and helps to explain our having a sense of justice. Justice as fairness is a theory of our moral sentiments as manifested by our considered judgments in reflective equilibrium. These sentiments presumably affect our thought and action to some degree. So while the conception of the original position is part of the theory of conduct, it does not follow at all that there are actual situations that resemble it. What is necessary is that the principles that would be accepted play the requisite part in our moral reasoning and conduct.

One should note also that the acceptance of these principles is not conjectured as a psychological law or probability. Ideally anyway, I should like to show that their

---

[6]*Manuel d'économie politique* (Paris, 1009), ch. III, §23. Pareto says: "L'équilibre résulte précisément de cette opposition des goûts et des obstacles."

acknowledgment is the only choice consistent with the full description of the original position. The argument aims eventually to be strictly deductive. To be sure, the persons in the original position have a certain psychology, since various assumptions are made about their beliefs and interests. These assumptions appear along with other premises in the description of this initial situation. But clearly arguments from such premises can be fully deductive, as theories in politics and economics attest. We should strive for a kind of moral geometry with all the rigor which this name connotes. Unhappily the reasoning I shall give will fall far short of this, since it is highly intuitive throughout. Yet it is essential to have in mind the ideal one would like to achieve.

A final remark. There are, as I have said, many possible interpretations of the initial situation. This conception varies depending upon how the contracting parties are conceived, upon what their beliefs and interests are said to be, upon which alternatives are available to them, and so on. In this sense, there are many different contract theories. Justice as fairness is but one of these. But the question of justification is settled, as far as it can be, by showing that there is one interpretation of the initial situation which best expresses the conditions that are widely thought reasonable to impose on the choice of principles yet which, at the same time, leads to a conception that characterizes our considered judgments in reflective equilibrium. This most favored, or standard, interpretation I shall refer to as the original position. We may conjecture that for each traditional conception of justice there exists an interpretation of the initial situation in which its principles are the preferred solution. Thus, for example, there are interpretations that lead to the classical as well as the average principle of utility. These variations of the initial situation will be mentioned as we go along. The procedure of contract theories provides, then, a general analytic method for the comparative study of conceptions of justice. One tries to set out the different conditions embodied in the contractual situation in which their principles would be chosen. In this way one formulates the various underlying assumptions on which these conceptions seem to depend. But if one interpretation is philosophically most favored, and if its principles characterize our considered judgments, we have a procedure for justification as well. We cannot know at first whether such an interpretation exists, but at least we know what to look for.

The Nature and Soundness of the Contract and Coherence Arguments

David Lyons

III

Rawls' main argument for his principles ... involves the notion of a "social contract." He asks us to imagine that a number of individuals who realize that they can benefit from cooperation seek agreement on the distributive ground rules for their social arrangements. If they can all agree on one set of principles, then, Rawls claims, these are certified as *the* principles of justice. And he argues, of course, that his principles would be selected. I shall deal with the nature of this argument first, and later turn to the soundness of Rawls' specific claims on behalf of his own principles. ...

What bearing could a Rawlsian social contract, an imaginary agreement, have on us? Why should we think ourselves in any way bound by it, obliged to judge our institutions by the principles agreed to, and to act accordingly? I shall try to suggest some answers to these questions by putting together the Rawlsian idea of a contract argument in stages.

An obvious difficulty for a hypothetical contract argument is that any group of individuals is likely to be misinformed about, or at least ignorant of, some relevant facts. How absurd to suppose ourselves bound by principles that may be grounded on ignorance or bad reasoning! Rawls avoids these objections by assuming that the deliberators have full knowledge of all the relevant general facts and scientific laws ... and that they also are rational, at least in the sense that they can decide on the basis of their long-term self-interest ...

Even so, an arbitarily selected group of individuals are unlikely to agree, or may well agree on distributive ground rules that specially favor some rather than others. Each person will seek principles to serve him best, given his own special talents, interests, needs, and condition in society. To avoid this source of contention, Rawls places the deliberators behind a "veil of ignorance" that deprives them temporarily of information about themselves, their specific conditions, and their social circumstances ... Then they cannot serve their separate, divergent interests, so they must select principles on the basis of their general knowledge of human beings and social institutions. Accordingly, they consider only the distribution of the primary goods.

These features of Rawls' hypothesis simplify the argument enormously, for they mean that the deliberators reason alike from the exact same premises. An incidental effect is that this is a "contract argument" in the most attenuated sense, since no room is left for disagreement, bargaining, or even relevant differences among the parties. At any rate, an important consequence is that unanimity is guaranteed if any of the hypothetical deliberators can rank alternative principles on the information that is made available to him ...

The problem of choice would still be extremely complex, and Rawls simplifies it further, increasing the likelihood that it has a rational solution. For example, instead of considering all questions of social justice, the deliberators limit their attention to the basic institutions of society. . . ; instead of choosing principles to suit all possible circumstances, they initially assume that their society actually conforms to whatever principles they select and that everyone there tries his best to serve justice . . .

When all such qualifications[1] are imposed, deliberations can proceed. Rawls has the deliberators compare alternative principles. He argues, first, that, given the special conditions that have been imposed, rational individuals who are choosing basic distributive ground rules would adopt a "maximin" strategy, which aims at guaranteeing that the worst condition one might find oneself in is the least undesirable of the alternatives . . . Given this connecting link, Rawls reasons that his principles would be preferred to others, since they favor the least advantaged members of society.[2]

Let us now step back and ask what all this accomplishes. Although Rawls provides only an elaborate sketch, he suggests that a relatively rigorous argument is possible. If that is right, then, from a logical standpoint, the contract argument is more powerful than a standard coherence argument. More important for us here, it might also be thought to possess greater justificatory force, because it avoids the suspicious circularity of the coherence argument by grounding principles, not on moral convictions that we happen to have, but on the independent theory of (self-interested) rational choice and facts about the human condition. Rawls, at any rate, claims that this argument justifies his principles. . . .

However, it is not transparently obvious that the principles of justice are to be viewed as the solution to a problem of (self-interested) rational choice—or that, when they are so viewed, they have been certified as *moral* principles. Rawls does not seem to explain this aspect of his argument adequately. And there are at least some possible grounds for thinking that he may have missed the mark and brought forward something other than a conception of justice.

The reason is that one can construe Rawls' principles as a rational (self-interested) departure from an egalitarian norm, where equality (and not Rawls' explicit principles of distribution) serves as the conception of justice *per se*. This interpretation is encouraged by the fact that one can find in Rawls the suggestion of an argument for egalitarianism plus another argument, on rational (self-interested) grounds, to depart from that norm. In the first place, Rawls maintains that distributions flowing from or based on natural or social contingencies alone are "arbitrary from a moral point of view" . . . Although he seems to believe there is a valid distinction between just and unjust distributions, he seems at first to deny that there is any valid *moral* basis for *discriminating* among persons when conferring benefits and imposing burdens. This

---

[1]For example, the principles actually concern the condition of "representative persons in the various social positions" I am ignoring here . . . many features of Rawls' theory that seem irrelevant to the present argument.

[2]I am glossing over complex problems here. For example, the maximin rule favors the worst-off, but the general conception of justice does not, requiring instead that all benefit from inequalities; and the Difference Principle (in the special conception) sometimes seems to favor the least advantaged, sometimes not. The gaps between these alternative conceptions, or formulations, are undoubtedly mediated by Rawls' "natural assumptions," "chain-connection" and "close-knittedness". . . .; which seem more controversial than he suggests. The upshot seems to be that favoring-the-worst-off is theoretically basic in Rawls' system, benefiting-all turning upon further contingent assumptions. Confusion arises in part because Rawls never formulates the general conception in the basic way, favoring the worst-off, though he takes pains to do this for the Difference Principle.

points (at least on the surface) to a strict egalitarianism. But, in the second place, Rawls also believes that devices such as incentives can benefit all, though they do so unequally . . . When they do, it seems rational to accept them and irrational (from a self-interested point of view) to refuse them. Thus, it seems rational, in general, from a self-interested point of view, to accept such departures from strict egalitarianism. One cannot lose: one stands only to gain. In this way, Rawls' position can seem like the amalgam of a moral egalitarianism and a non-moral acceptance of beneficial inequalities.[3]

The temptation so to view Rawls' principles is reinforced by (what I imagine would be) our shared, considered moral judgment of a test case: Suppose that a society has been organized on egalitarian lines by unanimous agreement, freely entered into. Suppose, further, that its members realize they could improve their material conditions by accepting Rawlsian inequalities, which benefit everyone. But, despite this, they freely and unanimously reaffirm their commitment to egalitarian institutions, thus refusing possible benefits. Now, from a self-interested standpoint, they might well be regarded as irrational. But there seems little reason to call them, or their institutions, unjust, or in any way defective from the standpoint of justice. Since they would be defective, according to Rawls' principles,[4] those principles seem miscast as principles *of justice,* even if they can be supported by the argument from rational self-interest in the original position.

There is, of course, another notion of social justice that is closer to the surface, and more faithful to the official spirit, of Rawls' principles. This is what he calls "reciprocity". . . , which corresponds closely to the notion of a "fair exchange." It seems a fair exchange, indeed, for the less advantaged to allow others extra benefits when everyone will profit as a consequence; and for the more advantaged to restrict their extra benefits to whatever will be useful to others. But Rawls' principles go well beyond this intuitive notion of fairness too. The intuitive notion merely *allows* such fair exchanges and does not require them; Rawls' principles require them, in the name of justice.[5]

These remarks are intended here, not as objections to Rawls' substantive principles, but as suggestions that his contract argument lacks moral force. It must be granted, however, that I have only given reasons for doubting that Rawls' principles fall neatly into the traditional category of *justice;* even if these were true, it would not follow that they do not describe the most important virtue of social institutions, as Rawls claims they do. Furthermore, I believe that much can be said in defense of Rawls' idea of a contract argument.

Let me deal with a couple of unsatisfactory defenses of it first. Someone might concede that the contract argument does not generate moral principles and hold that it is not supposed to. The coherence argument identifies certain principles as express-

---

[3]The general conception is at one point said to be arrived at by a similar agreement that begins differently . . . But I am uncertain how this squares with my reconstruction of Rawls' argument for the general conception . . . and accepted by Rawls in our 1972 Eastern Division APA symposium.

[4]Rawls' principles require any departure from equality that will benefit everyone (see note [5] below). But his special terminology seems to acknowledge our contrary intuitions. Thus, egalitarian arrangements when inequalities would benefit all are to be called "just throughout, but not the best just arrangement" . . .

[5]Unless his principles required such "reciprocity," thus guaranteeing that prospects under them would be better than under egalitarianism, they might also compare unfavorably with utilitarianism and thus fail to be selected in the original position.

ing our shared sense of justice, and the contract argument is supposed only to confer on those principles independent rational force, not moral certification. But, if nothing more were said, even that rational force would be problematic, since none of us seems likely to be found in the original position.

Alternatively, it might be held that the contract argument has moral force because of certain constraints imposed on it that I have not yet mentioned. For example, Rawls restricts the alternatives that are to be considered by the hypothetical deliberators to what he calls "recognizably ethical" conceptions ... But this would not help the argument at all. It would not explain how such principles are binding on us, or at least rational for us, here and now. Indeed, from a self-interested point of view, such restrictions would only serve to weaken the contract argument, for they would limit the choices of deliberators and might exclude principles that would otherwise be favored. Finally, these restrictions might account for and thus reinforce the impression that I have already described, that Rawls' principles are an amalgam of morality and self-interest.

To develop a more satisfactory account of the contract argument, one must combine some suggestions made by Rawls that are either never explicitly put together, sufficiently emphasized, or adequately developed. Rawls maintains that the principles of justice can be regarded as emerging from a fair procedure; the original position is supposed to guarantee just that ... But, to understand the force of this claim, one must exploit what Rawls has to say about "pure procedural justice". Finally, one must take seriously Rawls' assertion that we can enter the original position at any time ...

"The idea of the original position," Rawls says, "is to set up a fair procedure so that any principles agreed to will be just. The aim is to use the notion of pure procedural justice as a basis of theory" ... In the original position, no one enjoys an unfair advantage over another; no one is able, for example, to exploit his knowledge of the facts in order to serve his own special interests at others' cost. The veil of ignorance prevents that. When full knowledge of general facts and sound reasoning ability are also conferred on the deliberators, they all stand us equals. If they freely concur, that agreement will be fair. But what they agree to is how goods should be distributed in their society. In this way, a fair procedure is used to determine just distributions. That, I take it, is the root idea of "justice as fairness."

Let us suppose, for the sake of argument, that a fair agreement is reached in the original position. Why should it follow that distributions flowing from it are unjust? Or, rather, why should we say that distributions conflicting with the principles accepted there are unjust? According to Rawls, "pure procedural justice obtains when there is no independent criterion for the right result: instead there is a correct or fair procedure such that the outcome is likewise correct or fair, whatever it is, provided that the procedure has been properly followed. This situation is illustrated by gambling" ... We might try another example: Suppose that during an epidemic medical supplies are scarce relative to need; they cannot usefully be divided among all the persons who need them. We can think of everyone in need having an equal claim; or, if this violates the conditions assumed for pure procedural justice, we can suppose that no one has any claim to the supplies. In such circumstances, a fair lottery might legitimately be used to decide who shall obtain the medicine. Whatever the procedure chosen, if it is fair and properly followed, then the outcome can be regarded as "fair, or not unfair" ... Rawls' idea must then be that his hypothetical deliberators cannot invoke any independent criterion of just distribution. If they are to have one, they must forge their own. They themselves must choose among the possible bases for social organization.

But this seems to imply that *there simply are no* independent criteria of social justice. It is not that the veil of ignorance deprives one of, or prevents one from discovering, moral knowledge, but rather that it must be *created*. To see the weight of these remarks, we must apply them to our own case.

My reconstruction of Rawls' idea of a contract argument does not yet explain how it could have a bearing on us. We are not in the original position; we are imperfect reasoners; we lack full general knowledge; and we know at least some of our own special circumstances. Why should we suppose that the principles some imaginary deliberators would accept under conditions very different from ours are the principles of justice that *we* should judge with, and act by, here and now? Why should we suppose they have any rational force for us? Rawls' reply seems to be, that we can enter the original position at any time, and that the contract argument represents needed complaints upon, as well as ingredients for, our own satisfactory deliberations concerning the principles of justice . . .

Can we truly enter the original position, in the sense that we can assume the corresponding conditions for our moral arguments? Rawls seems to suggest that we can do so if we have the will, and, to some extent, this may be possible; for we can, perhaps, constrain ourselves to reason and deliberate impartially. In our own deliberations, for example, we must not allow ourselves to be swayed by considerations of special interest. (This mirrors the veil of ignorance and is, presumably, part of its justification.) But it is not true that we can reproduce at will other central features of the original position. Even with the best will in the world we cannot simply confer on ourselves either full rationality or full knowledge of all the general facts and scientific laws. I do not believe, however, that these limitations indicate defects in the contract argument idea. They acknowledge, in effect, that even our best efforts at deliberation are subject to correction in the light of scientific discovery and better reasoning. One would expect some such room for error in an account of anything aspiring to be moral knowledge. We should therefore think of the hypothetical contract argument (as distinct from Rawls' claims about the principles it generates) as an ideal that we can approximate in practice.

So far, I think, so good. Let us suppose that we can, so to speak, enter the original position. What significance does that have for us? I am not asking what (nonmoral) reason we might have for *participating* in fair deliberations designed to generate distributive principles. I am asking what reason we have for *believing* that the outcome of such deliberations are *the* principles of justice. Rawls answers this question by invoking the notion of pure procedural justice. But what can that mean for us? I see two ways of understanding it: (a) Outside the contract argument (or our approximations of it), there is no objective basis for social justice, (b) There is no alternative mode of argument for principles of social justice.

(a) We have noted that Rawls regards distributions flowing from or based on natural or social contingencies alone as morally arbitrary, not eligible to serve as valid bases for just distributions. And I suggested that this view seems at first to imply a strict egalitarianism. My point now is that Rawls avoids such a conclusion by invoking the notion of pure procedural justice. We will not—cannot—find the principles of justice in the natural world; we cannot discover them, for there is nothing to be discovered. There is no objective basis for just distributions—outside the contract argument. For the contract argument incorporates a fair procedure, and (the notion of pure procedural justice tells us) when there is no independent criterion of justice, we must turn to fair procedures if we are to have just, or fair, distributions at all. In other words, we must make our own moral principles. Moral skeptics conclude that our principles must be arbitrary. But, on Rawls' view, this does not follow. We can not only make our principles, we can also certify them ourselves, at least in the sense that we can rationally choose among the alternatives. Indeed, if Rawls is right about what is "morally arbitrary," then this is the *only* way we can validly get moral principles—and that alone entitles us to use it, for that allows us to invoke the notion of pure procedural justice.

It is unfortunate, therefore, that Rawls merely claims, without supporting argument, that distributions flowing from natural or social contingencies alone are arbitrary from a moral point of view. An adequate defense of this claim is required for the very idea of a contract argument, that is, to warrant the notion that pure procedural justice is relevant to our case. Rawls evidently believes that the claim would be accepted as one of our more general, abstract considered moral judgments. But there is room for disagreement here. As I understand Rawls' claim, so that it entitles him to invoke the notion of pure procedural justice, considerations of, say, merit or desert based on such qualities as talent or intelligence are not morally basic. More important, Rawls' dismissal of the notion of desert seems sometimes confused. He says, for example, that we do not deserve the advantages or disadvantages we receive in the "natural lottery" or as a consequence of social accident. It does not follow, however, as Rawls seems to suggest ... that some features of the natural or social "lotteries" could not serve as the *just basis* of deliberate distributions: one need not deserve what is itself a ground of desert. But I wish only to point out that difficult problems remain here, and I shall not pursue the matter further; it requires and will undoubtedly receive careful attention.

(b) Rawls' use of the notion of pure procedural justice also seems to assume that no alternative mode of argument for moral principles is possible. Suppose another line of reasoning were possible; then the principles emerging from the contract argument might clash with those certified in other ways. The problem here is not merely that of conflict between principles (though Rawls, unlike some other philosophers, is unprepared to accept it). It is, roughly, this: a sound argument for moral principles employing premises other than those found in the contract argument amounts, in effect, to an *independent* criterion of social justice. But the very possibility of such an independent criterion is contrary to the conditions of pure procedural justice. If there are grounds external to the contract agreement for judging the justice of social arrangements, then Rawls' "justice as fairness" notion would seem to be discredited.

As we have seen, however, Rawls seems to embrace the coherence argument too. But if the notion of pure procedural justice is to do its job of validating the contract agreement, then Rawls cannot regard the coherence argument as anything like a justification of defense of moral principles. It may be seen as an explication of our shared sense of justice, but its conclusions cannot be regarded as rationally binding. In fact, if the contract argument serves to justify moral principles, while the coherence argument is used to define our actual convictions, the results of the former cannot be applied in criticism of the latter.

This does not seem to be Rawls' view of the relations between these arguments, however ... His method is, instead, to design the contract argument so that its results agree with the outcome of the coherence argument, or at least to provide the best fit possible between our considered moral judgments and plausible premises for the argument, mediated by the principles of justice. On my attempt to suggest how the contract argument could have justificatory force, however, Rawls' approach looks as if it puts the cart before the horse.

One can go even further. Rawls may not merely try to fit the contract and coherence arguments together into a larger, consistent view. It is possible to conceive of Rawls' contract argument as a special branch of the coherence argument, that is to say, as a means of working out the implications of certain very basic values that we happen to share. I have refrained from suggesting this before because of my qualms about coherence arguments and my fear that such a way of viewing the contract argument would compromise it, undermining its independence and integrity, stripping it entirely of justificatory force. But, as I am not at all confident that Rawls would accept my view of these matters, I must suggest this way of looking at them now.

Suppose it can be said that justice rests on fairness, as Rawls believes. The contract argument *presupposes* the value of fairness (which, in turn, commits us, on Rawls' view, to other values, such as impartiality). The significance of this presupposition can be understood as follows. It sometimes looks as if the contract argument shows that, given general contingent facts about the human condition, certain principles of justice are, so to speak, rationally inescapable; at least that reason prefers them to the alternatives. But, on the alternative account that I am now suggesting, the contract argument shows, instead, that one who accepts the *prior* claims of fairness (impartiality, etc.) is rationally committed (given the relevant facts) to certain principles of justice.

In the contract argument, of course, fairness is initially construed, not as a way of dispensing benefits and burdens, but as a set of constraints upon arguments, deliberation, reasoning, and procedures generally; and this may seem to mitigate the argument's evaluative presuppositions. But this is misleading, for, under the notion of pure procedural justice, procedural fairness is valued precisely because it leads to social outcomes.

At any rate, the contract argument rests upon an unargued commitment to fairness and impartiality. On the assumption, then, that these are among the most "fixed" or least "provisional" of the "fixed points" in our system of shared values—perhaps fundamental to our (or a) moral outlook—the contract argument can retain some force. But it would nevertheless appear to be fundamentally weakened by its subordination to the coherence argument. It remains to be seen whether such evaluative assumptions are unavoidable; and, if so, whether it is reasonable to regard the resulting principles as justified.

Bargaining Our Way Into Morality: A Do-It-Yourself Primer

David Gauthier

1. "The theory of justice," according to John Rawls, "is a part, perhaps the most significant part, of the theory of rational choice."[1] Let us reflect on the significance of this claim.

Choice is the endeavour to realize one among several alternative possible states of affairs. The *rationality* which may be exhibited in choice is conceived in *maximizing* terms. A numerical measure is applied to the alternative possibilities, and choice among them is rational if and only if one endeavours to realize that possibility which has been assigned the greatest number. This measure is associated with *preference;* the alternative possible state of affairs are ordered preferentially, and the numerical measure, which is termed *utility,* is so established that greater utility indicates greater preference. The complications of this procedure need not concern us here.[2] What is important is that rational choice is conceived as *preference-based* choice, so that the rationally chosen state of affairs is the most preferred among the alternative possibilities.

John Rawls' claim, therefore, is that the theory of justice is the most significant part of the theory of preference-based choice. But this claim must seem quite implausible. Justice is moral virtue—indeed, some would claim that justice is the central moral virtue.[3] The theory of justice must be a part, and perhaps the most significant part, of the theory of morality. How can morality be part of preference-based choice?

The point of morality is surely to *override* preference. Were we to suppose that one should always endeavor to realize his or her most preferred state of affairs, then what need would we have for moral concepts? Why use the language of morality, of duties and obligations, of rights and responsibilities, when one might appeal directly to each person's greatest interest?

You offer me a choice among pieces of cake. I, greedily but perfectly rationally, basing my choice strictly on my preferences, select the largest piece. "That isn't fair," someone complains. "Of course not," I reply. My concern was not to be fair. My concern was to get the largest piece of cake—and I did. Surely here the appeal to *fairness,* to a consideration related to justice, is intended to override, or at least to constrain, preference-based choice. If you suppose that I should have chosen with fairness in mind, then you believe that I should not have acted simply to gratify my greed, even though my preference was for the largest piece of cake. You believe that I should have considered, not only my own desires, but also the desires of others.

---

[1]John Rawls, *A Theory of Justice,* Cambridge, Mass., 1971, p. 16.

[2]For further discussion of preference and utility, see R. D. Luce & Howard Raiffa, *Games and Decisions,* Wiley, New York, 1957, Chap. 2.

[3]Cf. Aristotle, *Ethica Nicomachea,* 1129b25ff.

Reprinted from *Philosophic Exchange,* vol. 2, no. 5, 1979, pp. 14–27.

Do examples such as this show that Rawls is wrong to treat the theory of justice as part of the theory of rational choice? Not at all. I shall argue that his claim is sound. Not that I agree with Rawls' theory of justice—that is quite another matter.[4] But justice provides a fundamental link between morality and preference, a link which, I believe, we are able to formulate in a precise and definitive way.

Indeed, I shall go farther than Rawls. In coming to understand how justice links morality and preference, one also realizes that our framework of moral concepts is seriously outmoded. Morality has been traditionally conceived as embracing the entire range of justifiable constraints on preference-based choice. But this range will be seen, in the light of my argument, to include at least two distinct, and apparently disparate, parts. One part, which I shall treat under the heading of *distributive justice,*[5] proves to be a constraint on preference-based choice which is based on the *structure* of some of the situations in which we make choices. This constraint is generated internally, within the theory of rational choice. That a *constraint* on preference can be justified by an *appeal* to preferences may appear paradoxical, but I shall endeavour to remove the air of paradox as we proceed. And as the upshot of my argument I shall insist that the distributive justice is not problematic in principle; it may be removed from the area of speculative enquiry, and established securely within rational choice. The age-old philosophical problems about the rationality of morality are *solved* for the case of distributive justice.

But the firm foundation provided for the constraints on preference-based choice required by distributive justice does not extend to those other constraints which are embraced in our traditional conception of morality. This is why our framework of moral concepts is outmoded. We must distinguish those constraints on preferences which can be justified by an appeal to preference itself from other, external constraints. The latter remains, at least for the present, within the area of speculative enquiry. And here the philosophical problems about the rationality of morality press with renewed vigour. . . .

3. The link which justice provides between morality and rational choice is discovered by reflection on a phenomenon long of concern to economists, but only recently receiving explicit attention from philosophers. The perfectly competitive market, the ideal of economic theory, is frequently marred by the presence of external inefficiencies. Here is a simple example of an inefficiency.

Several factories must each choose a method of waste disposal. Suppose that air is a free good, so that each factory may discharge effluents into the atmosphere without payment or restriction. Each may then find that it minimizes disposal costs by using the atmosphere as a sink for its wastes. But each factory may also suffer from the pollution occasioned by the effluents discharged. Indeed, it may be that the total cost to all factories, of atmospheric pollution caused by their wastes, exceeds the total net benefit in discharging those wastes into the atmosphere, rather than employing the

---

[4]For some of my disagreements with Rawls, see my paper "Justice and Natural Endowment: Toward a Critique of Rawls' Ideological Framework," *Society Theory and Practice,* 3, 1974, pp. 3–26.

[5]Why *distributive* justice? Because my concern is with justice in contexts in which a distribution of benefits and costs is part of the object of choice. In my view, distributive justice contrasts with acquisitive justice; the first constrains modes of cooperation, the second constrains the baseline from which cooperation proceeds. The Lockean proviso (see n. 19 *infra.*) concerns acquisitive justice, and falls in the realm of speculation which is *not* my concern in this paper.

least costly non-polluting method of disposal. The use of the atmosphere as a sink then constitutes an external inefficiency—*external,* in that each user displaces the costs of pollution onto others, and *inefficient,* in that the total costs of pollution exceed the total increase in disposal costs which would be required by an alternative non-polluting method of waste disposal. But no factory has any incentive to adopt such an alternative; each correctly minimizes its own costs by discharging its effluents into the atmosphere.

An external inefficiency creates a severe problem for rational choice. We may show this by considering an ideal case, in which each person involved in a situation is able to choose his or her course of action in the light of the actions selected by others.[6] Then, if the persons are rational, each will select that course of action which he or she expects will minimize his or her own utility, given the actions selected by the others. Each action will then be a *best reply* by the agent to the other's actions. If in any situation the action of each is a best reply to the actions of the others, then the set of actions is a *best reply* set.

In the presence of an external inefficiency, the outcome of any best reply set of actions is *sub-optimal,* which is to say that there is at least one other outcome possible in the situation which would better satisfy the preferences of *every person.*[7] Thus rational choice, given an external inefficiency, leads to an outcome which is *mutually disadvantageous,* in comparison with some other outcome which the persons could achieve if at least some were to choose differently.

In our example, each factory's best reply to the adoption of waste disposal methods by the others, is to discharge its own wastes into the atmosphere. But if each were to adopt some non-polluting alternative, then all would benefit. It may therefore seem that there is a straightforward solution to this problem created by the external inefficiency—a *cooperative* solution based on mutual *agreement.* All of the factories should agree to the least costly non-polluting method of waste disposal. It may then be urged that each factory's *true* best reply to the others consists in such mutual agreement, and since its outcome is optimal, the inefficiency disappears and there is no problem for rational choice.

Alas, matters are not so simple and straightforward. First, although a non-polluting method of waste disposal reduces total net costs, yet each factory need not benefit. Some factories may suffer greatly from the pollution caused by others, or may find some non-polluting method of waste disposal only slightly more costly than using the atmosphere as a sink, but other factories may suffer very little from pollution, or may find the increased costs of any alternative disposal method very great. Thus an agreement to adopt a non-polluting method of waste disposal, although beneficial on balance, may increase net costs for some factories. To avoid this, the agreement must provide for transfer payments, from those factories which would otherwise benefit most from non-pollution to those which would otherwise not benefit at all. But the amount of compensation is not easily determined. In general, many possible arrange-

---

[6]It may seem that if each person is to choose his or her course of action in the light of the actions chosen by the others, a regress is involved. But in fact the requirement may be operationalized quite straightforwardly. Suppose that each person were to announce his or her proposed action to the others, that after each announcement any other person might announce a new or changed proposal, and that no one were to act until, everyone having made some proposal, no one had announced any change.

[7]Strictly, an outcome is sub-optimal if there is at least one other possible outcome which would better satisfy the preferences of some persons without lessening the satisfaction of any.

ments will leave each factory better off than if all pollute, so that reaching a specific agreement, which each would rationally choose, raises difficulties not ony in practice, but for the theory of choice.

Furthermore, although the outcome of an agreement not to pollute may be optimal, and although the outcome of an agreement which includes transfer payments may be mutually advantageous, yet *adherence* to any agreement need not be the best reply course of action for any factory. Each factory would most prefer that all others cease using the atmosphere as a sink, while it continues polluting. Hence each will be tempted to defect from any agreement, however beneficial the agreement may be. Adherence to an agreement not to pollute, and to compensate any who would not otherwise benefit, is not, in the absence of penalties for violation, the most preferred course of action for any factory, whether the other factories adhere to the agreement, or violate it. Mutual violation thus makes up the best reply set of actions.

External inefficiencies thus raise two problems for rational choice. First, how are we to formulate a specific, optimal, mutually advantageous agreement, or mode of co-operation, for overcoming an inefficiency, which each person affected will consider it rational to accept? Second, how are we to ensure that rational persons will comply with an agreement so formulated and accepted? These problems may be related, in that we may suppose that compliance with an agreement is rational if acceptance of the agreement is also rational. But this is not evident, and I shall return to the problem of rational compliance in section 6.

4. Let us now focus on the problem of formulating a rational agreement. An agreement consists of a set of actions, one for each person party to it. I assume for the present that compliance is assured, so that no restriction to best reply sets of actions is involved. Now we may say that an agreement takes effect if and only if each party selects the same set of actions. Hence we may represent the problem of formulating agreement as a problem of rational choice—the problem of choosing among alternative possible states of affairs, each the outcome of a set of actions, one for each person involved, subject to the condition that the choice takes effect only if all parties select the same alternative.

This problem arises for anyone who may find him or herself in situations so structured that external inefficiencies arise, or in other words, so structured that no best reply set of actions is optimal. Although not all situations involving interaction among persons have this structure, there can be no assurance against finding oneself in such situations, as long as each individual's preference orderings among alternative possibilities are independent of the orderings of others. So this is a general problem which we all face. Its resolution is not to be found in the particular circumstances in which an individual finds him or herself. Rather its answer must be a general policy applicable to all such circumstances—and, obviously, applicable to all individuals. The policy which any person should adopt, who seeks to cooperate with his or her fellows in the face of external inefficiencies, is and must be identical with the policy every other person should adopt. The content of an agreed set of actions will of course vary with persons, their capacities, preferences, and circumstances, but the form which their agreement takes will be perfectly general.

Consider then the reasoning of a supposedly rational agent—myself—faced with this problem of rational choice. Given an external inefficiency, I must be willing to enter into some agreement with my fellows. Its expected utility to me must exceed the expected utility of failing to agree, which is the utility of my best reply to the actions I should expect others to perform in the absence of agreement. Its expected utility cannot exceed the greatest utility which would be compatible with others receiving only minimally more than they would in the absence of agreement. Thus a utility range is defined, with its lowest point the utility of no agreement, and its highest point the maximum utility compatible with others receiving their "no-agreement" utility. Each person will define such a utility range for him or herself, and only sets of actions which assure everyone a utility within his or her range will be candidates for agreement.

In choosing among candidates some compromise will be required. I must recognize that I am involved in a *bargaining situation,* and must make some *concession.*[8] How do I decide the magnitude of the concession which my agreement to some set of actions would require? The answer is implicit in the conception of a utility range. The lowest point of my range represents my point of *total concession,* in which I gain everything. Any intermediate point may be represented as a proportion of my total concession. Not only will this measure my concession; it will relate it to the concessions of others. Two persons make *equal concessions* in a situation if and only if each concedes the *same proportion* of his or her total concession.

Each set of actions which is a candidate for agreement may be represented also as a set of concessions, one for each person. Each such set must have a largest member—*the maximum* concession required for agreement to be reached on that set. Some possible set of concessions must have a largest member which is *no* greater than the largest member of any alternative set. This is the *minimax* concession—the smallest, or minimum, among all possible largest, or maximum concessions.

If there is to be agreement, then someone must make a concession at least equal to the minimax. Now if it is not rational for me to make such a concession, then, since the policy which is rational for me is rational for everyone, it is not rational for any person to make such a concession, and there can be no rational agreement. But it is rational for me to enter into an agreement; hence it must be rational for me to make a minimax concession. Furthermore, since agreement can be reached without any person making a larger concession, and since it cannot be rational for me to make a greater concession than necessary, it cannot be rational for me to make a concession larger than the minimax. Hence it is rational for me to enter into any agreement requiring at most the minimax concession from me. Since everyone reasons similarly, bargaining among rational persons proceeds on the *principle of minimax concession.* And this solves the problem of rational choice occasioned by external inefficiencies.

We have now characterized a *rational bargain.* I must next argue that the principle of minimax concession captures our conception of distributive justice, in characterizing a bargain which is fair as well as rational. And I must also argue that the principle constitutes a constraint on preference-based choice, even though it is, as I have shown, itself the outcome of a preference-based choice. Thus I must show that in acting on the principle of minimax concession, we enter into bargains which are fair,

[8]Discussions of bargaining theory may be found in J. F. Nash, "The Bargaining Problem," *Econometrica,* 18, 1950, pp. 155–162; E. Kalai & M. Smorodinsky, "Other Solutions to Nash's Bargaining Problem," *Econometrica,* 43, 1975, pp. 513–518; and my paper "The Social Contract: Individual Decision or Collective Bargain?," in C. A. Hooker, J. J. Leach, and E. F. McClennan (eds.), *Foundations and Applications of Decision Theory,* Vol. II, Reidel, Dordrect & Boston, 1978, pp. 47–67. The account I provide here of a rational bargain parallels a solution offered by Kalai and Smorodinsky.

and which constrain preference—or in other words, we bargain our way into morally binding arrangements.

One word of warning is in place before proceeding. Although we may literally bargain our way into moral constraints in some contexts, references to bargains and agreements are to be understood hypothetically. We face externalities and, if we are rational, we cooperate to overcome them. We may then assess our mode of cooperation *as if* it were the outcome of a bargain. But we need suppose no actual bargain or agreement.

5. Under what conditions is a state of affairs *distributively just?* The presence of more than one person (or perhaps of more than one sentient being) gives rise to a "distribution" of utilities, but this is not sufficient to raise issues of justice. If a state of affairs is said to be just or unjust, there must be at least one alternative to it, the variation in the utility-levels of different persons among alternatives must be at least partially interdependent, and the selection among alternatives must be at least partially a matter of human choice. These conditions are required if any comparison of the utilities received by different persons is to have moral significance. For distributive justice to have significance, distributive considerations must be relevant to the choice among the alternatives. If that choice is adequately represented by a best reply set of actions, then although the choice has distributive effects, these are of no concern to the choosers. It is, therefore, only when all best reply sets lead to sub-optimal outcomes, so that there are mutual advantages to be found in agreement or cooperation among persons, that considerations of distributive justice arise. Other moral considerations may arise in other contexts, but in restricting distributive justice in the context of mutually advantageous cooperation, we are following in the footsteps of Hobbes, Hume, and Rawls.[9]

This restriction on the scope of considerations of distributive justice suggests that a state of affairs is just, if and only if those involved in it would justly have agreed to the set of actions bringing it about. We must make any reference to agreement hypothetical, since as I have pointed out, much of our social interaction which is at least partially cooperative involves no actual agreement or bargain. But we may replace our question about the justice of states of affairs by one about the justice of agreements, provided we recognized that "Would we agree. . . ?" rather than "Did we agree. . . ?" is the appropriate way to introduce reference to such agreements.

The justice of an agreement may be supposed to have two dimensions—one concerning the matter of agreement, the other concerning the matter or content of agreement. But we cannot strictly distinguish these dimensions since in the case of hypothetical agreement, manner reduces to matter. We might say that, *ceteris paribus,* an agreement is just in manner if and only if it is genuinely voluntary. But the nearest approximation to what is voluntary in the case of hypothetical agreement, must be what is rationally acceptable. And so rationality and justice are inextricably intertwined in our account.

But we may still reflect on the matter of agreement. And here, although rationality and justice are still intertwined, the connection is less direct. For we may say, quite without reference to rationality, that a non-optimal agreement, in depriving someone

[9]Cf. discussions in Thomas Hobbes, *Leviathan,* Ch. 15; David Hume, *An Enquiry Concerning the Principles of Morals,* Sec. III, Pt.I; John Rawls, *A Theory of Justice,* pp. 126–130.

of benefit unnecessarily, without gain to anyone else, is unfair to the person so deprived. It is unfair for me to be allowed to profit at another's expense, no doubt, but it is equally unfair to me not to be allowed to profit, if no one is worsened thereby. Thus optimality is a requirement of fairness, and so of justice, as well as a requirement of rationality.

And this is not all. It is unfair to profit at another's expense. How is this unfairness expressed in the context of agreement? Each person's utility range represents his or her possible gain. The expected utility of any proposed agreement may be represented as a proportion of that gain, and so represented, constitutes the *relative advantage* of the agreement to the person. Now one profits at another's expense insofar as one's own relative advantage can arise only if he or she accepts, not merely a lesser relative advantage, but one less than anyone need accept. Thus one would arrive at a fair agreement by maximizing the minimum relative advantage received by anyone. But the measure of relative advantage is such that for any agreement, the sum of one's relative advantage and one's concession equal unity. Thus maximin relative advantage is equivalent to minimax concession. And so the requirements of fairness and rationality coincide. A hypothetical agreement which is just in manner and fair in manner is a rational agreement.

The justice of an agreement has been characterized *relatively* to the set of possible agreements. In other words, a state of affairs is distributively just (or unjust) in relation to alternatives. The set of possible agreements is itself defined relatively to the expected outcome of no agreement. Thus the justice or injustice of a state of affairs is determined against a baseline which provides a certain expected utility to each person, but which itself is not characterized as just or unjust. Any assessment, either of the range of possibilities, or of the baseline, falls outside the scope of considerations of distributive justice, except insofar as the assessment refers to other cooperative arrangements treated in terms of hypothetical agreement. Such assessment thus constitutes part of the realm of speculative enquiry from which distributive justice is freed by its identification with rational choice.

6. Why does a rational bargain, or a mode of cooperation which could be rationalized in terms of a bargain, involve a moral constraint on action? An objector might plausibly argue that insofar as the point of a bargain is to benefit all parties to it, morality has no place. Agreement and cooperation simply constitute an extension of rational prudence.

The apparent strength of this objection rests on ignoring the problem of compliance. This problem has received attention from earlier theorists of justice; although my concern here is not to discuss texts, a quotation from Hume may be illuminating. Hume, I should note, holds a general view of morality strongly opposed to the one I have assumed; he supposes it to further, rather than to constrain, each individual's pursuit of his own interests.[10] But on this view he finds that justice presents a problem:

"Treating vice with the greatest candour, . . . there is not, in any instance, the smallest pretext for giving it the preference above virtue, with a view of self-interest; except, perhaps, in the case of justice, where a man, taking things in a certain light,

[10]". . . what theory of morals can ever serve any useful purpose, unless it can show, by a particular detail, that all the duties which it recommends, are also the true interest of each individual!" *An Enquiry Concerning . . . Morals,* Sec. IX, Pt.II.

may often seem to be a loser by his integrity.... a sensible knave, in particular incidents, may think that an act of iniquity or infidelity will make a considerable addition to his fortune, without causing any considerable breach in the social union and confederacy. That *honesty is the best policy,* may be a good general rule, but is liable to many exceptions; and he, it may perhaps be thought, conducts himself with most wisdom, who observes the general rule, and takes advantage of all the exceptions."

"I must confess that, if a man think that this reasoning much requires an answer, it would be a little difficult to find any which will to him appear satisfactory and convincing."[11]

Hume states the problem of compliance very clearly. Grant that it is rational—or, to use his terminology, preferred with a view to self-interest—to agree on a particular mode of cooperation in situations in which otherwise external inefficiencies would prevent an optimal outcome. Grant that one should adhere to such agreements as a general rule, so that one avoids penalties, maintains one's reputation, and sets others a good example. Yet it is nevertheless advantageous to act on whatever opportunities will prove maximally profitable to oneself, including opportunities to violate one's agreements. And so it is in some cases rational to violate agreements, even though it is unjust.

I reject this conclusion. Adherence to one's agreements does indeed in some situations constitute a genuine constraint on preference-based choice. Were this not so, adherence would not be morally significant. But it is not contrary to reason to adhere, insofar as one is adhering to what is or would be a rational bargain. If one is to overcome inefficiencies by bargaining, then one must be able to expect everyone to adhere to the bargained outcome. It is advantageous to overcome inefficiencies, advantageous to do this by bargaining, advantageous therefore to be able to expect adherences to the outcome, and so, I maintain, *rational* to adhere to the outcome. Rationality is transmitted from making an agreement, to keeping the agreement.

Elsewhere I discuss this matter at greater length, arguing that the conclusion I have just reached requires a modification in the maximizing conception of rationality—a modification which, however, it is rational to choose.[12] Thus rationality and morality are brought into harmony. Adherence to a rational bargain, one resting on the principle of minimax concession, is just, and justice is both a requirement of reason, rightly understood, and an imperative of morality, constraining our preference-based choices.

The principle of minimax concession is thus both the object of rational choice for any person faced with external inefficiencies, and a ground of moral constraint. Characterizing all rational bargains and all modes of rational cooperation, it may itself be conceived as the outcome of a meta-bargain—of a supreme hypothetical agreement among all human beings who must interact in situations in which best reply sets of actions are sub-optimal. In accepting the principle of minimax concession, we bargain our way, not into particular moral arrangements, but into morality itself—or at least, into that part of morality constituted by distributive justice.

7. The principle of minimax concession is applied against a baseline situation, and a range of possibilities which must each be mutually advantageous in relation to that

---

[11]*An Enquiry Concerning . . . Morals,* Sec. IX, Pt.II.

[12]Cf. my paper "Reason and Maximization," *Canadian Journal of Philosophy,* 4, 1975, especially pp. 426–430.

baseline. In effect, both the characteristics and the existing circumstances of the persons involved are taken for granted; they provide a framework which determines whether the principle of justice has any application. As Hume noted, the relation between human beings and other creatures who, though rational, lack power to express effectively any resentment against human behaviour, does not involve the restraints of justice. Humans may act as they will, and "as no inconvenience ever results from the exercise of a power, so firmly established in nature, the restraints of justice and property, being totally *useless,* would never have place in so unequal a confederacy."[13] Hume insisted that animals in relation to humans, barbarous Indians in relation to civilized Europeans, and in many nations the female sex in relation to the male, are in a position of inferiority such that questions of justice and injustice simply do not arise.

Hobbes, who saw in morality a rational response to the horrendous external inefficiencies of the state of nature, and Rawls, who supposed the principles of justice to be the objects of rational choice in circumstances "under which human cooperation is both possible and necessary," have both insisted that one must reason from an initial situation of equality.[14] But this is no part of the present account—or of Hume's theory. Human beings are equally rational, and so all must choose the same principle to regulate their interaction. The worry that one might tailor principles to his or her particular advantage can be seen to be unfounded, once the formal constraints on choice are properly understood. The real worry is that the principle applies to whatsoever situations do arise, so that, although we bargain our way into moral constraints, we do so from a purely amoral stance. When we eliminate from our account all factors which do not fall within the domain of rational choice—when we eliminate, for example, either Rawls' specially favoured or Hobbes' specially disfavoured no agreement point—we find that distributive justice is an extremely weak constraint on preference-based choice.

An example—quite fictitious, of course—will help to clarify my point. Suppose a planet, the land mass of which consists of two large islands, widely separated by stormy seas. On each, human life—or life close enough to human for our purposes—has developed in complete independence and ignorance of the other. On one island, the Purple People have developed an ideally just society. Knowing the extent of their natural resources, they have adopted policies governing population, conservation, and development, to ensure, as far as they are able, that the worst-off person shall benefit, relative to his or her personal characteristics and the possible modes of social cooperation, as much as possible, not only in the present generation, but throughout their foreseeable future. On the other island, the Green People live in totally chaotic squalor. Taking no thought for the morrow, they have propagated their kind and squandered their resources so that they are on the brink of catastrophic collapse. At this point in their respective histories, an exploration party from the Purple People discovers the Green People, and reports back on their condition.

Consensus among the Purple People is reached on the following points. First, any contact between Purple and Green will require Purple's initiative, since the Greens lack means of both transportation and communication across the ocean. Sec-

---

[13]*An Enquiry Concerning ... Morals,* Sec. III, Pt.I.

[14]"If Nature ... have made men equal, that equalitie is to be acknowledged: or if Nature have made men unequal; yet because men think that themselves equal, will not enter into conditions of Peace, but upon Equal terms, such equalitie must be admitted." *Leviathan,* Ch. 15. "It seems reasonable to suppose that the parties in the original position are equal," *A Theory of Justice,* p. 19. The words quoted in the text are from p. 126.

ond, the combined resources of the two islands cannot support the combined populations at the level achieved by Purple society. Third, maximization of the average
absolute level of planetary well-being would require a massive but technologically
feasible transfer of resources from Purples to Greens. And fourth, the Purple People
have the capacity to eliminate the Green People, without any possibility of significant
retaliation.

Four parties develop among the Purple People. The first, whom I shall call Utilitarians, demand that the Purples give up their comfortable way of life to rescue the
Greens from impending catastrophe and maximize overall well-being. The second
group propose that existing levels of well-being in the two societies be taken as a
baseline, and the possibilities of mutually advantageous interchange be explored, in
line with the principle of minimax concession.[15] This policy, members of the group
urge, will maximize the minimum gain relative to existing circumstances, and so will
be just. The third group argue that the strains of the continuing inequality between
Purple and Greens envisaged in the policy proposed by the second group will outweigh any advantages from interchanges, and urge therefore that no contact be established with the Greens. Finally, the fourth group, whom I shall call Hobbists, argue
that the others mistakenly identify the baseline with the existing situation rather than
with the outcome of no agreement. Whatever the Greens may seek to do, the best action for the Purples is to eliminate the Greens and appropriate their resources. There
is no place for mutually advantageous agreement, and so for consideration of justice.

Let us reflect on these proposals. In my view, many existing moral theories accept far too strong constraints on the maximization of individual utility. Advocates of
such theories would find themselves committed to the individually and socially sacrificial policies of the Utilitarian Purples. But not one of us acts on the counterpart of
such policies. It is, however, a long step between supposing that one would be literally mad if one took utilitarianism seriously *in practice,* and supposing that we should
accept only that part of morality which can be salvaged with our theory of distributive
justice. For we should then be committed to the annihilative policies of the Hobbist
Purples, since they recognize that the Purples have no reason to cooperate in any way
with the Greens, but rather every reason to eliminate them and acquire their resources.

Of course, it is possible that humanitarian feelings would not only hold the Purple People back from the Hobbist policy, but would make that policy actually less satisfying than one of the alternatives. But surely we should want to say that it would be
wrong for the Purples to annihilate the Greens, even if the Purples take no interest
whatsoever in the Greens' interests, or feel no emotional concern at all. The Greens,
we might even say, have rights, which would be violated were the Purples to annihilate them.[16] There are moral constraints which the Purples should recognize, stronger
than any which are generated by mutual advantage.

Either the Purple People should cooperate with the Greens, taking their present
situations as the baseline, or they should leave them alone. Which they should do de-

---

[15]I shall leave the second and third parties unnamed. I do however believe that the second party could fairly
be called Humean, but I cannot defend this claim here.

[16]The reader may (should) be reminded of: "Individuals have rights, and there are things no person or
group may do to them (without violating their rights)." Robert Nozick, *Anarchy, State and Utopia,* Basic
Books, New York, 1974, p. ix.

pends, in my view, on empirical, psychological considerations about the strains of a continuing, unequal relationship. This is an issue in moral psychology, but not directly in moral philosophy. But to defend this position, I require something akin to Nozick's well-known Lockean proviso, as a constraint on the baseline from which mutual advantage is to be determined.[17] In the absence of such a constraint, I see no defense against the Hobbist who insists that the inequality in power between Purples and Greens makes any moral relationship, any moral constraint, irrational.

Thus I come to both an optimistic and a pessimistic conclusion. The optimistic conclusion is that the argument which I have presented grounds a part, and a not unimportant part, of traditional morality, on a strictly rational footing. Using only the weak conceptions of value as individual preference-satisfaction, and of rationality as maximizing preference-satisfaction, I have established the rationality of distributive justice, as that constraint on preference-based choice required by minimax concession.

The pessimistic conclusion is that no similar argument will put the remainder, or any important part of the remainder, of traditional morality on a similarly rational footing. I have not shown this, but we may easily see that the only constraints on preference-based choice which are compatible with our conceptions of value and reason must be those which it is mutually advantageous for us to accept, and these are simply the constraints required by minimax concession. Having abandoned all religious or metaphysical props for morality, we are left with no justification for principles some of which, at least, we are unwilling to abandon.

Related to these conditions are two opposed views of our society. The optimistic view is that modern Western society is, so far, unique in its recognition that the sole purposes for which coercive authority is justified among human beings are, first, to overcome the force and fraud which are the great external inefficiencies in the state of nature, thus making possible the emergence of the free, competitive market, and second, to assure the efficacy of those modes of cooperation which are required to avoid those public bads and attain those public goods which the free activity of the market will not provide. Until corrupted by the utilitarian and egalitarian ideas which have led to the welfare state, our society was beginning, for the first time in human history, to make it possible for human affairs to be guided by reason and justice.

The pessimistic view is that modern Western society has abandoned every justification for coercive authority and for constraints on preference-based choice save that which stems from consideration of mutual advantage, thereby opening the way to the dissolution of all those genuinely social bonds among human beings which are the necessary cement of any viable public order. That there is a rational resolution of the problem of compliance is of little concern to human beings for whom reason is the slave of the passions, and who, freed from traditional constraints, face a rapid decline into the state of nature conceived as the war of every person against every person.[18]

There is a schizophrenia in these conclusions which I find haunting the core of my moral and political theory. Perhaps we exceed both our hopes and our fears in bargaining our way into morality.

[17]"Locke's proviso ... is meant to ensure that the situation of others is not worsened." *Anarchy, State and Utopia,* p. 175. Clearly the Hobbist policy would worsen the situation of the Greens.

[18]Cf. my paper "The Social Contract as Ideology," *Philosophy and Public Affairs,* 6, 1977, especially pp. 159–164.

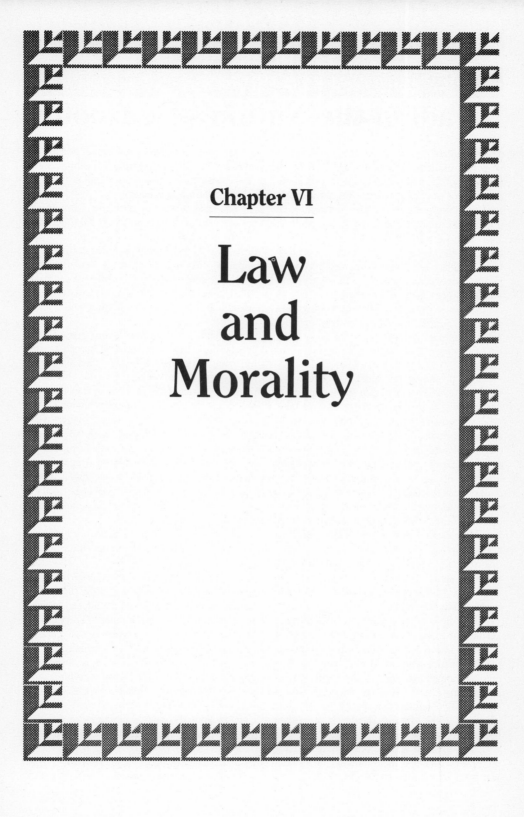

Chapter VI

Law
and
Morality

FRED BRUNING

Invading the Nation's Bedrooms

Determined to keep the empire from crumbling, a majority of U.S. Supreme Court justices recently proclaimed themselves squarely against the private practice of homosexuality. Their declaration no doubt will profoundly diminish the moral confusion and sexual rambunctiousness that so threaten the American nation and, for all we know, might even prompt the misguided to repent. As everyone is aware, homosexuals want nothing more dearly in life than to be like the rest of us, if only the poor souls knew how. With the Supreme Court providing guidance, gays at last can get back on track. By autumn San Francisco most likely will be a forgotten city.

What prompted the court to act with such vigor in regard to a Georgian antisodomy law is difficult to say. Did the magistrates once take a field trip and stumble mistakenly into an unseemly bar? AIDS, perhaps, has the judges on edge or maybe they are tired of all those male skin magazines cluttering the newsstands. There is, of course, just so much chest hair and leather haberdashery a respected jurist can be expected to tolerate while searching for the latest edition of *Reader's Digest*. Let the American Psychiatric Association assert, as it did recently, that homosexuality is not a mental disorder. Like many of their countrymen, the justices seem singularly unconvinced. You don't fool the Supreme Court of the United States quite that easily.

Regardless of the numerous subliminal concerns that might have affected the majority's decision, one is led to believe that the five assenting justices were, in the main, grossed out, as the children say, by the sordid matters confronting them. At issue was the Georgia law and two gentlemen snared by its provisions. In 1982 Michael Hardwick, an Atlanta bartender, was in the bedroom of his home with a companion when a police officer arrived on other business. Said officer peeked into Hardwick's chamber and there spied the bartender and his friend performing fellatio—a transaction that so threatened the foundations of Western civilization that the officer promptly arrested both practitioners.

The case never was tried, but when the local prosecutor hinted he might take action in the future, Hardwick, 32, challenged Georgia's antisodomy law. A federal circuit court agreed with the bartender, ruling, in essence, that while the state could quite properly repair potholes, assess air quality and issue traffic citations, it had no business dictating adult sexual activity.

Certainly, if state lawmakers possess any special expertise in the area of human sexuality, they have been reluctant thus far to acknowledge their skills. To the contrary, politicians would have us believe that they live like monks during those unbearably long legislative sessions—dreary times, really, when the diligent public servant must spend long evenings away from home pondering budget figures or drafting speeches on Americanism. Better that these humble friars absent themselves from discussions of bedroom manners lest they increase their risk of cardiopulmonary disorder.

While the lower court saw the merit of Hardwick's plea, the five intrepid Supreme Court jurists were not to be swayed. A dissenting judge sought to remind his colleagues that a citizen's most precious right is "the right to be left alone," but the majority thundered forward and upheld that Georgia statute. "The proposition that any kind of private sexual conduct between consenting adults is constitutionally insulated from state proscription is unsupportable," quoth Mr. Justice Byron R. White, writing for the majority. Oddly, White said in a footnote that while a state, indeed, had the right to limit the sexual practices of citizens, gay or straight, the court was expressing "no

Reprinted from *Maclean's*, Aug. 11, 1986. © 1986 by Fred Bruning. By permission of the author.

opinion" on heterosexual acts of sodomy. Only single-sex adventures perturbed the court's majority. In Georgia and the 23 other states with similar laws, we are led to believe, males and females are free to proceed undeterred.

The distinction was not lost on gays and their supporters, who responded in language exceedingly more vivid than White's. In New York, homosexuals held a traffic-blocking rally after the decision was announced and heard one speaker accuse the high court of going on a "judicial rampage." The state human rights commissioner decried the court's endorsement of "Gestapo or KGB tactics," and a man from the New Jersey Gay and Lesbian Alliance Against Defamation warned, "The first one who sticks his nose in my bedroom gets it broken off." So far as gays were concerned, the ruling meant one thing and one thing only: the Supreme Court had declared homosexuality illegal.

The high court's technique makes perfectly good sense, of course. From now on, magistrates have only to brand unconstitutional any conduct they view as deviant, and we will be relieved forever of this or that antisocial scourge. Surely, for instance, there must be justification for imposing a ban on the smutty practice of sleeping in the nude. Also, there are certain degenerates who pound mercilessly on their television sets when the New York Mets suffer defeat, and those individuals demand immediate attention. Alarming numbers of our people persist in playing old Little Richard records at high volume—here, let the court be swift and sure in its judgment!—while others think nothing at all of eating peanut butter and banana sandwiches well past the hour of midnight. And what of the misfits who sit in their living rooms and laugh hysterically all the way through President Reagan's press conferences? We can only hope that the justices are equal to the difficult task ahead.

As for the rest of us, we have only to sit back and await the millennium. Ours will be a truly splendid homeland at that point—purged by the court of all influences that do not enhance "family, marriage or procreation," as Justice White said in his sodomy decision. What happens to those who have no great interest in family, marriage or procreation—those who, for better or worse, interpret their needs differently from those that the justices deem appropriate—remains to be seen. Could be that the culprits will seek rehabilitation and, after a decent interval of penance and supplication, assume their rightful place in American society. Or it could be they will continue living precisely as they see fit and, legal precedent aside, call themselves American just the same.

Law and Morality

Throughout this text we have been working under the assumption that ethics plays an important role in our social life. In fact, without considering the issue carefully, we have assumed that the ethical principles we have been seeking are important enough that they could be the basis for rules enforced by social coercion—they could be the basis for laws in a society. This in part justifies the technique employed in the last two chapters. There we used the idea that ethical principles could be found by considering some theories in political philosophy. We assumed a close connection between ethical principles and a system of just laws. In this chapter we will take a serious look at this assumption.

While the last two chapters suggest a strong relationship between law and morality, perhaps the relationship is not as close as it seems. To be sure, we believe that laws against murder, theft, fraud and other serious crimes are firmly grounded in ethics. For the most part, the reason we have laws against murder and the rest is our strong belief that such actions are morally wrong. It might be tempting, then, to state the connection between law and morality strongly as follows: There should be legislation against all actions considered morally wrong. While this would certainly draw a tight connection between law and morality, such a connection is probably too tight. There are a number of actions that are clearly morally wrong, but we would not want to pass laws against them. Rudeness is such an action. One would hope that a proper ethical theory would classify rudeness as morally wrong. Yet, although rudeness is morally wrong, it would seem absurd to have a law against it. Imagine people being arrested on a charge of "criminal rudeness." Thus, we must admit that some morally wrong actions ought to be the basis for punitive laws. It is likely that we do not have laws against rudeness since rudeness is a comparatively trivial offense. Yet the example of rudeness raises the question of a possible limit to the enforcement of moral principles.

Historically there has been an influential position that draws a principled distinction between actions that should and should not fall under the purview of the law. John Stuart Mill, whom we know from his work on utilitarianism, was also concerned with the relations of law and morality. In *On Liberty,* a portion of which is our first selection, Mill argues for a position on law and morality that has come to be known as *liberalism*. Put simply, Mill distinguishes between actions that concern other people (other-regarding actions) and actions that concern only oneself (self-regarding actions). For example, the sort of food I choose to eat, even if others find my diet disgusting, is a self-regarding action. Murder and theft, however, are actions that clearly are other-regarding. Mill argues that it is proper for law to regulate other-regarding actions, specifically those actions that harm other people. However, the law has no business regulating self-regarding actions—those actions that affect only ourselves. Quite simply, if some of our actions affect only ourselves, then it is no one else's business whether or not we do them. Since we value our liberty to make decisions about our own lives, the law ought not prohibit any self-regarding actions. It should be mentioned that in *On Liberty* Mill sounds much like one of the rights theorists we studied in Chapter IV. Mill argues that we should be granted certain "rights," domains of liberty, to do as we please so long as we do not intrude on other people's rights (or liberties).

As mentioned above, Mill's position on the relation of law and morality has come to be called "liberalism." The central tenet of the position is that law ought not meddle with people's private lives—and it ought not meddle even in cases where a certain lifestyle is morally condemned by society at large—so long as this lifestyle does not actually harm anyone else. Yet, although this position is called "liberalism," one should not assume that all or only people we call "liberals" in our own society share this philosophical view. It is perhaps safe to say that current "liberals" often subscribe to the idea that laws should not restrict private behavior; however, "liberals" also tend to promote governmental welfare programs or oppose defense spending—two areas that have little to do with the philosophical idea of liberalism. By the same token, people we call "political conservatives" often argue, rather like Mill, that government should "get off our backs" in matters that concern only ourselves. The point of these remarks is that we should be careful not to assume that Mill's notion of "liberalism" is the same as the current political position of "liberalism" or necessarily different from the political position of conservatives. The truth of the matter is that on different issues political liberals and political conservatives will endorse Mill's idea of "liberalism."

As we have seen with other "philosophical" theses, liberalism is simply a more sophisticated expression of an attitude that can be found in ordinary contexts. Fred Bruning in our lead essay criticizes, by way of irony, a recent Supreme Court decision that let stand a Georgia law against sodomy. Bruning's criticism is much in the spirit of Mill. What is at issue is a kind of sexual practice (sodomy) performed in private by consenting adults. Bruning's argument is that the legal system has no more business regulating this sort of private behavior than it does passing laws against sleeping in the nude or pounding on one's television. Bruning (like Mill) believes that sexual activities performed in private by consenting adults affect only the parties involved. Because they only affect the parties involved, there is no good reason to enforce punitive laws against such activities.

A number of comments are in order concerning the Bruning article and Mill's position. First, allowing to let stand that Georgia law against sodomy has been seen as an attack against homosexuality, since sodomy is a common homosexual practice. However, it should be pointed out that the law is quite general. It prohibits any couples (homosexual, heterosexual, married, or unmarried) from the practice of sodomy. Nonetheless, it is safe to say that homosexuals were the group that the Supreme Court had in mind most when making its ruling. Second, it might be thought acts of sodomy are not a good example to illustrate Mill's point about self-regarding actions. Sodomy clearly does not concern only one person. What is at issue is a sexual practice between *two* consenting adults. It is easy enough, however, to extend Mill's basic idea to account for this. We can extend the notion of self-regarding actions to include not only those actions that literally concern only onself, but also ones that concern oneself and other *consenting* adults. It is not just one's own, private business that ought to be protected from legal tampering, but also business that is private among agreeing parties.

There is another, more difficult, question, however, concerning the suitability of the sodomy case as an illustration of Mill's point. It can be questioned whether sodomy, particularly homosexual sodomy, is genuinely an action that concerns only the parties consenting to the practice. Bruning suspects that the Supreme Court's ruling may reflect current worries about the spread of AIDS. Someone might argue as follows in favor of antisodomy laws. Sodomy is a sexual practice that contributes to the spread of AIDS. The spreading of AIDS is a public-health concern that threatens to affect a number of people. Thus, homosexual sodomy is not an action that is solely the business of the consenting adults engaging in it but threatens to harm a far greater number of people. As such, there are good grounds for prohibiting it.

It is important to point out that whatever the merits of the above argument, it is not the argument used by the Supreme Court. Officially, the public-health risks of homosexual practices was not an issue before the court. One should also be careful about such reasoning. It would seem that a similar argument could be made against heterosexual behavior on the grounds of the health risks of syphilis, herpes, and other sexually transmitted diseases—including AIDS. The worrisome issue about unpopular sexual practices—an example frequently used in our readings—is that the Supreme Court argues that it is permissible to pass laws against unpopular sexual practices simply because people regard these practices as immoral. It is specifically this sort of argument that Mill complains against. He argues that harming others is the only good reason for incorporating our moral dos and don'ts into law. If there are practices that people condemn as immoral but do not harm other (unconsenting) people, then the law has no business enforcing such moral views.

In actuality, Mill's attempt to restrict the power of law over people's private behavior is a bit broader than we have portrayed so far. There are really two reasons for restricting self-regarding actions that Mill criticizes—paternalistic and moralistic reasons. Sometimes laws are proposed to restrict a person's self-regarding actions on the grounds that such restrictions are for people's own good. Regulating a people's actions for their own good is called "paternalism," since the law acts like a concerned parent (or "father") toward its citizens. Motorcycle helmet and seat-belt laws are recent examples of laws criticized as paternalistic. Not wearing a helmet or seat belt dramatically increases the risk of serious injury. However, Mill would argue, while it may indeed be poor judgment to go without seat belt or helmet, such choices are for individuals to make since the effects of the actions go no farther than the person making the choice. Again, such self-regarding actions should be the business of the individual exclusively.

The argument that most concerns us in this chapter is the moralistic argument for prohibiting self-regarding actions. It is often argued that some actions should be prohibited not because they harm other people or even because they are dangerous to the individual, but simply because they are immoral. Homosexuality, bigamy, drinking, and gambling have all at one time or another been made illegal because these actions, while only self-regarding, are considered immoral. Simply because they are considered immoral, it is reasoned, they ought to be made against the law. It is the latter argument that will be of primary concern in our readings. Should "immoral," self-regarding actions be made illegal? Mill's answer is squarely negative. No self-regarding actions on whatever grounds ought to be illegal. If we made them illegal, then government would be allowed to intrude into people's own, private business.

Mill's position is appealing. There seems to be something basically correct in saying that we should be let alone in matters that concern only ourselves or ourselves and other consenting adults. However, there are some theoretical kinks that must be straightened out if Mill's position is to be accepted. Basically, two problem areas exist that will concern us in the following readings. First, is it really true that there is a class of purely self-regarding actions? Or, if there is, then does that class include the sorts of actions Mill wants to protect from legal intervention? There is reason to be skeptical here. Mill typically defines self-regarding actions as those actions that do not harm other people. Yet, unless this definition is considerably refined, it covers more ground than Mill would like. Consider kinds of actions typically used for illustration by our writers—eccentric sexual practices performed in private between consenting adults. Given the fact that such actions are performed in private, one might think that they are a perfect example of self-regarding actions. As such, they should not be outlawed even if people in our society consider them to be "nasty and immoral." This would surely be Mill's position.

However, an argument can be made that eccentric sexual practice done in private by consenting adults may indeed harm other people. For some people the bare knowledge that others are doing "nasty and immoral" things in their bedroom is enough to cause them consternation. For example, some people become distressed just thinking about the fact that a number of Americans engage in homosexual acts, even if they have had no acquaintance with homosexuals. I take it that Mill's defenders would still argue that eccentric sexual acts should not be outlawed. The argument might be that the "harm" these actions cause should not count in the same way that harm from theft or battery counts in favor of legal prohibition. The claim would be that the harm from some actions (so-called "self-regarding actions") should not justify legal prohibition, while the harm from other actions (so-called "other-regarding actions") can justify prohibition. Notice that this argument is different, however, from the one Mill initially gives. Mill thinks a distinction can be made between eccentric sexual practices and theft by distinguishing between actions that do and do not cause harm. The new distinction is in terms of justifying and nonjustifying kinds of harm. We would need to know just what this distinction involves.

A second, and more direct, challenge to Mill's position exists: We might grant that some acceptable definition of self-regarding acts can be given. Such a definition would count eccentric sexual practices, drinking, gambling, and so on, as self-regarding actions. We can yet challenge Mill's substantive claim that self-regarding actions ought not be legally prohibited when people condemn these actions as immoral. Lord Patrick Devlin in a famous lecture makes just this argument. Devlin's criticism is this: Mill holds that some actions, considered immoral by most of society, ought not be legally condemned. This cannot be permitted as a general doctrine, however, since a common moral outlook is crucial to the very existence of a society. Devlin argues that we cannot always permit actions generally regarded as immoral since such permission can threaten the foundations of society. Devlin argues that if there were no common moral outlook we might expect an "anything goes" attitude. A society cannot long survive such rampant permissiveness, however. Thus, just as we may prohibit treason because it threatens the existence of society, so may we prohibit action regarded as immoral since it, too, threatens the foundations of society.

H. L. A. Hart contributes to the discussion of law and morality in two ways. Hart addresses the first problem we identified with Mill's position—the problem that even so-called "self-regarding actions" can cause harm. Additionally, at the end of his paper Hart offers objections to Devlin's argument in favor of outlawing "immoral" actions. To the first problem Hart offers the following modification of Mill's basic position: As we have seen, Mill wants to insulate a group of actions (self-regarding actions) from legal prohibition on the grounds that these actions cause no harm to others. Hart considers prostitution, homosexuality, and bigamy as examples of such actions. The difficulty is that even if these acts are done in private, some people will be greatly offended (harmed) simply knowing that they go on. As such, they no longer seem like purely self-regarding actions. Hart's strategy is to distinguish two sorts of harm: public offenses and mere nuisances. Actions publicly observable cause direct harm and may be regulated by law. What Hart calls "nuisances," however, are actions done in private that only cause the psychological harm of knowing that certain unsavory things are going on. This latter class of actions, Hart argues, ought not be regulated by law. The difference between actions done in public versus in private is important, says Hart. To use one of his examples, we find nothing wrong with married couples having sexual intercourse in their bedroom, but we do find it objectionable if couples have sex in their front yard. It would be wrong to prohibit sexual intercourse in private, but appropriate to prohibit the same action when done in public.

Hart not only attempts to meet the first objection to Mill's theory, but also responds to Devlin's criticism. Hart has three criticisms of Devlin. First, Devlin offers no factual data to support his claim that a shared moral outlook is necessary to a society's social existence. What is the evidence that lack of a common outlook causes a society to crumble? This sounds reasonable, but we need to know if it is really true. Second, Devlin does not distinguish between the need for a common moral outlook concerning other-regarding versus self-regarding actions. We can admit, perhaps, that a society cannot survive unless most people agree that murder, battery, and theft (other-regarding actions) ought to be prohibited. However, a society may be able to tolerate a rather wide range of beliefs about sexual practices, drinking, and gambling (self-regarding actions). And, finally, Hart argues that Devlin cannot account for the fact that societies change their attitudes on the morality of self-regarding acts. It is safe to say that attitudes in our society have changed over the years, from considering premarital sex as strictly immoral, for example, to considering it as permissible in a range of cases. Although some people might disagree, this change in attitude has occurred without threatening the foundation of society. This tends to show that not only can differing views on the morality of self-regarding acts be allowed, it can even happen that views that were once unpopular can become the views of most people.

Ronald Dworkin also finds fault with Devlin's position, but believes that it has more merit than people think. In fact, Dworkin argues that while it may not be reasonable to say that a common outlook on self-regarding actions is necessary to the survival of a society, it may yet be justifiable for a society to resist changes in moral attitudes. The chief fault Dworkin finds with Devlin's position is that he is not overly careful about how he identifies a society's moral outlook on actions like homosexuality, and so on. Devlin seems to think that to discover a society's moral view on homosexuality and gambling, all one needs to do is take a poll and observe the results. Dworkin argues that this procedure is more likely to uncover people's prejudices than it is to identify well-considered moral judgments. Perhaps Devlin's position would be easier to accept if it held that the law can prohibit actions that society's *well-considered* judgments condemn.

In our final reading, Earnest Nagel reconsiders Mill's distinction between self- and other-regarding actions and Hart's way of defending the distinction. Generally speaking, Nagel supports Mill's position but recognizes the problem of identifying a class of actions that should be exempt from legal prohibitions. Nagel (like Hart) argues that Mill's distinction between actions that do and do not cause harm will not work. In all the controversial cases (sexual morality and the rest), it is typical that *some* kind of harm is caused. Nagel is not convinced, however, that Hart improves upon Mill's distinction. Arguing that it is permissible to ban public offenses but not nuisances conflicts with the spirit of Mill's liberalism. Consider the category of public offenses. As we have seen, Hart argues that it is permissible to ban public actions when they harm people. If Mill's point is to allow people freedom to act despite the "moral" disapproval of others, however, it is not clear that Hart's distinction will do the job. Hart and Nagel each use the example of bigamy (the practice of having two wives or two husbands at the same time). In the spirit of Mill, bigamy ought not be prohibited simply because people disapprove. However, if we use Hart's idea that actions can be prohibited if they cause public harm, bigamy is in trouble. A bigamous trio will want to go out to dine, go out shopping, and so on. People who believe that bigamy is immoral, however, will be greatly offended by "seeing" a bigamous trio. The same can be said of homosexuals in public or public drinking. The reason people are "harmed" in these cases is due to the fact that their moral attitudes toward homosexuality, bigamy, or drinking are offended by the thought of such activities going on. However, one can argue that this kind of "harm" does not justify prohibiting the acts mentioned.

The proper relation between law and morality continues to be a lively issue. There is an important sense in which law and morality are related. We feel justified in prohibiting actions that cause grave and unwanted harm to other people on the grounds that these actions are morally wrong. However, we may not want to prohibit every action that we morally condemn. Some attitudes about morality tell us how best to live our own lives, even when we do not significantly affect other people. Perhaps, as Mill argues, the law ought not incorporate these moral views into law. The theoretical challenge we face with this recommendation is to find an acceptable way to classify actions that do not "significantly affect other people."

On Liberty

John Stuart Mill

OF THE LIMITS TO THE AUTHORITY OF SOCIETY OVER THE INDIVIDUAL

What, then, is the rightful limit to the sovereignty of the individual over himself? Where does the authority of society begin? How much of human life should be assigned to individuality, and how much to society?

Each will receive its proper share if each has that which more particularly concerns it. To individuality should belong the part of life in which it is chiefly the individual that is interested; to society, the part which chiefly interests society.

Though society is not founded on a contract, and though no good purpose is answered by inventing a contract in order to deduce social obligations from it, everyone who receives the protection of society owes a return for the benefit, and the fact of living in society renders it indispensable that each should be bound to observe a certain line of conduct toward the rest. This conduct consists, first, in not injuring the interests of one another, or rather certain interests which, either by express legal provision or by tacit understanding, ought to be considered as rights; and secondly, in each person's bearing his share (to be fixed on some equitable principle) of the labors and sacrifices incurred for defending the society or its members from injury and molestation. These conditions society is justified in enforcing at all costs to those who endeavor to withhold fulfillment. Nor is this all that society may do. The acts of an individual may be hurtful to others or wanting in due consideration for their welfare, without going to the length of violating any of their constituted rights. The offender may then be justly punished by opinion, though not by law. As soon as any part of a person's conduct affects prejudicially the interests of others, society has jurisdiction over it, and the question whether the general welfare will or will not be promoted by interferring with it becomes open to discussion. But there is no room for entertaining any such question when a person's conduct affects the interests of no persons besides himself, or needs not affect them unless they like (all the persons concerned being of full age and the ordinary amount of understanding). In all such cases, there should be perfect freedom, legal and social, to do the action and stand the consequences.

It would be a great misunderstanding of this doctrine to suppose that it is one of selfish indifference which pretends that human beings have no business with each other's conduct in life, and that they should not concern themselves about the well-doing or well-being of one another, unless their own interest is involved. Instead of any diminution, there is need of a great increase of disinterested exertion to promote the good of others. But disinterested benevolence can find other instruments to persuade people to their good than whips and scourges, either of the literal or the metaphorical sort. I am the last person to undervalue the self-regarding virtues; they are only second in importance, if even second, to the social. It is equally the business of education to cultivate both. But even education works by conviction and persuasion as well as by compulsion, and it is by the former only that, when the period of education is passed, the self-regarding virtues should be inculcated. Human beings owe to each

Excerpted from John Stuart Mill, *On Liberty* (1859), Chapter IV.

other help to distinguish the better from the worse, and encouragement to choose the former and avoid the latter. They should be forever stimulating each other to increased exercise of their higher faculties and increased direction of their feelings and aims toward wise instead of foolish, elevating instead of degrading, objects and contemplations. But neither one person, nor any number of persons, is warranted in saying to another human creature of ripe years that he shall not do with his life for his own benefit what he chooses to do with it. He is the person most interested in his own well-being: the interest which any other person, except in cases of strong personal attachment, can have in it is trifling compared with that which he himself has; the interest which society has in him individually (except as to his conduct to others) is fractional and altogether indirect, while with respect to his own feelings and circumstances the most ordinary man or woman has means of knowledge immeasurably surpassing those that can be possessed by anyone else. The interference of society to overrule his judgment and purposes in what only regards himself must be grounded on general presumptions which may be altogether wrong and, even if right, are as likely as not to be misapplied to individual cases, by persons no better acquainted with the circumstances of such cases than those who look at them merely from without. In this department, therefore, of human affairs, individuality has its proper field of action. In the conduct of human beings toward one another it is necessary that general rules should for the most part be observed in order that people may know what they have to expect; but in each person's own concerns his individual spontaneity is entitled to free exercise. Considerations to aid his judgment, exhortations to strengthen his will may be offered to him, even obtruded on him, by others; but he himself is the final judge. All errors which he is likely to commit against advice and warning are far outweighed by the evil of allowing others to constrain him to what they deem his good. . . .

What I contend for is that the inconveniences which are strictly inseparable from the unfavorable judgment of others are the only ones to which a person should ever be subjected for that portion of his conduct and character which concerns his own good, but which does not affect the interest of others in their relations with him. Acts injurious to others require a totally different treatment. Encroachment on their rights; infliction on them of any loss or damage not justified by his own rights; falsehood or duplicity in dealing with them; unfair or ungenerous use of advantages over them; even selfish abstinence from defending them against injury—these are fit objects of moral reprobation and, in grave cases, of moral retribution and punishment. And not only these acts, but the dispositions which lead to them, are properly immoral and fit subjects of disapprobation which may rise to abhorrence. Cruelty of disposition; malice and ill-nature; that most antisocial and odious of all passions, envy; dissimulation and insincerity, irascibility on insufficient cause, and resentment disproportioned to the provocation; the love of domineering over others; the desire to engross more than one's share of advantages (the *pleonexia*[1] of the Greeks); the pride which derives gratification from the abasement of others; the egotism which thinks self and its concerns more important than everything else, and decides all doubtful questions in its own favor—these are moral vices and constitute a bad and odious moral character; unlike the self-regarding faults previously mentioned, which are not properly immoralities and, to whatever pitch they may be carried, do not constitute wickedness. They may be proofs of any amount of folly or want of personal dignity and self-respect, but they are

[1]Greed.

only a subject of moral reprobation when they involve a breach of duty to others, for whose sake the individual is bound to have care for himself. What are called duties to ourselves are not socially obligatory unless circumstances render them at the same time duties to others. The term duty to oneself, when it means anything more than prudence, means self-respect or self-development, and for none of these is anyone accountable to his fellow creatures, because for none of them is it for the good of mankind that he be held accountable to them.

The distinction between the loss of consideration which a person may rightly incur by defect of prudence or of personal dignity, and the reprobation which is due to him for an offense against the rights of others, is not a merely nominal distinction. It makes a vast difference both in our feelings and in our conduct toward him whether he displeases us in things in which we think we have a right to control him or in things in which we know that we have not. If he displeases us, we may express our distaste, and we may stand aloof from a person as well as from a thing that displeases us; but we shall not therefore feel called on to make his life uncomfortable. We shall reflect that he already bears, or will bear, the whole penalty of his error; if he spoils his life by mismanagement, we shall not, for that reason, desire to spoil it still further; instead of wishing to punish him, we shall rather endeavor to alleviate his punishment by showing him how he may avoid or cure the evils his conduct tends to bring upon him. He may be to us an object of pity, perhaps of dislike, but not of anger or resentment; we shall not treat him like an enemy of society; the worst we shall think ourselves justified in doing is leaving him to himself, if we do not interfere benevolently by showing interest or concern for him. It is far otherwise if he has infringed the rules necessary for the protection of his fellow creatures, individually or collectively. The evil consequences of his acts do not then fall on himself, but on others; and society, as the protector of all its members, must retaliate on him, must inflict pain on him for the express purpose of punishment, and must take care that it be sufficiently severe. In the one case, he is an offender at our bar, and we are called on not only to sit in judgment on him, but, in one shape or another, to execute our own sentence; in the other case, it is not our part to inflict any suffering on him, except what may incidentally follow from our using the same liberty in the regulation of our own affairs which we allow to him in his.

The distinction here pointed out between the part of a person's life which concerns only himself and that which concerns others, many persons will refuse to admit. How (it may be asked) can any part of the conduct of a member of society be a matter of indifference to the other members? No person is an entirely isolated being; it is impossible for a person to do anything seriously or permanently hurtful to himself without mischief reaching at least to his near connections, and often far beyond them. If he injures his property, he does harm to those who directly or indirectly derived support from it, and usually diminishes, by a greater or less amount, the general resources of the community. If he deteriorates his bodily or mental faculties, he not only brings evil upon all who depended upon him for any portion of their happiness, but disqualifies himself for rendering the services which he owes to his fellow creatures generally, perhaps becomes a burden on their affection or benevolence; and if such conduct were very frequent hardly any offense that is committed would detract more from the general sum of good. Finally, if by his vices or follies a person does no direct harm to others, he is nevertheless (it may be said) injurious by his example, and ought to be compelled to control himself for the sake of those whom the sight or knowledge of his conduct might corrupt or mislead.

And even (it will be added) if the consequences of misconduct could be confined to the vicious or thoughtless individual, ought society to abandon to their own
guidance those who are manifestly unfit for it? If protection against themselves is confessedly due to children and persons under age, is not society equally bound to afford
it to persons of mature years who are equally incapable of self-government? If gambling, or drunkenness, or incontinence, or idleness, or uncleanliness are as injurious
to happiness, and as great a hindrance to improvement, as many or most of the acts
prohibited by law, why (it may be asked) should not law, so far as is consistent with
practicability and social convenience, endeavor to repress these also? And as a supplement to the unavoidable imperfections of law, ought not opinion at least to organize a
powerful police against these vices and visit rigidly with social penalties those who are
known to practice them? There is no question here (it may be said) about restricting
individuality, or impeding the trial of new and original experiments in living. The only
things it is sought to prevent are things which have been tried and condemned from
the beginning of the world until now—things which experience has shown not to be
useful or suitable to any person's individuality. There must be some length of time and
amount of experience after which a moral or prudential truth may be regarded as established; and it is merely desired to prevent generation after generation from falling
over the same precipice which has been fatal to their predecessors.

I fully admit that the mischief which a person does to himself may seriously affect, both through their sympathies and their interests, those nearly connected with
him and, in a minor degree, society at large. When, by conduct of this sort, a person is
led to violate a distinct and assignable obligation to any other person or persons, the
care is taken out of the self-regarding class and becomes amenable to moral disapprobation in the proper sense of the term. If, for example, a man, through intemperance
or extravagance, becomes unable to pay his debts, or, having undertaken the moral
responsibility of a family, becomes from the same cause incapable of supporting or
educating them, he is deservedly reprobated and might be justly punished; but it is for
the breach of duty to his family or creditors, not for the extravagance. If the resources
which ought to have been devoted to them had been diverted from them for the most
prudent investment, the moral culpability would have been the same. George Barnwell[2] murdered his uncle to get money for his mistress, but if he had done it to set
himself up in business, he would equally have been hanged. Again, in the frequent
case of a man who causes grief to his family by addiction to bad habits, he deserves
reproach for his unkindness or ingratitude; but so he may for cultivating habits not in
themselves vicious, if they are painful to those with whom he passes his life, or who
from personal ties are dependent on him for their comfort. Whoever fails in the consideration generally due to the interests and feelings of others, not being compelled
by some more imperative duty, or justified by allowable self-preference, is a subject of
moral disapprobation for that failure, but not for the cause of it, nor for the errors,
merely personal to himself, which may have remotely led to it. In like manner, when
a person disables himself, by conduct purely self-regarding, from the performance of
some definite duty incumbent on him to the public, he is guilty of a social offense. No
person ought to be punished simply for being drunk; but a soldier or policeman
should be punished for being drunk on duty. Whenever, in short, there is a definite
damage, or a definite risk of damage, either to an individual or to the public, the case
is taken out of the province of liberty and placed in that of morality or law.

<hr />

[2]*The London Merchant: or, the History of George Barnwell* was a melodrama by George Lillo.

But with regard to the merely contingent or, as it may be called, constructive injury which a person causes to society by conduct which neither violates any specific duty to the public, nor occasions perceptible hurt to any assignable individual except himself, the inconvenience is one which society can afford to bear, for the sake of the greater good of human freedom. If grown persons are to be punished for not taking proper care of themselves, I would rather it were for their own sake than under pretense of preventing them from impairing their capacity or rendering to society benifits which society does not pretend it has a right to exact. But I cannot consent to argue the point as if society had no means of bringing its weaker members up to its ordinary standard of rational conduct, except waiting till they do something irrational, and then punishing them, legally or morally, for it. Society has had absolute power over them during all the early portion of their existense; it has had the whole period of childhood and nonage in which to try whether it could make them capable of rational conduct in life. The existing generation is master both of the training and the entire circumstances of the generation to come; it cannot indeed make them perfectly wise and good, because it is itself so lamentably deficient in goodness and wisdom; and its best efforts are not always, in individual cases, its most successful ones; but it is perfectly well able to make the rising generation, as a whole, as good as, and a little better than, itself. If society lets any considerable number of its members grow up mere children, incapable of being acted on by rational consideration of distant motives, society has itself to blame for the consequences. Armed not only with all the powers of education, but with the ascendency which the authority of a received opinion always exercises over the minds who are least fitted to judge for themselves, and aided by the *natural* penalties which cannot be prevented from falling on those who incur the distaste or the contempt of those who know them—let not society pretend that it needs, besides all this, the power to issue commands and enforce obedience in the personal concerns of individuals in which, on all principles of justice and policy, the decision ought to rest with those who are to abide the consequences. Nor is there anything which tends more to discredit and frustrate the better means of influencing conduct than a resort to the worse. If there be among those whom it is attempted to coerce into prudence or temperance any of the material of which vigorous and independent characters are made, they will infallibly rebel against the yoke. No such person will ever feel that others have a right to control him in his concerns, such as they have to prevent him from injuring them in theirs; and it easily comes to be considered a mark of spirit and courage to fly in the face of such usurped authority and do with ostentation the exact opposite of what it enjoins, as in the fashion of grossness which succeeded, in the time of Charles II, to the fanatical moral intolerance of the Puritans. With respect to what is said of the necessity of protecting society from the bad example set to others by the vicious or the self-indulgent, it is true that bad example may have a pernicious effect, especially the example of doing wrong to others with impunity to the wrongdoer. But we are now speaking of conduct which, while it does no wrong to others, is supposed to do great harm to the agent himself; and I do not see how those who believe this can think otherwise than that the example, on the whole, must be more salutary than hurtful, since, if it displays the misconduct, it displays also the painful or degrading consequences which, if the conduct is justly censured, must be supposed to be in all or most cases attendant on it.

But the strongest of all the arguments against the interference of the public with purely personal conduct is that, when it does interfere, the odds are that it interferes wrongly and in the wrong place. On questions of social morality, of duty to others, the opinion of the public, that is, of an overruling majority, though often wrong, is likely to be still oftener right, because on such questions they are only required to judge of their own interests, of the manner in which some mode of conduct, if allowed to be practiced, would affect themselves. But the opinion of a similar majority, imposed as a law on the minority, on questions of self-regarding conduct is quite as likely to be wrong as right, for in these cases public opinion means, at the best, some people's opinion of what is good or bad for other people, while very often it does not even mean that—the public, with the most perfect indifference, passing over the pleasure or convenience of those whose conduct they censure and considering only their own preference. There are many who consider as an injury to themselves any conduct which they have a distaste for, and resent it as an outrage to their feelings; as a religious bigot, when charged with disregarding the religious feelings of others, has been known to retort that they disregard his feelings by persisting in their abominable worship or creed. But there is no parity between the feeling of a person for his own opinion and the feeling of another who is offended at his holding it, no more than between the desire of a thief to take a purse and the desire of the right owner to keep it. And a person's taste is as much his own peculiar concern as his opinion or his purse. It is easy for anyone to imagine an ideal public which leaves the freedom and choice of individuals in all uncertain matters undisturbed and only requires them to abstain from modes of conduct which universal experience has condemned. But where has there been seen a public which set any such limit to its censorship? Or when does the public trouble itself about universal experience? In its interferences with personal conduct it is seldom thinking of anything but the enormity of acting or feeling differently from itself; and this standard of judgment, thinly disguised, is held up to mankind as the dictate of religion and philosophy by nine-tenths of all moralists and speculative writers. These teach that things are right because they are right; because we feel them to be so. They tell us to search in our own minds and hearts for laws of conduct binding on ourselves and on all others. What can the poor public do but apply these instructions and make their own personal feelings of good and evil, if they are tolerably unanimous in them, obligatory on all the world?

The evil here pointed out is not one which exists only in theory; and it may perhaps be expected that I should specify the instances in which the public of this age and country improperly invests its own preferences with the character of moral laws. I am not writing an essay on the aberrations of existing moral feeling. That is too weighty a subject to be discussed parenthetically, and by way of illustration. Yet examples are necessary to show that the principle I maintain is of serious and practical moment, and that I am not endeavoring to erect a barrier against imaginary evils. And it is not difficult to show, by abundant instances, that to extend the bounds of what may be called moral police until it encroaches on the most unquestionably legitimate liberty of the individual is one of the most universal of all human propensities.

As a first instance, consider the antipathies which men cherish on no better grounds than that persons whose religious opinions are different from theirs do not practice their religious observances, especially their religious abstinences. To cite a rather trivial example, nothing in the creed or practice of Christians does more to envenom the hatred of Mohammedans against them than the fact of their eating pork. There are few acts which Christians and Europeans regard with more unaffected disgust than Mussulmans regard this particular mode of satisfying hunger. It is in the first place, an offense against their religion; but this circumstance by no means explains either the degree or the kind of their repugnance; for wine also is forbidden by their religion, and to partake of it is by all Mussulmans accounted wrong, but not disgusting. Their aversion to the flesh of the "unclean beast" is, on the contrary, of that peculiar character, resembling an instinctive antipathy, which the idea of unclearness, when once it thoroughly sinks into the feelings, seems always to excite even in those whose personal habits are anything but scrupulously cleanly, and of which the sentiment of religious impurity, so intense in the Hindus, is a remarkable example. Suppose now that in a people of whom the majority were Mussulmans, that majority should insist upon not permitting pork to be eaten within the limits of the country. This would be nothing new in Mohammedan countries.[3] Would it be a legitimate exercise of the moral authority of public opinion, and if not, why not? The practice is really revolting to such a public. They also sincerely think that it is forbidden and abhorred by the Deity. Neither could the prohibition be censured as religious persecution. It might be religious in its origin, but it would not be persecution for religion, since nobody's religion makes it a duty to eat pork. The only tenable ground of condemnation would be that with the personal tastes and self-regarding concerns of individuals the public has no business to interfere.

To come somewhat nearer home: the majority of Spaniards consider it a gross impiety, offensive in the highest degree to the Supreme Being, to worship him in any other manner than the Roman Catholic; and no other public worship is lawful on Spanish soil. The people of all southern Europe look upon a married clergy as not only irreligious, but unchaste, indecent, gross, disgusting. What do Protestants think of these perfectly sincere feelings, and of the attempt to enforce them against non-Catholics? Yet, if mankind are justified in interfering with each other's liberty in things which do not concern the interests of others, on what principle is it possible consistently to exclude these cases? Or who can blame people for desiring to suppress what they regard as a scandal in the sight of God and man? No stronger case can be shown for prohibiting anything which is regarded as a personal immorality than is made out for suppressing these practices in the eyes of those who regard them as impieties; and unless we are willing to adopt the logic of persecutors, and to say that we may persecute others because we are right, and that they must not persecute us because they are wrong, we must beware of admitting a principle of which we should resent as a gross injustice the application to ourselves. . . .

Under the name of preventing intemperance, the people of one English colony, and of nearly half the United States, have been interdicted by law[4] from making any use whatever of fermented drinks, except for medical purposes, for prohibition of their sale is in fact, as it is intended to be, prohibition of their use. And though the impracticability of executing the law has caused its repeal in several of the States which had adopted it, including the one from which it derives its name, an attempt has notwithstanding been commenced, and is prosecuted with considerable zeal by many of the professed philanthropists, to agitate for a similar law in the country. The associa-

---

[3]The case of the Bombay Parsees is a curious instance in point. When this industrious and enterprising tribe, the descendants of the Persian fire-worshipers, flying from their native country before the Caliphs, arrived in western India, they were admitted to toleration by the Hindu sovereigns, on condition of not eating beef. When those regions afterward fell under the dominion of Mohammedan conquerors, the Parsees obtained from them a continuance of indulgence, on condition of refraining from pork. What was at first obedience to authority became a second nature, and the Parsees to this day abstain both from beef and pork. Though not required by their religion, the double abstinence has had time to grow into a custom of their tribe; and custom, in the East, is a religion.

[4]A precursor of prohibition, called the Marine Law, after the state that first adopted it in 1815.

tion, or "Alliance," as it terms itself, which has been formed for this purpose, has acquired some notoriety through the publicity given to a correspondence between its secretary and one of the very few English public men who hold that a politician's opinions ought to be founded on principles. Lord Stanley's[5] share in this correspondence is calculated to strengthen the hopes already built on him by those who know how rare such qualities as are manifested in some of his public appearances unhappily are among those who figure in political life. The organ of the Alliance, who would "deeply deplore the recognition of any principle which could be wrested to justify bigotry and persecution," undertakes to point out the "broad and impassable barrier" which divides such principles from those of the association. "All matters relating to thought, opinion, conscience, appear to me," he says, "to be without the sphere of legislation; all pertaining to social act, habit, relation, subject only to a discretionary power vested in the State itself, and not in the individual, to be within it." No mention is made of a third class, different from either of these, viz., acts and habits which are not social, but individual; although it is to this class, surely that the act of drinking fermented liquors belongs. Selling fermented liquors, however, is trading, and trading is a social act. But the infringement complained of is not on the liberty of the seller, but on that of the buyer and consumer; since the State might just as well forbid him to drink wine as purposely make it impossible for him to obtain it. The secretary, however, says, "I claim, as a citizen, a right to legislate whenever my social rights are invaded by the social act of another." And now for the definition of these "social rights": "If anything invades my social rights, certainly the traffic in strong drink does. It destroys my primary right of security by constantly creating and stimulating social disorder. It invades my right of equality by deriving a profit from the creation of a misery I am taxed to support. It impedes my right to free moral and intellectual development by surrounding my path with dangers and by weakening and demoralizing society, from which I have a right to claim mutual aid and intercourse." A theory of "social rights" the like of which probably never before found its way into, distinct language: being nothing short of this—that it is the absolute social right of every individual that every other individual shall act in every respect exactly as he ought; that whosoever fails thereof in the smallest particular violates my social right and entitles me to demand from the legislature the removal of the grievance. So monstrous a principle is far more dangerous than any single interference with liberty; there is no violation of liberty which it would not justify; it acknowledges no right to any freedom whatever, except perhaps to that of holding opinions in secret, without ever disclosing them; for the moment an opinion which I consider noxious passes anyone's lips, it invades all the "social rights" attributed to me by the Alliance. The doctrine ascribes to all mankind a vested interest in each other's moral, intellectual, and even physical perfection, to be defined by each claimant according to his own standard. . . .

I cannot refrain from adding to these examples of the little account commonly made of human liberty the language of downright persecution which breaks out from the press of this country whenever it feels called on to notice the remarkable phenomenon of Mormonism. Much might be said on the unexpected and instructive fact that an alleged new revelation and a religion founded on it—the product of palpable imposture, not even supported by the *prestige* of extraordinary qualities in its founder—

[5]Edward Henry Stanley (1826–1893) had a long and distinguished career in the foreign service and diplomacy.

is believed by hundreds of thousands, and has been made the foundation of a society in the age of newspapers, railways, and the electric telegraph. What here concerns us is that this religion, like other and better religions, has its martyrs: that its prophet and founder was, for his teaching, put to death by a mob; that others of its adherents lost their lives by the same lawless violence; that they were forcibly expelled, in a body, from the country in which they first grew up, while, now that they have been chased into a solitary recess in the midst of a desert, many in this country openly declare that it would be right (only that it is not convenient) to send an expedition against them and compel them by force to conform to the opinions of other people. The article of the Mormonite doctrine which is the chief provocative to the antipathy which thus breaks through the ordinary restraints of religious tolerance is its sanction of polygamy; which, though permitted to Mohammedans, and Hindus, and Chinese, seems to excite unquenchable animosity when practiced by persons who speak English and profess to be a kind of Christian. No one has a deeper disapprobation than I have of this Mormon institution; both for other reasons and because, far from being in any way countenanced by the principle of liberty, it is a direct infraction of that principle, being a mere riveting of the chains of one half of the community, and an emancipation of the other from reciprocity of obligation toward them. Still, it must be remembered that this relation is as much voluntary on the part of the women concerned in it, and who may be deemed the sufferers by it, as in the case with any other form of the marriage institution; and however surprising this fact may appear, it has its explanation in the common ideas and customs of the world, which, teaching women to think marriage the one thing needful, make it intelligible that many a woman should prefer being one of several wives to not being a wife at all. Other countries are not asked to recognize such unions, or release any portion of their inhabitants from their own laws on the score of Mormonite opinions. But when the dissentients have conceded to the hostile sentiments of others far more than could justly be demanded; when they have left the countries to which their doctrines were unacceptable and established themselves in a remote corner of the earth, which they have been the first to render habitable to human beings, it is difficult to see on what principles but those of tyranny they can be prevented from living there under what laws they please, provided they commit no aggression on other nations and allow perfect freedom of departure to those who are dissatisfied with their ways. A recent writer, in some respects of considerable merit, proposes (to use his own words) not a crusade, but a *civilizade,* against this polygamous community, to put an end to what seems to him a retrograde step in civilization. It also appears so to me, but I am not aware that any community has a right to force another to be civilized. So long as the sufferers by the bad law do not invoke assistance from other communities, I cannot admit that persons entirely unconnected with them ought to step in and require that a condition of things with which all who are directly interested appear to be satisfied should be put an end to because it is a scandal to persons some thousands of miles distant who have no part or concern in it. Let them send missionaries, if they please, to preach against it; and let them, by any fair means (of which silencing the teachers is not one), oppose the progress of similar doctrines among their own people. If civilization has got the better of barbarism when barbarism had the world to itself, it is too much to profess to be afraid lest barbarism, after having been fairly got under, should revive and conquer civilization. A civilization that can thus succumb to its vanquished enemy must first have become so degenerate that neither its appointed priests and teachers, nor anybody else, has the capacity, or will take the trouble, to stand up for it. If this be so, the sooner such a civilization receives notice to quit, the better. It can only go on from bad to worse until destroyed and regenerated (like the Western Empire) by energetic barbarians.

≝ ≝ ≝

Morals and the Criminal Law
Lord Patrick Devlin

The Report of the Committee on Homosexual Offences and Prostitution, generally known as the Wolfenden Report, is recognized to be an excellent study of two very difficult legal and social problems. But it has also a particular claim to the respect of those interested in jurisprudence; it does what law reformers so rarely do; it sets out clearly and carefully what in relation to its subjects it considers the function of the law to be.[1] Statutory additions to the criminal law are too often made on the simple principle that "there ought to be a law against it." The greater part of the law relating to sexual offences is the creation of statute and it is difficult to ascertain any logical relationship between it and the moral ideas which most of us uphold. Adultery, fornication, and prostitution are not, as the Report[2] points out, criminal offences: homosexuality between males is a criminal offence, but between females it is not. Incest was not an offence until it was declared so by statute only fifty years ago. Does the legislature select these offences haphazardly or are there some principles which can be used to determine what part of the moral law should be embodied in the criminal? There is, for example, being now considered a proposal to make A.I.D., that is, the practice of artificial insemination of a woman with the seed of a man who is not her husband, a criminal offence; if, as is usually the case, the woman is married, this is in substance, if not in form, adultery. Ought it to be made punishable when adultery is not? This sort of question is of practical importance, for a law that appears to be arbitrary and illogical, in the end and after the wave of moral indignation that has put it on the statute book subsides, forfeits respect. As a practical question it arises more frequently in the field of sexual morals than in any other, but there is no special answer to be found in

---

[1] The Committee's "statement of juristic philosophy" (to quote Lord Pakenham) was considered by him in a debate in the House of Lords on 4 December 1957, reported in *Hansard Lords Debates,* vol. ccvi at 738; and also in the same debate by the Archbishop of Canterbury at 753 and Lord Denning at 806. The subject has also been considered by Mr. J. E. Hall Williams in the *Law Quarterly Review,* January 1958, vol. lxxiv, p. 76.

[2] Para. 14.

From Lord Patrick Devlin, *The Enforcement of Morals* (Oxford: Oxford University Press, 1965). Reprinted by permission.

that field. The inquiry must be general and fundamental. What is the connexion between crime and sin and to what extent, if at all, should the criminal law of England concern itself with the enforcement of morals and punish sin or immorality as such? . . .

Early in the Report[3] the Committee put forward:

Our own formulation of the function of the criminal law so far as it concerns the subjects of this enquiry. In this field, its function, as we see it, is to preserve public order and decency, to protect the citizen from what is offensive or injurious, and to provide sufficient safeguards against exploitation and corruption of others, particularly those who are specially vulnerable because they are young, weak in body or mind, inexperienced, or in a state of special physical, official or economic dependence.

It is not, in our view, the function of the law to intervene in the private lives of citizens, or to seek to enforce any particular pattern of behaviour, further than is necessary to carry out the purposes we have outlined.

The Committee preface their most important recommendation.[4]

that homosexual behaviour between consenting adults in private should no longer be a criminal offence [by stating the argument[5]], which we believe to be decisive, namely, the importance which society and the law ought to give to individual freedom of choice and action in matters of private morality. Unless a deliberate attempt is to be made by society, acting through the agency of the law, to equate the sphere of crime with that of sin, there must remain a realm of private morality and immorality which is, in brief and crude terms, not the law's business. To say this is not to condone or encourage private immorality.

Similar statements of principle are set out in the chapters of the Report which deal with prostitution. No case can be sustained, the Report says, for attempting to make prostitution itself illegal.[6] The Committee refer to the general reasons already given and add: "We are agreed that private immorality should not be the concern of the criminal law except in the special circumstances therein mentioned." They quote[7] with approval the report of the Street Offences Committee,[8] which says: "As a general proposition it will be universally accepted that the law is not concerned with private morals or with ethical sanctions." It will be observed that the emphasisis on *private* immorality. By this is meant immorality which is not offensive or injurious to the public in the ways defined or described in the first passage which I quoted, in other words, no act of immorality should be made a criminal offence unless it is accompanied by some other feature such as indecency, corruption, or exploitation. This is clearly brought out in relation to prostitution: "It is not the duty of the law to concern

[3]Para. 13.
[4]Para. 62.
[5]Para. 61.
[6]Para. 224.
[7]Para. 227.
[8]Cmd. 3231 (1928).

itself with immorality as such ... it should confine itself to those activities which offend against public order and decency or expose the ordinary citizen to what is offensive or injurious."[9] ...

Morals and religion are inextricably joined—the moral standards generally accepted in Western civilization being those belonging to Christianity. Outside Christendom other standards derive from other religions. None of these moral codes can claim any validity by virtue of the religion on which it is based. Old Testament morals differ in some respects from New Testament morals. Even within Christianity there are differences. Some hold that contraception is an immoral practice and that a man who has carnal knowledge of another woman while his wife is alive is in all circumstances a fornicator; others, including most of the English-speaking world, deny both these propositions. Between the great religions of the world, of which Christianity is only one, there are much wider differences. It may or may not be right for the State to adopt one of these religions as the truth, to found itself upon its doctrines, and to deny to any of its citizens the liberty to practise any other. If it does, it is logical that it should use the secular law wherever it thinks it necessary to enforce the divine. If it does not, it is illogical that it should concern itself with morals as such. But if it leaves matters of religion to private judgement, it should logically leave matters of morals also. A State which refuses to enforce Christian beliefs has lost the right to enforce Christian morals.

If this view is sound, it means that the criminal law cannot justify any of its provisions by reference to the moral law. It cannot say, for example, that murder and theft are prohibited because they are immoral or sinful. The State must justify in some other way the punishments which it imposes on wrong-doers and a function for the criminal law independent of morals must be found. This is not difficult to do. The smooth functioning of society and the preservation of order require that a number of activities should be regulated. The rules that are made for that purpose and are enforced by the criminal law are often designed simply to achieve uniformity and convenience and rarely involve any choice between good and evil. Rules that impose a speed limit or prevent obstruction on the highway have nothing to do with morals. Since so much of the criminal law is composed of rules of this sort, why bring morals into it at all? Why not define the function of the criminal law in simple terms as the preservation of order and decency and the protection of the lives and property of citizens, and elaborate those terms in relation to any particular subject in the way in which it is done in the Wolfenden Report? The criminal law in carrying out these objects will undoubtedly overlap the moral law. Crimes of violence are morally wrong and they are also offences against good order; therefore they offend against both laws. But this is simply because the two laws in pursuit of different objectives happen to cover the same area. Such is the argument. ...

In jurisprudence, as I have said, everything is thrown open to discussion and, in the belief that they cover the whole field, I have framed three interrogatories addressed to myself to answer:

1. *Has society the right to pass judgement at all on matters of morals? Ought there, in other words, to be a public morality, or are morals always a matter for private judgement?*

[9]Para. 257.

2. *If society has the right to pass judgement, has it also the right to use the weapon of the law to enforce it?*
3. *If so, ought it to use that weapon in all cases or only in some; and if only in some, on what principles should it distinguish?*

I shall begin with the first interrogatory and consider what is meant by the right of society to pass a moral judgement, that is, a judgement about what is good and what is evil. The fact that a majority of people may disapprove of a practice does not of itself make it a matter for society as a whole. Nine men out of ten may disapprove of what the tenth man is doing and still say that it is not their business. There is a case for a collective judgement (as distinct from a large number of individual opinions which sensible people may even refrain from pronouncing at all if it is upon somebody else's private affairs) only if society is affected. Without a collective judgement there can be no case at all for intervention. Let me take as an illustration the Englishman's attitude to religion as it is now and as it has been in the past. His attitude now is that a man's religion is his private affair; he may think of another man's religion that it is right or wrong, true or untrue, but not that it is good or bad. In earlier times that was not so; a man was denied the right to practise what was thought of as heresy, and heresy was thought of as destructive of society.

The language used in the passages I have quoted from the Wolfanden Report suggests the view that there ought not to be a collective judgement about immorality *per se.* Is this what is meant by "private morality" and "individual freedom of choice and action"? Some people sincerely believe that homosexuality is neither immoral nor unnatural. Is the "freedom of choice and action" that is offered to the individual, freedom to decide for himself what is moral or immoral, society remaining neutral; or is it freedom to be immoral if he wants to be? The language of the Report may be open to question, but the conclusions at which the Committee arrive answer this question unambiguously. If society is not prepared to say that homosexuality is morally wrong, there would be no basis for a law protecting youth from "corruption" or punishing a man for living on the "immoral" earnings of a homosexual prostitute, as the Report recommends.[10] This attitude the Committee make even clearer when they come to deal with prostitution. In truth, the Report takes it for granted that there is in existence a public morality which condemns homosexuality and prostitution. What the Report seems to mean by private morality might perhaps be better described as private behaviour in matters of morals.

This view—that there is such a thing as public morality—can also be justified by *a priori* argument. What makes a society of any sort is community of ideas, not only political ideas but also ideas about the way its members should behave and govern their lives; these latter ideas are its morals. Every society has a moral structure as well as a political one: or rather, since that might suggest two independent systems, I should say that the structure of every society is made up both of politics and morals. Take, for example, the institution of marriage. Whether a man should be allowed to take more than one wife is something about which every society has to make up its mind one way or the other. In England we believe in the Christian idea of marriage and therefore adopt monogamy as a moral principle. Consequently the Christian institution of marriage has become the basis of family life and so part of the structure of

[10]Para. 76.

our society. It is there not because it is Christian. It has got there because it is Christian, but it remains here because it is built into the house in which we live and could not be removed without bringing it down. The great majority of those who live in this country accept it because it is the Christian idea of marriage and for them the only true one. But a non-Christian is bound by it, not because it is part of Christianity but because, rightly or wrongly, it has been adopted by the society in which he lives. It would be useless for him to stage a debate designed to prove that polygamy was theologically more correct and socially preferable; if he wants to live in the house, he must accept it as built in the way in which it is.

We see this more clearly if we think of ideas or institutions that are purely political. Society cannot tolerate rebellion; it will not allow argument about the rightness of the cause. Historians a century later may say that the rebels were right and the Government was wrong and a percipient and conscientious subject of the State may think so at the time. But it is not a matter which can be left to individual judgement.

The institution of marriage is a good example for my purpose because it bridges the division, if there is one, between politics and morals. Marriage is part of the structure of our society and it is also the basis of a moral code which condemns fornication and adultery. The institution of marriage would be gravely threatened if individual judgements were permitted about the morality of adultery; on these points there must be a public morality. But public morality is not to be confined to those moral principles which support institutions such as marriage. People do not think of monogamy as something which has to be supported because our society has chosen to organize itself upon it; they think of it as something that is good in itself and offering a good way of life and that it is for that reason that our society has adopted it. I return to the statement that I have already made, that society means a community of ideas; without shared ideas on politics, morals, and ethics no society can exist. Each one of us has ideas about what is good and what is evil; they cannot be kept private from the society in which we live. If men and women try to create a society in which there is no fundamental agreement about good and evil they will fail; if, having based it on common agreement, the agreement goes, the society will disintegrate. For society is not something that is kept together physically; it is held by the invisible bonds of common thought. If the bonds were too far relaxed the members would drift apart. A common morality is part of the bondage. The bondage is part of the price of society; and mankind, which needs society, must pay its price. . . .

You may think that I have taken far too long in contending that there is such a thing as public morality, a proposition which most people would readily accept, and may have left myself too little time to discuss the next question which to many minds may cause greater difficulty: to what extent should society use the law to enforce its moral judgements? But I believe that the answer to the first question determines the way in which the second should be approached and may indeed very nearly dictate the answer to the second question. If society has no right to make judgments on morals, the law must find some special justification for entering the field of morality: if homosexuality and prostitution are not in themselves wrong, then the onus is very clearly on the lawgiver who wants to frame a law against certain aspects of them to justify the exceptional treatment. But if society has the right to make a judgement and has it on the basis that a recognized morality is as necessary to society as, say, a recognized government, then society may use the law to preserve morality in the same way as it uses it to safeguard anything else that is essential to its existence. If therefore the first proposition is securely established with all its implications, society has a prima facie right to legislate against immorality as such. . . .

Society is entitled by means of its laws to protect itself from dangers, whether from within or without. Here again I think that the political parallel is legitimate. The law of treason is directed against aiding the king's enemies and against sedition from within. The justification for this is that established government is necessary for the existence of society and therefore its safety against violent overthrow must be secured. But an established morality is as necessary as good government to the welfare of society. Societies disintegrate from within more frequently than they are broken up by external pressures. There is disintegration when no common morality is observed and history shows that the loosening of moral bonds is often the first stage of disintegration, so that society is justified in taking the same steps to preserve its moral code as it does to preserve its government and other essential institutions.[11] The suppression of vice is as much the law's business as the suppression of subversive activities; it is no more possible to define a sphere of private morality than it is to define one of private subversive activity. It is wrong to talk of private morality or of the law not being concerned with immorality as such or to try to set rigid bounds to the part which the law may play in the suppression of vice. There are no theoretical limits to the power of the State to legislate against treason and sedition, and likewise I think there can be no the-

---

[11]It is somewhere about this point in the argument that Professor Hart in *Law, Liberty and Morality* discerns a proposition which he describes as central to my thought. He states the proposition and his objection to it as follows (p. 51). "He appears to move from the acceptable proposition that *some* shared morality is essential to the existence of any society [this I take to be the proposition on p. 12] to the unacceptable proposition that a society is identical with its morality as that is at any given moment of its history so that a change in its morality is tantamount to the destruction of a society. The former proposition might be even accepted as a necessary rather than an empirical truth depending on a quite plausible definition of society as a body of men who hold certain moral views in common. But the latter proposition is absurd. Taken strictly, it would prevent us saying that the morality of a given society had changed, and would compel us instead to say that one society had disappeared and another one taken its place. But it is only on this absurd criterion of what it is for the same society to continue to exist that it could be asserted without evidence that any deviation from a society's shared morality threatens its existence." In conclusion (p. 82) Professor Hart condemns the whole thesis in the lecture as based on "a confused definition of what a society is."

I do not assert that *any* deviation from a society's shared morality threatens its existence any more than I assert that *any* subversive activity threatens its existence. I assert that they are both activities which are capable in their nature of threatening the existence of society so that neither can be put beyond the law.

For the rest, the objection appears to me to be all a matter of words. I would venture to assert, for example, that you cannot have a game without rules and that if there were no rules there would be no game. If I am asked whether that means that the game is "identical" with the rules, I would be willing for the question to be answered either way in the belief that the answer would lead to nowhere. If I am asked whether a change in the rules means that one game has disappeared and another has taken its place, I would reply probably not, but that it would depend on the extent of the change.

Likewise I should venture to assert that there cannot be a contract without terms. Does this mean that an "amended" contract is a "new" contract in the eyes of the law? I once listened to an argument by an ingenious counsel that a contract, because of the substitution of one clause for another, had "ceased to have effect" within the meaning of a statutory provision. The judge did not accept the argument: but if most of the fundamental terms had been changed, I daresay he would have done.

The proposition that I make in the text is that if (as I understand Professor Hart to agree, at any rate for the purposes of the argument) you cannot have a society without morality, the law can be used to enforce morality as something that is essential to a society. I cannot see why this proposition (whether it is right or wrong) should mean that morality can never be changed without the destruction of society. If morality is changed, the law can be changed. Professor Hart refers (p. 72) to the proposition as "the use of legal punishment to freeze into immobility the morality dominant at a particular time in a society's existence. "One might as well say that the inclusion of a penal section into a statute prohibiting certain acts freezes the whole statute into immobility and prevents the prohibitions from ever being modified.

oretical limits to legislation against immorality. You may argue that if a man's sins affect only himself it cannot be the concern of society. If he chooses to get drunk every night in the privacy of his own home, is any one except himself the worse for it? But suppose a quarter or a half of the population got drunk every night, what sort of society would it be? You cannot set a theoretical limit to the number of people who can get drunk before society is entitled to legislate against drunkenness. The same may be said of gambling. The Royal Commission on Betting, Lotteries, and Gaming took as their test the character of the citizen as a member of society. They said: "Our concern with the ethical significance of gambling is confined to the effect which it may have on the character of the gambler as a member of society. If we were convinced that whatever the degree of gambling this effect must be harmful we should be inclined to think that it was the duty of the state to restrict gambling to the greatest extent practicable."[12]

In what circumstances the State should exercise its power is the third of the interrogatories I have framed. But before I get to it I must raise a point which might have been brought up in any one of the three. How are the moral judgements of society to be ascertained? By leaving it until now, I can ask it in the more limited form that is now sufficient for my purpose. How is the law-maker to ascertain the moral judgements of society? It is surely not enough that they should be reached by the opinion of the majority; it would be too much to require the individual assent of every citizen. English law has evolved and regularly uses a standard which does not depend on the counting of heads. It is that of the reasonable man. He is not to be confused with the rational man. He is not expected to reason about anything and his judgement may be largely a matter of feeling. It is the viewpoint of the man in the street—or to use an archaism familiar to all lawyers—the man in the Clapham omnibus. He might also be called the right-minded man. For my purpose I should like to call him the man in the jury box, for the moral judgement of society must be something about which any twelve men or women drawn at random might after discussion be expected to be unanimous. This was the standard the judges applied in the days before Parliament was as active as it is now and when they laid down rules of public policy. They did not think of themselves as making law but simply as stating principles which every right-minded person would accept as valid. It is what Pollock called "practical morality," which is based not on theological or philosophical foundations but "in the mass of continuous experience half-consciously or unconsciously accumulated and embodied in the morality of common sense." He called it also "a certain way of thinking on question of morality which we expect to find in a reasonable civilized man or a reasonable Englishman, taken at random. . . ."[13]

I return now to the main thread of my argument and summarize it. Society cannot live without morals. Its morals are those standards of conduct which the reasonable man approves. A rational man, who is also a good man, may have other standards. If he has no standards at all he is not a good man and need not be further considered. If he has standards, they may be very different; he may, for example, not disapprove of homosexuality or abortion. In that case he will not share in the common morality; but that should not make him deny that it is a social necessity. A rebel may be rational in thinking that he is right but he is irrational if he thinks that society can leave him free to rebel.

[12](1951) Cmd. 8190, para. 159.
[13]*Essays in Jurisprudence and Ethics* (1882), Macmillan, pp. 278 and 353.

A man who concedes that morality is necessary to society must support the use of those instruments without which morality cannot be maintained. The two instruments are those of teaching, which is doctrine, and of enforcement, which is the law. If morals could be taught simply on the basis that they are necessary to society, there would be no social need for religion; it could be left as a purely personal affair. But morality cannot be taught in that way. Loyalty is not taught in that way either. No society has yet solved the problem of how to teach morality without religion. So the law must base itself on Christian morals and to the limit of its ability enforce them, not simply because they are the morals of most of us, nor simply because they are the morals which are taught by the established Church—on these points the law recognizes the right to dissent—but for the compelling reason that without the help of Christian teaching the law will fail.

Law, Liberty, and Morality

H. L. A. Hart

THE LEGAL ENFORCEMENT OF MORALITY

The lectures are concerned with one question about the relations between law and morals. I say, advisedly, "one question," because in the heat of the controversy often generated when law and morals are mentioned in conjunction, it is often overlooked that there is not just one question concerning their relations but many different questions needing quite separate consideration. So I shall start by distinguishing four such questions and identifying the one with which I shall be here concerned.

The first is a historical and a causal question: Has the development of the law been influenced by morals? The answer to this question plainly is "Yes"; though of course this does not mean that an affirmative answer may not also be given to the converse question: Has the development of morality been influenced by law? This latter question has scarcely been adequately investigated yet, but there are now many admirable American and English studies of the former question. These exhibit the manifold ways in which morality has determined the course of the law, sometimes covertly and slowly through the judicial process, sometimes openly and abruptly through legislation. I shall say no more here about this historical causal question, except to utter the warning that the affirmative answer which may be given to it, and to its converse, does not mean that an affirmative answer is to be given to other quite different questions about the relations of law and morals.

Reprinted from Lecture I, II *Law, Liberty and Morality* by H. L. A. Hart © 1963 Stanford University Press. By permission of Stanford University Press and H. L. A. Hart.

The second question may be called an analytical or definitional one. Must some reference to morality enter into an adequate definition of law or legal system? Or is it just a contingent fact that law and morals often overlap (as in their common proscription of certain forms of violence and dishonesty) and that they share a common vocabulary of rights, obligations, and duties? These are famous questions in the long history of the philosophy of law, but perhaps they are not so important as the amount of time and ink expended upon them suggests. Two things have conspired to make discussion of them interminable or seemingly so. The first is that the issue has been clouded by use of grand but vague words like "Positivism" and "Natural Law." Banners have been waved and parties formed in a loud but often confused debate. Secondly, amid the shouting, too little has been said about the criteria for judging the adequacy of a definition of law. Should such a definition state what, if anything, the plain man intends to convey when he uses the expressions "law" or "legal system"? Or should it rather aim to provide, by marking off certain social phenomena from others, a classification useful or illuminating for theoretical purposes?

A third question concerns the possibility and the forms of the moral criticism of law. Is law open to moral criticism? Or does the admission that a rule is a valid legal rule preclude moral criticism or condemnation of it by reference to moral standards or principles? Few perhaps of this audience would find any contradiction or paradox in the assertion that a rule of law was valid and yet conflicted with some binding moral principle requiring behaviour contrary to that demanded by the legal rule. Yet in our own day Kelsen[1] has argued that there is a logical contradiction in such an assertion, unless it is interpreted merely as an autobiographical statement or psychological report by the speaker of his divergent inclinations both to obey the law and to disobey it by following the moral principle.

Within this third question there are many subordinate ones. Even if we admit, as most would, the possibility of a moral criticism of law, we may ask whether there are any forms of moral criticism which are uniquely or exclusively relevant to law. Does criticism in terms of Justice exhaust all the relevant forms? Or does "good law" mean something different from and wider than "just law"? Is Justice, as Bentham seems to have thought, merely a name for the efficient distribution of Utility or Welfare, or is it otherwise reducible to them? Plainly the adequacy of Utilitarianism as a moral critique of social institutions is in issue here.

The fourth question is the subject of these lectures. It concerns the legal enforcement of morality and has been formulated in many different ways: Is the fact that certain conduct is by common standards immoral sufficient to justify making that conduct punishable by law? Is it morally permissible to enforce morality as such? Ought immorality as such to be a crime?

To this question John Stuart Mill gave an emphatic negative answer in his essay *On Liberty* one hundred years ago, and the famous sentence in which he frames this answer expresses the central doctrine of his essay. He said, "The only purpose for which power can rightfully be exercised over any member of a civilized community against his will is to prevent harm to others."[2] And to identify the many different things which he intended to exclude, he added, "His own good either physical or moral is not a sufficient warrant. He cannot rightfully be compelled to do or forbear because it

---

[1]Hans Kelsen, *General Theory of Law and State,* pp. 374–76, 407–10.
[2]*On Liberty,* Chapter I.

will be better for him to do so, because it will make him happier, because in the opinions of others, to do so would be wise or even right."[3]

This doctrine, Mill tells us, is to apply to human beings only "in the maturity of their faculties": it is not to apply to children or to backward societies. Even so, it has been the object of much academic criticism on two different, and indeed inconsistent, grounds. Some critics have urged that the line which Mill attempts to draw between actions with which the law may interfere and those with which it may not is illusory. "No man is an island"; and in an organised society it is impossible to identify classes of actions which harm no one or no one but the individual who does them. Other critics have admitted that such a division of actions may be made, but insist that it is merely dogmatic on Mill's part to limit legal coercion to the class of actions which harm others. There are good reasons, so these critics claim, for compelling conformity to social morality and for punishing deviations from it even when these do not harm others.

I shall consider this dispute mainly in relation to the special topic of sexual morality where it seems *prima facie* plausible that there are actions immoral by accepted standards and yet not harmful to others. But to prevent misunderstanding I wish to enter a *caveat;* I do not propose to defend all that Mill said; for I myself think there may be grounds justifying the legal coercion of the individual other than the prevention of harm to others. But on the narrower issue relevant to the enforcement of morality Mill seems to me to be right. It is of course possible simply to assert that the legal enforcement by society of its accepted morality needs no argument to justify it, because it is a morality which is enforced. But Mill's critics have not fallen back upon this brute assertion. They have in fact advanced many different arguments to justify the enforcement of morality, but these all, as I shall attempt to show, rest on unwarranted assumptions as to matters of fact, or on certain evaluations whose plausibility, due in large measure to ambiguity or vagueness or inaccuracy of statement, dwindles (even if it does not altogether vanish) when exposed to critical scrutiny.

CONSPIRACY TO CORRUPT PUBLIC MORALS

In England in the last few years the question whether the criminal law should be used to punish immorality "as such" has acquired a new practical importance; for there has, I think, been a revival there of what might be termed *legal moralism.* Judges both in their judicial capacity and in extra-judicial statements have gone out of their way to express the view that the enforcement of sexual morality is a proper part of the law's business—as much as its business, so one judge has argued, as the suppression of treason. It is not clear what has provoked this resurgence of legal moralism: there must have been many factors at work, and among them, perhaps, has been the idea that a general stiffening of the sanctions attached to any form of immorality may be one way to meet the general increase in crime by which we are all vastly disturbed. But whatever its cause, this movement of judicial opinion has gone far. Last year the House of Lords in the case of *Shaw* v. *Director of Public Prosecutions*[4] conjured up, from what many had thought was its grave in the eighteenth century, the conception (itself a creature of the Star Chamber) that "a conspiracy to corrupt public morals" is

[3]*Ibid.*
[4](1961) 2 A.E.R. 446. (1962) A.C. 223.

a common law offence. As a result of this decision the prosecuting authorities in England can now face the complex problems equipped with Lord Mansfield's dictum of 1774 which some of the judges in Shaw's case invoked in their speeches.

> Whatever is *contra bonos mores et decorum* the principles of our laws prohibit and the King's Court as the general censor and guardian of the public morals is bound to restrain and punish.[5]

Of course the penal code of California, like that of many states of the Union, includes in its calendar of crimes a conspiracy to injure public morals, and it may seem strange to Americans to hear the recognition of this offence by the English House of Lords represented as a new development. But Americans are accustomed, as the English are not, to the inclusion among their statutes of much legal lumber in the form of penal provisions no longer enforced, and I am assured that, in California at least, the provision making a conspiracy to corrupt public morals a crime may safely be regarded as a dead letter. This is now not so with the English, and both the use actually made of the law in Shaw's case and the future use envisaged for it by the House of Lords are worth consideration.

The facts in Shaw's case are not such as to excite sympathy for the accused. What Shaw had done was to compose and procure the publication of a magazine called the *Ladies Directory* giving the names and addresses of prostitutes, in some cases nude photographs, and an indication in code of their practices. For this Shaw was charged and found guilty of three offences: (1) publishing an obscene article, (2) living on the earnings of the prostitutes who paid for the insertion of their advertisements in the *Ladies Directory,* (3) conspiring to corrupt public morals by means of the *Ladies Directory.*

All this may seem a somewhat ponderous three-handed engine to use merely to ensure the conviction and imprisonment of Shaw; but English law has always preferred the policy of thorough. The judges in the House of Lords not only raised no objection to the inclusion of the charge of conspiracy to corrupt public morals, but with one dissentient (Lord Reid) they confirmed the prosecution's contention that this was an offence still known to English law and insisted that it was a salutary thing that this should be so. They made indeed an excursion, rare for English judges, into the area of policy in order to emphasise this.

To show the contemporary need for the newly resuscitated penal law one of the judges (Lord Simonds), a former Lord Chancellor, made the following remarkable statement:

> When Lord Mansfield speaking long after the Star Chamber had been abolished said that the Court of King's Bench was the *custos morum* of the people and had the superintendency of offences *contra bonos mores,* he was asserting, as I now assert, that there is in that Court a residual power, where no statute has yet intervened to supersede the common law, to superintend those offences which are prejudicial to the public welfare. Such occasions will be rare, for Parliament has not been slow to legislate when attention has been sufficiently aroused. But gaps remain and will always remain, since no one can foresee every way in which the

---

[5]Jones v. Randall (1774). Lofft, at p. 385

wickedness of man may disrupt the order of society. Let me take a single instance . . . Let it be supposed that at some future, perhaps early, date homosexual practices between adult consenting males are no longer a crime. Would it
not be an offence if even without obscenity such practices were publicly advocated and encouraged by pamphlet and advertisement? Or must we wait till Parliament finds time to deal with such conduct? I say, my Lords, that if the common
law is powerless in such an event then we should no longer do her reverence.
But I say that her hand is still powerful and that it is for her Majesty's Judges to
play the part which Lord Mansfield pointed out to them.[6]

This is no doubt a fine specimen of English judicial rhetoric in the baroque manner.
Later judges may dismiss much of it as *obiter dictum*. But the interpretation given by
the House of Lords to the exceedingly vague and indeed obscure idea of corrupting
public morals has fashioned a very formidable weapon for punishing immorality as
such. For it is clear from the form of direction to the jury which the House of Lords
approved in this case that no limits are in practice imposed by the need to establish
anything which would be ordinarily thought of as a "conspiracy" or as "corruption."
These strong words have, as Lord Reid said, been "watered down," and all that has to
be established is that the accused agreed to do or say something which in the opinion
of a jury might "lead another morally astray."[7] There need moreover be no approach
to the "public" nor need the morality in question be "public" in any sense other than
being the generally accepted morality.

Legal writers in England have not yet worked out the relation between this vastly
comprehensive common law offence and those statutes which define certain specific
offences concerned with sexual morality. But it is certainly arguable that the prosecuting authorities may now avail themselves of this common law offence to avoid the restrictions imposed by statute or statutory defences. Thus the statute[8] under which the
publishers of D. H. Lawrence's *Lady Chatterley's Lover* were unsuccessfully prosecuted
in England last year provides that the interests of science, literature, and art or learning shall be taken into consideration, and if it is proved that on these grounds publication is justified as being for the public good, no offence under the statute is
committed. Evidence as to these merits was accordingly received in that case. Had the
publishers been charged with conspiring to corrupt morals, the literary or artistic
merits of the book would have been irrelevant, and the prosecution might very well
have succeeded. In the same way, though Parliament in recent legislation has refrained from making prostitution itself a crime, as distinct from soliciting in a street or
public place,[9] it seems that it is open to the Courts under the doctrine of Shaw's case
to do what Parliament has not done. Some apprehension that it may be so used has already been expressed.[10]

The importance attached by the judges in Shaw's case to the revival of the idea
that the Courts should function as the *custos morum* or "the general censor and
guardian of the public manners" may be gauged from two things. The first is that this

[6]Shaw v. Director of Public Prosecutions (1961) 2 A.E.R. at pp. 452–53. (1962) A.C. at p. 268.
[7](1961) 2 A.E.R. at pp. 461, 466. (1962) A.C. at p. 282.
[8]The Obscene Publications Act 1959.
[9]The Street Offences Act 1959.

[10]*Manchester Guardian,* January 31, 1962; comment on Weisz v. Monahan (1962) 2 W.L. R. 262. Cf. also R. V.
Quinn (1961) 3 W.L.R. 611.

revival was plainly a deliberate act of policy; for the antique cases relied upon as pre-
cedents plainly permitted, even under the rigorous English doctrine of precedent, a
decision either way. Secondly, the judges seemed willing to pay a high price in terms
of the sacrifice of other values for the establishment—or re-establishment—of the
Courts as *custos morum*. The particular value which they sacrificed is the principle of
legality which requires criminal offences to be as precisely defined as possible, so that
it can be known with reasonable certainty beforehand what acts are criminal and what
are not. As a result of Shaw's case, virtually any cooperative conduct is criminal if a jury
consider it *ex post facto* to have been immoral. Perhaps the nearest counterpart to this
in modern European jurisprudence is the idea to be found in German statutes of the
Nazi period that anything is punishable if it is deserving of punishment according "to
the fundamental conceptions of a penal law and sound popular feeling."[11] So while
Mill would have shuddered at the law laid down in Shaw's case as authorising gross
invasions of individual liberty, Bentham[12] would have been horrified at its disregard of
the legal values of certainty and its extension of what he termed "ex post facto law."[13]

PROSTITUTION AND HOMOSEXUALITY

There are other points of interest in Shaw's case. What after all is it to corrupt *morals*
or a *morality?* But I shall defer further consideration of this point in order to outline
another issue which in England has recently provoked discussion of the law's enforcement of morality and has stimulated efforts to clarify the principles at stake.

Much dissatisfaction has for long been felt in England with the criminal law relating to both prostitution and homosexuality, and in 1954 the committee well known as
the Wolfenden Committee was appointed to consider the state of the law. This committee reported[14] in September 1957 and recommended certain changes in the law on
both topics. As to homosexuality they recommended by a majority of 12 to 1 that homosexual practices between consenting adults in private should no longer be a crime;
as to prostitution they unanimously recommended that, though it should not itself be
made illegal, legislation should be passed "to drive it off the streets" on the ground
that public soliciting was an offensive nuisance to ordinary citizens. The government
eventually introduced legislation[15] to give effect to the Committee's recommendations
concerning prostitution but not to that concerning homosexuality, and attempts by
private members to introduce legislation modifying the law on this subject have so far
failed.

What concerns us here is less the fate of the Wolfenden Committee's recommendations than the principles by which these were supported. These are strikingly sim-

[11]Act of June 28, 1935.

[12]*Principles of the Civil Code,* Part I, Chapter 17 (I [Bowring ed.] *Works* 326).

[13]Shaw's case has been criticised on these grounds by Glanville Williams, "Conspiring to Corrupt," *The Lis-
tener,* August 24, 1961, p. 275; Hall Williams, 24 *Mod. L.R.* 631 (1961): "judicial folly"; D. Scaborne Davies,
"The House of Lords and the Criminal Law," *J. Soc. Public Teachers of Law* (1961), p. 105: "an egregious
performance." It was welcomed as "an important contribution to the development of the criminal law" by
A. L. Goodhart, 77 *Law, Q.R.* 567 (1961).

[14]Report of the Committee on Homosexual Offences and Prostitution (CMD 247) 1957.

[15]The Street Offences Act 1959.

ilar to those expounded by Mill in his essay *On Liberty*. Thus section 13 of the Committee's Report reads:

> [The] function [of the criminal law], as we see it, is to preserve public order and decency, to protect the citizen from what is offensive or injurious and to provide sufficient safeguards against exploitation or corruption of others, particularly those who are specially vulnerable because they are young, weak in body or mind or inexperienced. . . .

This conception of the positive functions of the criminal law was the Committee's main ground for its recommendation concerning prostitution that legislation should be passed to suppress the offensive public manifestations of prostitution, but not to make prostitution itself illegal. Its recommendation that the law against homosexual practices between consenting adults in private should be relaxed was based on the principle stated simply in section 61 of the Report as follows: "There must remain a realm of private morality and immorality which is, in brief and crude terms, not the law's business."

It is of some interest that these developments in England have had near counterparts in America. In 1955 the American Law Institute published with its draft Model Penal Code a recommendation that all consensual relations between adults in private should be excluded from the scope of the criminal law. Its grounds were *(inter alia)* that "no harm to the secular interests of the community is involved in atypical sex practice in private between consenting adult partners";[16] and "there is the fundamental question of the protection to which every individual is entitled against state interference in his personal affairs when he is not hurting others."[17] This recommendation has been approved by the Advisory Committee of the Institute but rejected by a majority vote of its Council. The issue was therefore referred to the annual meeting of the Institute at Washington in May 1955, and the recommendation, supported by an eloquent speech of the late Justice Learned Hand, was, after a hot debate, accepted by a majority of 35 to 24.[18]

It is perhaps clear from the foregoing that Mill's principles are still very much alive in the criticism of law, whatever their theoretical deficiencies may be. But twice in one hundred years they have been challenged by two masters of the Common Law. The first of these was the great Victorian judge and historian of the Criminal Law, James Fitzjames Stephen. His criticism of Mill is to be found in the sombre and impressive book *Liberty, Equality, Fraternity*,[19] which he wrote as a direct reply to Mill's essay *On Liberty*. It is evident from the tone of this book that Stephen thought he had found crushing arguments against Mill and had demonstrated that the law might justifiably enforce morality as such or, as he said, that the law should be "a persecution of the grosser forms of vice."[20] Nearly a century later, on the publication of the Wolfenden Committee's report, Lord Devlin, now a member of the House of Lords and a most distinguished writer on the criminal law, in his essay on *The Enforcement of*

---

[16]American Law Institute Model Penal Code, Tentative Draft No. 4, p. 277.
[17]*Ibid.*, p. 278.
[18]An account of the debate is given in *Time*, May 30, 1955, p. 13.
[19]2nd edition, London, 1874.
[20]*Ibid.*, p. 162.

Morals[21] took as his target the Report's contention "that there must be a realm of morality and immorality which is not the law's business" and argued in opposition to it that "the suppression of vice is as much the law's business as the suppression of subversive activities."

Though a century divides these two legal writers, the similarity in the general tone and sometimes in the detail of their arguments is very great. I shall devote the remainder of these lectures to an examination of them. I do this because, though their arguments are at points confused, they certainly still deserve the compliment of rational opposition. They are not only admirably stocked with concrete examples, but they express the considered views of skilled, sophisticated lawyers experienced in the administration of the criminal law. Views such as theirs are still quite widely held especially by lawyers both in England and in this country; it may indeed be that they are more popular, in both countries, than Mill's doctrine of Liberty. . . .

PRIVATE IMMORALITY AND PUBLIC INDECENCY

So far, scrutiny of two examples used by the writers we have considered has established two important distinctions: the distinction between paternalism and the enforcement of morality, and that between justifying the practice of punishment and justifying its amount. Our third example is the crime of bigamy. This is not discussed by Stephen or Lord Devlin, but the punishment of polygamy is cited as an example of the legal enforcement of morality by Dean Rostow in his essay defending Lord Devlin against his critics.[22] It is, however, a curiously complex case, and an examination of it shows that punishment of bigamy is not to be classed unambiguously as an attempt to enforce morality. In the short discussion of it which follows I shall attempt to show that in this case, as in the two already discussed, those who would wish to retain this rule of criminal law are not thereby committed to the policy of punishing immorality as such; for its punishment can be supported on other reasonable grounds.

In most common law jurisdictions it is a criminal offence for a married person during the lifetime of an existing husband or wife to go through a ceremony of marriage with another person, even if the other person knows of the existing marriage. The punishment of bigamy not involving deception is curious in the following respect. In England and in many other jurisdictions where it is punishable, the sexual cohabitation of the parties is not a criminal offence. If a married man cares to cohabit with another woman—or even several other women—he may do so with impunity so far as the criminal law is concerned. He may set up house and pretend that he is married: he may celebrate his union with champagne and a distribution of wedding cake and with all the usual social ceremonial of a valid marriage. None of this is illegal; but if he goes through a ceremony of marriage, the law steps in not merely to declare it invalid but to punish the bigamist.

Why does the law interfere at this point, leaving the substantial immorality of sexual cohabitation alone? Various answers have been given to this question. Some

---

[21]Oxford University Press, 1959.

[22]"The Enforcement of Morals," 174 *Cambridge L.J.* (1960) at p. 190. Dean Rostow mainly discusses polygamy "based on sincere religious belief" rather than "bigamy contracted for pleasure." He asks (rhetorically) "Should we not conclude that monogamy is so fundamental a theme in the existing common morality of the United States that the condemnation of polygamy as a crime is justified even though the law rests on 'feeling' and not on 'reason'?"

have suggested that the purpose of the legal punishment of bigamy is to protect public records from confusion, or to frustrate schemes to misrepresent illegitimate children as legitimate. The American Law Institute suggests in its commentary on the draft Model Penal Code that bigamous adultery, even where it does not involve deception, might call for punishment because it is a public affront and provocation to the first spouse, and also because cohabitation under the colour of matrimony is specially likely "to result in desertion, non-support, and divorce."[23] These, it is urged, are harms to individuals which the criminal law may properly seek to prevent by punishment.

Some at least of these suggested grounds seem more ingenious than convincing. The harms they stress may be real enough; yet many may still think that a case for punishing bigamy would remain even if these harms were unlikely to result, or if they were catered for by the creation of specific offences which penalized not the bigamy but, for example, the causing of false statements to be entered into official records. Perhaps most who find these various justifications of the existing law unconvincing but still wish to retain it would urge that in a country where deep religious significance is attached to monogamous marriage and to the act of solemnizing it, the law against bigamy should be accepted as an attempt to protect religious feelings from offence by a public act desecrating the ceremony. Again as with the two previous examples, the question is whether those who think that the use of the criminal law for these purposes is in principle justified are inconsistent if they also deny that the law may be used to punish immorality as such.

I do not think that there is any inconsistency in this combination of attitudes, but there is a need for one more important distinction. It is important to see that if, in the case of bigamy, the law intervenes in order to protect religious sensibilities from outrage by a public act, the bigamist is punished neither as irreligious nor as immoral but as a nuisance. For the law is then concerned with the offensiveness to others of his public conduct, not with the immorality of his private conduct, which, in most countries, it leaves altogether unpunished. In this case, as in the case of ordinary crimes which cause physical harm, the protection of those likely to be affected is certainly an intelligible aim for the law to pursue, and it certainly could not be said of this case that "the function of the criminal law is to enforce a moral principle and nothing else." It is to be noted that Lord Devlin himself, unlike his defender Dean Rostow, seems to attend to this distinction; for he does not include bigamy in his list of crimes which the principles of the Wolfenden Report would compel us to reject. This is not an oversight, for he specifically says of those which are included in the list that "they are all acts which can be done in private and without offence to others."[24]

It is perhaps doubtful whether Mill's principles as stated in the essay *On Liberty* would have allowed the punishment of bigamy, where no deception was involved, on the ground that it was a public act offensive to religious feelings. For although it is clear that he thought consideration might be due to the "feelings" as well as to the "interests" of others, and an act causing offence to feelings might deserve at least moral blame, he both asserts this and qualifies it in language which is notoriously very difficult to interpret. He seems to have thought that blame and punishment for offence to feelings were justified only if at least two conditions were satisfied: first that some

[23]See p. 220.

[24]*The Enforcement of Morals*, p. 9. Nonetheless Lord Devlin warmly endorses Dean Rostow's defence. See "Law, Democracy, and Morality," 110 *University of Pennsylvania L.R.* (1962) at p. 640.

close association and special relationship existed between the parties making consideration an obligation to "assignable" individuals; and secondly that the harm should not be "merely contingent" or "constructive."[25]

If we disregard the first of these conditions as too restrictive, and interpret the second to mean only that the offence to feelings should be both serious and likely, the question whether or not to punish bigamy will depend on comparative estimates (over which men may of course differ) of the seriousness of the offence to feelings and of the sacrifice of freedom and suffering demanded and imposed by the law. Supporters of the law could certainly argue that very little sacrifice or suffering is demanded by the law in this instance. It denies only one, though doubtless the most persuasive, item of the appearance of legal respectability to parties who are allowed to enjoy the substance and parade all the other simulacra of a valid marriage. The case is therefore utterly different from attempts to enforce sexual morality which may demand the repression of powerful instincts with which personal happiness is intimately connected. On the other hand, opponents of the law may plausibly urge, in an age of waning faith, that the religious sentiments likely to be offended by the public celebration of a bigamous marriage are no longer very widespread or very deep and it is enough that such marriages are held legally invalid.

The example of bigamy shows the need to distinguish between the immorality of a practice and its aspect as a public offensive act or nuisance. This is of general importance; for English law has often in the course of its development come to view in just this light conduct previously punished simply because it was forbidden by accepted religion or morality. Thus any denial of the truths of the Christian religion was once punished in England as blasphemy, whereas now it is only punishable if it is made in an offensive or insulting manner, likely to cause a breach of the peace. Those who support this modern form of the punishment of blasphemy are not, of course, committed to belief in the religion of those whose feelings are thereby protected from insult. They may indeed quite consistently oppose any attempt to enforce conformity with that or any religion.

In sexual matters a similar line generally divides the punishment of immorality from the punishment of indecency. The Romans distinguished the province of the Censor, concerned with morals, from that of the Aedile, concerned with public decency, but in modern times perhaps insufficient attention has been given to this distinction.[26] Indeed, Lord Simonds in his speech in the House of Lords in Shaw's case went out of his way to profess indifference to it.

> It matters little what label is given to the offending act. To one of your Lordships it may appear an affront to public decency, to another considering that it may succeed in its obvious intention of provoking libidinous desires it will seem a corruption of morality.[27]

But the distinction is in fact both clear and important. Sexual intercourse between husband and wife is not immoral, but if it takes place in public it is an affront to public decency. Homosexual intercourse between consenting adults in private is im-

[25]*On Liberty,* Chapter 4.
[26]But see "The Censor as Aedile," *Time Literary Suppl.,* August 4, 1961.
[27](1961) 2 A.E.R. at 452.

moral according to conventional morality, but not an affront to public decency, though it would be both if it took place in public. But the fact that the same act, if done in public, could be regarded both as immoral and as an affront to public decency must not blind us to the difference between these two aspects of conduct and to the different principles on which the justification of their punishment must rest. The recent English law relating to prostitution attends to this difference. It has not made prostitution a crime but punishes its public manifestation in order to protect the ordinary citizen, who is an unwilling witness of it in the streets, from something offensive.

It may no doubt be objected that too much has been made in this discussion of the distinction between what is done in public and what is done in private. For offence to feelings, it may be said, is given not only when immoral activities or their commercial preliminaries are thrust upon unwilling eyewitnesses, but also when those who strongly condemn certain sexual practices as immoral learn that others indulge in them in private. Because this is so, it is pointless to attend to the distinction between what is done privately and what is done in public; and if we do not attend to it, then the policies of punishing men for mere immorality and punishing them for conduct offensive to the feelings of others, though conceptually distinct, would not differ in practice. All conduct strongly condemned as immoral would then be punishable.

It is important not to confuse this argument with the thesis, which I shall later examine, that the preservation of an existing social morality is itself a value justifying the use of coercion. The present argument invokes in support of the legal enforcement of morality not the values of morality but Mill's own principle that coercion may be justifiably used to prevent harm to others. Various objections may be made to this use of the principle. It may be said that the distress occasioned by the bare thought that others are offending in private against morality cannot constitute "harm," except in a few neurotic or hypersensitive persons who are literally "made ill" by this thought. Others may admit that such distress is harm, even in the case of normal persons, but argue that it is too slight to outweigh the great misery caused by the legal enforcement of sexual morality.

Although these objections are not without force, they are of subsidiary importance. The fundamental objection surely is that a right to be protected from the distress which is inseparable from the bare knowledge that others are acting in ways you think wrong, cannot be acknowledged by anyone who recognises individual liberty as a value. For the extension of the utilitarian principle that coercion may be used to protect men from harm, so as to include their protection from this form of distress, cannot stop there. If distress incident to the belief that others are doing wrong is harm, so also is the distress incident to the belief that others are doing what you do not want them to do. To punish people for causing this form of distress would be tantamount to punishing them simply because others object to what they do; and the only liberty that could coexist with this extension of the utilitarian principle is liberty to do those things to which no one seriously objects. Such liberty plainly is quite nugatory. Recognition of individual liberty as a value involves, as a minimum, acceptance of the principle that the individual may do what he wants, even if others are distressed when they learn what it is that he does—unless, of course, there are other good grounds for forbidding it. No social order which accords to individual liberty any value could also accord the right to be protected from distress thus occasioned.

Protection from shock or offence to feelings caused by some public display is, as most legal systems recognise, another matter. The distinction may sometimes be a fine one. It is so, in those cases such as the desecration of venerated objects or ceremonies where there would be no shock or offense to feeling, if those on whom the public display is obtruded had not subscribed to certain religious or moral beliefs. Nonetheless the use of punishment to protect those made vulnerable to the public display by their own beliefs leaves the offender at liberty to do the same thing in private, if he can. It is not tantamount to punishing men simply because others object to what they do.

THE MODERATE AND THE EXTREME THESIS

When we turn from these examples which are certainly disputable to the positive grounds held to justify the legal enforcement of morality it is important to distinguish a moderate and an extreme thesis, though critics of Mill have sometimes moved from one to the other without marking the transition. Lord Devlin seems to me to maintain, for most of his essay, the moderate thesis and Stephen the extreme one.

According to the moderate thesis, a shared morality is the cement of society; without it there would be aggregates of individuals but no society. "A recognized morality" is, in Lord Devlin's words, "as necessary to society's existence as a recognized government,"[28] and though a particular act of immorality may not harm or endanger or corrupt others nor, when done in private, either shock or give offence to others, this does not conclude the matter. For we must not view conduct in isolation from its effect on the moral code: if we remember this, we can see that one who is "no menace to others" nonetheless may by his immoral conduct "threaten one of the great moral principles on which society is based."[29] In this sense the breach of moral principle is an offence "against society as a whole,"[30] and society may use the law to preserve its morality as it uses it to safeguard anything else essential to its existence. This is why "the suppression of vice is as much the law's business as the suppression of subversive activities."[31]

By contrast, the extreme thesis does not look upon a shared morality as of merely instrumental value analogous to ordered government, and it does not justify the punishment of immorality as a step taken, like the punishment of treason, to preserve society from dissolution or collapse. Instead, the enforcement of morality is regarded as a thing of value, even if immoral acts harm no one directly, or indirectly by weakening the moral cement of society. I do not say that it is possible to allot to one or other of these two theses every argument used, but they do, I think, characterise the main critical positions at the root of most arguments, and they incidentally exhibit an ambiguity in the expression "enforcing morality as such." Perhaps the clearest way of distinguishing the two theses is to see that there are always two levels at which we may ask whether some breach of positive morality is harmful. We may ask first, Does this act harm anyone independently of its repercussion on the shared morality of society? And secondly we may ask, Does this act affect the shared morality and thereby weaken society? The moderate thesis requires, if the punishment of the act is to be justified, an affirmative answer at least at the second level. The extreme thesis does not require an affirmative answer at either level.

[28]*The Enforcement of Morals*, p. 13.
[29]*Ibid.*, p. 8.
[30]*Ibid.*
[31]*Ibid.*, p. 15.

Lord Devlin appears to defend the moderate thesis. I say "appears" because, though he says that society has the right to enforce a morality as such on the ground that a shared morality is essential to society's existence, it is not at all clear that for him the statement that immorality jeopardizes or weakens society is a statement of empirical fact. It seems sometimes to be an *a priori* assumption, and sometimes a necessary truth and a very odd one.The most important indication that this is so is that, apart from one vague reference to "history" showing that "the loosening of moral bonds is often the first stage of disintegration."[32] no evidence is produced to show that deviation from accepted sexual morality, even by adults in private, is something which, like treason, threatens the existence of society. No reputable historian has maintained this thesis, and there is indeed much evidence against it. As a proposition of fact it is entitled to no more respect than the Emperor Justinian's statement that homosexuality was the cause of earthquakes.[33] Lord Devlin's belief in it, and his apparent indifference to the question of evidence, are at points traceable to an undiscussed assumption. That is that all morality—sexual morality together with the morality that forbids acts injurious to others such as killing, stealing, and dishonesty—forms a single seamless web, so that those who deviate from any part are likely or perhaps bound to deviate from the whole. It is of course clear (and one of the oldest insights of political theory) that society could not exist without a morality which mirrored and supplemented the law's proscription of conduct injurious to others. But there is again no evidence to support, and much to refute, the theory that those who deviate from conventional sexual morality are in other ways hostile to society.

There seems, however, to be central to Lord Devlin's thought something more interesting, though no more convincing, than the conception of social morality as a seamless web. For he appears to move from the acceptable proposition that *some* shared morality is essential to the existence of any society to the unacceptable proposition that a society is identical[34] with its morality as that is at any given moment of its history, so that a change in its morality is tantamount to the destruction of a society. The former proposition might be even accepted as a necessary rather than an empirical truth depending on a quite plausible definition of society as a body of men who hold certain moral views in common. But the latter proposition is absurd. Taken strictly, it would prevent us saying that the morality of a given society had changed, and would compel us instead to say that one society had disappeared and another one taken its place. But it is only on this absurd criterion of what it is for the same society to continue to exist that it could be asserted without evidence that any deviation from a society's shared morality threatens its existence.

It is clear that only this tacit identification of a society with its shared morality supports Lord Devlin's denial that there could be such a thing as private immorality and his comparison of sexual immorality, even when it takes place "in private," with treason. No doubt it is true that if deviations from conventional sexual morality are tolerated by the law and come to be known, the conventional morality might change in a permissive direction, though this does not seem to be the case with homosexuality in those European countries where it is not punishable by law. But even if the conven-

---

[32]*The Enforcement of Morals,* pp. 14–15.
[33]*Novels,* 77 Cap. 1 and 141.

[34]See, for this important point, Richard Wollheim, "Crime, Sin, and Mr. Justice Devlin," *Encounter,* November 1959, p. 34.

tional morality did so change, the society in question would not have been destroyed or "subverted." We should compare such a development not to the violent overthrow of government but to a peaceful constitutional change in its form, consistent not only with the preservation of a society but with its advance.

ᴱᴱ ᴱᴱ ᴱᴱ

Liberty and Moralism

Ronald Dworkin

No doubt most Americans and Englishmen think that homosexuality, prostitution, and the publication of pornography are immoral. What part should this fact play in the decision whether to make them criminal? This is a tangled question, full of issues with roots in philosophical and sociological controversy. It is a question lawyers must face, however, and recent and controversial events—publication of the Wolfenden Report in England,[1] followed by a public debate on prostitution and homosexuality, and a series of obscenity decisions in the United States Supreme Court[2]—press it upon us.

Several positions are available, each with its own set of difficulties. Shall we say that public condemnation is sufficient, in and of itself, to justify making an act a crime? This seems inconsistent with our traditions of individual liberty, and our knowledge that the morals of even the largest mob cannot come warranted for truth. If public condemnation is not sufficient, what more is needed? Must there be some demonstration of present harm to particular persons directly affected by the practice in question? Or is it sufficient to show some effect on social customs and institutions which alters the social environment, and thus affects all members of society indirectly? If the latter, must it also be demonstrated that these social changes threaten long-term harm of some standard sort, like an increase in crime or a decrease in productivity? Or would it be enough to show that the vast bulk of the present community would deplore the change? If so, does the requirement of harm add much to the bare requirement of public condemnation?

In 1958 Lord Devlin delivered the second Maccabaean Lecture to the British Academy. He called his lecture "The Enforcement of Morals," and devoted it to these issues of principle.[3] His conclusions he summarized in these remarks about the prac-

---

[1]*Report of the Committee on Homosexual Offences and Prostitution,* Cmd. no. 247 (1957).

[2]*Memoirs* v. *Massachusetts (Fanny Hill),* 383 U.S. 413 (1966), *Ginzburg* v. United States, 383 463 U.S. (1966), *Mishkin* v. *New York,* 383 U.S. 502 (1966).

[3]Devlin, *The Enforcement of Morals* (1959). Reprinted in Devlin, *The Enforcement of Morals* (1965). [The latter is hereinafter cited as Devlin.]

---

tice of homosexuality: "We should ask ourselves in the first instance whether, looking at it calmly and dispassionately, we regard it as a vice so abominable that its mere presence is an offence. If that is the genuine feeling of the society in which we live, I do not see how society can be denied the right to eradicate it."[4]

The lecture, and in particular this hypothetical position on punishing homosexuals, provoked a tide of rebuttal that spilled over from academic journals into the radio and the almost-popular press.[5] Lord Devlin has since republished the Maccabaean Lecture, together with six further essays developing and defending the views there expressed, a preface to the whole, and some important new footnotes to the original lecture.[6]

American lawyers ought to attend to Lord Devlin's arguments. His conclusions will not be popular, although the swaggering insensitivity some of his critics found disappears with careful reading. Popular or not, we have no right to disregard them until we are satisfied that his arguments can be met. One of these arguments—the second of the two I shall discuss—has the considerable merit of focusing our attention on the connection between democratic theory and the enforcement of morals. It provokes us to consider, more closely than we have, the crucial concept upon which this connection depends—the concept of a public morality.

LORD DEVLIN'S DISENCHANTMENT

The preface to the new book contains a revealing account of how Lord Devlin came to his controversial opinions. When he was invited to prepare his Maccabaean Lecture the celebrated Wolfenden Committee had recently published its recommendation that homosexual practices in private between consenting adults no longer be criminal. He had read with complete approval the Committee's expression of the proper division between crime and sin:

> In this field, its [the law's] function, as we see it, is to preserve public order and decency, to protect the citizen from what is offensive or injurious, and to provide sufficient safeguards against exploitation and corruption of others. . . . It is not, in our view, the function of the law to intervene in the private lives of citizens, or to seek to enforce any particular pattern of behaviour, further than is necessary to carry out the purposes which we have outlined. . . .
>
> [T]here must remain a realm of private morality and immorality which is, in brief and crude terms, not the law's business.[7]

Lord Devlin believed that these ideals, which he recognized as derived from the teachings of Jeremy Bentham and John Stuart Mill, were unquestionable. He decided to devote his lecture to a painstaking consideration of what further changes, beyond the changes in the crime of homosexuality that the Committee recommended, would

---

[4]Devlin 17. This position was carefully stated as hypothetical. Apparently Lord Devlin does not now think that the condition is met, because he has publically urged modification of the laws on homosexuality since the book's publication.

[5]Lord Devlin includes references to these comments in a bibliography. Devlin xiii.

[6]Devlin.

[7]*Report of the Committee on Homosexual Offences and Prostitution*, 9–10, 24.

be necessary to make the criminal law of England conform to them. But study, in his words, "destroyed instead of confirming the simple faith in which I had begun my task"[8] and he ended in the conviction that these ideals were not only questionable, but wrong.

The fact of his disenchantment is clear, but the extent of his disenchantment is not. He seems sometimes to be arguing the exact converse of the Committee's position, namely that society has a right to punish conduct of which its members strongly disapprove, even though that conduct has no effects which can be deemed injurious to others, on the ground that the state has a role to play as moral tutor and the criminal law is its proper tutorial technique. Those readers who take this to be his position are puzzled by the fact that distinguished philosophers and lawyers have concerned themselves to reply, for this seems a position that can safely be regarded as eccentric. In fact he is arguing not this position, but positions which are more complex and neither so eccentric nor so flatly at odds with the Wolfenden ideals. They are nowhere summarized in any crisp form (indeed the statement on homosexuality I have already quoted is as good a summary as he gives) but must be taken from the intricate arguments he develops.

There are two chief arguments. The first is set out in structured form in the Maccabaean Lecture. It argues from society's right to protect its own existence. The second, a quite different and much more important argument, develops in disjointed form through various essays. It argues from the majority's right to follow its own moral convictions in defending its social environment from change it opposes. I shall consider these two arguments in turn, but the second at greater length.

THE FIRST ARGUMENT: SOCIETY'S RIGHT TO PROTECT ITSELF

The first argument—and the argument which has received by far the major part of the critics' attention—is this:[9]

(1) In a modern society there are a variety of moral principles which some men adopt for their own guidance and do not attempt to impose upon others. There are also moral standards which the majority places beyond toleration and imposes upon those who dissent. For us, the dictates of particular religion are an example of the former class, and the practice of monogamy an example of the latter. A society cannot survive unless some standards are of the second class, because some moral conformity is essential to its life. Every society has a right to preserve its own existence, and therefore the right to insist on some such conformity.

(2) If society has such a right, then it has the right to use the institutions and sanctions of its criminal law to enforce the right—"[S]ociety may use the law to preserve morality in the same way it uses it to safeguard anything else if it is essential to its existence."[10] Just as society may use its law to prevent treason, it may use it to prevent a corruption of that conformity which ties it together.

(3) But society's right to punish immorality by law should not necessarily be exercised against every sort and on every occasion of immorality—we must recognize

[8]Devlin vii.
[9]It is developed chiefly in Devlin 7–25.
[10]*Ibid.* 11.

the impact and the importance of some restraining principles. There are several of these, but the most important is that there "must be toleration of the maximum individual freedom that is consistent with the integrity of society."[11] These restraining principles, taken together, require that we exercise caution in concluding that a practice is considered profoundly immoral. The law should stay its hand if it detects any uneasiness or half-heartedness or latent toleration in society's condemnation of the practice. But none of these restraining principles apply, and hence society is free to enforce its rights, when public feeling is high, enduring and relentless, when, in Lord Devlin's phrase, it rises to "intolerance, indignation and disgust."[12] Hence the summary conclusion about homosexuality: if it is genuinely regarded as an abominable vice, society's right to eradicate it cannot be denied.

We must guard against a possible, indeed tempting, misconception of this argument. It does not depend upon any assumption that when the vast bulk of a community thinks a practice is immoral they are likely right. What Lord Devlin thinks is at stake, when our public morality is challenged, is the very survival of society, and he believes that society is entitled to preserve itself without vouching for the morality that holds it together.

Is this argument sound? Professor H. L. A. Hart, responding to its appearance at the heart of the Maccabaean lecture,[13] thought that it rested upon a confused conception of what a society is. If one holds anything like a conventional notion of a society, he said, it is absurd to suggest that every practice the society views as profoundly immoral and disgusting threatens its survival. This is as silly as arguing that society's existence is threatened by the death of one of its members or the birth of another, and Lord Devlin, he reminds us, offers nothing by way of evidence to support any such claim. But if one adopts an artificial definition of a society, such that a society consists of that particular complex of moral ideas and attitudes which its members happen to hold at a particular moment in time, it is intolerable that each such moral status quo should have the right to preserve its precarious existence by force. So, Professor Hart argued, Lord Devlin's argument fails whether a conventional or an artificial sense of "society" is taken.

Lord Devlin replies to Professor Hart in a new and lengthy footnote. After summarizing Hart's criticism he comments, 'I do not assert that *any* deviation from a society's shared morality threatens its existence any more than I assert that *any* subversive activity threatens its existence. I assert that they are both activities which are capable in their nature of threatening the existence of society so that neither can be put beyond the law."[14] This reply exposes a serious flaw in the architecture of the argument.

It tells us that we must understand the second step of the argument—the crucial claim that society has a right to enforce its public morality by law—as limited to a denial of the proposition that society never has such a right. Lord Devlin apparently understood the Wolfenden Report's statement of a "realm of private morality . . . not the law's business" to assert a fixed jurisdictional barrier placing private sexual practices forever beyond the law's scrutiny. His arguments, the new footnote tells us, are designed to show merely that no such constitutional barrier should be raised, because it is possible that the challenge to established morality might be so profound that the

---

[11]*Ibid.* 16.
[12]*Ibid.* 17.
[13]H. L. A. Hart, *Law, Liberty and Morality* 51 (1963).
[14]Devlin 13.

very existence of a conformity in morals, and hence of the society itself, would be threatened.[15]

We might well remain unconvinced, even of this limited point. We might believe that the danger which any unpopular practice can present to the existence of society is so small that it would be wise policy, a prudent protection of individual liberty from transient hysteria, to raise just this sort of constitutional barrier and forbid periodic re-assessment of the risk.

But if we were persuaded to forego this constitutional barrier we would expect the third step in the argument to answer the inevitable next question: Granted that a challenge to deep-seated and genuine public morality may conceivably threaten society's existence, and so must be placed above the threshold of the law's concern, how shall we know when the danger is sufficiently clear and present to justify not merely scrutiny but action? What more is needed beyond the fact of passionate public disapproval to show that we are in the presence of an actual threat?

The rhetoric of the third step makes it seem responsive to this question—there is much talk of "freedom" and "toleration" and even "balancing." But the argument is not responsive, for freedom, toleration and balancing turn out to be appropriate only when the public outrage diagnosed at the second step is shown to be overstated, when the fever, that is, turns out to be feigned. When the fever is confirmed, when the intolerance, indignation and disgust are genuine, the principle that calls for "the maximum individual freedom consistent with the integrity of society" no longer applies. But this means that nothing more than passionate public disapproval is necessary after all.

In short, the argument involes an intellectual sleight of hand. At the second step, public outrage is presented as a threshold criterion, merely placing the practice in a category which the law is not forbidden to regulate. But offstage, somewhere in the transition to the third step, this threshold criterion becomes itself a dispositive affirmative reason for action, so that when it is clearly met the law may proceed without more. The power of this manoeuvre is proved by the passage on homosexuality. Lord Devlin concludes that if our society hates homosexuality enough it is justified in outlawing it, and forcing human beings to choose between the miseries of frustration and persecution, because of the danger the practice presents to society's existence. He

---

[15]This reading had great support in the text even without the new footnote: "I think, therefore, that it is not possible to set theoretical limits to the power of the State to legislate against immorality. It is not possible to settle in advance exceptions to the general rule or to define inflexibly areas of morality into which the law is in no circumstances to be allowed to enter." (Devlin 12–13).

The arguments presented bear out this construction. They are of the *reductio ad absurdum* variety, exploiting the possibility that what is immoral can in theory become subversive of society. "But suppose a quarter or a half of the population got drunk every night, what sort of society would it be? You cannot set a theoretical limit to the number of people who can get drunk before society is entitled to legislate against drunkenness. The same may be said of gambling." (*Ibid.* 14).

Each example argues that no jurisdictional limit may be drawn, not that every drunk or every act of gambling threatens society. There is no suggestion that society is entitled actually to make drunkenness or gambling crimes if the practice in fact falls below the level of danger. Indeed Lord Devlin quotes the Royal Commission on Betting, Lotteries, and Gaming to support his example on gambling: "If we were convinced that whatever the degree of gambling this effect [on the character of the gambler as a member of society] must be harmful we should be inclined to think that it was the duty of the state to restrict gambling to the greatest extent practicable." (Cmd. no. 8190 at para. 159 (1951), quoted in Devlin 14). The implication is that society may scrutinize and be ready to regulate, but should not actually do so until the threat in fact exists.

manages this conclusion without offering evidence that homosexuality presents any danger at all to society's existence, beyond the naked claim that all "deviations from a society's shared morality . . . are capable in their nature of threatening the existence of society" and so "cannot be put beyond the law."[16]

THE SECOND ARGUMENT: SOCIETY'S RIGHT TO FOLLOW ITS OWN LIGHTS

We are therefore justified in setting aside the first argument and turning to the second. My reconstruction includes making a great deal explicit which I believe implicit, and so involves some risk of distortion, but I take the second argument to be this:[17]

(1) If those who have homosexual desires freely indulged them, our social environment would change. What the changes would be cannot be calculated with any precision, but it is plausible to suppose, for example, that the position of the family, as the assumed and natural institution around which the educational, economic and recreational arrangements of men center, would be undermined, and the further ramifications of that would be great. We are too sophisticated to suppose that the effects of an increase in homosexuality would be confined to those who participate in the practice alone, just as we are too sophisticated to suppose that prices and wages affect only those who negotiate them. The environment in which we and our children must live is determined, among other things, by patterns and relationships formed privately by others than ourselves.

(2) This in itself does not give society the right to prohibit homosexual practices. We cannot conserve every custom we like by jailing those who do not want to preserve it. But it means that our legislators must inevitably decide some moral issues. They must decide whether the institutions which seem threatened are sufficiently valuable to protect at the cost of human freedom. And they must decide whether the practices which threaten that institution are immoral, for if they are then the freedom of an individual to pursue them counts for less. We do not need so strong a justification, in terms of the social importance of the institutions being protected, if we are confident that no one has a moral right to do what we want to prohibit. We need less of a case, that is, to abridge someone's freedom to lie, cheat or drive recklessly, than his freedom to choose his own jobs or to price his own goods. This does not claim that immorality is sufficient to make conduct criminal; it argues, rather, that on occasion it is necessary.

(3) But how shall a legislator decide whether homosexual acts are immoral? Science can give no answer, and a legislator can no longer properly turn to organized religion. If it happens, however, that the vast bulk of the community is agreed upon an answer, even though a small minority of educated men may dissent, the legislator has a duty to act on the consensus. He has such a duty for two closely connected reasons: (a) In the last analysis the decision must rest on some article of moral faith, and in a democracy this sort of issue, above all others, must be settled in accordance with democratic principles. (b) It is, after all, the community which acts when the threats and sanctions of the criminal law are brought to bear. The community must take the moral

---

[16]Devlin 13, n.1.

[17]Most of the argument appears in Devlin chs. 5, 6 and 7. See also an article published after the book: "Law and Morality," 1 *Manitoba* L.S.J. 243 (1964/65).

responsibility, and it must therefore act on its own lights—that is, on the moral faith of its members.

This, as I understand it, is Lord Devlin's second argument. It is complex, and almost every component invites analysis and challenge. Some readers will dissent from its central assumption, that a change in social institutions is the sort of harm a society is entitled to protect itself against. Others who do not take this strong position (perhaps because they approve of laws which are designed to protect economic institutions) will nevertheless feel that society is not entitled to act, however immoral the practice, unless the threatened harm to an institution is demonstrable and imminent rather than speculative. Still others will challenge the thesis that the morality or immorality of an act ought even to count in determining whether to make it criminal (though they would no doubt admit that it does count under present practice), and others still will argue that even in a democracy legislators have the duty to decide moral questions for themselves, and must not refer such issues to the community at large. I do not suppose to argue now for or against any of these positions. I want instead to consider whether Lord Devlin's conclusions are valid on his own terms, or the assumption, that is, that society does have a right to protect its central and valued social institutions against conduct which the vast bulk of its members disapproves on moral principle.

I shall argue that his conclusions are not valid, even on these terms, because he misunderstands what it is to disapprove on moral principle. I might say a cautionary word about the argument I shall present. It will consist in part of reminders that certain types of moral language (terms like "prejudice" and "moral position," for example) have standard uses in moral argument. My purpose is not to settle issues of political morality by the fiat of a dictionary, but to exhibit what I believe to be mistakes in Lord Devlin's moral sociology. I shall try to show that our conventional moral practices are more complex and more structured than he takes them to be, and that he consequently misunderstands what it means to say that the criminal law should be drawn from public morality. This is a popular and appealing thesis, and it lies near the core not only of Lord Devlin's, but of many other, theories about law and morals. It is crucial that its implications be understood.

THE CONCEPT OF A MORAL POSITION

We might start with the fact that terms like "moral position" and "moral conviction" function in our conventional morality as terms of justification and criticism, as well as of description. It is true that we sometimes speak of a group's "morals," or "morality," or "moral beliefs," or "moral positions" or "moral convictions," in what might be called an anthropological sense, meaning to refer to whatever attitudes the group displays about the propriety of human conduct, qualities or goals. We say, in this sense, that the morality of Nazi Germany was based on prejudice, or was irrational. But we also use some of these terms, particularly "moral position" and "moral conviction," in a discriminatory sense, to contrast the positions they describe with prejudices, rationalizations, matters of personal aversion or taste, arbitrary stands, and the like. One use—perhaps the most characteristic use—of this discriminatory sense is to offer a limited but important sort of justification for an act, when the moral issues surrounding that act are unclear or in dispute.

Suppose I tell you that I propose to vote against a man running for a public of-

fice of trust because I know him to be a homosexual and because I belive that homosexuality is profoundly immoral. If you disagree that homosexuality is immoral, you
may accuse me of being about to cast my vote unfairly, acting on prejudice or out of a
personal repugnance which is irrelevant to the moral issue. I might then try to convert
you to my position on homosexuality, but if I fail in this I shall still want to convince
you of what you and I will both take to be a separate point—that my vote was based
upon a moral position, in the discriminatory sense, even though one which differs
from yours. I shall want to persuade you of this, because if I do I am entitled to expect
that you will alter your opinion of me and of what I am about to do. Your judgment of
my character will be different—you might still think me eccentric (or puritanical or
unsophisticated) but these are types of character and not faults of character. Your
judgement of my act will also be different, in this respect. You will admit that so long
as I hold my moral position, I have a moral right to vote against the homosexual, because I have a right (indeed a duty) to vote my own convictions. You would not admit
such a right (or duty) if you were still persuaded that I was acting out of a prejudice or
a personal taste.

I am entitled to expect that your opinion will change in these ways, because
these distinctions are a part of the conventional morality you and I share, and which
forms the background for our discussion. They enforce the difference between positions we must respect, although we think them wrong, and positions we need not respect because they offend some ground rule of moral reasoning. A great deal of
debate about moral issues (in real life, although not in philosophy texts) consists of arguments that some position falls on one or the other side of this crucial line.

It is this feature of conventional morality that animates Lord Devlin's argument
that society has the right to follow its own lights. We must therefore examine that discriminatory concept of a moral position more closely, and we can do so by pursuing
our imaginary conversation. What must I do to convince you that my position is a
moral position?

(a) I must produce some reasons for it. This is not to say that I have to articulate
a moral principle I am following or a general moral theory to which I subscribe. Very
few people can do either, and the ability to hold a moral position is not limited to
those who can. My reason need not be a principle or theory at all. It must only point
out some aspect or feature of homosexuality which moves me to regard it as immoral:
the fact that the Bible forbids it, for example, or that one who practices homosexuality
becomes unfit for marriage and parenthood. Of course, any such reason would presuppose my acceptance of some general principle or theory, but I need not be able to
state what it is, or realize that I am relying upon it.

Not every reason I might give will do, however. Some will be excluded by general criteria stipulating sorts of reasons which do not count. We might take note of
four of the most important such criteria:

(i) If I tell you that homosexuals are morally inferior because they do not have
heterosexual desires, and so are not "real men," you would reject that reason as showing one type of prejudice. Prejudices, in general, are postures of judgment that take
into account considerations our conventions exclude. In a structured context, like a
trial or a contest, the ground rules exclude all but certain considerations, and a prejudice is a basis of judgment which violates these rules. Our conventions stipulate some
ground rules of moral judgment which obtains even apart from such special contexts,

the most important of which is that a man must not be held morally inferior on the basis of some physical, racial or other characteristic he cannot help having. Thus a man whose moral judgments about Jews, or Negroes, or Southerners, or women, or effeminate men are based on his belief that any member of these classes automatically deserves less respect, without regard to anything he himself has done, is said to be prejudiced against that group.

(ii) If I base my view about homosexuals on a personal emotional reaction ("they make me sick") you would reject that reason as well. We distinguish moral positions from emotional reactions, not because moral positions are supposed to be unemotional or dispassionate—quite the reverse is true—but because the moral position is supposed to justify the emotional reaction, and not vice versa. If a man is unable to produce such reasons, we do not deny the fact of his emotional involvement, which may have important social or political consequences, but we do not take this involvement as demonstrating his moral conviction. Indeed, it is just this sort of position—a severe emotional reaction to a practice or a situation for which one cannot account—that we tend to describe, in lay terms, as a phobia or an obsession.

(iii) If I base my position on a proposition of fact ("homosexual acts are physically debilitating") which is not only false, but is so implausible that it challenges the minimal standards of evidence and argument I generally accept and impose upon others, then you would regard my belief, even though sincere, as a form of rationalization, and disqualify my reason on that ground. (Rationalization is a complex concept, and also includes, as we shall see, the production of reasons which suggest general theories I do not accept.)

(iv) If I can argue for my own position only by citing the beliefs of others ("everyone knows homosexuality is a sin") you will conclude that I am parroting and not relying on a moral conviction of my own. With the possible (though complex) exception of a deity, there is no moral authority to which I can appeal and so automatically make my position a moral one. I must have my own reasons, though of course I may have been taught these reasons by others.

No doubt many readers will disagree with these thumbnail sketches of prejudice, mere emotional reaction, rationalization and parroting. Some may have their own theories of what these are. I want to emphasize now only that these are distinct concepts, whatever the details of the differences might be, and that they have a role in deciding whether to treat another's position as a moral conviction. They are not merely epithets to be pasted on positions we strongly dislike.

(b) Suppose I do produce a reason which is not disqualified on one of these (or on similar) grounds. That reason will presuppose some general moral principle or theory, even though I may not be able to state that principle or theory, and do not have it in mind when I speak. If I offer, as my reason, the fact that the Bible forbids homosexual acts, or that homosexual acts make it less likely that the actor will marry and raise children, I suggest that I accept the theory my reason presupposes, and you will not be satisfied that my position is a moral one if you believe that I do not. It may be a question of my sincerity—do I in fact believe that the injunctions of the Bible are morally binding as such, or that all men have a duty to procreate? Sincerity is not, however, the only issue, for consistency is also in point. I may believe that I accept one of these general positions, and be wrong, because my other beliefs, and my own conduct on other occasions, may be inconsistent with it. I may reject certain Biblical injunctions, or I may hold that men have a right to remain bachelors if they please or use contraceptives all their lives.

Of course, my general moral positions may have qualifications and exceptions. The difference between an exception and an inconsistency is that the former can be supported by reasons which presuppose other moral positions I can properly claim to hold. Suppose I condemn all homosexuals on Biblical authority, but not all fornicators. What reason can I offer for the distinction? If I can produce none which supports it, I cannot claim to accept the general position about Biblical authority. If I do produce a reason which seems to support the distinction, the same sorts of question may be asked about that reason as were asked about my original reply. What general position does the reason for my exception presuppose? Can I sincerely claim to accept that further general position? Suppose my reason, for example, is that fornication is now very common, and has been sanctioned by custom. Do I really believe that what is immoral becomes moral when it becomes popular? If not, and if I can produce no other reason for the distinction, I cannot claim to accept the general position that what the Bible condemns is immoral. Of course, I may be persuaded, when this is pointed out, to change my views on fornication. But you would be alert to the question of whether this is a genuine change of heart, or only a performance for the sake of the argument.

In principle there is no limit to these ramifications of my original claim, though of course, no actual argument is likely to pursue very many of them.

(c) But do I really have to have a reason to make my position a matter of moral conviction? Most men think that acts which cause unnecessary suffering, or break a serious promise with no excuse, are immoral, and yet they could give no reason for these beliefs. They feel that no reason is necessary, because they take it as axiomatic or self-evident that these are immoral acts. It seems contrary to common sense to deny that a position held in this way can be a moral position.

Yet there is an important difference between believing that one's position is self-evident and just not having a reason for one's position. The former presupposes a positive belief that no further reason is necessary, that the immorality of the act in question does not depend upon its social effects, or its effects on the character of the actor, or its proscription by a deity, or anything else, but follows from the nature of the act itself. The claim that a particular position is axiomatic, in other words, does supply a reason of a special sort, namely that the act is immoral in and of itself, and this special reason, like the others we considered, may be inconsistent with more general theories I hold.

The moral arguments we make presuppose not only moral principles, but also more abstract positions about moral reasoning. In particular, they presuppose positions about what kinds of acts can be immoral in and of themselves. When I criticize your moral opinions, or attempt to justify my own disregard of traditional moral rules I think are silly, I will likely proceed by denying that the act in question has any of the several features that can make an act immoral—that it involves no breach of an undertaking or duty, for example, harms no one including the actor, is not prescribed by any organized religion, and is not illegal. I proceed in this way because I assume that the ultimate grounds of immorality are limited to some such small set of very general standards. I may assert this assumption directly or it may emerge from the pattern of my argument. In either event, I will enforce it by calling positions which can claim no support from any of these ultimate standards *arbitrary,* as I should certainly do if you said that photography was immoral, for instance, or swimming. Even if I cannot articulate this underlying assumption, I shall still apply it, and since the ultimate criteria I recognize are among the most abstract of my moral standards, they will not vary much from those my neighbors recognize and apply. Although many who despise homosexuals are unable to say why, few would claim affirmatively that one needs no reason, for this would make their position, on their own standards, an arbitrary one.

(d) This anatomy of our argument could be continued, but it is already long enough to justify some conclusions. If the issue between us is whether my views on homosexuality amount to a moral position, and hence whether I am entitled to vote against a homosexual on that ground, I cannot settle the issue simply by reporting my feelings. You will want to consider the reasons I can produce to support my belief, and whether my other views and behavior are consistent with the theories these reasons presuppose. You will have, of course, to apply your own understanding, which may differ in detail from mine, of what a prejudice or a rationalization is, for example, and of when one view is inconsistent with another. You and I may end in disagreement over whether my position is a moral one, partly because of such differences in understanding, and partly because one is less likely to recognize their illegitimate grounds in himself than in others.

We must avoid the skeptical fallacy of passing from these facts to the conclusion that there is no such thing as a prejudice or a rationalization or an inconsistency, or that these terms mean merely that the one who uses them strongly dislikes the positions he describes this way. That would be like arguing that because different people have different understandings of what jealousy is, and can in good faith disagree about whether one of them is jealous, there is no such thing as jealousy, and one who says another is jealous merely means he dislikes him very much.

LORD DEVLIN'S MORALITY

We may now return to Lord Devlin's second argument. He argues that when legislators must decide a moral issue (as by hypothesis they must when a practice threatens a valued social arrangement), they must follow any consensus of moral position which the community at large has reached, because this is required by the democratic principle, and because a community is entitled to follow its own lights. The argument would have some plausibility if Lord Devlin meant, in speaking of the moral consensus of the community, these positions which are moral positions in the discriminatory sense we have been exploring.

But he means nothing of the sort. His definition of a moral position shows he is using it in what I called the anthropological sense. The ordinary man whose opinion we must enforce, he says, ". . . is not expected to reason about anything and his judgment may be largely a matter of feeling."[18] "If the reasonable man believes," he adds, "that a practice is immoral and believes also—no matter whether the belief is right or wrong, so be it that it is honest and dispassionate—that no right-minded member of his society could think otherwise, then for the purpose of the law it is immoral."[19] Elsewhere he quotes with approval Dean Rostow's attribution to him of the view that "the common morality of a society at any time is a blend of custom and conviction, of

[18]Devlin 15.
[19]*Ibid.* 22–3.

reason and feeling, of experience and prejudice."[20] His sense of what a moral conviction is emerges most clearly of all from the famous remark about homosexuals. If the ordinary man regards homosexuality "as a vice so abominable that its mere presence is an offence,"[21] this demonstrates for him that the ordinary man's feelings about homosexuals are a matter of moral conviction.[22]

His conclusions fail because they depend upon using "moral position" in this anthropological sense. Even if it is true that most men think homosexuality an abominable vice and cannot tolerate its presence, it remains possible that this common opinion is a compound of prejudice (resting on the assumption that homosexuals are morally inferior creatures because they are effeminate), rationalizaiton (based on assumptions of fact so unsupported that they challenge the community's own standards of rationality), and personal aversion (representing no conviction but merely blind hate rising from unacknowledged self-suspicion). It remains possible that the ordinary man could produce no reason for his view, but would simply parrot his neighbor who in turn parrots him, or that he would produce a reason which presupposes a general moral position he could not sincerely or consistently claim to hold. If so, the principles of democracy we follow do not call for the enforcement of the consensus, for the belief that prejudices, personal aversions and rationalizations do not justify restricting another's freedom itself occupies a critical and fundamental position in our popular morality. Nor would the bulk of the community then be entitled to follow its own lights, for the community does not extend that privilege to one who acts on the basis of prejudice, rationalization, or personal aversion. Indeed, the distinction between these and moral convictions, in the discriminatory sense, exists largely to mark off the former as the sort of positions one is not entitled to pursue.

A conscientious legislator who is told a moral consensus exists must test the credentials of that consensus. He cannot, of course, examine the beliefs or behavior of individual citizens; he cannot hold hearings on the Clapham omnibus. That is not the point.

The claim that a moral consensus exists is not itself based on a poll. It is based on an appeal to the legislator's sense of how his community reacts to some disfavored practice. But this same sense includes an awareness of the grounds on which that reaction is generally supported. If there has been a public debate involving the editorial columns, speeches of his colleagues, the testimony of interested groups, and his own correspondence, these will sharpen his awareness of what arguments and positions are in the field. He must sift these arguments and positions, trying to determine which are prejudices or rationalizations, which presuppose general principles or theories vast parts of the population could not be supposed to accept, and so on. It may be that

[20]Rostow, "The Enforcement of Morals," 1960 *Camb. L.J.* 174, 197; reprinted in E. V. Rostow, *The Sovereign Prerogative* 45, 78 (1962). Quoted in Devlin 95.

[21]*Ibid.* 17.

[22]In the preface (*Ibid.* viii) Lord Devlin acknowledges that the language of the original lecture might have placed "too much emphasis on feeling and too little on reason," and he states that the legislator is entitled to disregard "irrational" beliefs. He gives as an example of the latter the belief that homosexuality causes earthquakes, and asserts that the exclusion of irrationality "is usually an easy and comparatively unimportant process." I think it fair to conclude that this is all Lord Devlin would allow him to exclude. If I am wrong, and Lord Devlin would ask him to exclude prejudices, personal aversions, arbitrary stands and the rest as well, he should have said so, and attempted to work some of these distinctions out. If he had, his conclusions would have been different and would no doubt have met with a different reaction.

when he has finished this process of reflection he will find that the claim of a moral consensus has not been made out. In the case of homosexuality, I expect, it would not be, and that is what makes Lord Devlin's undiscriminating hypothetical so serious a misstatement. What is shocking and wrong is not his idea that the community's morality counts, but his idea of what counts as the community's morality.

Of course the legislator must apply these tests for himself. If he shares the popular views he is less likely to find them wanting, though if he is self-critical the exercise may convert him. His answer, in any event, will depend upon his own understanding of what our shared morality requires. That is inevitable, for whatever criteria we urge him to apply, he can apply them only as he understands them.

A legislator who proceeds in this way, who refuses to take popular indignation, intolerance and digust as the moral conviction of his community, is not guilty of moral elitism. He is not simply setting his own educated views against those of a vast public which rejects them. He is doing his best to enforce a distinct, and fundamentally important, part of his community's morality, a consensus more essential to society's existence in the form we know it than the opinion Lord Devlin bids him follow.

No legislator can afford to ignore the public's outrage. It is a fact he must reckon with. It will set the boundaries of what is politically feasible, and it will determine his strategies of persuasion and enforcement within these boundaries. But we must not confuse strategy with justice, nor facts of political life with principles of political morality. Lord Devlin understands these distinctions, but his arguments will appeal most, I am afraid, to those who do not.

The Enforcement of Morals

Ernest Nagel

1

An adequate account of the different ways in which moral principles enter into the development, the operation, and the evaluation of legal systems would require an examination of a broad spectrum of difficult issues. Such an account is certainly not a task to which a relatively short paper can do justice, and the present paper is not an attempt to do the impossible. I am therefore restricting myself in it almost entirely to but one issue that arises in considering the relation of law to morality—to the question whether there is a sharply delimited domain of human conduct that is by its very nature excluded from justifiable legal control, and in particular whether a society is ever warranted in using the law to enforce what are held to be widely accepted moral

This article first appeared in *The Humanist,* May/June (1968). Reprinted by permission of *The Humanist.*

rules. The question has a long ancestry in discussions of moral and political theory, and is closely related to issues raised in historical doctrines of natural law and inalienable rights. However, the question can be examined without reference to natural law theory, and in any case it is not simply of antiquarian interest, but is of vital interest to humanist writers. It is also directly relevant to a number of currently debated social problems, among others to problems created by changing attitudes toward euthanasia, obscenity, and deviant sexual practices; and it received considerable attention in recent years from legislators, judges, sociologists, and psychologists, as well as from philosophers and writers on jurisprudence.

Many current philosophical and jurisprudential discussions of the question I want to consider take as their point of departure a challenging essay by Lord Patrick Devlin—a distinguished British judge, who was for many years a Justice of the High Court, Queen's Bench, and subsequently a Lord of Appeal in Ordinary. Devlin's essay, entitled "The Enforcement of Morals" and published in 1959, tried to show that a fundamental principle to which many moral theorists subscribe and which had been recently invoked in support of certain recommendations for amending the English criminal law, is untenable—for reasons I will presently mention. Devlin's views have found some defenders, but have also been the subject of much severe criticism. Since my paper is for the most part a commentary on the main points in dispute between Devlin and his critics—especially H. L. A. Hart in the latter's *Law, Liberty, and Morality* (1963)—I must describe briefly the problem to which Devlin's essay was addressed, and the context in which the debate over his views has its locus.

In 1954, in response to widespread cricitism of the provisions of the English criminal law dealing with prostitution and homosexual practices, a committee was appointed, headed by Sir John Wolfenden, to look into the matter and to recommend needed changes in the law. The Report of the Committee was issued in 1957, and proposed a number of modifications in the existing law relating to various kinds of sexual offenses. The factual findings and the detailed proposals of the Committee are not pertinent here. What is of interest is that the Wolfenden Committee based its recommendations on the view that

> ... the function of the criminal law ... is to preserve public order and decency, to protect the citizen from what is offensive or injurious, and to provide sufficient safeguards against exploitations and corruption of others, particularly those who are specially vulnerable because they are young, weak in body or mind, inexperienced, or in a state of special physical, official or economic dependence.
>
> It is not the function of the law [the report went on] to intervene in the private lives of citizens, or to seek to enforce any pattern of behavior, further than is neceessary to carry out the purposes we have outlined.

Moreover, in recommending that solicitation of the young should continue to be punishable by law, but that "homosexual behavior between consenting adults should no longer be a criminal offence," the Wolfenden Report offered what it called a "decisive" reason, namely:

> ... the importance which society and the law ought to give to individual freedom of choice and action in matters of private morality. Unless a deliberate at-

tempt is to be made by society, acting through the agency of the law, to equate the sphere of crime with that of sin, *there must remain a realm of private morality and immorality which is, in brief and crude terms, not the law's business.* To say this is not to condone or encourage private immorality.[1]

Some of the Report's proposals were eventually adopted by Parliament. However, it is not my aim to examine either the merits of these recommendations or the recent history of English legislation. The question I do want to discuss is the adequacy of the general principle underlying the specific proposals of the Wolfenden Committee—that there is a realm of conduct which, irrespective of its morality or immorality, is not the law's business and by its very nature falls outside the legitimate concerns of the law. It is this principle that Devlin challenged on grounds that I will presently describe, even though he eventually expressed himself as being in agreement with some of the Report's specific recommendations; and it is largely to a critique of Devlin's stand on this principle that Hart's own book previously mentioned is devoted.

However, as the Wolfenden Report explicitly notes, the principle is stated by it only in brief and crude terms, without any attempt to articulate it clearly or to give supporting reasons for it. But there is little doubt that in its statement of the principle the Report was invoking the far more inclusive political doctrine which John Stuart Mill expounded at some length in his classic essay *On Liberty* (1859), and was simply applying that doctrine to the particular problem of the legal regulation of sexual practices. Accordingly, since both Devlin and Hart make constant reference to Mill's views on individual liberty, and since I want to discuss the principle exposed by the Wolfenden Committee when it is stated in its most general and influential form, it is desirable to quote the passage in which Mill expressed the central idea of his political philosophy. Mill declared that

> . . . The sole end for which mankind is warranted, individually or collectively, in interfering with the liberty of action of any of their number is self-protection. That the only purpose for which power can be rightfully exercised over any member of a civilized community, against his will, is to prevent harm to others. His own good, whether physical or moral, is not a sufficient warrant. He cannot rightfully be compelled to do or forbear because it will be better for him to do so, because it will make him happier, because, in the opinion of others, to do so would be wise, or even right. These are good reasons for remonstrating with him, or reasoning with him or persuading him, or entreating him, but not for compelling him, or visiting him with any evil in case he do otherwise. To justify that, the conduct from which it is desired to deter him must be calculated to produce evil to someone else. The only part of the conduct of anyone, for which he is amenable to society, is that which concerns others. In the part which merely concerns himself, his independence is, of right, absolute.[2]

---

[1]Patrick Devlin, *The Enforcement of Morals* (New York: Oxford University Press, 1965), pp. 2–3 [my italics]. All references to Devlin are to this book.

[2]J. S. Mill, *Utilitarianism, Liberty, and Representative Government* (New York: Dutton, 1950, Everyman's Library edition), p. 73.

Mill thus advanced a comprehensive rule for determining the limits of warranted interference with men's conduct through the use of *any* agency of social control and compulsion—not only through the operation of the law, whether civil or criminal, but also through other institutions, such as religious organizations, economic associations, or more temporary groups that may be formed to achieve particular ends. But in any event, the rule appears to provide a firm support for the recommendations of the Wolfenden Report, for on the face of it the general principle Mill enunciates excludes the use of the machinery of the law to enforce what the Report calls "private morality."

Nevertheless, the principle is not as determinate as it is often alleged to be; and it is debatable whether, in view of the complications involved in attempts to apply it to concrete cases, it suffices to define categorically a realm of conduct that is inherently outside the scope of the law. I propose to enter into this debate, by reviewing some of the problems confronting a doctrine such as Mill's that seeks to circumscribe the area of conduct into which no measure of social control can be justifiably introduced. I am afraid that little if anything I have to say will be unfamiliar, for the problems have been repeatedly canvassed; nor do I have a neat resolution for the controversy over the legal enforcement of morals, for if I am right there can be no wholesale answer to the question. But I hope that by distinguishing several issues that are often confounded, I will succeed in placing the controversy in clearer light.

2

Mill offers two formulations—a broader and a narrower one—for his principle to distinguish between conduct that does and conduct that does not fall within the scope of permissible social control. *1.* According to the broad formulation, a person's actions are matters for legitimate social scrutiny only if they are of "concern" to others, but not if they "merely concern himself." On this criterion for deciding on the justifiability of social control, the relevant question to ask is not whether an action is performed in private (e.g., within the walls of a man's home) or in public, but whether it has *consequences* that in some way may affect other men. However, as has often been noted, there are few if any actions, even when done in private, which can be guaranteed to have no effects whatsoever on others than the actors themselves, so that on this formulation of the principle the domain of conduct that is reserved for the exercise of individual liberty is at best extremely narrow.

2. In point of fact, it is not upon this broad formulation of his principle that Mill relies, but on the narrower one according to which no adult member of a civilized community can be rightfully compelled to perform or to desist from performing an act, unless the action or the failure to perform it is likely to produce *harm* or *evil* to others. But it takes little to see that even on this narrower injunction relatively few human actions are in principle excluded from social regulation. For example, a successful courtship may bring joy to a lover but acute anguish to his rival; the acclaim won by a musician or a scientist may produce self-destructive feelings of inferiority in those who do not achieve such distinction; and the vigorous expression of heterodox opinions may cause severe distress in those hearing them. Mill himself was fully aware of this, and qualified his principle by excluding from the class of actions he regarded as "harmful to others" (in the sense that they are subject to social control) many actions which, though they may affect others adversely by causing them physical or mental pain, he designated as merely "inconveniences"; and he maintained that society should tolerate such inconveniences, without attempting to control the actions that are their source, on the ground that this is the price men must be prepared to pay for the enjoyment of individual liberty. . . .

I do not believe it is possible to state a firm rule underlying Mill's selection of conduct for inclusion in the category of actions whose consequences for others are merely annoying inconveniences, rather than serious evils that justify the adoption of some form of social regulation. Indeed, it is obvious that his principle for demarcating a realm of behavior which is exempt from social control excludes virtually *nothing* from the scope of justifiable legal enactment—*unless* some argument is first reached on what to count as "harm or evil to others." But two points are no less clear: (1) an explication of what is to be understood as harmful to others (in the sense of warranting some type of social control), cannot escape reference to some more or less explicit and comprehensive system of moral and social assumptions—more fully articulated than Mill's, whether or not the moral theory involved in the explication is one about which reasonable men may differ; and (2) even when agreement on general moral principles can be taken for granted, it may be difficult to decide whether a given type of conduct is indeed harmful to others, especially if the circumstances under which the actions take place may vary considerably, or if the number of individuals who engage in them should increase. . . .

3

In the light of these reflections, I want now to examine the grounds on which Lord Devlin defends the thesis that under certain conditions the enforcement of morals through the agency of criminal law is justifiable. Devlin bases his argument on the premise that a society is constituted not only by individuals with certain more or less concordant habits of behavior which they exhibit despite differences in personal aims, but also by a "community of ideas"—and in particular moral ideas "about the way its members *should* behave and govern their lives."[3] The shared convictions of a community concerning what is the "right" mode of conduct in such matters as marriage or the protection of life and property make up what he calls the "public morality" or the "moral structure" of a society. And according to him, every threat to the moral order of a society is a threat to the continued existence of the society itself. But since on this view "society has the right to make a judgment [on morals], and has it on the basis that a recognized morality is as necessary to society as . . . a recognized government," Devlin concludes that "society may use the law to preserve morality in the same way as it uses it to safeguard anything else that is essential to its existence" (p. 11). To be sure, he believes that "there must be toleration of the maximum individual freedom that is consistent with the integrity of society" (p. 16), and also recognizes that "the extent to which society will tolerate . . . departures from moral standards varies from generation to generation" (p. 18). He nevertheless maintains that if in the collective but deliberate judgment of society some practice, even though it is carried on in private, would be gravely injurious to the moral order were it to become widespread, then society may well be justified *as a matter of general principle* in outlawing that "immoral" conduct—just as it is justified in taking steps to preserve its government by enacting laws against treason (p. 13).

[3]Devlin, *op. cit.,* p. 9 [my italics].

In my opinion, Devlin makes out a strong case for the impossibility of constructing a firm and enduring boundary between conduct that is a matter for individual conscience or private morality, and conduct that properly belongs to the domain of public concern. On the other hand, although I also think that this argument for the conclusion that under certain conditions the state may be justified in using the criminal law to enforce rules of public morality is *formally* sound, the conclusion rests on premises whose content is unclear and whose merits appear to me doubtful. Let me mention some of my difficulties.

1. In the first place, while Devlin seems to me to be on firm ground in claiming that every social system involves a community of certain ideas among its members, he does not explain what is to be understood by the "preservation" or "destruction" of a social order (as distinct from the persistence or collapse of its form of government), or just how one is to distinguish between the supposition that a social order has been *destroyed* and the supposition that there has been only a *change* in some pervasive pattern of institutionalized behavior. Much talk about societies continues to be based on the model which compares them to living organisms, and there is a point to the analogy. But the analogy is misleading if it leads us to assume that a society can die or flourish in the same sense that a biological organism does. Thus, an organism is usually defined to be a living one, if its so-called "vital functions"—such as respiration or assimilation of food—are being maintained, and to be dead when these processes no longer continue. In the case of societies, there are also processes (such as the maintenance of the food supply or the education of the young) that are sometimes compared with biological vital functions; and a society could therefore be said to have perished when these processes have ceased or, in the extreme instance, when its members have been permanently dispersed or have died without leaving any progeny. But with the possible exception of this extreme case, there appears to be no general agreement on the activities that *define* what it is for a society to be destroyed, rather than to be undergoing some alteration in its modes of organizing human conduct. It is therefore difficult to know what Devlin is asserting when he says that a given society fails or succeeds in preserving itself.

2. But secondly, Devlin does not establish his claim that any *specific tenet* of public morality—that is, any concrete moral conviction most members of a community ostensibly share about how men should behave and govern their lives in connection with some determinate activity, such as the conviction that marriages should be monogamous or that animals should not be mistreated—is *actually included* in the community of ideas whose maintenance he thinks is *indispensable* for the preservation of a social order. There is considerable evidence for believing that members of a given community do have in common a variety of more or less *general* ideas and attitudes as to what are the proper ways in which men should conduct themselves—for example, in many societies if not in all, most men expect others to have some regard for the sanctity of the lives of fellow members in their society, to comply with current laws or customs and the rules for changing them, or to make allowances for differences in the conduct of others because of differences in age and capacity. Moreover, it is quite plausible to hold that human societies would be impossible without the existence of a community of such general moral ideas. Indeed, given the biological makeup of men, their common desire to live and to procreate, and their dependence on the services rendered by others, it would be surprising if this were not so. But however this may be, and assuming that the notion of what it is for a society to be destroyed has been clarified, neither logic nor history appears to support the supposition that the violation of any *specific* moral standards prescribed by public morality may threaten the life of a social order.

An example may help to make the point clearer. Assume for the sake of the argument that no society can exist if it does not have *some* form of private property and if its members do not in the main believe that *some* ways of acquiring private property are morally justifiable. On this assumption, the preservation of a given society therefore requires the preservation of the conviction among its members that private ownership is morally warranted. But suppose further that in a particular society slavery is legal during a certain period, that during this period most of its members think it is entirely moral to own human beings as articles of private property, but that because of widespread protests against the institution of slavery the conviction that the institution is moral becomes seriously weakened. However, it does not follow from the basic premise of the argument that a weakening of *this* particular conviction is a threat to the social order—for on that premise, a necessary condition for the preservation of society is not the continued commitment to the morality of *human slavery,* but rather the continued commitment to the justifiability of *private property* in some form; and it is evident that this latter commitment is entirely compatible with the rejection of the former one.

Moreover, it is difficult to find in the historical record unquestionable instances in which a society collapsed because some one specific tenet of public morality had been extensively violated in actual practice, or because widely held beliefs in such a tenet had been seriously weakened. Human societies do not appear to be such fragile systems that they cannot survive a successful challenge to some established norm of conduct, nor are they such rigid structures that they are unable to accommodate their institutions to deviations from customary patterns of behavior and approved moral standards. Thus, since the end of the eighteenth century there have been radical transformations in the U.S. not only in commonly held ideas about the morality of various kinds of individual conduct—including sexual practices, the treatment of children by parents, and personal attitudes toward members of minority groups. On the face of it, at any rate, the society (or societies) occupying the territory of the U.S. during this period has adjusted itself to these changes in public morality. Or ought one to say that because of these changes in what were at various times deeply felt moral beliefs, American society has failed to preserve itself? In the absence of an unambiguous characterization of what constitutes the American social order and what is essential for its continuing existence, the question can be answered to suit one's preference. But if this is so, Devlin's major premise is either unproven (so that it cannot serve as a reason for accepting his conclusion), or the premise is so indeterminate in its content that a conclusion different from the one he reaches can also be drawn from it. There is therefore only a farfetched analogy at best between violations of public morality and treasonable actions—for there is no clear sense in which a social order is alleged to be capable of destruction by the former, while the downfall of established political authority can sometimes be correctly attributed to the latter. Accordingly, to build a case for the enforcement of morals on this analogy, as Devlin in effect does, is to build it on insubstantial foundations.

3. There are two other related assumptions in Devlin's argument that require brief notice. (a) Although he recognizes that public morality is subject to change, he appears to have no doubt that there is a quite definite community of moral ideas among members of a society during a given period. Moreover, he believes that the content of this morality can be ascertained without inordinate difficulty; and he suggests that for the purposes of the law, immorality is what any so-called "right-minded person" or "man in the Clapham omnibus," any jury of twelve men or women selected at random, is presumed to consider to be immoral.

However, neither assumption seems to me plausible. There have been communities in the past, and there are still some in the present, which were exposed to but a single intellectual and moral tradition, and were unaccustomed to the exchange and criticism of ideas on diverse subjects; and for such communities, the notion of a public morality which directs the energies of men into definite channels makes good sense. But in large urban societies such as our own, in which divergent ideals of life (often based on new scientific discoveries) are widely discussed, and technological advances in medicine as well as industry create opportunities for developing novel patterns of behavior, men differ widely in what they take to be moral conduct, and are in some measure tolerant of moral ideals which they do not themselves espouse. It is by no means evident whether in such pluralistic societies the notion of a public morality as Devlin conceives it is strictly applicable. For example, he declares that "The Institution of marriage would be gravely threatened if individual judgments were permitted about the morality of adultery; on [this matter] there must be a public morality" (p. 10). But there is reason to believe that Devlin overestimates the extent of current agreement on the immorality of extramarital relations and, as recent discussions of proposed reforms of divorce laws suggest, it is by no means certain that there is a real consensus on the immorality of adultery upon which the persistence of the institution of marriage is alleged to be contingent. Moreover, the educative and transformation function of the law must not be ignored. For while the effectiveness of a legal system undoubtedly depends on the support it recieves from the prevailing moral convictions of a community, the law does not simply *reflect* those convictions, but is in turn frequently an agency for *modifying* accepted moral standards. The supposition that even during a relatively brief period there is a determinate and clearly identifiable public morality is not a realistic picture of modern societies.

(b) Devlin's recommendation on how to ascertain the content of public morality is certainly simple. But is it also sound? If the moral convictions of members of contemporary societies are as diverse and divergent as I have suggested they are, what reason is there to suppose that the unanimous judgment of a dozen individuals drawn at random to serve on a jury is representative of the moral standards (for what may be to them an unfamiliar type of conduct) that are entertained throughout the society? Moreover, since on Devlin's view actions judged to be criminal because they are held to be immoral are actions which threaten the safety of the social order, why should we assume that twelve "right-minded persons" in a jury box—who presumably have no specialized training for evaluating the effects on others of some form of deviant behavior, nor the opportunity to undertake a careful study of what is already known about them—are more qualified to make competent judgments on what may be complex moral issues, than they are to pass on the significance of a scientific idea or on the merits of a surgical technique? To be sure, Devlin does not intend, as some commentators accuse him of doing, that the snap decisions of unreflective morality based on mere feelings of dislike and indignation are to be the ground on which a practice is to be made criminal. Thus he declares that "before a society can put a practice beyond the limits of tolerance [and hence make it a criminal offense], there must be a *deliberate* judgment that the practice is injurious to society" (p. 17, my italics). Nor does he maintain, as some critics have suggested, that "the arm of the law" should always be used to enforce society's judgment as to what is immoral—on the contrary, he presents a number of important prudential considerations which severely restrict the use of the criminal law to eradicate such immoral behavior. But except for the suggestion that a reliable symptom of practices that could destroy a social order is whether they generate in all members of a jury (and inferentially, in a majority of "right-minded persons" in the community) strong feelings of reprobation and intolerance (p. 17), he gives no reasons for supposing that the "deliberate judgments" he has emphasized as essential can be obtained by the procedure he recommends for ascertaining whether some conduct is detrimental to the social order; and he does not even discuss obvious alternatives to his proposal, such as the use of special commissions like the Wolfenden Committee itself to determine whether a practice does indeed have adverse consequences for society.

In short, while Mill's attempt to delimit a cateory of conduct which is permanently immune to legal as well as other forms of social control seems to me unsuccessful, I also think the difficulties I have been surveying make inconclusive Devlin's argument that the use of the criminal law to enforce moral standards for so-called "private conduct" is justifiable, if it is essential for preserving the integrity of society.

4

However, Devlin has been criticized by Professor Hart and others for disavowing Mill's doctrine on the justifiable limits of interference with an individual's freedom, and especially for dissenting from Mill's view that it is never warranted to compel a person to do or refrain from doing an action merely for the sake of his own welfare. I want therefore to examine briefly the main line of Hart's defense of Mill.

There are a variety of practices which are illegal in many countries, though on the face of it only the parties directly involved in their performance are affected by them. I have already noted that Mill himself approved a number of such laws; but despite the doubtful consistency of his doing so, he offered no clear rationale for them. On the other hand, Devlin maintains that the existence of such laws can be explained only on the assumption that they illustrate society's efforts "to enforce a moral principle and nothing else."[4] But Hart rejects this interpretation, and in his discussion of several examples of such laws, he proposes what he claims to be a different one. I will comment on his views as he presents them in the context of two examples.

1. Bigamy is a crime in many countries. Why should it be made a criminal offense, especially since in most jurisdictions a married man is doing nothing illegal if, while his legal spouse is alive, he lives with another woman and appears in public with her as husband and wife—*unless* he also goes through a marriage ceremony with her? Hart denies that the law is justified as an attempt "to enforce private morality as such"; and after expressing some sympathy for the view that the law might be "accepted as an attempt to protect religious feelings from offence by a public act desecrating the ceremony" of marriage, he declares that on this view "the bigamist is punished neither as irreligious nor as immoral but as a *nuisance.* For the law is then concerned with the *offensiveness to others* of his *public conduct,* not with the immo-

---

[4]H. L. A. Hart, *Law, Liberty, and Morality* (Stanford, Cal.: Stanford University Press, 1963), p. 7.

rality of his private conduct."[5] However, as Devlin has been quick to note, a marriage ceremony can be performed in the privacy of some civil servant's office, with no one but the celebrants and their intimate friends any the wiser; and it is therefore difficult to make sense of Hart's suggestion that the bigamist is being punished for the offense created by a public act, if there was no such offense because the bigamous marriage ceremony was in fact performed in private. But however this may be, there is a more fundamental point to be made. Hart is begging the question if he assumes that to judge an action to be a nuisance (or offensive) to others, is always independent of any judgment of its morality. If bigamous marriages and other kinds of public conduct are crimes in the U.S. because they are offensive to others in America, they are in fact not offensive to members of other cultures in which Puritanical conceptions of moral behavior are not widespread; and such examples make it difficult to deny that some conduct is regarded as a nuisance to others, just because those others regard the conduct as immoral. Accordingly, if bigamy is a crime because it is a nuisance to others, it does not follow without further argument that the bigamist is not punished because he is judged by society to be immoral, but for some other reason. This further argument Hart does not supply; but without it, he has not presented a clear alternative to the claim that in the case of bigamy at any rate the law is being used to enforce morals.

2. Hart's second example is as follows. With some exceptions such as rape, the criminal law does not permit, and has never permitted, the consent of the victim in a case involving physical injury to be used as an argument for the defense. But if one person makes a pact with a second to be beaten or even be killed, and the second one does as he promised, why should he be liable to punishment by society, if the parties to the agreement were of sane mind when they made it, both entered into it voluntarily, and no one else was injured by the transaction? (Incidentally, the example is not as grotesque as it may seem—it states the situation covered by current laws forbidding voluntary euthanasia.) To punish the defendant in this case is in direct conflict with Mill's explicit injunction that the law must never be used to interfere with an individual's freedom to make his "private" arrangements as he thinks best, even though as others see the matter his best interests are not served by his actions. Can this rule of law be justified? Devlin thinks it can, but only in one way; and he offers the justification that will by now be familiar, namely, that "there are certain standards of behavior or moral principles which society requires to be observed; and the breach of them is an offence not merely against the person who is injured but against society as a whole."[6] On the other hand, Hart denies this claim. How then does he justify this rule of law? He maintains that "The rules excluding the victim's consent as a defence to charges of murder or assault may perfectly well be explained as a piece of *paternalism,* designed to protect individuals against themselves."[7] In consequence, he finds fault with Devlin for failing to distinguish between what Hart calls "legal moralism" (the doctrine he attributes to Devlin and which justifies the use of the law to enforce positive morality), and "legal paternalism" (the doctrine which justifies using the law to protect people against themselves). According to Hart, Mill's principle of liberty excludes legal moralism. But while in general he aligns himself with Mill's principle, he believes that if it is to accommodate such rules of law as the one under discussion, the principle must be amended; and although he does not present a formulation of the re-

---

[5]*Ibid.,* p. 41 [my italics].
[6]Devlin, *op. cit.,* pp. 6–7.
[7]Hart, *op. cit.,* p. 31 [my italics].

vised principle, he suggests that the amended form must be consonant with legal paternalism.

However, Hart does little to make clear just how legal moralism differs from legal paternalism, and that it is not a distinction without difference. He suggests that while a legal moralist justifies a law regulating actions that are allegedly not harmful to others, on the ground that its aim is to enforce morality "as such"—whatever the phrase "as such" may signify—a legal paternalist who endorses the law will justify it on the ground that it seeks to protect people against themselves. But is there a substantive difference here? Can there be a rule of law that is compatible with legal moralism, but which is necessarily excluded by legal paternalism? Could not any law that is said to be simply an attempt to enforce morality be also construed as an attempt to protect men against themselves? Thus, Hart argues that the English law making the sale of narcotics a criminal offense is not concerned with punishing the seller for his immorality, as legal moralists claim, but with protecting the would-be purchaser.[8] But could not a legal paternalist offer an analogous support for *any* law endorsed by a legal moralist? And conversely, in endorsing the narcotics law on the ground that it punishes the seller for his immorality, the legal moralist can maintain that the seller is immoral *because* he makes available to others an article that is harmful to its users.

Hart also defends the distinction between legal paternalism and legal moralism by claiming that the former is a sounder moral policy than the latter. For according to him, the conceptions of men's best interests that legal paternalism seeks to enforce are the products of what he calls "critical morality," while the conceptions legal moralism would enforce are the creatures of blind custom and unexamined tradition. If there is this difference, it is undoubtedly an important one. But even if there is, Hart's claim presupposes that the distinction between legal moralism and legal paternalism has already been established; and it assumes without argument that there is a unique system of critical morality which underlies the proposals of legal paternalism, and that this system is a sound one. It is plain, however, that many systems of critical morality have been developed, and that their conceptions of what is to men's best interests do not always agree. There is certainly no consensus even among deeply reflective men as to which system of critical morality is the most adequate one, so that legal paternalists are likely to differ among themselves as well as with legal moralists as to the rules that should guide men's conduct. It surely does not follow that because legal paternalism is based on a critical morality, its proposals for regulating men's actions are necessarily sounder than the proposals of legal moralists.

But however this may be, if legal paternalism is a justifiable policy in the law—as Hart appears to hold—its adoption as a principle of legislation destroys the possibility of establishing a permanent division between conduct that is only of private concern and conduct that is of legitimate public interest. Adoption of the policy certainly permits the introduction of legal controls at which Mill would have been aghast.

5

I have taken much time to belabor the simple point that Mill's principle is not an adequate guide to legal and other forms of social control of men's behavior. My excuse

[8]*Ibid., p. 32.*

for doing so is that the principle is still very much alive in current discussions of legal and social philosophy, as the controversy between Devlin and his critics makes evident. Moreover, though the limitations of Mill's views on liberty have been often noted, they stress an important component in a reasonable ideal of human life—a component that needs to be stressed, if it is not to be swept aside by more insistent demands directed to realizing other human aspirations. But while I think Mill overdid the stress, how the ideal of individual freedom can be adjusted to competing aspirations is to me a question of perennial interest.

Like Tocqueville, Mill feared some of the leveling tendencies in modern democracies, and was apprehensive of the intolerance that custom-bound and unenlightened majorities can exhibit toward new ideas, fresh sensibilities, and intellectual as well as artistic excellence. He prized these achievements above all else, and believed they are indissolubly linked with the possession of maximum individual freedom that is compatible with life in society as he knew it. He therefore sought to secure the continuance of these achievements; and his principle of liberty was not only an expression of his conception of the human good, but also a protective wall to safeguard its pursuit.

As in the case of other political philosophers who saw in the pursuit of a multiplicity of objectives a danger to the realization of what they prized highly, Mill thus made individual freedom an absolute good to which he formally subordinated all other objectives—though his actual evaluations of social practices and his recommendations of changes in them are not always consonant with his formal principle. However, the elevation of individual liberty to the rank of the supreme good is clearly arbitrary. Most men do not cherish personal freedom above all else, even after prolonged and careful reflection; and in any case, they prize other things as well—indeed, sometimes as indispensable to a satisfactory and well-ordered life—such as health, some measure of worldly success and security, friendship and family, achievement and recognition by one's peers, or influence in the affairs of men. Moreover, maximum personal freedom is in general neither a necessary condition for the realization of all other legitimate objectives, nor is it compatible with some of them.

Accordingly, since many different interests, some of which may be conflicting ones, must be recognized in dealing with social problems, and since no one interest dominates the others permanently and in all contexts, it does not seem possible to set fixed limits to justifiable legal control of men's conduct. On the other hand, though it is frequently claimed that a compromise must be effected between the interests involved in a given problem, how the compromise should be made and in conformity with what rules, are questions to which I know no satisfactory answer. To be sure, broad rules have been proposed for dealing with this issue—for example, that the domain of personal freedom should be diminished as little as possible, or that the compromise should be so made as to maximize the expected social utility. But the proposed rules are vague and do not carry us very far. For in the absence of effective techniques for assessing the relative importance (or the utilities) of the various interests involved in the problem, it is not clear how the rules are to be applied; and despite the development of modern decision theory, there is no prospect that the needed techniques will soon be available.

There is then no general answer to the question whether certain categories of actions should be legally controlled and whether certain standards of conduct should be legally enforced. The question can be resolved only case by case, and though the proposed answers cannot be guaranteed to be the best ones possible, they are often the best ones available. And I cannot do better by way of a conclusion to this reflection than to quote a brief passage from Learned Hand:

> We shall never get along in matters of large public interest, if we proceed by generalization, indeed, if you insist, by principles, put forward as applicable in all circumstances. . . . The only way that public affairs can be successfully managed is by treating each case by itself; even so, the trouble is far from ended. We must ask what a proposed measure will do in fact, how all the people whom it touches react and respond to it? . . . Then—and this is the more difficult part—one must make a choice between the values that will be affected, for there are substantially always conflicts of group interest.[9]

---

[9]Learned Hand, *The Spirit of Liberty* (New York: Alfred A. Knopf, Inc., 1960), pp. 172–73.